BUSINESS LAW
a practical approach

BUSINESS LAW
a practical approach

FRANCES E. ZOLLERS   GAIL H. FOREMAN

DELMAR PUBLISHERS
COPYRIGHT ©1978
BY LITTON EDUCATIONAL PUBLISHING, INC.

LIBRARY OF CONGRESS CATALOG CARD NUMBER: 76-44036

Printed in the United States of America
Published simultaneously in Canada by
Delmar Publishers, A Division of
Van Nostrand Reinhold, Ltd.

To Mike and our three sons
G.H.F.
To my family
F.E.Z.

Foreword

BUSINESS LAW: A PRACTICAL APPROACH has been written to bring the complicated and sometimes highly detailed subject of business law to an understandable level. Students, business people, and consumers can all benefit by a careful study of its material.

We caution the reader at the outset that our purpose is not to train lawyers. We have provided only a taste of the entire body of law. Our hope is that the text will provide a basic course of study for those with this need, and spur others on to further inquiry and more comprehensive study.

A further caution is that the textbook is not meant to replace consultation with a lawyer. It can, however, help the reader to avoid serious legal difficulties by providing information which is presented in a comprehensive manner. When armed with this knowledge, the lay person can personally handle many legal problems and also know when it is advisable to seek the advice of an attorney.

It is the language barrier which often separates professional attorneys from consumers of legal services. Legal words and phrases, when clearly defined, can turn foreign sounding jargon into understandable legal language. We have used terms of art where they apply, since they have definite meanings in the law context. Each chapter of the textbook begins with a list of these new words and phrases which are introduced and defined for the reader in that chapter. There is also a complete glossary at the end of the book with definitions and page references for further information on the words and phrases.

Examples are used frequently throughout the text to provide an additional explanation of ideas being discussed. In addition, case examples appear in almost every chapter. These are actual court cases (usually edited to some extent) which show the reader how the theory of law works — how it is put into practice and used by individuals and businesses in varied situations.

It is recommended that this text be retained as a reference source in the reader's own library, since a topic that is studied today may require in-depth examination or re-evaluation when the theory must be put into actual practice.

Frances E. Zollers

Gail H. Foreman

Preface

It can no longer be said that the study of law is the sole province of prospective lawyers. Aspects of business law affect a variety of individuals involved in the day-to-day operation of business. The employee of a large business or corporation, the business operator and owner, and the consumer all have a need for an understanding of the basics of business law in a world where law and the legal system affect our lives daily.

Business Law: A Practical Approach fills the need for a comprehensive but understandable guide to the study of business law. Although the text was developed for the secondary, two-year college, and continuing education student, it can also be used by individuals currently involved in business who wish to become informed about current theories and practices of business law.

The format of the text complements the authors' lucid approach to legal theory. Performance objectives before each chapter state what the student should be able to accomplish before procceeding to the next concept. Since legal language can sometimes cloud issues with its complexity, special care has been taken to present the material in such a way that it is clear and easily understood. Legal words and phrases are listed before each chapter and defined therein upon first usage. Examples presented after the introduction of theories provide additional explanation for better understanding. Case examples, from actual court cases, illustrate how legal concepts are applied to courtroom practices. Self-evaluation sections following each chapter provide a tool by which individual comprehension of chapter material may be gauged. Included in this chapter-end material are cases for study, which give students the opportunity to apply newly learned concepts to a variety of factual settings. Suggested activities further involve the student in the legal environment.

An extensive glossary at the end of the text provides definitions of legal words and phrases. Page references indicate where a more thorough discussion of the term may be found in the text. An appendix to the text reproduces for the reader Articles 1, 2, 3, 4, and 9 of the Uniform Commercial Code, the Uniform Partnership Act, and the Uniform Limited Partnership Act.

An instructor's guide accompanying the text is available. Where applicable, the guide to each chapter begins with notes to the instructor concerning text material. Answers to self-evaluation sections are given, including suggestions relating to chapter-end activities. Additional activities and an analysis of cases for study are also provided. Dissenting opinions of certain court cases which appear in the text are presented for further class discussion. A final addition to the guide is a post-test which can be used to evaluate individual understanding of the text material.

Frances E. Zollers is presently an Assistant Professor of Law at the School of Management of Syracuse University, in Syracuse, New York. She received her B.A. from DePauw University and her J.D. from Syracuse University College of Law. Professor Zollers is a member of various professional organizations, including the American Business Law Association, the New York State Bar Association, and the American Legal Studies Association.

Gail Foreman has done extensive work as a free-lance writer for various private companies. Mrs. Foreman is currently employed in personnel management for a large petroleum corporation in Dewitt, New York, specializing in the formulation and writing of personnel programs. She received her B.A. degree from Syracuse University, Syracuse, New York.

Business Law: A Practical Approach is the latest addition to Delmar's Midmanagement/Marketing Series. Other texts currently include *Small Business Management* by William D. Hailes and Raymond T. Hubbard and *Effective Business Communications* by Bonnie D. Phillips.

Contents

Preface. vi

Section 1 Law and the Legal Process 1

   Chapter   1   History and Types of Law 3
   Chapter   2   The Legal Process. 14

Section 2 Contracts. 31

   Chapter   3   Types of Contracts 33
   Chapter   4   Requirements of a Legal Contract 51
   Chapter   5   The Assignment and Termination of
                  Contracts 78

Section 3 Consumer Dealings with Personal Property . . . 95

   Chapter   6   The Contract of Sale 97
   Chapter   7   The Secured Credit Sale 112
   Chapter   8   Consumer Protection: Warranties, Product
                  Liability, and Legislation 123
   Chapter   9   Bailments 146

Section 4 Real Property 171

   Chapter 10   Ownership of Real Property. 173
   Chapter 11   Real Property Transactions: Purchasings
                  and Leasing 190

Section 5 Torts 221

   Chapter 12   Torts – Intentional and Unintentional. . . 223

Section 6 Organizing Businesses 251

   Chapter 13   Agency. 253
   Chapter 14   The Partnership 277
   Chapter 15   The Corporation 294

Section 7 Commercial Paper 327

   Chapter 16 Commercial Paper 329

Appendix A 381
Appendix B 498
Appendix C 511
Acknowledgments 519

Section 1

Law and the Legal Process

Law by definition is a set of principles and regulations. It is established to define the relationships of people with each other and with their governments.

Almost every business person must consult a *lawyer* (also known as an *attorney-at-law,* or simply *attorney*) at some time. The person who seeks the advice of a lawyer is called a *client.* Business people are sometimes involved in cases which are brought into court. In law, a *case* is a controversy between two or more persons who, as a last resort, have turned to a court system to resolve their dispute. The party who begins the proceedings (the one who is alleging that a wrong has been committed) is known as the *plaintiff.* The party being brought into court to defend against the claim is known as the *defendant.*

In early America, there were no schools which offered training in legal matters. Students learned from practicing attorneys by acting as their apprentices. Today, there are many qualified law schools that admit college graduates. After earning a law degree, the student must pass a state examination and then obtain a license to practice the profession in that state. The behavior and duties of attorneys are regulated by strict standards set by the American Bar Association, a professional organization of lawyers.

Perhaps because of the influence of the media, the average citizen often thinks that a lawyer spends a great deal of time trying cases in court. Actually, this is only a small part of the job. Attorneys also have the legal knowledge necessary to organize businesses, write business documents, manage real estate dealings, draw up wills, and give advice on tax situations.

Section 1 expands upon the definition of *law* as a set of principles and regulations. It also includes an explanation of the origin of American law and the *legal system;* that is, how the law is used in various courts throughout the country.

Chapter 1

History and Types of Law

OBJECTIVES

After studying this chapter, the student will be able to

- explain what law is and where it originated.
- list the duties of a lawyer.
- identify several types of law which comprise the body of American law.
- differentiate between civil law and criminal law.
- define the following words and phrases.

law	legislature
lawyer	legislation
attorney	statutory law
client	act of Congress
law apprentice	ordinance
American Bar Association	uniform laws
case	Uniform Commercial Code
plaintiff	administrative agencies
defendant	administrative regulations
precedent	civil law
case or common law	criminal law
constitutional law	business law
legislate	

THE HISTORY OF LAW

Historians have found proof that ancient Egyptians had a form of law to govern their civilization over 6,000 years ago. Throughout every other culture since that time, laws have regulated people under many different forms of government.

One of the biggest tasks of early American settlers was to organize a new government and establish laws for their new land. Since most of the settlers were from England, it was natural for them to rely a great deal on English laws. The English laws which formed the basis for American law can be traced back to about 1066 A.D. when the Normans conquered England. The new Americans used many principles basic to English law, but placed a great deal more power in the hands of ordinary citizens.

SOURCES OF AMERICAN LAW

Some of the basics of American law were established when the country was formed. Other laws are being passed almost daily. To understand the entire body of American law, it is necessary to divide law into four categories, figure 1-1.

Common Law

American colonists adopted a form of law that had been used in England for hundreds of years; that is, relying on previous legal decisions when a similar problem arose. When a decision on a point of law is reached, that case becomes a *precedent*, or model for future cases which have the same features as the first. These precedents, decided in local, state, and federal courts, comprise what is called *common law*. Common law is also referred to as *case law* since it is derived from previously decided cases.

In 1966, the United States Supreme Court (the highest court in the land) decided a landmark case which involved the rights of criminal defendants. *Miranda* v. *Arizona*. The parties in the case had made confessions to the police, but were never informed that they did not have to answer questions or that they could have an attorney present during the questioning. Upon hearing the case, the Supreme Court decided that persons accused of a crime must be informed prior to any questions that they have a right to remain

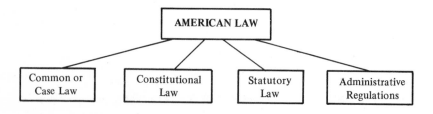

Fig. 1-1 Categories of American law

1. You have a right to remain silent and refuse to answer questions.
2. Anything you do or say may be used against you in a court of law.
3. As we discuss this matter you have a right to stop answering my questions at any time that you desire.
4. You have the right to a lawyer before speaking to me, to remain silent until you can talk to him, and to have him present during the time you are being questioned.
5. If you desire a lawyer but you cannot afford one, the Public Defender will be provided to you without cost.
6. Do you understand each of these rights as I have explained them to you?
7. Now that I have advised you of your rights, are you willing to answer my questions without an attorney?

Fig. 1-2 Miranda Rights card carried by police officers

silent; that if the right to remain silent is given up, statements made can be used against them; that they may have an attorney present during questioning; and that an attorney can be appointed to their case if they cannot afford to retain one of their own. The warnings read by police officers upon arrest have become known as the *Miranda Warnings,* figure 1-2.

The *Miranda* decision acted as a precedent in the following case, which deals with the same issue. Notice the extent to which the second case relies upon the *Miranda* case.

SWICEGOOD v. STATE

Criminal Court of Appeals of Alabama, 1973
50 Ala. App. 105, 277 So. 2d 380

[The defendant, Henry Ford Swicegood, was charged with grand larceny. He was convicted and sentenced, and brought the following appeal based on the *Miranda* decision.]

. . .The trial judge heard evidence outside the presence of the jury and determined that [Swicegood's statements to the police] were voluntarily made. The State at this hearing propounded [offered for consideration] a question to the witness and received an answer as follows:

Q. "Did you advise him of his rights?"
A. "Yes sir."

Before the jury, the same question was propounded and answered as follows:

A. "Yes, we did."

The admissibility of the evidence was raised by defendant's objection. The question is ambiguous, uncertain, and very general, with a marked absence of specificity. It may be that the prosecuting attorney had in mind the mandates of *Miranda* v. *Arizona,* 384 U.S. 436, 86 S. Ct. 1602, 16 L. Ed. 2d 694, 10 A.L.R.3d 974, wherein the Supreme Court of the United States impressed certain guidelines to be followed by a police officer when questioning a detained suspect in an effort to obtain inculpatory or confessory statements. *Miranda* explicates the precise warnings which the officer must give the defendant and the consequence of failure to give such "warnings."

• • •

It does not appear in the appeal record before us that the defendant was effectively and fairly informed of his rights under *Miranda,* nor was he warned of the consequence accruing to him if he confessed. . . .Because of such failure of proof,. . .none of the confessory answers. . .should have been admitted. It was the duty of the State to spell out with clarity and reasonable precision the warnings the officers gave the defendant, if any, as mandated in *Miranda.*   A general question, as here does not meet the requirements of law.

• • •

Reversed.

This system of following a precedent, or previous case decision, helps to keep cases from going needlessly to court. When a precedent has been set, lawyers are able to advise their clients of the probable outcome of the case. If the precedent is not favorable, the client may avoid costly court expenses by attempting to settle the problem by another method.

Example.   A case brought before a court involving an automobile accident denied the plaintiff recovery when it was proved that the plaintiff was slightly at fault, even though the defendant was more at fault. Knowing that such negligence on the part of the plaintiff completely barred recovery of damages, the potential plaintiff in a similar situation might be advised to reconsider a suit.

A legal system that relies on precedents provides a great benefit to all citizens, not just to attorneys. Such a system lends stability and predictability to law. If individuals know for what actions they are legally responsible, they can conform their conduct accordingly. No one need act at his or her peril since the results of a given act are predictable. For example, citizens can drive recklessly, but they know that if they do, they will be held responsible for any and all consequences of the action.

Of course, individuals cannot rely totally on precedents. Many times, a precedent is altered or overruled because it becomes outdated.

Example. At one time, a series of precedents stated that members of the same family could not sue each other when one family member unintentionally injured another family member. It was thought that allowing law suits within a family would disrupt family unity. Furthermore, it was thought that dishonest claims might be made when members of the same family were involved. Many courts now recognize that this type of suit will not necessarily break up families because of the almost universal coverage of individuals by insurance. They now feel that it is more important to assure payment for injuries, no matter who caused them.

Many courts now allow suits between members of the same family; the old precedents are no longer followed. In this case, the rule of law no longer exists because the reasons for the old rule no longer exist.

Constitutional Law

Laws which are found in state and federal constitutions form the basis of *constitutional law*. These laws make up a large part of this country's legal system. Constitutions usually are stated in very broad terms so that they can be used throughout the years, even as times change.

In 1789, the United States Constitution went into effect as the "supreme law of the land." The person involved in writing the Constitution granted certain powers to the federal government and at the same time placed certain limitations on it. Article I of the Constitution gave the United States government control over matters that concerned all of the states. This included the power to declare war, to coin money and regulate its value, to fix a standard of weights and measures, and to establish post offices.

Each of the states was free to control matters within its own borders that did not affect the other states.

Example. In the United States Constitution, the federal government is granted the power to regulate commerce (trade) between the states. Each state has the power to control commerce which is conducted only inside its own borders.

Whatever powers not specifically granted to the federal government were reserved for the states.

Example. Each state has the power to devise its own laws for punishing crimes such as murder or theft. These laws affect only the people in the state in which the crime takes place. The power to prosecute for violation of state crimes is not stated in the Constitution since it is not given to the federal government; however, it is reserved for, or belongs to, the individual states.

Each state has an established constitution, which is the supreme law in that state. The constitution of a state specifies areas in which that state holds power. It cannot, of course, conflict with the federal constitution.

Fig. 1-3 The New York State Senate, a legislative body in session

Statutory Law

The makers of the Constitution established the United States as a *republic*, a form of government in which the citizens elect people to represent them at all levels of government. At the federal level, senators and members of Congress are elected. States have elected senators and delegates or representatives. Local governments also have elected representatives.

Each of these elected officials represents the people from his or her district and votes with their interests in mind, figure 1-3. The major job of these elected officials is to *legislate*, which is to make or pass laws. Thus, the group to which they belong is called a *legislature*, and the laws which they pass are known as *legislation*. The entire group of laws or legislation passed by these legislatures is called *statutory law*.

Federal Statutes.   Federal statutes are those passed by the federal government. They are often called *acts of Congress*.

Example. The following statute was passed by Congress in 1974 to punish recording industry "pirates," people who reproduce recordings without proper permission and for a profit. Prior to this statute, such persons were not guilty of a federal crime. Legislation was necessary since the underground record business was so extensive that record companies and artists were losing millions of dollars in revenue every year. The statute: *Whoever knowingly and with fraudulent intent transports, causes to be transported, receives, sells, or offers for sale in interstate or foreign commerce any phonograph record, disk, wire, tape, film, or other article on which sounds are recorded, to which or upon which is stamped, pasted or affixed any forged or counterfeited label, knowing the label to have been falsely made, forged, or counterfeited, shall be fined not more than $25,000 or imprisoned for not more than one year, or both, for the first offense, and shall be fined not more than $50,000 or imprisoned for not more than two years, or both, for any subsequent offense.*

State Statutes.   Statutory law also includes all laws passed by state legislatures.

Example. Each state passes laws regarding the age when a person may begin driving a car. They also pass laws that set speed limits on all state highways.

With all fifty states passing legislation, great confusion could result. This is especially true in the area of business dealings because of the enormous growth of interstate trade and the operation of national industries in many states, which can result in conflicting state laws having an impact on one transaction.

To help eliminate the resulting confusion, there was a move in the early 1900s to make many of the state laws uniform. To do this, a National Conference of Commissioners on Uniform State Laws was established. The most important result of the commission was the establishment of the *Uniform Commercial Code* (UCC). The Code, as it is often called, contains uniform laws concerning the operation of business. By 1971, every state except Louisiana had adopted the UCC.

Regulations and rules for almost every phase of a business transaction are covered in the Code. It is used, therefore, as a guideline throughout this text when discussing laws which refer to business.

Local Statutes (Ordinances). Local laws passed by town, city, or county legislative bodies are usually called *ordinances.*

Example. Builders must be aware of local ordinances before doing any type of construction. A town may have an ordinance that requires that each new house be set back at least thirty feet from the edge of the road. Another local ordinance might restrict the size and placement of signs on property.

Administrative Regulations

Legislatures at all levels of government have enacted laws establishing administrative agencies and delegating rule-making powers to these agencies. These groups have the power to conduct hearings, require witnesses to appear, and issue orders which have the force of law. These orders or rulings have been grouped together and called *administrative regulations.* In recent years, there has been a great increase in this type of law.

There are hundreds of these administrative agencies at all levels of government. Some of the more active ones at the federal level are the Securities and Exchange Commission (SEC), the Food and Drug Administration (FDA), the Federal Communications Commission (FCC), and the Federal Trade Commission (FTC). At the state level, there are public utility commissions, state environmental agencies, drug control boards, and mental health administrations. Administrative agencies at the local level include water authorities, zoning boards, and recreation commissions.

Example. The following FDA ruling regarding labeling has the force of law even though it is not a statute passed by a legislative body: *(Dec. 1955) (a) Because methyl salicylate (wintergreen oil) manifests no toxicity in the minute amounts in which it is used as a flavoring, it is mistakenly regarded by the public as harmless even when taken in substantially large amounts. Actually, it is quite toxic when taken in quantities of a teaspoonful or more. Wintergreen oil and preparations containing it have caused a number of deaths through accidental misuse by both adults and children. Children are particularly attracted by the odor and are likely to swallow these products when left within reach.*

(b) To safeguard against fatalities from this cause, the Department of Health, Education and Welfare will regard as misbranded under the provisions of the Federal Food, Drug, and Cosmetic Act any drug containing more than 5 percent methyl salicylate (wintergreen oil), the labeling of which fails to warn that use otherwise than as directed therein may be dangerous and that the article should be kept out of the reach of children to prevent accidental poisoning.

(c) This statement of interpretation in no way exempts methyl salicylate (wintergreen oil) or its preparations from complying in all other respects with the requirements of the Federal Food, Drug, and Cosmetic Act.

Civil Law and Criminal Law

Civil law and criminal law are not types or categories of law such as those previously defined. Rather, they can be called subdivisions of law. There may be both civil and criminal laws in each of the categories into which American law is divided, figure 1-4.

Civil law defines the rights of individuals and protects their persons and property. Civil law concerns the relationship of one person to another; civil actions are brought by individuals against other individuals. Civil cases include automobile accidents, divorces, adoptions, and contract disputes — basically, anything that is not criminal.

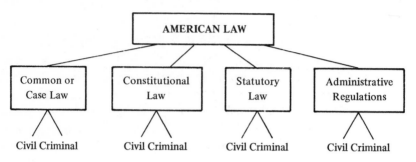

Fig. 1-4 Subdivisions of American law

Example. While crossing the street, Barbara Snead is hit by a car driven by Benjamin Grossman. She brings a civil suit against Grossman for damages she incurred as a result of the accident. (Individual v. another individual)

Criminal law was established to protect society as a whole from harmful acts of an individual and to maintain peace and order. Criminal law concerns the relationship of an individual to the community; that is, the entire organized group to which the person belongs, such as a town, state, or country. Examples of crimes are murder, theft, kidnapping, and treason and less serious crimes such as disturbing the peace.

Criminal actions are brought against an individual by the state. The word *state* in this sense is the organized government which issued the law that was broken. A criminal action regarding a local law is brought by the local authority, a state law by the state, and a federal law by the United States. In criminal law, the individual is always presumed innocent until proven guilty.

Example. Joseph Reed is accused of committing murder in Idaho. The case reads *The State* (or *The People*) *of Idaho* v. *Reed.* (A state criminal law is involved, so it is the state versus the individual.)

Example. Patrick Kline is accused of robbing a bank, which is a federal crime. A criminal action results, stated the *United States* v. *Kline.* (A federal law is involved; therefore, it is the United States government bringing the action against the individual.)

Business Law

Business law can be traced back to the dealings of the earliest merchants. It is not a separate subdivision of law; rather, it can be included in all four categories in figure 1-4. Business law concerns actions between individuals, between corporations, between government and an individual, and between government and a corporation. It can involve civil as well as criminal laws. This textbook describes business laws and how they affect each individual as a citizen, as a consumer, and as a member of the business world.

SELF-EVALUATION

Provide a brief explanation for each of the following.

1. What is law and why was it established?

2. Upon what did American settlers rely when they formed the laws of the early colonies?

3. What comprises common law?

4. What was a major result of the *Miranda* v. *Arizona* case?

5. According to the United States Constitution, which legal matters does the federal government control and which legal matters do the states control?

6. What is a republic?

7. What are acts of Congress and ordinances called?

8. What are administrative agencies?

9. What is the Uniform Commerical Code?

10. In which type of law, civil or criminal, is a person presumed innocent until proven guilty?

11. In what categories of law is business law found? Be specific.

SUGGESTED ACTIVITIES

1. Bring in a newspaper article involving an administrative agency at any level of government.

2. Interview an attorney. Report on the necessary training and the requirements for practicing law in your state. Ask the attorney to describe different functions performed during a typical week.

Chapter 2

The Legal Process

OBJECTIVES

After studying this chapter, the student will be able to

- define the five types of jurisdiction.

- outline the organization of the federal court system.

- explain various courts at state and local levels.

- list the various stages of court procedure by following a court case.

- define the following words and phrases.

public law	U.S. Supreme Court
private law	state court system
court	state lower courts
jurisdiction	state higher courts
subject matter jurisdiction	inferior courts
personal jurisdiction	municipal courts
original jurisdiction	justice of the peace courts
trial court	summons
appellate court	complaint
record	damages
judge	answer
Canons of Judicial Ethics	reply
circuit	pleadings
U.S. District Court	discovery
concurrent jurisdiction	litigate
exclusive jurisdiction	trial
U.S. Court of Appeals	

DEFINITION OF TERMS

Court as a legal term may be used in three different ways. It most frequently denotes the arm of government that administers justice. It may also indicate the place in which justice is administered. Figure 2-1 shows such a place, the United States Supreme Court building in Washington, D.C.

Court is also used to refer to the judge in many legal papers and discussions. For example, during a trial, an attorney sometimes begins a statement with "May it please the court. . . ." In this situation, the lawyer is actually talking to the judge in the courtroom and is asking permission to address the judge.

The purpose of courts of law is to protect the rights of citizens individually and as a unit. People cannot exist without having some disagreements. The court is a common meeting place in which these disputes are settled by the use of laws as discussed in Chapter 1.

Fig. 2-1 The United States Supreme Court Building, Washington, D.C.

Jurisdiction refers to the power of a certain court to hear a particular case and to interpret and apply the law. The court may be limited by subject matter or by its ability to force a defendant to appear.

Subject matter jurisdiction is the power of a court to hear a particular type of case. The subject matter jurisdiction of courts is usually specified in statutes. For example, federal statutes define which types of cases federal courts may hear. If a court hands down a decision but lacks subject matter jurisdiction to hear the case in the first place, the decision is absolutely void. The fact that the two parties might agree to allow that court to hear the case makes no difference; the judgment is still void because the court lacked subject matter jurisdiction.

Example. A certain court may not be able to handle cases involving traffic violations outside village or town limits. Such cases may be beyond its jurisdiction, or outside the limit of its power.

Example. A court might be limited by the amount of money involved in the case. For example, a local court may be able to deal only with cases in which $1,000 or less is involved.

Example. The types of cases that a court can hear may also reflect a limitation of its power. For example, a *probate court* is limited to cases involving the property which remains after an individual dies; a murder case is outside its jurisdiction.

Personal jursidiction is the power a court may exert to force a defendant to appear before it and to be subject to its decision. The method by which a court exercises personal jurisdiction is through service of a *summons* or *process.*

Example. A resident of Maine who has never been outside that state and does not transact any business outside that state cannot be forced to go to California to defend a suit, since the California courts do not have personal jurisdiction over this individual. In this situation, the plaintiff must go to Maine to begin the suit.

At one time, the only circumstances under which a court could exercise personal jurisdiction over a defendant in a civil case included:

- Residence. The courts of the state of an individual's residence have jursidiction over that resident. This is one of the obligations of residency.

- Presence. If a defendant is served with a summons while visiting or passing through a state, the courts in that state may exercise jurisdiction over that defendant.

- Consent. Even though a defendant is not a resident of a state and has not been in that state, the defendant may agree to be subject to suit in the state. Note that the parties can give the court personal jurisdiction in this instance, whereas subject matter jurisdiction can never be conferred by the parties to a suit.

These traditional bases of jurisdiction became too strict in an age of high mobility when goods and people began to move much more freely from state to state. In an effort to keep pace with the time, the law now recognizes additional bases of personal jurisdiction that are not as strict as the three mentioned above. Some of these include:

- Ownership of real property in the state attempting to exercise jurisdiction.
- Doing business within the state.
- Committing a wrongful act within the state.
- Committing a wrongful act outside the state that causes injury to a resident within the state.

This newer approach to personal jurisdiction is designed to aid plaintiffs. If injured plaintiffs were forced to rely solely on the traditional bases of personal jurisdiction, they might have to travel great distances before finding a court that could exercise jurisdiction over the defendant.

Example. A Massachusetts resident driving in Missouri causes an accident which injures a Missouri resident. The day after the accident, the Massachusetts resident returns home. By the time the plaintiff is ready to sue the defendant, it would not be possible under the former rules of jurisdiction. Under the newer rules, however, Missouri can exercise jurisdiction over the defendant, thereby aiding the plaintiff. By serving a summons on defendant in Massachusetts, plaintiff can force him to return to Missouri to defend the claim.

Example. A manufacturer of power tools in Michigan places a defectively made drill on the market. The drill is purchased by a resident of Oregon who is injured when the drill fails to operate properly. The wrongful act occurred in Michigan when the drill was improperly manufactured. However, the injury was caused to an Oregon resident within that state. Under the newer rules of jurisdiction, the Oregon courts have personal jurisdiction over the manufacturer.

Original jurisdiction is the power of a court to hear a case when it is first brought into court. In many instances, this means that a trial is held. *Trial courts* are courts in which decisions are made by a jury, or, if there is no jury, by a judge, after calling witnesses and hearing testimony. Trial courts have original jurisdiction to hear cases.

Appellate courts or *courts of appeal* review decisions of lower courts or courts of original jurisdiction. This occurs when an appeal (claim) is made that the lower court was in error in some way. In appellate courts there are no juries, and no new witnesses are introduced. A decision is made by a judge or panel of judges based on the *record* of the lower court trial. The record includes a copy of witness testimony, exhibits, and any papers that were used at the trial. The attorneys for both plaintiff and defendant may appear before the judges to argue the cases again, but they are not allowed to introduce any new facts. Therefore, an appeal may be made when

there is an error at law; not when one of the parties disputes the facts presented in the original case.

Judges or **justices** are public officials, either appointed or elected, who preside in court and administer the law. That is, they dispense or distribute justice by the use of laws. Judges make decisions on questions of law based on the information presented by both sides of the dispute.

According to the federal Constitution, the President of the United States appoints all federal judges, with the approval of the Senate, including United States Supreme Court justices. The term of federal judges is generally considered to be for life, unless their behavior is unacceptable. Many state and local judges are elected by the voting public for definite periods, varying by state and by position. Guidelines for the behavior of all judges are contained in the *Canons of Judicial Ethics* from the American Bar Association. These are not actual laws, but are generally accepted rules for judges to follow both in court and in their personal lives.

The United States is unique among countries in that it has fifty-one separate court systems; one at the federal level and one for each of the states.

THE COURT SYSTEM

The Federal Courts

Article III of the United States Constitution states that there shall be a Supreme Court and such other courts as Congress sees fit to establish at the federal level. Using this authority, Congress has established a complete federal court system by areas called *circuits*, figure 2-2.

Each circuit has one United States Court of Appeals. There are ninety United States District Courts (trial courts), with at least one in each state and as many as four in some of the more populated states. There are also several courts established for special purposes. These include the Court of Claims, the Tax Court, the Court of Customs, and the Court of Patent Appeals.

The federal courts hear all cases in which federal laws are involved. This includes selective service, bankruptcy, federal tax and patent laws, and crimes defined by federal law such as counterfeiting and treason. Their jurisdiction also includes all admiralty and maritime cases; that is, cases dealing with water borders on the east and west coasts of the country, all navigable rivers, and all rivers that

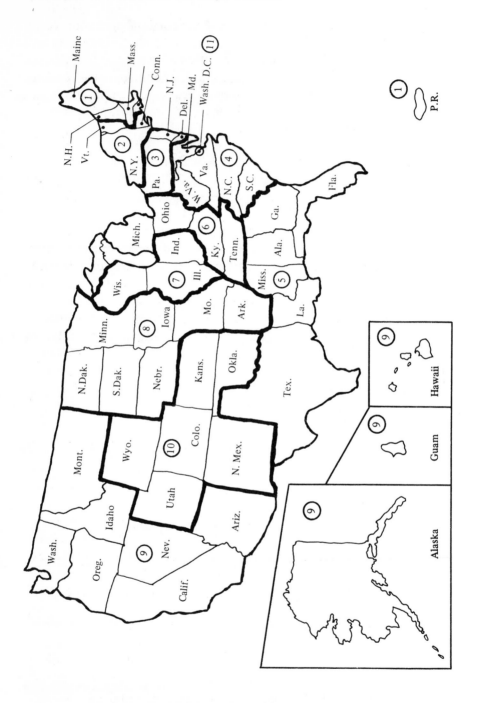

Fig. 2-2 Circuits of the Federal Court System

form state borders.   The federal court also acts in cases between states, between citizens of different states, and in cases which involve a state and citizens of another state.

To lighten the case load of federal courts, Congress has limited the subject matter jurisdiction of federal courts in civil law suits to amounts of over $10,000.   Certain exceptions do exist, however; these are stated in federal statutes.

The United States District Courts.   Each of the ninety federal district courts is a trial court and almost always the court of *original jurisdiction.*

Example.   Ralph Malone is arrested for making counterfeit twenty-dollar bills in San Francisco, California, and for distributing the money throughout the state.   Malone's case is heard in a federal district court located in California.   Even though the crime took place within the borders of that one state, a federal law (counterfeiting) was broken.

Some cases may be brought to either a federal district court or a state court since both courts have the power to hear the case. This is known as *concurrent jurisdiction.* In these cases, the choice of courts is the decision of the plaintiff.

Example.   A truck being driven by Richard Rowland, a resident of Vermont, is passing through New Hampshire when it is struck by a car driven by Kenneth Prescott, a New Hampshire resident.   The personal injury and property damage claim of Rowland amounts to $120,000.   A claim such as this could be taken to the federal district court in New Hampshire, since the claim is between residents of two different states, and the amount is over $10,000.   The case could also be brought to either state court, since it falls within their jurisdiction.   Since there is concurrent jurisdiction, Rowland, the plaintiff, decides in which court the case is to be heard.

There are often cases in which courts have *exclusive jurisdiction.* This means that there is only one court which has the power to hear the case.

Example. Mary Ann Gordon's creditors want to force her to declare bankruptcy. A federal statute provides that all bankruptcy matters be brought to a federal district court. Therefore, Gordon's creditors can take action only in a federal court. Neither the residency of the parties nor any amount of money involved in the controversy has any bearing on whether the federal court can declare Gordon bankrupt. The jurisdiction here is said to be *exclusive.*

The United States Courts of Appeals. One United States Court of Appeals is found in each of the eleven circuits. As an appellate court, most of the cases presented to it originate in the federal district courts within its circuit. This court also reviews rulings on appeal from the federal administrative agencies as described in Chapter 1.

If a party is involved in a case in a federal district court and feels at the end of the trial that an error of law was committed, the party may appeal to the United States Court of Appeals. The only higher court to which a case can go from this court is the United States Supreme Court.

The United States Supreme Court. The United States Supreme Court was established as the highest court in the land by the federal Constitution. Congress was given the duty of deciding upon the number of judges to serve on this court. Although the number has changed throughout history, the current number, and the number that has existed for many years, is nine.

The Supreme Court has original jurisdiction on rare occasions. Cases tried for the first time in that court include those involving foreign ambassadors or suits between two states. Normally, however, the Supreme Court handles only appeals from the federal system or a state court system. Figure 2-3 illustrates the course than an appeal can take through the court system.

For a citizen to appeal a case to the Supreme Court directly after it has been heard in the highest court in their state, the case must have challenged a point in the Constitution or a federal law. Even if a case meets this criteria, the Supreme Court may choose not to hear it, since it usually has the power to select cases it will hear.

In recent years, the Supreme Court has often taken several appeals from state appeals courts which are similar in nature and treated them as a single case. In these instances, one decision is reached and then applied to all the appeals to which it pertains.

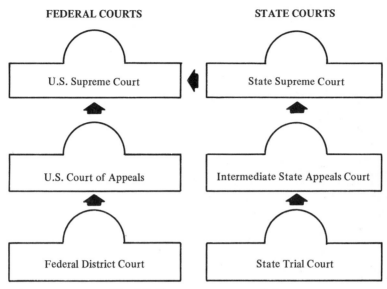

FEDERAL COURTS

STATE COURTS

U.S. Supreme Court

State Supreme Court

U.S. Court of Appeals

Intermediate State Appeals Court

Federal District Court

State Trial Court

Fig. 2-3 How cases are appealed

Example. A ruling of the United States Supreme Court held that students must be given a hearing before they are suspended from a public school for a given length of time. The case involved a number of student suspensions. The ruling applied to all such cases, as well as to any future suspensions.

Example. In the *Miranda* case, discussed in Chapter 1, there were actually several appeals to the United States Supreme Court on the same subject — the unconstitutionality of certain confessions. All the cases were so similar that they were treated as one. The ruling applied to all of the cases, as well as to any future cases.

Decisions made by the Supreme Court are considered final and are rarely *reversed,* or made void. At times, the legislature passes a law immediately following a Supreme Court decision which deals with the same matter. The effect is to establish statutory law from case law.

State Courts

Each state court system is entirely independent of any other state government and the federal government. The jurisdiction or power of the state courts is usually defined by state laws and the rights of citizens in that state, as found in the state constitution. The jurisdiction of state courts includes, among other things, cases which deal with crimes committed in the state and controversies over ownership of land located in the state.

Example. A wants to sue B for injuries received when A slipped on a sidewalk on B's property. Both are residents of the state of X. The courts of the state of X have jurisdiction to hear the case.

Most state court systems are organized in the same pattern as the federal court system. The state systems are divided into lower courts, including trial courts and higher courts which hear appeals. The highest court in the state is usually called the *state supreme court,* although it is also known by other names in some states. There are also many state courts set up for special purposes, such as juvenile courts and family courts.

Inferior Courts

Inferior courts include all courts at the local level in counties, cities, towns, and villages. Inferior courts are often called *municipal courts* or *justice of the peace courts (J.P. courts),* depending on the area they serve. These courts generally have very limited jurisdiction. They serve an important job at a local level, however, by enforcing local traffic, zoning, police, and fire regulations.

Inferior courts are different from most other courts in that they do not keep records of the proceedings. Therefore, if there is an appeal from such a court, there must first be a completely new trial in a higher trial court that does maintain records. (As noted earlier, an appeal court relies solely on the record of the trial from the lower court in reaching its decision.)

COURT PROCEDURE

Business people may occasionally find that they must go to court. They may be bringing an action against another party, or someone may be bringing an action against them. In other instances, they may be called before the court as a witness. For the average citizen, this may be a frightening experience, only because the legal terms, as well as what is happening in the courtroom, are usually so unfamiliar.

The remaining part of this chapter defines the various stages of court procedure by examining a case which involves two business people. This includes an explanation of how a case is prepared before it goes to trial and a definition of terms, procedures, and persons involved in civil court action.

The Facts

Samual Squires and Michael Morse enter into an agreement whereby Squires is to buy a carload of grain from Morse for $1,000 when the crop is harvested. Squires is in the business of making cereal, a fact of which Morse is aware at the time of the contract. It is a bad year for corn and the price continually rises as crop yields drop. Morse could demand much more than $1,000 a carload for his grain if he had not already contracted with Squires.

The time for delivery arrives and Squires sends Morse instructions for shipment, only to learn that Morse has sold his entire crop to other buyers at the going rate (considerably higher than $1,000 a carload). Squires decides to institute a lawsuit against Morse for damages he incurred as a result of Morse's breach of contract.

The Pleadings

Squires hires Lawrence Luft as his attorney. After discussing the facts, Luft determines that Squires has a valid claim and that there is a good chance that a lawsuit will be decided in Squires' favor. The first step in the process involves drawing up a summons and complaint that is sent to Morse to notify him of the suit being brought against him. The title of the case is *Squires* v. *Morse.* Note that the plaintiff's name is listed first in the case title.

The *summons,* figure 2-4, besides providing notice to the defendant of the suit against him, is the device which grants the court power over the person of the defendant. It literally summons the defendant into court.

The *complaint* is a statement of the plaintiff's claims set out in numbered paragraphs and drafted by the plaintiff's attorney. Squires' complaint alleges that he and Morse had a contract for the sale of a carload of corn at $1,000; that Squires performed his part of the contract; and that Morse refused to hold up his end of the bargain. The final clause of the complaint alleges the amount of the *damages,* the sum for which Squires is suing to compensate for his loss.

Index No.

SAMPLE

against

Plaintiff

Defendant

𝔖𝔲𝔪𝔪𝔬𝔫𝔰

**Action not based upon a
Consumer Credit Transaction**

Attorney(s) for Plaintiff

Office, Post Office Address and Tel. No.

DESCRIPTION
USE WITH
1 *or* 3 ☐   Deponent describes the individual served
as follows: sex: ☐ *male*   ☐ *female;*

☐ White Skin	☐ Under 5'	☐ Under 100 Lbs.
☐ Black Skin	☐ 5' 0" - 5' 3"	☐ 100 - 130 Lbs.
☐ Yellow Skin	☐ 5' 4" - 5' 8"	☐ 131 - 160 Lbs.
☐ Brown Skin	☐ 5' 9" - 6' 0"	☐ 161 - 200 Lbs.
☐ Red Skin	☐ Over 6'	☐ Over 200 Lbs.

☐ Black Hair	☐ 14 - 20 Yrs.
☐ Brown Hair	☐ 21 - 35 Yrs.
☐ Blond Hair	☐ 36 - 50 Yrs.
☐ Gray Hair	☐ 51-65 Yrs.
☐ Red Hair	☐ Over 65 Yrs.
☐ White Hair	
☐ Balding	

Other identifying features:

Sworn to before me on

Fig. 2-4A Front of Summons

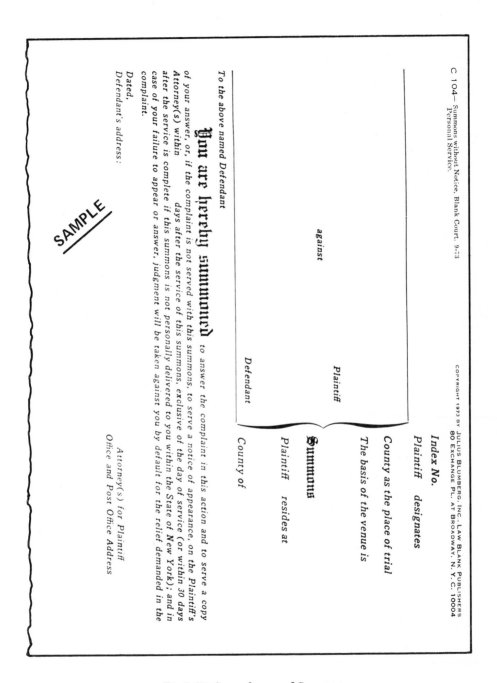

C 104— Summons without Notice, Blank Court. 9–73
Personal Service.

COPYRIGHT 1973 BY JULIUS BLUMBERG, INC.; LAW BLANK PUBLISHERS
80 EXCHANGE PL. AT BROADWAY, N. Y. C. 10004

Index No.

Plaintiff   designates

County as the place of trial

The basis of the venue is

against

𝔖𝔲𝔪𝔪𝔬𝔫𝔰

Plaintiff

Plaintiff   resides at

Defendant

County of

To the above named Defendant

𝔜𝔬𝔲 𝔞𝔯𝔢 𝔥𝔢𝔯𝔢𝔟𝔶 𝔰𝔲𝔪𝔪𝔬𝔫𝔢𝔡 to answer the complaint in this action and to serve a copy
of your answer, or, if the complaint is not served with this summons, to serve a notice of appearance, on the Plaintiff's
Attorney(s) within   days after the service of this summons, exclusive of the day of service (or within 30 days
after the service is complete if this summons is not personally delivered to you within the State of New York); and in
case of your failure to appear or answer, judgment will be taken against you by default for the relief demanded in the
complaint.

Dated,
Defendant's address:

SAMPLE

Attorney(s) for Plaintiff
Office and Post Office Address

Fig 2-4B Second page of Summons
(Form available from Julius Blumberg, Inc., 80 Exchange Place, NYC 10004.)

To determine the amount of damages, Squires must calculate the sum of money necessary to repay him for his loss. He was not able to buy corn from another seller because of the shortage. Since there was no corn, he was not able to produce a corn-based cereal for sale to consumers. He incurred other expenses in attempting to buy more corn from another source. He also had other contracts that he was forced to break because he did not receive the corn. Squires has calculated his damages to be $20,000. This sum is stated in the complaint. It may happen that the jury will award a lesser sum in damages should Squires win the suit, but the jury cannot award more than $20,000.

Once Morse receives the summons and complaint, he must take steps to answer Squires' allegations. He must do this in a given period of time as stated in the summons (usually twenty to thirty days), or he will not be allowed to participate in the suit. In this situation, the proceedings would he held without him. Morse's attorney then drafts an answer. Legally, an *answer* is a way by which a defendant resists a plaintiff's demands. This is done by either denying various statements in the complaint, or by introducing new matter that the plaintiff has not mentioned in the complaint.

In his answer, Morse alleges that the contract is not enforceable because the two parties had an understanding that if the price of corn rose above a certain price because of a shortage, Morse would not have to sell at the lower price. Morse would also like to dispute lost profits to Squires as part of the damages.

Morse's two claims seem inconsistent. The first states that there is no enforceable contract because the price of corn rose so dramatically. The second claim states that there is a contract, but that Morse does not owe Squires $20,000. The inconsistent statements do not hurt Morse's chances in the suit, because it is so early in the proceedings. At this point, Morse has not had an opportunity to fully investigate Squire's claim.

Morse sends a copy of the answer to Squires who sends a reply to Morse's claims. In a legal sense, a *reply* is an answer to allegations that a defendant (in this case, Morse) has made. All of the paper that has passed back and forth thus far are collectively known as the *pleadings.*

Discovery

The next step involves a period of *discovery* during which both parties exchange information which was previously unknown. Morse may want a more complete itemization of damages or proof that Squires is now liable for other contracts because the corn was not delivered. This discovery period cuts down on surprises during the trial; better prepares the parties to *litigate* (try in court) the suit; and gives the parties a chance to assess their respective claims.

The Trial

When the case is ready for trial, it is placed on the court calendar. It is not unusual for cases to go to trial three or more years after the suit was begun. In this case, there is a right to a trial by jury if either party desires one. When the case comes to trial, the jury is chosen and the case begins.

A *trial* is a process of proving claims. Witnesses are called and evidence which tends to substantiate contentions of both parties is offered. The jury listens to all the evidence and decides questions of fact, such as whether a contract was broken and the amount of damages, based on the evidence they have seen and heard.

Plaintiff presents evidence in an attempt to prove the existence of the contract; in this case, the order blank. He also brings in witnesses to establish his damages. Defendant has the opportunity to cross-examine any of plaintiff's witnesses. When the plaintiff thinks he has established his case, he rests. By *resting* the case, the party is saying in effect that he has presented all the evidence that he intends to offer at that stage of the trial.

Defendant then presents his case. This may consist of calling the plaintiff's evidence into question and proving his claim that there was no contract. Plaintiff then has an opportunity to cross-examine the defendant's witnesses. When all of his evidence is presented, the defendant rests his case. Generally, all the examining and cross-examining is done by the attorneys for both parties.

The judge then instructs the jury on the laws which apply specifically to the case. It is the task of the jury to search out the facts. The jury then leaves the courtroom to *deliberate* — talk about what they have seen and heard, weigh the evidence, and make a decision. A decision in favor of plaintiff includes a dollar amount representing the damages owed by defendant to plaintiff.

SELF-EVALUATION

Provide a brief explanation for each of the following.

1. How is the word *court* used in three different ways as a legal term?

2. How does subject matter jursidiction differ from personal jurisdiction?

3. Jones loses his case in court. A month later, certain new facts come to light. Can he bring his case to a court of appeals on the basis of the new facts? Why or why not?

4. How do federal judges obtain their positions? What types of judges are sometimes elected?

5. How was the federal court system established?

6. How many U.S. Courts of Appeal are there? How many U.S. District Courts?

7. How does concurrent jurisdiction differ from exclusive jurisdiction?

8. How many judges sit on the U.S. Supreme Court?

9. What steps must be taken for a case from a state trial court to reach the U.S. Supreme Court?

10. Smith commits a federal crime in her home state and does not leave her state after the crime is committed. Which court has jurisdiction over the case? Why?

11. Why can a trial in an inferior court not be brought to a court of appeals?

12. Are a summons and a complaint the same thing? Explain any difference between the two.

13. In a court case, which party submits an answer? Which party submits a reply?

14. What are the pleadings of a case?

15. What does the discovery period during preparation of a court case involve?

16. In a civil case in which damages are involved, who is responsible for deciding the amount of damages to be awarded once the case is in trial? Can this amount be more or less than the figure submitted by plaintiff?

17. Why is the sample case given in the chapter (*Squires* v. *Morse*) a civil case?

18. In what federal circuit are you now located?

Section 2

Contracts

An *agreement* is defined as a state of being in accord, or being of one mind. People enter into agreements every day. These may range from a mutual understanding to a binding obligation. Some agreements into which people enter daily are social agreements. For example, a person may invite a friend to dinner. The guest accepts the invitation and a date and time are arranged. This type of agreement is a mutual understanding and neither party intends that it be legally binding.

Agreements generally involve an exchange of promises. The person who makes the promise is the *promisor;* the one to whom the promise is made is the *promisee.* Almost every phase of business depends on these promises.

Example. A bank agrees to loan a manufacturer money to produce a new product. A retail firm agrees to buy the product from the manufacturer for a certain price. Finally, a consumer promises to pay for that item when the retailer delivers it. Each of the transactions in this chain of business events involves an exchange of promises.

The type of agreement used in business dealings is known as a *contract*. A contract is a promise or set of promises relating to business transactions, voluntarily made by the parties involved. It is usually enforceable in a court of law. Contracts are used for bank loans, for hiring employees, for performing services, and for manufacturing products.

The chart below is a basic illustration of how law can be divided into two categories, public law and private law, and some of the types of law that are included under each heading. For example, a crime is an unlawful act that is a threat to society as a whole and thus is classified under *public law*. A murderer may kill an individual, but it is the state that is responsible for arresting and bringing the offender to trial. Other examples of public law as shown on the chart include regulations of administrative agencies as described in Chapter 1 and any other laws that are designed to regulate the relationship between the individual and the state, local, and federal governments.

Private law, on the other hand, involves the relationship between individuals. Most of the business transactions discussed in this text concern the area of private law. The chart shows contract law as the first of the subdivisions under private law.

There are several different types of contracts that may be used by business people. They all require certain elements to make them legal. This section explains various types of contracts, how they are made, and how they are terminated, or ended.

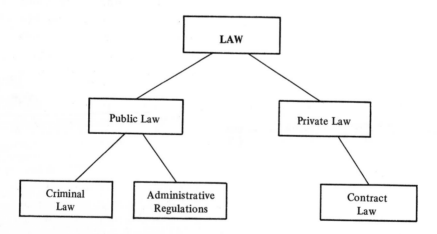

Chapter 3

Types of Contracts

OBJECTIVES

After studying this chapter, the student will be able to

- list and explain five classifications of contracts.
- explain the reason for, and requirements of, the statute of frauds.
- outline the statute of limitations.
- define the following words and phrases.

agreement	Types of Contracts:
social agreement	formal and simple
promisor	unilateral and bilateral
promisee	express, implied, and quasi
contract	valid, void, voidable, and
seal	unenforceable
Statute of Frauds	executed and executory
fraudulent	
perjury	
real property	
lease	
executor	
memorandum	
statute of limitations	

TYPES OF CONTRACTS

Legal agreements used in business can be divided into five categories, with distinct features in each of the groups. The categories include formal and simple contracts; unilateral and bilateral contracts; express and implied contracts; valid, void, voidable, and unenforceable contracts; and executed and executory contracts.

Formal and Simple Contracts

A *formal contract* is in written form. At one time, formal contracts required a seal. In England and early America, the seal was a wax impression. Seals were placed on documents to serve as a person's signature. Seals used today are usually embossed directly into the paper, figure 3-1.

According to the UCC (Uniform Commercial Code), a seal is no longer required to make contracts enforceable. Instead, courts accept several substitutes for the seal on a formal document. The word *seal* may appear, or the letters *L.S.* (representing Latin words meaning *place of seal*) may be placed after the signature. Documents having a seal or one of its substitutes are referred to as being *under seal.* These include deeds for land, leases, and stock certificates.

Simple contracts are not under seal. They may be oral or written. Most of the contracts discussed in this section are classified as simple contracts.

Fig. 3-1 The official seal of the Supreme Court of the United States

Unilateral and Bilateral Contracts

In a *unilateral contract,* one party makes a promise and desires an act or performance, rather than a promise, in return from another party.

Example. Robin McCarthy offers a reward of fifty dollars to anyone finding her watch. Brad Summers returns the watch and collects the fifty dollars. Robin has made a promise and expects an act to be performed; Brad performs the act. This is a unilateral contract.

A unilateral contract is a one-way contract in that there is only one promise. There is no contract until the act has been fully performed.

Case Example. The following case is taken from English law, but has been used as a precedent for contract cases in American law. Carlill won the case in the lower courts. This is the opinion of three judges at the appeal. The original decision was upheld. Notice that the contract involved is a unilateral one. What was the promise and by whom was it made? What acts constituted performance by the promisee?

CARLILL v. CARBOLIC SMOKE BALL CO.
Court of Appeal, 1893
1 Q.B. 256

The defendants, who were the proprietors and vendors of a medical preparation called the Carbolic Smoke Ball, inserted in the *Pall Mall Gazette* of November 13, 1891, and in other newspapers, the following advertisement:" 100 £ [100 pounds in English currency] reward will be paid by the Carbolic Smoke Ball Company to any person who contracts the increasing epidemic influenza, colds, or any disease caused by taking cold, after having used the ball three times daily for two weeks according to the printed directions supplied with each ball. 100 £ is deposited with the Alliance Bank, Regent Street, showing our sincerity in the matter.

"During the last epidemic of influenza many thousand carbolic smoke balls were sold as preventives against this disease, and in no ascertained case was the disease contracted by those using the carbolic smoke ball.

"One carbolic smoke ball will last a family several months, making it the cheapest remedy in the world at the price 10s. [10 shillings], post free. The ball can be refilled at a cost of 5s. Address, Carbolic Smoke Ball Company, 27 Princess Street, Hanover Square, London."

The plaintiff, a lady, on the faith of this advertisement, bought one of the balls at a chemist's, and used it as directed, three times a day, from November 20, 1891, to January 17, 1892, when she was attacked by influenza. Hawkins, J. [Judge], held that she was entitled to recover the 100 £. The defendants appealed.

LINDLEY, L.J. . . .The first observation I will make is that we are not dealing with any inference of fact. We are dealing with an express promise to pay 100 £ in certain events. Read the advertisement how you will, and twist it about as you will, here is a distinct promise expressed in language which is perfectly unmistakable — "100 £ reward will be paid by the Carbolic Smoke Ball Company to any person who contracts the influenza after having used the ball three times daily for two weeks according to the printed directions supplied with each ball."

We must first consider whether this was intended to be a promise at all, or whether it was a mere puff which meant nothing. Was it a mere puff? My answer to that question is No, and I base my answer upon this passage: "100 £ is deposited with the Alliance Bank, showing our sincerity in the matter." Now, for what was that money deposited or that statement made except to negative the suggestion that this was a mere puff and meant nothing at all? The deposit is called in aid by the advertiser as proof of his sincerity in the matter — that is, the sincerity of his promise to pay this 100 £ in the event which he has specified. I say this for the purpose of giving point to the observation that we are not inferring a promise; there is the promise, as plain as words can make it.

Then it is contended that it [the promise] is not binding. In the first place, it is said that it is not made with anybody in particular. Now that point is common to the words of this advertisement and to the words of all other advertisements offering rewards. They are offers to anybody who performs the conditions named in the advertisement, and anybody who does perform the condition accepts the offer. In point of law this advertisement is an offer to pay 100 £ to anybody who will perform these conditions, and the performance of the conditions is the acceptance of the offer.

We, therefore, find here all the elements which are necessary to form a binding contract enforceable in point of law, subject to two observations. First of all it is said that this advertisement is so vague that you cannot really construe it as a promise — that the vagueness of the language shows that a legal promise was never intended or contemplated. The language is vague and uncertain in some respects, and particularly in this, that the 100 £ is to be paid to any person who contracts the increasing epidemic after having used the balls three times daily for two weeks. It is said, When are they to be used? According to the language of the advertisement no time is fixed, and, construing the offer most strongly against the person who has made it, one might infer that any time was meant. I do not think that was meant, and to hold the contrary would be pushing too far the doctrine of taking language most strongly against the person using it. I do not think that business people or reasonable people would understand the words as meaning that if you took a smoke ball and used it three times daily for two weeks you were to be guaranteed against influenza for the rest of your life, and I think it would be pushing the language of the advertisement too far to construe it as meaning that. But if it does not mean that, what does it mean? It is for the defendants to show what it does mean: and it strikes me that there are two, and possibly three, reasonable constructions to be put on this advertisement, any one of which will answer the purpose of the plaintiff. Possibly it may be limited to persons catching the "increasing epidemic" (that is, the then prevailing epidemic), or any colds or disease caused by taking cold, during the prevalence of the increasing epidemic. That is one suggestion, but it does not commend itself to me. Another suggested meaning is that you are warranted free from catching this epidemic, or colds or other diseases caused by taking cold, whilst you are using this remedy after using it for two weeks. If that is the meaning, plaintiff is right, for she used the remedy for two weeks and went on using it till she got the epidemic. Another meaning, and the one which I rather prefer, is that the reward is offered to any person who contracts the epidemic or other disease within a reasonable time after using the smoke ball. Then it is asked, What is a reasonable time? It has been suggested that there is no standard of reasonableness; that it depends upon the reasonable time for a germ to develop! I do not feel pressed by that. It strikes me that a reasonable time may be ascertained in a business sense and in a sense satisfactory to a lawyer, in this way; find out from a chemist what the ingredients are; find out from a skilled physician how long the effect of such ingredients on the system could be reasonably expected to endure so as to protect a person from an epidemic or cold, and in that way you will get a standard to be laid before the jury, or a judge without a jury, by which they might exercise their judgement as to what a reasonable time would be. It strikes me, I confess, that the true construction of this advertisement is that 100 £ will be paid to anybody who uses this smoke ball three times daily for two weeks according to the printed directions, and who gets influenza or cold or other diseases caused by taking cold within a reasonable time after using it; and if that is the true construction, it is time enough for the plaintiff. . . .

It appears to me, therefore, that the defendants must perform their promise, and, if they have been so unwary as to expose themselves to a great many actions, so much the worse for them.

BOWEN, L.J. I am of the same opinion.

. . .One cannot doubt that, as an ordinary rule of law, an acceptance of an offer made ought to be notified to the person who makes the offer, in order that the two minds may come together.

•   •   •

[However,] if the person making the offer, expressly or impliedly intimates in his offer that it will be sufficient to act on the proposal without communicating acceptance of it to himself, performance of the condition is a sufficient acceptance without notification.

Now, if that is the law, how are we to find out whether the person who makes the offer does intimate that notification of acceptance will not be necessary in order to constitute a binding bargain? In many cases you look to the offer itself. In many cases you extract from the character of the transaction that notification is not required, and in the advertisement cases it seems to me to follow as an inference to be drawn from the transaction itself that a person is not to notify his acceptance of the offer before he performs the condition, but that if he performs the condition notification is dispensed with. It seems to me that from the point of view of common sense no other idea could be entertained. If I advertise to the world that my dog is lost, and that anybody who brings the dog to a particular place will be paid some money, are all the police or other persons whose business it is to find lost dogs to be expected to sit down and write me a note saying that they have accepted my proposal? Why, of course, they at once look after the dog, and as soon as they find the dog they have performed the condition. The essence of the transaction is that the dog should be found, and it is not necessary under such circumstances, as it seems to me, that in order to make the contract binding there should be any notification of acceptance. It follows from the nature of the thing that the performance of the condition is sufficient acceptance without the notification of it, and a person who makes an offer in an advertisement of that kind makes an offer which must be read by the light of that common sense reflection. He does, therefore, in his offer impliedly indicate that he does not require notification of the acceptance of the offer.

•   •   •

A.L. SMITH, L.J. It was argued that if the advertisement constituted an offer which might culminate in a contract if it was accepted, and its conditions performed, yet it was not accepted by the plaintiff in the manner contemplated, and that the offer contemplated was such that notice of the acceptance had to be given by the party using the carbolic ball to the defendants before used, so that the defendants might be at liberty to superintend the experiment. All I can say is, that there is no such clause in the advertisement, and that in my judgment, no such clause can be read into it; and I entirely agree with what has fallen from my Brothers, that this is one of those cases in which a performance of the condition by using these smoke balls for two weeks three times a day is an acceptance of the offer.

Lastly, it was said that there was no consideration, and that it was nudum pactum. There are two considerations here. One is the consideration of the inconvenience of having to use this carbolic smoke ball for two weeks three times a day; and the other more important consideration is the money gain likely to accrue to the defendants by the enhanced sale of the smoke balls, by reason of the plaintiff's use of them. There is ample consideration to support this promise. I have only to add that as regards the policy and the wagering points, in my judgment, there is nothing in either of them.

Appeal dismissed.

In a *bilateral contract,* both parties make a promise. Both are binding themselves to certain performances. This is usually a more effective type of contract than the unilateral, since both parties have an obligation. The unilateral contract needs performance of an act in order for the contract to exist. The promisor could retract the promise before the act was completed. In the bilateral contract, the contract comes into existence when both parties exchange promises.

Example. Mr. Barton agrees to paint Mrs. Lorrison's house. Mrs. Lorrison agrees to pay Mr. Barton $400. (Both parties have made a promise.)

Example. Mr. Homeowner says to the nurseryman, "I will pay you seventy-five dollars to deliver and plant a ten-foot Norway spruce on the left corner of my property." Mr. Nurseryman says, "I will deliver and plant the spruce exactly where you want it." (A promise is made by both parties.)

Express and Implied Contracts

In an *express contract,* the terms are clearly stated or expressed, and both parties intend to carry out the terms. Express contracts

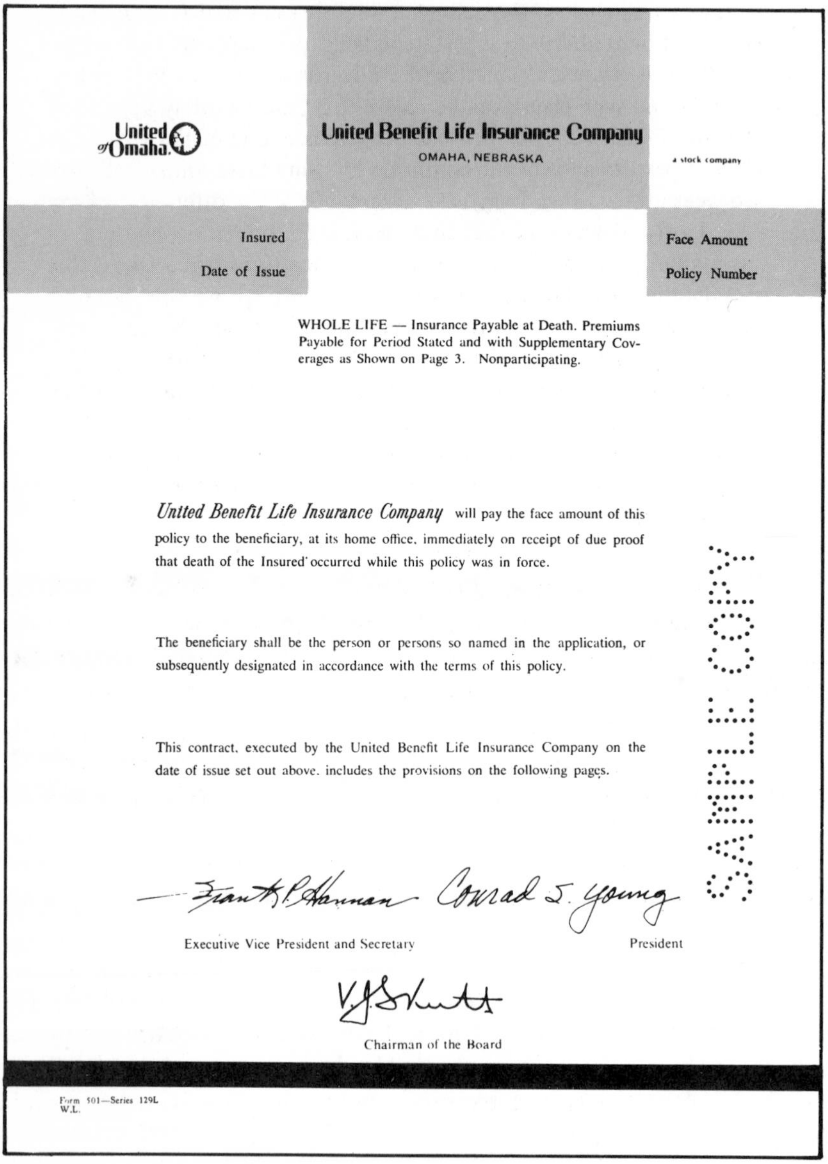

United of Omaha

United Benefit Life Insurance Company

OMAHA, NEBRASKA

a stock company

Insured

Date of Issue

Face Amount

Policy Number

WHOLE LIFE — Insurance Payable at Death. Premiums Payable for Period Stated and with Supplementary Coverages as Shown on Page 3. Nonparticipating.

United Benefit Life Insurance Company will pay the face amount of this policy to the beneficiary, at its home office, immediately on receipt of due proof that death of the Insured occurred while this policy was in force.

The beneficiary shall be the person or persons so named in the application, or subsequently designated in accordance with the terms of this policy.

This contract, executed by the United Benefit Life Insurance Company on the date of issue set out above, includes the provisions on the following pages.

SAMPLE COPY

Executive Vice President and Secretary

President

Chairman of the Board

Form 501—Series 129L
W.L.

Fig. 3-2 Insurance policies are express contracts

may be oral or written. Most simple contracts are made by such express agreement, including insurance policies and purchase and sale agreements, figure 3-2.

In an *implied contract,* promises are not stated directly by the parties. Instead, their acts or conduct only suggest that they are both in agreement.

Example. A driveway contractor mistakenly brings all his workers, materials, and equipment to Mr. Costanza's home and proceeds to put in a completely new tarred driveway. Actually, the job was ordered by the homeowner next door. Mr. Costanza watches from inside all day and makes no attempt to stop the workers. Legally, Costanza must pay a reasonable amount for the driveway. (There is an implied contract since the conduct of each suggests agreement.)

Example. Mrs. Henderson goes to a beauty shop where her hair is washed and set by the owner. When the job is complete, she must pay the amount due to the owner. (An implied contract exists since the conduct of each party suggests agreement.)

A *quasi-contract* is a type of implied contract. The phrase *quasi-contract* means *as if there were a contract.* Actually, a quasi-contract is not a true contract, but, rather, one created by law. There may be a quasi-contract when one party has money or property that belongs to another, or when one party confers a benefit on another party when there was no actual contract made. In these cases, the court rules that a contract was implied and in this way attempts to administer justice to the innocent party. A person who pays out a certain amount of money because of an error in facts may be able to recover the sum or part of it if the court decides the case based on a quasi-contract.

Example. An elderly man moves in with his child and promises to remember the child in his will. After the man's death, the will is read and there is no special provision for the child. The child may recover reasonable expenses of caring for the man based on a quasi-contract, even though no actual contract exists.

Valid, Void, Voidable, and Unenforceable Contracts

A *valid contract* has all the requirements of a legal contract and is enforceable in court. Most contracts are valid contracts.

A *void contract,* on the other hand, is illegal or contrary to public policy and simply has no legal effect. Neither party is bound to perform. Contracts to commit murder or involving illegal gambling are void, since they involve breaking a law.

Example. A and B make a bet on the Super Bowl football game in a state where gambling is against the law. B wins the bet and A refuses to pay. B is not able to bring an action against A in a court of law since a void contract, a contract which required the breaking of a law, is involved.

A *voidable contract* binds one party to a contract but allows the other party the choice of either carrying out the agreement or withdrawing from it without liability. There may be several reasons why there would be a right to withdraw from the contract. The party may have been under legal age or mentally incapable when the contract was signed. A party also may withdraw if a contract was obtained by any one of several *fraudulent* (dishonest) methods.

Example. Martin's Marina sells a boat to Pete Fish, who is seventeen years old. Pete promises to pay for the boat in twelve monthly payments. After ten months, Pete has no more money. He asks Martin's to return his money, saying that he will return the unused boat. If the Marina refuses and action is brought, the court would require the Marina to return the money to Pete. (Pete was under the legal age when he signed the contract, so the contract was voidable — he could keep the agreement or not, and he chose not to.)

Example. The Hammons sell their home to the Rays. The Hammons clearly state that the basement was dry during the ten years they had owned the home. After the Rays live in the house a short time, the basement begins leaking profusely. Close examination reveals watermarks from many previous basement floodings. The Rays sue the Hammons. The Rays are awarded the money they had paid and return the house to the Hammons. (The original contract of sale was voidable due to the fraudulent statement that the basement did not leak.)

An *unenforceable contract* cannot be enforced in a court of law for any one of several reasons. For example, the contract may not meet legal requirements, such as a contract made orally that is required by law to be in writing. An unenforceable contract can still be a legal contract. If both parties realize that their oral contract is not enforceable in court, they can still make a contract, complete it, and have a legal agreement. *Unenforceable* means only that the contract cannot be enforced in court.

Executed and Executory Contracts

A contract is *executed* when all the terms have been fulfilled by both parties. There is nothing else to be done; the transaction is completed.

Example. A meat market agrees to deliver beef to a restaurant at a certain price. The meat is delivered and the restaurant pays for it. This illustrates an executed contract since the promises were fulfilled and the transaction is completed.

An *executory contract* is a contract that has not yet been completed or fulfilled. One party may have completed its part of the contract, while the other party has not. In such cases, the first party's side of the contract is executed, or completed; the second party's side is executory, or unfulfilled.

Example. In the example above, the meat market has delivered the beef to the restaurant, but the restaurant has not yet paid for it. Therefore, the contract is executed by the market and executory on the restaurant.

Each party may still have some part of the contract terms to perform. In that case, the contract is executory on both sides.

Example. The meat market in the example above delivered half of the beef one day and is going to deliver the rest the next day. The restaurant pays for the half it receives the first day. The contract is considered executory at this point, since all of the meat has not yet been delivered and complete payment has not been made.

ORAL AND WRITTEN CONTRACTS

As stated earlier, simple contracts can be either oral or written and still be valid. In early English law, most contracts were made orally since many people could not read or write. This presented problems for courts when hearing cases in which the only evidence was based on promises that were made orally. There were many fraudulent claims made by parties that were almost impossible to prove. There was also perjury in many cases, which made accurate decisions difficult. *Perjury* is committed when a false statement is made under oath.

Example. A wife claims that her husband, who has recently died, had promised her all of his money. The man's brother claims that he has been promised half of the money. With no written proof, it is merely the word of the wife against the word of the brother.

To correct these abuses, a law called the Act for the Prevention of Frauds and Perjuries was passed in England in the late 1600s. This act carried over into American law and is used in some form by every state under the name Statute of Frauds.

Statute of Frauds

There is not a uniform Statute of Frauds throughout the United States, but the basic features are included by every state. About 25 percent of the Uniform Commercial Code is related to this important area of contract law.

The most important element of the Statute of Frauds is that it defines certain contracts which must be in writing and signed by the party being bound in order to be enforceable in court. The Statute of Frauds applies only to executory contracts in which performance has not been completed by one or both parties. The requirement of a writing is a technical one, and there is a fear by the courts that parties may try to use the statute of frauds as a defense to a contract action to simply avoid having to perform under a contract. This is possible under certain circumstances.

Example. Valdez and Moleski enter into an oral contract for the sale of real property; both intend to complete the transaction. Valdez makes preparations for purchasing the house by applying for a mortgage and placing his present residence on the market. A few days before the date set for the sale, Moleski finds a second buyer who is willing to pay a higher price, and refuses to sell the house to Valdez. Valdez brings action against Moleski. Moleski, however, has a defense under the Statute of Frauds. Although both parties had originally agreed on the sale, it was merely an oral agreement for the sale of real property — this type of sale requires a writing to be enforceable in court. The missing element of a writing allows Moleski to avoid the sale to Valdez, an action which would not be possible if the subject matter were not real property.

However, if a contract has been performed or partially performed, there can be no claim that the contract should have been in writing. The parties are acting as if they had contracted; their actions are more weighty than the formal requirement of a writing.

For instance, if Valdez and Moleski in the previous example completed the sale without incident, Moleski could not use the statute of frauds to void the contract at a later date. The contract should have been in writing; nonetheless, it was carried out by both parties as if it were. The courts would unnecessarily upset individual agreements if parties were allowed to bring action and have contracts set aside on the minor point of the lack of a writing after contracts have already been performed. If the parties act as if there is a contract in carrying out an agreement, this action is of greater significance to the courts than a formal writing.

These types of contracts, if made orally, are not illegal. They can be oral and executed, and be legal contracts. However, if there is a claim made by one of the parties, the court does not enforce the contract. The key here is being able to enforce the contract in court. Types of contracts or promises included in the Statute are as follows:

1. *A contract that cannot be performed within one year of the date of signing.* Long-term oral contracts can be ineffective since the terms are apt to be forgotten or confused by one or both parties as time passes.

   Example. Mr. Davidson, a motel owner, talks with a local contractor, Jeff Samuels, about adding on a wing to his motel for a certain price. Samuels agrees to take the job and estimates it will take eighteen months to complete. There should be a written contract, since the job will take longer than one year.

2. *Contracts for the Sale or Lease of Real Property. Real property* is land and/or anything attached to it, such as buildings, growing trees or crops, and minerals. When *leases* (rental agreements) are for a time period of more than one year, they must be in writing, according to the Statute.

    Example. Phillips orally agrees to sell his lakeside cabin to a neighbor for $18,000. Before he is paid, Phillips changes his mind. The neighbor brings action against Phillips to force him to carry out the agreement. The court does not enforce the neighbor's claim because it was an oral agreement for the sale of real property.

    Example. The Midstate Paper Company agrees to lease 2,000 acres of property belonging to Shea for three years. The company agrees to pay Shea a certain sum of money for lumber cut from live timber on that land. A written contract should be drawn up for two reasons; the contract is for longer than one year, and the company is leasing real property in the form of live trees.

3. *Promises to Pay the Debts of Another.* Business people often agree to pay the debts of another person. This exchange of an obligation must be in writing to be enforceable.

    Example. Bob visits a store with his employer, Dick, to buy a set of tires for Bob's car. Dick tells the clerk that if Bob cannot make all six payments, he, Dick, will make them. Unless this promise is expressed in writing and Dick signs it, the store cannot collect from Dick through the courts at a later time.

4. *Promises of Executors.* An *executor* is a person who handles the estate of an individual who has died. For example, the deceased may have debts that must be paid with money from the estate; the executor would see that this is done. The executor may promise a company to whom the estate owes money that the amount will be taken from the executor's own personal account, if necessary. This does not occur very frequently but when it does, the contract should be in writing and signed by the executor if the company expects to collect through a court action.

5. *Contracts in Consideration of Marriage.* This involves a promise by one party to give another party something of value if they marry. Although this is not commonly done today, historically, the promising of dowries was an important part of marriage plans.

Example. John agrees to give Mary a new car if she agrees to marry him. If Mary wants to be able to enforce this promise in a court of law after the marriage, she must have John's promise in writing and signed by him.

6. *Sale of a Specified Value.* The Statute of Frauds states that an agreement for the sale of goods over a certain value must be in

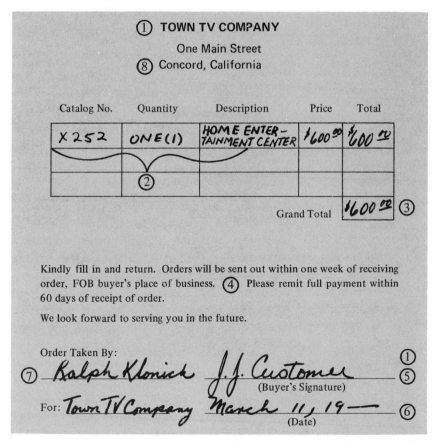

Fig. 3-3 An order blank: one type of memorandum. This form could serve as a legal writing in court, forcing the customer to pay for the article.

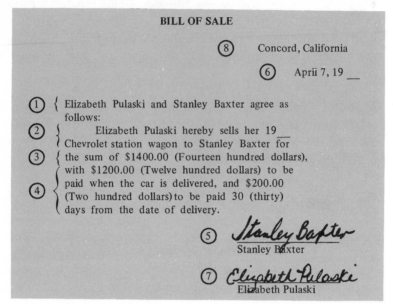

Fig. 3-4 A Bill of Sale: One type of memorandum

writing and signed by the person who is bound by the contract. The UCC restates this requirement, specifying $500 as the amount over which there must be a signed, written agreement for the sale of goods.

Example. A customer signs an order for a $600 home entertainment center from Town TV Company. Since the order is for more than $500, according to the UCC there must be a writing signed by the party purchasing the set. If the customer refuses to accept the unit and pay for it when it arrives, the order blank with the customer's signature could serve as a writing.

Under the UCC, the writing may take the form of an informal note or *memorandum.* Figure 3-3 illustrates a memorandum that would be applicable in the example concerning the promise to purchase the home entertainment center. Figure 3-4 is another type of memorandum, a bill of sale for a car. The requirements for memorandums, indicated in both illustrations by number, are: (1) the names of both parties; (2) the subject matter; (3) the price to be paid; (4) credit terms if any; and (5) the signature of the party assuming the obligation.   Other items, although not required, are generally included as a matter of common practice. These include: (6) the date; (7) the signature of the other party; and (8) the place where the memorandum was written.

Statute of Limitations

The *statute of limitations* sets a time limit regarding when an action can be brought by one party against another party, concerning a particular contract between the two. When the time limit expires, the contract becomes unenforceable in court. Every state has such statutes, although the time period varies from state to state, usually four to ten years.

Example. Mrs. Homeowner buys carpeting from a local store and signs a six-month contract to pay for it. She does not pay. The store must bring an action to collect within the time period of the statute of limitations in that state. If the state had a six-year limitation, the store could not wait for seven years after the breach and still expect to collect. The contract becomes unenforceable after six years.

In the previous situation, the time period starts from the end of the six months when the last payment was due but unpaid. If a payment is made after the last payment is due but within the statute period, a new statute period begins from the date of the payment.

Example. Harry borrows $200 from Don on July 2, 1976, and promises to pay it back in full in one year, on July 2, 1977. On the due date, Harry has paid nothing. Using the six-year statute period, Don has until July 1, 1983 to bring an action to collect the money. Presume, however, that Harry pays $100 on July 2, 1980. Don now has six years from that date, or until July 1, 1986, to bring action to collect the remaining $100.

SELF-EVALUATION

1. Identify the types of contracts in Column A by matching each one with the proper item(s) in Column B.

A	B
1) void contract	a) enforceable in court
2) valid contract	b) only one party is bound
3) voidable contract	c) is not enforceable in court
4) unenforceable contract	d) illegal contract

Provide a brief explanation for each of the following.

2. What is a contract?

3. What type of contract contains some form of seal or its equivalent?

4. How does a bilateral contract differ from a unilateral contract?

5. In *Carlill* v. *Carbolic Smoke Ball Co.,* what type of contract is under discussion? Explain.

6. What type of contract occurs when the acts of both parties suggest that they are in agreement?

7. Who issues a quasi-contract? When is it issued?

8. What is a contract that has been fulfilled by both parties known as?

9. What is the major purpose of the Statute of Frauds?

10. List four types of contracts that must be in writing as outlined in the Statute of Frauds.

11. What are the five elements that a memorandum must contain?

12. What is the purpose of the statute of limitations?

13. Provide a definition for: fraudulent, perjury, real property, promisor.

SUGGESTED ACTIVITY

1. Extract several examples of unilateral contracts from a newspaper for class discussion.

CASES FOR STUDY

1. *A* agrees to purchase $1,000 worth of stereo equipment from *B*. *A* and *B* live in different states so they communicate by mail. The contents of the letters mention the brand and style of the equipment and the price which has been agreed upon. Can *A* avoid the contract because no formal written contract was ever signed by both parties?

2. Fredericks purchases land from Grainer and the deed is transferred (given to Fredericks). The contract to purchase is never written, but the deal is closed anyway. Can either Fredericks or Grainer cancel the sale at a later time?

Chapter 4

Requirements of a Legal Contract

OBJECTIVES

After studying this chapter, the student will be able to
- list and explain the six legal requirements of a contract.
- define the following words and phrases.

binding contract	correspondence
offer	mutual assent
offeror	consideration
offeree	pre-existing obligation
intent	competent
bid	minor
certainty of terms	age of majority
termination	ratify
revocation	cosign
lapse of time	legal purpose
intervening illegality	usury
rejection	usurious
counteroffer	option
acceptance	

There are six elements that must be present to make a contract binding on all parties. In a *binding* contract, all parties must legally carry out their obligations.

The first two elements, the offer and the acceptance, together form the third element, mutual assent. When an offer is made by one party and an acceptance of that offer is made by the other party, there is *mutual assent,* or agreement by both parties. The final creation of the contract then relies on the presence of the other three elements, consideration, competent parties, and legal purpose. If a contract falls within the Statute of Frauds, a seventh element, a writing (discussed in Chapter 3), might be involved.

OFFER

The offer is the first step in the creation of a binding contract. An *offer* is a promise by one person to do something upon the acceptance of the terms by the other person involved. The party making the offer is the *offeror;* the party to whom the offer is made is the *offeree.*

There are three items for which courts look to determine whether or not an offer has in fact been made: intent, certainty of terms, and communication.

Intent

The offeror must *intend* (mean) to make the offer to the offeree.   It must be an offer made in good faith, not as a joke; and the parties must intend that their promises could be enforced by law.

Example.   After his new car had suffered several breakdowns, Dan became very disgusted with his purchase.   While in a service station, he said to the owner, "For two cents, I'd sell this car."   The station owner replied, "I'll take it!"   There was obviously no real intent on Dan's part to sell the car for two cents, so this is not considered an offer to sell.   There is no basis for a contract here.

Case Example.   In this appeal, the judgment was in favor of the defendant, the husband.   The element of intent is the major factor in the decision.

BALFOUR v. BALFOUR
Court of Appeal (1919)
2 K.B. 271.

The plaintiff sued the defendant (her husband) for money which she claimed to be due in respect of an agreed allowance of 30 £ [30 pounds, English currency] a month.   The alleged agreement was entered into under the following circumstances.   The parties were married in August, 1900.   The husband, a civil engineer, had a post under the Government of Ceylon as Director of Irrigation, and after the marriage he and his wife went to Ceylon, and lived there together until the year 1915, except that in 1906 they paid a short visit to this country, and in 1908 the wife came to England in order to undergo an operation, after which she returned to Ceylon.   In November, 1915, she came to this country with her husband, who was on leave. They remained in England until August 1916, when the husband's leave was up and he had to return. The wife however on the doctor's advice remained in England. On August 9, 1916, the husband being about to sail, the alleged parol [oral] agreement sued upon was made. The plaintiff, as appeared from the judge's note, gave the following evidence of what took place: "In August, 1916, defendant's leave was up. I was suffering from rheumatic arthritis. The doctor advised my staying in England for some months, not to go out till November 4. On August 8 my husband sailed. He gave me a cheque from 8th to 31st for 24 £, and promised to give me 30 £ per month till I returned." Later on she said: "My husband and I wrote the figures together on August 8; 34 £ shown. Afterwards he said 30 £." In cross-examination she said that they had not agreed to live apart until subsequent differences arose between them, and that the agreement of August 1916, was one which might be made by a couple in amity. Her husband in consultation with her assessed needs, and said he would send 30 £ per month for her maintenance. She further said that she then understood that the defendant would be returning to England in a few months, but that he afterwards wrote to her suggesting that they had better remain apart. In March, 1918, she commenced proceedings for restitution of conjugal [marital] rights, and on July 30 she obtained a [judgment.] On December 16,·1918, she obtained an order for alimony.

Sargant, J. [Judge] held that the husband was under an obligation to support his wife, and the parties had contracted that the extent of that obligation should be defined in terms of so much a month. The consent of the wife to that arrangement was a sufficient consideration to constitute a contract which could be sued upon.

He accordingly gave judgment for the plaintiff.

The husband appealed.

• • •

WARRINGTON, L.J. Those being the facts we have to say whether there is a legal contract between the parties, in other words, whether what took place between them was in the domain of a contract or whether it was merely a domestic arrangement such as may be made every day between a husband and wife who are living together in friendly intercourse. It may be, and I do not for a moment say that it is not, possible for such a contract as is alleged in the present case to be made between husband and wife. The question is whether such a contract was made. That can only be determined either by proving that it was made in express terms, or that there is a necessary implication from the circumstances of the parties, and the transaction generally, that such a contract was made. It is quite plain that no such contract was made in express terms, and there was no bargain on the part of the wife at all. All that took place was this: The husband and wife met in a friendly way and discussed what would be necessary for her support while she was detained in England, the husband being in Ceylon, and they came to the conclusion that 30 £ a month would be about right, but there is no evidence of any express bargain by the wife that she would in all the circumstances treat that as in satisfaction of the obligation of the husband to maintain her. Can we find a contract from the position of the parties? It seems to me it is quite impossible. If we were to imply such a contract in this case we should be implying on the part of the wife that whatever happened and whatever might be the change of circumstances while the husband was away she should be content with this 30 £ a month, and bind herself by an obligation in law not to require him to pay anything more; and on the other hand we should be implying on the part of the husband a bargain to pay 30 £ a month for some indefinite period whatever might be his circumstances. Then again it seems to me that it would be impossible to make any such implication. The matter really reduces itself to an absurdity when one considers it, because if we were to hold that there was a contract in this case we should have to hold that with regard to all the more or less trivial concerns of life where a wife, at the request of her husband, makes a promise to him that is a promise which can be enforced by law. All I can say is that there is no such contract here. These two people never intended to make a bargain which could be enforced in law. The husband expressed his intention to make this payment, and he promised to make it, and was bound in honour to continue it so long as he was in a position to do so. The wife on the other hand, so far as I can see, made no bargain at all. That is in my opinion sufficient to dispose of the case.

It is unnecessary to consider whether if the husband failed to make the payments the wife could pledge his credit or whether if he failed to make the payments she could have made some other arrangements. The only question we have to consider is whether the wife has made out a contract which she has set out to do. In my opinion she has not.

I think the judgment of Sargant, J. cannot stand, the appeal ought to be allowed and judgment ought to be entered for the defendant.

DUKE, L.J. I agree. This is in some respects an important case, and as we differ from the judgment of the Court below I propose to state concisely my views and the grounds which have led me to the conclusion at which I have arrived. Substantially the question is whether the promise of the husband to the wife that while she is living absent from him he will make her a periodical allowance involves in law a consideration on the part of the wife sufficient to convert that promise into a binding agreement. In my opinion it does not. . . . [We] have to see whether there is evidence of any such exchange of promises as would make the promise of the husband the basis of an agreement. It was strongly argued by Mr. Hawke that the promise being absolute in form ought to be construed as one of the mutual promises which make an agreement. It was said that a promise and an implied undertaking between strangers such as the promise and implied undertaking alleged in this case would have founded an action on contract. That may be so, but it is impossible to disregard in this case what was the basis of the whole communications between the parties under which the alleged contract is said to have been formed. The basis of their communications was their relationship of husband and wife, a relationship which creates certain obligations, but not that which is here put in suit.

· · ·

ATKIN, L.J. The defense to this action on the alleged contract is that the defendant, the husband, entered into no contract with his wife, and for the determination of that it is necessary to remember that there are agreements between parties which do not result in contracts within the meaning of that term in our law. The ordinary example is where two parties agree to take a walk together, or where there is an offer and an acceptance of hospitality. Nobody would suggest in ordinary circumstances that those agreements result in what we know as a contract, and one of the most usual forms of agreement which does not constitute a contract appears to me to be the arrangements which are made between husband and wife. It is quite common, and it is the natural and inevitable result of the relationship of husband and wife, that the two spouses should make arrangements between themselves — agreements such as are in dispute in this action — agreements for allowances, by which the husband agrees that he will pay to his wife a certain sum of money, per week, or per month, or per year, to cover either her own expenses or the necessary expenses of the household and of the children of the marriage, and in which the wife promises either expressly or impliedly to apply the allowance for the purpose for which it is given. To my mind those agreements, or many of them, do not result in contracts at all, and they do not result in contracts even though there may be what as between other parties would constitute consideration for the agreement. The consideration, as we know, may consist either in some right, interest, profit or benefit accruing to one party, or some forbearance, detriment, loss or responsibility given, suffered or undertaken by the other. That is a well-known definition, and it constantly happens, I think that such arrangements made between husband and wife are arrangements in which there are mutual promises, or in which there is consideration of form within the definition that I have mentioned. Nevertheless they are not contracts, and they are not contracts because the parties did not intend that they should be attended by legal consequences. To my mind it would be of the worst possible example to hold that agreements such as this resulted in legal obligations which could be enforced in the Courts. It would mean this, that when the husband makes his wife a promise to give her an allowance of 30s. or 2 £ a week, whatever he can afford to give her, for the maintenance of the household and children, and she promises so to apply it, not only could she sue him for his failure in any week to supply the allowance, but he could sue her for non-performance of the obligation, express or implied, which she had undertaken upon her part. All I can say is that the small Courts of this country would have to be multiplied one hundredfold if these arrangements were held to result in legal obligations. They are not sued upon, not because the parties are reluctant to enforce their legal rights when the agreement is broken, but because the parties, in the inception of the arrangement, never intended that they should be sued upon. Agreements such as these are outside the realm of contracts altogether. The common law does not regulate the form of agreements between spouses. . . . The consideration that really obtains for them is that natural love and affection which counts for so little in these cold Courts. . . . In respect of these promises each house is a domain into which the King's writ does not seek to run, and to which his officers do not seek to be admitted. The only question in this case is whether or not this promise was of such a class or not. For the reasons given by my brethren it appears to me to be plainly established that the promise here was not intended by either party to be attended by legal consequences. I think the onus was upon the plaintiff, and the plaintiff has not established any contract. The parties were living together, the wife intending to return. The suggestion is that the husband bound himself to pay 30 £ a month under all circumstances, and she bound herself to be satisfied with that sum under all circumstances, . . .whatever might be the development of her illness, and in whatever expenses it might involve her. To my mind neither party contemplated such a result. . . .

Appeal allowed.

Some statements which may appear to be offers are not considered by the courts to be the first item comprising a contract. A party may not be intending to make an offer, but only extending an invitation to another party to make an offer. Most advertisements are only invitations to consumers.

Example. A supermarket lists several canned food items on sale for three for one dollar during one specific week. They are not bound by this offer if, for example, they run out of one of the items. This type of advertisement is only inviting the public to purchase the items. The offer in this case is made by a customer who brings the items to the checkout counter.

One form of advertising, the type which states that a reward is to be given for the return of an item, is a legal offer. This type of ad leads to a unilateral contract since it is a promise (the reward) for an act (performing what is necessary to receive the reward). Sometimes, however, an advertisement can be worded in such a way that it does constitute an offer.

Case Example. In the case which follows, the Great Minneapolis Surplus Store, Inc. printed two advertisements that the court determined were offers which were accepted by Mr. Lefkowitz. Compare this case with the *Carbolic Smoke Ball* case in Chapter 3. What do the ads have in common?

LEFKOWITZ v. GREAT MINNEAPOLIS SURPLUS STORE, INC.

Supreme Court of Minnesota, 1957
251 Minn. 188, 86 N.W.2d 689

MURPHY, J.   . . .

This case grows out of the alleged refusal of the defendant to sell to the plaintiff a certain fur piece which it had offered for sale in a newspaper advertisement. It appears from the record that on April 6, 1956, the defendant published the following advertisement in a Minneapolis newspaper:

"Saturday 9 A.M. Sharp
3 Brand New
Fur
Coats
Worth to $100.00
First Come
First Served
$1
Each"

On April 13, the defendant again published an advertisement in the same newspaper as follows:

"Saturday 9 A.M.
2 Brand New Pastel
Mink 3-Skin Scarfs
Selling for $89.50
Out they go
Saturday. Each $1.00
1 Black Lapin Stole
Beautiful,
worth $139.50 . . . .$1.00
First Come
First Served"

. . .[O] n each of the Saturdays following the publication of the above-described ads the plaintiff was the first to present himself at the appropriate counter in the defendant's store and on each occasion demanded the coat and the stole so advertised and indicated his readiness to pay the sale price of $1. On both occasions, the defendant refused to sell the merchandise to the plaintiff, stating on the first occasion that by a "house rule" the offer was intended for women only and sales would not be made to men, and on the second visit that plaintiff knew defendant's house rules.

•   •   •

. . .[T] he trial court held that the value of this article was established and granted judgment in favor of the plaintiff for that amount less the $1 quoted purchase price.

The defendant contends that a newspaper advertisement offering items of merchandise for sale at a named price is a "unilateral offer" which may be withdrawn without notice. He relies upon authorities which hold that, where an advertiser publishes in a newspaper that he has a certain quantity or quality of goods which he wants to dispose of at certain prices and on certain terms, such advertisements are not offers which become contracts as soon as any person to whose notice they may come signifies his acceptance by notifying the other that he will take a certain quantity of them. Such advertisements have been construed as an invitation for an offer of sale on the terms stated, which offer, when received, may be accepted or rejected and which therefore does not become a contract of sale until accepted by the seller; and until a contract has been so made, the seller may modify or revoke such prices or terms. [Citations omitted.]

· · ·

The test of whether a binding obligation may originate in advertisements addressed to the general public is "whether the facts show that some performance was promised in positive terms in return for something requested." [Citation omitted.]

The authorities above cited emphasize that, where the offer is clear, definite, and explicit, and leaves nothing open for negotiation, it constitutes an offer, acceptance of which will complete the contract. . . .

Whether in any individual instance a newspaper advertisement is an offer rather than an invitation to make an offer depends on the legal intention of the parties and the surrounding circumstances. [Citation omitted.] We are of the view on the facts before us that the offer by the defendant of the sale of the Lapin fur was clear, definite, and explicit, and left nothing open for negotiation. The plaintiff having successfully managed to be the first one to appear at the seller's place of business to be served, as requested by the advertisement, and having offered the stated purchase price of the article, he was entitled to performance on the part of the defendant. We think the trial court was correct in holding that there was in the conduct of the parties a sufficient mutuality of obligation to constitute a contract of sale.

The defendant contends that the offer was modified by a "house rule" to the effect that only women were qualified to receive the bargains advertised. The advertisement contained no such restriction. This objection may be disposed of briefly by stating that, while an advertiser has the right at any time before acceptance to modify his offer, he does not have the right, after acceptance, to impose new or arbitrary conditions not contained in the published offer. [Citation omitted.]

Affirmed.

An advertisement for a *bid* (a price for which an individual or a company will do a certain job) is not considered an offer to enter into a contract, but rather an invitation to make offers. Parties then submit bids in reply to the ad. Statutes rather than contract law generally regulate bidding for jobs in most states.

Example. A city has a highway to be resurfaced. They advertise the job in its entirety and ask for firms to send in bids. The lowest responsible bid is usually accepted. However, since a request for bids is only an invitation to an offer, the city is not obligated to take the lowest bid if it is much higher than originally anticipated.

An auctioneer presenting items at auctions for sale to the highest bidder constitutes only an invitation for an offer. This is not considered to be an offer of a contract unless the auction is specifically stated to be "without reserve." (This is outlined by the UCC in its rules for auctions. See § 2-328.)

Certainty of Terms

The courts require that offers be clearly and completely stated. There must be no chance of misunderstanding on the part of the person to whom the offer is made. This is known as *certainty of terms.*

Example.   Williamson owns two sailboats of different sizes and values. He makes an offer to Brown as follows: "I will sell you my sailboat for $450." This is not a proper offer because Brown has no clear understanding of which of the two sailboats Williamson is offering at that price.

Communication

For an offer to be valid, it must be communicated (made known) by the offeror to the offeree. The offeree must be aware that an offer has been made. If an offer is made in a letter, that letter must be received by the offeree before the offer becomes effective. If the letter is lost in the mail, no offer is made. Only the offeree has the right to accept the offer.

Example.   Gonzales offers to sell an item to Henderson. Sheehan, standing nearby, says, "I'll take it!" The offer was not made to Sheehan, so Sheehan has no right to accept. At the same time, Gonzales is not bound to sell the item to Sheehan.

TERMINATION OF AN OFFER

An offer which has been properly communicated to an offeree can be *terminated* (ended) in several ways.

Revocation of the Offer

Generally, an offer can be *revoked* (withdrawn) at any time before it is accepted, with the requirement that proper notice is given to and received by the offeree. Before the adoption of the UCC, this could be done even if the offeror had promised to hold the offer open for a certain period of time, unless the offeree paid additional money for the promise of keeping the offer open for a stated period of time. UCC Section 2-205, which applies to the sale of goods, states that if a merchant offeror promises to keep the offer open, it must be done.

Example. Mary Ann offers to sell Gini her set of golf clubs for fifty dollars and gives her two weeks to decide whether or not to accept the offer. One week after the offer is made and Gini not having accepted, Mary Ann changes her mind. She calls Gini and tells her that she is withdrawing the offer. No offer now exists, since Mary Ann has properly communicated her revocation to Gini. Mary Ann is not in the business of selling golf clubs, and therefore is not considered a merchant. She is not bound by Section 2-205 of the UCC.

In a public offer, such as the offer of a reward listed in a newspaper, it is necessary to provide a public notice of withdrawal which states that the offer is no longer in effect. This is usually done by placing another advertisement. Even if the offeree does not see the withdrawal, the offer is considered to be revoked as soon as the public withdrawal notice appears.

Example. John advertises that a $100 reward will be paid for the return of his dog. A month later, he places another ad withdrawing the offer. Two months later, Harry returns John's dog and attempts to claim the $100 reward. Harry says that he has not seen the second ad revoking the offer. John does not have to pay since his withdrawal was properly made, even though Harry did not see it.

The offeror and the offeree sometimes make an agreement, with all the required elements of a contract, to hold the offer open for a specified period of time. This is known as an *option.* It includes a separate binding element such as payment of money. When an option exists, the offeror cannot revoke the offer until the stated period has expired. The offeror also cannot revoke the offer if it is under seal until the stated period has expired.

Example. Suppose that in the example in which Mary Ann offered her golf clubs to Gini, Gini paid Mary Ann ten dollars to hold the clubs for two weeks. Gini now has an option to purchase the clubs. Mary Ann could not revoke the offer before the two-week period had expired.

Lapse of Time

If an offer has a specified time stated in which it can be accepted and it is not accepted during that time, the offer is said to have *lapsed* (expired) and the offer is terminated. The offer is no longer in effect, and the offeree can no longer act on it.

Example. Mr. Houston offers his lawnmower for sale to Mrs. Mason for fifteen dollars and gives her ten days in which to decide whether or not to accept the offer. In ten days, Mr. Houston hears nothing from Mrs. Mason. The offer to Mrs. Mason has then lapsed.

If the offer does not specify the time within which it must be accepted, the offer lapses after a reasonable amount of time. The court decides what a reasonable time is by taking all the circumstances into consideration.

Example. A offers to sell a carload of bananas at ten cents a pound to a fruit and vegetable dealer. Since bananas are highly destructible and spoil easily, it would not be reasonable for the vendor to assume that the offer will still be open six months from the time at which the agreement was made.

Death or Insanity

An offer is terminated if death or insanity of either the offeror or the offeree occurs before the acceptance is made. When both parties understand and agree to all terms of a contract, there is a *meeting of the minds.* In a case of death or insanity, there can be no meeting of the minds. The death or insanity of one party or the other does not have to be communicated to the other party to end the offer.

Example. On May 20, Margolis offers to rent Johnson her motor home for the summer. On May 29, Johnson sends a letter to Margolis accepting the offer. Johnson is unaware that Margolis has died on May 22. The offer automatically terminates on May 22, even though Johnson has not been notified.

Destruction of Subject Matter

If the subject matter of an offer is destroyed before an acceptance is made, the offer is terminated. No notice of such destruction is required.

Example. On February 3, Mr. Landowner offers to sell the live timber from his property to the Western Lumber Company. On February 4, there is a fire and all of the trees are destroyed. On February 6, the lumber company gives notification of their acceptance. No offer exists on that date, since the subject matter had been destroyed two days earlier.

Intervening Illegality

If the subject matter of an offer becomes illegal between the time of the offer and the acceptance, the offer is terminated. Originally, the offer might have been legal, becoming illegal after the passing of the law. The new law intervenes between the time the offer is made and the acceptance is given, making the offer illegal. (To *intervene* means to come between.)

Example. An insecticide firm offers to sell a certain insecticide to a farmer and dust his crops with it. Before the farmer accepts, there is a law passed banning the use of that insecticide. The offer is automatically terminated.

Rejection by the Offeree

If the offeree rejects the offer, the offer is terminated. The offeree cannot accept that same offer at a later time.

Example. On May 21, Browning offers to sell a book to Harding for five dollars. Upon hearing the offer, Harding refuses it. On May 25, however, Harding changes his mind and says, "I'll take that book for five dollars now." An offer has been made and refused. From that point on, the offer no longer exists. Browning must renew the offer before Harding can accept it.

Counteroffers

When an offeree replies to an offer by making changes in the terms, a *counteroffer* is made. The counteroffer terminates the original offer.

Example. The Daltons offer to sell their home to the Zanes for $30,000. The Zanes accept all the terms, except the price; they offer to pay only $28,000. The Dalton's original offer is terminated. The Zanes have made a counteroffer and can no longer accept the $30,000 offer, unless the offer is remade.

THE ACCEPTANCE OF THE OFFER

The second step in creating a binding contract is the acceptance of the offer by the offeree. In the *acceptance*, the offeree acknowledges the offer and agrees to be bound by its terms. As with the offer, the acceptance must meet certain requirements. Although the UCC has modified some of these requirements concerning the sale of goods, the basic elements of an acceptance are necessary for the other areas of contract law. (See Section 2-207 of the UCC in Appendix.)

Silence and Words or Actions

As a general rule, silence does not indicate acceptance. Acceptance should be communicated to the offeror by words or by actions, according to the terms of the offer.

Example. Brown says to Gray, "I will sell you this truckload of pumpkins for seventy-five dollars if you will pay for it and unload it right now." Gray says, "I will take the truckload. Here is the money. My workers will start unloading it at once." Gray has accepted the offer by his words and by his actions.

One situation in which silence may indicate acceptance occurs when parties have dealt with each other over a period of time, so that their agreements become almost automatic. In these instances, if the offeror makes the usual offer and the offeree does not reject the offer, a contract is formed. (See Section 2-208 in Appendix.)

	OFFER	ACCEPTANCE	WHEN EFFECTIVE
(1)	By mail; no terms	By mail	When acceptance is mailed (Offeree used same method of communication)
(2)	By telegram; no terms	By mail	When received by offeror (Offeree used own method of communication)
(3)	By mail, stating: "Effective when acceptance sent by telegram and received in this office."	By telegram	When received in office of offeror (as per terms)

Fig. 4-1 Correspondence of an acceptance. Assume that all acceptances were made within the stated time limits.

Performance

Acceptance may be indicated by performance. This is done in unilateral contracts; most commonly when an offer of a reward is made.

Example. An individual advertises in a newspaper that a reward will be paid for the return of a lost item. (An offer has been made.) When another party returns the item, the reward is collected. (An acceptance by the performance of the second party.)

Correspondence

There can sometimes be confusion as to the effective date of a contract, especially when the parties are not dealing face to face. If the acceptance requires a return promise, it must be *corresponded* (sent) by some manner to the offeror. The contract itself usually becomes effective and is binding when the acceptance becomes effective.

There are certain ways in which an acceptance can be relayed, figure 4-1. In the table, assume that all acceptances have been made within the specified time limit. In (1), the offer is sent by mail, with no terms regarding how the acceptance should be returned. In such a case, the United States Postal Service becomes the *agent* of (is acting for) the offeror. The offeree has the right to use the same agent for the acceptance. When the acceptance is delivered to that agent, by placing it in a mailbox, it becomes effective. This is known as the mailbox rule. The same rule holds true if the offer is sent by telegram. When the offeree delivers the acceptance to the telegraph office, the acceptance takes effect.

In (2), there are also no terms as to how the acceptance should be returned. The offeree, however, has chosen an agent other than the one used by the offeror. If the acceptance becomes lost in the mail, there is no contract. If the acceptance is delayed in the mail and does not arrive within the stated time, there is no contract.

Since situation (1) and (2) can create misunderstandings, a better way is shown in (3). The offeror is protected by stating clearly how the acceptance must be sent and when the offer becomes effective.

The UCC has altered these correspondence rules to some degree to simplify the process involved in the sale of goods. Section 2-206 allows acceptance in any reasonable manner by any reasonable method. The UCC rules do not apply to all other contracts, however.

MUTUAL ASSENT

If there is an offer and an acceptance which meet all of the requirements, there is *mutual assent,* the next step in the creation of a binding contract. Mutual assent occurs when both parties have had a meeting of the minds; they have voluntarily agreed to all the terms and accepted all the obligations of the contract. There is a contract situation on the condition that the other requirements are met.

CONSIDERATION

All contracts involve promises. In a legal contract, there must be something to bind the promises and act as a basis for enforcement. This binding element, the formation of which is the fourth step in contracting, is known as consideration. *Consideration* is the price that a promisor specifies or demands for the promise. Without consideration, the transaction is a gift from one party to another rather than the exchange situation, which is so essential to contract law.

In this stage of contracting, there is an exchange of values. Each party receives something for something. Consideration may be money, the performance of an act, the refraining from the performance of an act, or the waiver of a legal right. There are several factors involved in consideration.

Adequacy

Legally, the degree of the consideration or its value has no importance. If the parties both agree on a consideration, then it is adequate (sufficient), according to the courts. The courts do not examine the monetary worth, since the value of the consideration may not be the same to every person. The parties are free to bargain on this term, unless the bargaining power of one of the parties is so unequal that it is obvious that one has taken advantage of the other.

Example. Susan needs forty dollars to purchase textbooks for one semester of school. She has a coat that is worth about ninety dollars which she offers to sell to Kathy for forty dollars. Kathy buys the coat for that price. Susan cannot later bring action to collect fifty dollars, claiming that this sum, plus the original forty dollars, comprises the value of the coat. Since both parties agreed on the consideration in the original offer of forty dollars, the courts would consider it adequate. In this case, the forty dollars is the binding factor in the contract.

Pre-existing Obligation

A party cannot make a second promise to do the same thing which that party has already promised to do or is already obligated to do, as consideration. This cannot be done because there is a *pre-existing obligation* already in effect. This often applies to duties of public officials.

Example. A homeowner with small children is concerned about cars speeding on the road past his house. He offers to pay a local police officer fifty dollars to watch the road especially carefully for speeders. There can be no binding contract here. The police officer, in accepting the duties as an officer of the law, has already made a promise to watch for speeders.

Past Performance

Consideration must be made at the same time at which contracts are drawn up. If a promise is made or an act is completed and consideration is requested at a later time, it will not pass as consideration in court.

Example. White helps his friend, Simms, move from one apartment to another without any mention of payment. Later, after an argument, White demands that Simms pay him $100 for his services. White cannot collect in court, since the consideration was requested after the performance of the act.

Charitable Subscriptions

An exception to the rule that consideration must be given to bind a promise occurs in the case of charitable subscriptions. A *charitable subscription* is a promise to give a gift of value to an organization that operates for a nonprofit or charitable purpose. Such organizations include churches, private colleges, or charity funds. Many times, institutions rely on gifts and form certain obligations in anticipation of receiving them. In these cases, the courts would enforce payment of the gift.

Example. Mrs. Bender signs a subscription form pledging a contribution to her church for the hymnal fund. On the basis of this pledge, the church orders the hymnals. Mrs. Bender cannot withdraw her subscription, since the church has already obligated itself based on her pledge.

COMPETENT PARTIES

A *competent party* is one that has the capacity to (is able to) enter into a contract. This element is step five leading to a binding contract. Most persons are considered legally competent. There are some groups of people, however, that are protected by the law. Legally, they are known as *incompetents*; the law presumes that they do not have the proper judgment to enter into contracts.

Minors

A *minor,* sometimes referred to as an *infant,* is any person who has not reached the legal age (the age of majority) as provided by the laws of the state in which they hold legal residence. At one time, the age of majority was twenty-one in most states. With the lowering of the voting age to eighteen, however, many states are enacting laws to change the legal age to eighteen. Minors are not considered to have the capacity to be fully responsible for their acts; they are incompetents in contract law.

If minors make a contract, they have the right to void their obligations at any time until they reach majority. Such a contract by a minor can be declared void. An adult who forms a contract with a minor, does not have the option to avoid the contract. The adult is released from the obligation, however, if the minor avoids the contract. If a minor chooses to withdraw from a contract, all benefits from the contract must be returned by that minor before any money can be collected by him or her.

Example. Linda, who is seventeen, signs up for a six-month sky-diving course. The total cost is $300, which includes books, equipment, and instruction. After three months, she decides to leave the course and requests a refund. She offers to return the books and equipment. When the school refuses to refund the money, Linda brings action against it. The school must return the money to Linda, since she is a minor and has chosen to withdraw from the contract.

If minors lie about their age, they can still avoid any contracts they make. In such situations, courts today usually allow the adult involved to deduct a certain amount for damages from the money they return to the minor. In some states, an adult may avoid a contract with a minor if the minor has used fraudulent means to obtain the contract, such as lying about his or her age.

Example. Suppose that in the previous case, Linda, age seventeen, had claimed to be twenty-two years of age. She could still withdraw from the contract. The court, however, might deduct $100, or some other equitable sum, from the amount that the skydiving school was forced to return, since Linda did have three months of lessons.

Minors are liable (must pay) for necessities supplied them when they require the necessities to survive. Such necessities include food, shelter, and medical attention.

Example. While on a two-week camping trip in the mountains, a sixteen-year-old boy breaks his wrist. He goes to a doctor in a near-by town, who treats him and charges him the normal fee. The boy is liable for that bill, even though he is a minor.

When minors reach the age of majority they may *ratify* (affirm or agree to) contracts they made as minors. If a reasonable time passes after they become of age, and they have said nothing, the contract is considered ratified.

Example. Ray is seventeen years old when he purchases a motorcycle. (Legal age in his state is eighteen.) Payment for the motorcycle is scheduled for two years. Ray continues making the regular payments after he turns eighteen. At this point, he is bound by the contract he made as a minor. He cannot wait until he is nineteen and then decide to withdraw from the agreement.

Business people can protect themselves and still have dealings with minors. When making contracts with minors they can require that the contract be signed by an adult. The adult then enters into the contract with the minor. The adult is said to be *cosigning* the contract, thus taking on all its obligations. If the minor chooses to withdraw, the cosigner is still responsible for the terms of the contract.

The Insane

People judged to be insane do not have sufficient judgment powers to make legal decisions because of mental deficiency. They have rights similar to those of minors in contract law. Contracts they make while in a state of mental illness are voidable, so they have the option to withdraw if they choose. As in the case of minors, mentally impaired persons are liable for necessities supplied to them. Contracts made when persons are judged legally insane may be ratified when they regain their health.

Intoxicated Persons

Legally intoxicated persons are those who have had so many alcoholic drinks that their judgment is impaired. The amount of alcohol which produces this result varies from individual to individual. Intoxicated persons are not able to have a meeting of the minds; therefore, they are not competent parties. Rules regarding intoxicated persons entering into contracts are similar to rules for minors and the insane.

LEGAL PURPOSE

The final element needed to produce a binding contract is *legal purpose,* or lawful reason for the contract in the subject matter of that contract. Legal purpose ensures that the contract is not illegal or harmful to the public welfare. If the subject matter does not have legal purpose, the contract is void, and, as noted in Chapter 3, unenforceable in court. No contract exists.

Breaking Statutory Laws

If a contract breaks statutory laws it is illegal and thus does not have a legal purpose. For example, many states have statutes forbidding gambling. In those states, any contract that has to do with gambling is void.

Usurious Contracts

Usury is the charging of interest which is over the legal rate on loans. Such a transaction is said to be *usurious*. Most states have statutes which limit interest rates that can be charged on loans. These rates, however, are not uniform throughout the states.

Usurious contracts have no legal purpose and are therefore void. Penalties for usury vary widely. In some states, there is no penalty at all. Other states require the return of the overcharged interest or the return of the entire interest and loan amount.

Example. A needs money very badly. *B* loans *A* the amount at 25 percent interest, a rate far surpassing state maximum rates. This is a usurious contract. *B* cannot bring court action against *A* if the money is not paid.

Contracts Which Are Harmful to the Public Welfare

Any contract which hurts the public as a whole is void, since it is not considered to have a legal purpose. For example, contracts in restraint of trade are illegal since such an agreement tends to limit competition and force prices up, thereby harming the public.

Example. Jackson sells his bakery to Lopez. As part of the deal, Jackson signs an agreement saying he will never open another bakery within the town limits. The next month, Jackson opens a bakery across the street and Lopez brings action to force Jackson to cease doing business. The original contract, in restraint of trade, is void and cannot be legally enforced.

There are instances when contracts of this type are enforceable. When an individual possessing a unique skill or classified information leaves a business, he or she may be bound by a provision which limits the use of the skill or information. However, the provision must be very narrowly worded in terms of time or area. The courts will not enforce broadly written clauses which would prevent the individual from earning a living. For instance, in the previous example, if Jackson had signed an agreement promising not to open a bakery within the town limits for a period of two years, the contract could be legally enforced.

Many people must by law have licenses to practice their professions. This includes doctors, dentists, real estate agents, and others. A contract made with a person who should be licensed, but is not, is without legal effect or void, since such an unlicensed person may be dangerous to the public.

Example. John Bush, an unlicensed doctor, treats Susan Morrey for two months, saying that his treatment will cure her of cancer. When her health does not improve, Morrey refuses to pay the bill. Bush cannot collect through a court action, since the contract is void. By practicing as an unlicensed doctor, his actions are considered harmful to the public.

Contracts which tend to interfere with good government are harmful to the public welfare and are void.

Example. XYZ Construction Company wants to build a shopping center in an area of the city that is zoned for homes only. They pay three of the five zoning board members substantial sums to vote to change the law. The final vote is 5-0 against the change. The XYZ Company cannot sue the three members whom they paid to vote in their favor, but did not. There is no legal contract here, since the company was attempting to interfere with proper governmental administration by offering bribes. The zoning board was established to enforce the zoning laws and protect the citizens from careless land use. This governmental purpose would be ignored if the courts recognized and enforced the contract.

SELF-EVALUATION

Provide a brief explanation for each of the following.

1. What are the six steps leading to a binding contract?

2. What are three elements that must be present in an offer?

3. In *Balfour* v. *Balfour,* what does Judge Atkin say about agreements concerning allowances between husbands and wives? What is the reason for his conclusion? What element necessary to a contract does he imply is missing in this case?

4. When can an offer not be revoked by the offeror?

5. Mary dies after she makes an offer to Susan. Can Susan still accept the offer? Why or why not?

6. What is a counteroffer?

7. In what type of contract is the acceptance made by performance?

8. If an offer is received by mail, how should the acceptance be made if there are no specific terms included? When does this acceptance become effective?

9. An offer not involving the sale of goods is sent by telegram. The acceptance is sent by mail. Is there a contract if the letter is lost in the mail? When does this contract become effective?

10. What is a meeting of the minds?

11. What element binds the parties in a contract to that contract?

12. What are three types of persons considered incompetent by the law?

13. When are incompetents bound by a contract?

14. If a minor lies about his or her age, is the contract enforceable?

15. How can business people protect themselves when dealing with minors?

16. Carter sells Simpson's home and attempts to collect a commission. Simpson learns that Carter is not licensed. Why can Simpson refrain from paying Carter a commission? What contract element is missing?

SUGGESTED ACTIVITY

1. Write a binding contract in everyday language. Identify each of the six elements that are present in the contract.

CASES FOR STUDY

1. Aunt Mamie promises her favorite niece, Judy, that she will provide for Judy's education by willing her $10,000. Aunt Mamie dies without ever writing a will. Can Judy collect $10,000 from the estate, based on the promise made before her Aunt's death? Assume that otherwise, Judy does not receive any inheritance.

2. Tom receives an offer to purchase three new books at bargain rates. He sends a check to the book company and attaches a note which requests three other books, rather than the ones described in the brochure. Does a contract exist? If so, for which set of books? If not, what has transpired in the course of the correspondence?

3. *X* sends an offer on June 1 through the mail to *Y*. It reaches *Y* on June 3. *Y* accepts the offer by letter, which is mailed June 5 and reaches *X* on June 8. In the meantime, *X* thinks again of the offer and sends a revocation through the mail on June 4, which reaches *Y* on June 7. Does a contract exist between *X* and *Y*?

4. When reading the following case, consider the element of intention to be bound in forming a contract. Sometimes it is difficult for the court to discover what was actually in the minds of the parties when the promises were made, so it must rely on outward appearances as evidence of intent. Compare this case with Balfour v. Balfour beginning on page 52.

LUCY v. ZEHMER

Supreme Court of Appeals of Virginia, 1954
196 Va. 493, 84 S.E.2nd 516

[Most citations have been omitted.]

BUCHANAN, J. This suit was instituted by W.O. Lucy and J.C. Lucy, complainants, against A.H. Zehmer and Ida S. Zehmer, his wife, defendants, to have specific performance of a contract by which it was alleged the Zehmers had sold to W.O. Lucy a tract of land owned by A.H. Zehmer in Dinwiddie County containing 471.6 acres, more or less, known as the Ferguson farm, for $50,000. J.C. Lucy, the other complainant, is a brother of W.O. Lucy, to whom W.O. Lucy transferred a half interest in his alleged purchase.

The instrument sought to be enforced was written by A.H. Zehmer on December 20, 1952, in these words: "We hereby agree to sell to W.O. Lucy the Ferguson Farm complete for $50,000.00, title satisfactory to buyer," and signed by the defendants A.H. Zehmer and Ida S. Zehmer.

The answer of A.H. Zehmer admitted that, at the time mentioned, W.O. Lucy offered him $50,000 cash for the farm, but that he, Zehmer, considered that the offer was made in jest; that so thinking, both he and Lucy having had several drinks, he wrote out "the memorandum" quoted above and induced his wife to sign it; that he did not deliver the memorandum to Lucy, but that Lucy picked it up, read it, put it in his pocket, attempted to offer Zehmer $5 to bind the bargain, which Zehmer refused to accept, and realizing for the first time that Lucy was serious, Zehmer assured him that he has no intention of selling the farm and that the whole matter was a joke. Lucy left the premises insisting that he had purchased the farm.

Depositions were taken and the decree appealed from was entered holding that the complainants had failed to establish their right to specific performance, and dismissing their bill. The assignment of error is to this action of the court.

• • •

The defendants insist that the evidence was ample to support their contention that the writing sought to be enforced was prepared as a bluff or dare to force Lucy to admit that he did not have $50,000; that the whole matter was a joke; that the writing was not delivered to Lucy and no binding contract was ever made between the parties.

It is an unusual, if not bizarre, defense. When made to the writing admittedly prepared by one of the defendants and signed by both, clear evidence is required to sustain it.

In his testimony Zehmer claimed that he "was high as a Georgia pine," and that the transaction "was just a bunch of two doggoned drunks bluffing to see who could talk the biggest and say the most." That claim is inconsistent with his attempt to testify in great detail as to what was said and what was done. It is contradicted by other evidence as to the condition of both parties, and rendered of no weight by the testimony of his wife that when Lucy left the restaurant she suggested that Zehmer drive him home. The record is convincing that Zehmer was not intoxicated to the extent of being unable to comprehend the nature and consequences of the instrument he executed, and hence that instrument is not to be invalidated on that ground. [Citations omitted] It was in fact conceded by defendant's counsel in oral argument that under the evidence Zehmer was not too drunk to make a valid contract.

The evidence is convincing also that Zehmer wrote two agreements, the first one beginning, "I hereby agree to sell." Zehmer first said he could not remember about that, then that "I don't think I wrote but one out." Mrs. Zehmer said that what he wrote was "I hereby agree," but that the "I" was changed to "We" after that night. The agreement that was written and signed is in the record and indicates no such change. Neither are the mistakes in spelling that Zehmer sought to point out readily apparent.

The appearance of the contract, the fact that it was under discussion for forty minutes or more before it was signed; Lucy's objection to the first draft because it was written in the singular, and he wanted Mrs. Zehmer to sign it also; the rewriting to meet that objection and the signing by Mrs. Zehmer; the discussion of what was to be included in the sale, the provision for the examination of the title, the completeness of the instrument that was executed, the taking possession of it by Lucy with no request or suggestion by either of the defendants that he give it back, are facts which furnish persuasive evidence that the execution of the contract was a serious business transaction rather than a casual, jesting matter as defendants now contend.

• • •

If it be assumed, contrary to what we think the evidence shows, that Zehmer was jesting about selling his farm to Lucy and that the transaction was intended by him to be a joke, nevertheless the evidence shows that Lucy did not so understand it but considered it to be a serious business transaction and the contract to be binding on the Zehmers as well as on himself. The very next day he arranged with his brother to put up half the money and take a half interest in the land. The day after that he employed an attorney to examine the title. The next night, Tuesday, he was back at Zehmer's place and there Zehmer told him for the first time, Lucy said, that he wasn't going to sell and he told Zehmer, "You know you sold that place fair and square." After receiving the report from his attorney that the title was good he wrote to Zehmer that he was ready to close the deal.

Not only did Lucy actually believe, but the evidence shows he was warranted in believing, that the contract represented a serious business transaction and a good faith sale and purchase of the farm.

In the field of contracts, as generally elsewhere, "We must look to the outward expression of a person as manifesting his intention rather than to his secret and unexpressed intention. 'The law imputes to a person an intention corresponding to the reasonable meaning of his words and acts.' "

• • •

. . .The mental assent of the parties is not requisite for the formation of a contract. If the words or other acts of one of the parties have but one reasonable meaning, his undisclosed intention is immaterial except when an unreasonable meaning which he attaches to his manifestations is known to the other party. . . .

". . .The law, therefore, judges of an agreement between two persons exclusively from those expressions of their intentions which are communicated between them. . . ."

An agreement or mutual assent is of course essential to a valid contract but the law imputes to a person an intention corresponding to the reasonable meaning of his words and acts. If his words and acts, judged by a reasonable standard, manifest an intention to agree, it is immaterial what may be the real but unexpressed state of his mind.

So a person cannot set up that he was merely jesting when his conduct and words would warrant a reasonable person in believing that he intended a real agreement.

Whether the writing signed by the defendants and now sought to be enforced by the complainants was the result of a serious offer by Lucy and a serious acceptance or was a serious offer by Lucy and an acceptance in jest by the defendants, in either event it constituted a binding contract of sale between the parties.·

.   .   .

The complainants are entitled to have specific performance of the contract sued on. The decree appealed from is therefore reversed and the cause is remanded for the entry of a proper decree requiring the defendants to perform the contract in accordance with the prayer of the bill.

Reversed and remanded.

Chapter 5

The Assignment and Termination of Contracts

OBJECTIVES

After studying this chapter, the student will be able to

- explain how contracts are assigned to third parties.
- differentiate between assignable and unassignable contracts.
- outline the various ways in which contracts are terminated.
- define the following words and phrases.

assignment	alteration
assignor	waiver
assignee	breach
delegated	injured party
executor	remedy
trustee	damages
satisfactory performance	liquidated damages
substantial performance	specific performance
tender	injunction
impossibility of performance	

ASSIGNMENT OF CONTRACTS

An *assignment* of a contract is the transfer of the rights held by one party to a third party not originally involved in the contract. The *assignor* transfers his or her rights to the *assignee*. The UCC rules on assignments are similar to standard contract laws regarding the same.

Unassignable Contracts

Some contracts by nature are not assignable. The UCC states that contracts cannot be assigned if the assignment would increase or alter the obligation of the other party. [See Section 2-210.]

Example. Tex Cassidy, owner of a dude ranch, agrees to purchase, for a certain sum, ten horses from the Lazy Stables to be delivered in May. The price includes the cost of the one-hundred mile delivery. Cassidy's ranch goes out of business in April, so he assigns the contract to Slim Rogers, a dude rancher who is another two hundred miles away from the stables. This contract is not assignable since there would be more costs involved for the stables to deliver to Rogers, who is farther away. The obligation of the stables has been increased.

Legal agreements which involve special personal skills or personal judgment are not assignable.

Example. George contracts with Mr. Pro for ten ski lessons for fifty dollars. Mr. Pro breaks his leg before the lessons begin. Mr. Pro cannot assign this contract to another instructor. George has contracted with him because he is the best in the area. No one else has the same skills as Mr. Pro; therefore, the contract is unassignable.

Delegated Contracts

Contracts which require the performance of a duty and in which that duty does not involve a special skill also cannot be assigned. The duty, however, can be delegated to another party. When a contract is *delegated,* the original party is still responsible for seeing that the obligation is performed, and is still liable for it.

Example.   Brad contracts to rake Mrs. Lambert's lawn for two months in the fall. He makes the school football team and does not have the time to do the job, so he delegates the job to his brother Scott. Since both brothers are capable of doing the job, the contract can be delegated. Brad, however, is responsible for seeing that the job is done the way that the contract requires.

Assignable Contracts

The most common type of assignable contract is one which involves a promise to pay money. In these contracts, there is no increase or change in the obligation, and there is no personal skill involved.

Example.   Colleen purchases a car from Ajax Used Car Company. She has a contract to pay Ajax $1,500 in cash in exchange for the car.   Ajax assigns the contract to Security Savings Bank.   This bank notifies Colleen, so she now owes the money to the bank. This is an assignable contract.

Rights of the Assignee

The assignee, to whom the contract is assigned, takes over all the rights of the assignor — no more and no less. The assignee actually takes the place of the assignor. To be sure that the rights of the contract are received, the assignee must properly notify the other party in the contract.

Example. If Colleen in the above example had agreed to pay 6 percent interest to Ajax Used Car Company, the assignee, the bank, could not raise the interest to 7 percent. By the same token, Colleen could not lower the interest rate to 5 percent. The rights of the bank are the same as those of the used car company.

Assignments Imposed by Law

At times, assignments of contracts are imposed or *granted* by law. Executors must by law see that most of the contracts of the deceased are carried out.

Another assignment imposed by law occurs when persons or firms go *bankrupt* (declare that they have far greater *liabilities,* or debts, than *assets,* or property which could be sold to pay debtors). When bankruptcy is declared, an individual, often called a *trustee,* is assigned to take over the contracts of the bankrupted and handle them in the proper way.

TERMINATION OF A CONTRACT

A contract can be terminated, or *discharged,* in several ways.

Performance

The most obvious and common way for a contract to be discharged is for both parties to fulfill their promises or perform their acts according to the terms. When this is done, the contract is *terminated by performance.* Figure 5-1 illustrates a loan that has been paid in full — a contract which has been terminated by performance.

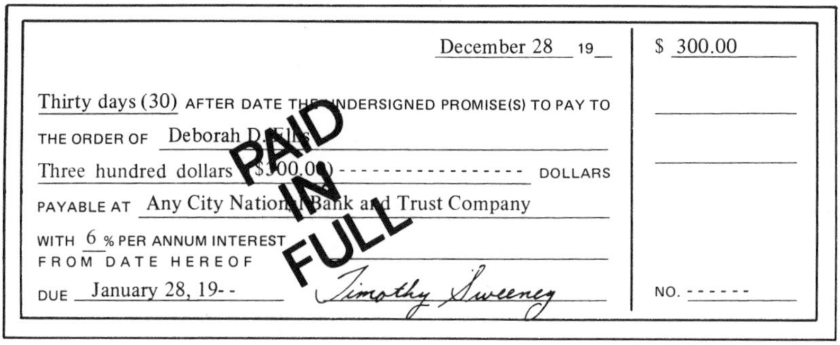

```
                                    December 28  19__    │ $ 300.00
                                                         │
Thirty days (30) AFTER DATE THE UNDERSIGNED PROMISE(S) TO PAY TO
THE ORDER OF  Deborah Davis
Three hundred dollars ($300.00) ---------------- DOLLARS
PAYABLE AT  Any City National Bank and Trust Company
WITH 6 % PER ANNUM INTEREST
FROM DATE HEREOF
DUE  January 28, 19--        Timothy Sweeney          │ NO. ------
```

PAID IN FULL

Fig. 5-1   A loan which has been paid in full, one example of a contract terminated by performance.

Example. *B* offers to sell his car to *C* for $900. *C* agrees. *C* pays *B* the $900 and drives away in the car. The contract is terminated by performance; both parties have fulfilled their promises.

An act required by a contract may be performed either completely or almost completely, depending upon the nature of the agreement. *Satisfactory performance* occurs when exact completion of the terms as stated in the contract is required. The completion must be to the satisfaction of the other party involved in the contract.

When payment of money is stipulated by a contract, satisfactory performance is usually required.

Example. Beth lends Kay fifty dollars. Satisfactory performance to terminate the contract requires that Kay pay back the fifty dollars to Beth. Payment of any sum less than that would not be sufficient.

Substantial performance requires slightly less than complete or satisfactory performance. In many agreements, a slight variation from the exact terms is allowed to terminate the contract. The contracts are then said to require only substantial performance.

Substantial performance is designed to prevent hardship to one party who must undertake a long and complicated performance. In a construction contract, for example, the builder may require months or years to complete the structure, while the buyer completes his or her performance simply by turning over the money. If the law required exact compliance on the part of the builder, any slight deviation from the specifications would give the buyer grounds to refuse performance. If the case were brought to court, a slight deviation would probably not be grounds for excusing payment altogether; rather, the buyer would have to pay the contract price less any allowance for the deviation from the specifications. Consider the following case. What would have been the effect of the decision if the court had required letter-perfect performance?

Case Example. In the following case, judgment is based on the meaning of substantial performance.

JACOB & YOUNGS v. KENT

Court of Appeals of New York, 1921
230 N.Y. 239, 129 N.E. 889

CARDOZO, J. The plaintiff built a country residence for the defendant at a cost of upwards of $77,000, and now sues to recover a balance of $3,483.46, remaining unpaid. The work of construction ceased in June 1914, and the defendant then began to occupy the dwelling. There was no complaint of defective performance until March, 1915. One of the specifications for the plumbing work provides that "all wrought iron pipe must be well galvanized, lap welded pipe of the grade known as 'standard pipe' of Reading manufacture." The defendant learned in March, 1915, that some of the pipe, instead of being made in Reading, was the product of other factories. The plaintiff was accordingly directed by the architect to do the work anew. The plumbing was then encased within the walls except in a few places where it had to be exposed. Obedience to the order meant more than the substitution of other pipe. It meant the demolition at great expense of substantial parts of the completed structure. The plaintiff left the work untouched, and asked for a certificate that the final payment was due. Refusal of the certificate was followed by this suit.

The evidence sustains a finding that the omission of the prescribed brand of pipe was neither fraudulent nor willfull. It was the result of the oversight and inattention of the plaintiff's subcontractor. Reading pipe is distinguished from Cohoes pipe and other brands only by the name of the manufacturer stamped upon it at intervals of between six and seven feet. Even the defendant's architect, though he inspected the pipe upon arrival, failed to notice the discrepancy. The plaintiff tried to show that the brands installed, though made by other manufacturers, were the same in quality, in appearance, in market value and in cost as the brand stated in the contract — that they were, indeed the same thing, though manufactured in another place. The evidence was excluded, and a verdict directed for the defendant. The Appellate Division reversed, and granted a new trial.

We think the evidence, if admitted, would have supplied some basis for the inference that the defect was insignificant in its relation to the project. The courts never say that one who makes a contract fills the measure of his duty by less than full performance. They do say, however, that an omission, both trivial and innocent, will sometimes be atoned for by allowance of the resulting damage, and will not always be a breach of a condition to be followed by a forfeiture. [Citations omitted.] The distinction is akin to that between dependent and independent promises, or between promises and conditions. Some promises are so plainly independent that they can never by fair construction be conditions of one another. Others are so plainly dependent that they must always be conditions. Others, though dependent and thus conditions when there is departure in point of substance, will be viewed as independent and collateral when the departure is insignificant. Considerations partly of justice and partly of presumable intention are to tell us whether this or that promise shall be placed in one class or in another. The simple and uniform will call for different remedies from the multifarious and the intricate. The margin of departure within the range of normal expectation upon a sale of common chattels will vary from the margin to be expected upon a contract for the construction of a mansion or a "skyscraper." There will be harshness sometimes and oppression in the implication of a condition when the thing upon which labor has been expended is incapable of surrender because united to the land, and equity and reason in the implication of a like condition when the subject-matter, if defective, is in shape to be returned. From the conclusion that promises may not be treated as dependent to the extent of their uttermost minutiae without the sacrifice of justice, the progress is a short one to the conclusion that they may not be so treated without a perversion of intention. Intention not otherwise revealed may be presumed to hold in contemplation the reasonable and probable. If something else is in view, it must not be left to implication. There will be no assumption of a purpose to visit venial faults with oppressive retribution.

Those who think more of symmetry and logic in the development of legal rules than of practical adaptation to the attainment of a just result will be troubled by a classification where the lines of division are so wavering and blurred. Something, doubtless, may be said on the score of consistency and certainty in favor of a stricter standard. The courts have balanced such considerations against those of equity and fairness, and found the latter to be the weightier. The decisions in this state commit us to the liberal view, which is making its way, nowadays, in jurisdictions slow to welcome it. Where the line is to be drawn between the important and the trivial cannot be settled by a formula. "In the nature of the case precise boundaries are impossible." The same omission may take on one aspect or another according to its setting. Substitution of equivalents may not have the same significance in fields of art on the one side and in those of mere utility on the other. Nowhere will change be tolerated, however, if it is so dominant or pervasive as in any real or substantial measure to frustrate the purpose of the contract. There is no general license to install whatever, in a builder's judgment, may be regarded as "just as good." The question is one of degree, to be answered, if there is doubt, by the triers of the facts and, if the inferences are certain, by the judges of the law. We must weigh the purpose to be served, the desire to be gratified, the excuse for deviation from the letter, the cruelty of enforced adherence. Then only can we tell whether literal fulfillment is to be implied by law as a condition. This is not to say that the parties are not free by apt and certain words to effectuate a purpose that performance of every term shall be a condition of recovery. That question is not here. This is merely to say that the law will be slow to impute the purpose, in the silence of the parties, where the significance of the default is grievously out of proportion to the oppression of the forfeiture. The willful transgressor must accept the penalty of his transgression. For him there is no occasion to mitigate the rigor of implied conditions. The transgressor whose default is unintentional and trivial may hope for mercy if he will offer atonement for his wrong.

In the circumstances of this case, we think the measure of the allowance is not the cost of replacement, which would be great, but the difference in value, which would be either nominal or nothing. Some of the exposed sections might perhaps have been replaced at moderate expense. The defendant did not limit his demand to them, but treated the plumbing as a unit to be corrected from cellar to roof. In point of fact, the plaintiff never reached the stage at which evidence of the extent of the allowance became necessary. The trial court had excluded evidence that the defect was unsubstantial, and in view of that ruling there was no occasion for the plaintiff to go farther with an offer of proof. We think, however, that the offer, if it had been made, would not of necessity have been defective because directed to difference in value. It is true that in most cases the cost of replacement is the measure. The owner is entitled to the money which will permit him to complete, unless the cost of completion is grossly and unfairly out of proportion to the good to be attained. When that is true, the measure is the difference in value. Specifications call, let us say, for a foundation built of granite quarried in Vermont. On the completion of the building, the owner learns that through the blunder of a subcontractor part of the foundation has been built of granite of the same quality quarried in New Hampshire. The measure of allowance is not the cost of reconstruction. "There may be omissions of that which could not afterwards be supplied exactly as called for by the contract without taking down the building to its foundations, and at the same time the omission may not affect the value of the building for use or otherwise, except so slightly as to be hardly appreciable." The rule that gives a remedy in cases of substantial performance with compensation for defects of trivial or inappreciable importance, has been developed by the courts as an instrument of justice. The measure of the allowance must be shaped to the same end.

The order should be affirmed, and judgment absolute directed in favor of the plaintiff upon the stipulation, with costs in all courts.

An offer to satisfy a debt or obligation is called *tender.* Tender may be an offer in the form of money or services. When tender is given and refused, the party making the tender is no longer obligated to perform under the terms of the contract. The contract is terminated.

Example. Mr. Barnsley delivers a load of gravel to Mr. Voorman according to the terms of their contract. Voorman refuses to accept the gravel. Barnsley is no longer obligated to deliver the gravel. The contract is terminated.

Impossibility of Performance

The phrase *impossibility of performance* indicates that the obligation of a party cannot be fulfilled. It does not mean that the party will not perform, but that the party cannot perform. Performance may have become more difficult since the signing of the contract, or a greater hardship may result because of it. However, this does not usually end or discharge the party's obligation. The party is still held liable for the inability to perform, and usually has to compensate the other party.

Example. A band is hired on May 1 to play at a dance on October 16. The band is to be paid $500 to play for four hours. In the intervening months, the band loses its lead singer. They notify the dance organizer, who must now locate another band. Even though it is virtually impossible for the first band to live up to its contract, they are liable for damages caused to the dance organizer, such as the difference in cost if another band is hired at a higher price.

The courts recognize only three reasons for which a promisor can be excused from failure to perform due to impossibility.

Death or Disability.   A contract may be discharged by the death or disability of the promisor.   This is true only if the contract is of a personal nature and the duties therefore cannot be delegated to another party.

Example.   Mrs. Ross contracts to design and make a wedding dress for Nancy.   One week later, Mrs. Ross dies. The contract is terminated because of impossibility of performance.   The duties can not be delegated since no one else has exactly the talents of Mrs. Ross.

Intervening Illegality.   Between the time that a contract is made and performed, there may be a change in a law which makes the contract illegal.   This terminates the contract due to impossibility of performance.

Example.   Sam's Super Store contracts to buy a truckload of laundry soap, which lists a phosphate as one of the ingredients.   Before delivery is made, the state in which the store is located declares that the sale of phosphate soaps is illegal.   The contract is terminated due to the intervening change in the law.

Destruction of Subject Matter.   If the subject matter of the contract is destroyed between the time of the contract and the performance and it is not the fault of the promisor, the contract is terminated due to impossibility of performance.   In these cases, it is impossible to fulfill a promise or perform an act if there is no subject matter.

Example.   Robert contracts to construct a new roof on Bill's garage. Before the job is started, the garage burns to the ground.   The contract is terminated because it is then impossible to fulfill; Robert cannot construct a roof on a building that no longer exists.

Agreement

A contract can be discharged before complete performance if both parties agree to the termination. When this is done, both parties give up any rights they may have had in the contract.

Alteration

Alterations can be made in contracts, but only if both parties agree to the changes. A contract is terminated if one party purposely or innocently makes an alteration (change) in the contract without the other party either being aware of it or agreeing to it. The other party is free from any and all obligations in the contract.

Example.   Hanrahan contracts with Santiago to plow Santiago's driveway all winter for seventy-five dollars. According to the contract, Hanrahan is to plow the driveway every time there is a snowfall of at least six inches. Hanrahan changes the contract, without the knowledge of Santiago, to read "every time there is a snowfall of at least sixteen inches." Since Hanrahan has altered the contract, the contract is terminated, and Santiago has no obligation to continue to employ Hanrahan's services or to pay him.

If a party not involved in the contract alters the document in some way, there is no change in the rights or duties of the parties.

Waiver

The rights of one party in a contract may be given up by that party by means of a *waiver*. For example, if the performance of one party does not meet all the terms of the contract, the other party can

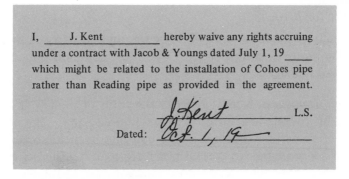

I,   J. Kent   hereby waive any rights accruing under a contract with Jacob & Youngs dated July 1, 19____ which might be related to the installation of Cohoes pipe rather than Reading pipe as provided in the agreement.

J. Kent   L.S.

Dated: Oct. 1, 19

Fig. 5-2 One form of a waiver

accept the performance anyway by waiving the right to an exact performance of terms, and accepting the performance as given. The contract is then discharged. Figure 5-2 is an example of a typical waiver that could have been used in the case of *Jacob & Youngs* v. *Kent* if Kent had agreed to the change in pipe.

Example.   Constantine agrees to build a five-foot fence around Jordan's home. When he finishes and the fence is measured, they find that the fence is only three feet high. Jordan is actually happier with that height than the proposed height, and waives the right to the five-foot fence. The contract is discharged.

Statute of Limitations

A contract is discharged if it is not enforced within the time limit of the statute of limitations of its state. The time limit varies by state, as discussed in Chapter 3. If the time period runs out, action can no longer be taken on the contract, and the contract is considered discharged.

Breach

When one party of a contract does not perform his or her obligation, that party is said to *breach* (break) the contract. This is another way in which contracts are terminated.

When one party breaches a contract, the other is known as the *injured party*. The injured party in a breached contract has no more obligations to the contract and can sue for his or her loss. Contract law and the UCC both state that an injured party should be in as secure a position as it would be if the other party had performed. This is done by giving remedies to the injured party.

Remedies for Breach

Legally, a *remedy* is a relief for the injured party; a means by which the injury is compensated. The most common remedy is the payment of damages.

Damages.   *Damages,* usually given in the form of money, are meant to make up for the loss suffered by the injured party. The parties in a contract sometimes outline in the contract itself reasonable damages that are to be paid if there is nonperformance. These are known as *liquidated damages.* The party who is to be paid damages must make every effort to keep the damages minimal.

Example. Mike has a one-year employment contract with his company at a salary of $12,000. After six months, through no fault of his, he is fired. Mike is entitled to the $6,000 in wages that remain in his contract. He must attempt however, to locate another job, and not expect to live off the remaining $6,000 for six months. If, after four months, Mike finds a similar job at the same salary, he would then be able to collect $4,000 from his first employer, for the four months he did not have a job.

Specific Performance. Another remedy for breach of contract is known as specific performance. *Specific performance* is an insistance that the exact terms of the original agreement be carried out. It is used when the subject matter of the contract is unique and when money payments would not be a sufficient remedy for the injured party, such as in situations involving land or works of art.

Example. Mrs. Mitchell offers to sell a piece of sculpture to Mr. Russell, an art collector. He agrees and pays her the price of $20,000. At the last minute, Mrs. Mitchell says she will not deliver. She has breached the contract by not performing. Since Russell does not want his money back or a different piece of sculpture, he could bring court action to demand specific performance. That is, he demands in court that Mrs. Mitchell sell him the sculpture for $20,000.

Case Example. The complainant in this case seeks specific performance.

CURTICE BROS. CO. v. CATTS

Court of Chancery of New Jersey, 1907
72 N.J. Eq. 831, 66 A. 935

Complainant is engaged in the business of canning tomatoes and seeks the specific performance of a contract wherein defendant agreed to sell to complainant the entire product of certain land planted with tomatoes. Defendant contests the power of this court to grant equitable relief.

LEAMING, V.C. The fundamental principles which guide a court of equity in decreeing the specific performance of contracts are essentially the same whether the contracts relate to realty or to personalty. By reason of the fact that damages for the breach of contract for the sale of personalty are, in most cases, easily ascertainable and recoverable at law, courts of equity, in such cases withhold equitable relief. Touching contracts for the sale of land the reverse is the case. But no inherent difference between real estate and personal property controls the exercise of the jurisdiction. Where no adequate remedy at law exists specific performance of a contract touching the sale of personal property will de decreed with the same freedom as in the case of a contract for the sale of land. Professor Pomeroy, in referring to the distinction, says:

"In applying these principles, taking into account the discretionary nature of the jurisdiction, an agreement for the sale of land is . . . presumed to come within their operation so as to be subject to specific performance, but a contrary presumption exists in regard to agreements concerning chattels [items of personal property] ."

Judge Story urges that there is no reasonable objection to allowing the party who is injured by the breach of any contract for the sale of chattels to have an election either to take damages at law or to have a specific performance in equity. While it is probable that the development of this branch of equitable remedies is decidedly toward the logical solution suggested by Judge Story, it is entirely clear that his view cannot at this time be freely adopted without violence to what has long been regarded as accepted principles controlling the discretion of a court of equity in this class of cases. The United States Supreme Court has probably most nearly approached the view suggested by Judge Story. In *Mechanics Bank of Alexandria* v. *Seton,* Mr. Justice Thompson, delivering the opinion of that court, says: "But not withstanding this distinction between personal contracts for goods and contracts for lands is to be found laid down in the books as a general rule, yet there are many cases to be found where specific performance of contracts relating to personalty have been enforced in chancery, and courts will only view with greater nicety contracts of this description than such as related to land." In our state contracts for the sale of chattels have been frequently enforced and the inadequacy of the remedy at law, based on the characteristic features of the contract or peculiar situation and needs of the parties, have been principal grounds of relief. . . .

I think it clear that the present case falls well within the principles defined by the cases already cited from our own state. Complainant's factory has a capacity of about one million cans of tomatoes. The season for packing lasts about six weeks. The preparations made for this six weeks of active work must be carried out in all features to enable the business to succeed. These preparations are primarily based upon the capacity of the plant. Cans and other necessary equipments, including labor, must be provided and secured in advance with reference to the capacity of the plant during the packing period. With this known capacity and an estimated average yield of tomatoes per acre the acreage of land necessary to supply the plant is calculated. To that end the contract now in question was made, with other like contracts, covering a sufficient acreage to insure the essential pack. It seems immaterial whether the entire acreage is contracted for to insure the full pack, or whether a more limited acreage is contracted for and an estimated available open market depended upon for the balance of the pack; in either case a refusal of the parties who contract to supply a given acreage to comply with their contracts leaves the factory helpless except to whatever extent an uncertain market may perchance supply the deficiency. The condition which arises from the breach of the contracts is not merely a question of the factory being compelled to pay a higher price for the product; losses sustained in that manner could, with some degree of accuracy, be estimated. The condition which occasions the irreparable injury by reason of the breaches of the contracts is the inability to procure at any price at the time needed and of the quality needed the necessary tomatoes to insure the successful operation of the plant. If it should be assumed as a fact that upon the breach of contracts of this nature other tomatoes of like quality and quantity could be procured in the open market without serious interference with the economic arrangements of the plant, a court of equity would hesitate to assume to interfere, but the very existence of such contracts proclaims their necessity to the economic management of the factory. The aspect of the situation bears no resemblance to that of an ordinary contract for the sale of merchandise in the course of an ordinary business. The business and its needs are extraordinary in that the maintenance of all of the conditions prearranged to secure the pack are a necessity to insure the successful operation of the plant. The breach of the contract by one planter differs but in degree from a breach by all.

The objection that to specifically perform the contract personal services are required will not divest the court of its powers to preserve the benefits of the contract. Defendant may be restrained from selling the crop to others, and if necessary, a receiver can be appointed to harvest the crop.

Injunction. Another remedy for breach of contract is known as an injunction. An *injunction* is a court order that forbids the performance of an act. Injunctions are usually issued to prevent hardship or injury in cases where there is a threat of a breach of contract.

Example. Mr. Jaski, a chemist, is one of only two people in the Coats Coating Company who knows the formula for their most successful paint product. He has promised in his employment contract that he will not give the formula to a rival company, or use it to start his own company. To obtain a raise, Jaski threatens to sell the formula to the company's biggest competitor. Coats Coating Company asks the court to issue an injunction barring Jaski from selling the formula.

SELF-EVALUATION

Provide a brief explanation for each of the following.

1. What is an assignable contract?

2. When can a contract be delegated?

3. How do satisfactory performance and substantial performance differ?

4. Define tender.

5. What are three situations in which courts allow contracts to be terminated by impossibility of performance?

6. If both parties agree to discharge a contract, can it be discharged? What happens if part of the contract has been performed?

7. *B* owes *C* money. *C* changes the date on the contract to specify payment one week earlier without notifying *B*. What happens?

8. By what means can one party give up some of his or her rights in a contract?

9. What are liquidated damages?

10. When are specific performance and injunctions likely to be used as contract remedies?

11. Who was awarded the decision in *Jacob & Youngs* v. *Kent?* How does the judge compare the situation in the Vermont granite case to this case?

12. Why does the judge in *Curtice Bros. Co.* v. *Catts* believe that specific performance is the only remedy available to the plaintiff?

SUGGESTED ACTIVITY

1. Locate a case in a previous chapter in which the remedy was specific performance. Explain what the judge required the defendants to do.

CASES FOR STUDY

1. Mullin's Furniture Makers contracts to buy its yearly lumber requirements from Ace Lumber Yard. Ace defaults when it is time to deliver the lumber. Can Mullin's Furniture Makers require Ace to deliver the goods?

2. Lopez agrees to pay Winn $150 to use Winn's camper for a weekend. Before the weekend, the camper is involved in an accident and is a total loss. Must Lopez pay the $150? Why or why not?

3. Scott loans Cheryl $500 at the rate of 8 percent interest to be repaid in one year. Six months into the year Scott assigns the contract to Chris for the remaining $450. When Cheryl discovers that she must now make her payments to Chris instead of Scott, she wants to get out of the contract. Can she?

Section 3

Consumer Dealings with Personal Property

Goods and services are being constantly produced and provided for people to use. Every human being is a *consumer* — one who uses these goods and services. Consumers are an important part of the business process, since most products are made and services provided with the consumer in mind. For this reason, a great part of business law deals with the consumer. This involves regulating consumer methods of buying and selling, as well as the institution of rules for the protection of the consumer.

Property is something which is the subject of ownership. Ownership of property includes the right to have and dispose of the items or rights of value. Property is divided into two major classifications, real property, and personal property. *Real property* (or *realty*) is land and anything that is firmly attached to it, including growing trees, crops, and minerals. *Personal property* is everything else that is not realty. This includes such items as clothing, cars, stocks, and cash. Also included in personal property are certain rights such as the right to be paid a debt that is owed. Some items may be real property at one point and personal property at another.

Example. Marble is real property when it is in the ground. When it is quarried (taken out), it becomes personal property. It may then be used in the construction of a building and become real property once again. If the building is destroyed and a sculptor takes a piece of the marble to chisel into an art object, it again becomes personal property.

Chapters 6 through 9 deal with the consumer's relation to personal property. Goods that are bought and sold involve the use of sales contracts. While similar to all other types of contracts, they do have some special requirements under the provisions of the Uniform Commercial Code that are discussed in Chapter 6.

Many consumer dealings with personal property require an understanding of the use of credit. *Credit* is the promise of future payment. Again, the UCC outlines quite clearly the methods for such transactions, which are the topic of Chapter 7.

In the twentieth century, unlike early America, much is being done to protect the consumer. Chapter 8 explains various product guarantees and laws that are in existence for that purpose.

Finally, there are business transactions in which one person gives personal property to another person for a special purpose, with the understanding that the property is to be returned. [See UCC 2-106.] This type of transaction involves a legal relationship called a *bailment.* There are many types of bailments. In each type, there are certain duties and rights of the parties involved. Chapter 9 discusses bailments and their relationship to the consumer.

Chapter 6

The Contract of Sale

OBJECTIVES

After studying this chapter, the student will be able to

- explain various contracts of sale that are enforceable in court.
- describe how and when title and risk of loss are transferred.
- list remedies for sellers and buyers for breach of contract.
- define the following words and phrases.

consumer	risk of loss
property	sale on approval
real property	sale or return
personal property	bulk transfer
sale	conforming goods
contract to sell	incidental damages
contract of sale	insolvent
merchant	cover
nonmerchant	unique goods
title	FOB

THE CONTRACT

In general, a *sale* is the transfer of goods or services from one party to another for a consideration. Buying and selling is the basis of our entire economy. All sales require the use of contracts. There are two types of contracts used in the sale of personal property. The first is called a *contract to sell,* which is a promise to transfer ownership at a future time.

A *contract of sale* (also called a *present sale* or *sale*) is a transfer of ownership at the present time. The rights of the buyers and sellers in both types of contracts are the same according to the UCC. Contracts for the sale of goods are the subject of Chapter 6.

Example. Diaz contracts to sell his entire orange crop to the Great Markets Company. The oranges are to be delivered in about four months, after they are ripe enough to pick. This is a contract to sell — a promise to transfer ownership at a future time.

Example. The Haywards, while touring in California, stop at the Diaz Citrus Groves. They select and pay for a bushel of oranges, and continue on their way. This is a contract of sale, a present sale, or a sale — the transfer of ownership takes place at that very time.

THE UNIFORM COMMERCIAL CODE

The UCC has devoted an entire section (Article 2) to the sale of goods. When the Code came into effect, some important changes in contract law were made, and some existing laws were clarified.

Many of the changes were made to simplify dealings between two merchants, two nonmerchants, or a merchant and a nonmerchant. A *merchant* is defined by the Code as a professional buyer and/or seller having specialized knowledge or skills; *nonmerchants* are consumers, casual buyers or sellers.

Example.

- Dealing between two merchants: A furniture store purchases a truckload of dining room sets from a furniture manufacturer.

- Dealing between nonmerchant and merchant: A homeowner purchases one dining room set from the furniture store.

- Dealing between two nonmerchants: The homeowner sells an old dining room set to a neighbor.

The UCC clarifies many of the business practices involving consumers in the Statute of Frauds. Section 2-201 of Article 2. (For a discussion of the Statute of Frauds rulings on contracts, see Chapter 3.) It has been noted that one contract which must be in writing to be enforceable in court is a contract for a sale of goods of $500 or more. The UCC outlines several ways to satisfy this requirement and several exceptions to that rule.

Written Contract or Memorandum

A contract for a sale of goods of $500 or more is enforceable in court if there is a written contract containing all the necessary

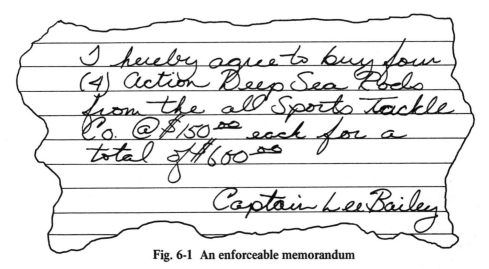

I hereby agree to buy four (4) Action Deep Sea Rods from the all Sports Tackle Co. @ $150⁰⁰ each for a total of $600⁰⁰

Captain Lee Bailey

Fig. 6-1 An enforceable memorandum

elements. A memorandum is acceptable, providing that it is signed by the party against whom enforcement is sought, indicates a contract for the sale of goods, and specifies a quantity of goods. (The correct quantity does not have to be given, but recovery is limited to the amount stated.)

Example. Captain Lee Bailey wants to purchase four Action Deep Sea fishing rods at $150 each for his charter boat from the All Sports Tackle Company. The Company must order them from the manufacturer. A memorandum jotted on a piece of scrap paper and signed by Captain Bailey, figure 6-1, is enforceable in court. Moreover, under the UCC requirements, an acknowledgment signed by Captain Bailey when he receives the goods indicating that he accepts the four fishing rods would be sufficient.

Enforceable Oral Contracts

The UCC makes certain exceptions to the requirement of a writing for a sale of goods over $500. There are several situations in which an oral contract may be enforced. For example, if there is an oral agreement and the buyer has received and accepted all or part of the goods, the agreement is enforceable. Receipt of the goods alone is not enough; the buyer must accept the goods with the intention of taking ownership. [See UCC § 2-201 (3)(c).]

Example.   Suppose that in the previous example, Captain Bailey picks up the rods the same day he visits the store.   There is no written contract or memorandum.   Bailey agrees to pay the following week.   Bailey puts his own fishing line on the rods, and uses them for a week on his charter boat. He has received the goods, and by his actions shows that he has the intention of taking ownership. He is liable for the bill, although there is an oral contract for the sale of goods over $500.

This section of the Code allows that if only part of the goods in an oral contract of $500 or more are received and accepted, the buyer is liable for that part of the goods, but is not liable for the remaining part.

Example.   Using the same example, presume that Captain Bailey orally agrees to purchase the four rods. The All Sports Tackle Company has only two rods in the store; they expect the other two later in the week. Captain Bailey takes the two available rods with him and uses them on his boat. There is no contract of sale or memorandum. In this case, Bailey is legally liable for payment for the two rods which he receives and accepts. He does not, however, have to accept and pay for the other two rods if he so chooses.

An oral contract for a sale of goods of $500 or over is enforceable if a partial payment is made by the buyer. The buyer in such a situation is liable only for that part of the goods for which payment is made.

Example.   Mrs. Komak agrees orally to purchase two hundred lobsters from the Maine Fish Store at three dollars each, for a total of $600. She pays the store a partial payment of $300. After seventy lobsters are delivered (worth $210), she cancels the order and asks for her ninety dollars to be returned to her. (She has received and accepted seventy lobsters worth $210. Since she paid $300 to the store, she still has ninety dollars at the store − $300 minus $210.) The store does not have to return the ninety dollars. She is liable to either accept thirty more lobsters or forfeit the money. The store, however, cannot force her to take the additional one hundred lobsters, either − only that which was paid for by her partial payment.

The statute section allows as enforceable oral contracts for goods which are manufactured for a certain buyer and are not suitable for sale to others. The manufacturer must have begun production of the goods or made commitments to obtain the goods from another source for the contract to be enforced. [See UCC § 2-201 (3)(a).]

Example. The Silo Restaurant orally agrees to have Calico Draperies custom make and install drapes for all the windows in the restaurant for a total of $1,200. Calico Draperies buys $800 worth of fabric that the Silo has chosen and begins cutting it. The Silo attempts to cancel the agreement. The courts enforce the contract, since the company has already obligated itself and the draperies are not suitable for sale to anyone else.

Finally, if one party admits in court that there was an oral contract, the oral contract is enforceable in a sale of goods of $500 or more.

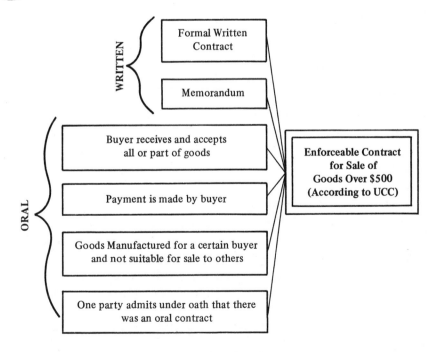

Fig. 6-2 Various types of enforceable written and oral contracts for a sale of goods of $500 or more.

Example.   *B* brings court action to collect payment from *C* for $1,000 worth of goods sold to *C.*   *C* claims that there was no written contract and that the agreement is therefore not enforceable under the Statute of Frauds.   Under oath, however, *C* admits that there was an oral contract with *B* to avoid committing perjury.   The contract is now enforceable.

TITLE

A *title* represents legal ownership of property.   This includes the right to possess, to use, and to dispose of the property.

Transfer of Title and Risk of Loss

In contracts of sale, there is a transfer of title.   This means that the ownership shifts from one party to another.   Rules for the passing of title are included in the UCC.

If the goods in a contract of sale are damaged or destroyed, there is a question as to who must absorb the loss, the buyer or the seller.   This is known as the *risk of loss.*   Prior to the Code, it was often difficult to determine who actually had title at the time of loss, which in turn made court decisions difficult.

Under the UCC, parties may decide to divide the risk of loss.   In the absence of such an agreement, the Code clarifies various times at which risk of loss passes in business transactions.

Example.   Beth contracts to purchase a coffee table which Mac agrees to produce by hand to certain specifications.   Title does not pass until the table is in existence and identified as belonging to Beth.

For example, unless otherwise agreed, title passes to the buyer when the seller's performance is completed.   [See UCC § 2-401.] If the contract requires the seller to ship the goods, title passes when the seller delivers the goods to the carrier.   This is identified by the shipping term known as *FOB (free on board) the place of shipment.* The buyer must bear the risk of loss if something happens to the goods in transit.   If, however, the contract requires the seller to deliver the goods to the buyer, title passes when the goods are delivered.   Up to that point, the loss is the responsibility of the seller.   This is identified by the phrase *FOB place of destination.*   [See UCC § 2-319 (1).]   Upon delivery to the buyer, the buyer assumes the risk.

The seller must have clear title (definite ownership) to transfer that title. Therefore, someone who sells stolen goods is not transferring the title, since that title legally belongs to the original owner. It was not legally transferred to the thief.

Example. Jensen unknowingly buys a stolen television set. The television was stolen from Mitchell. Mitchell still retains title to the television and can reclaim it from Jensen. Jensen does not have title to the television, since the thief never legally had the title to pass.

Sales on Approval. Goods may be delivered to a buyer with the agreement that the buyer may use the goods for a period of time to determine whether he or she wants to purchase them or not. This is known as *sale on approval.* [See UCC §§ 2-326(1) and 2-327(1).] The transfer of title and risk of loss do not pass until the buyer actually accepts the goods. Acceptance is considered to be given if the buyer keeps the goods; if the buyer does not notify the seller of nonacceptance within a reasonable time; or if the buyer fails to notify the seller that the goods will be returned. The seller must accept the risk and expense for the return of the goods.

Example. Carol purchases a painting on approval from a local artist. She wants to hang it in her living room for a week to decide if she really likes it. The artist still has title and risk of loss of the painting. If Carol pays for the painting after the week has passed, she will then have title and risk of loss.

Sale or Return. Goods are sometimes sold under a *sale or return* agreement; in this arrangement, the buyer may resell some of the goods to the seller within the time limits of the contract. To distinguish the sale or return from the sale on approval, the Code offers a rule of thumb in Section 2-326(3). If the goods are purchased primarily for resale, the transaction is said to be a sale or return. Upon delivery and acceptance, the buyer has title and risk of loss of all the goods. The buyer is responsible for the cost and risk of return to the seller. When the goods are returned, the seller regains title and risk.

Example. Stan buys 100 boxes of greeting cards from Big Cards, Inc. on a sale or return arrangement. He has three months to return any number of boxes he has not sold by that time. He is responsible for the boxes while he has them. After two months, he has twenty-five boxes remaining unsold. In returning them to Big Cards, he pays for the shipping. Since there are no damages or loss, the money is returned to him for the twenty-five boxes.

Bulk Transfers.   Dishonest merchants at times might sell all of a store's *inventory* (goods on hand), keep the money, and not pay the debts owed to creditors. Under Article 6 of the Code, creditors are protected from this possibility by a ruling on bulk transfers. A *bulk transfer* is a sale which occurs when the major part of the materials or supplies of a business are sold, usually to a new owner. The seller must give the buyer a list of all debts and creditors, and the buyer in turn must give the creditors ten days notice of the sale.

PERFORMANCE

The rules regarding performance of a contract of sale are basically the same as the rules in performance for all contracts. These are included in Article 2 of the UCC. Sales contracts can be assigned and duties in the contract can be delegated. As with other contracts of law, the original party to the contract is still liable for the contract even though duties have been delegated. Some of the Code rulings deal specifically with sales transactions.

Delivery

It is the seller's duty to deliver goods according to the terms of the contract of sale [See UCC § 2-301.] If the seller is required only to ship the goods, but not to deliver them to a specific destination, the seller must see that the goods reach the carrier and notify the buyer of shipment. [See UCC § § 2-308 and 2-503.] When the seller properly delivers the goods to a carrier or to a destination, the buyer is obligated to accept and pay for them.

Inspection and Payment

The buyer usually has the right to inspect the goods before accepting and paying for them. The time and place for the inspection may be included in the agreement; if it is not, it may be made after arrival of the goods. Unless there is a credit agreement, payment must be made by the buyer after inspection and upon delivery. [See UCC § § 2-512 and 2-513.]

Acceptance and Rejection

Acceptance of goods occurs when, after inspection, the buyer indicates to the seller that the goods will be kept. If the goods conform to the contract, the buyer must accept them or be liable for breach of contract. If the goods do not conform to the agreement, the buyer may reject them. The seller then has the expense of returning the goods. [See UCC §§ 2-206 and 2-607.]

Example. Mr. Holmes orders two truckloads of # 1 size gravel to be delivered for his driveway. When the trucks arrive, Holmes inspects the gravel and finds that it is size # 3. He rejects the delivery. The gravel company is responsible for the expense involved in the delivery of a second load of gravel.

REMEDIES FOR BREACH

Seller's Remedies

In all of the following remedy situations, it is presumed that the goods of the seller conform to contract specifications.

Recovery of Purchase Price. The seller is entitled to be paid the purchase price if the goods have been delivered to and accepted by the buyer. If the risk of loss has passed to the buyer and the goods are then damaged, the seller still has the right to receive payment of the purchase price. [See UCC § 2-709.]

Example. Disk Sounds delivers four hundred records to the Corner Record Shop, with payment due in ten days. The title has been transferred as well as the risk of loss. Two days after delivery, there is a flood in the storage celler of the shop, and all four hundred records are ruined. The seller has the right to collect the amount owed on the records, since the risk of loss was upon the buyer.

If the buyer wrongfully refuses to accept and pay for the goods, the seller must attempt to reduce the loss by trying to resell the goods, an act known as *cover.* If they cannot be resold, the seller is entitled to the purchase price. [See UCC § 2-708.]

Recovery of Damages. The seller is entitled to payment of damages to compensate for the loss which results from a breach by the buyer by nonacceptance of the goods. Under the UCC, if the buyer refuses the goods, the amount of the damages is the difference between the market price at the time and place of tender, and the unpaid contract price. Also included in damages due the seller are *incidental damages,* which include such items as expenses to the seller for shipping of goods and their storage. [See UCC § 2-710.]

Example. Seaside Inn orders twelve sets of outdoor furniture from the Casual Chair Company for $2,400. The Inn wrongfully refuses to accept the goods when delivered, thus breaching the contract. Meanwhile, as this occurs at the end of the season, the market value of the furniture drops to $1,800. Casual Chair Company can bring action for damages in the amount of $600 ($2,400 minus $1,800), plus the cost of shipping the chairs back and forth and storing them in the warehouse (incidental damages).

The seller may *cover,* or resell the goods that a buyer has wrongfully refused to accept. The seller must make the resale in good faith and in a commercially reasonable manner; in other words, honestly. In addition, the buyer must be notified of the sale. If the seller makes more from the resale than the original contract price of the goods, the seller keeps the profit. If, however, the resale brings less than the contract price, the seller can sue for damages for the difference and incidental damages. [See UCC § 2-706.]

Example. Suppose that in the previous example, Casual Chair Company resells the furniture in the proper manner and receives only $1,000. They could then sue Seaside Inn for $1,400 ($2,400 minus $1,000) and for the incidental expenses they incur because of the breach.

It should be noted that the seller may sue for the difference in contract price and market value, for the price, or for the difference between contract price and resale price, but not a combination of these remedies. The action for the price set out in Section 2-709 is usually reserved for the instances in which the buyer has accepted the goods and not paid for them, or in which the goods cannot be resold on the market, as is the case with custom-made goods.

Example. In the situation involving the Seaside Inn, suppose that the furniture was embossed with the Seaside Inn trademark. If the

Inn took delivery of the goods and did not pay for them, Casual Chair Company would have an action for the price. Obviously, no resale is possible since the seller does not have the goods to sell to another buyer. If the Inn wrongfully refuses to accept the goods, Casual Chair is still able to sue for the price. It is doubtful that any new buyer could be found because of the Seaside Inn trademark on the goods. If the seller sues for the price, the goods must be held for the buyer.

Stopping Delivery or Shipment. The seller has the right to stop delivery or to order the carrier not to make delivery in several situations. If the buyer breaches the contract or fails to make payment that was due before delivery, or if the seller learns that the buyer is *insolvent* (unable to pay debts), the seller can stop delivery or shipment. [See UCC § 2-705.]

Example. Wild Lumber Company has a contract to deliver a truckload of siding to Bob White, a local builder, on a certain date. White is to pay the lumber company two days before delivery. There is no payment by White; therefore, Wild Lumber has the right to stop delivery.

Reclaiming of Goods. The seller may learn that the buyer is insolvent after the goods have been delivered. Since the buyer has no funds for payment, it would be useless to sue for the purchase price. The UCC allows the seller to reclaim the goods. A demand for the goods must be made within ten days of delivery, although the physical act of reclaiming the goods does not have to occur within that time period. [See UCC § 2-702(2).]

Buyer's Remedies

The buyer is entitled to receive *conforming goods;* that is, goods which are specified in the contract. If the goods do not conform to the contract or are not tendered (offered for acceptance), there are certain remedies for the buyer in the Code.

Damages for Nondelivery. If the seller wrongfully fails or refuses to deliver the goods, the buyer may sue for damages. The amount of damages is the difference between the contract price and the new market price at the time of the breach. [See UCC § 2-713.]

Example. Tony contracts to buy 200 pounds of butter at fifty cents per pound for use in his restaurant. The delivery is to be in two months. One week before that date, the dairy wrongfully refuses to deliver; they claim that the market price is now seventy-five cents per pound. Tony can sue for damages of fifty dollars (market price at time of breach, $150, minus the contract price of $100) and incidental damages.

If the seller fails or refuses to deliver the goods, the buyer can also cover, or purchase goods similar to those in the contract in good faith on the open market. The buyer can then sue for damages from the seller. The damages would be the difference in the cost of cover and the contract price, and any incidental damages incurred [See UCC § 2-712.]

Example. In the previous example, Tony had to have the butter to continue his business; therefore, he was able to cover, or purchase the 200 pounds elsewhere. Suppose that after comparing prices, Tony found that he was able to purchase the butter at seventy cents a pound. He could then sue for forty dollars (cover cost of $140 minus the contract price of $100) and any incidental damages.

Damages for Defective Goods. The buyer may accept goods without realizing that they are defective and do not conform to specifications in the contract. The buyer must notify the seller within a reasonable period of time. If the seller does nothing to replace them, the buyer may then sue for damages. The amount of the damages is the contract price minus the value of the goods actually received, and any incidental damages incurred.   [See UCC §§ 2-601, 2-602, 2-607 and 2-714.]

Example. Kilmer purchases a diamond ring for his wife for $2,500. When he has the ring appraised by two other dealers for insurance purposes, he finds that the diamond is defective and is worth only $100. The store refuses to replace the ring. Kilmer sues for $2,400 (contract price of $2,500 minus actual value of $100) and the cost of the other appraisals.

Recovering Goods. Buyers may recover goods through specific performance when the courts feel that the buyer would suffer hardship or if the goods are considered to be unique. Goods are *unique* when similar goods are not available from another source. Specific performance compels the seller to act according to the terms of the contract. [See UCC § 2-716.]

Example. Mrs. Ames contracts to purchase a large handmade wall hanging for her living room. She has the room painted and the furniture reupholstered to match the colors in the hanging. When the store wrongfully refuses to sell the hanging to Mrs. Ames, she sues to recover the goods through specific performance. In this case, the courts would most likely rule that the item is unique and grant recovery.

SELF-EVALUATION

Provide a brief explanation for each of the following.

1. Differentiate between a contract to sell and a contract of sale.
2. Is a consumer a merchant? Why or why not?
3. List four situations in which an oral contract for a sale of $500 or over is enforceable in court.
4. What is the legal meaning of *title* and what rights does it include?
5. How does completion of the seller's performance affect title and risk of loss?
6. Who has title and risk of loss when goods are delivered to a buyer for a sale on approval? When does it change?
7. Who is protected by the UCC in a bulk transfer situation?
8. When may a buyer reject goods and not be breaching a contract of sale?
9. What happens to the profit from a resale of goods that a buyer has refused to accept?
10. If goods have already been delivered to an insolvent buyer, what can the seller do?
11. When the seller does not deliver goods and the buyer's cost of cover is more than the contract price, what may the buyer do?
12. If a buyer is sold defective goods, what action is taken first? What else can then be done?
13. If a buyer does not want to collect damages, but instead wants the contract goods, what remedy is available?
14. For what do the letters *UCC* stand?

SUGGESTED ACTIVITIES

1. X contracts to sell Y $25,000 worth of gasoline.

   a. The day it is delivered, tanks belonging to Y leak and $10,000 of gasoline is lost. Y pays X $15,000 in ten days when he receives the bill. What can X do? Why?

   b. Prior to delivery, X learns that Y is insolvent. The delivery is canceled. What can Y do? Why?

2. Z contracts to sell M $2,100 worth of cut flowers.

   a. M refuses to accept the flowers. The next day, after notice is given to M that Z plans to sell to another buyer, Z trucks the flowers at a cost of forty dollars and is able to sell them at half price even though they are slightly wilted. What else can Z do?

   b. M refuses shipment. Z resells the flowers for $2,150. What can M do to recover the fifty dollars above the original contract price?

   c. M refuses to accept the flowers. Z finds no buyer and the flowers die. What can Z do?

   d. On the day M needs the flowers, they are not delivered. M covers at the cost of $2,500. What else can M do?

CASES FOR STUDY

1. A grocery store orders $450 worth of a new product by telephone. When the order arrives, the manager of the store refuses to pay for it, saying that the contract is unenforceable because it is not in writing. Is the manager correct? Why or why not?

2. M orders personalized stationery from a printer. When the order arrives, M notices that the address is incorrect and immediately sends the stationery back with a letter of explanation. Does M have to pay for the printing of new stationery? Why or why not?

3. A food processing company enters into a contract in November to purchase carrots from X in June at twenty-five cents a pound. By June, carrots are selling at fifteen cents a pound. The company buys carrots elsewhere at the lower price and refuses to buy any carrots from X. May X keep the carrots and recover twenty-five cents a pound? May X sell the carrots to other buyers and collect twenty-five cents a pound from the food processing company?

4. Custom Car, Incorporated takes an order for a custom car. Before the car is complete, the manufacturer hears of the customer's insolvency. What can Custom Car do?

5. *D* contracts to purchase goods from *L*. One of the provisions of the contract specifies that *L* ship the goods. If the goods are damaged in transit, who bears the risk of loss?

6. Prestige Furriers, Inc. contracts to sell ten full-length mink coats to Right Department Store on October 15. The seller requires payment by November 15 and the buyer complies. When the coats arrive on November 20 the store personnel discover that they are all three-quarter length. What should the department store do?

7. *T* buys a sofa on approval from a furniture store. When it is delivered, *T* discovers that the sofa is too large for the room and calls the furniture store to pick it up. The sofa is damaged on the return trip while in the hands of the delivery service. Who bears the risk of loss, *T* or the furniture store?

Chapter 7

The Secured Credit Sale

OBJECTIVES

After studying this chapter, the student will be able to

- list the various types of credit available to the consumer.
- explain what is involved in drawing up a security agreement and financing statement.
- outline possible consequences of a buyer defaulting on a secured credit sale.
- define the following words and phrases.

credit	debtor
unsecured credit	security payment
secured credit	default
security interest	financing statement
collateral	repossession
secured party	breach of peace

Credit is the power to buy or borrow on trust; that is, buying or borrowing on the promise of future payment. Consumers use credit for numerous purchases. Credit can be divided into two classes, unsecured and secured.

Unsecured credit entails the greatest risk for creditors. Articles or services are sold and payment is promised. Nothing assures that payment will be made except the promise of the person obtaining the credit. No specific article can be taken back to satisfy the claim of the creditor. When nonpayment occurs, there can be lengthy and costly court actions against the promisor, but the creditor runs the risk of there being no assets from which to collect. Department store charge accounts are often an example of unsecured credit transactions.

Secured credit is much less risky for creditors. The seller keeps a security interest in the goods which the buyer owns. The UCC defines *security interest* as an interest in personal property which secures (assures) payment or performance of an obligation. If the buyer fails to pay, the security interest allows the seller to repossess (take back) the goods. The financing of appliances and automobiles is usually done by secured credit.

Article 9 of the UCC is devoted entirely to secured credit transactions and gives definite rules on how they should be handled. By following the steps in a typical financed automobile purchase, the secured credit transaction can be more easily understood.

SECURITY INTEREST

As previously noted, a security interest assures the seller of payment for personal property. The personal property itself is known as *collateral.* Under the UCC, collateral may be documents, contract rights, or goods. The Code also clearly lists what goods can be used as collateral. Chapter 7 deals solely with goods as collateral for a security interest.

Consider the following situation. James King decides to buy a used car from Mace Motors. He has some cash, but not enough for the car he wants to purchase, so he decides to finance it. He plans to enter into a secured credit transaction and use the car as collateral. There are several steps to be taken before he takes possession of the car. For the purpose of this example, assume that King does not live in a title state. A title state issues certificates of title to show ownership of a vehicle. Section 9-302(3) of the UCC allows for slight differences in the procedure for a secured credit arrangement in such states.

SECURITY AGREEMENT

The party who is extending the credit is the *secured party;* the borrower is the *debtor.* If the collateral is in the possession of the debtor, the UCC requires that there be a written agreement, known as a *security agreement.* This document gives the secured party the security interest in the collateral.

King investigates several sources of credit before buying the car, since annual interest rates vary among banks, credit institutions, and car dealers. King decides the best way to finance his car is through Mace Motors. Since King will have the car (the collateral) in his possession, he must enter into a written security agreement with Mace Motors, figure 7-1.

Date _____   No. _____

$ _____

FOR VALUE RECEIVED, the undersigned ("Debtor", jointly and severally if more than one, promises to pay to the order of Mace Motors ("Mace"), the sum of _____ Dollars ($ _____) in accordance with the disclosures and pursuant to the schedules set forth below:

Insurance Coverage

| | 1. Amount to Customer | 1. _____ | Class 01 1. _____ |

The purchase of Group Credit Accident and Sickness Insurance is voluntary and not required by Mace. Such insurance, insuring the Debtor whose signature appears immediately below, may be obtained through Mace at the cost set forth providing this Debtor qualifies for such insurance.

Cost: $ _____

I desire Group Credit Accident and Sickness Insurance coverage at the cost set forth.

Signed: _____
               Covered by A & S Insurance

Date _____

For Class 01 loans, the purchase of Group Credit Life Insurance is voluntary and not required by Mace. Such insurance, insuring the life of the Debtor whose signature appears immediately below, may be obtained through Mace at the cost set forth providing this Debtor qualifies for such insurance.

Cost: $ _____

I desire Group Credit Life Insurance coverage at the cost set forth.

Signed: _____
               Covered by Life Insurance

Date _____

1. Amount to Customer   1. _____   1. _____

2. Filing Fee   +2. _____   +2. _____

3. Amount of Loan (1 + 2)   3. _____   3. _____

4. Credit Life Insurance   +4. _____   +4. _____

5. Credit A & S Insurance   +5. _____   +5. _____   ②

6. Amount Financed (3 + 4 + 5)   6. _____   6. _____

7. Finance Charge
   (a) Interest }7. _____ | Interest |
   (b) Credit Life Ins. }   7. _____

8. Total of Payments (6+7)   8. _____   8. _____

9. **Annual Percentage Rate**   9. _____   9. _____

Total of Payments shall be paid in _____ successive monthly installments of $ _____ each and a final installment of $ _____ commencing on _____, 19___, with payments due consecutively on the same date of each month. Debtor may at any time pay the unpaid balance in full or in part, any partial prepayments to be credited against amounts last falling due. Upon prepayment in full, or a default under section 2.E, Mace will refund (1) any unearned interest computed under the Rule of 78's, provided, however, that a minimum charge for interest of $10.00 may be retained; and (2) insurance premiums to the extent such premiums were not paid or payable by Mace or were refunded to it. No refund for interest will be made where the total interest payable was less than $10.00, and no refund of amounts less than $1.00 for interest or insurance will be made.   ②a

For each installment which is due and unpaid for a period in excess of 10 days, Debtor shall pay a late charge of 5% of the amount of each such delinquent installment, or $5.00, whichever is less. In the event of a default under this Note, Mace in its sole discretion may elect to make the unpaid balance of the Note immediately due and payable. If this Note is not paid pursuant to its terms, Debtor shall pay the actual expenditures, including reasonable attorneys fees, for necessary court process. Mace retains a security interest in the Collateral for this Note as provided below and on the reverse, and it may, in its sole discretion, foreclose this security interest in the event of Debtor's default. Upon Debtor's default, Mace may also set off against the amount due it any of Debtor's property then in its possession.   ③

This Note shall also be subject to and include the Terms and Conditions set forth below and on the reverse:

1. **Security Interest.** To secure the payment of this Note, and any and all other liabilities of Debtor to Mace whether now existing or hereafter arising, and any extensions, renewals, or modifications thereof, Debtor hereby grants to the Bank a security interest, as defined in the New York Uniform Commercial Code, in the goods described below together with all accessories, additions, accretions, substitutions and replacements, and all appurtenances, fixtures and furnishings, and standard and optional equipment added thereto, all of which shall be deemed personal property (individually and collectively-"the Collateral"):

Motor Vehicles:

Year	Factory Make	Type of Body	Model	Truck-Bus Cap. Wgt.	Serial Number	Motor Number	No. of Cyl.	New Used

①

Debtor irrevocably authorizes Secured Party to perfect this security interest by filing a financing statement without Debtor's signature or by such other procedures as Secured Party shall deem prudent. To the extent permitted by law, Debtor shall pay the costs of this perfection, and such costs may be added to the amount of this Note.

2. **Covenants:** The Debtor hereby warrants and covenants:

A. If checked here ( ), the Collateral is being acquired with the proceeds of the above note, which may be paid directly to the Seller thereof by Mace.

B. The Collateral is used primarily for personal, family or household use.

C. The Debtor's residence is as specified below, and the address at which the Collateral shall be kept is as follows:

_____
    (No. and Street)   (City, Village)   (County)   (State)   (Zip)

See reverse side for additional Terms and Conditions.

Debtor acknowledges receipt of an executed copy of this Note and Security Agreement at the time of execution.

MACE MOTORS, CO.

By _____   X _____   _____
        (Signature)   Debtor (Covered by Life Insurance)   Social Security Number

_____   Address _____
        (Title)

                                                 X _____   _____
_____ _____   Debtor   Social Security Number
Officer Code   Office Code

REMOVE CARBON AND SIGN ON REVERSE SIDE   Address _____

Fig. 7-1 Simplified version of security agreement (page 1)

3. **Further Covenants:** Debtor covenants and agrees (A) to keep the Collateral at the address set forth on the front of this Note and Security Agreement, and not to remove the Collateral from such address without the prior written consent of Mace, except for temporary and ordinary use of not more than 30 days; (B) not to sell, transfer, assign, lease, rent or convey said Collateral or any interest therein; (C) to use the Collateral in a careful and prudent manner and to keep it in good repair, free and clear of all liens and incumbrances, and to give immediate written notice to Mace of any loss or injury to the Collateral; (D) to insure the Collateral against such loss as required by Mace in a company or companies acceptable to Mace, and to make the loss or damage, if any, payable first to Mace and then to Debtor, as their respective interests may appear, and to deposit the policies with Mace; in the event Debtor fails to do so, Mace may insure the Collateral, but without any obligation to do so under any circumstances, and any sum so expended by it shall be deemed part of the indebtedness secured hereby, and shall be paid by Debtor to Mace on demand; Debtor hereby appoints Mace Debtor's agent with full authority to make any claim or settlement under such insurance, to cancel the same upon repossession or otherwise, to execute any and all instruments in connection therewith, to indorse any loss payment or returned premium check in Debtor's name and to apply the proceeds thereof to any sum owing hereon, and Debtor hereby directs any such insurance company to pay directly to Mace any sum payable thereunder; (E) in the event certificates of title or registration are issued or outstanding as to any one of the Collateral, to cause the interest of Mace to be properly noted thereon, if permitted or required by applicable law; (F) to permit Mace free access and right of inspection of the Collateral at all times; (G) to authorize Mace to insert herein the model, serial number(s) and similar information concerning the Collateral and to correct any patent errors or omissions herein or in any other instrument pertaining to this transaction; (H) in the event of repossession of Collateral registered as vehicles, Mace may use Debtor's license plates from point of repossession to Mace's place of storage; (I) to authorize, and does hereby authorize, Mace to file this agreement or any Financing Statement pertaining hereto with such filing officer(s) as it may deem necessary or advantageous, but without any obligation on its part to do so, and Debtor upon demand shall pay Mace the cost thereof, together with the cost of filing any Continuation Statement hereof, and to avoid additional filing expense, Debtor requests Mace not to file a Termination Statement hereof until Debtor so requests in writing and pays the cost thereof.

4. **Repossession and Resale:** Upon the happening of any of the following events, with respect to Debtor, or any person secondarily liable hereon, or any one of them, if more than one: (A) the making of any materially untrue statement, representation or warranty herein or in any loan application or other statement given to Mace; (B) failure to pay any sum of money owing to Mace and secured hereby, or to perform any obligation due Mace, whether contained herein or elsewhere; (C) loss or damage to the Collateral or abandonment thereof or failure to take proper care of the Collateral; (D) death or legal incapacity; (E) the termination of the lease of the premises where the Collateral is located; (F) the entry of judgment, the commencement of a proceeding supplementary to judgment, or the issuance of an attachment, execution, levy or other legal process; (G) insolvency, appointment of a receiver or commencement of any proceedings under any bankruptcy or insolvency statute; (H) Mace at any time deems itself, the indebtedness secured hereby, or the security interest herein created, to be insecure, unsafe or at any risk, then in any such event, Mace may accelerate the maturity of all or any part of the indebtedness secured hereby, which shall become due and payable immediately, without any demand or notice, and Debtor shall thereupon immediately pay the same to Mace. Mace shall have all the rights and remedies of a secured party provided by the New York State Uniform Commercial Code. Upon Mace's demand, Debtor will assemble the Collateral and make it available to Mace at a place designated by Mace which is reasonably convenient to Debtor and Mace. Mace may enter the premises where the Collateral, or any part thereof, is located and retake the same. Mace may thereafter sell the Collateral at public or private sale, as provided by said Code, and after deducting the expenses of retaking, holding, repairing, preparing for sale, sale and reasonable attorney fees of not less than fifteen per cent of the amount secured hereby and owing by Debtor, if referred to an attorney for collection and enforcement, apply the net proceeds thereof to the amount owing by Debtor to Mace and secured hereby. If the net proceeds from such sale remaining after paying such costs and expenses are not sufficient to pay the indebtedness secured hereby, Debtor shall pay any deficiency. Mace may bid and purchase the Collateral at any such sale. The surplus, if any, will be paid by Mace to Debtor. All claims, damages and demands against Mace arising out of such repossession, retention, removal or sale are hereby waived and released by Debtor, and Debtor agrees to indemnify and save Mace harmless from any and all loss suffered by it by reason thereof. Upon the happening of any of the above events of default, Mace may, at its option, terminate this Agreement in whole or in part, and may, without demand, and without notice, enter upon the premises where the Collateral is kept, take possession thereof and may remove the same, and any additions, accessions, accretions, equipment, parts, replacements or substitutions therein or thereto with or without process of law.

④

I HAVE READ AND AGREE TO THESE TERMS AND CONDITIONS

		X	
Debtor	(Signature)	Debtor	(Signature)

Fig. 7-1 Simplified version of security agreement (page 2)

This paper must describe the collateral clearly enough so that it can be identified (item (1), figure 7-1). The agreement then specifies the financial terms and conditions of the transaction. This usually includes a description of how the payments are to be made (items (2) and (2A), figure 7-1). There also might be an explanation of what constitutes default by the buyer and what recourse would be available to the seller. *Default* is failure to perform an obligation. King would default if he failed to comply with one or more terms in the agreement (item (3), figure 7-1). Additional reasons for default and remedies available to the secured party are listed in item on page 2 of the agreement. Failure to comply with terms could include failure to repair damaged collateral or failure to make prompt payments. The terms also include requirements by the secured party which would protect its interest in the collateral, such as the insurance requirement.

THE FINANCING STATEMENT

The secured party must further protect its interest in the collateral against other creditors of the debtor or against sale of the collateral by the debtor. Mace Motors needs to be protected if King decides to sell the car before all the payments are made. This is most commonly done by filing a *financing statement.* The purpose of the financing statement is to give public notice of the secured party's interest so that a later purchaser of the collateral cannot claim lack of knowledge of the security interest. The proper location for filing is included in state statutes, but is usually a county clerk's office. Most states use the Standard UCC Form-1, figure 7-2.

The financing statement must include the signature of the secured party and the debtor, the address of the secured party and the debtor, and a description of the collateral [See UCC § 9-402.] If a maturity date (which is optional) is not included, or if the debt is payable on demand, the filing is valid for five years. If a maturity date is given, the filing is valid for sixty days beyond the stated period, but still cannot exceed five years. Statements extending the maturity date can be filed. [See UCC § 9-403.]

When King completely pays off his debt for the car, he is entitled to receive a statement terminating the financing statement. A third carbon copy of the Standard UCC Form-1 usually contains such a statement, figure 7-3. The form is signed by the secured party and delivered to the filing location. At this point, the financing

Uniform Commercial Code – NY FINANCING STATEMENT – Form UCC-1

IMPORTANT – Read instructions on back before filling out form.

This FINANCING STATEMENT is presented to a Filing Officer for filing pursuant to the Uniform Commercial Code.

| No. of Additional Sheets Presented: | 3. Maturity Date (optional): |

2. Secured Party(ies): Name(s) and Address(es):

4. For Filing Officer: Date, Time, No. Filing Office

1. Debtor(s) (Last Name First) and Address(es)

6. Assignee(s) of Secured Party and Address(es)

5. This Financing Statement covers the following types (or items) of property:

☐ Proceeds are also covered.   ☐ Products of the Collateral are also covered.

7. ☐ The described crops are growing or to be grown on *
☐ The described goods are or are to be affixed to: *
* (Describe Real Estate Below):

8. Describe Real Estate Here:

9. Name(s) of Record Owner(s):

| No. & Street | Town or City | County | Section | Block | Lot |

10. This statement is filed without the debtor's signature to perfect a security interest in collateral (check appropriate box)
☐ under a security agreement signed by debtor authorizing secured party to file this statement.
☐ already subject to a security interest in another jurisdiction when it was brought into this state.
☐ which is proceeds of the original collateral described above in which a security interest was perfected:

By _____

By _____

_____
(Signature(s) of Debtor(s)

_____
Signature(s) of Secured Party(ies)

(1) Filing Officer Copy – Numerical

FIN-069A   (9/65) NY STANDARD FORM – FORM UCC-1 – Approved by John P. Lomenzo, Secretary of State of New York

Fig. 7-2 Standard UCC Form-1

Uniform Commercial Code – NY FINANCING STATEMENT – Form UCC-1

IMPORTANT – Read instructions on back before filling out form.

This FINANCING STATEMENT is presented to a Filing Officer for filing pursuant to the Uniform Commercial Code.

| No. of Additional Sheets Presented: | Maturity Date 3. (optional): |

1. Debtor(s) (Last Name First) and Address(es)

2. Secured Party(ies): Name(s) and Address(es):

4. For Filing Officer: Date, Time, No. Filing Office

6. Assignee(s) of Secured Party and Address(es)

5. This Financing Statement covers the following types (or items) of property:

☐ Proceeds are also covered.   ☐ Products of the Collateral are also covered.

7. ☐ The described crops are growing or to be grown on *
☐ The described goods are or are to be affixed to: *
* (Describe Real Estate Below):

9. Name(s) of Record Owner(s):

8. Describe Real Estate Here:

| No. & Street | Town or City | County | Section | Block | Lot |

TERMINATION STATEMENT: This Statement of Termination of Financing is presented to a Filing Officer for filing pursuant to the Uniform Commercial Code. The Secured Party certifies that the Secured Party no longer claims a security interest under the financing statement bearing the file number shown above.

Date ———— 19 ————

By: _____

(Signature of Secured Party or Assignee of Record Not Valid Until Signed)

(3) Filing Officer Copy – Acknowledgment Filing Officer is requested to note file number, date and hour of filing on this copy and return to the person filing as an acknowledgment.

Fig. 7-3 The third carbon copy of Form-1 usually contains a notice of termination of the financial statement.

statement is removed from the records and the secured party's interest in the collateral is released. [See UCC § 9-404.]

DEFAULT

A debtor is in *default* if he or she fails to comply with any of the terms of the security agreement. In addition to any remedies for a default situation that may be specified in the agreement, the Code also lists certain remedies.

Repossession

In most cases the secured party will want to *repossess* (regain possession of) the collateral as soon as possible after default by the debtor. This may be done on the condition that there is no *breach of peace;* that is, the secured party cannot take the goods back with threats of force or harm to the debtor or to the debtor's property. The debtor must voluntarily return the goods. If the debtor does not voluntarily give up the goods, the secured party must take legal action to have the goods returned. [See UCC § 9-503.]

LONG ISLAND TRUST COMPANY v. PORTA ALUMINUM, INC.

Supreme Court of New York, Appellate Division, 1975
49 App. Div. 2d 579, 370 N.Y.S. 2d 166

[Gilbalstan, Inc. executed a security agreement to Long Island Trust Company creating a security interest in motor vehicles owned by Gilbalstan to secure repayment of a loan in the amount of $23,952.24 loaned by the Trust Company. Gilbalstan sold some of the vehicles to Porta Aluminum, Inc. without the Trust Company's permission. Gilbalstan did not make payments on the loan. The Trust Company therefore decided to repossess the vehicles but discovered that the vehicles had been sold. They then attempted to repossess from the new owners. The new owners refused to turn over the trucks, and the Trust Company filed suit. According to the findings of the court, Porta was forced to turn over the vehicles to the Trust Company.]

MEMORANDUM BY THE COURT.

* * *

Unless otherwise agreed, a secured party has, on default, the right to take possession of the collateral. This right may be enforced against third parties in possession [the Aluminum Company]. Here, that right was denied to plaintiff by Porta's improper refusal to turn over the collateral when requested. Article 9 of the Uniform Commercial Code contains various provisions which specify what a secured party may do upon obtaining posssssion. For example, section 9-207 (subd. [4]) states that a "secured party may use or operate the collateral for the purpose of preserving the collateral or its value," and section 9-504 (subd. [1]) states that a "secured party after default may sell, lease or otherwise dispose of any or all of the collateral." In other words, the code recognizes that, depending upon the type of collateral involved, and other circumstances, the secured party has the right to use or lease or otherwise exercise dominion over it.

· · ·

. . .The vehicles here, which the jury found to have a collective value of $9,750, are in constant use in interstate commerce and, consequently, have a substantial use value. If they had been surrendered to [the Trust Company] immediately upon default and demand, it could have sold them and applied the proceeds to the debt. But [the Trust Company] was prevented from doing so by Porta, which used the vehicles for many months, subjecting them to daily wear and tear, despite plaintiff's superior right of possession. The vehicles are obviously worth less now than when defendant was first asked to return them. Furthermore, they are the type of collateral which can be leased [citation omitted]. They have a "usable" value which can be easily measured [citation omitted]. The burden of this loss of use sustained by plaintiff should fall upon Porta, the one directly responsible therefor.

Disposing of Collateral

Once the secured party has taken possession, the collateral may be disposed of, usually by sale. Generally, the secured party is more interested in the value the collateral represents than having possession of the collateral. The purpose of the sale is to convert the collateral into cash. If the debtor has paid for 60 percent or more of the collateral and the goods involved are consumer goods, the secured party must dispose of them within ninety days after taking possession. [See UCC § 9-505.] The repossessed collateral may be disposed of at a public or private sale. The secured party must notify the debtor of the sale and must take the necessary steps to receive the maximum amount for the property.

The debtor can redeem the goods at any time prior to the sale by paying all that is owed. This includes all the expenses incurred by the secured party as a result of the default and repossession. [See UCC § 9-506.]

If the sale results in a profit, the debtor is entitled to any money that remains after the debt and all expenses of the repossession and sale are paid. If the sale results in a *deficiency,* an amount that is less than the value of the debt and expenses, the debtor is expected to pay the difference. [See UCC § 9-504.] If the debtor refuses to pay, the secured party may bring legal action to collect. The amount of the deficiency would be unsecured, so a regular civil suit must be commenced, and there is a risk that the debtor will not have any assets with which to pay.

If the debtor has paid less than 60 percent of the price of the goods, the secured party does not have to sell the goods, but may keep the repossessed collateral in full satisfaction of the debt. In such cases, the debtor must be notified. The debtor then has thirty days to object. If there is such an objection, the goods must be sold.

SELF-EVALUATION

Provide a brief explanation for each of the following.

1. Differentiate between unsecured and secured credit.
2. What is collateral?
3. What is the purpose of a security agreement?
4. When is a security agreement required, according to the UCC?
5. When does a debtor default on a security agreement?
6. What protection does a financing statement give to a secured party?
7. What five elements must be included in a financing statement?
8. A debtor has paid $900 toward a $1,200 secured credit loan for consumer goods at the time that the collateral is repossessed. What three things must the secured party do?
9. Who receives any profit from a sale of repossessed goods?
10. A debtor has paid $200 toward a $1,200 secured credit loan when he defaults on payment. What may the secured party do? What may the debtor do?

SUGGESTED ACTIVITY

1. Visit a lending institution, as if you were about to enter into a secured credit transaction for the purchase of an automobile.

Obtain all necessary forms. Inquire about what limits the institution would place on your borrowing power.

CASES FOR STUDY

1. Seller allows buyer to purchase a large appliance on a layaway plan whereby the buyer pays a certain amount weekly toward the cost of the goods which seller has set aside. When the whole purchase price is paid, the buyer may then take the article home and make use of it. Is this a secured transaction? Why or why not?

2. City Bank takes a secured interest in ovens purchased by *X* when it loans *X* the money to purchase the ovens for the purpose of opening up a bakery. However, City Bank forgets to file a financing statement. In the meantime, an unsecured creditor of *X* attempts to take the ovens in satisfaction of a debt. Can the unsecured creditor defeat City Bank's interest in the ovens? Why or why not?

3. Consider a case in which the facts are the same as those in the previous case, with one difference: the second creditor of *X*, not knowing of City Bank's interest, takes a security interest in the ovens and files the financing statement. Can this creditor defeat City Bank's security interest?

4. Lucille Karl purchases a new television set on credit on September 1. The store keeps a security interest and files the financing statement with the debtor's name spelled Loucile Carl. Does this error make the security interest fatally defective concerning other creditors?

5. Debtor is in default and secured creditor looks to the collateral as security for payment. Debtor owes $1,500 of a $3,000 sesured loan to purchase a car. Secured creditor sells the car in a reasonable manner and is able to obtain $2,000 for the car. How are the funds dispersed?

6. Consider the facts in case number 5, with the difference that the sale of the car yields $800. What are the liabilities and rights of the respective parties?

7. Once again, consider case number 5. Is there any way that debtor could keep the car even after default?

8. *M* holds secured interest in equipment *O* uses in his business. *O* sells the equipment to *P*. Can *M* force *P* to pay off the security interest?

Chapter 8

Consumer Protection: Warranties, Product Liability, and Legislation

OBJECTIVES

After studying this chapter, the student will be able to

- explain three ways in which express warranties are created.
- describe three types of implied warranties and three situations in which implied warranties may be excluded by sellers.
- explain the provisions of the UCC regarding product liability.
- describe the function of state and local legislation in consumer protection.
- list six federal statutes or agencies which protect consumers.
- define the following words and phrases.

caveat emptor	merchantability
warranty	conspicuous
express warranty	product liability
implied warranty	remote purchaser
model	puffing
disclaim	

WARRANTIES

In early days, buyers and sellers dealt face to face. Traveling peddlers often sold items and then left for parts unknown. These were the days of the exaggerated sales pitch and a great deal of haggling between buyer and seller. It was somewhat of a game on which both parties thrived, with the seller attempting to obtain the highest price and the buyer attempting to obtain the best deal. It was the buyer's responsibility to differentiate between a sales pitch and an honest statement about an item. The doctrine of *caveat emptor* (Latin for "let the buyer beware") was especially applicable in this environment. The seller took little or no responsibility for the products sold. If a product did not do what the seller claimed, the buyer had no recourse.

As merchandising changed through the years, so did the rules regarding the responsibility for items sold. More and more protection is being provided today for the buyer by placing much of the responsibility for product reliability upon the seller. Even after consumers take all the proper steps in a sales transaction, they may still be faced with problems concerning the performance of the goods they have purchased. Questions then arise as to the claims of the seller and their validity.

Sellers, even today, are not held responsible for statements they make that are a part of a normal sales talk, or for statements they make which express their opinion of a product. Buyers are expected to understand this practice (called *puffing*) for what it is. The following are examples of allowable sales talk and statements of opinion made by sellers.

"This car will really make you and your family happy." (sales talk)

"This is a really good buy." (sales talk)

"You should be able to trade this boat in after a year for almost the amount you are now paying for it." (opinion)

"I expect the price of this stock to double in about sixty days." (opinion)

If sellers make promises or statements of fact about products, however, they are making warranties to the buyer. According to the UCC, *warranties* place the responsibility for the quality, character, or suitability of goods sold on the seller. Some warranties result from representations made by the seller at the time of the sale. These are called *express warranties.* Other warranties are imposed on the seller by the operation of law. These are called *implied warranties.*

Express Warranty

Since statements of fact which accompany a sale are considered express warranties, the seller must be as precise as possible when describing the product and what it can do. If the statements are not true, the buyer has an action for breach of warranty. Under the UCC,

No. 111111

KAHN CORPORATION

BLACK & WHITE PICTURE TUBE

NON-TRANSFERRABLE

FIVE-YEAR ADJUSTMENT WARRANTY

Covers Picture Tube Only — Service Charge and Labor Charge Extra*

In addition to its regular one year picture tube Warranty, Kahn will make available to the original purchaser a rebuilt picture tube of the same size as the original picture tube in exchange for a picture tube that becomes defective upon payment of the amount stated below determined by the screen size and the time elapsed from the date of original purchase of the television receiver per the following schedule, F.O.B. local Kahn distributor warehouse:

Screen Size   9"____   12"____   16"____   18"____   19"____   22"____

Diagonal
Measurement

	9"	12"	16"	18"	19"	22"
Within 1st yr.	No Charge	No Charge	No Charge	No Charge	No Charge	No Charge
Within 2nd yr.	6.00	7.00	9.00	11.00	13.00	16.00
Within 3rd yr.	11.00	13.00	15.00	16.00	18.00	21.00
Within 4th yr.	16.00	19.00	20.00	21.00	23.00	26.00
Within 5th yr.	21.00	24.00	26.00	26.00	28.00	31.00

Replacement picture tubes will be warranted for the unexpired portion of this warranty per the above schedule.

THIS ADJUSTMENT WARRANTY DOES NOT APPLY TO: (A) any claim or loss where the picture tube has been damaged through abuse; (B) service charges or labor of any kind*; (C) transportation charges of any kind; (D) any claim by anyone other than the original retail purchaser of the television set containing the picture tube warranted; (E) any claim or loss occurring on or after the expiration of the fifth year from the date of the original retail sale of the television set containing the picture tube warranted; (F) any picture tube that is returned which does not have the same Kahn serial number on it that is also on the WARRANTY REGISTRATION CARD.

The WARRANTY REGISTRATION CARD must be properly completed and mailed within sixty (60) days of the date of the retail purchase to: Kahn Corp., P.O. Box 22, Anytown, U.S.A.

*There is no service or labor charge during the first ninety (90) days after date of original purchase of the television receiver.

Form No. 0000

Fig. 8-1 A written express warranty

an express warranty can be created even though the words *warranty* or *guarantee* are not used. [See UCC § 2-313.] An express warranty may be written, as in figure 8-1, page 125, or oral.

The UCC outlines several ways in which an express warranty can be created. Express warranties are created when a seller makes a promise or a factual statement relating to the goods being sold. The buyer relies on such a statement from the seller. (As mentioned, this does not include puffing.)

Example. A seller of boats says to a buyer, "This boat and motor will pull a water skier weighing over 200 pounds." The buyer then relies on the boat and motor to perform to that standard. This is a factual statement, not just an opinion. An express warranty is created.

Express warranties can also be created when a description by the seller accompanies the sale. By using descriptive terms, drawings, or charts, the seller is expressly warranting that the goods match the description.

Example. Mrs. Wilton contracts with Kustom Kitchens to remodel her kitchen. The company presents scaled drawings of the job showing five overhead cabinets, six countertop cabinets, and one broom closet. When the work is complete, there is no broom closet. Mrs. Wilton brings action since there is an express warranty. By presenting the drawn plans for the job, Kustom Kitchens is warranting that the goods delivered will fit the description.

An express warranty also can be made by showing a sample or a model to the customer. The seller promises that the whole of the goods will conform to the sample or model. A *sample* is a part of the goods to be sold, such as one pan from a thirty-piece set of cookware. A *model* is a representation of the goods being sold, such as a furniture designer's scale model of an actual table.

Example. Jim Moore plans to have his couch reupholstered by the Pillow Shop. He selects the fabric from a sample piece of material at the store, thus creating an express warranty. Moore can expect that the same fabric will be used when his couch is reupholstered.

Implied Warranty

Implied warranties are classified very clearly in the UCC. They result because a sale has taken place, and not from representations made by the seller at the time of the sale. They are imposed by law. These warranties protect consumers who do not have a chance to inspect or test goods that they are buying. The Code holds that because of this, the sellers are in a better position to be responsible for the reliability of the goods before they are purchased. Responsibility for the goods is not just assumed by a seller in making promises, but rather, is imposed by law. There are three major types of implied warranties.

Warranty of Title.   Whereas most warranties deal with the quality of goods, the warranty of title protects the buyer's ownership of goods. *Warranties of title* guarantee that the seller has clear title to the goods and the right to transfer that title with the sale. It is also a guarantee by the seller that there are no outstanding claims on the goods. This includes an outstanding security interest or debts owed on the goods by the seller. [See UCC § 2-312.]

Example.   Smith has a business in which he sells televisions and stereo equipment. He owes a secured debt of $500 to the wholesaler from whom he buys, with the stereo equipment providing the security for that debt. Wayne, a customer, purchases a set from Smith's store. An implied warranty of title protects Wayne by assuring that Smith will take responsibility for settling with the wholesaler before he sells the stereo and transfers the title. If Smith does not discharge that debt, he is not transferring clear title. Wayne would then be able to bring action on the basis of breach of the implied warranty of title.

Warranty of Merchantability.   This type of implied warranty deals with the quality of goods sold. The Code clearly sets standards which determine whether or not goods are of *merchantable* (marketable) quality. For example, goods must be appropriate for the ordinary purpose for which such goods are used; they must be adequately packaged and labeled; and they must conform to any promises or statements of fact made on the container or label. The UCC establishes that food served in a restaurant or hotel is a sale and not a service. Servers of this food are liable under the warranty of merchantability for the quality of the food served. [See UCC § 2-314.]

Example. The Lions Club holds its monthly luncheon meeting at the Plaza Hotel. The luncheon menu includes tuna salad. Inadvertently, the salad is left unrefrigerated and spoils. All of the persons who eat the salad become violently ill. The ordinary purpose of tuna salad is consumption. This particular salad was not fit for consumption, so the hotel is liable to everyone who became ill for breach of the implied warranty of merchantability. The UCC makes it clear that the hotel serving the salad is selling a good (the tuna salad) and not a service, which is not covered by the Code.

A warranty of merchantability applies only to sales by merchants; the nonmerchant or casual seller is not liable for this type of warranty.

Example. Sarah makes jellies and jams for her family. She makes more than the family can use, so she sells her neighbor a dozen jars of homemade cherry preserves. The neighbor chips a tooth when she bites into a cherry pit in the preserves. The neighbor cannot take action for breach of an implied warranty of merchantability since this is a sale made by a nonmerchant.

Under the Code, sellers can *disclaim* (be relieved of) all liability for warranties of merchantability in contracts, if certain steps are taken. The word *merchantability* must be mentioned in the *disclaimer* (the statement made by the seller). Also, if in writing, the *exclusion* (elimination) must be conspicuous. The UCC defines *conspicuous* as meaning that the clause must be printed in larger type or letters, or in ink of a different color. This is to ensure that the buyer sees the clause when it is part of a larger contract or warranty. [See UCC § 2-316.]

Case Example. This case was decided before the UCC was adopted in New Jersey. The court determined that an implied warranty of merchantability accompanied the sale of the automobile in question. This is an important case in the development of warranties concerning the protection of consumers. The court relied on policy and case law from other areas of law in reaching its decision. Currently, the Uniform Commercial Code requires the same result, but at the time the case was decided, the concept was a new idea. Notice the reasons the court gives to support its decision. Also notice that the court refers to the Code as a proposed statute. Even though it was not yet in effect, the court cites its provisions as being a persuasive authority supporting its decision.

HENNINGSEN v. BLOOMFIELD MOTORS, INC.

Supreme Court of New Jersey, 1959.
32 N.J. 358, 161 A.2d 69
(Many citations have been omitted.)

FRANCIS, J. Plaintiff Claus H. Henningsen purchased a Plymouth automobile, manufactured by defendant Chrysler Corporation, from defendant Bloomfield Motors, Inc. His wife, plaintiff, Helen Henningsen, was injured while driving it and instituted suit against both defendants to recover damages on account of her injuries. Her husband joined in the action seeking compensation for his consequential losses. The complaint was predicated upon breach of express and implied warranties and upon negligence. At the trial the negligence counts were dismissed by the court and the cause was submitted to the jury for determination solely on the issues of implied warranty of merchantability. Verdicts were returned against both defendants and in favor of the plaintiffs. Defendants appealed. . . .

The facts are not complicated, but a general outline of them is necessary to an understanding of the case.

On May 7, 1955, Mr. and Mrs. Henningsen visited the place of business of Bloomfield Motors, Inc., an authorized DeSoto and Plymouth dealer, to look at a Plymouth. They wanted to buy a car and were considering a Ford or a Chevrolet as well as a Plymouth. They were shown a Plymouth which appealed to them and the purchase followed. The record indicates that Mr. Henningsen intended the car as a Mother's Day gift to his wife. He said the intention was communicated to the dealer. When the purchase order or contract was prepared and presented, the husband executed [signed] it alone. His wife did not join as a party.

The purchase order was a printed form of one page. On the front it contained blanks to be filled in with a description of the automobile to be sold, the various accessories to be included, and the details of the financing. The particular car selected was described as a 1955 Plymouth, Plaza "6," Club Sedan. The type used in the printed parts of the form became smaller in size, different in style, and less readable toward the bottom where the line for the purchaser's signature was placed. The smallest type on the page appears in the two paragraphs, one of two and one-quarter lines and the second of one and one-half lines, on which great stress is laid by the defense in the case. These two paragraphs are the least legible and the most difficult to read in the instrument, but they are most important in the evaluation of the rights of the contesting parties. They do not attract attention and there is nothing about the format which would draw the reader's eye to them. In fact, a studied and concentrated effort would have to be made to read them. De-emphasis seems the motive rather than emphasis. More particularly, most of the printing in the body of the order appears to be twelve point block type, and easy to read. In the short paragraphs under discussion, however, the type appears to be six point script and the print is solid, that is, the lines are very close together.

The two paragraphs are:

"The front and back of this Order comprise the entire agree-ment affecting this purchase and no other agreement or under-standing of any nature concerning same has been made or entered into, or will be recognized. I hereby certify that no credit has been extended to me for the purchase of this motor vehicle ex-cept as appears in writing on the face of this agreement.

"I have read the matter printed on the back hereof and agree to it as a part of this order and same as if it were printed above my signature. I certify that I am 21 years of age, or older, and here-by acknowledge receipt of a copy of this order."

On the right side of the form, immediately below these clauses and immediately above the signature line, and in 12 point block type, the following appears:

"CASH OR CERTIFIED CHECK ONLY ON DELIVERY."

On the left side, just opposite and in the same style type as the two quoted clauses, but in eight point size, this statement is set out:

"This agreement shall not become binding upon the Dealer until approved by an officer of the company."

The two latter statements are in the interest of the dealer and ob-viously an effort is made to draw attention to them.

The testimony of Claus Henningsen justifies the conclusion that he did not read the two fine print paragraphs referring to the back of the purchase contract. And it is uncontradicted that no one made any reference to them, or called them to his attention. With respect to the matter appearing on the back, it is likewise uncontradicted that he did not read it and that no one called it to his attention.

The reverse side of the contract contains 8 1/2 inches of fine print. It is not as small, however, as the two critical paragraphs de-scribed above. The page is headed "Conditions" and contains ten separate paragraphs consisting of 65 lines in all. The paragraphs do not have headnotes or margin notes denoting their particular subject, as in the case of the "Owner Service Certificate" to be referred to later. In the seventh paragraph, about two-thirds of the way down the page, the warranty, which is the focal point of the case, is set forth. It is as follows:

"7. It is expressly agreed that there are no warranties express or implied *made* by either the dealer or the manufacturer on the motor vehicle, chassis, or parts furnished hereunder except as follows.

" 'The manufacturer warrants each new motor vehicle (including original equipment placed thereon by the manufacturer except tires), chassis' or parts manufactured by it to be free from defects in material or workmanship under normal use and service. Its obligation under this warranty being limited to making good at its factory any part or parts thereof which shall, within ninety (90) days after delivery of such vehicle *to the original purchasers* or before such vehicle has been driven 4,000 miles, whichever event shall first occur, be returned to it with transportation charges prepaid and which its examination shall disclose to its satisfaction to have been thus defective; *this warranty being expressly in lieu of all other warranties expressed or implied, and all other obligations or liabilities on its part*, and it neither assumes nor authorized any other person to assume for it any other liability in connection with the sale of its vehicles. . . .' " (Emphasis ours.)

. . .The testimony shows that Chrysler Corporation sends from the factory to the dealer a "New Car Preparation Service Guide" with each automobile. The guide contains detailed instructions as to what has to be done to prepare the car for delivery. The dealer is told to "Use this form as a guide to inspect and prepare this new Plymouth for delivery." It specifies 66 separate items to be checked, tested, tightened or adjusted in the course of the servicing, but dismantling the vehicle or checking all of its internal parts is not prescribed. The guide also calls for delivery of the Owner Service Certificate with the car.

This certificate, which at least by inference is authorized by Chrysler, was in the car when released to Claus Henningsen on May 9, 1955. It was not made part of the purchase contract, nor was it shown to him prior to the consummation of that agreement. The only reference to it therein is that the dealer "agrees to promptly perform and fulfill all terms and conditions of the owner service policy." The Certificate contains a warranty entitled "Automobile Manufacturers Association Uniform Warranty." The provisions thereof are the same as those set forth on the reverse side of the purchase order, except that an additional paragraph is added by which the dealer extends that warranty to the purchaser in the same manner as if the word "Dealer" appeared instead of the word "Manufacturer."

. . .Mr. Henningsen drove [the car] from the dealer's place of business in Bloomfield to their home in Keansburg [on May 9, 1955]. On the trip nothing unusual appeared in the way in which it operated. Thereafter, it was used for short trips on paved streets about the town. It had no servicing and no mishaps of any kind before the event of May 19. That day, Mrs. Henningsen drove to Asbury Park. On the way down and in returning the car performed in normal fashion until the accident occurred. She was proceeding north on Route 36 in Highlands, New Jersey, at 20-22 miles per hour. The highway was paved and smooth, and contained two lanes for northbound travel. She was riding in the right-hand lane. Suddenly she heard a loud noise "from the bottom, by the hood." It "felt as if something cracked." The steering wheel spun in her hands; the car veered sharply to the right and crashed into a highway sign and a brick wall. No other vehicle was in any way involved. A bus operator driving in the left-hand lane testified that he observed plaintiffs' car approaching in normal fashion in the opposite direction; "all of a sudden (it) veered at 90 degrees. . .and right into this wall." As a result of the impact, the front of the car was so badly damaged that it was impossible to determine if any of the parts of the steering wheel mechanism or workmanship or assembly were defective or improper prior to the accident. The condition was such that the collision insurance carrier, after inspection, declared the vehicle a total loss. It had 468 miles on the speedometer at the time.

The insurance carrier's inspector and appraiser of damaged cars, with 11 years of experience, advanced the opinion, based on the history and his examination, that something definitely went "wrong from the steering wheel down to the front wheels" and that the untoward happening must have been due to mechanical defect or failure; "something down there had to drop off or break loose to cause the car" to act in the manner described.

.   .   .

[At this point the court commenced an extended and critical discussion of whether the purchaser, Claus Henningsen, had a claim of implied warranty against the manufacturer.]

Accordingly, we hold that under modern marketing conditions, when a manufacturer puts a new automobile in the stream of trade and promotes its purchase by the public, an implied warranty that is reasonably suitable for use as such accompanies it into the hands of the ultimate purchaser. Absence of agency between the manufacturer and the dealer who makes the ultimate sale is immaterial.

II.

The Effect of the Disclaimer and Limitation of Liability Clauses on the Implied Warranty of Merchantability.

Judicial notice may be taken of the fact that automobile manufacturers, including Chrysler Corporation, undertake large scale advertising programs over television, radio, in newspapers, magazines and all media of communication in order to persuade the public to buy their products. As has been observed above, a number of jurisdictions, conscious of modern marketing practices, have declared that when a manufacturer engages in advertising in order to bring his goods and their quality to the attention of the public and thus to create consumer demand, the representations made constitute an express warranty running directly to a buyer who purchases in reliance thereon. The fact that the sale is consummated with an independent dealer does not obviate that warranty. . . .

In view of the cases in various jurisdictions suggesting the conclusion which we have now reached with respect to the implied warranty of merchantability, it becomes apparent that manufacturers who enter into promotional activities to stimulate consumer buying may incur warranty obligations of either or both the express or implied character. These developments in the law inevitably suggest the inference that the form of express warranty made part of the Henningsen purchase contract was devised for general use in the automobile industry as a possible means of avoiding the consequences of the growing judicial acceptance of the theses that the described express or implied warranties run directly to the consumer.

In the light of these matters, what effect should be given to the express warranty in question which seeks to limit the manufacturer's liability to replacement of defective parts, and which disclaims all other warranties, express or implied? In assessing its significance we must keep in mind the general principle that, in the absence of fraud, one who does not choose to read a contract before signing it, cannot later relieve himself of its burdens. . ."

"And. . ." in applying that principle, the basic tenet of freedom of competent parties to contract is a factor of importance. But in the framework of modern commercial life and business practices, such rules cannot be applied on a strict, doctrinal basis. The conflicting interests of the buyer and seller must be evaluated realistically and justly, giving due weight to the social policy evinced by the Uniform Sales Act [the forerunner of the U.C.C.] the progressive decisions of the courts engaged in administering it, the mass production methods of manufacturer and distribution to the public, and the bargaining position occupied by the ordinary consumer in such an economy. This history of the law shows that legal doctrines, as first expounded, often prove to be inadequate under the impact of the later experience. . . .

•   •   •

. . .As we have said, warranties originated in the law to safeguard the buyer and not to limit the liability of the seller or manufacturer. It seems obvious in this instance that the motive was to avoid the warranty obligations which are normally incidental to such sales. The language gave little and withdrew much. In return for the delusive remedy of replacement of defective parts at the factory, the buyer is said to have accepted the exclusion of the maker's liability for personal injuries arising from the breach of the warranty, and to have agreed to the elimination of any other express or implied warranty. An instinctively felt sense of justice cries out against such a sharp bargain. But does the doctrine that a person is bound by his signed agreement, in the absence of fraud, stand in the way of any relief?

•   •   •

The traditional contract is the result of free bargaining of parties who are brought together by the play of the market, and who meet each other on a footing of approximate economic equality. In such a society there is no danger that freedom of contract will be a threat to the social order as a whole. But in present-day commercial life the standardized mass contract has appeared. It is used primarily by enterprises with strong bargaining power and position. . . . Such standardized contracts have been described as those in which one predominant party will dictate its law to an undetermined multiple rather than to an individual. They are said to resemble a law rather than a meeting of the minds.

•   •   •

The warranty before us is a standardized form designed for mass use. It is imposed upon the automobile consumer. He takes it or leaves it, and he must take it to buy an automobile. No bargaining is engaged in with respect to it. In fact, the dealer through whom it comes to the buyer is without authority to alter it; his function is ministerial — simply to deliver it. The form warranty is not only standard with Chrysler but, as mentioned above, it is the uniform warranty of the Automobile Manufacturers Association. . . .Of these companies, the "Big Three" (General Motors, Ford and Chrysler) represented 93.5% of the passenger-car production for 1958. . . .And for the same year the "Big Three" had 86.72% of the total passenger vehicle registrations. . . .

The gross inequality of bargaining position occupied by the consumer in the automobile industry is thus apparent. There is no competition among the car makers in the area of express warranty. Where can the buyer go to negotiate for better protection? Such control and limitation of his remedies are inimical to the public welfare and, at the very least, call for great care by the courts to avoid injustice through application of strict common-law principles of freedom of contract. . . .

• • •

The rigid scrutiny which the courts give to attempted limitations of warranties and of the liability that would normally flow from a transaction is not limited to the field of sales of goods. Clauses on baggage checks restricting the liability of common carriers for loss or damage in transit are not enforceable unless the limitation is fairly and honestly negotiated and understandingly entered into. If not called specifically to the patron's attention, it is not binding. It is not enough merely to show the form of a contract; it must appear also that the agreement was understandingly made. . . .   • • •

. . .Basically, the reason a contracting party offering services of a public or quasi-public nature has been held to the requirements of fair dealing, and, when it attempts to limit its liability, of securing the understanding consent of the patron or consumer, is because members of the public generally have no other means of fulfilling the specific need represented by the contract. Having in mind the situation in the automobile industry as detailed above, and particularly the fact that the limited warranty extended by the manufacturers is a uniform one, there would appear to be no just reason why the principles of all of the cases set forth should not chart the course to be taken here.

• • •

. . .Assuming that a jury might find that the fine print referred to reasonably served the objective of directing a buyer's attention to the warranty on the reverse side, and, therefore, that he should be charged with awareness of its language, can it be said that an ordinary layman would realize what he was relinquishing in return for what he was being granted? Under the law, breach of warranty against defective parts or workmanship which caused personal injuries would entitle a buyer to damages even if due care were used in the manufacturing process. Because of the great potential for harm if the vehicle was defective, that right is the most important and fundamental one arising from the relationship. . . . Any ordinary layman of reasonable intelligence, looking at the phraseology, might well conclude that Chrysler was agreeing to replace defective parts and perhaps replace anything that went wrong because of defective workmanship during the first 90 days or 4,000 miles of operation, but that he would not be entitled to a new car. It is not unreasonable to believe that the entire scheme being conveyed was a proposed remedy for physical deficiencies in the car. *In the context* of this warranty, only the abandonment of all sense of justice would permit us to hold that, as a matter of law, the phrase "its obligation under this warranty being limited to making good at its factory any part or parts thereof" signifies to an ordinary reasonable person that he is relinquishing any personal injury claim that might flow from the use of a defective automobile.   Such claims are nowhere mentioned.   The draftsmanship is reflective of the care and skill of the Automobile Manufacturers Association in undertaking to avoid warranty obligations without drawing too much attention to its effort in that regard. No one can doubt that if the will to do so were present, the ability to inform the buying public of the intention to disclaim liability for injury claims arising from breach of warranty would present no problem.

·   ·   ·

The task of the judiciary is to administer the spirit as well as the letter of the law.   On issues such as the present one, part of that burden is to protect the ordinary man against loss of important rights through what, in effect, is the unilateral act of the manufacturer.   The status of the automobile industry is unique.   Manufacturers are few in number and strong in bargaining position.   In the matter of warranties on the sale of their products, the Automotive Manufacturers Association has enabled them to present a united front.   From the standpoint of the purchaser, there can be no arms length negotiating on the subject.   Because of his capacity for bargaining is so grossly unequal, the inexorable conclusion which follows is that he is not permitted to bargain at all.   He must take or leave the automobile on the warranty terms dictated by the maker. He cannot turn to a competitor for better security.

Public policy is a term not easily defined.   Its significance varies as the habits and needs of a people may vary.   It is not static and the field of application is an ever increasing one.   A contract, or a particular provision therein, valid in one era may be wholly opposed to the public policy of another. . . .   Courts keep in mind the principle that the best interests of society demand that persons should not be unnecessarily restricted in their freedom to contract.   But they do not hesitate to declare void as against public policy contractual provisions which clearly tend to the injury of the public in some way. . . .

Public policy at a given time finds expression in the Constitution, the statutory law and in judicial decisions.   In the area of sale of goods, the legislative will has imposed an implied warranty of merchantability as a general incident of sale of an automobile by description. The warranty does not depend upon the affirmative intention of the parties. It is a child of the law; it annexes itself to the contract because of the very nature of the transaction. . . .The judicial process has recognized a right to recover damages for personal injuries arising from a breach of that warranty. The disclaimer of the implied warranty and exclusion of all obligations except those specifically assumed by the express warranty signify a studied effort to frustrate that protection. . . .The lawmakers did not authorize the automobile manufacturer to use its grossly disproportionate bargaining power to relieve itself from liability and to impose on the ordinary buyer, who in effect has no real freedom of choice, the grave danger of injury to himself and others that attends the sale of such a dangerous instrumentality as a defectively made automobile. In the framework of this case, illuminated as it is by the facts and the many decisions noted, we are of the opinion that Chrysler's attempted disclaimer of an implied warranty of merchantability and of the obligations arising therefrom is so inimical to the public good as to compel an adjudication of its invalidity.

[At this point, the Court cited the proposed Uniform Commercial Code as additional authority for its conclusion that the implied warranty of merchantability had not been properly disclaimed, and Mr. and Mrs. Henningsen were able to recover damages.]

Warranty of Fitness for Particular Purpose. A buyer may tell a seller that the goods being purchased are needed for a certain purpose. The buyer in such a case relies on the seller's skill and judgment to supply suitable goods. In this situation, a *warranty of fitness for particular purpose* arises. [See UCC § 2-315.]

Example. Newcombe, a home builder, plans to clear a lot for a new house. Knowing little about chain saws, he explains to Woody's Chain Saw Company that he needs a power saw to cut down trees that average four feet in diameter. Woody's sells him a saw. An implied warranty of fitness for particular purpose has been created — Newcombe is relying on the seller's knowledge of saws to select the proper one for his job. He can bring action for breach of such a warranty if he is sold a saw that does not do the job.

For this type of warranty to exist, two things must occur: (1) the seller has reason to know of the particular purpose for which the goods are required and (2) the buyer relies on the expertise of the seller.

An implied warranty of fitness for particular purpose arises whether the seller is a merchant or a nonmerchant. It does not arise if the buyer insists on certain goods by brand name or when definite specifications of the goods are given. In either of those cases, the buyer is not relying on the seller's judgment, so the seller is not liable.

Example.   In the previous example, suppose Newcombe tells the seller that he wants a Cut-E-Z Saw, model 25783 for some trees that he has to cut down. Newcombe is not relying on the seller's judgment as to whether or not the saw will do the job. He has specified a particular saw himself. Therefore, no implied warranty of fitness for particular purpose has been created.

Exclusions of Implied Warranties.   There are two other situations in which implied warranties, except warranties of title, may be excluded (eliminated) according to the UCC. If goods are clearly marked with the words *to be sold as is,* or a similar phrase, the seller is not liable for implied warranties. [See UCC § 2-316.]

Example.   Mitchell Sport Co. has a set of golf clubs that have gouges in most of the handles which it wants to sell. The company lowers the price of the clubs and puts a tag on the set which reads *on sale as is.* There is no implied warranty for quality or particular purpose on which the buyer can rely in this situation.

Before entering into a contract, a buyer may examine the goods or a sample or model of the goods for possible defects, or may refuse to examine them. In these cases, there is no implied warranty concerning defects which the buyer failed to notice and which would have been obvious from an inspection.

Example.   Sharon is interested in buying a set of encyclopedias on sale. She examines the set very carefully. When she approaches the cash register to pay for them, the store owner insists that she examine them again, which she does. She then purchases the books. After she leaves the store, she discovers Volume F and Volume S are missing. She cannot hold the seller responsible under breach of implied warranty, since her examination of the goods removed the seller's responsibility for defects.

PRODUCT LIABILITY

In earlier days, the consumer often bought goods directly from a producer. Candles were purchased from a candlemaker's shop; shoes were purchased from a shoemaker. If a problem with the goods arose, the consumer went directly to the producer, who was also the seller, for satisfaction. In the economic system of the twentieth century, a product passes through many hands from the point of manufacture to the eventual purchase by the consumer. If a consumer purchases a defective product and there has clearly been a breach of warranty, a question of responsibility (legally known as *liability for the product*) arises. Who is responsible to the consumer? Is it the manufacturer, who made the goods; the shipper, who delivered them; or the retailer, who sold them?

In the past, the retailer has been held legally responsible; the manufacturer had no product liability. In recent years, however, the courts have been changing their views on this. They now often hold the manufacturer responsible when the safety and interest of the *remote purchaser* (the eventual consumer) are endangered. Specifically, the UCC holds manufacturers liable when they make factual statements about products. The Code also requires manufacturers to use due care in the design, manufacture or production, inspection, packaging, and sale of goods. If manufacturers fail in any of these respects, with the result being that their products cause injury or property damage, consumers may bring court action directly against them.

LEGISLATION

The Uniform Commercial Code provisions for consumer warranties and the courts' actions on product liability are not enough to adequately protect the consumer. Many sellers still make false claims in advertising and selling their goods. Because of this, there has been a great deal of special legislation by states, localities, and the federal government to control such selling practices.

State and Local Legislation

Every state has consumer protection laws. State laws prohibit false advertising, forbid the sale of certain drugs without prescriptions, and regulate the purity of drinking water. They require licensing of such people as doctors, accountants, real estate agents, and insurance agents. State laws also require inspection of scales where goods are sold by weight, and inspection of food dispensing operations such as supermarkets and restaurants. States by law regulate financial institutions such as insurance companies, banks, and loan companies.

Example. Tom's Diner places the advertisement *Free Lunches on Wednesday* in a local paper. When customers come to the diner on Wednesday, they learn that there is only one free lunch for each group of four people. When four people order lunch, the least expensive meal is given free of charge. One customer brings action, claiming that this is false advertising according to state laws. The restaurant is liable, since what they advertised and what they actually offered were two different things.

There is a growing movement by many city and county governments to establish consumer protection agencies to hear and act on consumer complaints. These agencies deal with federal and state product safety laws regarding goods sold in their areas. They are also involved in consumer education, aimed at making citizens aware of what they should expect from businesses and what can be done if customers feel they have been treated unfairly.

Federal Regulations

There are many federal laws similar to state laws in their protection of the consumer, and others covering areas in which state governments are not involved. Federal regulation usually applies to goods moving from one state to another, known as interstate commerce.

The Consumer Product Safety Commission plays a very important role in consumer protection. The Commission sets safety standards for almost all consumer products. It has the power to ban hazardous products. It also keeps extensive records of products and injuries they have caused.

The Federal Trade Commission (FTC) was originally established by law to prevent unfair trade practices. It has since been given the power to administer several other laws enacted to protect the consumer. This includes regulations prohibiting fraudulent claims in printed or television ads.

Example. Miracle Cleanser Company decides to film a television advertisement testing their product against Brand X, a popular competitor. They plan to use both products on a certain grease stain. Legally, they cannot use a weaker stain to test their own product, nor can they dilute Brand X so that it does not perform as well as their product. FTC regulations declare that such practices comprise a dishonest presentation.

The FTC also administers several acts that require proper labeling of the content of products. For example, wool items must be accompanied by labels showing the percentages of different types of wool in the product. Fur products must be tagged to indicate the type of animal fur used and any processing which has taken place. There are stiff penalties for manufacturers who do not comply with these federal regulations.

Most recently, the FTC has been charged with monitoring the Magneson-Mass Warranty Act. This federal act places additional requirements on the form and content of express warranties beyond the UCC requirements.

The Food and Drug Administration (FDA) protects consumers from foods, drugs, or cosmetics which might be harmful. They set purity, quality, and inspection standards as well as instituting labeling and advertising practices for such goods. For example, the FDA requires that all drugs must be labeled and include the name of the drug (not just a brand name), directions for use, and precautions about use by children or use that might be habit forming.

Example. A manufacturer produces maple syrup made with 50 percent imitation maple flavoring. It cannot be labeled "100 percent Pure Maple Syrup." Such a statement would be deceptive to consumers.

The Truth-In-Lending Act, passed in 1968, was one of the biggest breakthroughs for protection of consumers in recent years. For th first time, the cost of credit must be clearly stated for borrowers so that consumers know what they pay for credit. Lenders must clearly type, print, or write on the credit agreement the finance charge in dollars and cents, as well as the annual percentage rate. Figure 8-2 is an example of a typical bank demand note with requirements of the Truth-In-Lending Act listed in items (1), (2), (3), and (4).

Anytown Bank – Anytown, U.S.A.   BANK COPY

INFORMATION REQUIRED BY FEDERAL LAW

Date of

The Note with respect to which this information is given is a _____ Note. Note _____
(Demand)   (Time)

The amount owing under a DEMAND NOTE is payable on demand. For the purpose of computing the Finance Charge, a Demand Note is considered, under Federal Law, to have a maturity of one-half year. However the actual amount of the Finance Charge and total of payments depends on the date the note is repaid, and will usually differ from the amounts disclosed on this statement.

If you have borrowed on a TIME NOTE, and fail to meet its maturity on _____ 19____ , in addition to interest, a late charge of $1.00 may be imposed. In the event of pre-payment any unearned finance charge will be refunded on a pro rata basis.

For the period during which the note remains outstanding, interest payments are due on _____ and the same day of each _____ thereafter.
(month)   (quarter)   (other period)

As security for the repayment of your loan and any other indebtedness now or hereafter due to the Bank, you have granted to the Bank a security interest in the following described property:

1. Amount Financed $ _____

2. FINANCE CHARGE $ _____

_____

_____

_____

3. Total of payments
   (1 plus 2) $ _____

4. ANNUAL PERCENT
   RATE   _____ %

I HEREBY ACKNOWLEDGE RECEIPT OF A COMPLETED COPY OF THIS STATEMENT.

Signed _____   Date _____

Signed _____   Date _____

COM-041A

Fig. 8-2 Bank Demand Note

The annual percentage rate or the true percentage rate can sometimes be two or three times greater than the rate of interest that the lenders state. For example, on an "8 percent loan," the borrower may actually be paying 16 to 20 percent over a three-year period. This is because the borrower has the use of the full amount of the loan for only the first month. After that, the installment payments are reducing the amount owed. The interest, however, continues to be paid on the original amount. Lenders who violate the Truth-In-Lending Act face criminal penalties of fines, prison, or both.

There are many other federal government agencies that regulate the sale of goods to protect consumers. For example, the sale of stocks and bonds is regulated by the Securities and Exchange Commission (SEC), and the quality and labeling of meats and agricultural products is handled by the Department of Agriculture. The *caveat emptor* policy is gradually changing, creating a trend which gives consumers more bargaining power than ever in their demand for better quality goods and services.

SELF-EVALUATION

Provide a brief explanation for each of the following.

1. Sellers today may make two types of statements concerning products for which they are not held responsible. What are they?

2. Define warranty.

3. Differentiate between an express warranty and an implied warranty.

4. List three situations in which an express warranty is created.

5. How does a warranty of title differ from other implied warranties?

6. What are three standards of merchantability as outlined in the UCC?

7. When may an individual sell goods and not be liable under warranty of merchantability?

8. Define a conspicuous clause.

9. Explain why the disclaimer in the purchase order signed by Mr. Henningsen in *Henningsen* v. *Bloomfield Motors, Inc.* would not be valid under today's UCC standards.

10. When a consumer tells a seller that the goods are being purchased for a certain purpose, what type of warranty is created?

11. Exactly when is a manufacturer liable for the defects in a product?

12. Which level of government is responsible for legislation requiring insurance agents to hold a license?

13. What agency administers laws requiring the proper labeling of wool and fur products?

14. In what way does the Consumer Product Safety Commission protect consumers?

15. If a cosmetic is not properly labeled, which federal agency should be notified?

16. What items must be included in all credit agreements?

SUGGESTED ACTIVITIES

1. Consider various labeling practices used today. Affected products include such items as imitation mayonnaise (required

to be specified as such because there is not enough oil in the product to call it mayonnaise) and cosmetics which may contain harmful additives. If the product pork and beans was not protected by a *grandfather clause* (i.e., the term was in common use before the regulation was enacted) would not current labeling practices require that it be called beans and pork? List other examples of changing labeling practices.

2. Bring monthly billing statements from oil companies, department stores, and banking institutions to class. Check to see how they comply with laws requiring disclosure of actual effective interest rates.

CASES FOR STUDY

1. Carol visits a hardware store to purchase wall hooks with which to hang a heavy mirror. She is not sure which hooks will support the weight of the mirror and asks the owner of the store for assistance. After learning the type of wall on which the mirror is to be hung and the size and weight of the mirror, the owner suggests a particular hook. Carol returns home with the purchase and hangs the mirror as directed, only to find that the type of hook suggested is not suited for the job. She returns to the hardware store the next day to complain. The owner then points out a disclaimer of all warranties on the bottom of the cash register tape. What warranties, if any, arise out of this transaction?

2. Consider the same situation with this difference: Carol asks for "Hang-Ups," a brand of hooks recommended to her by a friend without describing the purpose for which she is buying them. Is there a warranty of fitness for particular purpose accompanying the sale? Why or why not?

3. Is the statement *All warranties are excluded* printed in boldface type on a bill of sale effective as a disclaimer? Why or why not?

4. Ching purchases a large appliance on credit. The bill of sale, the contract covering the credit agreement, and the monthly billing notices all indicate that a finance charge is being added to the total price. Considering the Truth-In-Lending laws, are these sufficient measures?

5. Parents of high school band students hold a supper to help raise money for new band uniforms. The parents cook, prepare, and serve the food. A customer becomes ill shortly after consuming the supper and immediately notifies the parent group. Samples of the various menu items are sent to a laboratory and found to contain bacteria that can cause food poisoning. Have the band parents breached the implied warranty of merchantability?

Chapter 9

Bailments

OBJECTIVES

After studying this chapter, the student will be able to

- identify the three essential elements in the formation of bailments.
- describe the conditions and responsibilities of both parties involved in gratuitous bailments, mutual bailments, and special bailments.
- list the five reasons for which common carriers are excused from responsibility for damage to property.
- define the following words and phrases.

bailment	carrier
bailor	private carrier
bailee	common carrier
gratuitous bailment	interstate
contract bailment	intrastate
extraordinary bailment	insurers of property
ordinary care	act of God
negligent	act of a public enemy
pledge	demurrage
pawn	passenger
lien	public carrier
custody	baggage
fungible goods	transient

Consumers are involved daily in business transactions to obtain a variety of services. Cars are taken to garages to be repaired and clothing is taken to the cleaners. People ride in buses or taxicabs and stay in hotels overnight. In all of these situations, the consumer is involved in a bailment. A *bailment* is a legal relationship which provides for the delivery of goods by the owner for a specific purpose to another party. In a bailment, only possession is transferred; title and ownership are retained by the owner. When the purpose is fulfilled, the same goods are returned to the owner or otherwise disposed of as agreed. The owner of the good is the *bailor;* the party who is given possession of the good is the *bailee.*

Example. Lyn leaves her watch to be repaired at the Tick Tock Shop. By this action, a bailment is created. Lyn is the bailor and the shop is the bailee. Lyn still owns the watch, but she has transferred possession to the Tick Tock Shop. When the watch is repaired, she pays for the services and takes it home.

Services are divided into two categories. Some are considered personal in nature, these are performed by individuals who are specially skilled either artistically or professionally, such as painters, designers, doctors, dentists, and lawyers.

The second type of services includes those related to personal property, such as money, stock, cars, boats, and jewelry. It is these types of services to which the discussion of bailments in this chapter refers.

ELEMENTS OF A BAILMENT

There are three essential elements in the formation of a bailment.

Ownership

The bailor must have title and ownership of the property or a superior right to possession. The owner of an article usually has title, but it is not required for a bailment. All of the examples in this chapter presume that the bailor has ownership and title.

Possession

The bailee must have lawful possession without title. If title were transferred, there would be a sale.

Example. In the previous example, note that the Tick Tock Shop has possession only. It does not own the watch when Lyn leaves it.

Return

When the special purpose is accomplished, the bailee must return the property to the bailor or dispose of it as directed. The bailee's possssion is only temporary. Usually, the same goods are expected to be returned, although there are exceptions to this rule.

Example.   Consider once again the case of the watch repair. When the watch is repaired, the Tick Tock Shop must return it to Lyn. If she tells the shop that her sister will pick it up on a certain date and sign for it, the shop must give it to her sister as instructed.

Case Example.   In the following case, note the missing bailment element.

BLACK BERET LOUNGE AND RESTAURANT
v.
MEISNERE
District of Columbia Court of Appeals, 1975
336 A.2d 532

NEBEKER, Associate Judge. Appellee won a judgment in the amount of $90 in the Small Claims and Conciliation Branch for the loss of his coat at the appellant-restaurant. The trial judge based his award on a determination that a bailment of the coat had occurred. We granted appellant's application for allowance of appeal to review that conclusion. We reverse.

The record reveals that appellee hung his coat in an unattended cloakroom at the request of one of appellant's waitresses. Appellant made no charge for the use of this cloakroom and gave no claim check to appellee. A notice was posted in appellant's cloakroom disclaiming any responsibility for lost belongings. Appellee testified that he did not see any such notice.

We hold on these facts that there was not delivery of the coat to appellant resulting in a change of possession and control. Therefore, there was no bailment. [Citations omitted.] That the appellee used the cloakroom at a waitress' request, since the coat had fallen from a chair — a fact to which the trial judge attached considerable importance — has been held not to impose liability on the restaurant keeper for appellee's loss. [Citations omitted.]

Accordingly, we conclude that there was no bailment. The judgment of the trial court is reversed with instructions to enter judgment for appellant.

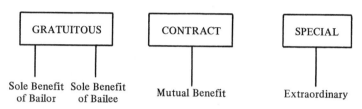

Fig. 9-1 Classification of bailments

CLASSIFICATION OF BAILMENTS

Bailments are classified according to benefits derived by the parties or according to special characteristics, figure 9-1. The first two classes are designated as either *for the sole benefit of the bailor* or *for the sole benefit of the bailee.* These are both known as *gratuitous bailments.* There is no consideration given. Neither party is paid for the services; the services are given as a courtesy. Therefore, only one party in the relationship receives benefits.

The third class is for the *mutual benefit of both parties.* Both the bailor and the bailee receive benefits from the relationship. This is called a *contract bailment.* Since consideration is given for services purchased from a bailee, all the elements necessary to create an enforceable contract are present.

There are also *special bailment* situations. These include bailments in which the same goods are not required to be returned to the bailor. They also include the *extraordinary bailment* which occurs when a bailee is subject to unusual duties or obligations that are imposed by law.

SOLE BENEFIT OF THE BAILOR

An agreement of bailment for the sole benefit of the bailor is only for the good of, or the advantage of, the bailor. The bailee gets little or no benefit from the transaction. There is no compensation or consideration for the services performed. Since there is no mutual consideration, which is a requirement of an enforceable contract, there is no contract. However, the bailee is still under certain obligations.

The bailee owes the duty of due care or ordinary care to prevent loss of or damage to the goods. *Due care* is care that the ordinary person would give in the same situation with the same property.

Example. Jeff asks Scott to care for his bike while he is away. Scott agrees. A bailment is created for the sole benefit of the bailor. Scott keeps his own bike locked in the garage overnight, but leaves Jeff's in the yard unlocked. Jeff's bike is stolen. Scott is held liable since he did not exercise ordinary care with Jeff's property.

The bailee is also under an obligation not to use the property without permission of the bailor. The property can only be used when it is necessary for the proper care or protection of the property.

Example. Rick receives permission to tie up his boat at Al's dock for the weekend. Al agrees to the arrangement. The day after Rick ties up his boat, Al hears hurricane warnings on the radio. He decides the boat would be safer at a nearby marina located in a protected cove, and moves the boat to that location. Even though Al has no permission to run the boat, he cannot be held liable, since he is doing what he feels is best to protect the boat from damage while it is in his possession.

In a bailment for the sole benefit of the bailor, the bailor has the duty to warn the bailee of any defects in the goods that might cause harm or injury. It is also the bailor's responsibility to examine the goods carefully for such defects before transferring possession. If there is no warning and there is injury to the bailee, the bailor is held responsible.

Example. Consider the previous example. Suppose the steering on Rick's boat was not functioning properly, but Rick did not tell Al about it. When Al takes the boat to safety, the steering fails and Al hits a rock. He is thrown against the windshield and breaks his arm. Rick is liable for Al's injury since he did not warn him about the steering.

This type of bailment can be terminated at will by either party. If, however, the bailee agrees to keep the property for a certain time or deliver it to a certain place, such an agreement must be carried out or the bailee is held responsible.

Example. Kane agrees to keep Lou's car for a week and leave it at the airport parking lot on Sunday night. When Lou arrives by plane on Sunday, the car is not there, and he must take a taxi home. Kane is liable for the cab fare, since he did not fulfill his promise to deliver the car.

SOLE BENEFIT OF THE BAILEE

A bailment for the sole benefit of a bailee is created when the owner of goods allows another party to use those goods free of charge. This usually occurs when one party lends goods to another party. There is no consideration, so there is no enforceable contract. The bailee in this situation owes a greater duty of care to the goods, more so than in the bailment for the sole benefit of the bailor. If the bailee fails in any respect to care for the goods and those goods are damaged or lost, the bailee is liable. The bailee also has no right to lend the goods to others without the bailor's permission.

Example. *B* lends *C* his power drill. *C* lends the drill to *D*. *D* breaks the drill. *C* is liable to *B* for the damages.

The bailee's use of the goods is limited strictly to the purpose for which they were given. Any departure from the agreed use makes the bailee liable.

Example. *B* lends *C* his power drill to build a wooden go-cart. *B* explains that it is a small drill and can only be used on wood. *C* builds the cart and then uses the drill to put some holes in a metal table top. The drill breaks. *C* is liable since he did not use the drill according to the instructions from *B*.

The bailor must warn the bailee of any known defect in the goods that might cause harm to the bailee. There does not have to be as careful an examination of the goods as in the previous type of bailment. However, if the bailor fails to warn the bailee and the bailee is harmed, then the bailor is held liable.

Example. Ann loans Pat her stereo. Ann tells her that the plug is loose and may cause an electrical shock when put into a socket. Pat has been warned, and therefore should repair it before she uses the stereo or take a chance on an injury. If Pat does not repair it and suffers an injury, she cannot hold Ann liable since there was a warning.

This type of bailment can also be terminated at will by either party. Of course, if the agreement is for a definite period, the parties must hold to that agreement.

MUTUAL BENEFIT

As the name implies, in a mutual benefit bailment, both the bailor and the bailee receive benefits from the relationship. This bailment is created when one party is given another party's property for a definite purpose and consideration is given. A bailee may hire the property of the bailor, or the bailor may deliver property to the bailee for a specified service. These bailments always involve a contract, since there is mutual consideration.

Example. Mrs. Lowe takes a floor lamp to the Fix-It Shop to be repaired. When the work is completed, she pays for it and takes it home. This is a mutual benefit bailment. Mrs. Lowe benefits by having the lamp returned in working order; the shop benefits by being paid for the work done.

The bailee in a mutual benefit bailment owes a duty of ordinary care, or such care as a responaible person would take with his or her own property. If this care is not taken, the bailee is said to be *negligent* and is liable for any damages to or loss of goods because of it. There are several types of mutual benefit bailments into which consumers enter.

Pledge or Pawn

A *pledge* is one type of mutual benefit bailment involving personal property. It is usually given to secure a loan. The pledge is created when one party gives any type of personal property to another as security for the payment of a debt or for the performance of an obligation. The *pledgor* is the bailor who gives the property. The *pledgee* is the bailee who receives possession but not title or ownership of the property.

If the pledgor defaults by failing to live up to the terms of the agreement, the pledgee has the right to sell the property after proper notification of the *pledgor.* If the sale results in an amount greater than the debt, including interest and expenses, the pledgor receives the excess. The pledgor must pay the difference if the sale results in an amount less than what is owed.

A loan made by a person based on some security left by the owner is called a *pawn*. The person making the loan is called a *pawnbroker*. Although similar to a pledge, these dealings are usually regulated by state statutes. In general, however, the same rules apply to these transactions as for the security pledge.

The pledgee in both situations must take ordinary care of the pledged property. If the care is negligent, then the pledgee is held liable for damage or loss.

Bailment for Hire

A *bailment for hire* is an agreement by which the bailor rents out property to be used by the bailee for a specific purpose and is paid a rental fee. The bailor impliedly warrants that the article is fit for the purpose for which it is to be used. This implied warranty of fitness for a particular purpose is similar to the one arising under the law of sales. The bailor is held responsible for any breach of this warranty and for any defects in the article that could cause injury unless the bailee has been warned.

Example. Ron and Rita rent motorbikes while on vacation. The rental agent fails to tell Ron that the chain on his bike is loose. Ron has an accident and holds the rental agency liable. Ron collects for damages since the bailor did not warn him about the chain.

Unless there is some other agreement, the bailee is responsible for repairs resulting from the ordinary care and use of the article. Repairs which are extraordinary are usually the responsibility of the bailor.

Example. Marshall rents Stock his tractor. Stock must pay for gas and oil as well as for a fan belt that breaks. Before returning the tractor, the fuel pump also breaks. This is considered an extraordinary repair; one which does not result from ordinary use. The bailor, Marshall, is responsible for replacement of the fuel pump.

Bailment for Service or Repair

Another type of mutual benefit bailment is the transfer of property to the bailee for repair or service. The property may sometimes change form or appearance, but it is still a bailment.

Example. Kathy delivers six yards of fabric to Judy's home to be made into a dress. In four weeks, Kathy picks up the dress and pays Judy for the labor involved. This is a mutual benefit bailment even though the property changes form.

When there is a bailment for service or repair, the bailee is required to take ordinary care of the property. The bailee is only held liable for damage or loss if there is negligent behavior on the part of the bailee. If there is damage or loss and the bailee is not negligent, the bailor must bear the loss. If, through no fault of the bailee, the goods are destroyed or stolen after services have been performed, the bailee has the right to receive payment for those services.

Example. Consider the previous case. Suppose that there is a fire in Judy's house the day Kathy delivers the fabric and the fabric is ruined. The fire occurs through no fault of Judy's. Since Judy did not act negligently, she cannot be held responsible for the expense of replacing Kathy's material; this would be Kathy's responsibility. If the fire occurs three weeks later, and it is through no fault of Judy's, Judy is still not liable for the material. In addition, if the dress is already completed and burns, Kathy must pay Judy for the labor charges.

If there is no credit agreement, the bailee has the right to be paid when the goods are repaired and ready for delivery. If the bailor does not pay, the bailee has a legal right to keep the goods in his or her possession until payment is made. This is known as a *lien* on the property.

Bailment for Hiring of Custody

A mutual benefit bailment called a *hiring of custody* (care) arises when one party engages another party to take care of his or her property. The bailee may perform no service other than storage.

A warehouse owner is a bailee who stores goods for others for profit. That bailee must take ordinary care of the property and is only liable for damage or loss when care is not taken.

Example. Cummings, a warehouse owner, stores the Dales' furniture under a leak in his warehouse roof. Much of the furniture is damaged by water. Cummings is held liable since the damage is a direct result of his negligence.

The bailee in a hiring of custody can expect payment from the bailor upon return of the goods. If the bailor does not pay, the bailee can exercise a right of lien and keep possession of the property until there is payment.

When garage or parking lot owners working for a fee park an individual's car, keep the keys, and then return the car when the party asks for it, a hiring of custody bailment is created. The lot owners are responsible for any damage to the car which is due to negligence by them or by their employees. Many state statutes hold the owners responsible for any damage or loss resulting from negligence even if the parking receipt contains a disclaimer relieving them of all liability. This is a true bailment situation since the parking lot exercises control over the car as a bailee would, and it should not be allowed to disclaim its own liability. There is no bailment created when drivers park their own vehicles in the parking lot and take their keys with them, even though there is a fee charged. It is thought that the parking lot operation does not exercise enough control in this situation to constitute a bailment.

Case Example. Consider the effect of a disclaimer of liability by a bailee as raised by the following case.

PICKER v. SEARCHER'S DETECTIVE AGENCY, INC.

United States Court of Appeals, District of Columbia Circuit, 1975
515 F.2d 1316

[A coin dealer sued the American Numismatic Association (ANA) and a private security agency for the loss of a coin collection which was missing from the security room at a convention. Plaintiff had signed an ANA form in October 1970 reserving display space at the August 1971 convention. The form told displayers to procure their own insurance and that ANA would not be responsible for any loss. When plaintiff checked two attache cases into the security room at the convention he was given a receipt for the cases which expressly limited ANA's liability to $25.00 for each item stored. The trial court dismissed the complaint alleging the simple negligence of both defendants and directed a verdict of $50.00 for plaintiff on the gross negligence claim.]

FAHY, Senior Circuit Judge. The American Numismatic Association (ANA), in connection with its annual national convention to be held at a hotel in Washington, D.C., arranged for the display and selling of coins, medals, paper money and like objects during the convention. Appellant Richard Picker, a professional coin dealer, completed an application form supplied by ANA in October 1970, and requested bourse (display and selling) space for his coin and currency collection at the convention, to be held the following August. His application was accepted in March 1971. On the afternoon of August 14, 1971, the last day of the convention, Picker placed his collection in two attache cases and checked them at the security room provided by the ANA at the hotel. He returned to repossess the two cases the following day. Delivery was not made, for the two cases had disappeared. He sued appellees ANA and Searcher's Detective Agency, Inc. (Searcher's) in the District Court for the value of the collection, alleged to be $135,000. Searcher's had entered into a contract with ANA under which it would furnish protection at the convention and security room for safekeeping of the displays when not on exhibit. During the convention period employees of both ANA and Searcher's were in attendance at the security room.

I

The delivery of the attache cases to appellees as bailees, and their failure to return the bailed property when duly claimed, raised a prime facie case of negligence under Count I [simple negligence]. [Citations omitted.] Appellees defend that Picker had released them of liability except for $25.00 for each article lost. Two documents are involved in their defense. One is the application form sent by ANA to Picker for participation in the bourse, which he signed and returned in October, 1970; the other is a three-part tag used by the appellees in operating the security room. The fifth of seven paragraphs in the application reads in pertinent part as follows:

A security room will be available for all officially registered ANA members during the convention period. Police protection and armed guards will be provided for the bourse and exhibit areas, but users thereof are expected to insure themselves against any loss sustained. The undersigned specifically releases the ANA, its officers, members and/or committees, either in their official, individual or personal capacities by reason of any loss, damage or injury whatsoever sustained, either directly or indirectly in connection with the bourse, security room exhibit and/or convention.

The tag used at the security room is in three parts, separated by perforations. Two parts contain only identical numbers and a place for the bailor to sign. One of these is signed and placed on the article when it is checked in. The other is retained by the bailor as his claim check and signed when he seeks to repossess the article. The center part, retained by the bailees in the security room file, is signed when the article is presented for safekeeping. This part reads as follows:

> In consideration for permitting me to use without charge the Security Room at the 19. . . . ANA Convention, I hereby agree that the liability of American Numismatic Association,
>
> . . . .
>
> and all officers, board members and other representatives of each of them shall be limited to the aggregate sum of $25.00 for loss, theft, damage and/or destruction (through negligence or otherwise) of all property held for me in said Security Room; provided, however, that the foregoing provision shall not limit the liability of any individual who may be personally guilty of theft, willful damage or destruction of my property.

———————————

Signature

II
The Liability of Searcher's for
Simple Negligence

[In Part II the court determined that a disclaimer of liability on the part of ANA did not also apply to Searcher's. Note that both documents in question specifically refer to the liability of the ANA. The court did not agree with Searcher's claim that since it was acting as the agent of ANA it should therefore benefit from the principal's immunity.]

· · ·

Searcher's also relies upon the language we have quoted from the part of the security room tag signed by appellant but retained in the file of the security room. Appellant testified, however, that when he checked his cases the security room was very busy, that he did not read the limitation of liability clause, was not asked to read it, and was not aware of its terms. The part retained by him, as we have noted, contained nothing but a number and place for signature.

We think the court erred in dismissing Picker's claim against Searcher's under Count I. A hurried transaction of this sort, with no special reference by the bailee to the provisions Searcher's relies upon, together with testimony the jury might believe that it was not even read by appellant, places the case in a different setting from contract cases which hold,

> The general rule in this jurisdiction is that one who signs a contract has the duty to read it and is obligated according to its terms. . . .[Citations omitted.]

Lucas v. *Auto City Parking* (1948) involved the theft of a car containing certain valuable articles, the loss of which was claimed. The car had been left in a parking lot. One phase of the case involved the contention of the proprietor of the lot, the defendant, that he was not responsible for the loss because of a limitation of liability printed on the claim check. The Court of Appeals stated:

> This Court has held that unless a customer knows of the terms of a limitation of liability on a ticket or claim check the limitation is not binding upon him but that when the customer does have knowledge of such terms he is bound thereby. In the circumstances of this case the question as to whether plaintiffs knew of the limitation was one of fact and the judge's finding thereon must stand, for there was sufficient evidence to support it.   •   •   •

In *Parking Management Incorporated* v. *Jacobson* (1969), the operator of the parking lot was held liable for damage to the plaintiff's car while in the operator's custody notwithstanding a notice of limited liability posted on the lot. The court stated:

> We hold the trial court did not err in rejecting appellant's contention that it had successfully limited its liability to damage claimed before leaving the parking lot. Plaintiff testified that he was not aware of such a condition of liability when he left the car at the lot. Absent proof that he expressly or impliedly agreed to such limitation at the time of the bailment contract, the effort to limit liability was unilateral and of no effect as between appellant and Jacobson. . . .

We conclude that as the law has developed in this jurisdiction the testimony as to the manner in which the checking of the two attache cases occurred at the security room, including testimony of appellant that he did not read and did not know of the limitation of liability written on that part of the tag retained by appellees, although signed by him, raised an issue for the jury on Count I of the complaint as to Searcher's, considered of course with the undisputed fact that the bailed articles taken in custody for appellant at the security room were not returned by the bailee when duly rerequested. In so concluding we have considered the cases presented by appellees, . . . and find they are not persuasive to the contrary in light of the factual differences which understandably led the courts in those cases to a different conclusion from that we reach in this case.

•   •   •

We decide the case respecting the liability of Searcher's without regard to the application of Picker of October, 1970, and its acceptance by ANA in March 1971. We thus limit our consideration of Searcher's defense to the actual transaction of bailment when the attache cases were checked at the security room. Accordingly, language in the formal contract cases cited by Searcher's which bear upon a contractual release or limitation of liability are not the criteria for decision as to Searcher's. The question turns upon whether Picker knew or in the circumstances of the checking of the attache cases should be charged with knowledge that Searcher's would be required to pay only $25.00 for each attache case it failed to return when duly requested rather than its actual value. We think the evidence required the question to be submitted to the jury.

III

The Liability of ANA for Simple
Negligence

Recognizing that if Picker was bound by the release of liability clause in the application form, or by the limitation clause of the tag used at the security room, gross negligence [extreme negligence] on appellees' part would not be excused, the District Court submitted the issue of such negligence to the jury. The result, as we have noted, was a verdict exonerating ANA and Searcher's of gross negligence. The question remains whether the court erred in entering a verdict for appellant against ANA for $50.00, thus limiting to that amount Picker's recovery from ANA for simple negligence, instead of also submitting that issue to the jury.

ANA relies upon the application letter signed and submitted by Picker in October, 1970, and its acceptance by ANA in March following, the convention to be held in August. We have noted that in the fifth of its seven paragraphs, the application refers to the availability of a security room, and states that police and armed guards would be provided for the "bourse and exhibit areas, but users thereof are expected to insure themselves against any loss sustained," no reference here being made to loss by the security room. Then comes the clause relied upon by ANA, that the applicant releases ANA of liability "by reason of any loss. . . in connection with the bourse, security room, exhibit and/or convention."

In ANA's March acceptance of the application mention was again made of a security room but there was no reference to a release of liability, although, in contrast to this omission, the acceptance communication called special attention to ANA's regulations governing the convention. Moreover, actual arrangements at the security room itself also omitted reference to the terms of the application. As we have noted, the part of the security room tag retained in the files there provided that the liability of ANA and "all officers, board members and other representatives of each of them shall be limited to the aggregate sum of $25.00" for loss of an article there.

We have held in Part II that the arrangement for, and the evidence with respect to the actual bailment at, the security room, did not obviate the need for submitting to the jury the issue of Searcher's liability for the true value of the two attache cases lost there. We noted in that connection that Picker testified he did not read or know of the provision printed on the portion of the tag retained by the bailees, although he had signed it.

With respect now to ANA, the use at the security room of the tag purporting to limit ANA's liability for loss to $25.00 for each article, long after the October application had been accepted, with no reference in the interim to its total release of liability clause, gives rise to a confused and uncertain factual situation as to the total arrangements with ANA respecting a loss at its hands. The application form provides for complete release of liability; the security room arrangements set out a monetary limit, and the efficacy of that limit turns upon the evidence concerning the actual circumstances at the time of the bailment. ANA does not rely on what occurred then, basing its defense for actual loss due to simple negligence solely upon the terms and acceptance of the application. Nevertheless, Picker's case against ANA does involve the actual bailment at the security room conducted by ANA and Searcher's. The two factual phases of the overall relationship between ANA and Picker as well as the two documents must be considered. For reasons similar to those set forth in Part II respecting the case against Searcher's, it follows that an issue for the jury is involved in the case against ANA insofar as the circumstances of the actual bailment are concerned. When to these circumstances is added the evidence residing in the application itself, and its acceptance, considered with Picker's testimony, together with the history of the application from its signing in October to the time of the loss of the attache cases in August, the jury issue embraces an enlarged evidentiary setting. . . .

• • •

[The court determined that the case should have been submitted to the jury at the trial level and sent the case back to the district court with a standard to govern the jury's deliberation. The standard was stated as follows.]

. . . to determine on the whole evidence whether it was or was not brought home to Picker with reasonable clarity that ANA was not to be accountable for the actual loss Picker might suffer through ANA's negligence in caring for the bailed attache cases.

SPECIAL BAILMENTS

Fungible Goods

In most bailment situations, the bailee is required to return the same goods that were originally received, even though they may be in a different form or have a different appearance. There is an exception, however, in the storage of fungible goods, which creates a special bailment situation. *Fungible goods* are goods which are so similar to other goods of their nature that they are indistinguishable. Such goods as stored grain are considered to be fungible goods.

If grain belonging to several persons is stored in the same elevator, and the operator contracts to return an equal amount of the same quality of grain to the depositor, a bailment of fungible goods is created.

Example. Calhoune delivers two truckloads of grain to a local storage elevator which is used by all the ranchers in that area. Several months later, he picks up two truckloads and pays the storage fee. This is a bailment of fungible goods. The grain he takes back does not have to be precisely the same grain that he brought in, providing it is of the same quality.

Transportation of Merchandise

The transportation of merchandise may be done by individuals or companies known as *carriers*. *Private carriers* agree to transport goods only under individual contracts. Their services are not offered to the general public, but only to those whom they select. Private carriers have the same responsibility as bailees for hire in a mutual benefit bailment. Private carriers may be moving van companies and private delivery services.

Example. The Coles are moving from Atlanta to Chicago. They contract with Ace Moving Company to move their furniture. Since Ace can either take the job or not, the company is considered to be a private carrier. If Ace does take the job, they have the same liability as a bailee for hire while the Cole's belongings are in their possession.

Common carriers are paid to transport the personal property of all who choose to employ them. Railroads, airlines, steamship companies, and trucking firms are all common carriers. Common carriers are known as *extraordinary bailees* because they have special duties and rights. They have a much greater responsibility to the consumer than private carriers or other standard bailees.

A common carrier usually cannot refuse to transport the goods of any shipper as long as the shipper meets the carrier's rules and regulations. Carriers can only refuse to carry goods which they do not usually transport; goods not properly packed; articles which are dangerous, such as explosives; or goods which are perishable when there are no refrigeration facilities available.

Example. West Tool Company decides to ship two properly crated boxes of tool parts by air freight with U.S. Airlines Company. As long as West complies with all the rules, the airlines must ship the goods. They cannot select only certain shippers at their own discretion, since they are a common carrier.

Common carriers of goods are controlled by the Interstate Commerce Commission (ICC) when they operate across state lines (*interstate*). State agencies regulate common carriers operating within state lines (*intrastate*).

The liability of common carriers begins when they accept the goods. The major reason that common carriers are involved in special bailment situations is that the carriers are held responsible as *insurers of the property*, guarantors of the safety of the goods in their care. Unlike bailees for hire who are only responsible for damage or loss due to negligence by them or by their employees, the obligations of common carriers extend to almost all causes of loss or damage. The carrier is relieved of responsibility only for the following reasons:

• An *act of God,* any natural cause that human beings could neither foresee nor avoid. This includes fire caused by lightning, snowstorms, floods, tornadoes, and hurricanes.

Example. Royal Steamship Company, already in possession of certain goods, is loading the goods when an unforecasted hurricane hits the area. Although they are able to return part of the goods to the warehouse or on board the ship, some of the goods that are left exposed on the dock are damaged. Royal is not held liable since damage was due to an act of God.

- An *act of a public enemy,* the damage or loss of goods caused by seizure by military forces of an opposing government. This does not include mobs, rioters, robbers, or strikers.

Example. While traveling from Spain to California, an American Overseas Transport Company plane stops to refuel in a foreign nation. The pilot is unaware that the friendly government has been overthrown. The freight on board the plane is seized by guerillas of the new government. The plane is then sent on its way. Overseas Transport is not liable for the loss of property.

- When loss is due to the *nature of the goods* and negligence is not a factor. This includes natural deterioration of foods, fermentation of liquids, or injury to animals.

Example. R.H. Trucking is carrying a shipment of apple cider properly stored in barrels. Several of the barrels burst due to fermentation of the cider. R.H. Trucking is not held liable due to the nature of the goods.

- When loss or damage is due to the *negligence of the shipper* This includes improper packing and fraudulent concealment of the nature or value of the goods.

Example. Bert's Book Store ships two crates of rare books worth over $2,000 by railroad. They state the value at $500 to receive a lower shipping rate. The railroad car is destroyed en route. The store enters claim for $2,000, stating that the cartons actually contained a rare first edition of books. The railroad is only liable for $500, since the shipper fraudulently concealed the true value of the goods.

- An *act of a public authority.* If an authorized government agency takes the goods by proper legal means, the carrier is not liable.

Example. A federal agency is alerted that there are drugs hidden inside mattresses in a truck in transit from Texas to Illinois. The agency seizes the truck by legal methods and removes the mattresses for further investigation. The trucker is not liable to the shipper for loss or damage to the goods.

Upon arrival at the destination, the common carrier either delivers the goods or they are picked up, according to the specifications of the contract. If the goods are not picked up, the common carrier's extraordinary responsibility as an insurer is ended. The liability from that point on is the same as in a bailment for hiring of custody in a warehouse storage situation. If the goods are not unloaded from the transportation vehicle and that vehicle is thus delayed from being used, the carrier can charge an additional fee to the shipper known as *demurrage.*

Transportation of Passengers

As in the transportation of goods, there are also private and public carriers of *passengers* (people being transported). The differentiation between these private and public carriers is the same as with private and common carriers of freight. Private carriers do not offer their services to the public; they can choose the people with whom they will do business under individual contracts. A company car, bus, or plane that carries only the firm's employees is considered a private carrier.

Example.   The Reynolds Oil Company transports workers from its main office to an offshore oil rig several miles out in the ocean. The plane is considered a private carrier since the only people who ride in it are Reynolds' employees, not the general public.

Public carriers must carry for hire all passengers who request their services, unless, of course, the passengers do not have the money to pay or their behavior is objectionable. Airlines, railroads, bus lines, taxicabs, subways, steamships, and ferries are among those carriers classified as public. They are known as *extraordinary bailees* because they have special duties and rights.

A person becomes a passenger upon entering the premises with the intention of using the carrier's services. At that point, the person is entitled to all the rights and privileges of a passenger even though a ticket has not yet been purchased. The carriers must use reasonable care in transporting their passengers safely to their destinations; they are held liable only for injuries resulting from their negligence or the negligence of their employees.

Public carriers are not responsible for any delay of their vehicles. They also are not responsible for the safety of the people who board their vehicle without permission to sell items to the passengers.

Example. While a bus is stopped at a station, a man boards the bus, without permission, to sell sandwiches and newspapers to the passengers. He trips on the steps as he leaves and is injured. The bus line cannot be held liable for injuries to the man.

The public carrier is obligated to carry a reasonable amount of baggage for each passenger at no extra cost. *Baggage* consists of articles necessary for the passenger's comfort during the trip or for the ultimate purpose of the trip. The carrier is not responsible for hand baggage carried by the passenger during the trip. When baggage is checked, however, the carrier becomes an insurer of those goods and thus becomes an extraordinary bailee. Carriers are responsible for all causes of loss or damage to the property except in the five instances listed earlier as exceptions for the common carrier of freight. Public carriers of passengers, however, may limit the amount of their liability by agreements with their passengers. These limitations are usually printed on the baggage checks and should be brought to the attention of the passenger.

Example. Al, prior to boarding a plane, checks one suitcase. He keeps one small briefcase with him at his seat. When he arrives at his destination, the briefcase is missing. In addition, the checked suitcase is not with the other baggage from the flight. The airline is only responsible for the loss of the missing suitcase that Al checked. Al is responsible for the loss of the briefcase that he took with him on the plane.

Hotel Owners and Innkeepers

Hotel owners and innkeepers are those who provide food and lodging to *transients* (guests who seek food and temporary lodging). Like common and public carriers, they are extraordinary bailees since they are obligated to serve the public, and thus have a greater responsibility than the ordinary bailee. They must, by law, receive all reputable transients who are able to pay the charges, provided there is room.

The hotel owner or innkeeper is not an insurer of the safety of the guest. They are only held liable for injury to a guest when they are negligent.

This is a special bailment situation because, in a strict sense, hotel owners and innkeepers are not bailees. They do not receive

---

Cornwall Inn

Cornwall, New York

LAWS OF NEW YORK

General Business Law—Section 200

SECTION 200. SAFES LIMITED LIABILITY. — Whenever the proprietor or manager of any hotel, inn or steamboat shall provide a safe in the office of such hotel or steamboat, or other convenient place for the safe keeping of any money, jewels, ornaments, bank notes, bonds, negotiable securities or precious stones belonging to the guests or travelers in such hotel, inn or steamboat, and shall notify the guests or travelers thereof by posting a notice stating the fact that such safe is provided, in which such property may be deposited, in a public and conspicuous place and manner in the office and public rooms and in the public parlors of such hotel or inn, or saloon of such steamboat, and if such guest or traveler shall neglect to deliver such property to the person in charge of such office for deposit in such safe, the proprietor or manager of such hotel or steamboat shall not be liable for any loss of such property, sustained by such guest or traveler by theft or otherwise: but no hotel or steamboat proprietor, manager or lessee shall be obliged to receive property on deposit for safe keeping, exceeding five hundred dollars in value; and if such guest or traveler shall deliver such property to the person in charge of such office for deposit in such safe, said proprietor, manager or lessee shall not be liable for any loss thereof, sustained by such guest or traveler by theft or otherwise, in any sum exceeding the sum of five hundred dollars, unless by special agreement in writing with such proprietor, manager or lessee.

Fig. 9-2   A sign typical of those posted in hotels and motels limiting liability.

possession of the property of the guest. Legally, however, it is still treated as a bailment, and the hotel owners and innkeepers are considered insurers of the property of their guests. The only exception to this strict liability of property are losses resulting from acts of God, public enemies, or from negligence by the guest or by a member of the guest's party.

Most states have statutes which allow hotels and inns to place a limit on this liability. This is done by providing a safe for guests and notifying the guests that they can use it for their property which is valued over a certain amount. There is usually a limit on the value of goods that can be placed in the safe at the responsibility of the hotel. If valuable goods that were not placed in the safe are stolen, the hotel is not liable. Also, if goods of a value greater than the maximum allowed are placed in the safe, the hotel cannot be held liable for the full amount. Such limitations are usually posted in each room for the guest to see, figure 9-2.

Example. Mrs. Hess, upon arrival at the Midcity Hotel, places her jewelry and cash totaling $2,500 in value in the hotel safe. She declares a value of $1,500, the maximum allowable by the hotel. The hotel safe is robbed during the night. Midcity Hotel is liable only for $1,500 of the $2,500 worth of cash and goods that Mrs. Hess deposited.

A hotel or inn has the right to a lien on all property brought in by a guest. If the guest does not pay the bill, the owner has the right to exercise the lien and keep the property until the bill is paid. If the bill is not paid within a reasonable time, the goods may be sold.

SELF-EVALUATION

Provide a brief explanation for each of the following.

1. What are the three elements of a bailment and how are they related to a bailment situation?

2. What is a gratuitous bailment? Give two examples.

3. Why is a mutual benefit bailment a contract bailment?

4. What is meant by the phrase *ordinary care* of property?

5. What must a bailor do before transferring possession in a bailment for the sole benefit of a bailor?

6. In which type of bailment is the bailee responsible for greater care of the goods, a bailment for the sole benefit of the bailor, or a bailment for the sole benefit of the bailee?

7. What type of bailment is a pledge? When is it created?

8. What type of warranty is issued in a bailment for hire? By whom is it issued?

9. When may a bailee exercise a right to lien?

10. What service must be performed by the bailee in a bailment for hiring of custody?

11. How does a bailment for hiring of custody differ from a bailment of fungible goods?

12. What do common carriers and public carriers have in common concerning liability for goods in their care?

13. If a common carrier is transporting perishable food in a properly refrigerated vehicle and the food spoils, is the carrier liable for the loss? Why or why not?

14. What is the term for an additional fee charged to a shipper by a carrier for goods that are not unloaded from a transporting vehicle?

15. What liability does a public carrier have for its passengers and the baggage that the passengers check?

16. What is a method by which hotels limit their liability for the property of a guest?

17. What recourse does a hotel owner or innkeeper have if a guest does not pay the bill?

SUGGESTED ACTIVITY

1. Collect samples of bailees and bailors attempting to avoid liability. Examples may be found in parking receipts, public carriers, passenger tickets, and rental car agencies. Discuss whether or not the samples seem effective in protecting the bailee or bailor from liability.

CASES FOR STUDY

1. *S* is the editor and photographer of the student newspaper at the State University. Some of his personal photographic equipment, stored in the paper's darkroom, is stolen. At the trial of *S* v. *State University,* the evidence tends to show that neither the security force nor any university official knew that *S*'s equipment was in the room. *S* offers evidence to the effect that by school policy, all persons leaving the building with property are to be stopped and checked for written permission to remove such property. *S*'s theory of liability is that State has been a negligent bailee of his property. Is he correct? Why or why not?

2. Brown asks an air carrier about rates, schedules, and special packing required to ship frozen food items from Virginia to California. In preparing the items for shipment, Brown places labels on the box marked *Fragile, Glass,* and *Store Frozen* before turning the parcel over to the carrier. The carrier pastes a shipping label over Brown's label marked *Store Frozen.* The recipient of the package is advised by Brown that the package is en route and must be refrigerated upon arrival. Brown also describes the package by referring to the labels. When the package arrives at the destination point, the recipient does not

recognize it as the package requiring special attention, since the label affixed by Brown was obscured by the carrier's shipping label. The recipient receives delivery of a number of additional packages sent by Brown, none of which required special storage. Is the carrier liable for spoilage of the food items? Explain.

3. Constantine delivers goods to Ace Trucking Lines. The goods are to be sent to a destination point in another state. The truck carrying the goods is struck by lightning, and both the truck and goods are consumed in flames. Is Ace liable for the loss of the goods? Why or why not?

4. Switz parks her car in a parking lot and leaves the keys with the attendant on duty. When she returns, the car is not in its parking space and the keys are missing from the attendant's post. The attendant remarks that he left the lot for only a minute when he walked to the corner to buy a paper. Can Switz recover the value of the car? Why or why not?

5. Miller takes a suit to the dry cleaners. He is told by an employee that the suit will be ready in three days, but if he should fail to pick up the suit within sixty days, it becomes the property of the dry cleaners. The same provision is printed on a large sign above the counter and also on the ticket given to the customer. Miller acknowledges that he understands, and leaves. He returns in six months to claim the suit. The employee at the counter advises Miller that the suit was given to charity three months ago as is the practice of the establishment. Can Miller recover the value of the suit? Explain.

6. Frank checks into the Sweet Dreams Hotel. He is asked by the desk clerk if he has anything to be deposited in the hotel safe. Frank declines. He reads a notice posted on the back of the door to his room which states that the hotel is not liable for damage to or loss of possessions valued at more than $500 which are left in the room. Frank leaves his room for dinner. When he returns, he discovers that someone has broken in and taken cash, a radio, a tape recorder, and a camera. The loss is estimated to be over $1,000. What is the hotel's responsibility?

7. Nastorri rents scaffolding from a rental agency. While using the scaffolding for its intended purpose, Nastorri is injured when one of the supports, and then the scaffolding, collapses. Is the rental agency liable? Explain.

8. *G* has agreed to take *H*'s diamond ring to a jeweler. *G* stops at a diner and leaves the box containing the ring on the counter while she goes to the register to pay the check. When she returns, the box and ring are missing. Does *H* have an action against *G*?

9. Altman ships bananas through Overland Railroad. The bananas are stored properly and the length of time en route is reasonable. When the bananas reach the destination point, however, they are spoiled. Is the carrier liable? Explain.

10. McGuire delivers goods to a trucking company with complete instructions for shipment. While the goods are with the carrier, they are destroyed by fire at the station. Is the carrier liable?

Section 4

Real Property

Real property is broadly defined as the crust of the earth and all things firmly attached to it. While in common usage the word *property* refers to a physical object, in a legal sense, *property* is the right to that physical object.

Example. Bob owns a house on Main Street. The house is therefore considered to be Bob's property. Legally speaking, however, the property is not the house itself, but rather Bob's right to use, enjoy, sell, or rent that house.

In the chart on page 172, which shows the basic divisions of law, the classification of property is now shown as one category of private law. Property includes personal property, as discussed in the previous section, and real property, as defined in this section.

Transactions involving real property are much more complicated than those dealing with personal property since there are a greater number of required legal documents and technical procedures. For this reason, most real property dealings call for the help of a competent, licensed attorney.

At one time or another, almost everyone deals with real property. Involvement in real property transactions may range from the renting of an apartment to the purchase of a large factory for a business.

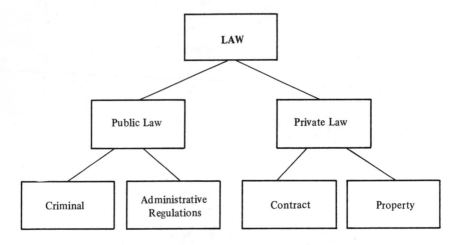

Chapter 10

Ownership of Real Property

OBJECTIVES

After studying this chapter, the student will be able to

- discuss the legal rights and limitations of owners imposed by the form of ownership, nonpossessory use, zoning ordinances, and eminent domain.

- outline the six forms of ownership, listing rules regarding the size of interest, the time and source of acquisition, and the rights of tenants which apply to each.

- list the five ways in which real property is conveyed from one owner to another.

- define the following words and phrases.

real property	sole tenant
fixture	concurrent ownership
reasonable man standard	tenancy in common
estate	deed
possessory interest	joint tenancy
fee simple	right of survivorship
life tenant	tenancy by the entirety
life estate	community property
remainder	condominium
easement	donor
license	donee
zoning ordinance	adverse possession
just compensation	tax sale
eminent domain	inheritance
tenancy	

Real property has been described as land and anything that is permanently attached to it. When personal property is affixed (attached) to or used with real property with the intention of it becoming a part of the realty, it is called a *fixture*. Fixtures are considered to be real property.

Example.   Brown cements a fourteen-foot flagpole into his front yard. Since Brown intends for the flagpole to be permanent, it is considered to be a fixture and part of the realty.

Example.   White hangs a tapestry on the wall of his living room. When he moves, he plans to take the tapestry with him. The tapestry is personal property; White did not intend for it to become a fixture when he hung it in his living room. It is therefore not considered realty.

In the absence of an agreement between parties, there can be a great deal of misunderstanding as to whether or not an item is a fixture. It is important to distinguish fixtures from items which are not fixtures, since a fixture is transferred to the new owner with real property when the former owner vacates the premises, while the original owner keeps the item if it is not a fixture.

To determine which items are fixtures, the courts apply the *reasonable man standard;* that is, would a reasonable man, familiar with the entire situation, assume that the person attaching the personal property intended it to become a fixture? In the court's determination, the key word is *intent.*

RIGHTS AND LIMITATIONS OF OWNERS

The owner of property has the right to posesss, use, enjoy, and dispose of that property. Ownership of real property involves both specific rights and limitations. Some limitations are created in contracts; others are imposed by law.

Estates

The rights of property owners differ according to the type of estate involved. In this sense, *estate,* or *possessory interest,* is the interest which a person has in lands.

Fee Simple Absolute.   The *fee simple absolute,* usually called *fee simple,* entitles an owner of real property to the entire property for an unlimited time; it is the absolute ownership of estate. This right to absolute ownership descends to any heirs of the owner, even if there is no will. The holder of fee simple may grant rights concerning the property to others without changing the nature of the original interest.

Example. Smith owns five acres of land. He leases it to the Stowe Rod and Gun Club for ten years. Smith still owns the land in fee simple. At the end of the ten years, Smith again has the right to do whatever he desires with the land.

Life Estate. In contrast to fee simple, a *life estate* is an interest in land that is limited in time. The interest is limited to the life of the person holding it or to the life of the person to whom it has been granted. The estate or interest remaining is the *remainder interest* or simply *the remainder,* which is usually a fee simple absolute. A life estate is not full ownership, so the individual holding it, a *life tenant,* cannot sell the property.

Example. *A* dies owning a fee simple estate in Blackacre. *A*'s will provides that *B* is to have a life estate in Blackacre with the remainder going to *C*. *A* had a fee simple and was thus able to dispose of the property as he saw fit. *B* has a life estate and is therefore able to use the land for as long as he lives. *C* has a fee simple subject to *B*'s life estate. Upon the death of *B*, *C* will have full ownership and use of the property; that is, he will own the full estate.

Nonpossessory Uses

Easement. An *easement* is the right of one party to use the land of another for a special purpose. There is no possession or ownership transferred. Since an easement is nonpossessory, it is not considered an estate in land.

There are many types of easements. They are usually created by contract for a long term. Easements might be the right to drive across land, install a sewer across land, or to restrain an adjoining landowner from erecting certain types of buildings.

Example. Murphy and Gomez live next door to each other. They have one driveway which branches off at the end to the right and to the left to each of their carports. Both parties have an easement for the part of the driveway that is located on both properties. Each individual has the right to use the driveway even though part of it is located on the other's property.

License. A *license,* created by mutual consent, is similar to an easement. It differs in that it creates only a temporary right to use another's land in a limited and specified manner and is revocable at the will of the licensor. Licenses are sometimes created orally. They may be used only by the party to whom the privilege is given. A license might be the permission to cross land or to hunt, fish, and trap on property belonging to another.

Example. Riley Lumber purchases trees from Daley. The trees are to be cut and carried away from Daley's property. Riley's right to enter Daley's property for that purpose is a license.

Example. When individuals patronize a theater, they enter the real property upon which the theater is located to be entertained. The license (in the form of the ticket) allows that use of the land, which is incidental to the main reason the patrons have purchased tickets, which is to see the play.

Case Example. Easements are not always created by deed. The appellant in the following case argues that an implied easement to use a portion of a lake over appellee's land was created when the land was divided, even though the deeds do not mention such an easement. His argument is based on the fact that the use of the lake is necessary to the enjoyment of his property. Notice the distinction the court makes between an easement and a license.

STORY v. HEFNER
Supreme Court of Oklahoma, 1975
540 P.2d 562

DOOLIN, Justice. The Apple Valley Recreational Club had its beginning in May of 1962. The Club maintained certain real estate which encompassed a large recreational lake developed by four tenants in common under the guidance of Robert Story, the defendant appellant, who initially held only an option to buy into the joint venture.

This initial agreement was terminated in September of 1964. In November of the same year, another agreement was executed also giving Story an option to purchase into the property and included a clause stating, "It is the intention of the parties that the premises be operated for the joint benefit of the parties and that each party shall contribute his proportionate share of the cost of maintaining and operating the premises."

In January of 1966, through the various buy-out agreements Story and Hefner, the plaintiff appellee, became sole tenants in common in the 260 acre tract.

From 1966 to 1974 Hefner and Story jointly utilized the lake for fishing and other recreational purposes. In May of 1967 the parties decided to divide the property into two individually owned tracts by the exchange of. . .deeds. Although there was testimony that both Story and Hefner believed that the lake itself could not be divided, the new property line created by the deeds did run through and divide the lake. However, both parties continued joint use of the lake after the [signing] of the deeds.

Seven years after this division, Hefner brought the present action to enjoin Story from using the portion of the lake covering Hefner's property and asked the court for a declaratory judgment declaring that the Storys had no right to use or enjoy this portion of the lake. A temporary injunction was issued and Hefner erected buoys across the lake preventing Story from entering the part of the lake that Hefner considered to be his.

Story answered and cross-petitioned claiming a right to reasonable use of the entire lake surface and asking for a permanent injunction prohibiting Hefner from interfering with his reasonable recreational use of the lake.

The trial court entered judgment for Hefner and granted each party exclusive right to the use of the lake over his own land and denied the existence of an easement or license,. . .which would allow the Storys to use the entire lake. Each party was permanently enjoined from trespassing upon the other's lake surface. The Storys appeal.

Hefner bases his claim on the unequivocality of the two. . . deeds. Story does not deny the deeds but rather bases his defense on evidence that the *consideration* for the deeds was the continued use of the entire lake, since no money changed hands. Story contends that the finding of the trial court that the deeds gave each party exclusive right to the use of the lake is erroneous. We agree.

At trial, Hefner offered into evidence the two. . .deeds which divided the property. In addition, he offered a map of the properties which showed that Story had access to all of his property without crossing the Hefner tract. Story, however, was not seeking access to or through Hefner's dry land. His defense was based on written and oral agreements, . . . and continuous recreational use that would tend to show that the intention of the parties at the time of the execution of the deeds was to allow the use of the entire lake surface to *both* parties, thus creating an implied easement. Story at no time sought to prohibit Hefner from using the entire lake.

Over the objection of Hefner, Story was allowed to introduce the prior agreements between the parties. His evidence also showed that after the . . . deeds were prepared, but before they were executed, each party prepared a written separation agreement. Both agreements included a provision that would allow both parties the common use of the lake. Because of a disagreement as to other parts of the document, neither of these agreements was adopted.

Story was properly allowed to offer evidence of these prior negotiations. The presence of a provision in the tentative contracts of *both* parties guaranteeing each party the right to reasonable use of the entire lake is evidence of their intention at the time of the division of the property to continue to use the lake jointly.

· · ·

. . .Evidence of the parties intentions and the prior agreements were properly admitted by the trial court and should be considered, for any competent and relevant evidence. . . is admissible to prove an easement by implication.

An easement is the right of one person to go onto the land of another and make a limited use thereof. Easements may be expressly created by deed or come about by necessity or prescriptive use or as in the present case may be implied into a deed.

An implied easement is a creature of common law. It is based on the theory that whenever one conveys property he includes or intends to include in the conveyance whatever is necessary for its beneficial use and enjoyment and to retain whatever is necessary for the use and enjoyment of the land retained. An easement by implication is a true easement having permanence of duration and should be distinguished from a "way of necessity" which lasts only as long as the necessity continues.

Ordinarily an easement being an interest in land requires compliance with the Statute of Frauds. However, an easement implied from pre-existing use arises by inference of the *intention* of the parties at the time of the conveyance which may be established by [oral evidence]. The inference is drawn from the circumstances under which the conveyance is made rather than from the language of the deed. The implication of an easement may always be prevented by language in the deed sufficiently explicit to negate it.

To establish an easement by implication there must first be a conveyance that divides one ownership into separately owned parts.

At the time of the conveyance one part of the property must be being used for the benefit of the other part, creating quasi-easement. The use must be apparent and continuous and must be reasonably necessary to the enjoyment of the . . .tract [requiring the easement].

In determining whether the circumstances under which a conveyance of land is made imply an easement we must also consider whether reciprocal benefits result and the manner in which the land was used prior to the conveyance as well as the extent of the necessity for the enjoyment of the land. [Citation omitted.]

According to the trial record the court was aware of the aforementioned requirements for the existence of an implied easement in favor of the Storys. It recognized that all of the elements were present except for the necessity to the full enjoyment of the Story's property. We hold that an adequate necessity does indeed exist.

The necessity requisite to the creation of an easement by implication is not an absolute necessity, a reasonable necessity is sufficient. . . .

In 1962, the parties stocked the lake with $3,000.00 worth of bass. Story introduced evidence and it was undisputed that if the injunction was continued, he would no longer be able to water ski on the lake or fish for bass which migrate to the deeper water near the dam in the summer. The dam is located at the north end of the lake and is included in Hefner's property. Story also agreed to maintain and has maintained a drain on the dam keeping it free from debris. If the drain is not properly cleared, his cabin, well house and other improvements would become flooded. The injunction prevents Story's access to the drain.

The lake is a recreational lake. It is used for skiing and fishing. The use of the entire lake surface is not merely a convenience, it is necessary for the fair enjoyment of the Storys' estate and a reservation of their right to continue such use arises by implication of the law.

Hefner. . .[claims] that Story's use of the Hefner portion of the lake after the exchange of the deeds was based on an oral license and thus was revocable at will. The Court defined a license in *Haas* v. *Brannon,* as "an authority to do a particular act upon another's land without possessing an estate therein. . . .It is distinguished from an easement which implies an interest in the land to be affected."

An oral license ordinarily can be revoked at the pleasure of the licensor with two exceptions: a license coupled with an interest is not revocable; first, where a continuation of such interest is necessary for him to make use of such interest; and second, where the licensee has incurred expenses in making permanent improvements to the property. [Citation omitted.]

In this case the use arose not from permission or even from prescriptive use, but from an absolute title to an undivided one-half interest in the lake and from the continued use of the lake prior to, as well as after the execution of the deeds. We hold that Story's use of the Hefner portion of the lake was not a revocable license, but rather an implied easement.

• • •

. . .Story, over the years has helped to develop and improve the lake, the primary use of which is for recreational purposes. He has used the entire lake for over ten years for fishing and skiing. Hefner, by erecting buoys, and by instituting this suit has sought to interfere with Story's continued use and enjoyment of the lake for the purpose for which it was intended.

A quasi-easement for use of the lake existed at the time of the separation. The deeds contained no express provision eliminating this use. Story's use has been continuous, apparent and necessary for his enjoyment. Thus, the deeds are ineffective to do away with Story's reasonable use of the entire lake for recreational purposes and an easement for such use must be implied by the deeds.

Story has cross-petitioned for an injunction to restrain Hefner from interference with his reasonable recreational use of the lake. He does not ask for access to Hefner's dry land. He does not desire to prohibit Hefner from using the entire lake, a relief the trial court granted, which Story did not seek. Trial Court is reversed except as to portion of judgment dividing costs one-half (½) to each party which is affirmed.

Appellant's cross petition to enjoin Hefner from interfering with his reasonable recreational use of the lake is granted.

Zoning Ordinances

There are several limitations imposed by law on owners of real property. State legislatures often delegate to communities the right to impose regulations designed to promote public health, safety, morals, and the general welfare of the citizens. These rules include *zoning ordinances,* which act to regulate the use of real property in specific areas.

Zoning ordinances control the use of various segments of land for houses, apartments, commercial development, and industry. They sometimes control the height of buildings as well as the distance that they are set back from roads or lot lines. They might also control the population density (the number of people who can be housed in a given area). This might be done by regulating the number of apartment units allowed per acre of land. Finally, zoning ordinances can restrict individuals by such actions as banning bill-boards or requiring houses in a subdivision to be of different styles or colors when the overall beauty of an area is being diminished.

Example. Winkle purchases a lot, planning to construct a profes-sional office building for local doctors and dentists. He fails to ex-amine the local zoning ordinances before making the purchase. When he submits his plans for the building to the proper authorities for approval, he discovers that the area in which his lot is located is zoned for one-family dwellings only. His alternatives at that point are to attempt to having the zoning ordinances changed, resell the lot, or use the property as required by the ordinances.

Eminent Domain

The United States Constitution protects American citizens by providing that private property cannot be taken for public use with-out *just compensation* (fair payment). This means that when there is just compensation for the owner, property may be taken for pub-lic use by the state. This is known as *eminent domain.* It makes possible the construction of highways, public housing, sewer lines, power projects, and urban renewal projects.

A major problem with eminent domain is deciding what is just compensation for the owner. It is usually determined through a panel study of the realty in the area and several appraisals of the property in question. What is considered to be a fair market value is then placed on the property.

Example. The federal government is building a highway through Gotham City. Richards is notified that the road will cross his prop-erty in such a way that his house must be torn down. A panel ex-amines the real estate values in the area and places a fair market price on Richards' house and land. The government pays Richards that amount. Richards has no choice but to accept the money, since the government is exercising its right of eminent domain and has given just compensation.

FORMS OF OWNERSHIP

Tenancy is the legal term for ownership of property. There are several forms of tenancy.

Sole Tenancy

If one individual has the title to property, the ownership is a *sole tenancy* and the owner is a *sole tenant.*

Example. Sam buys a cabin for himself in the woods. There are no other names on the title. Sam is a sole tenant.

Tenancy in Common

A *tenancy in common* is one form of coownership in which property is held concurrently (at the same time) by two or more persons. A tenancy in common is created when two or more persons acquire real property by a will or a *deed* (a written document which conveys title to a property). Upon the death of one of the tenants, the title passes to the heirs of that tenant. Tenants may sell their interests without the consent of the others. The new owner becomes a *tenant in common* with the other owners.

Tenants in common may own equal or unequal shares of real property. They contribute to expenses and taxes in proportion to their share of ownership. However, each tenant, not withstanding the size of the share, has a right to use the whole property. It is not necessary that all tenants in common obtain their interest in the property at the same time or from the same source.

Example. The Goods and the Shells buy a summer cottage together. The Goods own two-thirds and the Shells own one-third. They take title as tenants in common since they eventually want to leave their respective interests in the cottage to their children.

Example. The Goods buy a summer cottage. Some years later, they sell half the interest to the Shells. The Goods and the Shells then become tenants in common.

Joint Tenancy

A *joint tenancy* is concurrent ownership created when two or more persons own equal interests in real property. The interest is acquired at the same time and by the same instrument. The document conveying the property must clearly state that the parties are joint tenants. If the joint tenancy is not specified, the tenancy is interpreted to be a tenancy in common.

The main characteristic of joint tenancy is the *right of survivorship.* Upon the death of one of the joint tenants, the surviving tenants receive the interest of the one who died. The heirs of the deceased joint tenant receive nothing since the interest cannot be willed to them, as distinguished from the tenancy in common. The last surviving tenant has sole tenancy in the property. If any of the joint tenants transfers his or her interest, the joint tenancy is ended and a tenancy in common is created.

Example. Two brothers, Roger and Ben, each own one-half of an apartment building. The deed states that the arrangement is a joint tenancy. When Roger dies, his son claims Roger's half of the property. The courts deny the son's claim since a joint tenancy has been specified, thereby creating a right of survivorship. Roger's interest in the property goes to his brother, Ben, the survivor in the joint tenancy.

Tenancy by the Entirety

Tenants in a *tenancy by the entirety* must be husband and wife. This type of tenancy is not recognized in every state. It must be clearly stated to be effective. The tenants have the right of survivorship, and neither party can dispose of the property in a will. In addition, neither husband nor wife can sell the property without the consent of the other.

Example. Charles and Carol Bartell, husband and wife, purchase ten acres of land. The deed specifies a tenancy by the entirety. Charles, needing cash for his business, sells three acres of the land. Carol claims that a tenancy by the entirety exists and that she has not given her consent to the sale. The courts uphold Carol's claim, and declare the sale invalid.

Community Property

Several states use a system whereby all property that is acquired by either a husband or wife during marriage is considered *community property;* that is, both persons own equal interest in the property regardless of who earned it. This does not include property owned by either spouse before the marriage or property that is inherited by or given to either party individually during the marriage.

Example. Marcia and Don live in a state which provides for community property between husband and wife. Shortly after their marriage, Marcia uses her savings to buy a local craft shop. Some years later Don borrows money from a bank and takes out a mortgage on one-half of the shop. Marcia claims that he cannot do that since the property is in her name and she bought it with her own money. The courts uphold Don's right, since the store is considered to be community property. Even though Marcia paid for the store herself, the laws of most community property states hold that she and her husband both have an equal share in it.

Condominiums

In recent years, there has been an increase in a form of ownership known as the *condominium.* This arrangement states that the owner has sole tenancy (or that husband and wife have tenancy by the entirety) of an apartmentlike unit. At the same time, the owners are tenants in common with every other unit owner of parts of the realty that they use in common, such as the elevators, halls, recreational facilities, and parking areas. The owner is treated as the owner of a single-family dwelling as far as taxes and mortgages on the apartment are concerned. Each owner usually pays a monthly fee for maintenance of the common facilities. The owner of an apartment in a condominium can usually sell the unit without the approval of the other owners, unless it is stated otherwise in the deed.

Example. A and B own an apartment as tenants by the entirety in a condominium. A and B sell their apartment to C and D, who then take over the monthly payments for such things as maintenance. The other apartment owners cannot avoid the sale since A and B owned their apartment in fee simple and had absolute power to dispose of it. There is no argument that A and B could not dispose of their interest in the common facilities, since tenants in common can sell, lease, or mortgage their interests without affecting the tenancies of the others.

The chart in figure 10-1 outlines the forms of concurrent ownership of real property. By way of review, notice that the possessory interest in land or the estate is different from the type of ownership or the tenancy. Thus, it is possible to have joint tenants holding a life estate (measured by one life) or tenants in common of a fee simple.

	Interest in Property	Source of Acquisition	Time of Acquisition	Rights of Tenants
Tenancy in Common	May be equal or unequal	May be different for each tenant	May be different for each tenant	Each tenant may sell, give, or will interest without consent of others
Joint Tenancy	Must be equal	Must be from same source (will, deed, etc.) specifically stating joint tenancy	Must be at same time	Survivor(s) takes whole, no rights of inheritance
Tenancy by the Entirety	Equal (must be husband and wife)	Must be to both husband and wife	Persons must be spouses at time of conveyance	Each owns whole; survivor takes whole; no rights of inheritance. Cannot dispose of property without other's consent.
Community Property	Equal (must be husband and wife)	Property acquired during marriage by either spouse, except property inherited or given to only one or the other	Applies only to spouses	Each owns whole; upon death deceased's half may be willed

Fig. 10-1 Forms of concurrent ownership

ACQUIRING OWNERSHIP

There are five common ways by which real property is transferred from one owner to another in the United States, figure 10-2. The first two result from voluntary acts of the owner: by purchase or by gift. The other three are a result of the operation of the law: by adverse possession, by a tax sale, and by carrying out the provisions of a will.

Purchase

One of the rights of ownership is the right to dispose of the property by sale. Most real property today is acquired by purchase from another owner.

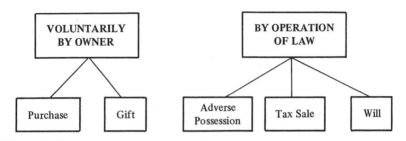

Fig. 10-2   Five common methods of acquiring ownership of real property

Gift

An individual (*donee*) may acquire real property as a gift from another party (*donor*).   In order to be a valid transfer by gift, the deed must be delivered to the donee or a third party acting for the benefit of the donee.

Example.   Faro puts a deed to his house in his safe-deposit box, with instructions in a·note that upon his death, the deed is to be delivered to his son.   The courts do not uphold this as a gift of real property since the deed was not properly delivered.   As an alternative, Faro could have given the deed to his attorney as a third party with instructions that upon his death, the deed is to be delivered to his son.   The property would then be considered a legal gift.

Adverse Possession

Title to real property may be acquired by adverse possession according to state statutory laws.   *Adverse possession* occurs when a person openly and continuously occupies land without the owner's permission for the statutory period, and pays the taxes on the land.   State statutory periods range from five to twenty years, but twenty years is the most common.

For original owners to avoid losing title by adverse possession, they must remove the trespassers from the property before the end of the statutory period.   Otherwise, the person who is occupying the land takes title.

Example.   Bliss owns a farm that has belonged to his family for two generations.   There are ten acres next to his land which his family has used for about thirty years for storage of their equipment and for growing of various crops.   Their tax bill has included the taxes on the adjoining ten acres.   When a developer offers to buy the ten acres from Bliss, Parker appears and shows a deed to the land in his name, which is duly recorded. Bliss claims the property is his by adverse possession since he and his father have occupied the land and paid taxes on it for a length of time far beyond the statutory period. The courts uphold Bliss and grant him title to the ten acres.

Tax Sale

Tax laws vary greatly from state to state. Generally, however, if taxes on real property are not paid, they become a lien on that property. If the taxes are still unpaid, after a specified period, the government body involved can sell the property at a tax sale. The purchaser at such a sale then acquires a valid title to the property, and the money paid is applied to the back taxes.

Inheritance

Another way that title is acquired through the operation of the law is by inheritance, in which ownership is transferred by a statement in an individual's will. Owners of real property, although subject to some restrictions, can dispose of real property by will. This does not hold true in tenancies where there is a right of survivorship. The will must be legally drawn according to the state laws to be valid. When owners die without wills, property descends to the heirs according to the laws of the state where the property is located. If there are no heirs and no will, the property becomes the state's.

SELF-EVALUATION

A. Provide a brief explanation of each of the following.

1. Differentiate between fee simple absolute and life estate.

2. Is an easement an estate in land? Why or why not?

3. In *Story* v. *Hefner,* what was the injunction that the Supreme Court of Oklahoma granted?

4. In which form of tenancy may tenants own equal or unequal shares of real property?

5. Define right of survivorship.

6. Under which doctrine may the state take land for public use, after giving the owner just compensation?

7. What is the major requirement of the tenants in a tenancy by the entirety?

8. What are the two types of tenancies held by husband and wife owners living in a condominium?

9. What are the two requirements of a valid transfer of real property as a gift?

10. How can an owner avoid conveying title to property by adverse possession to those occupying the land?

B. Which of the following items in a house would be legally considered fixtures?

   a. a four-foot evergreen tree planted in the yard
   b. a portable dishwasher
   c. a refrigerator
   d. custom-made drapery rods
   e. a furnace humidifier
   f. shutters
   g. an installed carpet
   h. a room-sized rug

SUGGESTED ACTIVITIES

1. Inquire at a local bank about any tax sales of property in the area. Evaluate several of the properties with the banker.

2. Investigate state regulations to see if (1) it is a community property state and (2) if state statutes permit tenancies by the entirety. Submit a report on the findings to the instructor.

CASES FOR STUDY

1. *A* dies, owning the Circle Ranch in fee simple. His will provides that upon his death his wife (*W*) is to have a life estate with the remainder going to his children. *W* is in need of money and wishes to sell the ranch. May she do so? Explain.

2. Referring to Case 1, could *A*'s children convey title to the Circle Ranch while *W* is still alive? (In a legal sense, to *convey* is to transmit title to property to another.)

3. *X* wills a life estate in Whiteacre to *Y*, with remainder going to *Z*. *Y* predeceases (dies before) *X*. Do *Y*'s heirs have any claim to the land? Why or why not?

4. *O* owns beach front property which he divides into six parcels:

①	②	③
④	⑤	⑥

Body of Water

O keeps parcel six for himself and finds prospective purchasers for the other five parcels. Of course, the value of the land is due mostly to its location. What should *O* do to provide access to the water for the owners of parcels one, two, and three?

5. Brothers *A* and *B* take title to property as *A and B, with the survivor to take the whole.* A question arises as to whether they are joint tenants or tenants in common. How can the issue be resolved?

6. Husband *H* and wife *W* reside in a community property state and the following transactions occur. Which transactions form part of their community property, or pool of common resources?

   a. *H* purchases a farm before he and *W* are married.
   b. *W* purchases a car during the marriage.
   c. *W* is willed $5,000 worth of stocks and bonds by an aunt.
   d. *H* gives *W* an Arabian horse as a birthday present.
   e. *W* sells the car and purchases more stock.
   f. *H* and *W* are divorced and agree to a property settlement. *H* purchases additional land adjoining the farm with some of the funds from the settlement.

7. Husband *H* and wife *W* purchase a home as tenants by the entirety. Some years later, *H* and *W* are divorced, but no changes are made in the form of ownership of the home, although only *W* lives in it. Do they still hold the property as tenants by the entirety? Explain.

8. *A, B,* and *C* hold rental property as tenants in common, each owning one-third. *B* sells her interest to *D,* who then demands one-third of the income from *A* and *C.* *A* and *C* do not trust *D* and would never have voluntarily associated with him in the venture. Must they turn over one-third of the income from the property to *D*? Do they have any recourse against *B*?

9. The city school district plans to build a new school on the corner of Main and First Streets. The residents of the area decide to band together and refuse to sell when the city tries to purchase the land. Are they likely to be successful? Why or why not?

10. *T* has rented a house from *O* for a number of years. *T* treats the house as his own; that is, he does exterior and interior painting when needed, shovels the sidewalk, and cares for the yard. If *T* remains at the house for the statutory period, does he become the owner by adverse possession? Why or why not?

Chapter 11

Real Property Transactions: Purchasing and Leasing

OBJECTIVES

After studying this chapter, the student will be able to

- outline the steps involved in the purchase of real property.
- identify the documents required for the purchase and explain the purpose of each.
- describe the conditions necessary to create and terminate a lease.
- list and describe the rights of the landlord and tenant in a leasing relationship.
- define the following words and phrases.

brokers	landlord/lessor
listing agreement	tenant/lessee
contract of sale	rent
purchase offer	long-term lease
title company	short-term lease
title search	covenant
abstract of title	habitable
survey	dispossess
deed	assignment of lease
grantor	assignor of lease
grantee	assignee of lease
quitclaim deed	sublet
bargain and sale deed	sublessor
warranty deed	sublessee
encumbrance	security
title closing	eviction
closing statement	constructive eviction
lease	

PURCHASING REAL PROPERTY

There are certain steps required by law in the purchase of real property, whether the property is a multimillion-dollar commercial development or a small plot of land. The legalities involve the use of formal documents and certain procedures for the transfer of title to be valid.

BROKERS

Owners of property may choose to sell their real estate themselves by posting *For Sale* signs and placing advertisements in local newspapers. Instead, they may decide to deal with a real estate *broker*, who is paid a fee to obtain possible buyers and to settle the details of the transaction. The seller negotiates a *listing agreement* with a broker, a written document that states the period of time of the listing and states the percentage, or amount of *commission*, that is to be paid to the broker upon the sale of the property.

The commission is customarily earned when a broker produces a buyer who is ready, willing, and able to purchase the property on the terms of the seller. The seller is usually responsibile for paying the broker's fee. If the broker fulfills the requirements and the seller decides not to go through with the sale, the seller is generally still responsible for the commission.

Example. Broker *B* finds a purchaser (*P*) for *S*'s home. *P* is ecstatic about the place and returns again and again to inspect it. On one such visit, *S* suggests to *P* that *P* not sign the sales contract *B* has prepared and pretend to lose interest in purchasing. *S* proposes to then sell the house to *P* for a lower price and thereby cut *B* out of his commission. If *P* and *S* decide to carry out the plan and *B* discovers this, he will most likely be able to collect from *S* for the lost commission.

PURCHASE OFFER

The formal agreement between a buyer and seller to purchase real property is a contract of sale called a *purchase offer.* It does not transfer title, but rather serves as evidence that there is agreement to transfer title at a definite time in the future.

Under the Statute of Frauds, the purchase offer must be in writing to be enforceable, figure 11-1. The statute also requires that the agreement include the following: (1) the names of the buyer and

Purchase Offer—Standard Form.

OFFER TO PURCHASE

TO THE OWNER OR PERSON EMPOWERED TO SELL THE PROPERTY DESCRIBED BELOW:

Property

I (We) agree to purchase the following property situated in the Town of Bucolia

County of Erehwon , State of ---- known as 101 First Street

being a single-family, two-story brick structure situate on a

one acre lot

For a more particular description of said premises reference is hereby made to the deed thereof.

Together with all lighting, heating and plumbing fixtures, window shades, screen and storm doors and windows, if any, water heater, water meter and all fixtures and fittings appurtenant to or used in the operation of the premises and owned by you.

Price

AT THE PRICE OF Forty Thousand and no/100------------------ $40,000.00
Dollars, payable as follows:

Deposit

$ 1,000.00 cash deposited with Sellers .to be held
until this offer is accepted, at which time it shall become part of the purchase price, or returned if not accepted.

Balance

$ 39,000.00 cash on or before July 1, 19__ on passing of deed.

This offer is expressly contingent upon the purchasers obtaining a purchase money mortgage in the principal amount of $35,000.00 with an interest rate of no more than 8½% per annum.

Searches

You are to deliver to me, or my attorney, at least five (5) days before closing, a forty year abstract of title and ten year search or tax receipts showing the property free and clear of all liens and encumbrances except as herein set forth, and except building and use restrictions, pole and wire easements of record, and subject to zoning ordinance and to any taxes for local improvements not now completed.

Deed

Transfer is to be completed at the office of the Erehwon County Clerk

on or before July 1, 19__ or as soon thereafter as abstracts can be brought to date, at

which time you are to convey to me by warranty deed, good title to
the property free of all liens and encumbrances, except as hereinabove set forth, subject to rights of tenants, if any.

Adjustments

Interest, insurance premiums, rents, and taxes to be pro-rated and adjusted as of July 1 , 19

City, State and County Taxes shall be adjusted and apportioned on a calendar year beginning Jan. 1, and ending Dec. 31. School Taxes outside the city shall be adjusted and apportioned for the fiscal year, beginning July 1st and ending the following June 30th, and Village Taxes shall be adjusted and apportioned for the fiscal year beginning June 1st and ending the last day of May following or as otherwise prescribed or authorized by law.

Possession

Possession of premises shall be delivered on or before July 1, 19__ on passing of deed

Upon any purchase money mortgage given, I (We) agree to pay the usual mortgage tax and recording fee and Revenue stamps on bond where required.

This offer may be assigned to an individual or corporation for the purpose of holding title thereto, except that the undersigned shall remain responsible for the faithful performance of the contract.

The risk of loss or damage to said premises by fire or other causes until the delivery of the deed is assumed by you.

XXXXXXXXXXXXXXXXXXXXXXXXXXXXXXXXXXXXXXXXXXXXXXXXXXXXXXXXXXXXXXXXX
XXXXXXXXXXXXXXXXXXXXXXXXXXXXXXXXXXXXXXXXXXXXXXXXXXXXXXXXXXXXXXXXX

This offer, when accepted shall constitute a binding contract of purchase and sale and it shall bind and inure to the benefit of the parties hereto and their respective executors, administrators, distributees, successors and assigns.

Dated April 1 , 19   (Signed) /s/ Jules V. Wright (L. S.)

Witness /s/ Seth Miller   (Signed) /s/ Elizabeth B. Wright (L. S.)

Fig. 11-1 Front side of standard purchase offer.

ACCEPTANCE

I (We) hereby accept this offer and agree to sell on the terms and conditions set forth, XXXXXXX

XXXXXXXXXXXXXXXXXXXXXXXXXXXXXXXXXXXXXXXXXXXXXXXXXXXXXXXXXXX
XXXXXXXXXXXXXXXXXXXXXXXXXXXXXXXXXXXXXXXXXXXXXXXXXXXXXXXXXXX

Dated April 1 ...., 19......   (Signed)/s/ Robert S. Ames .... (L. S.)

Witness/s/ Seth Miller ....   (Signed)/s/ Louise R. Ames .... (L. S.)

*Any item on a form that is not applicable may be x'd out. In
this transaction there is no broker or agent, so the clauses
pertaining to a broker have been deleted in such a manner.

PURCHASE OFFER

PROPERTY

Seller

Attorney Phone

TO Phone

Purchaser

Attorney Phone

Phone

Dated ...., 19

To be closed ...., 19

Fig. 11-1   Back side of standard purchase offer.   (Form available from Julius Blumberg, Inc., 80 Exchange Place, NYC 10004.)

seller; (2) a description of the property so that it can be identified; (3) the purchase price; and (4) the signatures of the persons bound by the agreement. Both parties usually sign the contract so that both are bound — one to sell and the other to purchase.

The purchase offer commonly identifies other terms of the agreement as well, such as the type of deed the purchaser will receive, or a listing of personal property which is to be transferred with the sale such as curtains and rugs. Items considered to be fixtures are not required to be listed since they are considered part of the realty.

Example. The Baylords sign a purchase offer to buy a home from the Coles. When the Coles move out, they take a fireplace screen that had been custom made and permanently attached to the fireplace. The Baylords bring action against them. The Coles claim that the screen was not listed in the purchase offer as property to be transferred to the Baylords. The court holds that the screen is not considered personal property, but rather a fixture, and thus did not have to be listed in the purchase offer. The Baylords' claim is upheld.

TITLE SEARCH

After the purchase offer has been signed, it is important for the buyer to determine that the seller has good title to the property so that it can be conveyed. County clerks or attorneys sometimes furnish this information. Another method involves the use of the services of a title company. For a fee, title companies search all the records of the property (usually located in the county clerk's office). They investigate all the transfers in the chain of title of the property in question. They also note any and all mortagages and liens that are outstanding on the property.

Upon completion of the investigation the title company submits a written report of its findings, known as an *abstract of title*. The seller pays for this abstract unless some other arrangement is made. An abstract of title is not legal proof that the seller is the actual owner of the property; an attorney must carefully examine the abstract to make that determination.

SURVEY

A *survey* is a formal examination that determines the true boundaries of a particular section of land and the position of structures on the land. If the seller does not have such a survey, a wise buyer has one made by a qualified engineer. Although the description of the property is given in the purchase offer, it may not be completely accurate. The buyer may find that the property purchased does not exactly fit the description.

Example. Wilkes contracts to buy a house from Connally. There is no survey of the land made. Wilkes examines the description in the purchase offer and paces off the measurements. There is just enough room for him to install the tennis court that he wants. After Wilkes takes possession and begins construction of the court, a neighbor brings action against Wilkes. The neighbor claims that Wilkes has been digging on land that is not his. A survey is then taken which proves that the neighbor is correct. A survey taken before the purchase would have saved Wilkes a great deal of disappointment and money.

DEEDS

Real property is generally conveyed or transferred from one party to another by the creation and delivery of a written document known as a *deed.* The party who conveys title is the *grantor;* the party receiving title is the *grantee.*

Forms of Deeds

Statutes which outline forms of deeds are not uniform in all states, but certain similarities do exist. A deed may be valid even if the suggested form is not used, but it is common practice to use the statutory forms. Figure 11-2 illustrates the front and the back of a warranty deed using the statutory form.

The statutory form includes the name of the grantee (item (1) on the form); the consideration (item (2) on the form); and a description of the property (item (3) on the form). To be recorded, the deed must be executed (signed) by the grantor (item (4) on the form) and usually must be witnessed by an authorized person such as a notary public (item (5) on the form). Any language that clearly explains the intent of the owner to transfer title may be used.

Delivery is always necessary for a deed to be valid. Title is not conveyed to another party unless the deed is delivered to the grantee or to a third party acting in behalf of the grantee.

685—Warranty Deed with Full Covenants, Individual.
Statutory Form A. Photostat Recording.

JULIUS BLUMBERG, INC., LAW BLANK PUBLISHERS
80 EXCHANGE PLACE AT BROADWAY, NEW YORK

THIS INDENTURE, made the   1st   day of   July   , nineteen hundred and

BETWEEN

④   ROBERT S. AMES AND LOUISE AMES, husband and wife,
101 First Street, Town of Bucolia, State of _____,
as tenants by the entirety,

part **ies** of the first part, and

①   JULES V. WRIGHT and ELIZABETH B. WRIGHT, husband and wife,
601 Main Street, City of Grayville, State of _____,

part **ies** of the second part,

WITNESSETH, that the part **ies** of the first part, in consideration of

②   One and more -- Dollars,

lawful money of the United States, and other good and valuable consideration

paid by the part **ies** of the second part do   hereby grant and release unto the part **ies** of the second part,

their heirs, distributees   and assigns, forever,

ALL   THAT TRACT OR PARCEL OF LAND, situate in the Town of Bucolia,
③   county of Erehwon and State of _____, and being known as
Lot 10 as shown on a map drawn by Charles A. Evans, C.E. which
map is entitled "Bucolia Farms" and is on file in the Erehwon
County Clerk's Office in Book 11 of Maps at Page 432.

TOGETHER with the appurtenances and all the estate and rights of the part **ies** of the first part in and to
said premises.

TO HAVE AND TO HOLD the premises herein granted unto the part **ies** of the second part,

and assigns forever.

AND the said part **ies** of the first part covenant   as follows:

⑥   **FIRST.**—That the part **ies**   of the first part **are** ------- seized of the said premises in fee simple, and
ha**ve** good right to convey the same;

⑦   **SECOND.**—That the part **ies** of the second part shall quietly enjoy the said premises;

⑧   **THIRD.**—That the said premises are free from incumbrances;

Fig. 11-2 Warranty deed in statutory form.

⑨ **FOURTH.**—That the part ies   of the first part will execute or procure any further necessary assurance of the title to said premises;

⑩ **FIFTH.**—That the part ies   of the first part will forever warrant the title to said premises;

SIXTH.—That the grantor, in compliance with Section 13 of the Lien Law, covenants that the grantor will receive the consideration for this conveyance and will hold the right to receive such consideration as a trust fund to be applied first for the purpose of paying the cost of the improvement and that the grantor will apply the same first to the payment of the cost of the improvement before using any part of the total of the same for any other purpose.

IN WITNESS WHEREOF, the parties   of the first part have hereunto set   their   hands and seal s the day and year first above written.

In presence of:

—————————————————————————————— L. S.
Robert S. Ames

—————————————————————————————— L. S.
Louise R. Ames

STATE OF _____ **COUNTY OF** Erehwon   **ss.:**

⑤
On the   1st   day of   July   , nineteen hundred and before me came

Robert S. Ames and Louise R. Ames, husband and wife

to me known and known to me to be the individual s described in, and who executed, the foregoing instrument, and acknowledged to me that they executed the same.

—————————————————————
Notary Public

Deed

WARRANTY — FULL COVENANTS

Dated, _____, 19____

The land affected by the within instrument lies in

Record and Return To

Reserve this space for use of Recording Office.

Fig. 11-2 Warranty deed in statutory form. (Con't) (Form available from Julius Blumberg, Inc., 80 Exchange Place, NYC   10004.)

T 693—Quitclaim Deed.—Individual.
Statutory Form D. Photostat Recording.

JULIUS BLUMBERG, INC., LAW BLANK PUBLISHERS
80 EXCHANGE PLACE AT BROADWAY, NEW YORK

THIS IS A LEGAL INSTRUMENT AND SHOULD BE EXECUTED UNDER SUPERVISION OF AN ATTORNEY

THIS INDENTURE, made the 1st   day of   July   , 19 ___

BETWEEN

ROBERT S. AMES and LOUISE R. AMES, husband and wife, 101 First Street, Town of Bucolia, State of _____ , as tenants by the entirety,

part ies of the first part, and

JULES V. WRIGHT and ELIZABETH B. WRIGHT, husband and wife, 601 Main Street, City of Grayville, State of _____ ,

parties of the second part,

WITNESSETH, that the part ies of the first part, in consideration of

One and more --- Dollars,

lawful money of the United States,   and other good and valuable consideration

paid by the parties of the second part does hereby remise, release and quitclaim unto the parties of the second part,

their heirs. distributees and assigns forever,

ALL THAT TRACT OR PARCEL OF LAND, situate in the Town of Bucolia,

County of Erehwon and State of _____ , and being known as

Lot No. 10 as shown on a map drawn by Charles A. Evans, C.E. which

map is entitled "Bucolia Farms" and is on file in the Erehwon

County Clerk's Office in Book 11 of Maps at Page 432.

Fig. 11-3 A quitclaim deed.

TOGETHER with the appurtenances and all the estate and rights of the party of the first part in and to said premises.

TO HAVE AND TO HOLD the premises herein granted unto the part ies of the second part, their heirs, distributees and assigns forever.

IN WITNESS WHEREOF, the part ies of the first part have hereunto set their hands and seals the day and year first above written.

In presence of

....L. S.
Robert S. Ames
....L. S.
Louise R. Ames

STATE OF _____ **COUNTY OF** Erehwon *ss.:*

On the 1st day of July , 19 __ before me came Robert S. Ames and Louise R. Ames, husband and wife to me known and known to me to be the individuals described in, and who executed, the foregoing instrument, and acknowledged to me that they executed the same.

_____
Notary Public

ROBERT S. AMES and
LOUISE R. AMES, husband and wife

TO

JULES V. WRIGHT and
ELIZABETH B. WRIGHT, husband and wife

Deed

QUITCLAIM — INDIVIDUAL

Dated, July 1 ...., 19........

The land affected by the within instrument lies in the Town of Bucolia, County of Erehwon

RECORD AND RETURN TO

Reserve this space for use of Recording Office.

Fig. 11-3 A quitclaim deed. (Con't) (Form available from Julius Blumberg, Inc., 80 Exchange Place, NYC 10004.)

Recording of Deeds

All states require that deeds to real property be recorded, although the place of recording may differ. Without such laws, there would be no way to prove clear title to any real property. When title is transferred, the deed should immediately be recorded by the purchaser or by the purchaser's attorney. If there are two deeds to the same property, the first deed recorded is generally considered to be the legal one.

Example. On May 21, Weiner and Gates each purchase and pay for a lot in a new area which is being sold by a dishonest land developer. They both unknowingly purchase the same lot. Weiner records her deed on the day of the purchase. On May 22, Gates attempts to record her deed and discovers that it is for the same lot that Weiner has already recorded. Since Weiner's deed was recorded first, it takes priority over Gates' deed and is considered to be the valid deed to the property.

Types of Deeds

There are three types of deeds that are commonly used in the United States. These include the quitclaim deed, the bargain and sale deed, and the warranty deed.

The Quitclaim Deed. The *quitclaim deed,* figure 11-3, pages 198 and 199, is generally used only to release claims that an individual has against the property. It releases any interest a grantor may have. The quitclaim deed is not usually used to transfer title, since grantors of quitclaim deeds do not claim to have clear title, or any title at all, to the property. In a quitclaim deed, grantors only promise to give whatever interest they have in the property, if any, to the grantee.

Example. *H* owns property in his own name which has been acquired during his marriage to *W.* They reside in a community property state. *H* conveys the property to *X* and fails to have *W* sign the deed to indicate that she is conveying her interest as well. *X* realizes some time later what has happened and wants to settle the matter; otherwise, *W* could claim an interest in the land. *W* has received part of the benefit from the sale; it is not as if *H* were trying to avoid the effects of community property by selling to *X.* The title can be cleared by *W* giving *X* a quitclaim deed to the same property, thereby releasing her interest.

Bargain and Sale Deed. A *bargain and sale deed* is used to transfer title to real property. Grantors in such deeds make no express guarantees that their title is clear; only that they have done nothing to affect that title. If a buyer makes no specific request for a certain type of deed, a bargain and sale deed is used.

Warranty Deed. The *full-covenant and warranty deed* (commonly known as the *warranty deed*) contains various covenants. *Covenants* are promises by the grantor that actually stand as guarantees. The covenant warrants to the grantee that the grantor has clear title to the property and has the legal right to sell it. (See item (6) in figure 11-2.)

A *covenant of quiet enjoyment* is usually given by the grantor in a warranty deed. (See item (7) in figure 11-2.) This promises to the grantees that no one will interfere with their right to enjoy ownership and use of the property by claiming title.

The grantor warrants by covenant that the property is free from encumbrances other than those listed in the deed. (See item (8) in figure 11-2.) An *encumbrance* is anything that adversely affects the property or the title, such as an outstanding mortgage or tax lien.

By covenant, the grantor promises to obtain any "further assurances" of title should they become necessary. (See item (9) in figure 11-2.) A promise to obtain further assurances of title assures that if anyone claims title, the grantor agrees to obtain any necessary documents, such as a quitclaim deed, to settle the claim.

There is usually a final covenant in a warranty deed which states that the grantor will forever warrant the title to the property. (See item (10) in figure 11-2.) However, there may be other covenants that apply to a particular property included in a warranty deed.

TITLE CLOSING

Upon completion of all documents, both parties to the sale and their attorneys meet for the title closing. The meeting takes place on a date mutually agreed upon and stated in the purchase offer. A *title closing* is the actual transference of the title, accomplished by delivery of a properly executed deed by the seller. At the closing, payment of the balance of the purchase price is made by the buyer with a certified check.

The final purchase price is determined by making a closing statement. A *closing statement* is actually a balance sheet showing

---

CLOSING STATEMENT

Robert S. Ames and Louise R. Ames, Sellers to
Jules V. Wright and Elizabeth B. Wright, Purchasers
     101 First Street, Town of Bucolia
     Closing Date: July 1, 19__

Purchase Price	$40,000.00
Tax Adjustments:	
County taxes Jan. 1 - July 1	
@ $240.00 per annum[1]	120.00
School taxes – no adjustment[2]	-0-
TOTAL AMOUNT DUE SELLER	$40,120.00

Purchaser:
    Downpayment $1,000.00
    Water adjustment[3]   20.00
                  $1,020.00

     BALANCE DUE   1,020.00
                                    39,100.00

Expenses of Seller		Expenses of Purchaser	
Revenue Stamps (Deed)[4]	$ 44.00	Recording Deed	$ 4.00
Survey	90.00	Recording Mortgage	7.00
Continuing Search	50.00	Mortgage Tax[5]	175.00
Attorney's Fees	300.00	Redate Search[6]	20.00
	$484.00	Attorney's Fees	200.00
			$406.00

Purchaser is receiving a $35,000.00 mortgage from Bucolia Savings and Loan, so final cash amount that Purchaser must have at closing:

                                $39,100.00
                              −35,000.00
                                4,100.00
                            +   406.00 (expenses)
    CASH PURCHASER MUST BRING TO CLOSING: $ 4,506.00

Seller therefore receives at the closing:

                                $39,100.00
                             −   484.00 (expenses)
    TOTAL CASH DUE SELLER AT CLOSING: $38,616.00

Fig. 11-4 Closing statement with footnotes

1. The tax year in Bucolia runs from January 1 – December 31 with taxes payable in January. So Sellers have paid a full year of taxes ($240.00) when actually Buyer will receive 6 months worth of benefit from those taxes. Half of the tax bill is a credit to Seller.

2. The school tax year in Bucolia runs from July 1 – June 30 with the taxes payable in September. The tax bill will come to the new owners who have owned the house since the first day of the tax year, so there is no adjustment. If the closing date were August 1, then the purchasers would have had 1/12 of the bill credited to them.

3. The water meter was read on the day of the closing or the day before. It showed $20.00 of water had been used since the last billing date, but the bill will not come until after the closing. So $20.00 is credited to the purchasers.

4. Revenue stamps are a tax imposed when real property changes hands. The tax is based on the purchase price and is usually an expense of the seller.

5. The mortgage tax is another form of revenue. It is figured on the principal loaned and is an expense of the purchaser.

6. Sellers have paid for the title examination since the property was last conveyed, but that was completed a month or more before closing. Purchaser pays for continuing the search from that day to the day of closing.

Fig. 11-4 Closing statement with footnotes (Con't)

adjustments that have been made to the amount of money owed by both parties, figure 11-4. Money may be due the seller for such items as insurance and taxes that have already been paid in advance. There may also be money due the buyer for such things as gas and electric bills that have not yet been paid. After the adjustments are made, the final amount due by the buyer is submitted on the statement.

The buyer acquires title immediately upon delivery of the deed. It must be recorded at the proper location as soon as possible after closing.

LEASING REAL PROPERTY

Owners of real property may allow others to use their property by issuing a contract called a *lease*. The owner becomes a *landlord*, also known as the *lessor*. The person renting the property is the *tenant* or the *lessee*. The consideration paid to the lessor by the lessee for the use of the property is called *rent*.

In early America, the landlord-tenant relationship usually involved the use of land for farming. The tenant had total responsibility for the property, including all buildings thereon. Today, leases are more commonly for apartment units or buildings used for business purposes. The courts today give more attention to the rights of tenants by assigning more of the responsibility for the property to the landlords.

LEASES

Since a lease concerns real property, it is subject to the Statute of Frauds and must be in writing. Most states, however, allow an oral contract for a lease when it is for a period of less than one year. A lease is a contract and is therefore subject to all the requirements of a legal contract. Any terms or conditions agreed upon by both parties must be included for the lease to be enforceable.

Example. Biggs rents an apartment from Searles and signs a two-year lease. She asks if she can use a portion of the basement for storage and Searles agrees, but this agreement is not included in the lease. After a year, Searles notifies Biggs that he intends to convert the basement space into an apartment. She refuses to move her belongings. Searles brings action against her. The court upholds Searles' claim and Biggs is forced to remove her belongings, since the agreement was not included in the lease.

According to the statutes of most states, *long-term leases* (five or ten years or longer, depending on the state) must be recorded. Such leases must be executed in the same formal manner as a deed. Because of the duration of these leases, they are often very detailed and carefully drafted to meet the parties' particular needs. Commercial leases are usually of this type and require expert counsel to assure full protection under the lease. *Short-term leases,* leases for over one year but not classified as long term by state statutes, do not require such procedures. Residential leases are usually of this type.

Form of the Short-term Lease

There are no formal requirements concerning the form of·a short-term lease for it to be valid, figure 11-5. The contents of the lease usually include (1) a description of the property; (2) the term for which the lease is to be effective; (3) the amount of the rent; (4) the manner in which the rent is to be paid; and (5) the signatures of both parties. There are also covenants or conditions included in most leases which give both the parties certain rights and impose certain obligations on them. These covenants might cover such matters as the use permitted by the tenant, which party is to make repairs, and whether or not the lease can be assigned. Item (6) of figure 11-5 shows several typical lease covenants.

RIGHTS AND DUTIES OF THE LANDLORD

There are certain rights and duties of landlords and tenants that are covered by common law rules. These, of course, are not enforceable if they have been eliminated or changed by clauses in the lease. These laws apply only when there is no clause in the lease or specific state statutes covering the situation.

Landlord Warrants

The landlord impliedly warrants that the tenant has the right to undisturbed possession of the premises. The landlord can only enter the premises to demand the rent, make repairs, show the unit to prospective tenants, or when the tenant abandons the premises. The landlord becomes a trespasser when entering for any other reason during the period of the lease, unless consent is given by the tenant.

172—Lease, Short Form.

JULIUS BLUMBERG, INC., LAW BLANK PUBLISHERS
80 EXCHANGE PLACE AT BROADWAY, NEW YORK

This Agreement,

Made the 1st *day of* September 19

BETWEEN

SARAH A. GOODMAN, 300 Maple Avenue, Apartment #1,
Springfield, Any State,

party *of the first part, and*

JAMES K. FISHER, 839 Euclid Street, Springfield,
Any State,

party *of the second part.*

WITNESSETH, *that the said part* y *of the first part ha* s *agreed to LET, and hereby doe* s
LET to the said part y *of the second part, and the said part* y *of the second part ha* s *agreed to*
TAKE, and hereby doe s *TAKE from the said party* *of the first part, the following premises, viz:*

① A two-bedroom, unfurnished apartment known as #300 Maple Avenue,
Apartment #2, City of Springfield, State of Any,

with the privileges and appurtenances for and during the term of one year
② *from the* 1st *day of* September 19 *which term will end* 31st day of
August, 19__ .

⑥ The party of the second part shall be responsible for all
utility bills, except water, that are charged to the premises
during the term.

AND *the said part* y *of the second part covenan* ts *that* *he* *will pay to the party of the first*
③ *part for the use of said premises, the* monthly *rent of* one hundred fifty & no/100 *Dollars*
④ *(* $150.00---*) to be paid* on the first day of each and every month of the
term.
And the said party of the second part has deposited with the
party of the first part the sum of one hundred fifty dollars ($150.00)
as security for damage caused during the term. It is mutually
⑦ understood and agreed that the party of the first part shall deduct
any amounts expended for the repair of such damage, normal wear and
tear excepted, from the security deposit, or, if no repairs are
necessitated, shall return same to the party of the second part at
the expiration of the term with 5% interest.
AND PROVIDED FURTHER, *if said part* y *of the second part shall fail to pay said rent, or*
any thereof when it becomes due,
it is agreed that said party *of the first part may sue for the same, or re-enter said premises, or resort*
to any legal remedy.

② *The part* y *of the* first *part agree* s *to pay all* city, sewer, school
taxes to be assessed on said premises during said term.

⑥ The party of the first part convenants that she will pay for all
major repairs during the term of the lease.

Fig. 11-5 Short-term lease.

(6) The part y   of the second part covenant s that at the expiration of said term   he   will surrender up said premises to the part y   of the first part in as good condition as now, necessary wear
and damage by the elements excepted.

WITNESS *the hands and seals of the said parties, the day and year first above written.*

IN PRESENCE OF

(5)

/s/ Sarah A. Goodman .... *(L. S.)*

/s/ James K. Fisher .... *(L. S.)*

𝕷𝖊𝖆𝖘𝖊

TO

Dated, ... *19.*

PREMISES

Begins .... *19.*

Expires .... *19.*

Rental $ .... *per.*

Payable ....

Fig. 11-5 Short-term lease. (Con't) (Form available from Julius Blumberg, Inc., 80 Exchange Place, NYC 10004.)

Landlord Liability

The landlord does not warrant the condition of the premises, nor is there any warrant that the premises are suitable for the purpose of the tenant. In recent years, however, there are several situations in which courts have begun to hold the landlord liable. For instance, landlords must use care in the common areas of the building such as the stairs, halls, and common entrance areas. Landlords are held liable for repairs which are negligently made, even though they may not have been required to make the repairs. Also, landlords are liable for injuries caused by defects which were not brought to the tenants' attention.

Example.   John Wicks rents Jane Snow an apartment which includes a gas stove. Wicks is aware that the gas line to the stove is defective, but does not notify Snow. Snow is badly burned in a gas explosion and brings action against Wicks. Wicks is held liable, since he knew of the defect in the stove and should have warned Snow.

Some states have enacted statutes or developed case law which impose a warranty on the landlord that the premises are *habitable;* that is, that they are fit to live in. The remedy for breach of this warranty is often a procedure whereby the tenant withholds a part of the rent until the premises are made habitable.

Case Example.   Under common law, the landlord had little obligation to the tenant other than to provide the leased premises. At that time, most rental property was made up of large parcels of land used for agricultural purposes; not dwellings. Today, contract principles are more frequently applied than common law real property principles in situations involving leases. Notice in the following case that the court implies a warranty of habitability from the landlord to the tenants. When the warranty is breached and the tenants move out, their obligation to pay rent is suspended. Under the common law, there would have been no warranty of habitability, and the tenants would have been obligated to pay rent for the full term of the lease.

PINES v. PERSSION
Supreme Court of Wisconsin, 1961
14 Wis 2d 590, 111 N.W.2d 409

Action by plaintiffs Burton Pines, Gary Weissman, David Klingenstein and William Eaglestein, lessees, against defendant

Leon Perssion, lessor, to recover the sum of $699.99, which was deposited by plaintiffs with defendant for the fulfillment of a lease, plus the sum of $137.76 for the labor plaintiffs performed on the leased premises. After a trial to the court findings of fact and conclusions of law were filed which determined that plaintiffs could recover the lease deposit plus $62 for their labor, but less one month's rent of $175. From a judgment to this effect defendant appeals. Plaintiffs have filed a motion for review of that part of the judgment entitling defendant to withhold the sum of $175.

At the time this action was commenced the plaintiffs were students at the University of Wisconsin in Madison. Defendant was engaged in the business of real estate development and ownership. During the 1958-1959 school year plaintiffs were tenants of the defendant in a student rooming house. In May of 1959 they asked the defendant if he had a house they could rent for the 1959-1960 school year. Defendant told them he was thinking of buying a house on the east side of Madison which they might be interested in renting. This was the house involved in the lease and is located at 1144 East Johnson Street. The house had in fact been owned and lived in by the defendant since 1951, but he testified he misstated the facts because he was embarrassed about its condition.

Three of the plaintiffs looked at the house in June, 1959 and found it in a filthy condition. Pines testified the defendant stated he would clean, and fix up the house, paint it, provide the necessary furnishing and have the house in suitable condition by the start of the school year in the fall. Defendant testified he told plaintiffs he would not do any work on the house until he received a signed lease and a deposit. Pines denied this.

The parties agreed that defendant would lease the house to plaintiffs commencing September 1, 1959 at a monthly rental of $175 prorated [distributed evenly] over the first nine months of the lease term, or $233.33 per month for September through May. Defendant was to have a lease drawn and mail it to plaintiffs. It was to be signed by the plaintiff's parents as guarantors and a deposit of three months' rent was to be made.

Defendent mailed the lease to Pines in Chicago in the latter part of July. Because the plaintiffs were scattered around the country. Pines had some difficulty in securing the necessary signatures. Pines and the defendant kept in touch by letter and telephone concerning the execution of the lease, and Pines came to Madison in August to see the defendant and the house. Pines testified the house was still in terrible condition and defendant again promised him it would be ready for occupancy on September 1st. Defendant testified he said he had to receive the lease and the deposit before he would do any work on the house, but Pines could not remember him making such a statement.

On August 28th Pines mailed defendant a check for $175 as his share of the deposit and on September 1st he sent the lease and the balance due. Defendant received the signed lease and the deposit about September 3rd.

Plaintiffs began arriving at the house about September 6th. It was still in a filthy condition and there was a lack of student furnishings. Plaintiffs began to clean the house themselves, providing some cleaning materials of their own, and did some painting with paint purchased by defendant. They became discouraged with their progress and contacted an attorney with reference to their status under the lease. The attorney advised them to request the Madison building department to inspect the premises. This was done on September 9th and several building code violations were found. They included inadequate electrical wiring, kitchen sink and toilet in disrepair, furnace in disrepair, handrail on stairs in disrepair, screens on windows and doors lacking. The city inspector gave defendant until September 21st to correct the violations, and in the meantime plaintiffs were permitted to occupy the house. They vacated the premises on or about September 11th.

The pertinent parts of the lease, which was dated September 4, 1959, are as follows:

"1. For and in consideration of the covenants and agreements of the Lessees hereinafter mentioned. Lessor does hereby devise, lease and let unto Lessees the following described premises, to-wit:

"The entire house located at 1144 East Johnson Street, City of Madison, Dane County, Wisconsin, including furniture to furnish said house suitable for student housing.

"2. Lessees shall have and hold said demised premises for a term of one (1) year commencing on first day of September 1959. . . .

"3. [Total annual rent was $2100, to be paid in monthly installments in advance, prorated over the first nine months of the term, or $233.33 per month. The deposit of three months' rent of $699.99 was to be applied for March, April and May of 1960.]

"4. The Lessees also agree to the following:. . .to use said premises as a private dwelling house only. . . .

"7. If Lessees shall abandon the demised premises, the same may be re-let by Lessor for such reasonable rent, comparable to prevailing rental for similar premises, and upon such reasonable terms as the Lessor may see fit; and if a sufficient sum shall not be realized, after paying the expenses of re-letting, the Lessees shall pay and satisfy all deficiencies. . . ."

The trial court concluded that defendant represented to the plaintiffs that the house would be in a habitable condition by September 1, 1959; it was not in such condition and could not be made so before October 1, 1959; that sec. 234.17, Stats. applied and under its provisions plaintiffs were entitled to surrender possession of the premises; that they were not liable for rent for the time subsequent to the surrender date, which was found to be September 30, 1959.

MARTIN, Chief Justice. We have doubt that sec. 234.17, Stats. applies under the facts of this case. In our opinion, there was an implied warranty of habitability in the lease and that warranty was breached by the appellant.

There is no express provision in the lease that the house was to be in habitable condition by September 1st. We cannot agree with respondents' contention that the provision for "including furniture to furnish said house suitable for student housing" constitutes an express covenant that the house would be in habitable condition. The phrase "suitable for student housing" refers to the "furniture" to be furnished and not to the general condition of the house.

•   •   •

The general rule is that there are no implied warranties to the effect that at the time a lease term commences the premises are in a tenantable condition or adapted to the purposes for which leased. A tenant is a purchaser of an estate in land, and is subject to the doctrine of *caveat emptor* [let the buyer beware]. His remedy is to inspect the premises before taking them or to secure an express warranty. Thus, a tenant is not entitled to abandon the premises on the ground of uninhabitability. [Citations omitted.]

There is an exception to this rule, some courts holding that there is an implied warranty of habitability and fitness of the premises where the subject of the lease is a furnished house. This is based on an intention inferred from the fact that under the circumstances the lessee does not have an adequate opportunity to inspect the premises at the time he accepts the lease. . . . In [*Collins* v. *Hopkins*, 2K.B. 617 (1923)] the English court said:

> "Not only is the implied warranty on the letting of a furnished house one which, in my own view, springs by just and necessary implication from the contract, but it is a warranty which tends in the most striking fashion to the public good and the preservation of public health. *It is a warranty to be extended rather than restricted.* (Emphasis supplied.)"

•   •   •

We have not previously considered this exception to the general rule. Obviously, however, the frame of reference in which the old common law rule operated has changed.

Legislation and administrative rules, such as the safeplace statute, building codes and health regulations, all impose certain duties on a property owner with respect to the condition of his premises. Thus, the legislature has made a policy judgment — that it is socially (and politically) desirable to impose these duties on a property owner — which has rendered the old common law rule obsolete. To follow the old rule of no implied warranty of habitability in leases would, in our opinion, be inconsistent with the current legislative policy concerning housing standards. The need and social desirability of adequate housing for people in this era of rapid population increases is too important to be rebuffed by that obnoxious legal cliche, *caveat emptor*. Permitting landlords to rent "tumbledown" houses is at least a contributing cause of such problems as urban blight, juvenile delinquency and high property taxes for conscientious landowners.

There is no question in this case but that the house was not in a condition reasonably and decently fit for occupation when the lease term commenced. Appellant himself admitted it was "filthy," so much so that he lied about owning it in the first instance, and he testified that no cleaning or other work was done in the house before the boys moved in. The filth, of course, was seen by the respondents when they inspected the premises prior to signing the lease. The had no way of knowing, however, that the plumbing, heating and wiring systems were defective. Moreover, on the testimony of the building inspector, it was unfit for occupancy, and:

> "The state law provides that if the building is not in immediate danger of collapse the owner may board it up so that people cannot enter the building. His second choice is to bring the building up to comply with the safety standards of the code. And his third choice is to tear it down."

The evidence clearly showed that the implied warranty of habitability was breached. Respondents' covenant to pay rent and appellant's covenant to provide a habitable house were mutually dependent, and thus a breach of the latter by appellant relieved respondents of any liability under the former.

Since there was a failure of consideration, respondents are absolved from any liability for rent under the lease and their only liability is for the reasonable rental value of the premises during the time of actual occupancy. That period of time was determined by the trial court in its finding No. 9, which is supported by the evidence.

Granting respondents' motion for review, we direct the trial court to find what a reasonable rental for that period would be and enter judgment for the respondents in the amount of their deposit plus the amount recoverable for their labor, less the rent so determined by the court.

Cause remanded with instructions to enter judgment for the respondents consistent with this opinion. . . .

RIGHTS AND DUTIES OF THE TENANT

Payment of Rent

The tenant's major duty is to pay rent at the specified time and place. If the lessee fails or refuses to pay the rent or in some other way breaches the terms of the lease, the landlord may bring a legal proceeding called a dispossess. A *dispossess* allows the lessor to evict (expel) the tenant and regain possession of the premises.

Repairs

The tenant has full responsibility for the care and upkeep of the property so that it is returned in the same condition as when rented, except for normal wear and tear. Formerly, this included all repairs, but the law currently gives more of that obligation to the landlord. Tenants today are generally responsible for minor repairs, and for major repairs when they have been negligent. Landlords must repair all common areas.

Example. Daley breaks a picture window in his apartment while swinging a golf club in the living room. He must replace the glass at his expense since it was broken due to his negligent behavior.

Example. Boys playing ball in the yard outside Daley's apartment hit a baseball into Daley's picture window. Most likely, Daley's landlord would have to replace the window since it is considered a major repair and was not due to the tenant's negligence.

Assignment and Subletting

A tenant's entire interest in real property may be transferred to another by *assignment* of the lease to a third party, unless the lease prohibits it. The new tenant, the *assignee,* has the interest in the property and is held liable to the landlord. The original tenant, as in the standard assignor-assignee relationship, still has the obligation of the contract and is held liable for the performance of the lease by the assignee.

Example. The Hales rent an apartment with a three-year lease. After one year, they are transferred to a different state. The Hales assign the two remaining years of their lease to the Mannings.

A tenant, if not prohibited in the lease, can transfer only a part interest to the premises by subletting. In *subletting,* the new tenant, the *sublessee,* is not liable to the landlord, but to the *sublessor,* the original tenant. The new tenant's relationship to the sublessor is that of landlord-tenant.

Example. Suppose that in the previous example, the transfer is only for a six-month period. The Hales do not want to have to pay rent on the apartment while they are gone, but want to inhabit the same unit when they return. They decide to sublet the unit to the Mannings for the six-month period. The Mannings now become liable to the Hales, who are the landlords to the sublessee.

Fire

In the event of fire, a lease usually requires the tenant to notify the landlord immediately. The landlord must repair the damage as soon as possible. If the tenant remains in the structure during the repairs, the rent continues. If the damage is so great that the tenant must vacate, the rent ceases until the property is repaired. If the entire building is damaged beyond repair, the lease is cancelled as of the time of the fire and the rent is due only up until that time.

Fixtures

Fixtures or improvements by tenants that are attached to the property and would cause damage if removed, are considered to be part of the real property and become the property of the landlord, unless there is a clause to the contrary in the lease. The courts normally exclude trade fixtures from this regulation. *Trade fixtures* are items that are added by the tenant for the purpose of carrying on a trade. The landlord has no right to possession of such fixtures on the condition that they are removed before the lease is up. Trade fixtures might include a built-in saw in a hardware store, sinks and chairs in a beauty or barber shop, or ovens in a pizza shop.

Example. Don's Donut Shop builds in three commercial deep-fat fryers in a building which is being rented. At the end of the lease, they plan to move to a new location. Shortly before the termination date, they begin disassembling the fryers. The landlord brings action, claiming that the fryers are a permanent fixture and must remain on the premises. The court rules in favor of Don's Donut Shop since the fryers are considered to be trade fixtures, and they were removed before the lease ended.

Security

The landlord may require the tenant to supply *security* to assure performance of the terms of the lease, such as payment of rent or return of the premises in good condition. The security, whether it is cash, bonds, or the like, is still considered to be the property of the tenant, even though it is in the landlord's possession. Many states now require the payment of interest on security deposits. Landlords who misuse security deposits are often subject to criminal penalties. (See item (7) in figure 11-5.)

TERMINATION OF THE LEASE

Normally, a lease, like other contracts, is terminated (ended) at the end of the lease period by the agreement of the parties. Death of the landlord or tenant does not terminate a lease. Since this is a contract situation, the obligation is binding on their estates.

Operation of Law

Termination of a lease can occur through the operation of law. This occurs if the premises are condemned by a public authority for reasons such as unsafe or unhealthy conditions. Leases are also terminated if the property is taken over by a government agency under its rights of eminent domain.

Example. Several tenants of an apartment building complain to the city health department that sewage is leaking into the pipes from which the tenants get their drinking water. The health department, after investigating, condemns the entire building and gives the tenants three days to vacate. All leases are terminated as of the date of the condemnation.

Breach

Termination of a lease may occur when there is breach of any of the terms by either of the parties. *Eviction* is one type of breach whereby the tenant is deprived of use of the premises. Eviction may be a result of actions by the tenant or the landlord. If the premises become uninhabitable and the landlord, after being notified, fails to correct the condition, a tenant may claim *constructive eviction.* The tenant may then move out within a reasonable time and not be liable for further payment of rent.

Example. In January, the heating system leading to Young's apartment in Bangor, Maine breaks down and Young immediately calls the landlord. There is still no heat after four weeks, so Young moves out. The landlord brings action against Young for breach of the lease. The court does not hold Young liable for continuing the lease or for further rent under the doctrine of constructive eviction, since the premises were judged to be uninhabitable.

Example. Suppose that Young in the previous example, remains in his apartment during January and February until the heating system is repaired. In July he moves out, claiming constructive eviction because of the faulty heating system. The landlord sues for breach of the lease. In this situation, the courts would uphold the landlord's claim. Since Young did not move out of the premises within a reasonable time, he could not claim constructive eviction at a later time, and thus is judged to have broken the lease.

As mentioned earlier, the landlord may bring action to evict a tenant if the tenant fails to pay the rent or breaches other terms of the lease.

Fire

It has already been mentioned that leases are automatically terminated if a building is totally destroyed by fire. Tenants are only liable for rent up to the time of the fire. Neither party is held liable for breach of the lease in such a situation if there is no negligence on the part of either party.

SELF-EVALUATION

Provide a brief explanation for each of the following.

1. What is the function of a real estate broker?

2. Define the term purchase offer.
3. Differentiate between a title search and a survey.
4. Must deeds be recorded? Why or why not?
5. What is the purpose of a quitclaim deed?
6. What is a limitation of a bargain and sale deed?
7. What are covenants in a warranty deed?
8. What paper is drawn up at a title closing? What does it include?
9. How does a long-term lease differ from a short-term lease?
10. A tenant sues a landlord for injury resulting from a fall on the front stairs of an apartment building that were in ill-repair. Will the tenant be able to collect? Why or why not?
11. What action can a landlord take if a tenant does not pay rent at the specified time and place?
12. *A* is assigned a lease by *T. A* fails to pay the rent to *L,* the landlord. Who is liable?
13. When only a part interest of a lease is transferred, what is the result?
14. A tenant panels a wall of a leased apartment. Before the lease is terminated, the tenant removes the paneling. Is this legal? Why or why not?
15. How does the death of a tenant affect a lease? Death of a landlord?

SUGGESTED ACTIVITY

1. Write a complete real estate purchase for the following, using document forms from the text as a guide.

   Buyers: Michael F. Gordon and Meryle H. Gordon
   Sellers: Alfonso T. Fruizzi and Rita T. Fruizzi
   Date: March 11, 19___
   Property: 407 Winding Road, Mayfield, Culver County, Any State
   Property Description: Tract of land in the Town of Mayfield, County of Culver, Any State, known as Lot 803 and 804, in block 75 as shown on a map filed in the office of the Clerk of Culver County, Any State, on May 21, 19___, drawn by Alvin Evers, Civil Engineer.
   Considerations: $43,000

CASES FOR STUDY

1. *A* purchases a parcel of land from *B* without examining the title to the property. It happens that a lien has been filed against the property during *B*'s ownership and the lienor now seeks to enforce it. Can *A* prevent this from happening?

2. Husband *H* and wife *W* own property as tenants by the entirety. *H* dies and the property is sold to *X* with the grantor's name appearing on the warranty deed as *E,* executor of the estate of *H.   X* contracts to sell the property to *Y.* When *Y* has a title examination done, he discovers the deed from *H*'s estate to *X.* Should he proceed with his plans to purchase from X?

3. *P* and *S* sign a purchase offer in which *P* agrees to purchase and *S* agrees to sell a piece of property owned by *S.* The document reads as the purchase offer in figure 11-1 of the text. *P*'s attorney advises *P* before the closing date that *S* cannot convey good title. Must *P* go through with the purchase?

4. *T* rents a house from *L* and signs a lease for a period of one year. Four months into the term, *T* finds a more comfortable apartment and vacates *L*'s property. What is *T*'s liability to *L?*

5. If *D* takes title to property under a quitclaim deed, what are the dangers involved in conveying the same property to another by warranty deed?

6. With a closing date of September 15, what tax adjustments must be made if county taxes are calculated from January 1 to December 31, payable in January, and village taxes are calculated from May 1 to April 30, payable on October 1?

7. *O* gives *X* a warranty deed to a parcel of land. *X* places the deed in a safe-deposit box, but does not record it. *O* then gives *Y* a warranty deed to the same parcel, but *Y* does not record his deed immediately. In the interim between the time *O* gives the deed to *Y* and the time *Y* takes the deed to the county clerk's office, *X* records his deed. Who owns the property, *X* or Y?

8. Use the same situation as in case 7, with this difference: before *Y* takes the deed from *O,* he goes to the property. While there, *Y* sees *X* building a cottage on the property. In response to questions, *X* mentions that he owns the property. *Y* goes to the clerk's office and can find no deed showing that the property belongs to *O.* Should *Y* go through with the sale?

9. *T* rents an apartment from *L*. There are no restrictions in the lease regarding subletting or assigning the apartment. *T* sublets to *Z*, who then defaults on the rent. Can *L* recover the rent from *T*?

10. *L* has a great number of land holdings throughout the city which he rents as residences. Many of the buildings have been struck by fires of "mysterious origin." *L* is arrested and charged with arson in connection with the fires in his own buildings. May the tenants in the remaining buildings legally cease their rent payments?

Section 5

Torts

Individuals acting as business people or consumers must be aware of wrongs they may commit against other individuals either intentionally (deliberately) or unintentionally. By the same token, if wrongs are committed against them, it is also necessary to know what legal relief can be expected.

Section 5 discusses civil wrongs (as opposed to criminal wrongs) committed by people in violation of the rights of other individuals, known as *torts*. Tort law is important in our society to assure that each individual has the greatest amount of freedom possible without infringing on the rights of others.

Chapter 12

Torts–Intentional and Unintentional

OBJECTIVES

After studying this chapter, the student will be able to

- explain the nature and purpose of tort law.

- identify eight types of intentional torts and the relief available to the victim in each case.

- identify two types of unintentional torts.

- outline two torts specifically connected with business transactions.

- define the following words and phrases.

intentional tort	malicious intent
unintentional tort	privilege
tort	malicious prosecution
tort feasor	conversion
duty	suit in conversion
breach of duty	trespass
proximate cause	nuisance
damage	negligence
assault	reasonable man standard
battery	contributory negligence
false imprisonment	comparative negligence
false arrest	respondeat superior
warrant	strict liability
defamation	trade secret
slander	patent
libel	copyright
published	

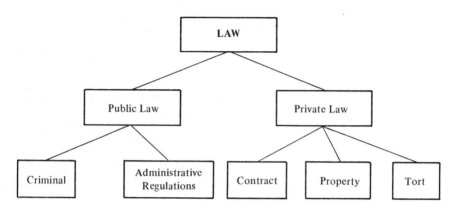

Fig. 12-1

The basic chart in figure 12-1 illustrating the two major classif-ications into which law can be divided now includes the third and final heading under private law — tort. *Tort* involves the violation of a right of one party by another party that is not covered by a contract.   The word *tort* is derived from a French word meaning *twisted.* There is no one definition of the word, but a useful syno-nym is *civil wrong.* It is believed that when one person causes an in-jury or loss to another, the *tortfeasor* (the person committing the tort) should compensate the injured party.

Each American citizen is guaranteed certain personal and pri-vate rights by constitutions and by federal and state laws. These include (1) the right to be free from bodily harm; (2) the right to a good reputation; (3) the right to enjoy and use one's property with-out interference from others; and (4) the right to conduct business without interference from others. A tort arises when there is a vio-lation of any of these rights that is not covered by a contract and that results in damage or injury. The injured party can then bring action for a recovery of damages.

Torts may be classified as either intentional or unintentional. *Intentional torts* are those which are purposely committed. This category includes intentional wrongs against a person and those against a person's property. *Unintentional torts,* those not done purposely, include negligent and strict liability torts. A more spe-cialized body of tort law exists in the area of business torts. These are torts which apply specifically to economic situations. They may be either intentional or unintentional.

ELEMENTS OF A TORT

Duty

A tort is committed when one person who owes a *duty* (obligatory conduct) to another breaches that duty, causing injury or damage to the victim. Duty is imposed by law. When a driver is traveling in a car, there is a duty owed to other travelers or pedestrians to exercise proper caution. Similarly, residents of a certain area owe a duty to their neighbors and other persons who are in that area.

This is not to say that the law imposes a duty on everyone to exercise caution for every other person at all times. For example, when the population was less dense and common law prevailed, there was no duty owed to trespassers. That meant that a person injured while on another individual's land without permission had no cause of action against the landowner. In a crowded society, it can be expected that even persons without permission will enter onto private property; with the prevalence of insurance, the law today does not take an absolute position that no duty is owed to trespassers.

One owes no duty to aid another who might be in danger unless it was the former who originally caused the latter to be in danger. An eyewitness to an accident is under no legal duty to render assistance, whatever moral obligation there might be. If the injuries are aggravated because of the delay in obtaining help, the victim does not look to the passerby for compensation. Duty is a flexible concept, one that changes as social conditions change.

Case Example. Consider the following case and what is said about duty. The court determined that a duty should not be imposed on the defendant to not rent the boat to the plaintiff or to rescue the plaintiff. What long range effects could you foresee if the court had imposed a duty?

OSTERLIND v. HILL

Supreme Judicial Court of Massachusetts, 1928
263 Mass. 73, 160 N.E. 301

BRALEY, J. This is an action of tort, brought by the plaintiff as administrator of the estate of Albert T. Osterlind to recover damages for the conscious suffering and death of his intestate [one who dies without leaving a will]. . . .The first count of the original declaration alleges that, on or about July 4, 1925, the defendant was engaged in the business of letting for hire pleasure boats and canoes to be used on Lake Quannapowitt in the town of Wakefield; that it was the duty of the defendant to have a reasonable regard for the safety of the persons to whom he let boats and canoes; that the defendant, in the early morning of July 4, 1925, in willful, wanton, or reckless disregard of the natural and probable consequences, let for hire, to the intestate and one Ryan, a frail and dangerous canoe, well knowing that the intestate and Ryan were then intoxicated, and were then manifestly unfit to go upon the lake in the canoe; that, in consequence of the defendant's willful, wanton, or reckless disregard of his duties, the intestate and Ryan went out in the canoe, which shortly afterwards was overturned and the intestate, after hanging to it for approximately one-half hour, and making loud calls for assistance, which calls the defendant heard and utterly ignored, was obliged to release his hold, and was drowned; that in consequence of the defendant's willful, wanton, or reckless conduct the intestate endured great conscious mental anguish and great conscious physical suffering from suffocation and drowning. Count 2 differs materially from count 1 only in so far as negligent conduct is alleged as distinguished from willful, wanton, or reckless conduct. . . .The amended declaration adds allegations to the effect that the plaintiff's intestate and Ryan were intoxicated and incapacitated to enter into any valid contract or to exercise any care for their own safety and that the condition of the intestate was involuntary and induced through no fault of his own.

The trial court [dismissed the action].

. . .The declaration must set forth facts which, if proved, establish the breach of a legal duty owed by the defendant to the intestate. Sweeney v. Old Colony & Newport Railroad, 10 Allen, 368, 372, 87 Am. Dec. 644. The plaintiff relies on Black v. New York, New Haven & Hartford Railroad, 193 Mass. 448, 79 N.E. 797, 7 L.R.A. (N.S.) 148, 9 Ann. Cas. 485, as establishing such a duty on the part of the defendant. In that case the jury would have been justified in finding that the plaintiff was "so intoxicated as to be incapable of standing or walking or caring for himself in any way. . . ." There was testimony to the effect that "when he fell, he did not seize hold of anything, his arms were at his side." The defendant's employees placed a helpless man, a man impotent to protect himself, in a dangerous position.

In the case at bar, however, it is alleged in every count of the original and amended declaration that after the canoe was overturned the intestate hung to the canoe for approximately one-half hour and made loud calls for assistance. On the facts stated in the declaration the intestate was not in a helpless condition. He was able to take steps to protect himself. The defendant violated no legal duty in renting a canoe to a man in the condition of the intestate. The allegation appearing in each count of the amended declaration that the intestate was incapacited to enter into any valid contract states merely a legal conclusion. [Citations omitted.] The allegations, therefore, in the courts of the amended declaration to the effect that the intestate was incapable of exercising any care for his own safety is controlled by the allegations in the same counts that he hung to the side of the canoe for approximately one-half hour, calling for assistance.

In view of the absence of any duty to refrain from renting a canoe to a person in the condition of the intestate, the allegations of involuntary intoxication. . . become immaterial. The allegations of willful, wanton, or reckless conduct also add nothing to the plaintiff's case. The failure of the defendant to respond to the intestate's outcries is immaterial. No legal right of the intestate was infringed. [Citations omitted.] The allegation common to both declarations that the canoe was "frail and dangerous" appears to be a general characterization of canoes. It is not alleged that the canoe was out of repair and unsafe.

[Affirmed.]

Breach of Duty

Once it is established that duty exists, the next element that must be present is *breach of duty*. Depending on the type of tort involved, this breach might occur by a negligent act or by an intentional act. The breach might also occur because of an act unrelated to the amount of care exercised by the tort feasor, as in the case of strict liability torts. Breach of duty in the sphere of intentional torts and strict liability requires little explanation other than that which is provided in figure 12-2. However, some discussion of negligence is necessary.

Everyone occasionally engages in careless conduct unintentionally. The waiter who drops a tray of hot food in the lap of an unsuspecting customer certainly does not intend to engage in careless conduct; a momentary lapse in attention or a failure to properly balance the weight on the tray causes such an accident to happen.

In a case which arises from this type of behavior, the jury decides whether the conduct in question is *negligent.* The standard against which the conduct is measured is the *reasonable man standard;* in other words, would a reasonable and prudent person have engaged in the same kind of conduct? If the answer is "yes," the

Types of Torts	Duty	Breach	Proximate Cause	Damage
Intentional	Yes (Required)	Intentional Act, e.g. striking or libeling another	Necessary	Necessary, with a few recognized exceptions
Unintentional	Yes (Required)	Negligent Act – tort feasor has not conformed to reasonable man standard	Necessary	Necessary
Strict Liability	Yes (Required)	Do not have to prove negligence or intent	Necessary	Necessary

Fig. 12-2 Elements of a tort

conduct is not considered to be negligent. If the act in question falls below the standard of care, the conduct is considered negligent. The reasonable and prudent person, for example, exercises caution in day-to-day behavior by not following the car ahead too closely when driving and not allowing ice to build up on front walks.

Proximate Cause

The third element required of a tort action is proximate cause. Defendant's negligence must be the *proximate* (next or nearest) *cause* of plaintiff's injuries. If too many other events or other acts of negligence intervene, the chain of causation is broken.

Courts today often refer to *Palsgraf* v. *The Long Island Railroad* (1928) when discussing proximate cause. In that case, a man carrying a package jumped aboard a car of a moving train at a station. He seemed as if he were about to fall, so a guard on the car reached forward to help him and another guard on the platform pushed him from behind. In doing so, both guards disobeyed company rules. During the process, the man's package was dislodged, fell on the tracks, and exploded. Mrs. Palsgraf, who stood on the platform many feet away, was injured by some scales which fell as the result of the explosion. She sued the railroad for negligence on the part of the guards, but was denied recovery on the grounds of proximate cause. The court held that the guard's negligence was to the holder of the package, not to Mrs. Palsgraf. According to the courts, the chain of causation was broken before it reached her.

Example. While walking one rainy day, Jim is splashed by a car driven by his neighbor that is traveling too near the curb. He has to have his new coat dry-cleaned as a result. The dry cleaner ruins the coat in the cleaning process by using the wrong fluids. Jim cannot expect reimbursement from the driver of the car, since the negligence of the dry cleaner intervened to break the chain of causation between the negligent driving and the loss of the coat.

Damage

The fourth element of a tort is *damage,* or loss. Except for a few situations in the intentional tort area, it is important to note that there must be damage or injury as a result of the wrong for there to be relief. Without damage or injury, there can be no recovery.

Example. Doris approaches a stop sign in her car but does not stop. Luckily, no one else is approaching the intersection at the same time, so no consequences result from the act. No tort has occurred, even though Doris was driving negligently, because no injury or damage resulted from her act. (Doris could, of course, receive a traffic ticket for her failure to obey the stop sign.)

The law of torts, then, can also be defined as a standard of conduct. All citizens, including those who operate businesses, must make sure that their conduct does not injure others. When it does, there are laws to give relief to those harmed.

The classifications of public and private law are not distinct and often overlap; the same act may be both a crime and a tort. A person convicted of a crime may still be held liable for damages to the individual who is harmed by the unlawful act.

Example. Janus is accused and convicted of the crime of kidnapping Mrs. Ross, the wife of a prominent banker. Mrs. Ross suffers physical and mental injury as a result of the kidnapping. She sues Janus in tort for $100,000 and presents proof with numerous hospital and doctor bills. The courts award the damages to Mrs. Ross. Even though Janus was already convicted of the crime, he is still held liable in tort to Mrs. Ross for her injuries that resulted from his unlawful conduct.

A person who commits a tort may cause injury to several people during the wrongful act, either directly or indirectly. The wrongdoer is held liable for all damage that proximately results from the act.

Example. Nojaim jumps on Bird in the street and begins to beat him. While Bird is attempting to defend himself, he accidentally trips Wein, who falls and breaks her leg. Nojaim, when found liable for the tort, is held responsible for the injuries to both Bird and Wein.

An individual is not responsible for damages when there is no tort committed. That is, if damage occurs from an act which is legal, the person causing the damage is not liable under tort law.

INTENTIONAL TORTS

Wrongs Affecting Personal Rights

There are several torts maliciously committed by individuals that affect the freedom and safety of other individuals. They are known as *intentional torts* against personal rights.

Assault and Battery. *Assault* and *battery* involve the violation of the right of individuals to be free from bodily harm. An *assault* is a threat with the intent to inflict bodily injury or harm. The threat must indicate a real or apparent ability to inflict bodily injury by force on the part of the person making it. The threatened person must have a reasonable fear of physical harm.

Example. Dave threatens to hurt Kathy, pulls a gun out of a drawer, and aims it at her. Kathy is able to escape from him before any more threats occur. Afterward, Kathy sues Dave in tort. Dave claims that the gun was not loaded. Kathy is awarded damages. Even though she was not hurt, she was reasonably fearful that she would be, since she had no way of knowing whether or not there were bullets in the gun. Dave is liable for the assault.

Battery is the intentional and wrongful touching of another person without the consent of that person. Battery always includes a threat or an assault.

Example. Bates and Kahn begin to argue about baseball in a local bar. Bates becomes so angry that he threatens, and then hits, Kahn.

Kahn suffers a broken jaw and a slight concussion. He sues Bates in tort for assault and battery and is awarded damages.

False Imprisonment. *False imprisonment,* sometimes referred to as *false arrest,* is the intentional confining of a person without that person's consent and where there is no means of safe escape. Unlawfully keeping an individual in a home, store, or vehicle constitutes false imprisonment.

Example. A cab driver drives Green to his destination, but refuses to let him out of the cab when Green offers him only a small tip. Green may sue the driver for false imprisonment.

An arrest can be made legally by a police officer with the proper authorized document, called a *warrant*. If the person arrested is later proven not guilty, there can be no action brought against the police department for false arrest or false imprisonment.

Defamation. *Defamation* is the injuring of another's good reputation without good reason. It is a violation of one of an American citizen's basic rights — the right to keep a good reputation.

There are two types of defamation, slander and libel. *Slander* is defamation by words or gestures. Defamation of good character by the use of information in the form of printing or pictures is known as *libel.*

For there to be a tort action, the slander or libel must be published. The term *published* in this instance means communicated or reproduced so that a third person hears or reads the statement.

Example. In a private conversation, Earl accuses Fred of cheating on his income tax statement. There is no case of slander here, since the defamation was not heard by anyone else.

For there to be recovery, there must be *malicious intent* (a desire to inflict injury), and damage to the reputation must be proved.

Example. Jacobs notices a steady decline in customers at his restaurant. He learns that Connors, a competitor, is telling people that Jacobs has been purchasing inferior meat and that his kitchens are unsanitary. Jacobs brings action for slander. He proves that the claims are false and that Connors, through his actions, is attempting to persuade Jacobs' customers that they should patronize Connors' establishment. Jacobs is awarded damages on the basis of malicious intent and injury to Jacobs' reputation.

There are a few situations in which it is not necessary to prove damage to the reputation — the charges are so great that damage is assumed. One of these slander situations in which proof of damage to the reputation is not necessary is one in which slander has injured a person in his or her occupation or profession. Other situations include false charges that a person has committed a crime, and claiming that a person has a loathsome disease.

Example. Ann is fired from her job at the supermarket. She learns that her boss has told the other employees that she has taken money from the cash register (which is false) and has given this as the reason for her firing. Ann brings action in tort for slander and collects damages. She does not have to prove that her reputation has been damaged, making it impossible to obtain another job. She must simply prove that the statements accusing her of committing a crime are false and that they were made maliciously to a third party.

If a statement can be proven to be true, it cannot be labeled slanderous or libelous. Therefore, the entire defense in a defamation case can be based on truth.

Example. Captain Mays and Captin Kent both operate charter fishing boats. Mays bring suit against Kent when a tourist informs him that Kent is telling people that his boat is unsafe. After investigation, it is found that Mays does not have the required life jackets and fire extinguishers on board. In addition, required lights are not in working order. Mays loses the suit since the statements that Kent made are found to be true.

Another defense in a defamation case is called *privilege,* which is a legal or justified excuse. This applies to lawyers, judges, and witnesses while in court, and to members of Congress speaking on the floor of Congress. They may make defamatory statements, but they are excused from being defamatory in those situations because of the position of the speaker.

Statements made about persons in the public eye are also ruled as privileged. They must, however, be honest opinions with no malice intended.

Malicious Prosecution. *Malicious prosecution* occurs when a person brings a criminal action against another without a valid reason and with the intent to cause injury or damage. The person upon whom the charges are made must be proven not guilty. That person must also show that damages or injury resulted because of the malicious action.

Example. Blount and Parisi are coowners of a hotel. Blount complains to the prosecutor's office, which results in the bringing of a criminal action against Parisi for misappropriation of a great deal of money from the hotel accounts. While awaiting trial, Parisi is imprisoned for some months and receives no income during that time. At the trial it is shown that Parisi never misused funds, and that Blount only wanted to get Parisi out of the business. When found not guilty, Parisi sues Blount in tort for malicious prosecution. Parisi proves that the criminal action was brought with malice and is awarded damages as a result of his imprisonment, loss of income, and injury to his reputation.

Right of Privacy. Individuals are also protected from invasion of their privacy. Pictures, names, or statements made by an individual cannot be used in any type of advertising or promotion without his or her permission. Laws prohibiting the tapping of telephones also serve to protect the right of privacy. It is thought that violations of this right cause mental anguish to the individual involved.

Example. A photograph of a well-known sports figure entering a certain restaurant is taken. The restaurant has the picture printed in a newspaper with the caption, *If he dines here, shouldn't you?* The sports figure sues in tort. He contends that the advertisement is an invasion of privacy since he had never given his written consent for his picture to appear in the ad. He is awarded damages.

Wrongs Affecting Property Rights

Americans have the right to enjoy and use their property, both personal and real, without interference from others. An action in tort can be brought when these rights are violated.

Conversion. *Conversion* is the unlawful seizure and use of the personal property of another. The nature of such an action is called a *suit in conversion.* Damages are paid to the owner in the amount of the loss suffered.

Example.   Linda is a collection agent for Dobbs, Inc., a local insurance office.   If she uses collected funds as her own, the company can bring action against her for conversion.   Notice that Linda's act may also give rise to criminal liability, but criminal prosecution would not serve to restore the money to the company.

Trespass.   *Trespass* is any violation of the right of people to enjoy and use their property without interference from others.   It may be entry onto land without permission and without privilege whether or not the trespasser is aware of being on private property.   Even if such entry does not result in monetary damages to the property, the owner can still collect nominal damages due to the violation of the right of use and enjoyment of property.   Trespass can also result from an act which affects the land or the use and enjoyment of it.

Example.   Jonick digs a hole as close to his property line as possible. The sides collapse and portions of Culver's land, next to Jonick's, also collapse.   Culver's rare rose bushes are irreparably damaged in the collapse.   Culver sues for trespass and is awarded damages.

Nuisance.   *Nuisance* is a tort which results from improper or unlawful use of one's own land which causes threatened or actual damage to others.   It is thought that the improper act could interfere with the individual's enjoyment of his or her personal property or even be harmful to health and safety.

Example.   Munson burns papers and garbage every day behind his store.   The odor is unbearable.   Donnally, who lives next door, brings a tort action, claiming that the burning is a nuisance and potentially dangerous.   Donnally is awarded damages and Munson is ordered to stop burning the garbage.

UNINTENTIONAL TORTS

Perhaps the most common basis for tort actions is negligence. *Negligence* occurs when proper care is not taken, resulting in injury or damage to other persons or property.   There must be resultant injury for there to be cause for action.

Negligence is classified as an unintentional tort.   The intent of the defendant is not an element of the tort, as it is in intentional torts.

Example. Edith Bruning drives her car through an intersection without stopping at the newly erected stop sign. She hits nine-year-old Susy Nastor who is riding her bike. Edith did not intend to go through the stop sign and did not intend to hit Susy. Even though Edith claims that she was not aware of the new stop sign, her behavior is held to be negligent and Susy is awarded damages.

Cases in this area of tort generally use the reasonable man standard to determine if there is negligent behavior. The measure of negligence asks the question, "Would a reasonable person of ordinary wisdom have acted the same way under the same or similar circumstances?"

Example. Apply the reasonable man standard to the previous example. It can be seen that a reasonable person would not have driven through the stop sign without stopping, as Edith did. Her ignorance was not a legal defense and her action was judged to be negligent. The reasonably prudent person looks for stop signs at intersections. Ignorance, honest mistakes, or physical disabilities are not legal excuses for negligent behavior. They do not relieve individuals from any liability for injury caused by the negligent action.

In many states, injured parties in negligence actions cannot collect damages if their own actions contributed to the injury. This is known as *contributory negligence.* The law holds that since a combined negligence caused the injury, neither party can recover damages.

Example. Falstaff installs a chain link fence around his swimming pool. The fence is not given proper support and is structurally weak in one area. Waghe, on his way home from school, climbs the fence and begins walking along the top of it when part of the fence collapses. He falls and injures himself on the concrete around the pool. Waghe sues Falstaff in tort for damages due to the negligent manner in which Falstaff kept the fence. Fallstaff argues that Waghe was negligent himself in walking along the fence. The jury might decide that both parties were negligent and that no damages would be awarded to either party, based on contributory negligence.

Some states have adopted the standard of *comparative negligence* instead of the stricter contributory negligence rule. Under the doctrine of comparative negligence, the plaintiffs are not barred from recovery, even if they were slightly negligent. The jury determines how negligent the plaintiff was and reduces the verdict by that amount. A plaintiff found to be 10 percent negligent would receive a verdict which is 10 percent less than full damages as determined by the jury.

Strict Liability

Strict liability occurs in certain special situations in which persons are held liable for the results of their actions without any reference to negligence. There are certain hazardous functions which are necessary to society and therefore are not forbidden. They are so potentially dangerous, however, that the law holds the performer liable for all resultant injuries, despite whose fault it is. Such situations include the use of explosives, the keeping of wild animals, and the spraying of crops.

Another example of strict liability involves the employer-employee relationship. The victim of an accident caused by the driver of a company truck can sue the company, even though the employer was not the negligent driver. The reasoning is that the employer is better able to bear the loss than the employee, the employer can take out insurance to protect against the negligence of employees, and the victim is more apt to be able to recover from an employer. This doctrine of holding the employer legally responsible for the negligent conduct of employees is known as *respondeat superior.*

Case Example. The doctrine of strict liability is also placed on sellers of products in a defective condition which renders them unreasonably dangerous to users or consumers. This case illustrates such strict liability. Was the store responsible for placing a flimsy sheath around the knife? If not, why then is the store considered responsible for the injuries caused by the knife?

DAVIS v. GIBSON PRODUCTS COMPANY
Court of Civil Appeals of Texas, 1974
505 S.W. 2d 682, rehearing denied 513 S.W. 2d 4
[Most citations have been omitted.]

CADENA, Justice. Plaintiff, Larry L. Davis, individually and as next friend in his minor son, Larry Mark Davis (referred to in this opinion as "Mark"), appeals from a judgment, based on a jury verdict, denying recovery against defendant, Gibson Products, Co., d/b/a/ Gibson Discount Store, for injuries suffered by Mark while he was examining a machete which was on display at defendant's store.

According to the petition, Mark picked up the machete, which was encased in a cloth sheath, to examine it. While holding the sheathed machete in his left hand, he began to withdraw the machete from its sheath. As he did so, the blade cut through the bottom of the sheath, and Mark suffered lacerations on the third and fourth fingers of his left hand. Recovery sought on the basis of "strict liability" and on several alleged negligent acts on the part of defendant.

Defendant's store is of the self-service type, and persons in the store are expected to handle and examine the goods on display and, if they decide to buy an item, to take their selection to a cash register station and pay for it. Defendant desires that people handle and examine the displayed merchandise if they want to buy it and also if they just want to look at it. No signs are displayed informing unescorted teenagers not to enter the store, nor are there any signs requesting those unescorted teenagers who are in the store to leave. A substantial portion of defendant's sales are made to teenagers.

Mark was thirteen years old at the time he was injured. Defendant's manager testified that it was anticipated that persons in the store, including boys thirteen years of age, would handle the machetes, which were on display on an open counter and within reach of customers, to examine them and that, in the course of such examination the machetes would be withdrawn from their sheaths.

It is undisputed that, immediately prior to, and at the time of, the injury, Mark was in the store accompanied by three boys of about the same age as Mark. After Mark had purchased some gum and one of the other boys had bought some popcorn, the boys went to the sporting goods department. While they were in the vicinity of an archery display, Ralph Schoenfeld, the manager of the department, asked if he could help them and was told that they were ". . .just looking."

Schoenfeld testified that the boys then proceeded down the aisle to the machete display, where one of the boys picked up a machete. He was joined by two other boys, and ". . .they were all handling them, fooling around." Schoenfeld said that when one of the boys ". . .acted like he was going to fence," Schoenfeld told him, "That's about enough now. Why don't you just put them back and leave?" The boys left the area of the machete display but, according to Schoenfeld, they soon returned at a time when Schoenfeld was attending to some customers, so that, according to Schoenfeld, he was unable to talk to them again. While Schoenfeld was attending to the customers, Mark cut his hand. Schoenfeld did not see the incident.

. . .Schoenfeld's testimony was contradicted by the boys. They denied that they were "playing around with the machetes" and denied Schoenfeld's statement relating to the "fencing" incident. They denied that Schoenfeld, or any other employee, had talked to them and denied that any of defendant's employees had commanded, directed or suggested that they put the machetes back "and leave." There is no evidence indicating that, at the time he was injured, Mark was "fooling around" with the machetes or that he was using them in an improper manner. Mark's testimony relating to the manner in which he cut himself is not a model of consistency, but it is sufficient to justify the conclusion that the injury occurred in the manner described in the petition.

The machete in question, and the sheath in which it was encased, were admitted into evidence. The operator of a testing laboratory testified that his test of the machete and sheath revealed that the blade of the machete was "sharp" and that it would cut through the sheath if withdrawn under 9 pounds' pressure, and that if it were withdrawn rapidly, the machete would cut through the sheath under 4 pounds' pressure. The jury found that Mark withdrew the machete from its sheath in a "sudden" manner.

The jury had an opportunity to examine the machete and witnessed the demonstration which showed that it was sharp enough to cut a sheet of paper. An examination of the sheath reveals that it consists of a single layer of cloth sewn together at the bottom by a single strand of thin thread. When the machete is withdrawn from its sheath, the sharp edge of the blade slides across the seam so formed. A simple examination of the sheath justifies describing it as flimsy.

It is undisputed that defendant did not inspect the machetes or the sheaths and subjected them to no tests. It is also undisputed that there were no signs or other warnings as to the existence of any danger to persons handling the machetes.

[The court then discusses whether the defendant was negligent and, if so, whether such negligence was a proximate cause of the injury.]

•   •   •

There remains for consideration only plaintff's complaint, embodied in his first point, of the refusal of the trial court to submit issues relating to plaintiff's claim under the doctrine of strict liability. The requested issues and the requested explanatory instructions, are substantially in the form described in *McKisson* v. *Sales Affiliates, Inc.* . . .Such requested issues and instructions incorporate the elements of the doctrine of strict liability as enunciated in Restatement, Torts, Section 402A (1966).

The doctrine of strict liability as set out in the Restatement was approved by our Supreme Court in *McKisson* and, again, in *Darryl* v. *Ford Motor Co.* . . .This formulation of the doctrine imposes strict liability on "one who sells" a product in a defective condition unreasonably dangerous to the "user" or "consumer" for harm caused to the "ultimate user or consumer" if the "seller" is engaged in the business of "selling" such a product and the product is expected to, and does, reach the "user or consumer" without substantial change in the condition in which it is "sold."

Defendant asserts that the tendered issues were properly refused because such issues ". . .assumed the machete was transferred. . ." by defendant to Mark ". . .as user or consumer within the meaning of the rule of strict liability, and this was a disputed fact issue. . . ." Defendant further defends the trial court's refusal to submit the tendered issues by pointing out that there was no "sale" of the product by the defendant.

Before discussing the question of the applicability of the doctrine of strict liability, it should be pointed out that the evidence establishes that one of the purposes of encasing the machetes in sheaths is to protect the hands of persons examining the machetes.

Although the Restatement's formulation speaks in terms of liability of the "seller" of chattels to "users and consumers," it is clear that the protection of the doctrine is not limited to users and consumers of the defective product. The framers of the Restatement. . ., made it clear that no opinion was expressed on whether the rules embodied in that section ". . .may not apply to harm to persons other than users or consumers. . . ." . . .there may be no reason for denying the protection of the doctrine to nonusers and nonconsumers ". . .other than that they do not have the same reasons for expecting such protection as the consumer who buys . . ." the product, since the development of the doctrine of strict liability was a response to "consumers' pressure."

The Restatement's "consumer expectation" rationale for denying recovery to nonusers and nonconsumers has not won judicial acceptance. Apparently with only one exception, the courts which have considered the problem have not limited its application to users and consumers. . .Perhaps the most influential case allowing nonusers and nonconsumers to recover is *Elmore* v. *American Motors Corp.* . . .where, in the course of holding that a casual bystander is protected by the doctrine, the Supreme Court of California pointed out that injury to a bystander is often foreseeable and that restriction of the doctrine to users and consumers

rests on what is but a vestige of the disappearing privity requirement often applied, and frequently mutilated, in cases where a sup-
plier of chattels was held liable on some theory of "warranty."

• • •

In *Darryl,* Texas rejected the limitation on the doctrine. . .
saying: "There is no adequate rationale or theoretical explanation
why non-users and non-consumers should be denied recovery against
the manufacturer of a defective product." . . .The statement concerning the absence of an "adequate" rationale for limiting recovery
to users and consumers is significant because it was made after the
Supreme Court had referred to the Restatement. . . .Clearly,
the "consumer-expectation" rationale was regarded as not "adequate,". . . .

The trial court's refusal to submit the requested issues cannot
be supported on the ground that Mark was not a user or consumer
of the product.

Defendant concedes that, despite the use in [the Restatement]
of such terms as "one who sells," "seller," "sells" and "sold," the
rule of strict liability is applicable even though there has been no
"sale" of the product by defendant. . . .

While recognizing that proof of a "sale" in the strict legal
sense of that term is not essential, defendant insists that the sup-
plier of a chattel is strictly liable only when he has transferred
possession of the chattel by sale, lease or similar commercial transaction. . . .

It is true that in most cases where the doctrine has been applied the facts have shown a sale, bailment, lease or . . .a gift of the
product for advertising purposes by defendant, and that, in such
cases, there has been a transfer of possession of the product by
defendant. But we have found no case which makes liability dependent on a transfer of possession by defendant.

The two cases involving facts most clearly similar to those in
the case before us were both decided by the highest tribunal of the
state of Kentucky. In both *Rogers* v. *Karem,* . . .and *Kroger Co.*
v. *Bowman,.* . .it was held that the operator of a self-service grocery
store was strictly liable to a person injured when, as she was lifting a
carton of soft drinks from a shelf, the bottles fell to the floor due
to the defective condition of the carton.

. . .Both decisions are based on the doctrine of strict liability
. . . .

Defendant argues that in each of the Kentucky cases there had
been sale of the product to the plaintiff, ". . .who accepted delivery
. . ." of the product ". . .as offered by the seller." It is clear that in
neither case had there been a "sale" of the product in the sense that

there had been a transfer of title, and it cannot be persuasively argued that, in either case, plaintiff and the retailer had entered into a contract of sale.   Nor do the facts of *Rogers* and *Kroger* suggest that there had been a transfer of possession such as that involved in the bailment or lease of a chattel.   If, in fact, the plaintiff in each of the two cases had possession of the carton of soft drinks, it was a unique sort of possession.   No definition of "possession" has been suggested which would justify the conclusion that a person who picks up a product from a shelf in a self-service establishment acquires, by such act, possession of the product or "has accepted delivery of" the product "as offered by the seller."   In any event, if plaintiffs in *Rogers* and *Kroger* had acquired possession of the cartons, it must be concluded that, unless we are prepared to rely on distinctions too abstruse to be understood, Mark had the same kind of possession here.

Since, as defendant points out, neither the *Rogers* nor the *Kroger* opinion discusses the question of whether there had been a "sale," in the sense of a transfer or delivery of possession of the product by defendant, it is necessary to consider the basis for the liability imposed by Section 402A, in order to determine the classes of persons upon whom liability is imposed and the classes of persons protected.

·   ·   ·

While the statement of the doctrine speaks of the liability of a "seller," it is clear that the term designates a class and is not a designation of limitation. . . .Our Supreme Court adopted this view in *Darryl,* when it spoke of the liability of one ". . .who places in commerce. . ." a product dangerous because of some defect. The stream of commerce includes the manufacture of the object and its distribution, including the activities of retailers. Unless it be argued that goods displayed for sale by a retailer are not in the stream of commerce, it is clear that continuation of the flow of commerce does not require transfers of possession.

Concerning the class of persons protected by the doctrine, Chief Justice Traynor. . .spoke of liability when the defective product causes injury not merely to a user or consumer, but ". . .to a human being."

·   ·   ·

The liability created by the doctrine of strict liability rests on foreseeability, and not on esoteric concepts relating to transfer or delivery of possession. . .As one recognized authority has pointed out, the effect of extending the protection of the doctrine to casual bystanders, as was done in *Darryl,*". . .is obviously to put strict liability on the same footing as negligence."

·   ·   ·

In this case, injury to a person in Mark's position was clearly foreseeable by defendant. It is undisputed that defendant foresaw that persons in the store, including persons of Mark's age, would handle the machetes and, in the process of examining them, would remove the machete from the sheath in order to examine the blade. Even without such testimony, the operator of a self-service establishment can certainly foresee that persons in his store will handle and examine the products displayed for sale.

We conclude that. . .the term "user or consumer" as interpreted by the courts, particularly in the bystander cases, is broad enough to bring Mark within the protection of the doctrine.

To impose liability of defendant here is not to make it an insurer. The scope of responsibility under Section 402A is limited by the "intended use" doctrine, which requires consideration of the defendant's marketing scheme and the foreseeability of harm. Defendant's marketing procedure contemplated, and, perhaps, made it inevitable, that persons in its store would handle and examine the items on display. The injury here was to a person who belongs to the class of persons who, because of defendant's marketing procedures, could be expected to use the machete and sheath. Mark, at the time of his injury, was using the product in at least one of the manners for which it was intended and exactly in the manner that defendant intended that he would use it. . . .Defendant's display of the product was essentially commercial in character, since it displayed the goods with the expectation of profiting from future sales. . . .

Defendant points out that, at the time of his injury, Mark had no present intention of buying the machete. However, Mark testified that, while he had no use for a machete, if he saw one he liked he might return later and buy it. He testified that, on prior occasions, he had gone into stores just to "look around," and, after seeing something that appealed to him, he had returned to the store later to purchase it. Defendant's manager testified that a substantial portion of the store's sales were "delayed" sales. That is, it is not uncommon for a person to walk into a store with no present intention of making a purchase, leave the store, and return later to purchase an item which caught his fancy on the first trip. There is sufficient evidence to support the conclusion that Mark was a prospective purchaser or potential customer and a member of the class of persons whom retailers welcome into their stores with the expectation that the "just looking" visit will result, then or at a later date, in a purchase of an item on display.

. . .[D]efendant. . .assert[s] that the strict liability issues were properly refused because there is no evidence which would support a finding that the sheath in which the machete was encased was defective in the sense that it created an unreasonable risk of injury when put to its intended purpose. We have already reviewed the evidence concerning the sharpness and the thinness of the sheath. While we concluded that the evidence was insufficient to establish the existence of a dangerous condition as a matter of the law, it is sufficient to support the conclusion that, considering the sharpness of the blade, the sheath was improperly designed and that, because of such defective design, it was unreasonably dangerous when put to one of its intended uses.

There is nothing in the record to suggest that Mark assumed the risk. Since the machetes were encased in sheaths, it was impossible to discover the sharpness of the blades without withdrawing the machetes from the sheaths.

We conclude that the pleadings and the evidence were sufficient to entitle plaintiff to a submission of the issues relating to strict liability.

The judgment of the trial courts is reversed and the cause is remanded for a new trial.

BARROW, C.J. concurs in result.

BUSINESS TORTS

One of the rights listed in the beginning of this chapter is the right of American citizens to conduct business without interference from others. As the field of business has grown in this country, so has this area of tort law. Business torts may be either intentional or due to negligence.

Deceitful Practices by Competitors

Competition is the basis of the free enterprise system. When performed legally, it is wholesome and healthy and advances our economic system. Unlawful competition, however, violates the rights of others and is punishable under tort law.

There are many deceitful practices that are not allowed by law. For example, a company may not publish false statements about the products or services of another company. A company may not use trademarks or other marks that are registered by someone else. A company also may not illegally force a competitor out of business either directly or indirectly.

Example. Company *B* and Company *C* are the two largest manufacturers of a waterproofing paint. They both use the same product, XYZ, as the major ingredient in their paints. Company *B* makes a deal with the producer of XYZ to stop delivery to Company *C*. Without XYZ, Company *C* goes out of business. Company *C* sues Company *B* for unfair competition and is awarded damages.

Unlawfully Copying Competitor's Products

The copying of a competitor's product is a widespread and lawful practice in American business. It becomes unlawful when the copying infringes on trade secrets, copyrights, or patents.

A *trade secret* is a formula, a pattern, or special information known only to a few individuals in a company and treated in a very confidential manner by those individuals. When such secrets become known to others by deceitful means such as bribery, theft, or blackmail, there is cause for action for damages or injunction.

Example. Benson applies for a job with a company which is in competition with his employer. He states that if he is given the very high salary he requests, he will bring the new designs for next year's product model with him. He is only one of three people in his present firm who know the designs. The firm hires him and, in effect, buys the designs from him. When Benson's original company discovers what has happened, they bring a suit in tort. They are awarded damages and an injunction is issued to halt further use of the design by the new company.

A *patent* may be issued by the United States Patent Office on any new invention of a process, machine, product, growing plant, or design. A patent is usually valid for seventeen years, after which the item may be copied by anyone. If any copy is made during the seventeen-year period, the copier is liable for any profits earned and for any damages suffered by the patentee.

Example. In 1955, a manufacturer developed a new camera that required the use of a special type of film. Both the camera and the film process were patented. It was not until 1972 that another large film manufacturer could produce and market the film.

A *copyright* gives an exclusive right to the holder to reproduce written material. It is valid for the lifetime of the author, plus an additional fifty years after the author's death (effective January 1, 1978). Copyrighted material can be reproduced by another party only with written permission, figure 12-3. If the material is copied without such permission, the copier is held liable if damages can be proved.

Example. Professor Alfred writes and publishes an article that Professor Bailey wants to use in her class. Rather than ordering fifty copies of the article, she instead has fifty photocopies made and passes them out to the class. Since the article was copyrighted and Professor Bailey used the material without permission, Professor

---

RANDALL
396 Lincoln Avenue
Crandale, Florida 10000

PERMISSION REQUEST

IDENTIFY:_____
Unit/Figure

To: From:

☐ Please send 8 x 10, black and white glossy photographs and grant permission to reprint, for world distribution, the photos from your publication or as described below:

☐ Please grant permission to reprint, for world distribution, material from your publication:

(insert author, title, and copyright date of the publication, and a specific description of the material to be reprinted)

_____

_____

_____

The requested material will be reprinted by RANDALL PUBLISHERS in a title described as follows:

(insert author, tentative title, and tentative copyright date)

_____

_____

_____

The credit line to acknowledge the use of your material will appear on a specially designed acknowledgment page.

Sincerely,

Date: _____

PUBLISHER'S REPLY

☐ Permission granted.

☐ 8 x 10 glossies unavailable but permission granted to copy illustration(s) from publication(s).

☐ Material in public domain, no permission needed.

☐ Publisher addressed does not hold copyright, request permission from:

By: _____

Date: _____ Title:_____

1

Fig. 12-3 **A request to reprint copyrighted material**

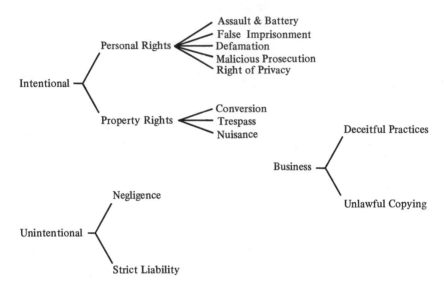

Fig. 12-4 Torts

Alfred has a cause of action. He can prove that there were damages because he was deprived of revenue when Professor Bailey did not purchase fifty copies of the article in its original form.

SELF-EVALUATION

Provide a brief explanation for each of the following.

1. Why is tort law classified as private law rather than public law?

2. What four personal rights are guaranteed to American citizens by federal and state constitutions and laws?

3. What are the four elements of a tort action?

4. Massey repairs Pyle's car and negligently leaves the steering wheel bolts loose, causing the steering to be defective. When leaving the garage, Pyle loses control of the car and runs into the side of the store which is next door to his garage. Who is liable for the damage to the car? Who is liable for the damage to the store? Why?

5. Why are assault and battery considered torts?

6. How can the tort of false arrest or false imprisonment be avoided by police officers?

7. In *Davis* v. *Gibson Products Company,* how does the judge relate the incident of the woman who was injured lifting the soft drink carton to Mark's situation?

8. Define the term *publish* in relation to slander and libel.

9. Define slander and libel.

10. In most cases involving a charge of defamation, what three elements must be present for there to be recovery of damages?

11. What defense can be used in a defamation case against a senator who has made a slanderous statement while speaking in the United States Senate?

12. Aunt Bessie's Baked Beans Company sponsors a television advertisement which states that Jensen, a famous actor, prefers Aunt Bessie's Baked Beans above all others. Jensen never made such a statement. What legal recourse does he have?

13. *B* brings a tort action against *C* for unlawful trespass on *B*'s land. There was no harm done to the land. Can *B* collect any damages? Why or why not?

14. For there to be a cause of action in a claim of negligence, what element must be proved, even if duty and negligence are admitted?

15. What standard of conduct is used to determine whether or not there can be a charge of negligent behavior in a case? Explain.

16. The injured party in a negligence case is shown to have also been negligent. Who is awarded damages in such a case, the injured party or the defendant? What principles are applied in such a situation? Explain.

17. *B* exercises great care while using explosives to blast some rock on a job site. Still, a nearby car is damaged. What tort, if any, can the car owner use to sue *B*? Explain. Does the car owner have to prove anything to recover damages?

18. When is the copying of a competitor's product unlawful?

19. For how long are patents and copyrights valid?

SUGGESTED ACTIVITIES

1. Consider situations involving lawful competition among business firms. Examine national brands versus store (or house) brands in supermarket and drugstore chains. Compile a list of instances in which house brands copy national brands with similar names and/or packaging. Discuss why you feel that these instances are lawful or unlawful, depending on how closely items are copied.

2. Identify several patented items by their patent number. Investigate one of them by writing to the United States Patent Office in Washington, D.C. to ascertain such things as when the patent was issued and when it expires.

CASES FOR STUDY

1. A doctor performs surgery without obtaining the consent of the patient or the patient's next of kin when it was reasonable to do so. Has a tort been committed? Explain.

2. Edison is prone to attacks of dizziness followed by a loss of consciousness. If Edison causes an accident by blacking out while driving, can she be said to have breached the standard of care required by drivers of automobiles? Why or why not?

3. Consider the situation presented in the previous case. Was Edison negligent if her first attack occurred while driving her car, causing an accident? She had no forewarning of the occurrence of the attack.

4. Bradley is a local artist of renown. Thomas tells a gathering of neighbors that Bradley is a bad credit risk and that she is deeply in debt. Assume that the statements are not true. Can Bradley take action against Thomas for injury to her business reputation without any proof of actual damages?

5. XYZ Company devises a product with the brand name of Bright Lustre. ABC Company manufactures a similar product with similar packaging and calls it Brite Luster. The packaging is distinguishable only on close inspection. ABC Company's product is definitely chemically inferior. Does XYZ have a tort action against ABC? Why or why not?

6. Lance is following Marlene too closely in his car. When Marlene must stop quickly to avoid hitting a child who has run into the

street, Lance runs into the rear of her car. The force of the impact ejects Marlene from the car. In a suit by Marlene against Lance, a safety engineer testifies that at the time of the accident, Marlene was not wearing a seat belt and that had she done so, she would not have been thrown from the car and her injuries would have been less severe. No one contradicted the testimony. Can Marlene still recover damages from Lance? Explain.

7. *Q* stores extra inventory in a back room of his store. A customer asks *Q* if he (the customer) can go into the back to search for a product that he cannot find on the shelves in the front of the store. *Q* tells the customer that it is dark in the back, making a search rather dangerous, and that he prefers that the customer stay in the front. The customer says that he is not concerned about injury and that he will be careful. The customer goes into the back room and runs into a shelf, suffering a broken nose. What are his chances of collecting damages from *Q*?

Section 6

Organizing Businesses

A *business* is any profit-seeking enterprise or concern. Businesses range from simple one-person operations to complex multibillion-dollar organizations. In the American free enterprise system, citizens may establish one of several types of businesses on their own, or seek employment in existing concerns.

The most basic type of business organization is the sole proprietorship. A *sole proprietorship* consists of one owner who provides all capital, assumes all risks, receives all profits, and incurs all losses that result from the business. The proprietor may hire other employees, but he or she remains the only owner. The major advantage of a sole proprietorship is that the owner is his or her own boss. The disadvantages are varied. It is often difficult to obtain adequate funds for operation or expansion. Illness or death usually results in termination of the business. Most importantly, however, a sole proprietorship requires a great deal of managerial skill. The failure rate of one-owner businesses is very high because of the lack of such skills.   Over half of such new businesses fail in the first two years, and after ten years, over 80 percent prove unsuccessful.

Several other forms of business organizations are closely examined in Section 6.   Each of these has advantages as well as disadvantages.   Organizers must first understand the goals and functions of their new business.   Then they must be aware of the structure of various types of business forms.   At that point, they can best organize their new business in the most appropriate way and thus increase their chances for success.

An understanding of the principles of agency is essential in the study of various business organizations.   These principles are discussed in Chapter 13.   *Agency* indicates a legally created, three-party relationship.   Agency relationships are becoming more and more prevalent in the economic world.   As will be examined in Section 6, the rules of agency law also enter into other forms of business.

A discussion of *partnerships,* businesses owned by two or more individuals, is also included in this section.   Partnerships resolve many of the problems of sole proprietorships, but are not as complex as corporations.

Chapter 15 takes a close look at the *corporation* — a familiar and sometimes awesome form of business that is currently the most influential organization in the American enterprise system.   The corporation is frequently more structured and certainly more regulated than either the sole proprietorship or the partnership.   However, the limited liability of the shareholders of the corporation makes it an attractive form of business organization to investors.   By studying the corporation from creation to termination, many of the complex terms and systems can be clarified and understood.

Chapter 13

Agency

OBJECTIVES

After studying this chapter, the student will be able to

- explain the nature, purpose, and historical development of the law of agency.
- identify four types of agents and their functions.
- describe the ways in which agencies are created and terminated.
- explain the various relationships which exist between principal and agent, principal and third party, and agent and third party.
- define the following words and phrases.

agency	agency by ratification
agent	scope of authority
principal	express authority
third party	implied authority
employee	apparent authority
employer	fiduciary duty
general agent	compensation
special agent	reimbursement
professional agent	disclosed principal
independent contractor	partially disclosed principal
express agency	undisclosed principal
power of attorney	revocation
implied agency	renouncement

Agency is a three-party, legally created relationship. An agency relationship is formed when one party, an *agent*, is granted the authority to act as a representative for another party, the *principal*, when dealing with a *third party*, figure 13-1. Legally, the act is considered to have been accomplished by the principal. Therefore, the principle, and not the agent, is obligated to and receives benefits from the third party.

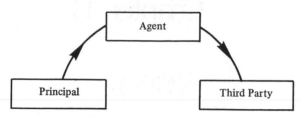

Fig. 13-1 The Agency Relationship

Agency relationships are actually very common in everyday life, even though they may not be labeled as such. Individuals often act as agents for one another when doing simple tasks.

Example. Tom drives to the stadium to purchase two tickets for the football game. His neighbor, Dwight, gives him ten dollars to purchase two tickets for him. Tom acts as an agent for Dwight, the principal, in dealing with a third party, the seller of the tickets to the football game.

The development of agency law into its modern form began in the days of the master-slave relationships. At times, a slave acted for the master, but the courts held that the master was responsible to the third party.

In early America, the small business owner usually performed all the tasks in the operation of the business. As mass production and expanding marketing areas developed in the early 1900s, business people found they could no longer handle all aspects of the business themselves. They began to hire other people, known as agents, to sell, deliver, and service their customers. The master-slave concepts of law were adapted to these situations and developed into agency law as it is known today.

TYPES OF AGENTS

Employees

Perhaps the most common type of agent is the employee. An *employee* is an individual who is contracted either in writing or orally to do work for another, the *employer*. When the employee is under the total control of the employer within the confines of the business, an employer-employee relationship is established. Very often, however, the employee acts in the name of the employer, thereby creating an agency relationship.

Example. Mary is a sales person at the Thrifty-Mart. She is authorized to make sales contracts with customers. Thus, she is acting as an agent for her employer in dealing with third parties. If an item is sold that is defective, her employer is obligated to make an adjustment to the customer. Mary may also have been instructed to stock shelves and set up the displays. In this function, Mary is acting only as an employee.

Example. Chris is a bookkeeper for Tony at Tony's Superior Service Center; he functions as an employee. In addition, however, Tony has authorized Chris to purchase needed supplies for the center from specified salespeople. Chris acts as an agent for Tony in the purchase of the supplies.

General and Special Agents

General agents act for their principals in a wide range of transactions — they may even be given complete control over all the principal's business matters. A *special agent,* on the other hand, may only be given the authority to act on a certain matter at a specific time and in a designated manner. General agents usually are allowed to exercise their own judgment to a greater extent than special agents.

Example. When he goes on vacation, Harry authorizes his employee, Clinton, to act as general agent for all purchasing for the furniture store. The owner leaves instructions to order 100 red and 100 blue director's chairs. When the order arrives, it is found that the company shipped 100 red, 50 blue, and 50 green chairs. Another order would take two months to fill and would mean missing the selling season. Clinton accepts the order for the store after deciding that they would probably sell more chairs with the extra color choice. As a general agent, it is within his power to make this decision.

Example. Consider the previous example. Suppose that the owner appoints Clinton as a special agent during his absence. The owner leaves instructions for Clinton to order 100 red and 100 blue director's chairs and sign the invoice when they arrive. If the incorrect order arrives, consisting of 100 red, 50 blue, and 50 green chairs, Clinton must refuse the shipment. The authority granted to him as a special agent does not include the power to change the order without further instructions.

Professional Agents

Some agents are in business for themselves; they are not employed by any specific individual. They may even hire others to work for them. These persons are known as *professional agents.* Manufacturer's representatives, one example of a professional agent, sell the goods of a principal in their own name, but are paid their *commission* (fee) by the principal. Real estate, insurance, and stock brokers are all agents for buyers or sellers and are paid by them. Auctioneers sell goods for others at public sales and thus act as agents. An attorney also acts as a professional agent in many instances.

Example. C is a defendant in a civil suit. She retains *L* as her attorney who, during the course of the litigation, submits papers, makes motions, and questions witnesses. It is not *L*'s personal suit. Rather, *L* is acting on behalf of *C* as a professional agent.

INDEPENDENT CONTRACTORS

A major relationship in business that is similar to agency but does not enter into the realm of agency law is established when an individual is hired as an independent contractor. The *independent contractor* performs a certain task according to a contract agreement. The hirer is concerned only with the end result and has no control over the way in which the independent contractor attains that result.

Any third parties dealing with the independent contractor are liable to and must seek recovery from that contractor, not the original hirer. Thus, there is no agency relationship, since the hirer is not held responsible for acts of the independent contractor or any others involved in the job.

It is often advantageous for individuals to have jobs done by independent contractors rather than by agents. This type of arrangement, for example, limits the liability of the hirer to the third party. It is important that the relationship is clarified so that confusion is avoided if claims are later made regarding a specific job.

Example. *B* is a builder of houses. *B* or his employees handle every aspect of the construction process but have no knowledge of landscaping. *B* contracts with one of the local nurseries to install the lawn, trees, and shrubs when a house is near completion. The nursery then brings in whatever employees of its own that are necessary to landscape the yard. If something is wrong with the landscaping, the new owner must seek reimbursement from the nursery and not *B*, since the nursery is an independent contractor and not an employee of *B*. The relationship is not as consistent nor as subject to *B*'s control as an employer-employee relationship would be. *B* does not pay a salary, but rather a fixed fee for the nursery's services.

If the new owner's complaint related to the construction of the house proper rather than landscaping, *B* would be liable. *B* has under his control people who work for him consistently, to whom he pays a salary, and who are directly answerable to *B*. In constructing the house, they acted for *B* and *B* is responsible for any negligent acts.

CREATING AN AGENCY

Who Can Be a Principal?

People who are considered legally competent usually have the right to act as principals and to appoint agents to act for them. In most states, minors may appoint agents. As with most other contracts, however, the appointments are voidable by the minor. The minor is only bound by the agent's acts if those acts are necessities.

Example. *B,* a patient commited to a mental institution, appoints Dr. *C* as his agent to handle his affairs. The bank refuses to allow Dr. *C* to sign checks from *B*'s account. The courts uphold the decision of the bank, since *B* is not considered legally competent and thus has no legal right to appoint an agent.

Who Can Be An Agent?

Anyone who is given the authorization by a competent principal may act as an agent, as long as that person is capable of performing whatever is required. Thus, a minor may be appointed as an agent, and often is. Minors acting as agents are contracting for their principals and not for themselves; therefore, the contracts are not voidable. However, the contract which establishes the agency between the principal and the agent is voidable by the minor agent.

Individuals may be disqualified from being agents for any one of several reasons. For example, agents cannot act for several different principals when there are conflicting interests. This might occur when all of the principals have the same purpose in hiring the agent. By seeking to help one principal, the agent may harm the other principals.

Example. Agent *M* has two principals looking for a similar type of property. Agent *M* locates the property. Which principal does he inform? This is a case of conflicting interests which could have been avoided if Agent *M* had not agreed to act for both principals.

Certain agents cannot be appointed if they lack the required licenses to perform the task. This includes stockbrokers, real estate brokers, and attorneys.

Example. Sue Daley applies to the Neill Realty Company in Buffalo, New York for a position as a real estate agent. She is well qualified for the position, having successfully sold real estate in Ohio for eighteen years. Sue, however, does not have a license to sell real estate in New York State when she applies for the position. Even though Neill wants to appoint her as an agent for his company, he cannot, since Sue lacks the legally required license.

Express Agencies

In most situations, an agency is created by express authority granted by the principal. Such authority can be either written or oral. If written, there is no particular form that is required, as long as all the elements of a binding contract are included.

Statutory Regulations. Statutory regulations often require agency relationships to be in writing. For example, the statute of frauds requires that contracts for services of an agent that cannot be completed in one year must be in writing. Contracts authorizing agents to sell and lease real property must also be in writing in most states.

Power of Attorney. One type of express written authorization which creates an agency is called a power of attorney. A *power of attorney* is power given by a principal to any competent person to act as an agent in business or in personal dealings. A person need not be a lawyer to be granted power of attorney.

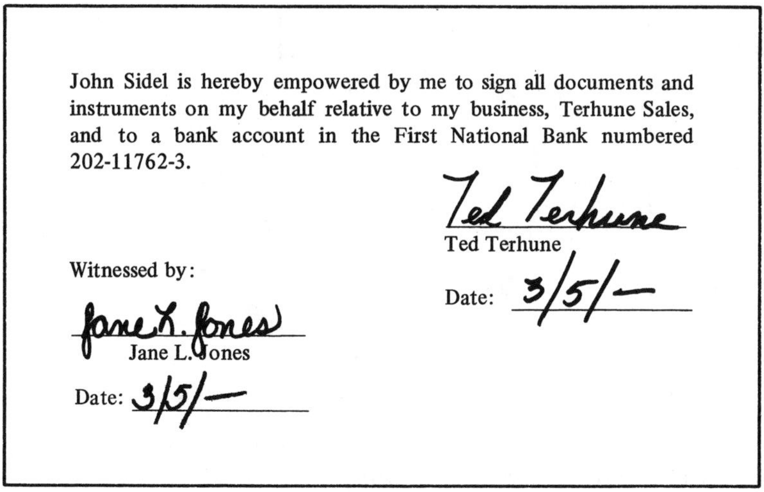

> John Sidel is hereby empowered by me to sign all documents and instruments on my behalf relative to my business, Terhune Sales, and to a bank account in the First National Bank numbered 202-11762-3.
>
> *Ted Terhune*
> Ted Terhune
>
> Witnessed by:
>
> Date: **3/5/—**
>
> *Jane L. Jones*
> Jane L. Jones
>
> Date: **3/5/—**

Fig. 13-2 Document granting power of attorney

Example. Ted Terhune is planning to visit Europe for six months. During that time, he is aware that many business decisions will have to be made, and that papers and bank checks will have to be signed. Ted gives a power of attorney to his business associate and friend, John Sidel. Figure 13-2 illustrates a form granting power of attorney. Again, there is no required form, as long as the necessary elements of a binding contract are included.

Implied Agencies

Courts may imply (assume) that an agency exists in situations where such an assumption seems just. The acts of the parties establish this type of agency. They are sometimes called *agencies of necessity,* since they usually arise when there is an emergency or very unusual circumstance.

Example. Jack, who is the sole support of his family, neglects for two weeks to give his wife, Joyce, money for food. Joyce finally visits a grocery store where she charges enough food to feed her children and herself. Jack refuses to pay the bill. The courts hold that an implied agency of necessity has been created. Joyce was acting as an agent for her husband. Jack, as the principal, is held liable for the bill.

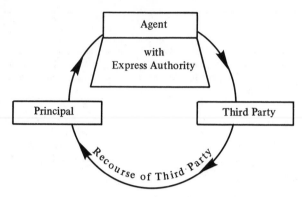

Fig. 13-3 Cycle of responsibility when express authority is granted

Courts sometimes rule that an implied agency of necessity has been created when there is a marine emergency. In such a situation, the master of a ship may authorize repairs or towing charges. The vessel's owner, as principal, is held responsible for the costs.

THE PRINCIPAL – AGENT RELATIONSHIP

Authority of the Agent

An agent has a *scope* (range) *of authority* that is granted by the principal when the agency is created. This authority may be express, implied, or apparent.

Express Authority. When a principal gives specific instructions either orally or in writing to an agent, *express authority* is granted, figure 13-3. The principal is liable to both the agent and the third party for damages or obligations resulting from an agent's express authority.

Example. Pauling directs Allen to purchase a tape recorder, sign the bill charging it to Pauling's account, and deliver it to Pauling's office. Allen has the express authority as an agent to make the purchase, sign the bill, and make the delivery.

Implied Authority. In most cases, every detail that an agent must perform in carrying out a job cannot be itemized by means of express authority. The agent is granted *implied authority* or *incidental authority* by the principal to do those things which are also necessary to accomplish the objective. As when express authority is granted, the principal is liable to both the agent and the third party for dam-

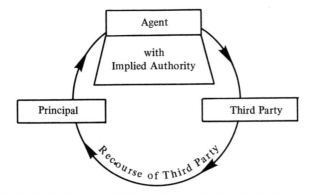

Fig. 13-4 Cycle of responsibility when implied authority is granted

ages and obligations resulting from an agent's implied authority, figure 13-4.

Example. Suppose that in the previous example, Allen is told that Pauling needs the tape recorder by later that same night for an important meeting. Allen is delayed in traffic. When he returns to the office building, Pauling has gone home. Knowing that Pauling lives only ten miles away, he delivers the tape recorder to Pauling's home. This is within the scope of his implied authority, since it is necessary in reaching the objective of delivering the tape recorder to Pauling in time for the meeting. Pauling is liable to Allen for the added expense of the trip.

Apparent Authority. *Apparent authority* is the extent of the power that the third party reasonably presumes that the principal has granted the agent. This presumption is based on the conduct or words of the principal, not the agent. The third party must rely on statements made or impressions given by the principal to presume that there is apparent authority. The extent of apparent authority may be less, the same, or greater than the actual authority of the agent. The principal is held liable to the third party even if the agent has not followed specific instructions, figure 13-5.

Example. City Lumber makes weekly deliveries of lumber products to Upstate Sales Company. Each week, John Doles signs the delivery receipt and all bills are paid by Upstate when due. Upstate tells Doles one day that he no longer has the authority to sign the delivery receipts. Four more weeks of deliveries are made, however, and

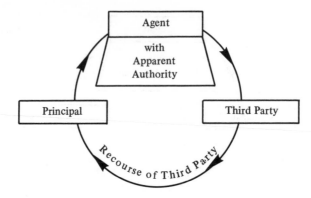

Fig. 13-5 Cycle of responsibility when there is apparent authority

Fig. 13-6 Cycle of responsibility when there is no ratification by the principal

Doles accepts them and signs the receipts since no one else is present to sign. Upstate refuses to pay the bill for those four weeks of deliveries, claiming that Doles was not authorized to accept the lumber products. The courts hold that Upstate is responsible for the bills on the basis of apparent authority. City lumber had not been notified that Doles no longer had authority to sign the receipts. He had been authorized to sign receipts all along; therefore, they could reasonably presume that he still had such authority.

Agency By Ratification.   An agent may sometimes act for a principal without authorization or beyond the authority that was granted. Such an act may later be *ratified* (approved) by the principal which then binds that principal and not the agent. This ratification may be expressed either orally or in writing, or simply implied by the actions of the principal.

To be valid, the principal must accept the entire unauthorized act of the agent. The third party may cancel the transaction any time before ratification, but not afterward. Ratification cannot occur unless the principal knows, or reasonably should know, about

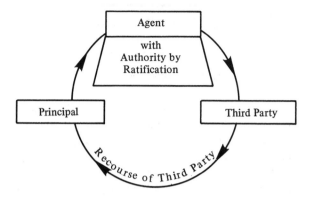

Fig. 13-7 Cycle of responsibility when there is ratification by the principal

the agent's unauthorized act and approves it. If there is no ratification, the principal is not held liable for acts of the agent. The third party must go to the agent for recourse, figure 13-6. If there is ratification by the principal, the responsibility and obligations return to the usual cycle, figure 13-7.

Example. White asks Jensen to locate a buyer for his car in return for 5 percent of the selling price. White instructs Jensen that he wants to receive a minimum of $2,500 for the car and that the payment must be by certified check. Jensen finds a buyer at White's asking price and accepts a certified check for $2,000 and the buyer's personal check for $500. Jensen then turns over the checks to White who cashes them and pays the agent his 5 percent commission. By so doing, White has ratified the act of the agent even though it was not in strict compliance with his directions. Note that the principal was aware that the agent acted in excess of his authority when he accepted a certified check in the amount of only $2,000, but decided to complete the transaction anyway.

Case Example. In the following case, the court must decide whether the principal is bound by the statements of an agent made to tenants indicating that the tenants would be allowed to cancel their lease. The defendants are two individuals who have promised to pay the rent in case the corporation which leased the premises fails to pay. Note the court's discussion of express, implied, and apparent authority and ratification.

PAILET v. GUILLORY
Court of Appeal of Louisiana
315 So. 2d 893 (1975)
[Most citations have been omitted.]

FRUGE, Judge. This is a suit based on a written contract of lease instituted by one of the lessors, Ruth E. Pailet, against Dr. Richard Michel and Twyman Guillory. . . .Plaintiff alleges that the lessee has vacated the leased premises and has failed to pay rent since December 1, 1973. The defendants contend that the lease has been validly cancelled and that no rent is due or owing. . . .

The trial court rendered judgment in favor of the plaintiff in the amount of $1,980 against both defendants jointly. . . .

The contract of lease out of which this action arises was signed in Marksville, Louisiana, on November 25, 1970, and had a five-year term. The leased premises is part of the Estate of Anne Elster whose surviving daughters, Rae Abramson and plaintiff Ruth E. Pailet, signed the lease as lessors. The lessee was the Cenla Equipment Company, Inc. In the lease Dr. Richard Michel and Twyman Guillory also bound themselves personally to guarantee the compliance of Cenla.

• • •

The present action was instituted by Ruth Pailet, one of the lessors, for her half of rents due under the lease. . . .

Defendants admit that no rent was paid after November of 1973. They contend, however, that the lease was cancelled and they are under no obligation to pay any rentals.

All matters concerning the leased property was [sic] handled for the lessors by Dr. Albert Abramson, who was the husband of Rae Abramson at the time the lease was entered into. The record shows that the defendants contacted Dr. Abramson about leasing the property, that they paid rent checks to Dr. Abramson (made out to the Estate of Anne Elster), and that Dr. Abramson handled minor repairs on behalf of the lessors on his own authority. The defendants have never had any direct contact with the lessors concerning the property. Their only contact was through Dr. Abramson.

Dr. Abramson made it clear to the defendants that he did not own the leased property and that on certain matters he could act only with the permission of the lessors. For instance, Dr. Abramson made it clear that he did not have authority to lease the premises. The lease was made only upon approval of the terms by the lessors and they signed the lease themselves. . . .

• • •

In March of 1973 Guillory approached Dr. Abramson and asked that the lease be cancelled. Dr. Abramson informed him that he would have to check with the lessors, Mrs. Abramson and Mrs. Pailet, as he did not have the authority to cancel. A few days later Dr. Abramson notified Guillory and Michel that the lessors had agreed to cancel the lease.

Mrs. Rae Abramson testified that she had been contacted by Dr. Abramson and had consented to the cancellation. The plaintiff, Mrs. Pailet, however, vigorously denied at trial that she had been contacted by Dr. Abramson and denied that she ever agreed to the cancellation. At trial Dr. Abramson testified that he did contact Mrs. Pailet but admitted that there may have been some "misunderstanding" regarding cancellation.

Guillory vacated the leased premises in 1973. The building had not yet been rented at the time of trial in December, 1974.

The trial judge rendered judgment for the plaintiff, finding that the lease had not in fact been cancelled. Defendants have appealed, contending that the trial court erred in holding that the plaintiff had not agreed to a cancellation of the lease and, in the alternative, in holding that plaintiff had not vested Dr. Abramson with implied or apparent authority to cancel the lease.

· · ·

The sole issue therefore is whether Mrs. Pailet. . .agreed [to the cancellation of the lease].

At trial Mrs. Pailet denied that she had ever been contacted by Dr. Abramson about cancelling the lease. She testified that had she been so contacted she would not have agreed to the cancellation because she needed the income from the rent. Dr. Abramson testified that he contacted Mrs. Pailet and thought she had agreed to the cancellation. He admitted that there had apparently been a misunderstanding.

· · ·

Appellants contend that even if Mrs. Pailet did not agree to cancellation of the lease, she is bound by the act of Dr. Abramson who was vested with the implied and the apparent authority to cancel the lease.

An agency relationship may be created through either express or implied authority. . . .Like an express agency, an implied agency is an actual agency. . . .Apparent authority, on the other hand, created no actual agency relationship. However, where the principal clothes an agent with apparent authority to perform certain acts and a third party, who has no knowledge of or reason to believe that there are limitations on that authority, deals with the agent, then the principal is bound by the acts of the agent, which although beyond the actual power delegated to him, are within his apparent authority. . . .

In the case before us, although there was never any express agency relationship between Mrs. Pailet and Dr. Abramson, he clearly had the authority to act as her agent in some matters concerning the leased property. Dr. Abramson was given the authority to collect rents, to make minor repairs, and to represent the lessors in preliminary negotiations regarding the lease.

However, the question before us is whether he had the implied authority to cancel the lease. Implied authority is actual authority which is inferred from the circumstances and nature of the agency itself. "An agent is vested with the implied authority to do all of those things necessary or incidental to the agency assignment." . . .In this case Dr. Abramson's agency authority included collecting the rent and making minor repairs. Certainly the authority to cancel the lease is not incidental or necessary to his authority to collect rent and make minor repairs. No such authority can be inferred in these circumstances, particularly where the authority to lease or permit assignment was not given.

We turn now to the issue of apparent authority. The concern here is whether the principal did anything to clothe the agent with apparent authority to perform the act though no actual authority was given. Because third persons [do not know] the actual terms of the agency agreement, they may rely upon the [appearances] of authority with which the agent is vested. . . .

•   •   •

We do not find that the lessors in this case clothed Dr. Abramson with the apparent authority to cancel the lease. Dr. Abramson himself denied that he had any authority to do so. The lease agreement. . .[was] signed by the lessors and not by Dr. Abramson. Thus all the indications were that Dr. Abramson did not have authority to cancel.

Appellants rely on the fact that all of their communications with the lessors concerning the leased property were through Dr. Abramson. This alone is not enough. The fact that Dr. Abramson failed to secure cancellation of the lease from Mrs. Pailet is not imputable to her, but rather to the appellants since they relied on Dr. Abramson to secure cancellation.

•   •   •

Appellants' final argument is that because Mrs. Pailet waited nine months before making any claim to the rent she ratified the cancellation made by Dr. Abramson. However, for ratification to occur the facts must indicate a clear and absolute intent to ratify the act. . . .In this case there is no evidence that Mrs. Pailet even had any knowledge that Dr. Abramson told the defendants that the lease was cancelled. In these circumstances there could be no intent to ratify.

For the reasons assigned the judgment of the trial court is affirmed. Costs are assessed to defendants-appellants.

Affirmed.

Torts and Crimes of the Agent

If an agent commits a tort while performing within the scope of the assigned authority, the principal is held liable. Any action by the third party, however, usually names both the agent and the principal. If the tort is committed on the agent's own time, or outside the scope of the agency, the principal is not held liable.

Example. Lomes, who installs washing machines for Home Services Company, neglects to seal the drain hose when hooking up a washer at the Giles home. Water leaks from the machine and causes extensive damage in a newly finished basement. The Giles bring action against Lomes and Home Services Company. Home Services Company, the principal, is held liable for Lomes' negligence and for payment of damages.

Example. Suppose that Lomes, in the previous example, helps a neighbor install his washer one night after work. If Lomes is negligent in his performance, the neighbor cannot bring an action naming Home Services Company. The action would be against Lomes alone, since the tort was committed on Lomes' own time, not while in the employ of his company.

A principal is generally not held liable for an agent's crime or intentional tort, even if they are committed within the scope of the assigned authority. If, however, the principal directs the agent to commit a crime or an intentional tort and the agent does so, both parties are held liable for that crime.

Example. Ames is traveling as an agent in Europe on a company assignment. He meets a man at his hotel who offers him a large sum of money to bring illegal drugs back into the United States. When arrested at customs, Ames is charged with a federal crime. His principal, the company, is not charged or held liable for Ames' crime.

Example. Ames' employer directs him to pick up illegal drugs in Europe and to bring them back with him when he returns to the United States. Both Ames and his employer are held liable for the crime.

Duties of the Agent

There are certain legal obligations that agents have to their principals. These are in addition to any specific requirements of the contract itself between the two parties.

Obedience. Agents are obligated to follow the instructions of their principals as closely as possible. Principals have the right to specify, within reasonable limits, the manner in which the assigned task is to be performed. If agents do not obey, or if they refuse to follow instructions, they may be held liable for losses that occur.

Example. Dan, an employee at Scott's Stationery Supply, is directed by the manager not to sell any more items on credit to the Maze Sales Company, as the firm has declared bankruptcy. Mr. Maze visits the store a few days later, selects seventy-eight dollars worth of supplies from Dan, and charges the merchandise to the company account. The manager holds Dan liable for the seventy-eight dollar bill since he has not followed the instructions given to him.

Loyalty. The agent's duty of loyalty requires that the agent be completely honest in all dealings with and for the principal. This is known as a *fiduciary duty*. The agent must always act in the best interest of the principal.

There is an adage concerning the fact that one cannot serve two masters and serve them both well. This applies especially well to agents. An agent cannot represent two principals in the same transaction without the consent of both. Such dealings without consent involve a conflict of interests. In such situations, the agent loses the right to be paid by either principal.

Example. Rosen is appointed as an agent to sell a certain tract of land. At that time, he is an agent for a company that is looking for a similar piece of property to purchase. If Rosen sells the land to the company without informing either party of his dual role as an agent, he is representing conflicting interests. As an agent for the seller, his obligation is to obtain the highest price possible for the land. As an agent for the buyer, his obligation is to purchase the property for the lowest price. As an agent for the two principals, he is unable to act with the best interests of both in mind. If Rosen proceeds with the sale without the consent of both principals, he will not be entitled to his fee from either one.

Agents must not buy or sell the goods of a principal to themselves without the knowledge and consent of the principal. This includes any dealings with themselves in the names of others. Agents who profit at the expense of their principals through such dealings are said to have breached their fiduciary duty. Such sales are voidable at the election (choice) of the principal.

Example. Baker sells cars for Two Corners Motors. She accepts a used model in trade for a new car, knowing that the car is worth almost double the price that the company allows for it. She buys the car herself, but records the sale in her sister's name. Bergen, the owner of Two Corners Motors, learns what Baker has done and reclaims the car, stating that the sale is voidable. The courts uphold Bergen. Baker has violated her fiduciary duty (duty of loyalty).

Accounting. Agents are required to keep accurate and up-to-date records of all the financial aspects of their job. Principals can request these records at any time. Any monies earned in a transaction for the principal must be paid to the principal, even if they are greater than expected.

Example. Emerson is appointed as an agent to sell Daley's boat. Daley prices the boat at $1,595. Emerson sells the boat for $1,795. The additional $200 belongs to Daley, not Emerson.

Funds or goods of principals must not be *commingled* (mixed with) funds or goods of agents. Agents should keep property of their principals separate from personal property to avoid confusion.

Care and Skill. Agents must use reasonable care and skill in performing their tasks. They may not always be successful, but they cannot be held liable for failure if reasonable care and skill are used.

Example. On June 15, Elms is appointed to purchase 2,500 pounds of prime beef for the Steak House Restaurant on or before July 2. On June 20, after checking the stock of several distributors, Elms purchases what he feels is the best meat at the best price for the restaurant. On June 30, beef prices drop considerably and quite unexpectedly. The restaurant cannot hold Elms liable for the difference in the higher prices that he has paid. Elms used his knowledge and took adequate care in the purchase.

Communication. It is the duty of every agent to communicate fully with the principal. All facts known by the agent concerning a transaction must be related to the principal. If any information is withheld, the agent can be held liable for resulting injuries or damages.

Example. Bales appoints Caine to purchase ten acres of land suitable for building lots for one-family homes. Caine locates a property at a good price. In his investigation, he discovers that almost every year, a nearby stream overflows and floods about two-thirds of the land. Since this is an important aspect in considering the land for use as building lots, Caine is obligated to inform Bales about the flooding. It is then Bales' decision as to whether or not the land should be purchased.

Duties of the Principal

Compensation. When most agencies are created, the contract states what compensation (fees) are to be paid to the agent by the principal for the services performed. If the compensation is not defined in the agreement, the agent is entitled to a reasonable rate for the service.

Reimbursement. The principal is obligated to reimburse (pay back) the agent for any expenses that the agent incurs while performing his or her duties. Such expenses may be either expressly or impliedly authorized as a necessity in the completion of the task. This is not a fee or compensation − it is simply returning to the agent money that has been spent in executing the actions of the principal.

Example. Hayes agrees to sell a piece of mountain property for Phillips. To properly show the acreage to a potential buyer, Hayes must have aerial photographs taken. Hayes pays for the photos and is then reimbursed by Phillips, the principal.

THE PRINCIPAL − THIRD PARTY RELATIONSHIP

Disclosed Principal

Usually, the third party in an agency relationship is aware that the agent is acting for a principal and knows the identity of that principal. In this situation, the principal is said to be *disclosed*. The third party is aware that the contract is being made with the principal, not the agent, and therefore, that the agent is not bound by the contract that is made.

Partially Disclosed Principal

Sometimes a third party is aware that an agent is acting for a principal, but does not know the identity of the principal, who is referred to as a *partially disclosed principal*. The agent may be held liable to the third party along with the principal unless it is otherwise clearly stated.

Undisclosed Principal

If a third party is not aware of the identify of the principal and does not know that the agent is acting as an agent, there is said to be an *undisclosed principal*. The agent becomes the contracting party and is liable for the contract. If, however, the third party discovers the agency and the identity of the principal, the third party can hold either the agent or the principal liable, but not both.

An agent often works for an undisclosed principal when purchasing land for real estate development. If owners knew of possible large development plans, they might automatically raise the price of the property.

Example. XYZ Company, a large, successful firm, plans to build an additional plant. They select five pieces of property which comprise the land necessary to build the plant. If they act as a disclosed principal, one key owner might hold out for a very high, inflated price, knowing that the firm must have each of the five properties to develop the plant. XYZ might choose, in this instance, to act through an agent as an undisclosed principal.

TERMINATION OF AN AGENCY

An agency may be terminated by the acts of one or both of the parties, or by operation of law.

Agreement

An agency may be terminated at any time by the agreement of the principal and the agent. Both parties may also agree in the terms of the contract that the agency will terminate at a certain time or when a specific task is performed.

Example. Principal contracts with agent to deliver one truckload of goods to a certain destination. When the goods are delivered, the agency is terminated by agreement, since the task has been completed.

Revocation by the Principal

A principal may *revoke* (end) an agency at any time. If, however, good cause for the termination cannot be shown and there is a breach of contract, the principal is held liable for damages to the agent.

Example. Kates is hired as a sales person for Hank's Hardware Store. Kates arrives late for work and leaves early, takes extensive coffee breaks and long lunch hours, and lounges in the back room while customers wait in the store. Hank's terminates the relationship by revocation since Kates' performance is not in accordance with the terms of the contract.

Renouncement by the Agent

An agent may *renounce* or abandon the agency. If, however, there is a breach of contract involved, the agent can be held liable to the principal for damages.

Example. Switz Architectural Company contracts with Mays to draw a finished set of plans for a large office building. Mays abandons the agency when the plans are half finished without good reason. Switz is forced to spend a great deal more money to have the plans redrawn from the beginning. Mays is held liable for the loss suffered by Switz due to a breach of contract.

Operation of Law

Certain events often cause the termination of an agency by operation of law:

- The death of either the principal or the agent
- Impossibility of performance

Example. Green contracts with Fine Portraits Company to have an oil painting of each member of his family done by the firm's foremost artist, Jim Doen. Doen breaks his arm in a car accident and is unable to paint. The contract is terminated due to impossibility of performance.

- Illegality of the work after formation of the agreement

Example. Benz contracts to distribute fireworks in his state for Explosives For Fun Company. Two months later, his state passes a law banning the sale of fireworks. The contract is terminated by operation of law due to the illegality of the work.

- Upon the bankruptcy of either party when the bankruptcy affects the subject matter of the agency

Example. King is an agent for New Form Door Company. The firm goes bankrupt and thus discontinues production of the doors. The agency is terminated by operation of law.

- When the subject matter of the agency is destroyed or no longer exists

Example. Van is an agent for the sale of a home. The home burns to the ground. The agency is terminated as the subject matter no longer exists.

NOTICE OF TERMINATION

Notice must be given to third parties upon the termination of agency relationships. If third parties who have dealt previously with the agent have not been notified of termination and therefore reasonably believe that an agent is performing an authorized act, the principal is still held liable because the agent is acting under apparent authority.

Such notice may be in either written or oral form. It is wise, however, for principals to send written notice to all third parties who have dealt with agents who have been terminated.

Example. For several years, Bert acts as an agent collecting rents on apartments for George. George terminates the relationship because he feels that Bert is unreliable. Bert continues to collect for a month and keeps the money himself. When George visits tenants to collect rent, the lessees say they have already paid and were not aware that Bert was no longer authorized to collect. The courts hold George liable for the acts of Bert since there had been no proper notification of termination. The lessees do not have to repay the rent.

Since death of the agent or principal automatically terminates the agency, a majority of jursidictions do not require that notice of the termination be given to third parties. In the above example, if George had died and Bert collected the rent from lessors, they would not be able to claim lack of notice to avoid repaying the rent to George's estate. This is a harsh result and, because of this, some jurisdictions now require that notice of death be given to terminate the agency.

SELF-EVALUATION

Provide a brief explanation for each of the following.

1. What is an agency relationship?
2. When does an employee become an agent?
3. How does a general agent differ from a special agent?
4. What is the difference between an employee and a professional agent?
5. Why is an independent contractor not an agent?
6. Can a minor be a principal and appoint agents?
7. Can a minor be an agent? Why or why not?
8. Who may be granted a power of attorney?
9. What type of agency is created when courts assume the existence of agency due to very unusual circumstances?
10. If an agent performs an act without authorization, what recourse does the principal have?
11. What liability does a principal have to the agent and to the third party for damages or obligations resulting from the agent's express and implied authority?
12. In *Pailet* v. *Guillory,* why did the court deny the appellant's argument that by waiting nine months before making a claim, Mrs. Pailet ratified the cancellation of the lease by Dr. Abramson?
13. Is the principal always liable for the torts of the agent? Why or why not?
14. When is a principal liable for the crime of an agent?
15. Name four of the five legal obligations that agents have to their principals.

16. Agent buys an item from principal without knowledge and consent of principal. What legal obligation is the agent violating? What recourse does the principal have?

17. How can agents avoid commingling their personal funds or goods with those of their principals?

18. In terms of an agency relationship, what is the difference between compensation and reimbursement?

19. What is the principal called if the third party is aware that the agent is acting for a principal, but does not know the identity of that principal?

20. When the principal is undisclosed, who is liable for the contract?

21. How would the death of an agent affect an agency relationship?

22. Why is it wise for the principal to send notice of termination to third parties?

SUGGESTED ACTIVITY

1. Interview an agent and submit a report of your meeting. In your report, include specifics such as the type of agent with whom you spoke, the various types of authority which the agent has, and how the agent is compensated. In an interview, it is usually wise to have several prepared questions before meeting with the individual.

CASES FOR STUDY

1. *P* asks *A* to sell *P*'s collection of rare books. *P* instructs *A* to have the books appraised and add on an additional 10 percent to the appraised value to determine the selling price. In return, *A* is to receive 5 percent of the selling price as a commission.

   a) When the bill arrives for the appraisal fee, *P* refuses to pay, stating that he never contracted for the charge. Must *P* pay the bill? Why or why not?

   b) *A* places an advertisement in a rare book collector's trade magazine describing *P*'s library and requesting interested buyers to submit offers. *A* pays for the ad and seeks reimbursement from *P*. *P* refuses to reimburse *A* arguing that he never intended that *A* expend money for advertising. Is *P* correct? Explain.

c) *A* pays a bribe to the appraiser to submit a low appraisal fee to *P*. *A* actually sells the books for a much larger figure and keeps the difference plus 5 percent of the amount *P* believes is the selling price. *P* discovers what has happened. What action does he have against *A*?

d) Assume *A* finds a buyer who is not willing to pay *P*'s asking price (10 percent over the appraised value). *A* tells the prospective buyer (*B*) that *P* will lower the price. Must *P* accept the new terms? Explain.

e) Consider the same facts as stated in part (d) except that *B* asks *P* directly whether the original selling price is firm. *P* acknowledges to *B* that if no one buys at a higher price, he will allow *A* to negotiate a price. At a later date, *A* agrees to *B*'s lower offer even though *P* has not as yet specifically told *A* he may do this. Is *P* bound? Why or why not?

f) *P* wants the books sold to a private collector and not to a dealer. *D* is a dealer as is indicated by her letterhead on which she writes a letter to *P* during the price negotiations. Can *P* revoke the sale based on the fact that *A* is acting outside the scope of his authority by allowing a dealer to enter into the negotiations? Explain.

2. *X* is a tenant in a building owned by *Y*. *X* performs minor repair work around the building, shovels the sidewalk, and maintains the lawn and shrubbery in exchange for reduced rent. One night, upon returning to the building, *X* sees someone he thinks is a prowler walking by the building. He runs to his apartment, picks up a pistol, returns, and shoots. When he does so, he wounds the suspect who, as it happens, is an innocent person out walking his dog. Does the victim have an action against *Y* as well as *X*? Explain.

3. *L* is the personnel manager for a company. She is directed to interview candidates and hire an office manager at an annual salary of $10,000. *L* finds a candidate, *C*, who seems well qualified and offers her $15,000 a year. *C* accepts and begins work on September 1. *C*'s first monthly paycheck is issued on October 1 and she notices that the gross amount of the check is one-twelfth of $10,000 instead of $15,000. When she learns what has happened, she sues the firm for an additional $5,000 a year, arguing that even though *L* had no authority to offer $15,000, the company had ratified the actions. Will *C* win in court? Why or why not?

Chapter 14

The Partnership

OBJECTIVES

After studying this chapter, the student will be able to

- describe the ways in which partnerships are created and terminated.
- list the three types of partners and describe their duties and rights.
- identify the liabilities of partners and partnerships.
- define the following words and phrases.

partnership	partnership capital
partner	trading partnership
Uniform Partnership Act	nontrading partnership
entity	dissolution
articles of partnership	winding up
general partner	receiver
silent partner	Uniform Limited Partnership Act
incoming partner	limited partner
partnership property	limited partnership

A *partnership* is a form of business created by the agreement of two or more persons to operate as coowners or *partners,* for the purpose of making a profit. It is not a new idea; the partnership concept can be traced back to ancient times. Modern partnership laws were clarified in 1914 by the Uniform Partnership Act (UPA), which has been adopted by almost every state.

Legally, a partnership is not an *entity;* that is, it is not something that has real existence in itself. Rather, according to the law, it is an *aggregation* (combination) of its members. For this reason, most law suits are brought in the names of the individual partners as well as in the name of the company. Business people and courts do, however, treat the partnership as an entity in some situations. For example, ownership of property can legally be in a firm's name.

Persons enter into partnerships for many reasons. One party may have a product and the other party the financial resources to produce it. Partners can share responsibility and work. The partnership may be able to obtain more credit than an individual and may pay less taxes than if the partners worked alone or became incorporated. In addition, the partnership is a very flexible business association.

CREATION OF THE PARTNERSHIP

A partnership can be created by the simple agreement of two or more parties either in writing or orally. All of the essentials of a valid contract must be present. Also, if the partnership is governed by the Statute of Frauds, it must be in writing.

If such an agreement is not in writing, the law usually holds that a partnership exists if the parties are sharing in the profits and management of the business. The UPA applies to partnership relationships which are not in writing, or to situations not covered in written agreements. Partners are free in most instances to modify the UPA by specific agreement.

Articles of Partnership

Most partnerships are formed by drawing up a written agreement known as *articles of partnership*, figure 14-1. This document usually includes (1) names of partners, (2) name of firm, (3) place of business, (4) nature of the business, (5) term of partnership, (6) equal or unequal duties of partners, (7) capital investment of each partner, (8) how profits and losses are to be shared, (9) bookkeeping methods. (10) drawing accounts, and (11) provisions for termination.

Capacity to be a Partner

Any person who is legally competent to make a binding contract may become a partner. Since a minor's contract is voidable, a minor has the right to disaffirm a partnership at any time prior to the age of majority. The capital investment of the minor, however, usually cannot be withdrawn until all debts of the partnership are satisfied.

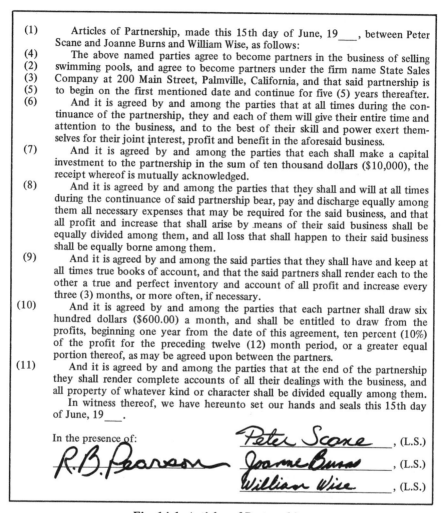

(1)   Articles of Partnership, made this 15th day of June, 19___ , between Peter Scane and Joanne Burns and William Wise, as follows:

(4)   The above named parties agree to become partners in the business of selling
(2) swimming pools, and agree to become partners under the firm name State Sales
(3) Company at 200 Main Street, Palmville, California, and that said partnership is
(5) to begin on the first mentioned date and continue for five (5) years thereafter.
(6)   And it is agreed by and among the parties that at all times during the continuance of the partnership, they and each of them will give their entire time and attention to the business, and to the best of their skill and power exert themselves for their joint interest, profit and benefit in the aforesaid business.

(7)   And it is agreed by and among the parties that each shall make a capital investment to the partnership in the sum of ten thousand dollars ($10,000), the receipt whereof is mutually acknowledged.

(8)   And it is agreed by and among the parties that they shall and will at all times during the continuance of said partnership bear, pay and discharge equally among them all necessary expenses that may be required for the said business, and that all profit and increase that shall arise by means of their said business shall be equally divided among them, and all loss that shall happen to their said business shall be equally borne among them.

(9)   And it is agreed by and among the said parties that they shall have and keep at all times true books of account, and that the said partners shall render each to the other a true and perfect inventory and account of all profit and increase every three (3) months, or more often, if necessary.

(10)   And it is agreed by and among the parties that each partner shall draw six hundred dollars ($600.00) a month, and shall be entitled to draw from the profits, beginning one year from the date of this agreement, ten percent (10%) of the profit for the preceding twelve (12) month period, or a greater equal portion thereof, as may be agreed upon between the partners.

(11)   And it is agreed by and among the parties that at the end of the partnership they shall render complete accounts of all their dealings with the business, and all property of whatever kind or character shall be divided equally among them.

      In witness thereof, we have hereunto set our hands and seals this 15th day of June, 19___ .

In the presence of:

R. B. Pearson   *Peter Scane* , (L.S.)

Joanne Burns , (L.S.)

William Wise , (L.S.)

Fig. 14-1 Articles of Partnership

Types of Partners

The articles of partnership usually define the role of each partner.

General Partners are actively engaged in the management of the partnership. They have full powers and full personal liability. In figure 14-1, all partners are general partners.

Silent Partners do not take an active role in the business. Their names are not used, and their relationship to the company is usually not known to the public. They are, however, fully liable for all partnership obligations.

Incoming Partners are brought into an established business as new partners. They are not personally responsible for old obligations of the firm, unless they agree otherwise. However, any capital contribution they make to the firm upon joining could be used to satisfy old debts.

PARTNERSHIP PROPERTY

Property, in one form or another, is the basis of most business transactions. When a partnership is formed, it is important to establish which property belongs to the partnership and which belongs to individuals of the partnership. If the relationship is dissolved and there are profits, they may be a question of how the assets are to be distributed. If there is insolvency by the partnership or by an individual of the partnership, *creditors* (persons to whom a debt is owed) must know which property they can claim to satisfy debts. Creditors of the partnership are entitled by law to have first claim on partnership property. Creditors of the individuals have first claim on the property of those individuals.

Generally, all property originally contributed by members of the firm is considered part of the partnership property. Also included is all property later acquired with partnership funds or as a result of partnership knowledge or services.

Example. Mary Ann owns a car when she becomes a partner in a firm. She transfers the car to the partnership. The value of the car is considered her capital contribution. The car is then considered partnership property.

Example. Mark purchases a car with company funds to use on company business. In this situation, also, the car is considered partnership property.

Rights of Partners in Specific Partnership Property

Each member of the partnership has an equal right to possess and use partnership property for purposes of the partnership, regardless of the amount of the individual's original investment. A partner does not have the right to use partnership property for personal use without the consent of the other partners.

Example. Consider the previous example on page 280. Mark's car can be used by any of his partners for company business. Mark, however, cannot take the car on vacation unless his partners agree.

Partnership Capital

Partnership capital is the amount of goods, money, or services contributed to the firm by each member. It may be an unequal sum; if so, it must be returned in the same proportion at the end of the partnership, although other assets may be divided equally.

Example. *B* and *C* form an equal partnership. *B* contributes $10,000 and *C* contributes a truck worth $2,000. At the termination of the relationship, the capital investment of $10,000 to *B* and $2,000 to *C* is paid first (after any creditors are paid). Any additional profits are then divided equally.

MANAGEMENT OF THE PARTNERSHIP

In the absence of another agreement, each partner has the right to an equal voice and an equal vote in the management of the business. This is true even if the capital investment of the partners is unequal. Partners may assign certain management tasks to certain partners, but they usually each have a vote on major decisions or changes.

Example. *B* and *C* in the previous example, unless otherwise stated in their agreement, have an equal voice in the business, even though *B* has a greater capital investment in the firm.

COMPENSATION OF PARTNERS

Salaries

Partners are not actually paid wages or a salary for carrying out partnership business, unless it is agreed upon between the partners. The monies paid partners are actually *draws* (funds drawn) against expected profits from the business. If one partner performs other services for the firm, there is no extra money paid without a prior agreement.

Profits and Losses

In the absence of an agreement stating otherwise, profits are divided equally, regardless of capital contribution. Partners are also equally liable for losses the business may encounter. If there is an agreement outlining unequal profit sharing, the same agreement applies to unequal responsibility for any losses incurred.

Example. Walker and Ames are partners in a distributing business. They agree that 60 percent of the profits are Walker's and 40 percent are Ames'. After eight months, the business is terminated due to insolvency. Walker claims that since they had a partnership, he and Ames are equally liable for the losses. The courts rule that the liability for losses is to be divided in the same proportion as the profits would have been — 60 percent of the loss is Walker's and 40 percent is Ames'.

DUTIES OF PARTNERS

Good Faith and Loyalty

A partnership is a relationship of mutual trust and confidence which requires good faith and loyalty on the part of each of the partners. Each partner is performing acts for which the other partners may be held liable. Partners are agents of the partnership and each other, and are held to a fiduciary duty.

All money earned by each partner while conducting company business must be returned to the partnership. Also, all information relative to the business must be communicated to the other partners.

Example. Baines, a partner in a trucking firm, makes a delivery two days early and receives a sizable bonus which he keeps for himself. When his partner, Lane, learns of the bonus, he claims that the money should have gone into company funds. The courts hold that Baines was on company business and therefore, that the bonus belongs to the company, not to Baines as an individual.

Reasonable Skill and Care

Each partner is responsible for using reasonable skill and care in conducting partnership business within the granted authority. If a partner makes an honest mistake in judgment which results in a loss, that partner is not liable to the other partners. If, however, the loss is due to negligent behavior, that partner must bear the loss.

Example. Baines, the partner in the previous example concerning the trucking firm, has the job of delivering a rush order that must arrive at its destination in two days. Baines stops to go fishing en route. When he arrives four days late, the order is refused. Baines is liable to pay his partner, Lane, for the loss due to his negligent behavior.

Example. Consider again the Baines and Lane partnership. Suppose Baines is delayed due to flooding of the roads he must travel and detours en route. He arrives late and the order is refused. He is not liable to Lane in this situation, since the delay was through no fault of his own.

Accounting

The Uniform Partnership Act requires that records of the partnership be kept and be made available at the place of business for inspection at any time by any of the partners. Partners must also keep an accurate accounting of business funds expended and profits made.

POWERS OF PARTNERS

In the absence of an agreement between partners, each partner has the power to act as an agent for the partnership. When there are limitations, third parties must be made aware of them. If they are not, the actions are still binding. The UPA limits the power of a partner without the authorization of all the other partners in such acts as selling all the partnership assets, paying or assuming a debt of a partner, or providing gratuitous (free) services.

Trading and Nontrading Partnerships

A *trading partnership* is one in which the partners engage in buying and selling for profit, such as in a store or manufacturing operation. In a *nontrading partnership,* the partners are engaged in providing a service, such as in law, medicine, or real estate. In trading partnerships, partners have much greater power to borrow money, buy on credit, and make binding contracts in the name of the partnership, with the partnership held liable for the transactions. In nontrading partnerships, partners generally have little or no power to bind the partnership in such credit or borrowing situations.

Example. Steve Cone, a partner of Cone and Sons Clothing Store, orders 200 men's suits for the store on credit from a manufacturer with whom he has dealt for years. Steve's father, another partner, refuses to pay for the suits. The courts hold Cone and Sons liable for the bill. Steve Cone has the power to bind the trading partnership to the purchase.

PARTNERSHIP LIABILITY
Contract Liability

Partners are jointly liable on all partnership contracts. A suit against a partnership names each partner, since a partnership is not a legal entity and does not protect the individuals from personal liability. A partner's individual assets may be claimed if the partnership assets cannot satisfy the debt.

Example. A creditor sues William Morgan, Robert Hayes, and their partnership, Morgan and Hayes Sales Associates, for the amount of a bill for office furniture bought by Morgan. Since Hayes is a member of the partnership, he is also liable for the bill and thus is also named in the suit.

Tort Liability

The same standards governing agency law apply to partnership law in determining liability for torts or wrongful acts of a partner. If the wrong is committed within a partner's scope of authority while he or she is conducting company business, the partnership is liable. Tort actions are always brought against the partners jointly and severally (individually). If judgment is attained, it is against assets of the partnership as well as the individual assets of each of the partners named.

Example. While driving his car on company business, Morgan, a partner in Morgan and Hayes Sales Associates described in the previous example, hits and injures a bike rider. The bike rider can name Morgan and Hayes Sales Associates as well as Morgan and Hayes individually in his suit for damages. The full amount of the judgment can be recovered from the partnership or either of the partners.

Criminal Liability

A partnership cannot be held liable for the crime of one partner even if the crime is committed while the partner is conducting company business. If however, the partnership or other partners authorized or participated in·the crime, they are held criminally liable.

Example. While on business at a client's home, Morgan, of Morgan and Hayes Sales Associates, steals a rare coin collection from a desk. Neither the partnership nor Hayes are held criminally liable. Only Morgan is charged with the crime.

TERMINATION OF THE PARTNERSHIP

A partnership is *dissolved* (ended) when there is a change in the relationship of the partners. A period of *winding up* then takes place during which the assets are *liquidated* (turned into cash). *Termination* takes place only after all partnership affairs are concluded.

Most businesses are worth more while in operation than if they liquidate. For that reason, most partnership agreements include plans for continuing the operation if a business partner withdraws or dies, since otherwise, the partnership is automatically dissolved under such circumstances.

Dissolution

Dissolution may take place because of expiration of the time period of the contract, or upon completion of a certain objective for which the partnership was created. Also, all the partners may vote unanimously to dissolve the partnership.

Any partner may dissolve the partnership by notifying the other partners of withdrawal. If, however, the partner withdraws and thus violates the original agreement, that partner may be held liable for damages for breach of contract. The UPA allows the other parties to continue the business themselves or locate new partners if there is such a breach.

According to the UPA, the death or bankruptcy of any partner automatically dissolves a partnership. Operation of law also dissolves a partnership if one partner becomes insane, or if the business can only be conducted at a loss.

Example. In an informal partnership with no written agreement, one of the two partners dies. The surviving partner must then wind up the business since the death of a partner terminates the business. The survivor may associate with someone else later, but that would create a new partnership.

Case Example. The following case demonstrates one way in which partners may attempt to avoid terminating a business should a partner die. In this case, the partners provided to purchase the deceased partner's interest for a fixed dollar amount.

MUNDY v. HOLDEN
Supreme Court of Delaware, 1964
204 A.2d 83

CAREY, J. This is an appeal from a decree of the Court of Chancery for Kent County directing specific performance of a contract for the sale of a deceased partner's share in the partnership.

In 1945, William C. Holden and Gilbert H. Mundy entered into an informal partnership in Dover, Delaware, as an automobile agency. During subsequent years, the partnership continued to prosper, and the parties, on January 25, 1954, executed a formal written partnership agreement.

After recitals indicating that the partners shared equally in all assets and interests of the partnership, the agreement provided, inter alia [among other things]:

"As a part of the consideration of this partnership agreement, IT IS MUTUALLY UNDERSTOOD AND AGREED that in the event of the death of one of the partners during the existence of the partnership, the surviving partner does covenant and agree to purchase from the estate of the deceased partner the share or interest of the deceased partner for the sum of Forty Thousand Dollars ($40,000) and to make settlement for the same within three months from the date of death and said partner, and the executor or administrator of the deceased partner is hereby authorized, empowered and directed to consummate said sale and to execute any and all papers necessary to be executed in order to carry out the provisions hereof to transfer and assign all of the right, title and interest of the partner so dying in and to the assets of said partnership, upon condition that the surviving partner shall assume and pay all of the then existing debts and obligations of said partnership. The surviving partner shall continue the operation of said business without interruption."

On April 14, 1959, the parties executed a written modification to the agreement which effected a change in the status of the financial reserves of the partnership but expressly reaffirmed the remaining terms of the original agreement. Following the death of Gilbert H. Mundy on May 31, 1963, William C. Holden, the surviving partner, tendered the sum of $40,000 to the Executor of the estate of the deceased partner, Holden having paid or assumed the debts due outside creditors. Tender of this sum was refused upon the ground that it was insufficient and, accordingly, plaintiff brought an action in the Court below seeking to compel an assignment of the interest of the deceased partner to him upon payment of $40,000. The Court below. . .[gave judgment to plaintiff and defendants appealed].

Before this Court, defendants urge that the tender of $40,000 was insufficient because they contend that plaintiff was also required to tender the amount of Mundy's share of capital and profits accumulated on the date of his death. In short, defendants argue that such capital investment is an "existing debt and obligation of said partnership" to be assumed and paid by the survivor.

•　　•　　•

These defendants, in the lower Court, urged that the tender of $40,000 was insufficient; in fact, the second affirmative defense in their answer avers that part of the retained capital was a separate debt and obligation owing to the deceased partner. . . .

Defendants initially contend that. . .the words "debts and obligations" are inherently ambiguous. Specifically, defendants contend that the invested capital of a partner may properly be considered a debt or obligation of the partnership. As stated by the Missouri Court of Appeals:

"It is the general rule that capital furnished by any partner, in the absence of agreement to the contrary, is a debt owing by the firm to the contributing partner, and necessarily is to be repaid him, if the firm assets are sufficient after paying the firm liabilities to outsiders. . . ." *Chapin's Estate* v. *Long*, 205 Mo. App. 414, 224 S.W. 1012, 1013 (1920).

But the mere recital of this legal principle does not resolve the question presented by this appeal. The rule set forth in Chapin's Estate and the other authorities cited supra [above] applies only in the absence of an agreement to the contrary. In the instant case, the parties have specifically provided for the manner of dissolution of the firm upon death of one partner and we must consider that entire agreement to determine whether the parties have expressed an intent not to treat capital as a "debt or obligation". . . .

[The Court then interpreted the partnership agreement to mean that the $40,000 figure included the deceased partner's original capital contribution, and that according to the agreement, plaintiff did not need to pay any additional sums to defendants.]

Defendants then contend that since the book value of each party's interest was substantially in excess of the $40,000.00 figure at the time of the agreement, it is unreasonable to presume that the parties would have contracted for a sale of the share of each for

$40,000.00. We do not know what the capital shares were when the parties reaffirmed their agreement in April, 1959; the excess was considerably smaller at the time of Mundy's death. In any event, this dissolution provision only applied upon the death of one partner, neither partner could predict who would survive to enjoy the benefits of these provisions. As stated by the Supreme Court of Pennsylvania:

"Neither could know to whom the option to purchase would fall; and if, during the running of the agreement, because of large additions or reductions, the price might become inequitable, either party had the remedy in his own hands, as without his assent they could not be made." In re *Rohrbacher's Estate*, 168 Pa. 158, 32 A. 30, 31 (1895).

The decision of the lower Court is affirmed.

Winding Up

After dissolution, the next step to termination of a partnership is the winding up process, during which assets are liquidated and creditors are paid. The remainder is distributed to the partners. The business may continue to operate although new contracts or new business is usually not accepted.

The partners may wind up the business themselves if the dissolution is friendly and all partners are available. If death or bankruptcy is a cause of dissolution, the surviving or solvent partners are responsible for the winding up. When a court decree causes dissolution, a person known as a *receiver* is usually appointed to handle the liquidation.

Distribution of Assets

If the results of the winding up process show a profit, the assets are distributed equally among the partners or as agreed upon. If, however, the liquidation results in a loss, the UPA establishes the order of distribution of funds. Creditors of the partnership have first claim on partnership assets; creditors of the individuals have first claim to the individual's assets. Figure 14-2 outlines a situation showing the distribution of funds from an insolvent partnership.

LIMITED PARTNERSHIPS

The Uniform Limited Partnership Act (ULPA), adopted by almost every state, sets out regulations for limited partnerships. A limited partnership is composed of one or more general partners and one or more limited partners.

Quinn and Bowles Company, a partnership, dissolves. After winding up, they end up with assets of $20,000. The firm owes $30,000 to creditors, so they wind up with a company liability of $10,000. Quinn has personal assets of $40,000 and personal liabilities of $5,000. Bowles has personal assets of $15,000 and personal liabilities of $15,000. Charted, this information is:

	Co. Assets	Co. Liab's	Pers. Assets	Pers. Liab
Quinn & Bowles Co.	$20,000	$30,000		
Quinn			$40,000	$ 5,000
Bowles			15,000	15,000

Following the UPA rule, partnership creditors take the $20,000 in partnership assets, leaving a partnership liability of $10,000. Quinn's creditors take $5,000 from his personal assets, leaving him $35,000. Bowles creditors take all of his $15,000, leaving him no personal assets. The chart as it now appears is:

	Co. Assets	Co. Liab's	Pers. Assets	Pers. Liab
Quinn & Bowles Co.	-0-	$10,000		
Quinn			$35,000	-0-
Bowles			-0-	-0-

Since the personal creditors had been satisfied, the partnership creditors could now go to Quinn's personal assets and claim $10,000, leaving him $25,000. Bowles is still liable to Quinn for one-half of that, or $5,000, since each partner is liable for an equal portion of the losses in this partnership. The final chart appears as:

	Co. Assets	Co. Liab's	Pers. Assets	Pers. Liab
Quinn & Bowles Co.	-0-	-0-		
Quinn			$25,000	-0-
Bowles			-0-	-0-

Fig. 14-2 Distribution of funds from an insolvent partnership

General partners are responsible for the operation and management of the business. They are subject to standard partnership liability.

Limited partners are only liable to the firm and its creditors to the extent of their original contributions. Limited partners cannot participate in the management of the company. Also, the firm name may not include the name of limited partners, since this might imply that they were general partners. Even though these restrictions exist against a limited partner, the appeal of that status is the limited liability.

Example. Badger, Cox, and Helms wish to form a limited partnership. Helms is to be a limited partner with Badger and Cox acting as general partners. Helms insists that the name of the firm be Helms, Badger and Cox, since he is contributing the greatest amount of cash for the venture. The law does not allow them to do this, since Helms is only a limited partner. No matter how great his investment, his name cannot appear in the title of the firm, with one exception as noted in Section 5 of the ULPA.

The statutory requirements are stricter in a limited partnership than in a general partnership due to the limited liability of one or more of the partners. According to the ULPA, a certificate must be filed with a designated authority in the county or state. This must include the name of the firm; the nature and address of the business; the term for which the business exists; the name and home address of each general partner; the name, home address, and amount of contribution of each limited partner; and the share of profits due to each limited partner. The purpose of this certificate is to make public the fact that one or more of the partners is only partially obligated for partnership liabilities.

Most other rules of general partnership apply to limited partnerships. For example, a limited partner has the right to inspect the accounting books of the partnership at any time and to be fully informed of all company affairs.

SELF-EVALUATION

Provide a brief explanation for each of the following.

1. Define partnership.
2. What limitation is placed on a minor when the minor disaffirms a partnership?
3. Explain the liability obligations of general partners, silent partners, and incoming partners.
4. What right do partners have concerning partnership property?
5. When a partnership is terminated, how is capital divided?
6. How is a partnership managed?
7. Describe how partners are paid.
8. If one partner is to receive 75 percent of the profits, for what percentage of the losses is that partner liable?
9. What are three duties of partners?
10. How does partnership relate to agency?

11. Differentiate between the powers of a partner in a trading and a nontrading partnership.

12. Can a partnership be sued? Why or why not?

13. Partners *B* and *C* are sued. There are not enough company funds to cover the claim. What recourse does the plaintiff have?

14. Is a partnership liable for torts and crimes of the partners?

15. What must occur before a partnership is terminated?

16. List five ways in which partnerships are dissolved.

17. What occurs during the winding up process?

18. In *Mundy* v. *Holden*, why didn't the UPA stipulation regarding the dissolution of a partnership upon the death of one partner automatically apply?

19. The partnership of *B* and *C* is $100,000 in debt. *B* has $100,000 in personal assets and $20,000 in personal liabilities. What happens to *B*'s assets? What must *C* do?

20. How does the creation of a limited partnership differ from that of a general partnership?

21. What is the liability of a limited partner to the partnership?

22. What are two ways in which a limited partner is restricted in a limited partnership?

23. What do the abbreviations UPA and ULPA mean?

24. Differentiate between silent partners and limited partners.

SUGGESTED ACTIVITIES

1. Wind up the partnership of Carter, Band and Munn Company, according to the following description, showing the distribution of funds.

Partnership assets: $1,550,000   Band assets: $140,000
Partnership liabilities: $2,650,000   Band liabilities: $140,000
Carter assets: $1,200,000   Munn assets: $5,400,000
Carter liabilities: $75,000   Munn liabilities: $100,000

2. Wind up Carter, Band and Munn Company with figures from the previous activity with this change: partnership assets are $3,650,000, and partnership liabilities are $1,550,000. (Disregard any capital investments in this problem.)

CASES FOR STUDY

1. Pickle and Hempel are in business together, but have never formalized their arrangement with a writing. They call their business Pickle-Hempel Company. Pickle contributes $20,000 at the outset and Hempel contributes $10,000. Both persons have been drawing $10,000 a year from the profits for five years.

   Answer the following questions regarding the relationship.

   a) Are Pickle and Hempel partners? Explain.

   b) If Hempel wants to end the relationship, can he do so? Explain.

   c) Hempel wants to leave because the partnership is heavily in debt. Can he withdraw to escape liability for the debt? Why or why not?

   d) The business goes bankrupt. Assuming that there are funds remaining after the creditors and capital contributions of Pickle and Hempel are paid, is Pickle correct in demanding twice a much in profit as Hempel, since he contributed twice as much money in the first place? Explain.

2. *X* and *Y* are partners in a consulting business. After two years of operation, *X* decides to take control of the hiring and firing of personnel, acceptance of clients, and supervision of the bookkeeping system, since she has had more business experience in these areas than *Y*. *Y* does not like the new arrangement. What arguments does *Y* have to support her position?

3. *C* loans money to *M* to purchase a new boat for personal use. *M* is a member of a partnership; *C* is aware of that association. If *M* is unable to make payments, may *C* look to the partnership for payment?

4. *G* is a general partner in a law firm comprised of four attorneys. She is concerned about the aspect of full liability in partnerships and decides that she wants to become a limited partner. The other three agree and the partnership agreement is modified to state that *G* is a limited partner. Aside from that, no procedures in the partnership change. Is *G* liable only to the extent of her capital contribution? Explain.

5. *D* and *E* form a partnership. *D* is driving a car which belongs to the partnership on partnership business when he is involved in an accident due to his own negligence. The injured party sues *D*, the partnership, and *E* for damages. Are the partnership and *E* obligated to pay damages when *D* was the negligent party? Why or why not?

6. Mason, a partner in a firm, is found guilty of driving while intoxicated (a crime), and is fined a large sum of money. Can the other partners in the firm be held liable for the fine? Explain.

Chapter 15

The Corporation

OBJECTIVES

After studying this chapter, the student will be able to

- identify five types of corporations.
- describe the formation of a corporation and the ways in which it may be terminated.
- discuss the powers of corporations.
- explain the role of shareholders and describe the way in which they are paid dividends.
- outline the management structure of corporations.
- define the following words and phrases.

corporation	treasury stock
legal entity	stock certificate
governmental corporation	par value
not-for-profit corporation	common stock
profit corporation	preferred stock
business corporation	cumulative stock
domestic corporation	bonds
foreign corporation	stock assignment form
promoter	proxy
Model Business Corporation Act	cumulative voting
articles of incorporation	dividends
certificate of incorporation	cash dividends
charter	stock dividends
bylaws	stock split
officer	reverse stock split
ultra vires	director
capital stock	inside director
retained earnings	outside director

securities	quorum
debt securities	minutes
equity securities	consolidation
stock	merger
issued stock	insolvency
nonissued stock	bankruptcy

The corporation is the predominant form of business organization in America today.   Unlike a partnership, the corporation is viewed as an artificial being referred to as a *legal entity*; it may sue and be sued in its corporate name, and it may acquire, hold, and convey property.   There must be governmental consent for its creation, and it is not dissolved by the withdrawal or death of one of its members.   This gives corporations a permanency not experienced by some other forms of business.

One of the most important characteristics of a corporation is that its members are exempt from personal liability of the firm beyond the amount of their individual shares.   This limited liability is perhaps one of the major advantages of a corporation.

The idea upon which the corporation is based dates back to the Romans and early English.   With the rapid development of business in early America, the concept of the corporation was used as a means of limiting the liability of a firm's members.   In 1811, New York State passed the first statute concerning corporations operating for profit, which established strict guidelines for the granting of charters and the procedures involved in their operation.   The statutes in most states today allow much greater flexibility in corporate operations than the 1811 statute.

TYPES OF CORPORATIONS

Corporations are generally divided into three classifications: governmental, not-for-profit, and profit.   Each of these types is usually regulated by a separate set of statutes.   A corporation is also classified as either domestic or foreign, depending on its place of incorporation.

Governmental Corporations

Governmental corporations are corporations organized for public purposes.   They are generally created by state or federal governments.   For example, cities, towns, state universities, and school districts may all be incorporated.

Not-For-Profit Corporations

A *not-for-profit corporation,* as its name implies, is a corporation in which there is no purpose of receiving a profitable return on the money invested. If there is a surplus of capital, it cannot be distributed among its members. Hospitals, churches, fraternities, charitable organizations, and schools may be not-for-profit corporations.

Profit Corporations

A *profit corporation* is a corporation created to transact business with the purpose of distributing returns to its shareholders in the form of dividends. Profit corporations include manufacturers, wholesalers and retailers, and construction businesses. They are often referred to as *business corporations.*

Domestic and Foreign Corporations

A corporation is *domestic* in the state in which it is chartered. When it functions in any other state, that same corporation is considered to be *foreign.* As a foreign corporation, it must follow special regulations in the state in which it is doing business. It may be taxed as a foreign corporation in addition to the taxes it pays in its own state. For this reason, it is wise for those planning a corporation to consider carefully in which state they wish to be incorporated.

CREATING A CORPORATION

Who May Incorporate

Most states require three or more parties to incorporate. In a few states, however, one person or a partnership may be an incorporator.

The Promoter

Much of the work done to promote or organize a corporation is done by a party called a *promoter.* The promoter may be an attorney, one of the incorporators, or an individual whose profession consists of organizing capital and business opportunities for a fee.

Promoters have many functions: they plan the organization, locate the financial backing for the company, negotiate all the necessary contracts and leases, incorporate the business, and get the new business going.

Promoters hold unique positions. They are not agents, since there is not yet a corporation to be the principal. They are, however, held to a fiduciary duty as if they were agents. It is usually necessary for the promoter to make contracts on behalf of the corporation which is to be formed, but as yet is not. The corporation is not bound by these contracts. Thus, the contracts made for such transactions as attorney's fees, purchase of property, and printing costs are actually the personal liability of the promoters. When the corporation is formed, it may agree to adopt such contracts and thus assume the liability.

If the new corporation does not agree to adopt the contracts, the promoters are held liable. Corporations would not, of course, agree to adopt contracts that were fraudulent or beyond their powers. In cases where the planned corporation does not come into being, the promoter is held personally liable for all pre-corporation contracts.

Example. Payne agrees to become a promoter for *A, B,* and *C's* new corporation. Payne signs a purchase contract in his own name on a warehouse for the corporation's use. The charter is not granted to *A, B,* and *C.* Payne sues them for the price of the warehouse. Judgment is against Payne, and he is judged liable for the price of the warehouse. As a promoter, this was one of his risks.

The Model Business Corporation Act

The Model Business Corporation Act, often called simply the Model Act, was adopted in 1946 by a committee of the American Bar Association. It was created to be used as a guide for states to update their statutes on corporate regulations. Most states today use all or part of the Model Act in their statutes.

Articles of Incorporation

The first step to incorporation is the preparation of the *articles of incorporation.* According to the Model Act, the provisions which must be included are:

1. Name of the proposed corporation, including the word *corporation, incorporated,* or *limited,* or an abbreviation of those words, *Corp., Inc.,* or *Ltd.*

2. The purpose or nature of the business, which in most states can be in general terms.

3. The city and county in which the principal office is to be located.

4. The duration of the corporation.

5. (a) The amount of authorized capital stock the corporation will issue and the number and types of shares into which the stock is to be divided; and (b) the amount of capital stock with which it will commence business.

---

1) The name of the proposed corporation is:
   BDS Associates, Incorporated

2) The purpose for which this corporation is formed is as follows:
   To engage in the manufacture and sale of garden tools.

3) The office of the corporation is to be located in the Town of Porterville, County of Easton, Any State.

4) The existence of this corporation is to be perpetual.

5) (a) The amount of total authorized capital stock of the corporation shall be Five Hundred Thousand Dollars ($500,000.00), which shall be divided into Fifty Thousand (50,000) shares of the par value of Ten Dollars ($10.00) each.

   (b) The amount of capital stock with which it will commence business is Two Hundred Thousand Dollars ($200,000.00), being Twenty Thousand (20,000) shares at Ten Dollars ($10.00) each.

6) The names and addresses of the incorporators and number of shares of stock subscribed by each are as follows:

Name	Address	Number of Shares of Common Stock
Bart Stahl	75 Homer Street Porterville, Any State	10,000
Douglas Frazer	R.F.D. No. 3, Box 12 Porterville, Any State	5,000
Sally Young	10 Johnson Street Porterville, Any State	5,000

7) The names and addresses of the initial directors are as follows:

Bart Stahl	Address above
Douglas Frazer	Address above
Sally Young	Address above
Alan Osgood, Attorney	43 Main Street Porterville, Any State

We, the undersigned, for the purpose of forming a Corporation under the laws of Any State do make and file this agreement and we have accordingly set our hands this 1st day of May 19___.

Witnessed:

_____ (L.S.)   _____ (L.S.)

_____ (L.S.)   _____ (L.S.)

_____ (L.S.)

Fig. 15-1 Articles of incorporation (simplified form)

6. Names and complete addresses of each incorporator, with the number of shares of stock for which each of them will subscribe.

7. Names and addresses of initial directors.

After the articles of incorporation are completed and signed, they must be mailed to the designated authority, usually the secretary of state. The appropriate fees outlined in the state regulations must be sent along with the form. Figure 15-1 illustrates a simplified form of articles of incorporation.

Certificate of Incorporation

When articles of incorporation have been approved and all necessary monies have been paid, the secretary of state issues a *certificate of incorporation,* also called a *charter.* This is basically composed of the articles of incorporation with the state seal affixed, and the signature of the appropriate state official.

Organizational Meeting

After the charter has been granted, the Model Act requires an organizational meeting by the directors named in the articles. The main purposes of the meeting are to elect the officers and adopt by-laws. The *officers* run the day-to-day operations of the business. The *bylaws* are regulations concerning duties and conduct of the members of the corporation.

The bylaws usually outline the time and place of annual meetings and board of directors meetings, the manner in which special meetings are called, how amendments are made, voting rights of the incorporators, dividend schedules of various classes of stock, and other rules regarding the conduct of the corporation business.

After this final step in the incorporation process is completed, the company can begin functioning to complete its purpose.

POWERS OF THE CORPORATION

Express Powers

A corporation obtains express powers from the statutes of the state in which it is chartered. These include the power to have a name and seal, to sue and be sued in the corporate name, to own and transfer property used in the business, to make certain contracts, and to make and alter the corporation's bylaws.

The articles of incorporation also outline express powers by defining the purpose and objectives of the corporation, which must, of course, be within the guidelines of the statutes. It is important that investors know the purposes of the corporation so that they are aware of how their money is to be used.

Example. Ace Homes Corp. has defined its purpose in broad terms as the construction of single and multiple family dwellings. One director wants to use some of the corporation's funds to *speculate* (risk capital in hope of gain) in an oil well project. This action is beyond the power of the Ace Homes Corp. and thus is considered illegal. The investors have placed their money in a construction company, not an oil well drilling company.

Implied Powers

Most corporations have adequate implied powers to accomplish the purposes stated in their articles of incorporation. The objectives outlined in the articles are often stated in general terms to allow the corporation to assume implied powers when necessary.

Example. An automobile sales corporation uses its implied power to sell accessories for the cars they sell. Being able to offer the customer popular accessories such as whitewall tires and FM radios helps them to sell more cars, which is their major purpose.

Ultra Vires

Originally, powers of corporations were quite strictly defined in statutes and in the articles of incorporation. Any act of a corporation outside of such authority was void, or *ultra vires* (beyond the power allowed). Today, however, most statutes and articles are stated in very general terms and corporations are given very broad powers. The result is that the doctrine of ultra vires is rarely cited in court cases today.

FINANCING THE CORPORATION

The initial funds for a corporation are usually provided by investors obtained by the promoter. It is normally easier to obtain such investors for an incorporated business than for an unincorporated business because those investing in an incorporated business risk only the amount of the investment; the investor's personal assets cannot be touched, as they can be in a partnership.

The initial investment is known as the *capital stock* and may be in the form of property, equipment, ideas, or money. The investors then receive shares of stock in proportion to their investment. Some states set a minimum figure for the capital that a corporation must have to begin business.

Example. In figure 15-1, the capital stock used to start BDS Associates, Incorporated is $200,000.00. (See item 5 (b).) In the same figure, item (6) shows the number of shares subscribed by each of the incorporators.

For most corporations, this initial capital is only enough to begin the business; usually, more funds are needed to operate it. Further financing may be accomplished by the use of *retained earnings* — investing profits earned by the business back into the business. Another method is to offer securities to outside investors. *Securities* are instruments which represent shares or interests in property or in enterprise which show an obligation of the issuer. There are *equity securities,* called *stocks,* and debt *securities,* called *bonds.*

Stock

Every corporation must issue some equity securities. The corporation charter specifies the total authorized capital stock that can be issued, and how it is to be divided.

Example. In figure 15-1, the total authorized capital stock as shown in item 5 (a) is $500,000.00, divided into fifty-thousand shares with the face value of $10.00 each.

All of the shares defined in the authorized capital stock do not have to be issued. That portion which is issued and owned by stockholders is called *issued stock.* That portion which is not is called *nonissued stock.*

Treasury stock is issued stock which has been bought back by the corporation. It can either be kept or reissued at any price. If it is held by the corporation, no dividends are paid on it and no one may vote the shares at a shareholder's meeting.

When an individual purchases one or more shares of stock in a corporation, a stock certificate is issued. A *stock certificate* represents a person's portion of interest in that corporation, figure 15-2.

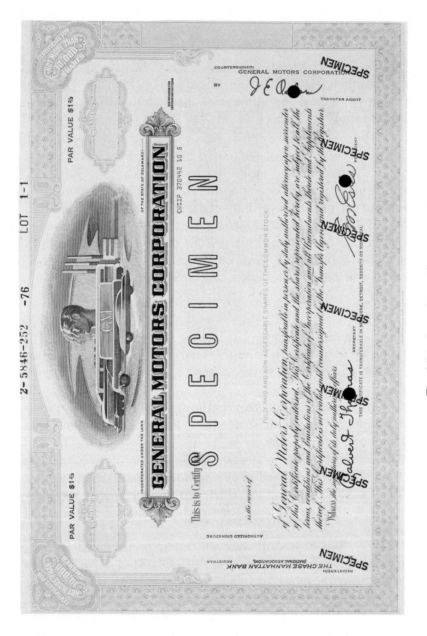

Fig. 15-2 A stock certificate

The stockholder is entitled to a share in the profits of the company and in the assets if the corporation is dissolved.

Par Value. Corporations place a monetary worth on each share of stock, called its *par value* (literally, its *face value*). This is specified in the articles of incorporation. (See figure 15-1, 5(a).) The stock must initially be sold by the corporation for the full par value. After the original issuance, buyers on the market, however, may buy or sell for the market price, which may be more or less than par value. This is why treasury stock, since it has already been issued once at par value, can be reissued at any price.

Common Stock. Holders of common stock have control of the corporation by virtue of their voting power. They have voting rights at all shareholders' meetings in proportion to the number of shares they own. With these votes, they elect the directors of the company. Common stock owners share the profits of the company with other common stock owners.

Common stock prices may vary greatly on the stock market. Thus, holders of such stock have a greater chance to gain if the company is successful than do holders of preferred stock. Common stock owners also have a greater risk, however, as they are usually the last on the list to be paid if the company has financial problems.

Preferred Stock. Preferred stockholders have, as the name implies, preferences or rights over other classes of stockholders. They have one of the first claims on profits. Also, on the distribution of assets upon dissolution, the preferred stockholder is usually paid first, even if there is nothing remaining for the common stockholder. Preferred stockholders usually do not have the right to vote, although they do have ownership in the corporation.

Preferred stock is more secure than common stock since there is generally less fluctuation in its price on the market. The potential for high profit, however, is usually more limited than for common stock.

Most preferred stock is *cumulative,* meaning that if dividends are not declared one year, the money is accumulated and is paid to the preferred shareholder the next year. Common stock is not cumulative and, therefore, dividends which are not paid one year are not paid in any succeeding years. However, there can also be noncumulative preferred stock.

The following abbreviations, when used in the inscription on the face of this certificate, shall be construed as though they were written out in full according to applicable laws or regulations:

TEN COM — as tenants in common

TEN ENT — as tenants by the entireties

JT TEN — as joint tenants with right of survivorship and not as tenants in common

UNIF GIFT MIN ACT — .... Custodian ....
                                              (Cust)   (Minor)
under Uniform Gifts to Minors
Act ....
                        (State)

Additional abbreviations may also be used though not in the above list.

For value received _____ hereby sell, assign and transfer unto

PLEASE INSERT SOCIAL SECURITY OR OTHER
IDENTIFYING NUMBER OF ASSIGNEE

(PLEASE PRINT OR TYPEWRITE NAME AND ADDRESS INCLUDING POSTAL ZIP CODE OF ASSIGNEE)

_____ Shares

represented by the within Certificate, and do hereby irrevocably constitute and appoint

_____ Attorney

to transfer the said Shares on the books of the within named Corporation with full power of substitution in the premises.

Dated _____ 19___

In presence of

NOTICE: THE SIGNATURE TO THIS ASSIGNMENT MUST CORRESPOND WITH THE NAME AS WRITTEN UPON THE FACE OF THE CERTIFICATE IN EVERY PARTICULAR WITHOUT ALTERATION OR ENLARGEMENT OR ANY CHANGE WHATEVER.

Fig. 15-3 Assignment form on back of stock certificate

Bonds

Corporations often raise money by issuing debt securities, commonly called bonds. *Bonds* are evidence of a debt. Bondholders are creditors of the corporation and receive interest on their loans. Corporations often prefer to issue bonds rather than stock since the interest paid on bonds is a tax deduction, but dividends paid on stock are not. Bondholders usually do not have voting rights in the corporation.

SHAREHOLDERS

Over thirty million Americans from all walks of life are shareholders. They may have become owners in any of several ways. Regulations for stock transfers are covered in Article 8 of the Uniform Commercial Code.

Purchasing Stock

Individuals usually buy stock through a broker at the daily market price and pay a commission to that broker. Daily closing prices for major stocks are listed in the stock market section of major newspapers.

Stock Transfers

According to the UCC, certain steps must be taken once ownership in stock is transferred. The stock certificate, as pictured in figure 15-2, is the evidence of ownership of an intangible share of stock, which is considered personal property. On the back of the certificate, figure 15-3, is an *assignment form* to be completed and signed by the seller when the stock is transferred.

The certificate must then be delivered to the buyer. The buyer surrenders the certificate to the transfer agent at the corporation. That agent is required to note the transaction in the corporate transfer records and issue a new certificate to the new owner. The corporate transfer records are an accurate record of all current shareholders in a corporation, figure 15-4, page 306. Such a transfer is normally handled through a broker.

Shareholders' Meetings

While the ownership of a corporation is in the hands of the shareholders, management of the company is the job of the directors. The shareholders elect or remove these directors at annual meetings that are required by the Model Act. Shareholders also may vote on other matters, as outlined in the Model Act. These may include amendment of the articles of incorporation, approval of loans to officers, and voluntary dissolution.

Notice. The Model Act and most state statutes require that written notice of the date, time, and place of the annual meeting and of special meetings be delivered not less than ten and not more than fifty days before the meetings to all shareholders eligible to vote. If notice is not given, all actions taken at the meeting may be canceled.

The Meeting. The chairman of the board of directors usually conducts the shareholders' meeting. The Model Act requires that at least one-third of the stockholders be represented for any business to be conducted. Many state statutes, however, set the minimum as a majority of the shareholders.

ATTACH CANCELLED CERTIFICATE HERE

CERTIFICATE NO.   FOR _____ SHARES

Use Form Below For Transfer From Original Issue

FROM WHOM TRANSFERRED:

ISSUED TO

DATED _____ 19 ____

DATED ____

ORIGINAL CERTIFICATE NUMBER	Number Original Shares	Number of Shares Transferred

RECEIVED CERTIFICATE

Record of Transfer of Surrendered Certificates

NO. ____ FOR ____ SHARES
THIS ____ DAY OF ____ 19 ____

NEW CERTIFICATES ISSUED TO:	Number of Shares Transferred	Number of New Certificates

DATED   19

Fig. 15-4 Page from a corporation transfer book

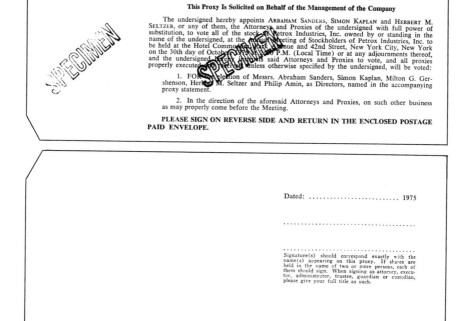

Fig. 15-5 A Proxy Statement (Front and Back)

Shareholders have the right to full participation in the meetings. They can ask questions, make proposals, or speak for or against a proposal.

Voting. Each share of stock entitles the holder to one vote at the shareholders' meeting, as defined in the articles of incorporation. Shareholders who cannot attend can vote by proxy. To vote *by proxy,* absentees must send a statement appointing an agent to vote for them. Figure 15-5 illustrates a proxy statement sent out by the management of a corporation. Opposition to management can also send out proxy statements to request that shareholders vote their way in an upcoming vote.

Most states provide for *cumulative voting* which allows minority shareholders to be represented on the board of directors. The number of shares held by each shareholder is multiplied by the number of directors to be elected. The shareholder can then accumulate

Presume that there are 900 shares of a corporation outstanding, owned by two people. *A* owns 790 shares and *B* owns 110 shares. There are 8 directors to be elected from a slate of 9 nominees.

Under straight voting, *A* elects all directors. Under cumulative voting, *B* is able to elect one director as shown below:

A is entitled to 790 (shares) x 8 (directors), or 6,320 votes
B is entitled to 110 (shares) x 8 (directors), or 880 votes

B casts all votes for one director, candidate 9, and *A* spreads his votes over his *8* candidates. (To simplify the problem, assume that *A* votes for candidates 1 and 8 as charted, to avoid a runoff situation.)

Candidate	Votes by A	Votes by B
1	785	0
2	790	0
3	790	0
4	790	0
5	790	0
6	790	0
7	790	0
8	795	0
9	0	880

By this method, directors 2 through 9 are elected, and a minority shareholder has representation on the board of directors.

Fig. 15-6 Cumulative voting problem

the votes and place them on one candidate or spread the votes among several candidates.

Example. There are three directors to be elected for the ZIP Corporation board. Sands has 500 shares. Cumulative voting is allowed, so Sands has 1,500 votes (number of shares times number of directors to be elected). Sands has many options; for example, he can place all 1,500 votes on Director *A*, 500 votes each on Director *A*, *B*, and *C;* or 1,000 on *A* and 250 each on Director *B* and *C*.

Figure 15-6 shows how cumulative voting can help a minority stockholder.

Inspection of Records

According to the Model Act, shareholders have the right to inspect many of the books and records of their corporations, if there is a good reason. They could not, of course, inspect the records to gain information for competitors, for their personal gain or for any unethical reason. The Model Act outlines penalties, including damages for which corporate officers who refuse proper requests to inspect corporate books are liable.

Example. Shareholder Kroll makes a request to inspect corporate records to identify his fellow shareholders. When the company secretary learns that Kroll wants to write each shareholder in an effort to replace some of the corporate directors, the request is refused. The courts uphold Kroll's request since it is for a proper purpose. Kroll, as a shareholder, is part owner of the company, with the right to elect management that he feels will best run the company.

DIVIDENDS

Business corporations exist to make a profit. Individuals become shareholders so that they can share these profits. This is done by distribution of *dividends,* which are funds from profits divided among the holders of certain types of stock.

Each year, the board of directors decides whether or not there are sufficient funds to declare and pay a dividend. They must follow statutory regulations as to the validity of such payments. For example, the Model Act and almost all state statutes forbid dividend payments which would cause insolvency.

Example. A corporation has $500,000 in assets (total property) and $700,000 in liabilities (total debts). They are not able to pay a dividend, since doing so would leave them insolvent (with more liabilities than assets).

State statutes vary regarding which funds can be used for payment of dividends. Sometimes, net profit for a certain year can be used, even though there were net losses from other years. At other times, surplus can be used. Surplus occurs when assets exceed liabilities plus stated capital. Dividends, when issued, are usually paid in either cash or stock.

Cash Dividends

Cash dividends are paid to the appropriate shareholders as decided upon by the board of directors. (They are actually not paid in cash, but rather in the form of corporate checks.)

Example. Jane has 100 shares of ABC, Inc. common stock. A sum of $100,000 is allotted by the board of directors of ABC, Inc. to be divided among the 50,000 common stockholders. (The preferred shareholders are paid separately.) Each shareholder receives $2.00 per share; hence, Jane receives a cash dividend check for $200.00.

Stock Dividends and Stock Splits

A *stock dividend* occurs when additional shares of corporation stock are distributed to shareholders instead of cash. The advantage to the shareholders is that if cash dividends are paid at the same rate per share at a later time, there are more shares on which dividends are paid.

Example. Jane, from the previous example, is issued ten shares of ABC, Inc. stock as a stock dividend on the 100 shares she already owns. The following year, a cash dividend of $2.00 per share is declared. Jane, who would have earned $200.00 on her 100 shares, now earns $220.00 because of the extra stock dividend she received the year before.

A *stock split* is different from a stock dividend in the sense that it is a change in the par value of the stock, but with the total capital remaining the same. The shareholders must approve an amendment to the articles to make a stock split, since the par value is specified in the articles. A stock split is normally used to lower a high market price per share to encourage new investors.

Example. A board of directors may propose a split from 2,000 shares of stock at $100.00 per share to 4,000 shares at $50.00. The capital amount of $200,000.00 remains the same (2,000 times $100.00 and 4,000 shares times $50.00). The market price has been lowered so that it is within the reach of more investors.

There may also be a *reverse split* of stock, which is a decrease rather than an increase in the number of shares. The capital again remains the same. This is often used to adjust the market price.

Example. The board of directors of Kemco, Inc. proposes a reverse stock split from 12,000 shares at $3.00 per share to 6,000 shares at $6.00. The capital amount of $36,000.00 remains the same (12,000 shares times $3.00 and 6,000 shares times $6.00). The market price has been raised to a more attractive figure for Kemco investors.

MANAGEMENT

Directors

One of the major functions of stockholders as owners of a corporation is to elect *directors,* who, as a group, are called the *board of directors.* Directors who are also company officers are called *inside directors.* They are familiar with affairs of the corporation since they are closely involved in management. *Outside directors* bring outside knowledge to the board by way of their expertise in law, finance, politics, or other fields. They are not connected in any other way with the corporation which they serve. Their function is to apply their knowledge to the corporation they represent.

The Model Act makes no requirements as to ownership of stock by directors, their residency, or the number of directors. However, these requirements may be specified in the articles. Some state statutes do require some of these specifications and provide that they must appear in the articles or the bylaws.

Statutory regulations give corporate directors the authority to manage all of the business affairs of the company and make major decisions concerning the company, except those which are reserved for the shareholders. Under the Model Act, certain corporate actions must be handled by the directors, such as declaring dividends and filling vacancies on the board. They also elect and assign duties to the officers, establish executive salaries, and approve company operating plans. Most directors are paid a nominal sum for their services.

Board of Directors Meetings. Directors gather at regular intervals as defined in the bylaws. They may also hold special meetings if proper notice is given. Each director has one vote, regardless of the amount of stock held. For the directors to act at a meeting, there must be a quorum present. A *quorum,* normally a majority of the directors, is specified in the bylaws or articles.

Example. The bylaws of Hempel Co. state that ten directors must be present at directors meetings before voting can take place. Between meetings, one director dies and one resigns. A board meeting is called, and of the eight remaining directors, five attend. Those present feel that five constitutes a quorum (a majority of the eight existing directors), but later learn that the business they transacted is void. The quorum must be a majority of the directors required by the bylaws which, for this corporation, is six (the majority of ten).

An accurate record, known as *minutes,* must be kept of all board meetings. They contain the time and place of the meeting, a list of those who attended, and the proposals that were made and their outcome. They should be safeguarded since they may be needed at a later time to prove what actions were or were not taken. They must also be kept available for shareholders to inspect so that they can learn what is taking place in their company.

Obligations.   Although directors are not strictly defined as agents, they are responsible to the corporation in much the same manner that agents are obligated to their principals. They must act within the authority given to the corporation by statutes, bylaws, and articles. They may be held liable for damaging acts if they act beyond this authority. They have a definite fiduciary duty to the corporation.

Case Example.   Courts carefully guard the fiduciary duty owed by directors to their corporations. Notice in the following case that the majority of the court is not willing to excuse competition with the corporation even when, according to the dissent, the business that defendant took over was of no value to the corporation. Two dissenting opinions are included with this case to show some additional views on the situation, although they do not, of course, change the outcome of the case.

ROBERT N. BROWN ASSOCIATES, INC.
v.
FILEPPO

**Supreme Court of New York, Appellate Division
38 A.D.2d 515, 327 N.Y.S.2d 133 (1971)**

PER CURIAM. [Majority of the Court agreed to this opinion without one particular judge taking credit for writing it.]
. . .The defendant Fileppo was employed by plaintiff [a printing company] as salesman pursuant to written contract dated December 31, 1960. Fileppo was made Vice President and Secretary and employed as salesman at a weekly salary of $150, later increased to $200, plus an expense account of $50, and one-third of plantiff's

profits. He resigned as employee on March 21, 1968, but remained an officer, director and stockholder of plaintiff. Fileppo was required to devote all his time to the business of the corporation and covenanted not to engage directly or indirectly in any other business. Fileppo was permitted to be "interested in any noncompetitive business." In 1965, Fileppo acquired stock and became the principal of Graphein Associates Ltd. Thereafter, and prior to his resignation from plaintiff's employ, Fileppo obtained printing orders from customers of the plaintiff and turned them over to Graphein. Fileppo's said conduct constituted a breach of his contractual obligation not to engage in any other business and to devote all his time to plaintiff's business. . . .Moreover, as an officer of the plaintiff he was under an obligation not to compete with or profit personally at the expense of the plaintiff. [Citation omitted.]

The provision in the employment contract that Fileppo might "be interested in any non-competitive business" is subject to the proviso that such interest "does not infringe upon (Fileppo's) duties and time under the terms of this agreement." It is not a grant to Fileppo either of the right to compete with plaintiff or to utilize his time and effort therefor.

. . .Fileppo does not deny that he did not disclose to plaintiff his interest in defendant, Graphein Associates Ltd., or that he was turning over to it printing orders he had obtained. Such covert conduct bespeaks guilty knowledge of Fileppo's obligation not to compete with plaintiff and to devote all his time to plaintiff's business. Even if Fileppo had first offered the orders to plaintiff and it had refused them, which is not the case, he was not free to divert them to a competitor for his profit without the express consent and approval of the plaintiff. . . .

It is not a matter of defense that the orders diverted to Graphein may have been of insignificance or no value to the plaintiff as claimed in substance by Fileppo. This may be a factor relevant on the damages, if any, sustained by plaintiff; it does not affect the plaintiff's right to an accounting.

Plaintiff-appellant is clearly entitled to an accounting based on the contract's definition of the relationship of the parties. The objections of our brethren to such an accounting really sum up to no more than objections to certain items of business of which, it is asserted without real contradiction, defendant-respondent deprived plaintiff by diverting them elsewhere. If these items are actually outside the contract's purview, the accounting will award plaintiff nothing for them, but their existence cannot deprive plaintiff of its contract-based right to have an accounting [of the business diverted by the defendant].

[Court decides Fileppo must account to plaintiff for any profits gained from his dealings with Graphein.]

KUPFERMAN, J. (dissenting):

The majority would foreclose analysis of the facts and of the real relationship, alleged by Fileppo, between his interest in Graphein Associates, Ltd. and his duty to the plaintiff. It is Fileppo's contention that rather than being competition, his other connection was beneficial to the plaintiff, because it meant that lesser assignments which plaintiff would consider of no value or an undesirable costly chore, could be handled by his other company, and the customer relationship thus satisfactorily sustained. Rather than being a breach of trust or a diversion of profit, it could be, depending on the facts proven, a benefaction to the employer, while still of comfort to the employee. Potiphar received no less from Joseph, but the judgment was also summary. Genesis, Chapter 39.

McGIVERN, Justice Presiding (concurring in the dissent):

The basic fallacy of the majority stance is that it preemptorily concludes that Fileppo has breached his obligation to plaintiff despite the permissive lee-way of his contract: ". . .except that he may be interested in any non-competitive business provided such interest does not impinge upon his duties and time under the terms of this agreement." This is a not unambiguous arrangement, and I do not see that on this submission, a court can conclude a transgression occurred as a matter of law. . . . And noteworthy is the development that although Fileppo avows that Graphein did not compete, that in fact it was complementary to the plaintiff, that plaintiff realized increasing profits, nevertheless the reply affidavit is not made by an interested party having personal knowledge of the pertinent and determinative facts, but by counsel. . . .As noted [above] the [record in this case] precludes a determination as a matter of law that there has been a breach of an agreement or of a fiduciary relationship. Thus, in my judgment, Special Term was correct, and we should affirm.

Directors must act with due care and skill in their functions for the corporation. If they act negligently, they are held liable for any resulting losses. As with agents, however, directors are not held liable for losses when they are caused by an error in judgment.

Directors must act in good faith and in loyalty to the corporation. The benefit of the company must be their major concern. They cannot profit at the expense of the corporation. Directors also cannot use knowledge that they have and which others do not have for personal gain.

Example. Horton, a director for Southern Paper Company, Inc., learns at a board meeting that the firm has just received an unusually large federal contract. The announcement is to be made public in one week. Knowing that this will substantially raise the value of the stock, Horton immediately buys a large block of shares at the low market price. After the announcement, he sells the shares for almost twice what he had paid. Horton is charged with not acting loyally and in good faith. He used information that was unavailable to other security holders for personal gain. Horton is forced to pay back the profits he made as a result of the information gained as a director.

The agency rule regarding torts and crimes also applies to corporations. Directors may be held liable for torts if they have participated in them. They are held liable for crimes if they have acted beyond their authority.

Officers

Officers of a corporation are responsible for the day-to-day operation of the business such as the hiring and firing of employees and office policy. They are hired, appointed, or elected by the board of directors. The Model Act provides that there is to be a president, one or more vice-presidents, a secretary, and a treasurer. Unless a state statute forbids it, two or more offices may be held by the same person, such as president and treasurer. It is common practice for the president, at least, to also be a director.

Officers are general agents of the corporation. They have express authority as granted by the board, the bylaws and/or the articles. They also have the implied authority to do what is necessary to carry out their functions.

Corporate officers have approximately the same liabilities for their actions as directors and are also held to a fiduciary duty. When they are acting for the corporation, it is wise for them to have the authority in writing.

Case Example. Consider the following case in which the president had the daily responsibility of management and the directors did not.

BATES v. DRESSER

U.S. Supreme Court, 1919
251 U.S. 524, 40 Sup. Ct. 247, 64 L. Ed. 388
[Most citations have been omitted.]

MR. JUSTICE HOLMES delivered the opinion of the court.

This is a bill in equity brought by the receiver of a national bank to charge its former president and directors with the loss of a great part of its assets through the thefts of an employee of the bank while they were in power. The case was sent to a master who found for the defendants; but the District Court entered a decree against all of them. . . .The Circuit Court of Appeals reversed this decree, dismissed the bill as against all except the administrator of Edwin Dresser, the president, cut down the amount with which he was charged and refused to add interest from the date of the decree of the District Court. . . .Dresser's administrator and the receiver both appeal, the latter contending that the decree of the District Court should be affirmed with interest and costs.

The bank was a little bank at Cambridge with a capital of $100,000 and average deposits of somewhere about $300,000. It had a cashier, a bookkeeper, a teller, and a messenger. Before and during the time of the losses Dresser was its president and executive officer, a large stockholder, with an inactive deposit of from $35,000 to $50,000. From July, 1903, to the end, Frank L. Earl was cashier. Coleman, who made the trouble, entered the service of the bank as messenger in September, 1903. In January, 1904, he was promoted to be bookkeeper, being then not quite eighteen but having studied bookkeeping. In the previous August an auditor employed on the retirement of a cashier had reported that the daily balance book was very much behind, that it was impossible to prove the deposits, and that a competent bookkeeper should be employed upon the work immediately. Coleman kept the deposit ledger and this was the work that fell into his hands. There was no cage in the bank, and in 1904 and 1905 there were some small shortages in the accounts of three successive tellers that were not accounted for, and the last of them, Cutting, was asked by Dresser to resign on that ground. Before doing so he told Dresser that someone had taken the money and that if he might be allowed to stay he would set a trap and catch the man, but Dresser did not care to do that and thought that there was nothing wrong. From Cutting's resignation on October 7, 1905, Coleman acted as paying and receiving teller, in addition to his other duty, until November, 1907. During this time there were no shortages disclosed in the teller's accounts. In May, 1906, Coleman took $2,000 cash from the vaults of the bank, but restored it the next morning. In November of the same year he began the thefts that come into question here. Perhaps in the beginning he took the money directly. But as he ceased to have charge of the cash in November, 1907, he invented another way. Having a small account at the bank, he would draw checks for the amount he wanted, exchange checks with a Boston broker, get cash for the broker's check, and, when his own check came to the bank through the clearing house, would abstract it from the envelope, enter the others on his book and conceal the difference by a charge to some other account or a false addition in the column of drafts or deposits in the depositors' ledger. He handed to the cashier only the slip from the clearing house that showed the totals. The cashier paid whatever appeared to be due and thus Coleman's checks were honored. So far as Coleman thought it necessary, in view of the absolute trust in him on the part of all concerned, he took care that his balances should agree with those in the cashier's book.

By May, 1907, Coleman had abstracted $17,000, concealing the fact by false additions in the column of total checks, and false balances in the deposit ledger. Then for the moment a safer concealment was effected by charging the whole to Dresser's account. Coleman adopted this method when a bank examiner was expected. Of course when the fraud was disguised by overcharging a depositor it could not be discovered except by calling in the pass-books, or taking all the deposits slips and comparing them with the depositors' ledger in detail. By November, 1907, the amount taken by Coleman was $30,100, and the charge on Dresser's account was $20,000. In 1908 the sum was raised from $33,000 to $49,671. In 1909 Coleman's activity began to increase. In January he took $6,829.26; in March, $10,833.73; in June, his previous stealing amounting to $83,390.94, he took $5,152.06; in July, $18,050; in August, $6,250; in September, $17,350; in October, $47,277.08; in November, $51,847; in December $46,956.44; in January, 1910, $27,395.53; in February, $6,473.97; making a total of $310,143.02, when the bank closed on February 21, 1910. As a result of this the amount of the monthly deposits seemed to decline noticeably and the directors considered the matter in September, 1909, but concluded that the falling off was due in part to the springing up of rivals, whose deposits were increasing, but was parallel to a similar decrease in New York. An examination by a bank examiner in December, 1909, disclosed nothing wrong to him.

In this connection it should be mentioned that in the previous semi-annual examinations by national bank examiners nothing was discovered pointing to malfeasance. The cashier was honest and everybody believed that they could rely upon him, although in fact he relied too much upon Coleman, who also was unsuspected by all. If Earl had opened the envelopes from the clearing house, and had seen the checks, or had examined the deposit ledger with any care he would have found out what was going on. The scrutiny of anyone accustomed to such details would have discovered the false additions and other indicia of fraud that were on the face of the book. But it may be doubted whether anything less than a continuous pursuit of the figures through pages would have done so except by a lucky chance.

The question of the liability of the directors in this case is the question whether they neglected their duty by accepting the cashier's statement of liabilities and failing to inspect the depositors' ledger. The statements of assets always were correct. A by-law that had been allowed to become obsolete or nearly so is invoked as establishing their own standard of conduct. By that a committee was to be appointed every six months "to examine into the affairs of the bank, to count its cash, and compare its assets and liabilities with the balances on the general ledger, for the purpose of ascertaining whether or not the books are correctly kept, and the condition of the bank is in a sound and solvent condition." Of course liabilities as well as assets must be known to know the condition and, as this case shows, peculations [embezzlements] may be concealed as well by a false understatment of liabilities as by a false show of assets. But the former is not the direction in which fraud would have been looked for, especially on the part of one who at the time of his principal abstractions was not in contact with the funds. A debtor hardly expects to have his liability understated. Some animals must have given at least one exhibition of dangerous propensities before the owner can be held. This fraud was a novelty in the way of swindling a bank so far as the knowledge of any experience had reached Cambridge before 1910. We are not prepared to reverse the finding of the master and the Circuit Court of Appeals that the directors should not be held answerable for taking the cashier's statement of liabilities to be as correct as the statement of assets always was. If he had not been negligent without their knowledge it would have been. Their confidence seemed warranted by the semiannual examinations by the government examiner and they were encouraged in their belief that all was well by the president, whose responsibility, as executive officer; interest, as large stockholder and depositor; and knowledge, from long daily presence in the bank, were greater than theirs. They were not bound by virtue of the office gratuitously assumed by them to call in the pass-books and compare them with the ledger, and until the event showed the possibility they hardly could have seen that their failure to look at the ledger opened a way to fraud. . . .We are not laying down general principles, however, but confine our decision to the circumstances of the particular case.

The position of the president is different. Practically he was the master of the situation. He was daily at the bank for hours, he had the deposit ledger in his hands at times and might have had it at any time. He had had hints and warnings in addition to those that we have mentioned, warnings that should not be magnified unduly, but still that taken with the auditor's report of 1903, the unexplained shortages, the suggestion of the teller, Cutting, in 1905, and the final seeming rapid decline in deposits, would have induced scrutiny but for an invincible repose upon the *status quo.* In 1908 one Fillmore learned that a package containing $150 left with the bank for safe keeping was not to be found, told Dresser of the loss, wrote to him that he could but conclude that the package had been destroyed or removed by someone connected with the bank, and in later conversation said that it was evident that there was a thief in the bank. He added that he would advise the president to look after Coleman, that he believed he was living at a pretty fast pace, and that he had pretty good authority for thinking that he was supporting a woman. In the same year or the year before, Coleman, whose pay was never more than twelve dollars a week, set up an automobile, as was known to Dresser and commented on unfavorably, to him. There was also some evidence of notice to Dresser that Coleman was dealing in copper stocks. In 1909 came the great and inadequately explained seeming shrinkage in the deposits. No doubt plausible explanations of his conduct came from Coleman and the notice as to speculations may have been slight, but taking the whole story of the relations of the parties, we are not ready to say that the two courts below erred in finding that Dresser had been put upon his guard. However little the warnings may have pointed to the specific facts, had they been accepted they would have led to an examination of the depositors' ledger, a discovery of past and prevention of future thefts.

. . .In accepting the presidency Dresser must be taken to have contemplated responsibility for losses to the bank, whatever they were, if chargeable to his fault. Those that happened were chargeable to his fault, after he had warnings that should have led to steps that would have made fraud impossible, even though the precise form that the fraud would take hardly could have been foreseen. We accept with hesitation the date of December 1, 1908, as the beginning of Dresser's liability, but think it reasonable that interest should be charged against his estate upon the sum found by the

Circuit Court of Appeals to be due. It is a question of discretion, not of right, . . .but to the extend that the decree of the District Court was affirmed,. . .it seems to us just upon all the circumstances that it should run until the receiver interposed a delay by his appeal to this Court. . . .Upon this as upon the other points our decision is confined to the specific facts.

Decree modified by charging the estate of Dresser with interest from February 1, 1916, to June 1, 1918, upon the sum found to be due, and affirmed.

TERMINATION

Consolidation

Two or more corporations can dissolve and form a single, completely new corporation. This is known as *consolidation.* Assets are not liquidated and distributed to shareholders. Instead, securities in the new corporation are given in exchange for the assets of the old corporations.

Merger

In a *merger,* one corporation stays in existence and absorbs one or more other corporations that dissolve. As in consolidation, assets in the dissolved corporations are not liquidated, but rather, securities in the surviving corporation are exchanged for these assets. Debts and liabilities of the dissolved companies are assumed by the surviving corporation.

Insolvency

Insolvency occurs when a corporation can no longer pay its debts. It is not a form of dissolution, but it often leads to it.

Sometimes, however, a careful analysis of the financial structure of a corporation reveals that the business is still sound and should be continued, even though it is insolvent. This could be done by obtaining additional capital or by completely reorganizing the management. Sometimes certain arrangements can be made with creditors to reduce or postpone the debts. Wise guidance should be obtained for help in making these decisions.

Dissolution

A corporation may be dissolved voluntarily if it was organized for a definite period of time and the charter then expires. Also, a majority of the stockholders may vote to dissolve a corporation.

SOME DISTINGUISHING FEATURES OF PARTNERSHIPS & CORPORATIONS	
GENERAL PARTNERSHIP	**CORPORATION**
1. Unlimited liability	1. Limited liability
2. Definite life (death, bankruptcy, withdrawal of partner causes dissolution)	2. Continued existence (does not end if shareholder, director, etc. withdraws)
3. Single taxation (partners are taxed)	3. Double taxation (corporation taxed and then shareholder taxed on dividends)
4. Cannot transfer interest without consent of all partners.	4. Interest freely transferable (shareholder can sell stock)
5. No formal requirements to bring into existence.	5. Must conform to statutes, etc., to form (additional paperwork to meet state and federal requirements)
6. Often difficult to raise capital (must borrow or find new partner which causes dissolution and new partnership arises)	6. Raise capital by selling stock

SOME WAYS TO AVOID DISADVANTAGES OF PARTNERSHIPS AND CORPORATIONS*
1. Limited partnership provides limited liability for some members. (partnership)
2. Provide in articles of partnership for continuation of business in the event of withdrawal of partner. This avoids winding up. (partnership)
3. The Internal Revenue Service allows single taxation of small corporations if certain specific criteria is met. (known as Subchapter Selection) (corporation)
6. Limited partner may provide capital without being exposed to full liability. (partnership)
*Numbers refer to numbers above.

Fig. 15-7 A and B

Most dissolutions of corporations result from insolvency that cannot be remedied and leads to bankruptcy. *Bankruptcy* is actually the systematic distribution of assets of an insolvent company. Most bankruptcies are handled under the federal Bankruptcy Act and thus are under the jurisdiction of the federal courts.

COMPARISON OF PARTNERSHIPS AND CORPORATIONS

Figure 15-7 provides a comparison of some of the features of partnerships and corporations. Organizers of a new business should evaluate their aims and goals and then utilize the form that best suits their particular purposes.

SELF-EVALUATION

Provide a brief explanation for each of the following.

1. What are three distinguishing factors of a corporation as a legal entity?

2. Differentiate between a domestic and a foreign corporation.

3. What must happen for promoters to be released from liability for contracts they make before a corporation is formed?

4. What are a corporation's bylaws, and when and by whom are they made?

5. What is the source of the express powers of a corporation?

6. Name three methods of obtaining funds to operate a corporation.

7. Define par value. Where is the par value of a share of stock specified? How can the par value of a share be changed?

8. What is the difference between cumulative preferred stock and cumulative voting rights?

9. What is the legal meaning of *bond?*

10. On March 1, a notice is sent to shareholders of PDQ Corporation which reads:

   "The annual Shareholders' Meeting of the PDQ Corp. will take place on March 5 at the City Hotel, Chicago, Ill."

   According to the Model Act, is this a valid notice? Explain.

11. A shareholder cannot attend the annual shareholders' meeting, but wants to vote for the directors. What can the shareholder do?

12. What group in a corporation is responsible for deciding to declare and pay a dividend?

13. Differentiate between a cash dividend and a stock dividend.

14. The Board of Directors of LMN Corp. vote to raise the market value of their stock with a reverse stock split. Is this valid? Explain.

15. L. Reeves, local bank president, is a director for the Acme Corporation. C. Hughes, president of that company, is also a director. What type of director is each individual?

16. Of the five directors of a corporation, four own 100 shares and one owns 200 shares. How many votes does each director have at the board meetings?

17. What offices does the Model Act require in a corporation?

18. In *Bates* v. *Dresser,* why did the Court feel that the president was responsible and the directors were not?

19. What term describes the result of one corporation remaining in existence and absorbing one or more corporations that dissolve? What is the result of two or more companies dissolving to form an entirely new corporation?

20. What courts have jurisdiction in bankruptcy cases?

SUGGESTED ACTIVITIES

1. Invest an imaginary $25,000 in the stock market for a period of time suggested by the instructor. Keep records of gains and/or losses. At the end of the designated period, analyze your overall record in a report. Report on economic, national, or world situations that may have influenced the movement of your stocks.

2. Select a U.S. corporation. Learn what the par value of its stock was at issue and its current value. Follow its progress on the stock market for a two- or three-week period.

CASES FOR STUDY

1. *A* and *B* establish a business together on a friendly basis. All agreements are oral. They call their business A & B, Inc. because they learned in a business law course that a corporation offers limited liability to its owners. Is their business a corporation and are they allowed to have limited liability?

2. *D,* a director of ABC, Inc., learns at a board of director's meeting that the corporation is interested in purchasing a certain plot of land upon which to build a plant. *D* buys the land in his own name and sells it to ABC, Inc. at a profit. Does the corporation have a cause of action against *D*? Explain.

3. The Board of Directors of Loew's Construction, Inc. determines that it would be wise to begin manufacturing interiors for recreational vehicles. Since its formation, Loew's has only operated in the housing industry which, as a whole, has fallen off drastically

in recent years. Meanwhile, the recreational vehicle business is booming. Two years into the new project, the recreational vehicle industry also begins to sag, and Loew's finds itself involved in two depressed product lines. The company has to withstand heavy losses which do not please the shareholders. Can the directors be found liable for the losses?

4. *CS* is a common shareholder of Electronics, Inc. *CS* invests in the corporation because it has a consistent record of dividend payments. After *CS* becomes a shareholder, earnings fall and dividends drop off. Can *CS* bring suit to force the board of directors to declare dividends?

5. *PS* is a preferred shareholder of Electronics, Inc. His stock is cumulative. In 1974, Electronics declared no dividend, and in 1975 it declared a dividend on common stock only. Can *PS* sue for dividends?

6. *X* is a self-employed printer. The printing business is incorporated with *X* as president, chairman of the board, and sole employee. A bank loaned money to the corporation when it was first formed, and it is now doubtful that the loan will be repaid. Can the bank sue *X* for repayment of the loan? The bank is arguing that the only reason *X* formed a corporation was to have limited liability and that they should be allowed to take action against *X* since *X* is such an integral part of the corporation.

7. XYZ, Inc. is a small corporation with only four shareholders. All of the shareholders are also officers and directors. One shareholders dies. Must the corporation dissolve? Explain.

8. Acme Supply, Inc. is incorporated in a state whose statutes require cumulative voting when shareholders elect directors. Acme, however, has a provision in its certificate of incorporation which states that the election of directors is to be by straight voting. Which provision controls?

9. *P* is considering establishing a recording business. She finds a site on which to locate the studio, arranges financing, and speaks to some musicians who agree to record. The owners of the property know of *P*'s plans and agree to a clause stating that the sale will not take place unless the corporation is formed and stating that the purchase price is strictly a corporate obligation. The bank requires *P* to sign the loan on behalf of the proposed corporation and in her individual capacity. The musicians have

dealt with *P* on an individual basis and the contract carries *P*'s name only. The recording business becomes a reality and the first item of business on the board of director's agenda is to adopt all of the above contracts. If the corporation defaults· on its obligations, what is *P*'s liability as a promoter?

Section 7

Commercial Paper

Once the basics of business organization are learned, it is necessary to become familiar with the day-to-day operations, many of which involve commercial paper.

Commercial paper refers to specific types of legal documents, sometimes called *instruments.* The four major types of commercial paper are discussed in this chapter. Also covered are the requirements necessary to make such documents *negotiable,* or transferable. The manner in which negotiable instruments are transferred by various types of holders is also detailed.

Commercial paper can be written evidence or proof of a debt. Thus, in these cases, it is a form of credit. *Credit* is a transfer of goods, services, or cash without immediate payment — the buyer is promising to pay at a future time. Commercial paper can also be a substitute for money. If commercial paper is negotiable, it can be transferred from one party to another, as if it were money.

Example. Dollars and coins are used every day as negotiable items. A customer gives five dollars and eighty three cents in cash to the grocer to pay for food. The customer is transferring negotiable items to another party, the grocer. The same transaction takes place if the customer uses a check, one form of commercial paper, to pay for the food. The grocer will, in turn, transfer the cash or the check to someone else to pay for goods or services he has purchased.

Chapter 16 describes negotiable documents that are used every day in the business world. Not all commercial paper is negotiable, such as the IOU. This chapter focuses on negotiable instruments, what makes them negotiable, and the rights and duties of the various parties to such instruments.

Chapter 16

Commercial Paper

OBJECTIVES

After studying this chapter, the student will be able to

- compare and contrast the three types of commercial paper.
- list the five elements that must appear on commercial instruments to make them negotiable.
- describe other terms that appear on commercial documents and some precautions to be taken when writing such papers.
- explain how commercial instruments are negotiated and the various types of endorsements that may be used.
- describe the requirements and rights of a holder in due course.
- explain how negotiable documents are discharged.
- define the following words and phrases.

commercial paper	bearer
negotiable	bearer paper
document	order paper
instrument	time instrument
credit	value received
drawer	antedate
drawee	postdate
payee	transferor
maker	transferee
check	endorser
note	endorsee
promissory note	blank endorsement
certificate of deposit	special endorsement
draft	restrictive endorsement
bill of exchange	qualified endorsement

transferable	holder
unconditional	holder in due course
sum certain	personal defenses
endorsement	real defense

THE CONCEPT OF NEGOTIABILITY

Since commercial paper is used in place of cash, it is used in a setting in which goods, services, or money are given to a party in exchange for the instrument. For example, a buyer purchases goods from a seller and gives the seller a check in the amount of the purchase price. The check is a substitute for cash, but is not exactly the same as cash since the check may be written on a nonexistent account or on an account with insufficient funds to cover the check. In such a case, the check may never be converted to cash. In this situation, the seller has an action against the buyer because the buyer has made a contract to exchange goods for value, and has not fulfilled the obligation of giving value.

It has become important in our economic system that credit be extended in place of cash. Especially for large business deals, cash would be burdensome, and many transactions would not occur at all if cash were required. Sellers are more willing to extend credit to buyers because of the concept of *negotiability*. The seller may transfer a negotiable instrument to a third party for value (usually a sum less than the amount of the instrument). In turn, the third party is willing to purchase the commercial paper because as the document is negotiated, the person holding the note has, in most instances, an almost absolute right to receive payment from the original debtor. In other words, all of the parties involved from the debtor on have greater rights than the seller, who may be liable on the contract that gave rise to the commercial paper in the first place.

Example.   Buyer *B* purchases stock from seller *S* for $2,000. Instead of giving *S* $2,000 in cash, *B* pays for the stock with a negotiable instrument in the amount of $2,000 plus interest. *S* sells (negotiates) the instrument to financier *F* for $1,900. *S* is willing to take $1,900 immediately rather than $2,000 plus interest later with the accompanying risk that *B* will not be able to pay later. *F* will be able to enforce payment from *B* even if something is wrong with the stock. Any defenses *B* has regarding the stock can be asserted against *S*, of course, based on their contract of sale. But the defenses do not prevent payment to *F* who has achieved greater rights in the paper than *S* had.

It can be seen that this negotiation is different than a straight assignment of contract. In an assignment, the assignee receives the same rights as the assignor — no more and no less. When commercial paper is negotiated, the transferee receives greater rights than the transferor. Commercial paper which is not negotiable can still be transferred, but the transferee receives only those rights that the transferor had.

TYPES OF NEGOTIABLE COMMERCIAL PAPER

Drafts

A *draft* is a written order by one individual directing another individual to pay a certain sum on demand, or at a definite time, to

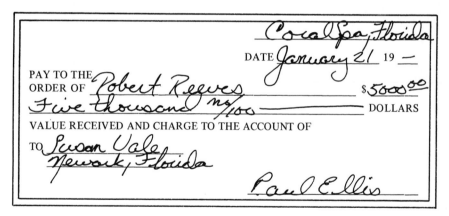

Fig. 16-1 A draft

the bearer or the specific person indicated on the draft. A draft includes any three-party instrument having a drawer, a drawee, and a payee. Drafts are used to exchange debts among three parties. Thus, they are sometimes called *bills of exchange*. Large businesses use drafts quite frequently. Small businesses and individuals do not usually have the need for any other draft except the check.

In the draft in figure 16-1, the drawer, Paul Ellis, orders the drawee, Susan Vale, to pay $5,000 to the payee, Robert Reeves.

Checks

The most common type of commercial paper is the check. It is used every day by business persons and consumers. A *check* is a written order used by a depositor instructing a bank to pay money drawn on his or her account to the bearer or a specific party indicated on the check. When properly filled out, it becomes an *order to pay,* meaning that it is a valid substitute for money and is negotiable.

There are three parties involved in the issuance of a check: the drawer, the drawee, and the payee, figure 16-1. In this example, the *drawer,* or the party drawing money from the bank is Donald Slutes. The *drawee,* or the bank on which the check is drawn, is Seneca Trust. Frederick King is the *payee,* or the party to whom the money is to be paid.

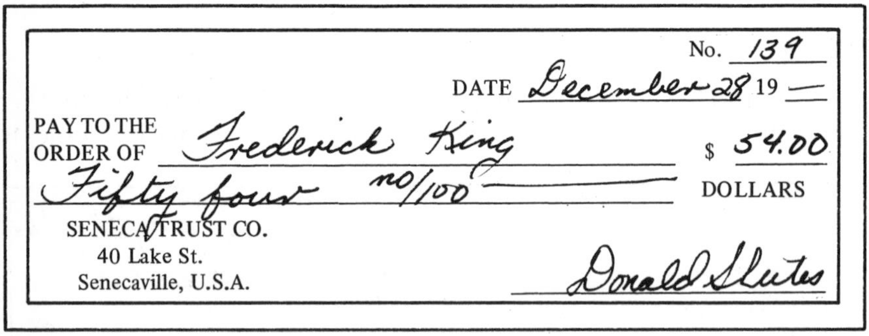

No. *139*

DATE *December 28* 19 —

PAY TO THE ORDER OF *Frederick King* $ *54.00*

Fifty four   *no/100* —————— DOLLARS

SENECA TRUST CO.
40 Lake St.
Senecaville, U.S.A.

Donald Slutes

Fig. 16-2 A check

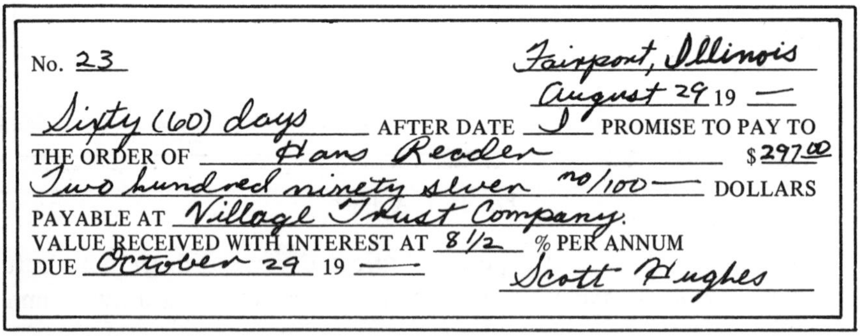

No. *23*

Fairport, Illinois

August 29 19 —

Sixty (60) days _____ AFTER DATE *J* PROMISE TO PAY TO

THE ORDER OF _____ *Hans Reader* _____ $ *297.00*

Two hundred ninety seven *no/100* — DOLLARS

PAYABLE AT *Village Trust Company.*

VALUE RECEIVED WITH INTEREST AT *8 1/2* % PER ANNUM

DUE *October 29* 19 —   *Scott Hughes*

Fig. 16-3 A promissory note

Notes

A *note* is a credit document. It is given by one person to another to obtain goods, services, or cash without paying for them at the time the transaction takes place. The person making a promise to pay at a later time, who issues or gives the note, is referred to as the *maker.* The party to whom the promise to pay is made is the *payee.* A note is sometimes called a *promissory note* because of the promise it contains.

In figure 16-3, Scott Hughes is the maker and Hans Reader is the payee. Such a note, when properly filled out, is negotiable. Whereas a check is a substitute for money, the note is a contract of credit. Both are forms of commercial paper.

Certificates of Deposit

A person may deposit money in a bank with the intent of leaving it there for a certain period of time. The bank promises to repay the depositor that money with interest if the money is left on deposit for the time stated on the *certificate of deposit.* The bank is the maker of the certificate, and the depositor is the payee.

Charles Mason deposits $500 into the Unity Savings Bank and receives a certificate of deposit, figure 16-4. The bank promises to pay Mr. Mason $500, plus interest at 5 percent in twelve months. This document, when properly filled out, is negotiable. Like a check, it can be used in place of cash.

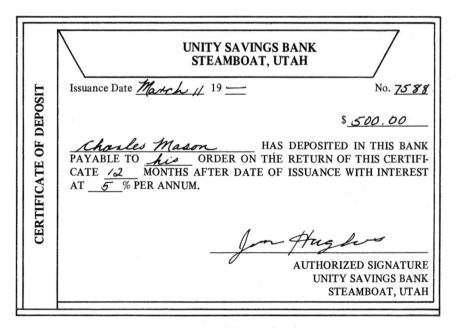

Fig. 16-4 A certificate of deposit

COMMERCIAL PAPER

NOTE	CERTIFICATE OF DEPOSIT	DRAFT (INCLUDING CHECKS)
Credit Document	Savings Document	Exchange of Debt Document
Maker Payee	Maker Payee	Drawer Drawee Payee

Fig. 16-5 The three types of commercial paper

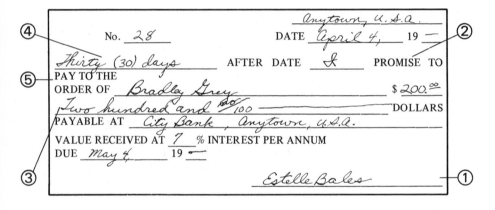

Fig. 16-6 A promissory note illustrating the five required items of commercial paper.

The chart in figure 16-5 outlines the three types of commercial paper, their uses, and the parties taking part in each transaction.

REQUIREMENTS OF COMMERCIAL PAPER

The UCC defines the five items that are required for commercial paper to be negotiable. As an example, a properly completed promissory note will be examined throughout the following discussion of the required items, figure 16-6.

Written and Signed

To be negotiable, the instrument must be in writing and signed. A note or a certificate of deposit must be signed by the maker; a check or draft must be signed by the drawer. See item (1) in figure 16-6. [See UCC § 3-104 (1)(a).]

The UCC in Article 1 clearly defines a signature. It includes "any symbol executed or adopted by a party with present intention to authenticate a writing." [See UCC § 1-201 (39).] This could include initials, an *X,* or any other symbol identifiable to an individual.

Promise to Pay or Order to Pay

On checks, drafts, and certificates of deposit, the words *order to pay,* or *pay to the order of* must appear. Notes must include an unconditional *promise to pay.* The UCC states that other similar wording is acceptable. It must be absolutely clear, however, that an unconditional order or promise to pay exists. To avoid error, it is wise to use the words *order* or *promise.* This section of the text deals only with that usage. [See UCC § 3-104 and § 3-105.] An *unconditional* promise is one that is not limited by conditions or other requirements for its fulfillment. An IOU is not negotiable because it is only evidence of a debt; it does not contain an unconditional promise or order to pay.

Example. The following are notes containing *conditions,* or events which must take place for the promise to be effective.

I promise to pay if I get the job in the gas station.

I promise to pay when I get my annual bonus.

Both of these statements prevent the notes from being negotiable because each places a condition on making the payment. In the first statement, if the individual does not get the job at the gas station, he does not have to pay. If the person in the second example does not get the annual bonus, she does not have to pay.

The proper wording of a promise to pay is illustrated in item (2) in figure 16-6.

Payment in Money or Sum Certain

The payment must be in money. Goods or services cannot be used to pay the amount due. In addition, the payment must be sum certain. *Sum certain* means that the amount must be stated exactly or can be computed from the information on the note itself. In other words, the interest might also be due, but the rate must be clearly stated. In figure 16-6, the sum certain is $200, plus 7 percent interest. [See UCC § 3-106 and § 3-107.]

In the event of a discrepancy between the written words and the figures on an instrument, the amount written in words is the amount payable unless the words are ambiguous. [See UCC § 3-118.] Refer to item (3) in figure 16-6.

Case Example.   The amount payable on the note in the following case is not certain because of a mix-up in the wording. The court attempts to clarify the meaning of the words by examining other statements printed on the face of the note. Notice, also, the court's citation of a rule of construction, i.e., that words control figures. Consider why this rule exists.

WALL v. EAST TEXAS TEACHERS CREDIT UNION
Court of Civil Appeals of Texas, 1975
526 S.W.2d 148

CORNELIUS, J.   Appellee, East Texas Teachers Credit Union, filed this suit against appellant, John L. Wall, to collect a promissory note. In a trial to the court, judgment was rendered for appellee for the sum of $29,949.63 representing principal, interest, and attorney's fees.

The note is as follows:

00
"Note No. 22724 Account No. 3329-99

$19,896.01   May 7, 1971

For Value Received, I/We jointly and severally, promise to pay to the EAST TEXAS TEACHERS CREDIT UNION Credit-Union, or order, at LONGVIEW, TEXAS the sum of Nineteen hundred eight hundred ninety-six ——— and 01/100 Dollars, payable in 1 installments of Seven thousand ——— and No/100 Dollars, and 1 installment of Seven thousand —— and No/100 Dollars
1 at $6,803.48 due September 15, 1971
(X)   which includes principal and interest
( )   plus interest
on the unpaid balance at the rate of One percent per month, both before and after maturity, the installments to be paid
(X) monthly   ( ) semi-monthly ( ) weekly ( ) bi-weekly beginning June 15, 1971
Collateral: Shares, 170 head mixed cattle

•   •   •

SIGNATURE OF	SIGNATURE OF MAKER	ADDRESS
WITNESSES	AND COMAKERS	
_____	X John L. Wall	_____

As indicated, there is a variance between the principal amount of the note as expressed in figures and as expressed in words, the figures providing for "19,896.01" and the words providing for "Nineteen hundred eight hundred ninety-six------------------ and 01/100" Dollars. Appellant's first three points of error contend that the trial court should have granted judgment for principal of only $2,796.01 (Nineteen hundred dollars plus eight hundred ninety-six dollars and one cent) rather than $19,896.01.

Section 3.118 of the Tex. Bus. & Comm. Code Ann., V.T.C.A. provides that in commercial paper words shall control figures, except that if the words are ambiguous, figures shall control. Appellant contends that the words "Nineteen hundred eight hundred ninety-six------------------ and 01/100," although awkward and somewhat unusual, are not ambiguous and therefore they should control over the figure $19,896.01. There are several accepted definitions of the term "ambiguous." It is sometimes said to mean words which are susceptible of more than one meaning. [Citations omitted.] On the other hand, the term has been defined as denoting uncertainty of meaning; wanting in clearness or definiteness; or of doubtful import. [Citations omitted.] Taken literally the words "Nineteen hundred eight hundred ninety-six------------------ and 01/100" may not be susceptible of more than one meaning, but considering that they constitute a grammatically incorrect or unorthodox use of words to express a monetary amount, and considering the additional provisions of the note calling for two payments of Seven Thousand Dollars each, *both also expressed in words,* we conclude that the wording of the note is uncertain of meaning and of doubtful import and therefore ambiguous within the meaning of the Tex. Bus. & Comm. Code Ann. Consequently, the trial court correctly ruled that the principal of the note was $19,896.01.

Judgment affirmed.

[The case was later reversed on other grounds by the Supreme Court of Texas. However, the court specifically agreed with the Court of Civil Appeals that the note was in the amount of $19,896.01. See 533 S.W.2d 918.]

Payable on Demand or at a Specific Time

Commercial paper must be payable on demand, or at a specific time to be negotiable. If it is stated as *on demand,* the paper is payable any time the payee presents the paper for payment. If no time is stated, it is presumed to be payable upon demand. [See UCC § 3-108.] Most checks are payable on demand.

It can also be due at a *specific time,* usually at a later date, which is stated in the document. [See UCC § 3-109.] Most notes and certificates of deposit are payable in the future and are thus called *time instruments.* Item (4) in figure 16-6 indicates that this is a time note. Figure 16-7 illustrates the wording for a demand note.

Payable to Order or Bearer

Negotiable commercial paper is either *payable to order* or *payable to bearer.* An instrument that states that it is payable to the bearer is called *bearer paper.* It can be negotiated simply by having the person who is bearing or holding the paper deliver it. [See UCC § 3-111.]

A paper with the words *order of* on it is called *order paper.* It can only be negotiated when it is endorsed, or signed by the payee. [See UCC § 3-110.]

Example. Louise Philips writes a check to Randal Holmes. When Randal Holmes cashes the check, he must endorse it on the back. This must be done because a check is order paper. The words *pay to the order of* appear on all checks. Item (5) in figure 16-6 illustrates that this note is an order paper.

COMMON PRACTICES NOT EFFECTING NEGOTIABILITY

The note in figure 16-7 is a common note form used in every-day business. Several items are usually included, but are not required by the UCC for the note to be negotiable.

Place Drawn and Place Payable

The note in figure 16-7 was drawn in Dallas, Texas, [item (1a)] and is payable at the East Dallas Savings and Loan, [item (1b)]. This information makes the note understandable for all parties and is most often included in commercial documents.

Date

The date, item (2) in figure 16-7, is not necessary to make the note negotiable. If left blank, the holder of the note can insert any

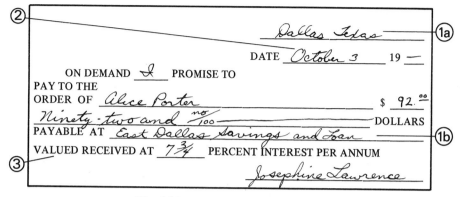

②   ①a

DATE *October 3* 19 —

ON DEMAND *I* PROMISE TO
PAY TO THE
ORDER OF *Alice Porter* $ 92.⁰⁰

Ninety-two and ⁿᵒ⁄₁₀₀ ——————— DOLLARS

PAYABLE AT *East Dallas Savings and Loan* —— ①b

VALUED RECEIVED AT *7¾* PERCENT INTEREST PER ANNUM

③   *Josephine Lawrence*

Fig. 16-7 A typical negotiable note

date and the note remains negotiable. The note can be *antedated* (dated earlier), or *postdated* (dated later). [See UCC § 3-114.] It is generally not wise for a business person to accept a postdated check since the money might not be collectable at a later date.

Value Received

It is common practice to include the words *value received* on negotiable paper. This indicates that the paper is issued or given in exchange for value or worth.

PRECAUTIONS WHEN WRITING COMMERCIAL PAPERS

Although not required legally, a writer of negotiable paper of any kind should remember certain basics. The check in figure 16-8, page 340, illustrates some correct and incorrect methods.

Correct Methods

1) A clearly written signature makes *forging* (signing by someone else with intent to defraud) more difficult.
2) Readable, well-formed numbers that fill the entire space make addition of other numbers more difficult.

Incorrect Methods

3) Never leave any lines blank, especially the name of the payee. Anyone could fill in his or her own name and cash it by endorsing it on the back.

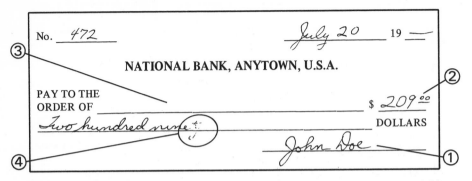

Fig. 16-8   Some correct (1, 2) and incorrect (3, 4) methods of writing negotiable papers.

4)   When writing the amount in words, keep the words close together to avoid additions or changes. In this check, the dotted lines indicate how easily the *nine* could be changed to *ninety*.

METHODS OF NEGOTIATION

The basic benefit of commercial paper is that it is negotiable — can be transferred from one party to another. When the maker or drawer transfers the paper to the payee, the payee becomes the *holder*.   The UCC specifies two requirements for such a transfer:

1)   If it is payable to bearer, it is negotiated by delivery alone.

2)   If the instrument is payable to order, it is negotiated upon delivery to the payee with any necessary endorsement. [See UCC § 3-202.]

By Delivery

When commercial paper is payable to bearer, cash, or other impersonal designation, it may be negotiated by delivery alone, in the same way money is transferred.   The bearer is known as the *transferor* and the one to whom it is delivered is called the *transferee*.

By Endorsement and Delivery

An instrument payable to the order of a particular person may be negotiated only by endorsement and delivery.   An *endorsement* is the signature of the person negotiating the instrument, who is the *endorser*.   If the endorser's name is misspelled on the instrument, the endorsement should be spelled in the same way with the correct spelling written directly underneath it. The party receiving such a paper is known as the *endorsee*. To be effective, an endorsement must transfer the entire instrument or any unpaid balance.

ENDORSEMENTS

Endorsements may be either blank, special, restrictive, or qualified.

Blank

A *blank endorsement* consists solely of the signature of the endorser on the back of the paper and specifies no particular endorsee, figure 16-9. It changes order paper to bearer paper so that any holder of the paper can negotiate it by delivery. [See UCC § 3-204 (2).]

Example. James Bernak endorses a check to L. Lydel with simply his name. Len Lydel loses the check and learns later from his bank that it has been cashed. Neither party can take action. The check became bearer paper and was negotiated as such.

Special

A *special* or *full* endorsement specifies the person to whom or to whose order the instrument is payable. It may then be negotiated

Fig. 16-9   A blank endorsement

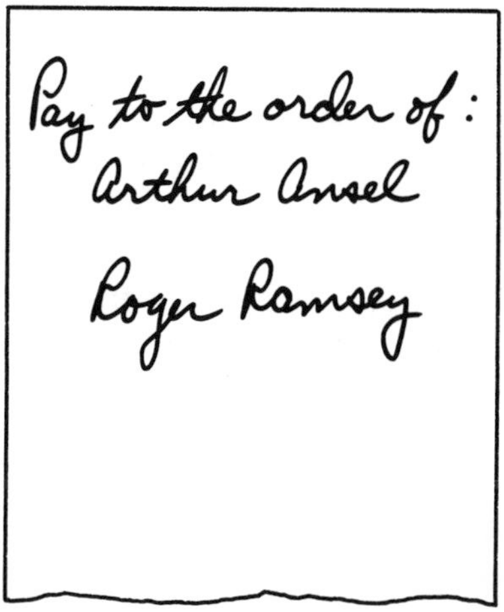

Fig. 16-10 A special or
full endorsement

only with an additional endorsement by that new endorsee. A special endorsement changes bearer paper to order paper and order paper continues as order paper. The holder of an instrument with a blank endorsement can convert it to an order instrument by adding a statement above the signature of the endorser, figure 16-10. [See UCC § 3-204 (1).]

Example. In the previous example, Lydel could have protected himself by adding *Pay to the order of Len Lydel* above Bernak's signature. The check would then have been an order paper and only negotiable by delivery and with his endorsement.

Restrictive

A *restrictive endorsement* prohibits further endorsements on the instrument but does not prevent further transfer. According to the Code, the restrictions may be either conditional or for a specific purpose. A conditional restriction makes the instrument payable only after the occurrence or nonoccurrence of a stated event. [See UCC § 3-205.]

Example. Palmer endorses a check to Richard's Roofing as follows: *Payable to Richard's Roofing only if new roof on my house is completed by October 31, 19 --.* This is a conditional clause which places a restriction on the negotiation of the check.

Restrictive endorsements can also specify a special purpose for the checks. They include such terms as *for collection, pay any bank,* and *pay to J. Rings for the support of Beth Wilsey.* The most common term is *for deposit only* which is used on instruments, especially those to be mailed, so that if they are lost or stolen they cannot be cashed as bearer paper.

Example. Donna Aldrick works during all the hours that her bank is open, so she has to mail her paychecks to the bank. She endorses them with her name, but adds the restrictive clause *for deposit only* for protection, figure 16-11. The bank receiving the check must deposit the check for the payee. It cannot cash the check for someone who presents the check to the bank for payment, representing herself as Donna Aldrick.

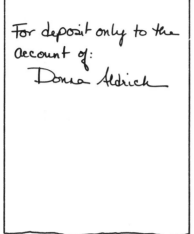

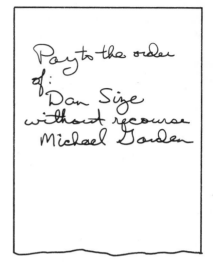

**Fig. 16-11 A restrictive
endorsement**

**Fig. 6-12 A qualified
endorsement**

Qualified

A *qualified endorsement* usually includes the words *without recourse.*   It permits a qualified endorser to disclaim any liability on the instrument if the maker or drawer fails to pay, as long as the endorser is not aware of any defenses the maker or drawer may have, figure 16-12.

HOLDER IN DUE COURSE

As mentioned earlier, the UCC defines *holders* as parties who are in possession of instruments which have been issued or endorsed to them.   When such holders enjoy superior rights to the former holders, they are called *holders in due course.*   [See UCC § 3-302.]   It is the holder in due course who can enforce payment on the note or draft without regard to the underlying contract that gave rise to the paper.

Requirements

There are certain requirements for a holder to become a holder in due course.   The paper must be taken (1) for value, (2) in good faith, and (3) without notice that the paper is overdue or dishonored or of any defense against it or claims to it on the part of any person. [See UCC § 3-302.]

Value. To qualify as a holder in due course, the party must give value for the instrument. Full value is not necessary; reasonable value is sufficient. For a holder in due course to give value, a promise must be actually carried out by such holder, or something must actually be given in exchange for the paper. [See UCC § 3-303.] An instrument given as a gift does not qualify the holder as a holder in due course, since no value is given for the paper.

Example. Benson wins a state lottery and gives Hines a promissory note for $1,000 of it as a gift. Hines in turn gives the note to his wife as an anniversary present. Neither Hines nor his wife is a holder in due course, since neither gave any value for the note.

Good Faith. The Uniform Commercial Code defines *good faith* as honesty in fact in the conduct or transaction concerned. [See UCC § 1-201 (19).] If a person acquires an instrument that is obviously suspicious in nature, that person is guilty of bad faith and cannot be considered a holder in due course.

Example. Brown purchases a promissory note from Clemens. Brown notices that there is writing over the numbers in the space for the amount, but says nothing. These writings are actually alterations in the amount changing it from $3,000 to $8,000. Brown cannot be considered a holder in due course since he purchased the note in bad faith, knowing that there were alterations made in it.

Overdue or Dishonored Paper. A party cannot become a holder in due course by accepting an instrument that is overdue or dishonored. A paper payable at a definite date becomes overdue at the beginning of the day after the due date. A demand note is overdue within a reasonable time, depending upon the nature of the situation. A dishonored instrument is one on which payment or acceptance has been refused.

Example. On October 8, Denvers purchases a promissory note with a due date of October 8. Denvers is still a holder in due course, since the note is not overdue until the next day, October 9.

Rights

Holders in due course have rights that are superior to ordinary holders of commercial paper. If they cannot collect from the maker or drawer, the parties primarily liable, they may collect from the endorsers. The primary parties have certain defenses, both personal and real.

Personal Defenses.   Holders in due course are free from *personal defenses* whereas holders are not. Makers or drawers have several personal defenses which can be used against the immediate parties to the instrument, but which cannot be used against holders in due course. They may claim fraud or duress during the making of the instrument, breach of the underlying contract, or nondelivery to the paper against the holder, but not against the holder in due course.

Case Example.   Without the holder in due course status, the holder is subject to many more defenses by the makers or drawers. The note is a contract between the maker and the payee, so contract defenses are available, such as duress. Notice how this point is illustrated in the following case.

SHURTLEFF v. GILLER
Court of Civil Appeals of Texas, 1975
527S.W.2d 214

McDONALD, Chief Justice.

This is an appeal by plaintiff Shurtleff from take-nothing judgment in suit on a note against defendant Giller.

Plaintiff sued defendant on a promissory note dated June 1, 1973, in amount of $67,136., bearing 9% interest, and payable September 30, 1973. Plaintiff alleged he is owner and holder of the note, that defendant refused to pay same, and sought judgment for the face of the note, interest and attorney's fees.

Defendant answered that he executed the note under duress applied by plaintiff, and but for such duress he never would have executed same.

Trial was to the court without a jury, which rendered judgment plaintiff take nothing.

The trial court filed Findings of Fact and Conclusions of Law, pertinent of which are summarized as follows:

1) Plaintiff Shurtleff sued defendant Giller on a note for $67,136., dated June 1, 1973, and payable September 30, 1973.

2) In 1970 Giller became an employee of Thorsen Tool Company.

3) At all pertinent times Shurtleff was Chief Operating Officer of Thorsen.

5) Shurtleff was Giller's superior.

6) In May, 1973, Shurtleff demanded Giller sign the note sued on.

7) Immediately prior to Giller's signing the note, Shurtleff advised Giller unless he signed the note his employment with Thorsen would be terminated.

8) Giller signed the note because of the threat of termination of his employment by Shurtleff, and but for such fact would not have signed it.

9) For several months prior to and at the time of signing the note Giller's daughter was hospitalized at a charge of $700 per week.

10) Shurtleff was aware of the fact Giller's daughter was hospitalized.

11) Giller's employment contract contained a covenant not to compete with his employer for five years following termination of his services for any reason.

12) Giller knew of his covenant not to compete with his employer at the time he signed the note.

13) The signing of the note was not related to the business of Thorsen, but to matters personal to Shurtleff and Giller.

14) In 1968, Shurtleff and Giller entered into an agreement whereby they participated in construction of apartments in Dallas; Shurtleff was to have 50% interest in the project, but was not to be out any money as a result of participation in the project.

16) In 1969, Giller and Shurtleff borrowed $170,000 from a bank for the project, and jointly signed a note for such funds.

17) The note was paid down by the project to $60,000.

20) Shurtleff paid the Bank the $60,000.

24) Giller has not paid Shurtleff the note sued on.

CONCLUSIONS OF THE LAW

Giller executed the note as a result of duress applied by Shurtleff. As a result of such duress, such transaction represented by said note is void and unenforceable, and Giller is not indebted to Shurtleff on the note.

Plaintiff appeals on 16 points, pertinent of which contend:

1) The evidence is insufficient as a matter of law to establish duress.

2) The evidence is insufficient to establish defendant signed the note because of the threat of termination of his employment.

3) The finding that plaintiff advised defendant if he did not sign the note his employment would be terminated is based on parol evidence which is inadmissible to vary the terms of the written note.

4) There is no evidence, and/or insufficient evidence to support the judgment, and the judgment is against the great weight and preponderance of the evidence.

Plaintiff was defendant's superior in the Thorsen Tool Company. Plaintiff and defendant formed a joint venture aside from their duties with Thorsen to construct apartment houses. Plaintiff and defendant signed a note at a bank for $170,000 to get funds for the project. The note was paid down to $60,000 by the project. Plaintiff and defendant dissolved the joint venture, and agreed that all assets of the venture be transferred to defendant and defendant be liable for all indebtedness. Thereafter the bank called on plaintiff to pay the $60,000 due on the $170,000 note plaintiff and defendant had signed. Plaintiff paid such note, and thereafter asked defendant to sign the note here sued on. Defendant testified plaintiff told him that his employment at Thorsen would be terminated unless he signed the note. Plaintiff denied the foregoing. Defendant knew of his covenant not to compete with his employer after termination of employment, and plaintiff knew of the hospitalization of defendant's daughter.

Duress is a question of fact and is the threat to do some act which the party threatening has no legal right to do. Such threat must be of such character as to destroy the free agency of the party to whom it is directed. It must overcome his will and cause him to do that which he would not otherwise do, and which he was not legally bound to do. The restraint caused by such threat must be imminent, and must be such that the person to whom it is directed has no present means of protection. [Citations omitted.]

Plaintiff could have sued defendant on the termination agreement for the $60,000 plaintiff paid to the bank, but instead chose to have defendant sign a note. The note is for more than $60,000 and bears 9% interest. Plaintiff did not have the right to threaten to terminate defendant's employment if he did not sign the note.

We think the evidence as a whole is ample and sufficient to establish that plaintiff did threaten to terminate defendant's employment if defendant did not sign the note, that duress has been established, and that the findings and judgment are not against the great weight and preponderance of the evidence. [Citations omitted.]

All plaintiff's points and contentions have been considered and are overruled.

Affirmed.

Assume that payment is made before maturity, but that the maker fails to obtain the canceled instrument from the holder.

The instrument can be negotiated and the holder in due course can still collect. The maker has no defense against the holder in due course. Likewise, lack of consideration in the original paper is no defense against a holder in due course.

Example.   Consider the example presented earlier in which Benson gives Hines a promissory note for $1,000 as a gift and Hines then gives it to his wife as a gift. Suppose that Mrs. Hines transfers the note for value to Watkins. Watkins, as a holder in due course, can collect from Benson. Benson has no defenses of lack of consideration against Watkins.

Real Defenses.   No one, including a holder in due course, may collect on commercial paper if the maker has one of several *real* or *absolute* defenses. This includes situations in which the maker is incompetent or when there is illegality which makes the contract void. [See UCC § 3-305 (2).] When there is alteration of the instrument it cannot be enforced as altered, but the holder in due course can enforce the paper according to the original provisions. [See UCC § 3-407 (3).]

Example.   Wells, a holder in due course, attempts to collect on an instrument from the maker, Hardy, in the amount of $3,000. Hardy claims and proves that the original paper was altered from the amount of $300. Wells can only collect $300.

Finally, the holder in due course cannot enforce an instrument which has been fraudulently conceived or has been forged.

The Federal Trade Commission recently enacted a regulation that cuts back on the rights of a holder in due course of commercial paper from a consumer transaction. The effect of the new regulation is to allow the consumer/buyer to assert defenses, even personal ones, against a holder in due course as if they were real defenses. The regulation only applies to consumer transactions and does not effect the protected status of the holder in due course in a commercial setting that does not include a consumer.

At times, a holder may enjoy the rights of a holder in due course even though he or she has not met the specific requirements of a holder in due course. By virtue of the shelter provision, UCC Section 3-201 (1), a transferee obtains the same rights in an instrument as the transferor had. Therefore, if a holder takes an instrument from a holder in due course without giving value, the holder will still be able to enforce the instrument as if he or she were a holder in due course, having received the same rights as the transferor who was a holder in due course. This shelter provision, however, does not protect a transferee who has taken part in a fraud or illegality which affects the instrument, or someone who held the instrument previously and could not have been a holder in due course at that time because of notice of some claim against the instrument.

Example. *A* is the maker on a note; *B* is the payee. *B* negotiates the note to *C* for value after which *C* achieves the status of holder in due course. *C* gives the note to *D* as a gift. *D* cannot be a holder in due course because of the lack of value, but can act as one, since *C,* the immediate transferor, had achieved holder in due course status.

Example. *A* is the maker on a note; *B* is the payee. *B* is not a holder in due course because *B* has dealt directly with *A* and would be subject to both real and personal defenses *A* might have. *B* sells the note to *C* (a holder in due course) who sells it back to *B.* *B* does not come within the shelter provision of Section 3-201 since *B* is a prior holder of the note and was subject to defenses at that time. The purchase from *C* was an attempt to improve *B*'s position and will not be successful.

WARRANTIES OF ENDORSERS AND TRANSFERORS

Any person who transfers a commercial paper makes certain implied warranties to the transferee. If the paper is endorsed, the endorser also makes the same warranties to any subsequent holder who takes the paper in good faith. [See UCC § 3-417.]

The warranties are:

- The transferor has good title to the instrument.
- All signatures are genuine or authorized.
- The instrument has not been materially altered.
- No defense of any party is good against the instrument.
- The transferor has no knowledge of any insolvency proceedings with respect to the maker, acceptor, or drawer of the instrument.

When there is a qualified endorsement (without recourse) of a paper, the warranties are the same except that instead of the warranty that no defense is good against the instrument (fourth item on page 349), the endorser warrants no knowledge of such defense. [See UCC § 3-417 (3).]

DISCHARGE OF COMMERCIAL PAPER

By Payment

Generally, commercial papers are discharged when the primary party pays the money to the holder [See UCC § 3-603.]

Example. Swenson has a note from Olsen in the amount of $287, due on July 1. On June 28, Olsen pays the amount due to Swenson. The note is now discharged, and Olsen obtains the canceled note for his records.

If the payment is made before maturity date, the maker should be sure to obtain possession of the canceled instrument so that it is not transferred to another holder in due course who could still collect on it.

Cancellation

The holder of a negotiable instrument may relieve the maker of the obligation at any time by cancellation. The holder can purposely destroy the paper or surrender it with the signature crossed out. The holder can also deliver a signed writing of cancellation to the obligated party. [See UCC § 3-605.]

Example. Swenson in the previous example decides to cancel the note which Olsen owes. He delivers a note to Olsen which states, "This writing cancels your obligation of the $287 note. Your note is enclosed which has been ripped and destroyed. (signed) C. Swenson."

Alteration

Negotiable paper is discharged if there has been *material alteration;* that is, alteration in the content, such as the date due or amount due. The holder in due course may still, however, enforce it according to its original terms. [See UCC § 3-407.]

Example. On May 1, Hemming takes an instrument from Galt and changes the due date from December 1 to August 15 of the same year. Such alteration discharges the paper canceling any obligation on Galt's part. If, however, Slater has purchased the instrument in good faith (without knowledge of the alteration) from Hemming, Slater can still enforce it with the original due date of December 1.

SELF-EVALUATION

1. What are the three types of commercial paper?

2. What are the three parties necessary to make a check negotiable?

3. What is meant by credit?

4. In a note, who is the maker and who is the payee?

5. Define the term *negotiable.*

6. Who issues a certificate of deposit?

7. Why is a check a type of draft?

8. Where can the requirements for making commercial papers negotiable be found?

9. Doug borrows five dollars from his roommate and says he will pay him back next week. Why is this promise not negotiable?

10. Define the term *sum certain.*

11. In *Wall* v. *East Texas Teachers Credit Union,* why did the court rely on the figures instead of simply the words in the agreement?

12. Brown borrows $200 from his neighbor and gives him a note in return. When the note is due in thirty days, Brown delivers $200 worth of potatoes to pay it off. Is this legal? Why or why not?

13. What are the two "times of payment" that may appear on a negotiable instrument?

14. If the words *pay to the order of* appear on a commercial paper, what is necessary before it can be negotiated?

15. How is a bearer paper negotiated?

16. List four items usually found on a commercial paper, but which are not required to make it legal.

17. When writing a negotiable instrument, what are the four points that the writer must remember?

18. When may negotiable paper be transferred by delivery alone?

19. A holder receives a paper with a blank endorsement and adds a phrase to make it a special endorsement. Is the paper now discharged due to alteration?

20. Alton mails a check to the bank and adds the words *for deposit only* above his signature. What type of endorsement is this?

21. Differentiate between a holder and a holder in due course.

22. What are three ways in which negotiable documents are discharged?

SUGGESTED ACTIVITIES

1. In the following check, identify the drawer, the drawee, and the payee.

No. *562*

DATE *December 18,* 19 —

PAY TO THE
ORDER OF *Samuel Higgins* $ *47.*⁰⁰

Forty-seven and 00/100 ————— DOLLARS

MERCHANTS TRUST
DILVILLE, U.S.A.

Robert Levine

Fig. 16-12

2. On June 10, Robert Dunn of St. Louis Missouri, borrows $65 from James Good. Dunn will repay the money to Good at 6 percent interest per annum, at the Union Bank, in sixty days. Draw up a legal note for Dunn, filling in any signature if necessary. Also include those items not required, but usually present in a note.

CASES FOR STUDY

1. Ace Distributors, Inc. purchases new stereos and televisions from manufacturers for resale to consumers. Ace pays for the appliances by delivering notes payable to the sellers. One seller negotiates the notes to a bank for an amount slightly less than the face value of the note. If Ace discovers that a shipment

of televisions from that seller is defective and returns the goods, can the company avoid paying the note that the bank now holds?

2. *G* gives *B* a note dated August 7, 1970 promising to pay to *B*'s order the sum of $2,500 one year after the date of the note without interest. On October 1, 1971, *B* endorses the note and hands it over to a bank. *G* now believes that he has a good defense of fraud to assert against *B*. When the bank sues *G* for payment on the note, may *G* assert the fraud defense?

3. *A* writes a $100 check payable to *B* with First National Bank as the drawee. A thief steals the check from *B*, forges *B*'s endorsement, and transfers the check to *C*. *C* uses the check to pay for goods purchased from *D*. First National Bank dishonors the check because of the forged endorsement. Of *C* and *D*, on whom does the loss fall? Explain.

4. *A* writes a check payable to *B*'s order with First National Bank as the drawee. *B* endorses the check to *C*'s order without recourse. *C* endorses the check in blank. A thief steals the check from *C* and cashes it at First National Bank. Who must bear the loss? Why?

5. When the warranties of transferors and endorsers are breached, the Uniform Commercial Code provides that actions based on the breach can be brought within a reasonable time. [See UCC § 4-207 (4).] A payee of a stolen check sues a bank for damages when the bank breached the warranty of genuineness of prior endorsements by cashing the check with a forged signature. The check was dated May 10, 1971 and was paid by the bank on May 19, 1971. The suit was not begun until September of 1974, more than three years later. During those three years, no action was taken against the thief by the payee, who was aware of the theft and knew the thief's identity. In early 1974, the thief moved out of the jurisdiction. Can the bank defend the action by saying that the payee has not brought the action within a reasonable time as provided in section of the UCC cited above?

6. *M* receives money on her sixteenth birthday with which to make a down payment on a new car. She finances the rest of the purchase price by signing a promissory note with the car dealership as payee. The dealer negotiates the note to the bank which becomes a holder in due course. After two months,

M disaffirms her contract with the dealer based on her incapacity to enter into a binding contract. Does this fact defeat the rights of the holder in due course?

7. *P* is the payee on a note from *Q*. *Q* gives *P* the note to evidence a debt incurred when *Q* bought goods from *P*. *P* knows that the goods are defective, so he immediately gives the note to his friend *R*. He explains the situation to *R* and persuades *R* to agree to say that he has purchased the note from *P*. *R* plans to then collect the debt and split the proceeds with *P*. Is the scheme legal?

Glossary

This glossary contains definitions of legal words and phrases found in the text. A page number notation follows each definition which refers to the first major usage of the term in the text. This reference usually includes a more complete discussion of the word or phrase.

abstract of title — the findings of a title search; not legal proof of clear title of the seller (p. 194)

acceptance — the taking or receiving of something offered; an element in creating a binding contract (p. 64)

act of Congress — statutes passed by the federal legislature, Congress (p. 9)

act of God — any natural event that human beings can neither foresee nor avoid (p. 162)

act of a public authority — seizure of goods by an authorized government agency (p. 163)

act of a public enemy — damage or loss of goods caused by seizure by military forces of an opposing government (p. 163)

administrative agencies — groups established by all levels of government to accomplish specific purposes and given the power to conduct hearings, require witnesses to appear, and issue orders which have the force of law (examples: FDA, FCC, drug commissions, zoning boards) (p. 10)

administrative regulations — orders or rulings of administrative agencies which have the force of law (p. 10)

adverse possession — a method of acquiring title to real property by continuously occupying realty without the owner's permission and paying taxes on that realty for the statutory period (p. 186)

age of majority — the legal age; the age at which minors reach maturity according to the laws of their state (p. 68)

agency — a three-party, legally created relationship in which one party is granted the authority to act as a representative for another when dealing with a third party (p. 253)

agency by ratification — a type of agency created by the principal's approval of acts performed by the agent without authorization or beyond granted authority; ratification binds the principal (not the agent) to the act (p. 262)

agent — the party in an agency who is granted authority to act as a representative of the principal (p. 253)

agreement — a state of being in accord, or being of one mind; ranging from a mutual understanding to a binding obligation (p. 31)

alteration — a change (p. 87)

American Bar Association — a national professional association of lawyers (p. 2)

answer — a statement drafted by a defendant's attorney in which the defendant admits or denies the statements made in the complaint; the answer must be served in a given period of time stated in the summons (p. 28)

antedate — to date earlier than the current date (p. 339)

apparent authority — the authority that the third party in an agency relationship reasonably assumes that the principal has granted to the agent based on impressions created by the principal (p. 261)

appellate court (court of appeals) — a court that reviews decisions of lower courts or courts of original jurisdiction when a claim is made that the lower court was in error in some way (p. 18)

articles of incorporation — the document outlining the powers and functions of a corporation, approved by the appropriate state official, which serves as public notice of the structure of a given corporation, its authorized capital, corporate address, and other required information (p. 297)

articles of partnership (partnership agreement) — a written agreement defining the rights and duties of partners and the provisions for carrying on the partnership (p. 278)

assault — a threat with the intent to inflict bodily injury or harm (p. 230)

assignee of a contract — the third party who receives the rights transferred in an assignment of a contract (p. 78)

assignee of a lease — the new tenant in an assignment of a lease on real property (p. 213)

assignment of a contract — a transfer of rights held by one party to a third party not originally involved in the contract (p. 78)

assignment of a lease — transferal of a tenant's entire interest in the real property; follows rules of standard assignor-assignee relationship (p. 213)

assignor of a contract — the transferor of rights in the assignment of a contract (p. 78)

assignor of a lease — a tenant who assigns a lease on real property to another (p. 213)

attorney — see *lawyer*

baggage — articles necessary for the passenger's comfort during the trip on a public carrier, or for the ultimate purpose of the trip (p. 165)

bailee — the party who is given possession in a bailment transaction (p. 147)

bailment — a legal relationship which provides for the delivery of goods by the owner for a specific purpose to another party; only possession is transferred — title and ownership are retained by the owner (p. 147)

bailor — the owner who transfers possession in a bailment transaction (p. 147)

bankruptcy — a systematic distribution of assets of an insolvent company, or individual; bankruptcies are handled under the Federal Bankruptcy Act, and thus are under the jurisdiction of the federal courts (p. 321)

bargain and sale deed — a document used to transfer title to real property; the grantor makes no express guarantees of clear title (p. 201)

battery — the intentional and wrongful touching of another person without the consent of that person; battery always includes a threat or an assault (p. 230)

bearer — a holder or carrier of commercial paper (p. 338)

bid — a price for which a person or company will do a certain job (p. 59)

bilateral contract — an agreement in which both parties make a promise; both bind themselves to certain performances (p. 39)

bill of exchange — see *draft*

binding contract — a legal agreement which requires all parties to carry out their obligations; six required elements must be present (p. 51)

blank endorsement — an endorsement on the back of commercial paper consisting solely of the endorser's signature (p. 341)

bonds — evidence of a debt; debt securities (p. 301)

breach — to break; also, a violation of the terms of a contract (p. 88)

breach of duty — a violation of expected conduct owed by one person to another which causes injury or damage to the victim (p. 227)

breach of peace — in the context of a secured credit sale, a situation in which threats of force or harm to the debtor or the debtor's property are used by the creditor in an attempt to repossess goods from a debtor who is in default (p. 119)

broker — in the context of real property transactions, a person who is paid a fee to obtain buyers and settle the details of real estate transactions (p. 191)

bulk transfer — the sale of the major part of a store's inventory, usually to a new owner; the buyer receives a list of the owner's debts and must notify the seller's creditors of the sale (p. 104)

business — any profit-seeking enterprise or concern (p. 251)

business corporation — see *profit corporation*

business law — laws found in the four major categories of law which regulate all business transactions (p. 13)

bylaws — the regulations of a corporation listing the duties and conduct of the members of the corporation, the annual meetings times and places, the amendment procedures, the dividend schedules, and so forth (p. 299)

Canons of Judicial Ethics — generally accepted rules of behavior issued by the American Bar Association for judges to follow both in court and in their personal lives (p. 19)

capital stock — initial funds to finance a corporation which can be in the form of property, equipment, ideas, or money (p. 301)

carrier — an individual or company that transports merchandise (p. 161)

case — a controversy between two or more persons who, as a last resort, have turned to the courts to resolve their dispute (p. 1)

case law — precedents decided in local, state, and federal courts (p. 4)

cash dividends — funds from profits of a corporation paid to the appropriate shareholders in amounts decided by the board of directors (actually paid in the form of corporate checks) (p. 309)

caveat emptor — Latin for "let the buyer beware"; seller takes no responsibility for the product (p. 123)

certainty of terms — one stipulation of a contract which requires that the offer be clearly and completely stated (p. 60)

certificate of deposit — a promise by a bank to repay a depositor money with interest if the money is left on deposit for the time stated; a form of commercial paper (p. 332)

certificate of incorporation — a document issued by the state in which the business is being incorporated; composed of the articles of incorporation with the state seal affixed, and the signature of the appropriate state official (p. 299)

charter (corporate) — see *certificate of incorporation*

check — a type of draft; an order to pay which is negotiable when properly filled out (p. 331)

circuit — one of the eleven areas into which the country is divided in the federal court system (p. 19)

civil law — law which defines the rights of individuals and protects their persons and property (p. 11)

client — one who seeks the advice of a lawyer (p. 1)

closing statement — in the context of a real estate transaction, a balance sheet showing adjustments that have been made in money that is owed by both the buyer and the seller in a real property sale; used at the title closing (p. 201)

Code, the — see *Uniform Commercial Code*

collateral — personal property used to secure a debt; may be documents, rights, or goods (p. 113)

commercial paper — negotiable documents or instruments including notes, certificates of deposit and drafts used for the payment of money (p. 327)

common carrier — transporter of personal property of all who choose to employ them (examples: railroads, trucking firms) (p. 161)

common law — see *case law*

common stock — owners of this type of corporation stock share with other common stock owners in the profits of the company; they have control of the corporation by virtue of their voting power (p. 303)

community property — a type of ownership in which all property that is acquired by either a husband or wife during a marriage belongs to both with equal interest; property owned before the marriage, or property that is inherited or given to either party individually during a marriage is excluded (p. 183)

comparative negligence — the rule in some states whereby the injured party is not barred from recovery of damages even though slightly negligent; the jury determines the degree of negligence of the plaintiff and reduces the verdict by that amount (p. 235)

competent — in the context of contract law, able to enter into a contract, both parties in a binding contract must be competent (p. 68)

complaint — a statement of the plaintiff's claims outlined in numbered paragraphs and drafted by the plaintiff's attorney; served with, or just after, the summons (p. 25)

concurrent jurisdiction — a situation in which two courts (such as a federal district court and a state court) both have the power to hear the case (p. 21)

concurrent ownership — coownership of property by two or more persons at the same time (p. 182)

condominium — a form of ownership of real property in which there is sole tenancy (or tenancy by the entirety by a husband and wife) in an apartment, and tenancy in common with the other apartment owners in the parts of the realty used in common (such as elevators and halls) (p. 184)

conforming goods — goods that meet the specifications of a contract (p. 107)

consideration — the element of a binding contract which binds the promises made in the contract; each party to a contract receives something for something such as a promise for a promise, a promise for an act, or an act for a promise (p. 66)

consolidation — two or more corporations dissolving and forming a single new corporation (p. 320)

conspicuous — readily attracting attention; often, being printed in larger type or ink of a different color (p. 128)

constitutional law — law which is based on federal and state documents called constitutions (p. 7)

constructive eviction — the right of a tenant to move out of premises within a reasonable time if they become uninhabitable and the landlord fails to correct the condition (p. 216)

consumer — user of goods and services for household purpose (p. 95)

contract — a promise or set of promises relating to business transactions, voluntarily made by the parties involved, which give rise to legal consequences (p. 32)

contract bailment — a bailment in which consideration is given for services purchased from a bailee; all elements of a contract are present, hence an enforceable contract is created (p. 149)

contract of sale (present sale or sale) — a transfer of goods and services at the present time from one party to another for consideration (p. 97)

contract to sell — a promise to transfer ownership at a future time (p. 97)

contributory negligence — the rule in many states whereby injured parties in negligence actions cannot collect damages if their own actions contributed to the injury; neither party collects any damages (p. 235)

conversion — the unlawful seizure and use of the personal property of another (p. 233)

copyright – the exclusive legal right to reproduce written material valid for the life of the author plus 50 years (p. 244)

corporation – a legal entity created only with government consent, whose members are exempt from personal liability of the firm beyond the amount of their individual shares (p. 295)

correspondence – agreement by communication; sometimes a requirement of the acceptance of an offer to make a contract binding (p. 65)

cosign – to sign a document jointly with another person, taking on responsibility for that contract (p. 70)

counteroffer – the reply made when an offeree does not accept all the terms of an offer, but changes the terms; terminates original offer (p. 64)

court – the arm of government that administers justice; the place where justice is administered; the judge (p. 15)

court of appeals – see *appellate court*

Court of Appeals, U.S. – an appellate court in the federal court system which hears cases from federal district courts within its circuit and reviews rulings on appeal from federal administrative agencies; one such court is located in each of the eleven circuits (p. 22)

court record – documents and papers kept at a court trial which include a copy of witnesses' testimony, exhibits, and any papers used in the trial; these records are used by judges in making decisions in appellate courts (p. 18)

covenant – a condition or guarantee; in leases, covenants give parties certain rights and impose on them certain obligations; in deeds, covenants are promises by the grantor that amount to guarantees that the grantor has clear title (p. 201)

cover – for a seller to resell goods wrongfully refused by a buyer; (p. 105) or for a buyer to purchase necessary goods from another seller when the seller with whom he or she originally contracted wrongfully refuses or fails to deliver those goods (p. 108)

credit – the power to buy or borrow on trust with a promise of future payment (p. 112)

criminal law – rulings which protect society as a whole from harmful acts of individuals and maintain peace and order (p. 12)

cumulative stock – a type of stock which accumulates unpaid dividends; if dividends are not paid in one year, the money is accumulated and paid to holders of this type of stock the next year (p. 303)

cumulative voting – a method of corporate voting provided for by most states which allows minority shareholders to be represented on the board of directors; the number of shares possessed by each shareholder is multiplied by the number of directors to be elected and the voter can then accumulate the votes and place them on one candidate or spread them among several (p. 307)

damage – loss or injury as a result of a wrong; element of a tort action (p. 229)

damages – the sum sued for by a plaintiff to compensate for a loss (p. 25) or a form of remedy for the loss suffered by an injured party (p. 88)

debt securities (bonds) – instruments issued by corporations which are evidence of a debt to the holder (p. 301)

debtor – borrower (p. 113)

deed – a written document that conveys title to property (p. 182)

defamation – injury to another's good reputation without good reason (p. 231)

default – failure to perform an obligation (p. 116)

defendant – the party being brought into court in a case to defend against the claim (p. 1)

delegated – when contract duties cannot be assigned they can sometimes be delegated, or committed, to another party; the original party is still responsible and liable (p. 79)

deliberation – the action of the jury when it leaves the courtroom; when the jury *deliberates*, they discuss what has been seen and heard, weigh the evidence, and make a decision (p. 29)

demurrage – an additional fee charged by a shipper for goods not unloaded from a transport vehicle which delays that vehicle from being used (p. 164)

director – an individual elected by the shareholders of a corporation to sit on the board which makes the major decisions in the corporation, except those reserved to the shareholders (p. 311)

disclaim – to renounce a claim; to deny; to disavow (p. 128)

disclosed principal – in an agency relationship, the designation of the principal when the third party is aware that the agent is acting for a principal and knows the identity of that principal (p. 270)

discovery – a period of time after the pleadings have been issued and before the trial begins during which both parties in a court proceeding exchange additional information (p. 28)

dispossess – a legal proceeding whereby the lessor can evict the lessee and regain possession of the premises (p. 213)

dissolution (of a partnership) — termination of a partnership as the result of a change in the relationship of the partners (p. 285)

District Court, U.S. — a trial court of the federal court system; there are ninety such courts with at least one per state and as many as four in some states (p. 21)

dividends — funds from profits of a corporation divided among the holders of certain types of stock (p. 309)

document — a legal paper (p. 327)

domestic corporation — a business functioning in the state in which it was created (p. 296)

donee — the receiver of a gift (p. 186)

donor — the giver of a gift (p. 186)

draft — a written order by one person directing another person or party to pay a certain sum on demand, or at a definite time, to the bearer or the specific person indicated on the draft; used to exchange debts among three parties; sometimes called a bill of exchange. A check is a type of draft (p. 332)

drawee — the bank or party on which a draft is drawn (p. 331)

drawer — the party who directs the payment of money to a payee by a draft (p. 331)

due (ordinary) care — the care a responsible person would give in the same situation with the same property (p. 150)

duty — actions or conduct expected of an individual in the treatment of other people in society; an obligation imposed by law (p. 225)

easement — the right of one party to use the land of another for a special purpose; no possession or ownership transferred (p. 175)

eminent domain — a doctrine which provides that property may be taken for public use by the state when there is just compensation paid to the owner (p. 181)

employee — an individual who is contracted either in writing or orally to do work for another (p. 254)

employer — an individual who contracts another either orally or in writing to do work for him or her (p. 254)

encumberance — anything that hurts property or title to property, such as outstanding mortgages or tax liens (p. 201)

endorsee — the person receiving commercial paper that has been signed or endorsed (p. 341)

endorsement — signature of a person negotiating a commercial instrument (p. 340)

endorser — the person signing commercial paper to negotiate it (p. 340) entity — see *legal entity*

equity securities — (stocks) instruments issued by corporations which are evidence of a credit interest of the holder (p. 301)

estate (possessory interest) — the interest a person or persons have in real property (p. 174)

eviction — one type of breach of any terms of a lease whereby the tenant is deprived of use of the premises; may be a result of the landlord's or the tenant's actions (p. 216)

exclusive jurisdiction — a situation in which only one type of court has the power to hear a case and the plaintiff has no choice of courts (p. 21)

executed contract — a legal agreement in which all the terms have been fulfilled by both parties (p. 43)

executor — an individual appointed by a will to handle the estate of one who has died (p. 46)

executory contract — a legal agreement that has not been completed or fulfilled by all parties; one party's terms may be complete (p. 43)

express agency — a relationship created by the actual authority granted by a principal to an agent (p. 258)

express authority — authority granted to an agent when a principal gives specific instructions either orally or in writing (p. 260)

express contract — a legal agreement in which the terms are clearly stated either orally or in writing and both parties intend to carry out those terms (p. 39)

express warranty — a promise arising from a representation concerning the product made by the seller at the time of the sale (p. 124)

extraordinary bailment — a bailment situation in which a bailee is subject to unusual duties or obligations that are imposed by law (p. 149)

false arrest — see *false imprisonment*

false imprisonment (false arrest) — intentional confining of a person without that person's consent or without justification (p. 231)

fee simple absolute — see *fee simple*

fee simple (fee simple absolute) — a type of estate which entitles a real property owner to the entire property for an unlimited time (p. 174)

fiduciary duty — an obligation to be completely honest in all dealings with and for the principal; the highest duty imposed by law (p. 268)

financing statement – a document protecting the secured party's interest in the collateral against other creditors of the debtor or against sale of the collateral by the debtor (p. 116)

fixture – personal property which is affixed to or used with real property with the intention of it becoming a part of the realty (p. 174)

FOB (free on board) place of shipment – a shipping term used when a contract calls for the seller to ship the goods; title passes when the seller delivers the goods to the carrier, and the buyer bears the risk of loss if the goods are damaged in transit (p. 102)

FOB place of destination – a shipping term used when a contract requires the seller to deliver the goods to the buyer; title passes when the seller delivers the goods to the buyer, and the seller bears the risk of loss if the goods are damaged in transit (p. 102)

foreign corporation – a business functioning in any state other than the one in which it was formed (p. 296)

formal contract – a legal agreement in writing which requires a seal or its substitute (such as the word *seal*, or the letters *L.S.*) (p. 34)

fraudulent – intentionally dishonest (p. 42)

full endorsement – see *special endorsement*

fungible goods – goods which are so similar to other goods of their nature that they are indistinguishable; thus any portion of the goods may be replaced by any other portion (p. 161)

general agent – in an agency relationship, a person authorized to act in a wide range of transactions for the principal (p. 255)

general partner – coowner of a partnership who is actively engaged in its management; a general partner has full powers and full liability (p. 279)

governmental corporation – a business form organized for public purposes (p. 295)

grantee – the party receiving title to real property (p. 195)

grantor – the party who conveys title to real property (p. 195)

gratuitous bailment – a bailment in which no consideration is given; either a bailment for the sole benefit of the bailor, or a bailment for the sole benefit of the bailee (p. 149)

habitable – fit to live in (p. 208)

holder – a party who is in possession of an instrument which has been issued or endorsed to him or her (p. 343)

holder in due course – holders of instruments endorsed or issued to them who enjoy superior rights to the former holders, as long as they have received the instrument for value, in good faith, and without notice of any defenses (p. 343)

implied agency (agency of necessity) – the assumption of the existence of an agency by the court in situations where such an assumption seems just; acts of the parties lead to implied agency (p. 259)

implied authority – authority beyond the actual expressed authority granted to an agent to do those things which are necessary to accomplish the principal's objective (p. 260)

implied contract – a situation in which the acts or conduct of individuals suggest that they are in agreement; the promises are not stated directly (p. 41)

implied warranty – a promise to buyer imposed on seller by the operation of law rather than by the express statements of seller (p. 124)

impossibility of performance – the inability of a party in a contract to perform an obligation of the contract (p. 85)

incidental damages – extra expenses, such as shipping or storage costs, incurred by an injured party as a result of a breached contract (p. 106)

incoming partner – a person joining an existing partnership as a new partner; not usually personally responsible for old obligations, unless it is so agreed (p. 280)

independent contractor – a party contracted to perform a specific task who has discretion in choosing the method to obtain the required results; not an employment relationship since the hirer is not liable for the acts of the independent contractor and does not control the acts (p. 256)

infant – see *minor*

inferior courts (municipal courts; justice of the peace courts) – all courts at the local level in counties, cities, towns, and villages which usually have limited jurisdiction and do not keep records of their proceedings (p. 24)

inheritance – a method of acquiring real property from one who has died (p. 187)

injunction – a court order that forbids the performance of an act (p. 91)

injured party – the party who suffers injury or loss in a contract that has been breached by another party (p. 88)

inside director – a director of a corporation who is also a company officer or employee (p. 311)

insolvency – when a person or firm can no longer pay its debts as they become due; or when liabilities exceed assets (p. 320)

instrument – a legal paper (p. 327)

insurers of property — guarantors of the safety of the goods in their care (p. 162)

intent — in reference to contract law, the required mental state necessary to form a contract (p. 52)

intentional tort — a civil wrong that is purposely committed (p. 224)

intervening illegality — a situation in which the subject of an offer becomes illegal between the time of the offer and the acceptance; the offer is automatically terminated (p. 63)

intrastate — within state lines (p. 162)

interstate — across state lines (p. 162)

issued stock — the portion of shares which is sold and owned by shareholders in a corporation (p. 301)

joint tenancy — concurrent ownership of real property in which all owners possess interest which is acquired at same time and by the same instrument; title is passed through right of survivorship (p. 182)

judge (justice) — a public official who is either appointed or elected to be in charge of a court and to administer the law (p. 19)

jurisdiction — the power of a certain court to hear a particular case and to interpret and apply the law (p. 16)

just compensation — fair payment (p. 181)

justice(s) — see *judge*

justice of the peace courts (J.P. courts) — see *inferior courts*

landlord (lessor) — a real property owner who promises use of his or her property to others in a lease (p. 204)

lapse of time — one reason for the termination of an offer of a contract; if the offer is not accepted during a specified time stated in the offer it is said to have *lapsed* (p. 62)

law — a set of principles and regulations that is established to define the relationships of people with each other and with their government (p. 1)

law apprenticeship — the system of education of lawyers in England and early America in which students learned the law by working with practicing attorneys (p. 1)

lawyer (attorney-at-law, attorney) — one whose profession is the law; one who handles cases in court, gives legal advice and aid (p. 1)

lease — a contract which enables owners of real property to allow others to use their property; usually, must be in writing (p. 204)

legal entity — something that has real existence in the eyes of the law; a natural or artifical person (p. 277)

legal purpose — an element in a binding contract; lawful reason or legality of the subject matter of a contract (p. 70)

legislate — to make or pass laws (p. 9)

legislature — a group of elected officials who enact laws (p. 9)

legislation — laws passed by legislatures (p. 9)

lessee — see *tenant*

lessor — see *landlord*

libel — defamation of good character in the form of writing, printing or pictures (p. 231)

license — a temporary right of one party to use another's land in a limited and specified manner which is revocable at the will of the licensor; no possession or ownership transferred (p. 176)

lien — in relation to a bailment, the legal right a bailee has to keep goods in his or her possession until payment is made (p. 154)

life estate — an interest in land that is limited in time to the life of the person holding it or the life of another; not full ownership (p. 175)

life tenant — the holder of a life estate (p. 175)

limited partner — a member of a partnership who is only liable to the firm and its creditors to the extent of his or her original contribution, but is limited in participation and management of the firm (p. 289)

limited partnership — a firm composed of one or more general partners and one or more limited partners (p. 288)

liquidated damages — a stated sum of money outlined in a contract that will be paid should there be nonperformance on the part of one of the parties (p. 88)

listing agreement — a written agreement between a seller and a broker of real property stating the period of time of the listing and the amount of commission that will be paid by seller to broker (p. 191)

litigate — to contest or dispute by judicial process (p. 29)

long-term lease — a lease for a period of five, ten, or more years, depending on state statutes; must be executed in a formal manner and recorded (p. 205)

maker — the party who makes a promise to pay and issues a note (p. 332)

malicious intent — a desire to inflict injury; must be present in an intentional tort action in order for there to be recovery (p. 231)

malicious prosecution — initiation of a criminal action against another without valid reason and with the intent to cause injury or damage (p. 233)

memorandum — an informal note which constitutes a writing under UCC rules for the sale of goods of $500 or more (p. 48)

merchant — a professional buyer or seller having specialized knowledge or skills (p. 98)

merchantability — the marketable quality of goods (p. 127)

merger — one corporation remaining in existence and absorbing one or more other corporations that dissolve (p. 320)

minor (infant) — any person who has not reached the legal age as provided by the laws of the state in which the person resides; an incompetent in contract law (p. 68)

minutes — an accurate record kept at meetings (such as board of directors meetings) which contains such things as time and place of meeting, list of those who attended, proposals made and their outcome, and so forth (p. 312)

model (of goods) — representation of goods to be sold (p. 126)

Model Act — see *Model Business Act*

Model Business Act (the Model Act) — a guide used by states to update their statutes on corporate regulations; adopted in 1949 by the American Bar Association and used completely or in part by almost every state today (p. 297)

municipal courts — see *inferior courts*

mutual assent — an element of a binding contract; the situation which exists when there is an offer and an acceptance that meet all the requirements; a meeting of the minds (p. 66)

negligence — failure to take proper care, resulting in injury or damage to other persons or property; basis for tort action (p. 234)

negligent — failing to exercise such care as a responsible person would under the same circumstances (reasonable man standard) resulting in injury or damage to other persons or property (p. 152,227)

negotiable — the quality of some types of commercial paper stipulating an unconditional promise or order to pay a sum certain on demand or in the future. The negotiating of commercial paper creates an almost absolute right to payment for holders who achieve the status of holder in due course.

nonissued stock — that portion of the shares of a corporation which are not issued and owned by shareholders (p. 301)

nonmerchant — a casual, as opposed to professional, buyer or seller; a consumer (p. 98)

nontrading partnership—one that engages in providing a service (p. 283)

note — a credit document given by one person to another to obtain goods or services with a promise of future payment; a form of commercial paper (p. 332)

not-for-profit corporation — a business not formed with the purpose of receiving a profitable return on money invested (p. 296)

nuisance — a tort which arises from improper or unlawful use of one's own land which results in threatened or actual damage to others (p. 234)

offer — an element of a binding contract; a promise by one person to do something upon the acceptance of the terms by the other person involved (p. 52)

offeree — the party to whom the offer or promise is made in a binding contract (p. 52)

offeror — the party making the offer or promise in a binding contract (p. 52)

officer (of a corporation) — an individual who takes care of the day-to-day running of the business; hired, appointed, or elected by the board of directors (p. 299)

option — an additional promise by the offeror in a contract to hold an offer open for a given period of time with a separate binding element, such as a payment of money (p. 61)

ordinance — a local law passed by a town, city, or county legislative body (p. 10)

original jurisdiction — the power of a court to hear a case when it is first brought into court (p. 18)

outside director — a director who brings knowledge to a corporation by way of expertise in such fields as politics, law, or finance; outside directors are not connected in any other way with the company they serve (p. 311)

par value — the monetary worth placed on each share of stock by a corporation in its articles of incorporation (p. 303)

partially disclosed principal — in an agency relationship, the designation of the principal when the third party is aware that the agent is acting for a principal, but does not know the identity of that principal (p. 271)

partner — a coowner of a partnership (p. 277)

partnership — a form of business created by agreement of two or more persons to operate a business as coowners (partners) for the purpose of making a profit (p. 277)

partnership capital — the amount of goods or money contributed by each member of a partnership to the firm; may be unequal amounts (p. 281)

partnership property — all property originally contributed, and all property later acquired with partnership funds or as a result of partnership knowledge or services (p. 280)

passenger — a person being tranported (p. 164)

patent — a guarantee against the copying of an idea; issued by the U.S. Patent Office on any new invention of a process, machine, product, growing plant, or design; valid for seventeen years (p. 244)

pawn — a loan made by a person based on some security left by the owner (p. 153)

payee — the party to whom the promise to pay is made on a note; or the party to whom a draft is written (p. 331)

perjury — making false statements under oath (p. 44)

personal defenses — the defenses that makers and drawers of commercial paper have against the immediate parties to the instrument, but which cannot be used against holders in due course, such as fraud or duress during the making of the instrument (p. 345)

personal jurisdiction — the power a court may exert to force a defendant to appear before it and to be subject to its decision (p. 16)

personal property — everything that is not realty, including clothes, cars, stocks, cash, and the right to be paid a debt (p. 95)

plaintiff — the party in a case who begins the proceedings (is alleging the wrong) (p. 1)

pleadings — the initial papers passed between plaintiff and defendant (or their attorneys) in a court procedure, including the summons, the answer, and the reply (p. 28)

pledge — a mutual benefit bailment created when one party gives any kind of personal property to another as security for the payment of a debt, or for the performance of an obligation (p. 152)

possessory interest -- see *estate*

postdate — to date later than the current date (p. 339)

power of attorney — power given in writing by a principal to any competent person to act as an agent in business or personal dealings (p. 258)

precedent — a case decision which serves as a model for all future cases with the same features (p. 4)

pre-existing obligation — an obligation already in effect; a party cannot make a second promise to do the same thing which that party has already promised to do (p. 67)

preferred stock — owners of this type of corporation stock have preferences or rights over other classes of stockholders, such as one of the first claims on profits; holders usually do not have the right to vote, although they do have ownership in the corporation (p. 303)

principal — the party who grants authority to an agent to act as the representative in an agency relationship (p. 253)

private carrier — transporter of goods under individual contracts; does not offer service to the general public, only those it selects (p. 161)

private law — a body of laws that deals with relationships between individuals (p. 32)

privilege — a legal or justified excuse (p. 232)

product liability — legal responsibility for the quality of a product (p. 139)

professional agent — an individual who acts as an agent but is not employed by any specific person; a professional agent may hire others to work for him or her (example: a lawyer) (p. 256)

profit corporation — a business form created to transact business with the purpose of distributing returns to its shareholders in the form of dividends (p. 296)

promisee — the one to whom a pledge or promise is made (p. 31)

promisor — the person who makes a pledge or promise (p. 31)

promissory note — another name for a note; a form of commercial paper (p. 332)

promoter — a person(s) who organizes a corporation (p. 296)

property — the subject of ownership; the right to have, use, and dispose of things or rights or value (p. 95)

proximate cause — the next or nearest cause of a plaintiff's injury in a tort action; an element of a tort action (p. 228)

proxy — a statement sent in by a shareholder of a corporation who cannot attend the shareholders' meeting which appoints an agent to vote for the absentee and directs how the vote shall be cast (p. 307)

public carrier — a carrier which must carry for hire all passengers who request their services, unless they do not have money to pay or their behavior is objectionable (p. 164)

public law — a body of laws that deals with acts that are a threat to society as a whole, such as crimes (p. 32)

published — communicated or reproduced so that a third person hears or reads the statement; slander or libel must be *published* for there to be a tort action (p. 231)

puffing — statements made by sellers that are a part of a normal sales talk, or statements they make which express their opinion about a product; do not give rise to express warranties (p. 124)

purchase offer — a contract of sale which is a formal agreement between a buyer and a seller to transfer ownership of real property at a definite time in the future (p. 191)

qualified endorsement — an endorsement which permits the endorser to disclaim any liability on an instrument if the maker or drawer fails to pay, as long as the endorser is not aware of any defenses the maker or drawer may have; usually includes the words *without recourse* (p. 343)

quasi-contract — a type of implied contract that is created by operation of law (p. 41)

quitclaim deed — a document used to release any outstanding claims against a property; it conveys only that interest that the grantor has the property (p. 200)

quorum (of a board of directors) — normally, the majority of the directors of a corporation that are required by the bylaws or articles to be present at a meeting before business can be transacted (p. 311)

ratify — affirm or agree to (p. 69)

real defenses — defenses makers or drawers of commercial paper have against both holders and holders in due course, such as the maker's incompetency, or alteration of the instrument (p. 348)

real property (realty) — land and anything that is firmly attached to it, including growing trees, crops, and minerals (p. 95)

reasonable man standard — the standard of care against which the conduct of a defendant in a tort action is measured (p. 227)

receiver — in the context of partnerships, a person appointed to handle the winding up of a partnership when a court decree causes dissolution (p. 288)

reimbursement — a paying back for funds spent; a principal is obligated to *reimburse* an agent for funds used in carrying out directives (p. 270)

rejection — a turning down; nonacceptance (p. 63)

remainder (remainder interest) — the estate or interest which is left after the life estate expires; usually a fee simple interest (p. 175)

remainder interest — see *remainder*

remedy — relief or means of compensation for an injured party (p. 88)

remote purchaser — the eventual consumer of a product which has passed through a series of sellers and buyers (p. 139)

renouncement — an abandonment or giving up; an agent may *renounce* an agency (p. 272)

rent — the consideration paid to the lessor by a lessee for the use of real property (p. 204)

reply — a response by the plaintiff to any allegations stated in defendant's answer (p. 28)

repossession — regaining possession; the taking back of collateral by the secured party from a debtor who defaults (p. 119)

respondeat superior — a doctrine which holds the employer responsible for the negligent conduct of an employee (p. 236)

restrictive endorsement — an endorsement which prohibits further endorsement on an instrument, but does not prevent further transfer; such restrictions may be either conditional or for a specific purpose (p. 342)

retained earnings — earned profits that are retained (kept) instead of paid out in dividends; one method of financing a corporation (p. 301)

reverse stock split — a change in the par value of the stock of a corporation by decreasing the number of shares but keeping the total capital amount the same (p. 310)

revocation — a taking back, a withdrawal; results in termination of prior agreements (p. 272)

revoke — to withdraw (an offer) (p. 60)

right of survivorship — referring to ownership of real property, upon the death of one tenant, the surviving tenants take the interest of the one who died; ownership cannot be willed (p. 183)

risk of loss — responsibility for compensation of a loss if goods in a contract of sale are damaged or destroyed (p. 102)

sale — the transfer of goods or services at the present time from one party to another for a consideration (p. 97)

sale on approval — a sale in which goods are delivered to a buyer with an agreement that the buyer may try or use the goods to determine whether that buyer wants to purchase them or not (p. 103)

sale or return — a sale agreement in which the buyer may resell some of the goods to the seller within the time limits of the contract (p. 103)

sample (of goods) — part of the goods to be sold (p. 126)

satisfactory performance — a standard of performance for contract obligations which demands exact completion of the terms of the contract to the satisfaction of the other party involved; for instance, when payment of a certain sum is required (p. 81)

scope of authority − the range of power given by a principal to an agent in an agency relationship (p. 260)

seal − impression on a document (originally made of wax) that serves as a person's signature; formerly required on all formal contracts (p. 34)

secured credit sale − a type of credit sale in which the seller retains a security interest in the goods; the buyer is allowed to take possession of the goods with a promise of future payment (p. 113)

secured party − a person or institution extending credit which is secured by collateral (p. 113)

securities − instruments which represent shares or interests in property or in enterprise which show an obligation of the issuer (p. 301)

security (in a lease) − a payment to assure performance of the terms of a lease (p. 215)

security agreement − a document giving a secured creditor a security interest in the collateral (p. 113)

security interest − an interest of the secured party in personal property which assures payment or performance of an obligation by the creditor (p. 113)

short-term lease − a rental agreement for over one year, but less than the statutory term for long-term leases; no formal requirements for its form (p. 205)

silent partner − coowner of a partnership who is inactive in conducting the business but has full liability for all partnership obligations (p. 279)

simple contract − a legal agreement not required to be under seal; may be oral or written (p. 34)

slander − defamation of good character by words or gestures (p. 231)

social agreement − a state of being in accord that does not affect society as a whole; a social agreement is not legally enforceable in court (p. 31)

sole proprietorship − a business owned soley by one person who supplies all capital, takes all risks, and receives all profits of the operation (p. 251)

sole tenant − an individual who has title to property alone (p. 182)

special agent − in an agency relationship, a person given only limited authority to act for the principal (p. 255)

special (full) endorsement — an endorsement which specifies the person to whom or to whose order the instrument is payable; (p. 341)

specific performance — a remedy for breach of contract which demands that exact terms of the original legal agreement be carried out (p. 89)

staie court system — the organization of courts established by each state, independent of any other state and the federal government, and given power relating to state law and rights of the citizens in that state (usually organized on the same pattern as the federal court system) (p. 23)

state lower courts — trial courts (courts with original jurisdiction) in the state court system (p. 24)

state higher courts — appellate courts in the state court system (p. 24)

Statute of Frauds — statutes which specify which contracts must be in writing to be enforceable (p. 44)

statute of limitations — a statute which sets a time limit regarding when an action can be brought by one party against another party (p. 49)

statutory law — the entire group of laws (legislation) passed by legislatures (p. 9)

stock (equity securities) — instruments which entitle holder to share in profits of the corporation, or in the assets at dissolution (p. 301)

stock assignment form — found on the back of a stock certificate and used in the transfer of ownership of the stock (p. 305)

stock certificate — a document issued to a person who buys one or more shares of stock in a corporation which represents the person's portion of interest in that corporation; evidence of an intangible share of stock (p. 301)

stock dividends — additional shares of the corporation stock distributed to shareholders instead of cash dividends (p. 310)

stock split — a change in par value of the stock of a corporation by increasing the number of shares, but keeping the total capital amount the same (p. 310)

strict liability — holding individuals liable in special situations for the results of their actions without any reference to negligence (p. 236)

subject matter jurisdiction — the power of a court to hear a particular type of case (usually specified in statutes) (p. 16)

sublessee — a new tenant in a subletting transaction, who is liable to the sublessor, the original tenant (p. 214)

sublessor — tenant who transfers a part interest to real property and becomes a landlord to the new tenant, the sublessee (p. 214)

sublet — transferral of a part interest in real property by a tenant (p. 214)

substantial performance — slightly less than complete or satisfactory performance of a contract; a situation in which a slight variation from the exact terms of a contract is allowed (p. 81)

suit in conversion — a civil action against one who unlawfully seizes and uses personal property of another (p. 233)

sum certain — an amount stated exactly or able to be computed from available information (p. 335)

summons — a device which provides notice to the defendant of the suit against him or her and grants the court power over the person of the defendant; it literally orders the defendant to appear in court (p. 25)

Supreme Court, U.S. — the highest court in the land as established by the federal constitution; it normally handles appeals cases from federal and state courts, but on rare occasions has original jurisdiction (p. 22)

survey — a formal examination (usually by an engineer) that determines the true boundaries of a particular section of land and the position of structures on the land (p. 194)

tax sale — sale of property by a government body after a stated period to compensate for unpaid taxes; purchaser acquires title and money paid is applied to the back taxes (p. 187)

tenancy — the ownership of property (p. 181)

tenancy by the entirety — concurrent ownership of real property in which the tenants must be husband and wife; right of survivorship applies; tenant must have consent of spouse to sell (p. 183)

tenancy in common — concurrent ownership of real property in which each tenant may sell, give, or will interest without consent of others; owners can have equal or unequal shares (p. 182)

tender — an offer to satisfy a debt or perform an obligation (p. 85)

tenant (lessee) — a person renting real property (p. 204)

terminate — to end; to cease to exist (p. 60)

third party — in agency relationship, the party who deals with the principal through an authorized agent (p. 253)

title — legal ownership of property including the right to possess, to use, and to dispose of the property (p. 102)

title closing — time agreed upon in the purchase offer for the actual transferring of the title by seller by delivery of a properly executed deed; attended by both parties to the sale and their attorneys (p. 201)

title company — a firm which is paid a fee to search all the records of a property, investigate all transfers in the chain of title and note any and all mortgages and liens that are outstanding; their report is called an abstract of title (p. 194)

title search — an investigation of all the transfers in the chain of title of a particular property, and any and all mortgages and liens outstanding on the property; usually paid for by the seller of the property (p. 194)

tort — a violation of a right of one party by another party that is not covered by a contract; a civil wrong (p. 224)

tortfeasor — a person who commits a tort against another (p. 224)

trade fixture — an item that is added by the tenant for the purpose of carrying on a trade; normally it does not become part of the property (p. 214)

trade secret — a formula, pattern, or special information known only to a few people in a company and treated very confidentially by those individuals (p. 244)

trading partnership — one that engages in buying and selling for profit (p. 283)

transferable — able to be exchanged; negotiable (p. 327)

transient — guest who seeks food and temporary lodging (p. 165)

treasury stock — issued stock which has been brought back by the corporation; these shares can be kept or reissued at any price (p. 301)

trespass — any violation of the right of people to enjoy and use their property without interference from others (p. 234)

trial — a process of proving claims of a plaintiff and a defendant; a jury or judge listens to all the evidence and decides questions of fact based on the evidence they have seen and heard (p. 29)

trial court — a court where decisions are made by a jury, or if there is no jury, by a judge, after calling witnesses and hearing testimony; trial courts have original jurisdiction to hear cases (p. 18)

trustee — a person assigned by law to take over the contracts and business affairs of those who have gone bankrupt (p. 80)

UCC – see *Uniform Commercial Code*

ULPA – see *Uniform Limited Partnership Act*

ultra vires – beyond the power allowed; formerly used to limit the powers of corporations, but rarely used in courts today (p. 300)

unconditional – without limitations, conditions or other requirements (p. 335)

undisclosed principal – in an agency relationship, the designation of the principal when the third party does not know that an agency relationship exists (is unaware the agent is acting in that capacity) (p. 271)

unenforceable contract – an agreement that cannot be enforced in a court of law (p. 43)

Uniform Commercial Code (the UCC, the Code) – uniform laws for the operation of business transactions adopted by every state except Louisiana (p. 10)

uniform laws – laws which make many of the state laws the same (p. 10)

Uniform Limited Partnership Act (ULPA) – a statute which establishes regulations for limited partnerships; adopted by almost every state (p. 288)

Uniform Partnership Act (UPA) – a statute which defines modern partnership laws; passed in 1914 and adopted by almost every state (p. 277)

unilateral contract – an agreement in which one party makes a promise and desires an act or performance, rather than a promise, in return from another party (p. 35)

unintentional tort – a civil wrong that is not purposely committed, including those resulting from negligence (p. 224)

unique goods – goods whose equivalent cannot be obtained from another source (p. 108)

unsecured credit – a type of credit sale in which articles or services are sold and payment is only promised (example: department store charge accounts) (p. 112)

UPA – see *Uniform Partnership Act*

usurious – a transaction in which a higher interest rate is charged than is legally allowed (p. 71)

usury – the charging of interest which is over the legal rate for loans (p. 71)

valid contract – an agreement containing all the legal requirements of a contract that is enforceable in court (p. 42)

value received — words that are usually included on commercial paper to indicate that it has been issued or exchanged for value or worth (p. 339)

void contract — an agreement that is illegal because it breaks the law or is contrary to public policy; not enforceable in court (p. 42)

voidable contract — an agreement that binds one party to a contract but allows the other party the choice of either carrying it out or withdrawing from it without liability (p. 42)

waiver — the intentional surrender of rights by one party of a contract (p. 87)

warrant — a document issued by a judge when probable cause has been shown; a warrant authorizes the arrest of a person or search of an area (p. 231)

warranty — an express or implied promise which places the responsibility of the quality, character, or suitability of the goods sold upon the seller (p. 124)

warranty deed (full covenant and warranty deed) — a deed used to transfer real property which contains covenants or guarantees by the grantor of clear title to the property (p. 201)

warranty of fitness for particular purpose — an implied warranty which arises when the buyer relies on the seller's judgment to supply suitable goods for a purpose specified by the buyer (p. 137)

warranty of merchantability — an implied warranty which guarantees that goods being sold meet established standards of quality (p. 127)

warranty of title — an implied warranty which guarantees the seller's clear title to the goods and the right to transfer that title with the sale (p. 127)

winding up — a period prior to termination during which the assets of a partnership are liquidated and creditors are paid (p. 285)

without recourse — see *qualified endorsement*

zoning ordinance — a ruling established by a community to regulate the use of real property in specific areas; designed to promote public health, safety, morals, and general welfare of the citizens; power delegated to community by the state (p. 180)

Appendix A

THE UNIFORM COMMERCIAL CODE

(Adopted in 51 jurisdictions: District of Columbia, Virgin Islands, and 49 States, all except Louisiana)

The Code consists of 10 Articles as follows:

Art.
1. General Provisions
2. Sales.
3. Commercial Paper
4. Bank Deposits and Collections
5. Letters of Credit
6. Bulk Transfers
7. Warehouse Receipts, Bills of Lading and Other Documents of Title
8. Investment Securities
9. Secured Transactions: Sales of Accounts, Contract Rights and Chattel Paper
10. Effective Date and Repealer

1972 OFFICIAL TEXT
[Including all Amendments to July 1, 1972]
ARTICLE 1
GENERAL PROVISIONS
PART 1
SHORT TITLE, CONSTRUCTION, APPLICATION AND SUBJECT MATTER OF THE ACT

§ 1–101. Short Title.

This Act shall be known and may be cited as Uniform Commercial Code.

§ 1–102. Purposes; Rules of Construction; Variation by Agreement.

(1) This Act shall be liberally construed and applied to promote its underlying purposes and policies.

(2) Underlying purposes and policies of this Act are

(a) to simplify, clarify and modernize the law governing commercial transactions;

(b) to permit the continued expansion of commercial practices through custom, usage and agreement of the parties;

(c) to make uniform the law among the various jurisdictions.

(3) The effect of provisions of this Act may be varied by agreement, except

as otherwise provided in this Act and except that the obligations of good faith, diligence, reasonableness and care prescribed by this Act may not be disclaimed by agreement but the parties may by agreement determine the standards by which the performance of such obligations is to be measured if such standards are not manifestly unreasonable.

(4)   The presence in certain provisions of this Act of the words "unless otherwise agreed" or words of similar import does not imply that the effect of other provisions may not be varied by agreement under subsection (3).

(5)   In this Act unless the context otherwise requires

> (a) words in the singular number include the plural, and in the plural include the singular;
> (b) words of the masculine gender include the feminine and the neuter, and when the sense so indicates words of the neuter gender may refer to any gender.

§ 1–103. Supplementary General Principles of Law Applicable.

Unless displaced by the particular provisions of this Act, the principles of law and equity, including the law merchant and the law relative to capacity to contract, principal and agent, estoppel, fraud, misrepresentation, duress, coercion, mistake, bankruptcy, or other validating or invalidating cause shall supplement its provisions.

§ 1–104. Construction Against Implicit Repeal.

This Act being a general act intended as a unified coverage of its subject matter, no part of it shall be deemed to be impliedly repealed by subsequent legislation if such construction can reasonably be avoided.

§ 1–105. Territorial Application of the Act; Parties' Power to Choose Applicable Law.

(1)   Except as provided hereafter in this section, when a transaction bears a reasonable relation to this state and also to another state or nation the parties may agree that the law either of this state or of such other state or nation shall govern their rights and duties. Failing such agreement this Act applies to transactions bearing an appropriate relation to this state.

(2)   Where one of the following provisions of this Act specifies the applicable law, that provision governs and a contrary agreement is effective only to the extent permitted by the law (including the conflict of laws rules) so specified:

Rights of creditors against sold goods. Section 2–402.

Applicability of the Article on Bank Deposits and Collections. Section 4–102.

Bulk transfers subject to the Article on Bulk Transfers. Section 6–102.

Applicability of the Article on Investment Securities. Section 8–106.

Perfection provisions of the Article on Secured Transactions. Section 9–103.

§ 1–106. Remedies to Be Liberally Administered.

(1)   The remedies provided by this Act shall be liberally administered to the end that the aggrieved party may be put

in as good a position as if the other party had fully performed but neither consequential or special nor penal damages may be had except as specifically provided in this Act or by other rule of law.

(2) Any right or obligation declared by this Act is enforceable by action unless the provision declaring it specifies a different and limited effect.

§ 1–107. Waiver or Renunciation of Claim or Right After Breach

Any claim or right arising out of an alleged breach can be discharged in whole or in part without consideration by a written waiver or renunciation signed and delivered by the aggrieved party.

§ 1–108. Severability.

If any provision or clause of this Act or application thereof to any person or circumstances is held invalid, such invalidity shall not affect other provisions or applications of the Act which can be given effect without the invalid provision or application, and to this end the provisions of this Act are declared to be severable.

§ 1–109. Section Captions.

Section captions are parts of this Act.

PART 2

GENERAL DEFINITIONS AND PRINCIPLES OF INTERPRETATION

§ 1–201. General Definitions.

Subject to additional definitions contained in the subsequent Articles of this Act which are applicable to specific Articles or Parts thereof, and unless the context otherwise requires, in this Act:

(1) "Action" in the sense of a judicial proceeding includes recoupment, counterclaim, setoff, suit in equity and any other proceedings in which rights are determined.

(2) "Aggrieved party" means a party entitled to resort to a remedy.

(3) "Agreement" means the bargain of the parties in fact as found in their language or by implication from other circumstances including course of dealing or usage of trade or course of performance as provided in this Act (Sections 1–205 and 2–208). Whether an agreement has legal consequences is determined by the provisions of this Act, if applicable; otherwise by the law of contracts (Section 1–103). (Compare "Contract".)

(4) "Bank" means any person engaged in the business of banking.

(5) "Bearer" means the person in possession of an instrument, document of title, or security payable to bearer or indorsed in blank.

(6) "Bill of lading" means a document evidencing the receipt of goods for shipment issued by a person engaged in the business of transporting or forwarding goods, and includes an airbill. "Airbill" means a document serving for air transportation as a bill of lading does for marine or rail transportation, and includes an air consignment note or air waybill.

(7) "Branch" includes a separately incorporated foreign branch of a bank.

(8) "Burden of establishing" a fact means the burden of persuading the triers of fact that the existence of the fact is more probable than its non-existence.

(9) "Buyer in ordinary course of business" means a person who in good faith and without knowledge that the sale

to him is in violation of the ownership rights or security interest of a third party in the goods buys in ordinary course from a person in the business of selling goods of that kind but does not include a pawnbroker. All persons who sell minerals or the like (including oil and gas) at wellhead or minehead shall be deemed to be persons in the business of selling goods of that kind. "Buying" may be for cash or by exchange of other property or on secured or unsecured credit and includes receiving goods or documents of title under a pre-existing contract for sale but does not include a transfer in bulk or as security for or in total or partial satisfaction of a money debt.

(10) "Conspicuous": A term or clause is conspicuous when it is so written that a reasonable person against whom it is to operate ought to have noticed it. A printed heading in capitals (as: NON-NEGOTIABLE BILL OF LADING) is conspicuous. Language in the body of a form is "conspicuous" if it is in larger or other contrasting type or color. But in a telegram any stated term is "conspicuous". Whether a term or clause is "conspicuous" or not is for decision by the court.

(11) "Contract" means the total legal obligation which results from the parties' agreement as affected by this Act and any other applicable rules of law. (Compare "Agreement".)

(12) "Creditor" includes a general creditor, a secured creditor, a lien creditor and any representative of creditors, including an assignee for the benefit of creditors, a trustee in bankruptcy, a receiver in equity and an executor or administrator of an insolvent debtor's or assignor's estate.

(13) "Defendant" includes a person in the position of defendant in a cross-action or counterclaim.

(14) "Delivery" with respect to instruments, documents of title, chattel paper or securities means voluntary transfer of possession.

(15) "Document of title" includes bill of lading, dock warrant, dock receipt, warehouse receipt or order for the delivery of goods, and also any other document which in the regular course of business or financing is treated as adequately evidencing that the person in possession of it is entitled to receive, hold and dispose of the document and the goods it covers. To be a document of title a document must purport to be issued by or addressed to a bailee and purport to cover goods in the bailee's possession which are either identified or are fungible portions of an identified mass.

(16) "Fault" means wrongful act, omission or breach.

(17) "Fungible" with respect to goods or securities means goods or securities of which any unit is, by nature or usage of trade, the equivalent of any other like unit. Goods which are not fungible shall be deemed fungible for the purposes of this Act to the extent that under a particular agreement or document unlike units are treated as equivalents.

(18) "Genuine" means free of forgery or counterfeiting.

(19) "Good faith" means honesty in fact in the conduct or transaction concerned.

(20) "Holder" means a person who is in possession of a document of title or an instrument or an investment security drawn, issued or indorsed to him or to his order or to bearer or in blank.

(21) To "honor" is to pay or to accept and pay, or where a credit so engages to purchase or discount a draft complying with the terms of the credit.

(22) "Insolvency proceedings" includes any assignment for the benefit of creditors or other proceedings intended to liquidate or rehabilitate the estate of the person involved.

(23) A person is "insolvent" who either has ceased to pay his debts in the ordinary course of business or cannot pay his debts as they become due or is insolvent within the meaning of the federal bankruptcy law.

(24) "Money" means a medium of exchange authorized or adopted by a domestic or foreign government as a part of its currency.

(25) A person has "notice" of a fact when

    (a) he has actual knowledge of it; or

    (b) he has received a notice or notification of it; or

    (c) from all the facts and circumstances known to him at the time in question he has reason to know that it exists.

A person "knows" or has "knowledge" of a fact when he has actual knowledge of it. "Discover" or "learn" or a word or phrase of similar import refers to knowledge rather than to reason to know. The time and circumstances under which a notice or notification may cease to be effective are not determined by this Act.

(26) A person "notifies" or "gives" a notice or notification to another by taking such steps as may be reasonably required to inform the other in ordinary course whether or not such other actually comes to know of it. A person "receives" a notice or notification when

    (a) it comes to his attention; or

    (b) it is duly delivered at the place of business through which the contract was made or at any other place held out by him as the place for receipt of such communications.

(27) Notice, knowledge or a notice or notification received by an organization is effective for a particular transaction from the time when it is brought to the attention of the individual conducting that transaction, and in any event from the time when it would have been brought to his attention if the organization had exercised due diligence. An organization exercises due diligence if it maintains reasonable routines for communicating significant information to the person conducting the transaction and there is reasonable compliance with the routines. Due diligence does not require an individual acting for the organization to communicate information unless such communication is part of his regular duties or unless he has reason to know of the transaction and that the transaction would be materially affected by the information.

(28) "Organization" includes a corporation, government or governmental subdivision or agency, business trust, estate, trust, partnership or association, two or more persons having a joint or common interest, or any other legal or commercial entity.

(29) "Party", as distinct from "third party", means a person who has engaged in a transaction or made an agreement within this Act.

(30) "Person" includes an individual or an organization (See Section 1–102).

(31) "Presumption" or "presumed" means that the trier of fact must find the existence of the fact presumed unless and

until evidence is introduced which would support a finding of its nonexistence.

(32) "Purchase" includes taking by sale, discount, negotiation, mortgage, pledge, lien, issue or re-issue, gift or any other voluntary transaction creating an interest in property.

(33) "Purchaser" means a person who takes by purchase.

(34) "Remedy" means any remedial right to which an aggrieved party is entitled with or without resort to a tribunal.

(35) "Representative" includes an agent, an officer of a corporation or association, and a trustee, executor or administrator of an estate, or any other person empowered to act for another.

(36) "Rights" includes remedies.

(37) "Security interest" means an interest in personal property or fixtures which secures payment or performance of an obligation. The retention or reservation of title by a seller of goods notwithstanding shipment or delivery to the buyer (Section 2–401) is limited in effect to a reservation of a "security interest". The term also includes any interest of a buyer of accounts or chattel paper which is subject to Article 9. The special property interest of a buyer of goods on identification of such goods to a contract for sale under Section 2–401 is not a "security interest", but a buyer may also acquire a "security interest" by complying with Article 9. Unless a lease or consignment is intended as security, reservation of title thereunder is not a "security interest" but a consignment is in any event subject to the provisions on consignment sales (Section 2–326). Whether a lease is intended as security is to be determined by the facts of each case; however, (a) the inclusion of an option to purchase does not of itself make the lease one intended

for security, and (b) an agreement that upon compliance with the terms of the lease the lessee shall become or has the option to become the owner of the property for no additional consideration or for a nominal consideration does make the lease one intended for security.

(38) "Send" in connection with any writing or notice means to deposit in the mail or deliver for transmission by any other usual means of communication with postage or cost of transmission provided for and properly addressed and in the case of an instrument to an address specified thereon or otherwise agreed, or if there be none to any address reasonable under the circumstances. The receipt of any writing or notice within the time at which it would have arrived if properly sent has the effect of a proper sending.

(39) "Signed" includes any symbol executed or adopted by a party with present intention to authenticate a writing.

(40) "Surety" includes guarantor.

(41) "Telegram" includes a message transmitted by radio, teletype, cable, any mechanical method of transmission, or the like.

(42) "Term" means that portion of an agreement which relates to a particular matter.

(43) "Unauthorized" signature or indorsement means one made without actual, implied or apparent authority and includes a forgery.

(44) "Value". Except as otherwise provided with respect to negotiable instruments and bank collections (Sections 3–303, 4–208 and 4–209) a person gives "value" for rights if he acquires them

> (a) in return for a binding commitment to extend credit or for the extension of immediately available credit whether or not drawn

upon and whether or not a charge-back is provided for in the event of difficulties in collection; or

(b) as security for or in total or partial satisfaction of a pre-existing claim; or

(c) by accepting delivery pursuant to a pre-existing contract for purchase; or

(d) generally, in return for any consideration sufficient to support a simple contract.

(45) "Warehouse receipt" means a receipt issued by a person engaged in the business of storing goods for hire.

(46) "Written" or "writing" includes printing, typewriting or any other intentional reduction to tangible form.

§ 1–202. Prima Facie Evidence by Third Party Documents.

A document in due form purporting to be a bill of lading, policy or certificate of insurance, official weigher's or inspector's certificate, consular invoice, or any other document authorized or required by the contract to be issued by a third party shall be prima facie evidence of its own authenticity and genuineness and of the facts stated in the document by the third party.

§ 1–203. Obligation of Good Faith.

Every contract or duty within this Act imposes an obligation of good faith in its performance or enforcement.

§ 1–204. Time; Reasonable Time; "Seasonably".

(1) Whenever this Act requires any action to be taken within a reasonable time, any time which is not manifestly unreasonable may be fixed by agreement.

(2) What is a reasonable time for taking any action depends on the nature, purpose and circumstances of such action.

(3) An action is taken "seasonably" when it is taken at or within the time agreed or if no time is agreed at or within a reasonable time.

§ 1–205. Course of Dealing and Usage of Trade.

(1) A course of dealing is a sequence of previous conduct between the parties to a particular transaction which is fairly to be regarded as establishing a common basis of understanding for interpreting their expressions and other conduct.

(2) A usage of trade is any practice or method of dealing having such regularity of observance in a place, vocation or trade as to justify an expectation that it will be observed with respect to the transaction in question. The existence and scope of such a usage are to be proved as facts. If it is established that such a usage is embodied in a written trade code or similar writing the interpretation of the writing is for the court.

(3) A course of dealing between parties and any usage of trade in the vocation or trade in which they are engaged or of which they are or should be aware give particular meaning to and supplement or qualify terms of an agreement.

(4) The express terms of an agreement and an applicable course of dealing or usage of trade shall be construed wherever reasonable as consistent with each other; but when such construction is unreasonable express terms control both course of dealing and usage of trade and course of dealing controls usage of trade.

(5) An applicable usage of trade in the place where any part of performance is to occur shall be used in interpreting

the agreement as to that part of the performance.

(6) Evidence of a relevant usage of trade offered by one party is not admissible unless and until he has given the other party such notice as the court finds sufficient to prevent unfair surprise to the latter.

§ 1–206. Statute of Frauds for Kinds of Personal Property Not Otherwise Covered.

(1) Except in the cases described in subsection (2) of this section a contract for the sale of personal property is not enforceable by way of action or defense beyond five thousand dollars in amount or value of remedy unless there is some writing which indicates that a contract for sale has been made between the parties at a defined or stated price, reasonably identifies the subject matter, and is signed by the party against whom enforcement is sought or by his authorized agent.

(2) Subsection (1) of this section does not apply to contracts for the sale of goods (Section 2–201) nor of securities (Section 8–319) nor to security agreements (Section 9–203).

§ 1–207. Performance or Acceptance Under Reservation of Rights.

A party who with explicit reservation of rights performs or promises performance or assents to performance in a manner demanded or offered by the other party does not thereby prejudice the rights reserved. Such words as "without prejudice", "under protest" or the like are sufficient.

§ 1–208. Option to Accelerate at Will.

A term providing that one party or his successor in interest may accelerate payment or performance or require collateral or additional collateral "at will" or "when he deems himself insecure" or in words of similar import shall be construed to mean that he shall have power to do so only if he in good faith believes that the prospect of payment or performance is impaired. The burden of establishing lack of good faith is on the party against whom the power has been exercised.

ARTICLE 2

SALES

PART 1

SHORT TITLE, CONSTRUCTION AND SUBJECT MATTER

§ 2–101. Short Title.

This Article shall be known and may be cited as Uniform Commercial Code – Sales.

§ 2–102. Scope; Certain Security and Other Transactions Excluded From This Article.

Unless the context otherwise requires, this Article applies to transactions in goods; it does not apply to any transaction which although in the form of an unconditional contract to sell or present sale is intended to operate only as a security transaction nor does this Article impair or repeal any statute regulating sales to consumers, farmers or other specified classes of buyers.

§ 2–103. Definitions and Index of Definitions

(1) In this Article unless the context otherwise requires

    (a) "Buyer" means a person who buys or contracts to buy goods.

    (b) "Good faith" in the case of a merchant means honesty in fact and the observance of reasonable commercial standards of fair dealing in the trade.

    (c) "Receipt" of goods means taking physical possession of them.

    (d) "Seller" means a person who sells or contracts to sell goods.

(2) Other definitions applying to this Article or to specified Parts thereof, and the sections in which they appear are:

"Acceptance". Section 2–606.

"Banker's credit". Section 2–325.

"Between merchants". Section 2–104.

"Cancellation". Section 2–106(4).

"Commercial unit". Section 2–105.

"Confirmed credit". Section 2–325.

"Conforming to contract". Section 2–106.

"Contract for sale". Section 2–106.

"Cover". Section 2–712.

"Entrusting". Section 2–403.

"Financing agency". Section 2–104.

"Future goods". Section 2–105.

"Goods". Section 2–105.

"Identification". Section 2–501.

"Installment contract". Section 2–612.

"Letter of Credit". Section 2–325.

"Lot". Section 2–105.

"Merchant". Section 2–104.

"Overseas". Section 2–323.

"Person in position of seller". Section 2–707.

"Present sale". Section 2–106.

"Sale". Section 2–106.

"Sale on approval". Section 2–326.

"Sale or return". Section 2–326.

"Termination". Section 2–106.

(3) The following definitions in other Articles apply to this Article:

"Check". Section 3–104.

"Consignee". Section 7–102.

"Consignor". Section 7–102.

"Consumer goods". Section 9–109.

"Dishonor". Section 3–507.

"Draft". Section 3–104.

(4) In addition Article 1 contains general definitions and principles of construction and interpretation applicable throughout this Article.

§ 2–104. Definitions: "Merchant"; "Between Merchants"; "Financing Agency".

(1) "Merchant" means a person who deals in goods of the kind or otherwise by his occupation holds himself out as having knowledge or skill peculiar to the practices or goods involved in the transaction or to whom such knowledge or skill may be attributed by his employment of an agent or broker or other intermediary who by his occupation holds himself out as having such knowledge or skill.

(2) "Financing agency" means a bank, finance company or other person who in the ordinary course of business makes advances against goods or documents of title or who by arrangement with either the seller or the buyer intervenes in ordinary course to make or collect payment due or claimed under the contract for sale, as by purchasing or paying the seller's draft or making advances against it or by merely taking it for collection whether or not documents of title accompany the draft. "Financing agency" includes also a bank or other person who similarly intervenes between persons who

are in the position of seller and buyer in respect to the goods (Section 2–707).

(3)   "Between merchants" means in any transaction with respect to which both parties are chargeable with the knowledge or skill of merchants.

§ 2–105. Definitions: Transferability; "Goods"; "Future" Goods; "Lot"; "Commercial Unit".

(1)   "Goods" means all things (including specially manufactured goods) which are movable at the time of identification to the contract for sale other than the money in which the price is to be paid, investment securities (Article 8) and things in action. "Goods" also includes the unborn young of animals and growing crops and other identified things attached to realty as described in the section on goods to be severed from realty (Section 2–107).

(2)   Goods must be both existing and identified before any interest in them can pass. Goods which are not both existing and identified are "future" goods. A purported present sale of future goods or of any interest therein operates as a contract to sell.

(3)   There may be a sale of a part interest in existing identified goods.

(4)   An undivided share in an identified bulk of fungible goods is sufficiently identified to be sold although the quantity of the bulk is not determined. Any agreed proportion of such a bulk or any quantity thereof agreed upon by number, weight or other measure may to the extent of the seller's interest in the bulk be sold to the buyer who then becomes an owner in common.

(5)   "Lot" means a parcel or a single article which is the subject matter of a separate sale or delivery, whether or not it is sufficient to perform the contract.

(6)   "Commercial unit" means such a unit of goods as by commercial usage is a single whole for purposes of sale and division of which materially impairs its character or value on the market or in use. A commercial unit may be a single article (as a machine) or a set of articles (as a suite of furniture or an assortment of sizes) or a quantity (as a bale, gross, or carload) or any other unit treated in use or in the relevant market as a single whole.

§ 2–106. Definitions: "Contract"; "Agreement"; "Contract for Sale"; "Sale"; "Present Sale"; "Conforming" to Contract; "Termination"; "Cancellation".

(1)   In this Article unless the context otherwise requires "contract" and "agreement" are limited to those relating to the present or future sale of goods. "Contract for sale" includes both a present sale of goods and a contract to sell goods at a future time.   A "sale" consists in the passing of title from the seller to the buyer for a price (Section 2–401). A "present sale" means a sale which is accomplished by the making of the contract.

(2)   Goods or conduct including any part of a performance are "conforming" or conform to the contract when they are in accordance with the obligations under the contract.

(3)   "Termination" occurs when either party pursuant to a power created by agreement or law puts an end to the contract otherwise than for its breach.   On "termination" all obligations which are still executory on both sides are discharged but any right based on prior breach or performance survives.

(4)   "Cancellation" occurs when either party puts an end to the contract

for breach by the other and its effect is the same as that of "termination" except that the cancelling party also retains any remedy for breach of the whole contract or any unperformed balance.

§ 2–107. Goods to Be Severed From Realty: Recording.

(1)   A contract for the sale of minerals or the like (including oil and gas) or a structure or its materials to be removed from realty is a contract for the sale of goods within this Article if they are to be severed by the seller but until severance a purported present sale thereof which is not effective as a transfer of an interest in land is effective only as a contract to sell.

(2)   A contract for the sale apart from the land of growing crops or other things attached to realty and capable of severance without material harm thereto but not described in subsection (1) or of timber to be cut is a contract for the sale of goods within this Article whether the subject matter is to be severed by the buyer or by the seller even though it forms part of the realty at the time of contracting, and the parties can by identification effect a present sale before severance.

(3)   The provisions of this section are subject to any third party rights provided by the law relating to realty records, and the contract for sale may be executed and recorded as a document transferring an interest in land and shall then constitute notice to third parties of the buyer's rights under the contract for sale.

PART 2

FORM, FORMATION AND READJUSTMENT OF CONTRACT

§ 2–201. Formal Requirements; Statute of Frauds.

(1)   Except as otherwise provided in this section a contract for the sale of goods for the price of $500 or more is not enforceable by way of action or defense unless there is some writing sufficient to indicate that a contract for sale has been made between the parties and signed by the party against whom enforcement is sought or by his authorized agent or broker. A writing is not insufficient because it omits or incorrectly states a term agreed upon but the contract is not enforceable under this paragraph beyond the quantity of goods shown in such writing.

(2)   Between merchants if within a reasonable time a writing in confirmation of the contract and sufficient against the sender is received and the party receiving it has reason to know its contents, it satis-fies the requirements of subsection (1) against such party unless written notice of objection to its contents is given within ten days after it is received.

(3)   A contract which does not satisfy the requirements of subsection (1) but which is valid in other respects is enforceable

(a)   if the goods are to be specially manufactured for the buyer and are not suitable for sale to others in the ordinary course of the seller's business and the seller, before notice of repudiation is received and under circumstances which reasonably indicate that the goods are for the buyer, has made either a substantial beginning of their manufacture or commitments for their procurement; or

(b) if the party against whom enforcement is sought admits in his pleading, testimony or otherwise in court that a contract for sale was made, but the contract is not enforceable under this provision beyond the quantity of goods admitted; or

(c) with respect to goods for which payment has been made and accepted or which have been received and accepted (Section 2–606).

§ 2–202. Final Written Expression: Parol or Extrinsic Evidence

Terms with respect to which the confirmatory memoranda of the parties agree or which are otherwise set forth in a writing intended by the parties as a final expression of their agreement with respect to such terms as are included therein may not be contradicted by evidence of any prior agreement or of a contemporaneous oral agreement but may be explained or supplemented.

(a) by course of dealing or usage of trade (Section 1–205) or by course of performance (Section 2–208); and

(b) by evidence of consistent additional terms unless the court finds the writing to have been intended also as a complete and exclusive statement of the terms of the agreement.

§ 2–203. Seals Inoperative.

The affixing of a seal to a writing evidencing a contract for sale or an offer to buy or sell goods does not constitute the writing a sealed instrument and the law with respect to sealed instruments does not apply to such a contract or offer.

§ 2–204. Formation in General.

(1)   A contract for sale of goods may be made in any manner sufficient to show agreement, including conduct by both parties which recognizes the existence of such a contract.

(2)   An agreement sufficient to constitute a contract for sale may be found even though the moment of its making is undetermined.

(3)   Even though one or more terms are left open a contract for sale does not fail for indefiniteness if the parties have intended to make a contract and there is a reasonably certain basis for giving an appropriate remedy.

§ 2–205. Firm Offers.

An offer by a merchant to buy or sell goods in a signed writing which by its terms gives assurance that it will be held open is not revocable, for lack of consideration, during the time stated or if no time is stated for a reasonable time, but in no event may such period of irrevocability exceed three months; but any such term of assurance on a form supplied by the offeree must be separately signed by the offeror.

§ 2–206. Offer and Acceptance in Formation of Contract.

(1)   Unless otherwise unambiguously indicated by the language or circumstances

(a) an offer to make a contract shall be construed as inviting acceptance in any manner and by any medium reasonable in the circumstances;

(b) an order or other offer to buy goods for prompt or current shipment shall be construed as inviting acceptance either by a prompt promise to ship or by the prompt or current shipment of conforming or nonconforming goods, but such a shipment of non-conforming goods does not constitute· an acceptance if the seller seasonably notifies the buyer that the shipment is offered only as an accommodation to the buyer.

(2) Where the beginning of a requested performance is a reasonable mode of acceptance an offeror who is not notified of acceptance within a reasonable time may treat the offer as having lapsed before acceptance.

§ 2–207. Additional Terms in Acceptance or Confirmation.

(1) A definite and seasonable expression of acceptance or a written confirmation which is sent within a reasonable time operates as an acceptance even though it states terms additional to or different from those offered or agreed upon, unless acceptance is expressly made conditional on assent to the additional or different terms.

(2) The additional terms are to be construed as proposals for addition to the contract. Between merchants such terms become part of the contract unless:

(a) the offer expressly limits acceptance to the terms of the offer;

(b) they materially alter it; or

(c) notification of objection to them has already been given or is given within a reasonable time after notice of them is received.

(3) Conduct by both parties which recognizes the existence of a contract is sufficient to establish a contract for sale although the writings of the parties do not otherwise establish a contract. In such case the terms of the particular contract consist of those terms on which the writings of the parties agree, together with any supplementary terms incorporated under any other provisions of this Act.

§ 2–208. Course of Performance or Practical Construction.

(1) Where the contract for sale involves repeated occasions for performance by either party with knowledge of the nature of the performance and opportunity for objection to it by the other, any course of performance accepted or acquiesced in without objection shall be relevant to determine the meaning of the agreement.

(2) The express terms of the agreement and any such course of performance, as well as any course of dealing and usage of trade, shall be construed whenever reasonable as consistent with each other; but when such construction is unreasonable, express terms shall control course of performance and course of performance shall control both course of dealing and usage of trade (Section 1–205).

(3) Subject to the provisions of the next section on modification and waiver, such course of performance shall be relevant to show a waiver or modification of any term inconsistent with such course of performance.

§ 2–209. Modification, Rescission and Waiver.

(1) An agreement modifying a contract within this Article needs no consideration to be binding.

(2) A signed agreement which excludes modification or rescission except by a signed writing cannot be otherwise modified or rescinded, but except as between merchants such a requirement on a

form supplied by the merchant must be separately signed by the other party.

(3) The requirements of the statute of frauds section of this Article (Section 2–201) must be satisfied if the contract as modified is within its provisions.

(4) Although an attempt at modification or rescission does not satisfy the requirements of subsection (2) or (3) it can operate as a waiver.

(5) A party who has made a waiver affecting an executory portion of the contract may retract the waiver by reasonable notification received by the other party that strict performance will be required of any term waived, unless the retraction would be unjust in view of a material change of position in reliance on the waiver.

§ 2–210. Delegation of Performance; Assignment of Rights.

(1) A party may perform his duty through a delegate unless otherwise agreed or unless the other party has a substantial interest in having his original promisor perform or control the acts required by the contract. No delegation of performance relieves the party delegating of any duty to perform or any liability for breach.

(2) Unless otherwise agreed all rights of either seller or buyer can be assigned except where the assignment would materially change the duty of the other party, or increase materially the burden or risk imposed on him by his contract, or impair materially his chance of obtaining return performance. A right to damages for breach of the whole contract or a right arising out of the assignor's due performance of his entire obligation can be assigned despite agreement otherwise.

(3) Unless the circumstances indicate the contrary a prohibition of assignment of "the contract" is to be construed as barring only the delegation to the assignee of the assignor's performance.

(4) An assignment of "the contract" or of "all my rights under the contract" or an assignment in similar general terms is an assignment of rights and unless the language or the circumstances (as in an assignment for security) indicate the contrary, it is a delegation of performance of the duties of the assignor and its acceptance by the assignee constitutes a promise by him to perform those duties. This promise is enforceable by either the assignor or the other party to the original contract.

(5) The other party may treat any assignment which delegates performance as creating reasonable grounds for insecurity and may without prejudice to his rights against the assignor demand assurances from the assignee (Section 2–609).

PART 3

GENERAL OBLIGATION AND CONSTRUCTION OF CONTRACT

§ 2–301. General Obligations of Parties.

The obligation of the seller is to transfer and deliver and that of the buyer is to accept and pay in accordance with the contract.

§ 2–302. Unconscionable Contract or Clause.

(1) If the court as a matter of law finds the contract or any clause of the contract to have been unconscionable at

the time it was made the court may refuse to enforce the contract, or it may enforce the remainder of the contract without the unconscionable clause, or it may so limit the application of any unconscionable clause as to avoid any unconscionable result.

(2) When it is claimed or appears to the court that the contract or any clause thereof may be unconscionable the parties shall be afforded a reasonable opportunity to present evidence as to its commercial setting, purpose and effect to aid the court in making the determination.

§ 2–303. Allocation or Division of Risks.

Where this Article allocates a risk or a burden as between the parties "unless otherwise agreed", the agreement may not only shift the allocation but may also divide the risk or burden.

§2–304. Price Payable in Money, Goods, Realty, or Otherwise.

(1) The price can be made payable in money or otherwise. If it is payable in whole or in part in goods each party is a seller of the goods which he is to transfer.

(2) Even though all or part of the price is payable in an interest in realty the transfer of the goods and the seller's obligations with reference to them are subject to this Article, but not the transfer of the interest in realty or the transferor's obligations in connection therewith.

§ 2–305. Open Price Term.

(1) The parties if they so intend can conclude a contract for sale even though the price is not settled. In such a case the price is a reasonable price at the time for delivery if

(a) nothing is said as to price; or
(b) the price is left to be agreed by the parties and they fail to agree; or
(c) the price is to be fixed in terms of some agreed market or other standard as set or recorded by a third person or agency and it is not so set or recorded.

(2) A price to be fixed by the seller or by the buyer means a price for him to fix in good faith.

(3) When a price left to be fixed otherwise than by agreement of the parties fails to be fixed through fault of one party the other may at his option treat the contract as cancelled or himself fix a reasonable price.

(4) Where, however, the parties intend not to be bound unless the price be fixed or agreed and it is not fixed or agreed there is no contract. In such a case the buyer must return any goods already received or if unable so to do must pay their reasonable value at the time of delivery and the seller must return any portion of the price paid on account.

§ 2–306. Output, Requirements and Exclusive Dealings.

(1) A term which measures the quantity by the output of the seller or the requirements of the buyer means such actual output or requirements as may occur in good faith, except that no quantity unreasonably disproportionate to any stated estimate or in the absence of a stated estimate to any normal or otherwise comparable prior output or requirements may be tendered or demanded.

(2) A lawful agreement by either the seller or the buyer for exclusive dealing in the kind of goods concerned imposes un-

less otherwise agreed an obligation by the seller to use best efforts to supply the goods and by the buyer to use best efforts to promote their sale.

§ 2–307. Delivery in Single Lot or Several Lots.

Unless otherwise agreed all goods called for by a contract for sale must be tendered in a single delivery and payment is due only on such tender but where the circumstances give either party the right to make or demand delivery in lots the price if it can be apportioned may be demanded for each lot.

§ 2–308. Absence of Specified Place for Delivery.

Unless otherwise agreed
  (a) the place for delivery of goods is the seller's place of business or if he has none his residence; but
  (b) in a contract for sale of identified goods which to the knowledge of the parties at the time of contracting are in some other place, that place is the place for their delivery; and
  (c) documents of title may be delivered through customary banking channels.

§ 2–309. Absence of Specific Time Provisions; Notice of Termination.

(1)   The time for shipment or delivery or any other action under a contract if not provided in this Article or agreed upon shall be a reasonable time.

(2)   Where the contract provides for successive performances but is indefinite in duration it is valid for a reasonable time but unless otherwise agreed may be terminated at any time by either party.

(3)   Termination of a contract by one party except on the happening of an agreed event requires that reasonable notification be received by the other party and an agreement dispensing with notification is invalid if its operation would be unconscionable.

§ 2–310. Open Time for Payment or Running of Credit; Authority to Ship Under Reservation.

Unless otherwise agreed
  (a) payment is due at the time and place at which the buyer is to receive the goods even though the place of shipment is the place of delivery; and
  (b) if the seller is authorized to send the goods he may ship them under reservation, and may tender the documents of title, but the buyer may inspect the goods after their arrival before payment is due unless such inspection is inconsistent with the terms of the contract (Section 2–513); and
  (c) if delivery is authorized and made by way of documents of title otherwise than by subsection (b) then payment is due at the time and place at which the buyer is to receive the documents regardless of where the goods are to be received; and
  (d) where the seller is required or authorized to ship the goods on credit the credit period runs from the time of shipment but postdating the invoice or delaying its dispatch will correspondingly delay the starting of the credit period.

§ 2–311. Options and Cooperation Respecting Performance.

(1)   An agreement for sale which is otherwise sufficiently definite (subsection (3) of Section 2–204) to be a contract is not made invalid by the fact that it leaves particulars of performance to be specified by one of the parties.   Any such specification must be made in good faith and within limits set by commercial reasonableness.

(2)   Unless otherwise agreed specifications relating to assortment of the goods are at the buyer's option and except as otherwise provided in subsections (1) (c) and (3) of Section 2–319 specifications or arrangements relating to shipment are at the seller's option.

(3)   Where such specification would materially affect the other party's performance but is not seasonably made or where one party's cooperation is necessary to the agreed performance of the other but is not seasonably forthcoming, the other party in addition to all other remedies

(a) is excused for any resulting delay in his own performance; and

(b) may also either proceed to perform in any reasonable manner or after the time for a material part of his own performance treat the failure to specify or to cooperate as a breach by failure to deliver or accept the goods.

§ 2–312. Warranty of Title and Against Infringement; Buyer's Obligation Against Infringement.

(1)   Subject to subsection (2) there is in a contract for sale a warranty by the seller that

(a) the title conveyed shall be good, and its transfer rightful; and

(b) the goods shall be delivered free from any security interest or other lien or encumbrance of which the buyer at the time of contracting has no knowledge.

(2)   A warranty under subsection (1) will be excluded or modified only by specific language or by circumstances which give the buyer reason to know that the person selling does not claim title in himself or that he is purporting to sell only such right or title as he or a third person may have.

(3)   Unless otherwise agreed a seller who is a merchant regularly dealing in goods of the kind warrants that the goods shall be delivered free of the rightful claim of any third person by way of infringement or the like but a buyer who furnishes specifications to the seller must hold the seller harmless against any such claim which arises out of compliance with the specifications.

§ 2–313. Express Warranties by Affirmation, Promise, Description, Sample.

(1)   Express warranties by the seller are created as follows:

(a) Any affirmation of fact or promise made by the seller to the buyer which relates to the goods and becomes part of the basis of the bargain creates an express warranty that the goods shall conform to the affirmation or promise.

(b) Any description of the goods which is made part of the basis of the bargain creates an express warranty that the goods shall conform to the description.

(c) Any sample or model which is made part of the basis of the bargain creates an express warranty that the whole of the goods shall conform to the sample or model.

(2) It is not necessary to the creation of an express warranty that the seller use formal words such as "warrant" or "guarantee" or that he have a specific intention to make a warranty, but an affirmation merely of the value of the goods or a statement purporting to be merely the seller's opinion or commendation of the goods does not create a warranty.

§ 2–314. Implied Warranty: Merchantability; Usage of Trade.

(1) Unless excluded or modified (Section 2–316), a warranty that the goods shall be merchantable is implied in a contract for their sale if the seller is a merchant with respect to goods of that kind. Under this section the serving for value of food or drink to be consumed either on the premises or elsewhere is a sale.

(2) Goods to be merchantable must be at least such as

(a) pass without objection in the trade under the contract description; and

(b) in the case of fungible goods, are of fair average quality within the description; and

(c) are fit for the ordinary purposes for which such goods are used; and

(d) run, within the variations permitted by the agreement, of even kind, quality and quantity within each unit and among all units involved; and

(e) are adequately contained, packaged, and labeled as the agreement may require; and

(f) conform to the promises or affirmations of fact made on the container or label if any.

(3) Unless excluded or modified (Section 2–316) other implied warranties may arise from course of dealing or usage of trade.

§ 2–315. Implied Warranty: Fitness for Particular Purpose.

Where the seller at the time of contracting has reason to know any particular purpose for which the goods are required and that the buyer is relying on the seller's skill or judgment to select or furnish suitable goods, there is unless excluded or modified under the next section an implied warranty that the goods shall be fit for such purpose.

§ 2–316. Exclusion or Modification of Warranties.

(1) Words or conduct relevant to the creation of an express warranty and words or conduct tending to negate or limit warranty shall be construed wherever reasonable as consistent with each other; but subject to the provisions of this Article on parol or extrinsic evidence (Section 2–202) negation or limitation is inoperative to the extent that such construction is unreasonable.

(2) Subject to subsection (3), to exclude or modify the implied warranty of merchantability or any part of it the language must mention merchantability and in case of a writing must be conspicuous, and to exclude or modify any implied warranty of fitness the exclusion must be by a writing and conspicuous. Language to exclude all implied warranties of fitness is sufficient if it states, for example, that "There are no warranties which extend beyond the description on the face hereof."

(3) Notwithstanding subsection (2)

(a) unless the circumstances indicate otherwise, all implied warranties are excluded by expressions like "as is", "with all faults" or other language which in common understanding calls the buyer's attention to the exclusion of warranties and makes plain that there is no implied warranty; and

(b) when the buyer before entering into the contract has examined the goods or the sample or model as fully as he desired or has refused to examine the goods there is no implied warranty with regard to defects which an examination ought in the circumstances to have revealed to him; and

(c) an implied warranty can also be excluded or modified by course of dealing or course of performance or usage of trade.

(4) Remedies for breach of warranty can be limited in accordance with the provisions of this Article on liquidation or limitation of damages and on contractual modification of remedy (Sections 2–718 and 2–719.

§ 2–317. Cumulation and Conflict of Warranties Express or Implied.

Warranties whether express or implied shall be construed as consistent with each other and as cumulative, but if such construction is unreasonable the intention of the parties shall determine which warranty is dominant. In ascertaining that intention the following rules apply:

(a) Exact or technical specifications displace an inconsistent sample . or model or general language of description.

(b) A sample from an existing bulk displaces inconsistent general language of description.

(c) Express warranties displace inconsistent implied warranties other than an implied warranty of fitness for a particular purpose.

§ 2–318. Third Party Beneficiaries of Warranties Express or Implied.

A seller's warranty whether express or implied extends to any natural person who is in the family or household of his buyer or who is a guest in his home if it is reasonable to expect that such person may use, consume or be affected by the goods and who is injured in person by breach of warranty. A seller may not exclude or limit the operation of this section.

§ 2–319. F.O.B. and F.A.S. Terms.

(1) Unless otherwise agreed the term F.O.B. (which means "free on board") at a named place, even though used only in connection with the stated price, is a delivery term under which

(a) when the term is F.O.B. the place of shipment, the seller must at that place ship the goods in the manner provided in this Article (Section 2–504) and bear the expense and risk of putting them into the possession of the carrier; or

(b) when the term is F.O.B. the place of destination, the seller must at his own expense and risk transport the goods to that place and there tender delivery of them in the manner provided in this Article (Section 2–503);

(c) when under either (a) or (b) the term is also F.O.B. vessel, car or other vehicle, the seller must in addition at his own expense and risk load the goods on board. If the term is F.O.B. vessel the buyer must name the vessel and in an appropriate case the seller must comply with the provisions of this Article on the form of bill of lading (Section 2–323).

(2)   Unless otherwise agreed the term F.A.S. vessel (which means "free alongside") at a named port, even though used only in connection with the stated price, is a delivery term under which the seller must

  (a) at his own expense and risk deliver the goods alongside the vessel in the manner usual in that port or on a dock designated and provided by the buyer; and

  (b) obtain and tender a receipt for the goods in exchange for which the carrier is under a duty to issue a bill of lading.

(3)   Unless otherwise agreed in any case falling within subsection (1) (a) or (c) or subsection (2) the buyer must seasonably give any needed instructions for making delivery, including when the term is F.A.S. or F.O.B. the loading berth of the vessel and in an appropriate case its name and sailing date.   The seller may treat the failure of needed instructions as a failure of cooperation under this Article (Section 2–311).   He may also at his option move the goods in any reasonable manner preparatory to delivery or shipment.

(4)   Under the term F.O.B. vessel or F.A.S. unless otherwise agreed the buyer must make payment against tender of the required documents and the seller may not tender nor the buyer demand delivery of the goods in substitution for the documents.

§ 2–320. C.I.F. and C. & F. Terms.

(1)   The term C.I.F. means that the price includes in a lump sum the cost of the goods and the insurance and freight to the named destination.   The term C. & F. or C.F. means that the price so includes cost and freight to the named destination.

(2)   Unless otherwise agreed and even though used only in connection with the stated price and destination, the term C.I.F. destination or its equivalent requires the seller at his own expense and risk to

  (a) put the goods into the possession of a carrier at the port for shipment and obtain a negotiable bill or bills of lading covering the entire transportation to the named destination; and

  (b) load the goods and obtain a receipt from the carrier (which may be contained in the bill of lading) showing that the freight has been paid or provided for; and

  (c) obtain a policy or certificate of insurance, including any war risk insurance, of a kind and on terms then current at the port of shipment in the usual amount, in the currency of the contract, shown to cover the same goods covered by the bill of lading and providing for payment of loss to the order of the buyer or for the account of whom it may concern; but the seller may add to the price the amount of the premium for any such war risk insurance; and

  (d) prepare an invoice of the goods and procure any other documents required to effect shipment or to comply with the contract; and

(e) forward and tender with commercial promptness all the documents in due form and with any indorsement necessary to perfect the buyer's rights.

(3) Unless otherwise agreed the term C. & F. or its equivalent has the same effect and imposes upon the seller the same obligations and risks as a C.I.F. term except the obligation as to insurance.

(4) Under the term C.I.F. or C. & F. unless otherwise agreed the buyer must make payment against tender of the required documents and the seller may not tender nor the buyer demand delivery of the goods in substitution for the documents.

§ 2–321. C.I.F. or C. & F.: "Net Landed Weights"; "Payment on Arrival"; Warranty of Condition on Arrival.

Under a contract containing a term C.I.F. or C. & F.

(1) Where the price is based on or is to be adjusted according to "net landed weights", "delivered weights", "out turn" quantity or quality or the like, unless otherwise agreed the seller must reasonably estimate the price. The payment due on tender of the documents called for by the contract is the amount so estimated, but after final adjustment of the price a settlement must be made with commercial promptness.

(2) An agreement described in subsection (1) or any warranty of quality or condition of the goods on arrival places upon the seller the risk of ordinary deterioration, shrinkage and the like in transportation but has no effect on the place or time of identification to the contract for sale or delivery or on the passing of the risk of loss.

(3) Unless otherwise agreed where the contract provides for payment on or after arrival of the goods the seller must before payment allow such preliminary inspection as is feasible; but if the goods are lost delivery of the documents and payment are due when the goods should have arrived.

§ 2–322. Delivery "Ex-Ship".

(1) Unless otherwise agreed a term for delivery of goods "ex-ship" (which means from the carrying vessel) or in equivalent language is not restricted to a particular ship and requires delivery from a ship which has reached a place at the named port of destination where goods of the kind are usually discharged.

(2) Under such a term unless otherwise agreed

(a) the seller must discharge all liens arising out of the carriage and furnish the buyer with a direction which puts the carrier under a duty to deliver the goods; and

(b) the risk of loss does not pass to the buyer until the goods leave the ship's tackle or are otherwise properly unloaded.

§ 2–323. Form of Bill of Lading Required in Overseas Shipment; "Overseas".

(1) Where the contract contemplates overseas shipment and contains a term C.I.F. or C. & F. or F.O.B. vessel, the seller unless otherwise agreed must obtain a negotiable bill of lading stating that the goods have been loaded on board or, in the case of a term C.I.F. or C. & F., received for shipment.

(2) Where in a case within subsection (1) a bill of lading has been issued in a set of parts, unless otherwise agreed if the documents are not to be sent from abroad

the buyer may demand tender of the full set; otherwise only one part of the bill of lading need be tendered. Even if the agreement expressly requires a full set

    (a) due tender of a single part is acceptable within the provisions of this Article on cure of improper delivery (subsection (1) of Section 2–508); and

    (b) even though the full set is demanded, if the documents are sent from abroad the person tendering an incomplete set may nevertheless require payment upon furnishing an indemnity which the buyer in good faith deems adequate.

(3) A shipment by water or by air or a contract contemplating such shipment is "overseas" insofar as by usage of trade or agreement it is subject to the commercial, financing or shipping practices characteristic of international deep water commerce.

§ 2–324. "No Arrival, No Sale" Term.

Under a term "no arrival, no sale" or terms of like meaning, unless otherwise agreed,

    (a) the seller must properly ship conforming goods and if they arrive by any means he must tender them on arrival but he assumes no obligaiton that the goods will arrive unless he has caused the non-arrival; and

    (b) where without fault of the seller the goods are in part lost or have so deteriorated as no longer to conform to the contract or arrive after the contract time, the buyer may proceed as if there had been casualty to identified goods (Section 2–613).

§ 2–325. "Letter of Credit" Term; "Confirmed Credit".

(1) Failure of the buyer seasonably to furnish an agreed letter of credit is a breach of the contract for sale.

(2) The delivery to seller of a proper letter of credit suspends the buyer's obligation to pay. If the letter of credit is dishonored, the seller may on seasonable notification to the buyer require payment directly from him.

(3) Unless otherwise agreed the term "letter of credit" or "banker's credit" in a contract for sale means an irrevocable credit issued by a financing agency of good repute and, where the shipment is overseas, of good international repute. The term "confirmed credit" means that the credit must also carry the direct obligation of such an agency which does business in the seller's financial market.

§ 2–326. Sale on Approval and Sale or Return; Consignment Sales and Rights of Creditors.

(1) Unless otherwise agreed, if delivered goods may be returned by the buyer even though they conform to the contract, the transaction is

    (a) a "sale on approval" if the goods are delivered primarily for use, and

    (b) a "sale or return" if the goods are delivered primarily for resale.

(2) Except as provided in subsection (3), goods held on approval are not subject to the claims of the buyer's creditors until acceptance; goods held on sale or return are subject to such claims while in the buyer's possession.

(3) Where goods are delivered to a person for sale and such person maintains a place of business at which he deals in goods of the kind involved, under a name

other than the name of the person making delivery, then with respect to claims of creditors of the person conducting the business the goods are deemed to be on sale or return. The provisions of this subsection are applicable even though an agreement purports to reserve title to the person making delivery until payment or resale or uses such words as "on consignment" or "on memorandum". However, this subsection is not applicable if the person making delivery

    (a) complies with an applicable law providing for a consignor's interest or the like to be evidenced by a sign, or

    (b) establishes that the person conducting the business is generally known by his creditors to be substantially engaged in selling the goods of others, or

    (c) complies with the filing provisions of the Article on Secured Transactions (Article 9).

(4) Any "or return" term of a contract for sale is to be treated as a separate contract for sale within the statute of frauds section of this Article (Section 2–201) and as contradicting the sale aspect of the contract within the provisions of this Article on parol or extrinsic evidence (Section 2–202).

§ 2–327. Special Incidents of Sale on Approval and Sale or Return.

(1) Under a sale on approval unless otherwise agreed

    (a) although the goods are identified to the contract the risk of loss and the title do not pass to the buyer until acceptance; and

    (b) use of the goods consistent with the purpose of trial is not acceptance but failure seasonably to

notify the seller of election to return the goods is acceptance, and if the goods conform to the contract acceptance of any part is acceptance of the whole; and

    (c) after due notification of election to return, the return is at the seller's risk and expense but a merchant buyer must follow any reasonable instructions.

(2) Under a sale or return unless otherwise agreed

    (a) the option to return extends to the whole or any commercial unit of the goods while in substantially their original condition, but must be exercised seasonably; and

    (b) the return is at the buyer's risk and expense.

§ 2–328. Sale by Auction.

(1) In a sale by auction if goods are put up in lots each lot is the subject of a separate sale.

(2) A sale by auction is complete when the auctioneer so announces by the fall of the hammer or in other customary manner. Where a bid is made while the hammer is falling in acceptance of a prior bid the auctioneer may in his discretion reopen the bidding or declare the goods sold under the bid on which the hammer was falling.

(3) Such a sale is with reserve unless the goods are in explicit terms put up without reserve. In an auction with reserve the auctioneer may withdraw the goods at any time until he announces completion of the sale. In an auction without reserve, after the auctioneer calls for bids on an article or lot, that article or lot cannot be withdrawn unless no bid is made within a reasonable time. In either

case a bidder may retract his bid until the auctioneer's announcement of completion of the sale, but a bidder's retraction does not revive any previous bid.

(4)   If the auctioneer knowingly receives a bid on the seller's behalf or the seller makes or procures such a bid, and notice has not been given that liberty for such bidding is reserved, the buyer may at his option avoid the sale or take the goods at the price of the last good faith bid prior to the completion of the sale. This subsection shall not apply to any bid at a forced sale.

PART 4

TITLE, CREDITORS AND GOOD FAITH PURCHASERS

§ 2–401. Passing of Title; Reservation for Security; Limited Application of This Section.

Each provision of this Article with regard to the rights, obligations and remedies of the seller, the buyer, purchasers or other third parties applies irrespective of title to the goods except where the provision refers to such title. Insofar as situations are not covered by the other provisions of this Article and matters concerning title became material the following rules apply:

(1)   Title to goods cannot pass under a contract for sale prior to their identification to the contract (Section 2–501), and unless otherwise explicitly agreed the buyer acquires by their identification a special property as limited by this Act. Any retention or reservation by the seller of the title (property) in goods shipped or delivered to the buyer is limited in effect to a reservation of a security interest. Subject to these provisions and to the provisions of the Article on Secured Transactions (Article 9), title to goods passes from the seller to the buyer in any manner and on any conditions explicitly agreed on by the parties.

(2)   Unless otherwise explicitly agreed title passes to the buyer at the time and place at which the seller completes his performance with reference to the physical delivery of the goods, despite any reservation of a security interest and even though a document of title is to be delivered at a different time or place; and in particular and despite any reservation of a security interest by the bill of lading

(a) if the contract requires or authorizes the seller to send the goods to the buyer but does not require him to deliver them at destination, title passes to the buyer at the time and place of shipment; but

(b) if the contract requires delivery at destination, title passes on tender there.

(3)   Unless otherwise explicitly agreed where delivery is to be made without moving the goods,

(a) if the seller is to deliver a document of title, title passes at the time when and the place where he delivers such documents; or

(b) if the goods are at the time of contracting already identified and no documents are to be delivered, title passes at the time and place of contracting.

(4)   A rejection or other refusal by the buyer to receive or retain the goods, whether or not justified, or a justified

revocation of acceptance revests title to the goods in the seller. Such revesting occurs by operation of law and is not a "sale".

§ 2-402. Rights of Seller's Creditors Against Sold Goods.

(1) Except as provided in subsections (2) and (3), rights of unsecured creditors of the seller with respect to goods which have been identified to a contract for sale are subject to the buyer's rights to recover the goods under this Article (Sections 2-502 and 2-716).

(2) A creditor of the seller may treat a sale or an identification of goods to a contract for sale as void if as against him a retention of possession by the seller is fraudulent under any rule of law of the state where the goods are situated, except that retention of possession in good faith and current course of trade by a merchant-seller for a commercially reasonable time after a sale or identification is not fraudulent.

(3) Nothing in this Article shall be deemed to impair the rights of creditors of the seller

(a) under the provisions of the Article on Secured Transactions (Article 9); or

(b) where identification to the contract or delivery is made not in current course of trade but in satisfaction of or as security for a pre-existing claim for money, security or the like and is made under circumstances which under any rule of law of the state where the goods are situated would apart from this Article constitute the transaction a fraudulent transfer or voidable preference.

§ 2-403. Power to Transfer; Good Faith Purchase of Goods; "Entrusting".

(1) A purchaser of goods acquires all title which his transferor had or had power to transfer except that a purchaser of a limited interest acquires rights only to the extent of the interest purchased. A person with voidable title has power to transfer a good title to a good faith purchaser for value. When goods have been delivered under a transaction of purchase the purchaser has such power even though

(a) the transferor was deceived as to the identity of the purchaser, or

(b) the delivery was in exchange for a check which is later dishonored, or

(c) it was agreed that the transaction was to be a "cash sale", or

(d) the delivery was procured through fraud punishable as larcenous under the criminal law.

(2) Any entrusting of possession of goods to a merchant who deals in goods of that kind gives him power to transfer all rights of the entruster to a buyer in ordinary course of business.

(3) "Entrusting" includes any delivery and any acquiescence in retention of possession regardless of any condition expressed between the parties to the delivery or acquiescence and regardless of whether the procurement of the entrusting or the possessor's disposition of the goods have been such as to be larcenous under the criminal law.

(4) The rights of other purchasers of goods and of lien creditors are governed by the Articles on Secured Transactions (Article 9), Bulk Transfers (Article 6) and Documents of Title (Article 7).

PART 5

PERFORMANCE

§ 2–501. Insurable Interest in Goods; Manner of Identification of Goods.

(1)   The buyer obtains a special property and an insurable interest in goods by identification of existing goods as goods to which the contract refers even though the goods so identified are non-conforming and he has an option to return or reject them.   Such identification can be made at ,any time and in any manner explicitly agreed to by the parties.   In the absence of explicit agreement identification occurs

    (a) when the contract is made if it is for the sale of goods already existing and identified;

    (b) if the contract is for the sale of future goods other than those described in paragraph (c), when goods are shipped, marked or otherwise designated by the seller as goods to which the contract refers;

    (c) when the crops are planted or otherwise become growing crops or the young are conceived if the contract is for the sale of unborn young to be born within twelve months after contracting or for the sale of crops to be harvested within twelve months or the next normal harvest season after contracting whichever is longer.

(2)   The seller retains an insurable interest in goods so long as title to or any security interest in the goods remains in him and where the identification is by the seller alone he may until default or insolvency or. notification to the buyer that the identification is final substitute other goods for those identified.

(3)   Nothing in this section impairs any insurable interest recognized under any other statute or rule of law.

§ 2–502. Buyer's Right to Goods on Seller's Insolvency.

(1)   Subject to subsection (2) and even though the goods have not been shipped a buyer who has paid a part or all of the price of goods in which he has a special property under the provisions of the immediately preceding section may on making and keeping good a tender of any unpaid portion of their price recover them from the seller if the seller becomes insolvent within ten days after receipt of the first installment on their price.

(2)   If the identification creating his special property has been made by the buyer he acquires the right to recover the goods only if they conform to the contract for sale.

§ 2–503. Manner of Seller's Tender of Delivery.

(1)   Tender of delivery requires that the seller put and hold conforming goods at the buyer's disposition and give the buyer any notification reasonably necessary to enable him to take delivery. The manner, time and place for tender are determined by the agreement and this Article, and in particular

    (a) tender must be at a reasonable hour, and if it is of goods they must be kept available for the period reasonably necessary to enable the buyer to take possession; but

    (b) unless otherwise agreed the buyer must furnish facilities reasonably suited to the receipt of the goods.

(2) Where the case is within the next section respecting shipment tender requires that the seller comply with its provisions.

(3) Where the seller is required to deliver at a particular destination tender requires that he comply with subsection (1) and also in any appropriate case tender documents as described in subsections (4) and (5) of this section.

(4) Where goods are in the possession of a bailee and are to be delivered without being moved

    (a) tender requires that the seller either tender a negotiable document of title covering such goods or procure acknowledgment by the bailee of the buyer's right to possession of the goods; but

    (b) tender to the buyer of a non-negotiable document of title or of a written direction to the bailee to deliver is sufficient tender unless the buyer seasonably objects, and receipt by the bailee of notification of the buyer's rights fixes those rights as against the bailee and all third persons; but risk of loss of the goods and of any failure by the bailee to honor the non-negotiable document of title or to obey the direction remains on the seller until the buyer has had a reasonable time to present the document or direction, and a refusal by the bailee to honor the document or to obey the direction defeats the tender.

(5) Where the contract requires the seller to deliver documents

    (a) he must tender all such documents in correct form, except as provided in this Article with respect to bills of lading in a set (subsection (2) of Section 2-323); and

    (b) tender through customary banking channels is sufficient and dishonor of a draft accompanying the documents constitutes non-acceptance or rejection.

§ 2-504. Shipment by Seller.

Where the seller is required or authorized to send the goods to the buyer and the contract does not require him to deliver them at a particular destination, then unless otherwise agreed he must

    (a) put the goods in the possession of such a carrier and make such a contract for their transportation as may be reasonable having regard to the nature of the goods and other circumstances of the case; and

    (b) obtain and promptly deliver or tender in due form any document necessary to enable the buyer to obtain possession of the goods or otherwise required by the agreement or by usage of trade; and

    (c) promptly notify the buyer of the shipment.

Failure to notify the buyer under paragraph (c) or to make a proper contract under paragraph (a) is a ground for rejection only if material delay or loss ensues.

§ 2-505. Seller's Shipment Under Reservation.

(1) Where the seller has identified goods to the contract by or before shipment:

(a) his procurement of a negotiable bill of lading to his own order or otherwise reserves in him a security interest in the goods. His procurement of the bill to the order of a financing agency or of the buyer indicates in addition only the seller's expectation of transferring that interest to the person named.

(b) a non-negotiable bill of lading to himself or his nominee reserves possession of the goods as security but except in a case of conditional delivery (subsection (2) of Section 2–507) a non-negotiable bill of lading naming the buyer as consignee reserves no security interest even though the seller retains possession of the bill of lading.

(2) When shipment by the seller with reservation of a security interest is in violation of the contract for sale it constitutes an improper contract for transportation within the preceding section but impairs neither the rights given to the buyer by shipment and identification of the goods to the contract nor the seller's powers as a holder of a negotiable document.

§ 2–506. Rights of Financing Agency.

(1) A financing agency by paying or purchasing for value a draft which relates to a shipment of goods acquires to the extent of the payment or purchase and in addition to its own rights under the draft and any document of title securing it any rights of the shipper in the goods including the right to stop delivery and the shipper's right to have the draft honored by the buyer.

(2) The right to reimbursement of a financing agency which has in good faith honored or purchased the draft under commitment to or authority from the buyer is not impaired by subsequent discovery of defects with reference to any relevant document which was apparently regular on its face.

§ 2–507. Effect of Seller's Tender; Delivery on Condition.

(1) Tender of delivery is a condition to the buyer's duty to accept the goods and, unless otherwise agreed, to his duty to pay for them. Tender entitles the seller to acceptance of the goods and to payment according to the contract.

(2) Where payment is due and demanded on the delivery to the buyer of goods or documents of title, his right as against the seller to retain or dispose of them is conditional upon his making the payment due.

§ 2–508. Cure by Seller of Improper Tender or Delivery; Replacement.

(1) Where any tender or delivery by the seller is rejected because non-conforming and the time for performance has not yet expired, the seller may seasonably notify the buyer of his intention to cure and may then within the contract time make a conforming delivery.

(2) Where the buyer rejects a non-conforming tender which the seller had reasonable grounds to believe would be acceptable with or without money allowance the seller may if he seasonably notifies the buyer have a further reasonable time to substitute a conforming tender.

§ 2–509. Risk of Loss in the Absence of Breach.

(1) Where the contract requires or authorizes the seller to ship the goods by carrier

(a) if it does not require him to deliver them at a particular destination, the risk of loss passes to the buyer when the goods are duly delivered to the carrier even though the shipment is under reservation (Section 2–505); but

(b) if it does require him to deliver them at a particular destination and the goods are there duly tendered while in the possession of the carrier, the risk of loss passes to the buyer when the goods are there duly so tendered as to enable the buyer to take delivery.

(2)   Where the goods are held by a bailee to be delivered without being moved, the risk of loss passes to the buyer

(a) on his receipt of a negotiable document of title covering the goods; or

(b) on acknowledgment by the bailee of the buyer's right to possession of the goods; or

(c) after his receipt of a non-negotiable document of title or other written direction to deliver, as provided in subsection (4) (b) of Section 2–503.

(3)   In any case not within subsection (1) or (2), the risk of loss passes to the buyer on his receipt of the goods if the seller is a merchant; otherwise the risk passes to the buyer on tender of delivery.

(4)   The provisions of this section are subject to contrary agreement of the parties and to the provisions of this Article on sale on approval (Section 2–327) and on effect of breach of risk of loss (Section 2–510).

§ 2–510. Effect of Breach on Risk of Loss.

(1)   Where a tender or delivery of goods so fails to conform to the contract as to give a right of rejection the risk of their loss remains on the seller until cure or acceptance.

(2)   Where the buyer rightfully revokes acceptance he may to the extent of any deficiency in his effective insurance coverage treat the risk of loss as having rested on the seller from the beginning.

(3)   Where the buyer as to conforming goods already identified to the contract for sale repudiates or is otherwise in breach before risk of their loss has passed to him, the seller may to the extent of any deficiency in his effective insurance coverage treat the risk of loss as resting on the buyer for a commercially reasonable time.

§ 2–511. Tender of Payment by Buyer; Payment by Check.

(1)   Unless otherwise agreed tender of payment is a condition to the seller's duty to tender and complete any delivery.

(2)   Tender of payment is sufficient when made by any means or in any manner current in the ordinary course of business unless the seller demands payment in legal tender and gives any extension of time reasonably necessary to procure it.

(3)   Subject to the provisions of this Act on the effect of an instrument on an obligation (Section 3–802), payment by check is conditional and is defeated as between the parties by dishonor of the check on due presentment.

§ 2–512. Payment by Buyer Before Inspection.

(1)   Where the contract requires payment before inspection non-conformity

of the goods does not excuse the buyer from so making payment unless

    (a) the non-conformity appears without inspection; or

    (b) despite tender of the required documents the circumstances would justify injunction against honor under the provisions of this Act (Section 5–114).

(2)   Payment pursuant to subsection (1) does not constitute an acceptance of goods or impair the buyer's right to inspect or any of his remedies.

§ 2–513. Buyer's Right to Inspection of Goods.

(1)   Unless otherwise agreed and subject to subsection (3), where goods are tendered or delivered or identified to the contract for sale, the buyer has a right before payment or acceptance to inspect them at any reasonable place and time and in any reasonable manner. When the seller is required or authorized to send the goods to the buyer, the inspection may be after their arrival.

(2)   Expenses of inspection must be borne by the buyer but may be recovered from the seller if the goods do not conform and are rejected.

(3)   Unless otherwise agreed and subject to the provisions of this Article on C.I.F. contracts (subsection (3) of Section 2–321), the buyer is not entitled to inspect the goods before payment of the price when the contract provides

    (a) for delivery "C.O.D." or on other like terms; or

    (b) for payment against documents of title, except where such payment is due only after the goods are to become available for inspection.

(4)   A place or method of inspection fixed by the parties is presumed to be exclusive but unless otherwise expressly agreed it does not postpone identification or shift the place for delivery or for passing the risk of loss. If compliance becomes impossible, inspection shall be as provided in this section unless the place or method fixed was clearly intended as an indispensable condition failure of which avoids the contract.

§ 2–514. When Documents Deliverable on Acceptance; When on Payment.

Unless otherwise agreed documents against which a draft is drawn are to be delivered to the drawee on acceptance of the draft if it is payable more than three days after presentment; otherwise, only on payment.

§ 2–515. Preserving Evidence of Goods in Dispute.

In furtherance of the adjustment of any claim or dispute

    (a) either party on reasonable notification to the other and for the purpose of ascertaining the facts and preserving evidence has the right to inspect, test and sample the goods including such of them as may be in the possession or control of the other; and

    (b) the parties may agree to a third party inspection or survey to determine the conformity or condition of the goods and may agree that the findings shall be binding upon them in any subsequent litigation or adjustment.

PART 6

BREACH, REPUDIATION AND EXCUSE

§ 2–601. Buyer's Rights on Improper Delivery.

Subject to the provisions of this Article on breach in installment contracts (Section 2–612) and unless otherwise agreed under the sections on contractual limitations of remedy (Sections 2–718 and 2–719), if the goods or the tender of delivery fail in any respect to conform to the contract, the buyer may

(a) reject the whole; or

(b) accept the whole; or

(c) accept any commercial unit or units and reject the rest.

§ 2–602. Manner and Effect of Rightful Rejection.

(1) Rejection of goods must be within a reasonable time after their delivery or tender. It is ineffective unless the buyer seasonably notifies the seller.

(2) Subject to the provisions of the two following sections on rejected goods (Sections 2–603 and 2–604),

(a) after rejection any exercise of ownership by the buyer with respect to any commercial unit is wrongful as against the seller; and

(b) if the buyer has before rejection taken physical possession of goods in which he does not have a security interest under the provisions of this Article (subsection (3) of Section 2–711), he is under a duty after rejection to hold them with reasonable care at the seller's disposition for a time sufficient to permit the seller to remove them; but

(c) the buyer has no further obligations with regard to goods rightfully rejected.

(3) The seller's rights with respect to goods wrongfully rejected are governed by the provisions of this Article on Seller's remedies in general (Section 2–703).

§ 2–603. Merchant Buyer's Duties as to Rightfully Rejected Goods.

(1) Subject to any security interest in the buyer (subsection (3) of Section 2–711), when the seller has no agent or place of business at the market of rejection a merchant buyer is under a duty after rejection of goods in his possession or control to follow any reasonable instructions received from the seller with respect to the goods and in the absence of such instructions to make reasonable efforts to sell them for the seller's account if they are perishable or threaten to decline in value speedily. Instructions are not reasonable if on demand indemnity for expenses is not forthcoming.

(2) When the buyer sells goods under subsection (1), he is entitled to reimbursement from the seller or out of the proceeds for reasonable expenses of caring for and selling them, and if the expenses include no selling commission then to such commission as is usual in the trade or if there is none to a reasonable sum not exceeding ten per cent on the gross proceeds.

(3) In complying with this section the buyer is held only to good faith and good faith conduct hereunder is neither acceptance nor conversion nor the basis of an action for damages.

§ 2–604. Buyer's Options as to Salvage of Rightfully Rejected Goods.

Subject to the provisions of the immediately preceding section on perishables if the seller gives no instructions within a reasonable time after notification of rejection the buyer may store the rejected goods for the seller's account or reship them to him or resell them for the seller's account with reimbursement as provided in the preceding section. Such action is not acceptance or conversion.

§ 2–605. Waiver of Buyer's Objections by Failure to Particularize.

(1)   The buyer's failure to state in connection with rejection a particular defect which is ascertainable by reasonable inspection precludes him from relying on the unstated defect to justify rejection or to establish breach

(a) where the seller could have cured it if stated seasonably; or

(b) between merchants when the seller has after rejection made a request in writing for a full and final written statement of all defects on which the buyer proposes to rely.

(2)   Payment against documents made without reservation of rights precludes recovery of the payment for defects apparent on the face of the documents.

§ 2–606. What Constitutes Acceptance of Goods.

(1)   Acceptance of goods occurs when the buyer

(a) after a reasonable opportunity to inspect the goods signifies to the seller that the goods are conforming or that he will take or retain them in spite of their nonconformity; or

(b) fails to make an effective rejection (subsection (1) of Section 2–602), but such acceptance does not occur until the buyer has had a reasonable opportunity to inspect them; or

(c) does any act inconsistent with the seller's ownership; but if such act is wrongful as against the seller it is an acceptance only if ratified by him.

(2)   Acceptance of a part of any commercial unit is acceptance of that entire unit.

§ 2–607. Effect of Acceptance; Notice of Breach; Burden of Establishing Breach After Acceptance; Notice of Claim or Litigation to Person Answerable Over.

(1)   The buyer must pay at the contract rate for any goods accepted.

(2)   Acceptance of goods by the buyer precludes rejection of the goods accepted and if made with knowledge of a non-conformity cannot be revoked because of it unless the acceptance was on the reasonable assumption that the nonconformity would be seasonably cured but acceptance does not of itself impair any other remedy provided by this Article for nonconformity.

(3)   Where a tender has been accepted

(a) the buyer must within a reasonable time after he discovers or should have discovered any breach notify the seller of breach or be barred from any remedy; and

(b) if the claim is one for infringement or the like (subsection (3) of Section 2–312) and the buyer is sued as a result of such a breach he must so notify the seller within a reasonable time after he receives notice of the litigation or be barred from any remedy over for liability established by the litigation.

(4) The burden is on the buyer to establish any breach with respect to the goods accepted.

(5) Where the buyer is sued for breach of a warranty or other obligation for which his seller is answerable over

(a) he may give his seller written notice of the litigation. If the notice states that the seller may come in and defend and that if the seller does not do so he will be bound in any action against him by his buyer by any determination of fact common to the two litigations, then unless the seller after seasonable receipt of the notice does come in and defend he is so bound.

(b) if the claim is one for infringement or the like (subsection (3) of Section 2–312) the original seller may demand in writing that his buyer turn over to him control of the litigation including settlement or else be barred from any remedy over and if he also agrees to bear all expense and to satisfy any adverse judgment, then unless the buyer after seasonable receipt of the demand does turn over control the buyer is so barred.

(6) The provisions of subsections (3), (4) and (5) apply to any obligation of a buyer to hold the seller harmless against infringement or the like (subsection (3) of Section 2–312).

§ 2–608. Revocation of Acceptance in Whole or in Part.

(1) The buyer may revoke his acceptance of a lot or commercial unit whose non-conformity substantially impairs its value to him if he has accepted it

(a) on the reasonable assumption that its non-conformity would be cured and it has not been seasonably cured; or

(b) without discovery of such non-conformity if his acceptance was reasonably induced either by the difficulty of discovery before acceptance or by the seller's assurances.

(2) Revocation of acceptance must occur within a reasonable time after the buyer discovers or should have discovered the ground for it and before any substantial change in condition of the goods which is not caused by their own defects. It is not effective until the buyer notifies the seller of it.

(3) A buyer who so revokes has the same rights and duties with regard to the goods involved as if he had rejected them.

§ 2–609. Right to Adequate Assurance of Performance.

(1) A contract for sale imposes an obligation on each party that the other's expectation of receiving due performance will not be impaired. When reasonable grounds for insecurity arise with respect to the performance of either party the other may in writing demand adequate assurance of due performance and until he receives such assurance may if commercially reasonable suspend any performance for which he has not already received the agreed return.

(2) Between merchants the reasonableness of grounds for insecurity and the

adequacy of any assurance offered shall be determined according to commercial standards.

(3) Acceptance of any improper delivery or payment does not prejudice the aggrieved party's right to demand adequate assurance of future performance.

(4) After receipt of a justified demand failure to provide within a reasonable time not exceeding thirty days such assurance of due performance as is adequate under the circumstances of the particular case is a repudiation of the contract.

§ 2–610. Anticipatory Repudiation.

When either party repudiates the contract with respect to a performance not yet due the loss of which will substantially impair the value of the contract to the other, the aggrieved party may

(a) for a commercially reasonable time await performance by the repudiating party; or

(b) resort to any remedy for breach (Section 2–703 or Section 2–711), even though he has notified the repudiating party that he would await the latter's performance and has urged retraction; and

(c) in either case suspend his own performance or proceed in accordance with the provisions of this Article on the seller's right to identify goods to the contract notwithstanding breach or to salvage unfinished goods (Section 2–704).

§ 2–611. Retraction of Anticipatory Repudiation.

(1) Until the repudiating party's next performance is due he can retract his repudiation unless the aggrieved party has since the repudiation cancelled or materially changed his position or otherwise indicated that he considers the repudiation final.

(2) Retraction may be by any method which clearly indicates to the aggrieved party that the repudiating party intends to perform, but must include any assurance justifiably demanded under the provisions of this Article (Section 2–609).

(3) Retraction reinstates the repudiating party's rights under the contract with due excuse and allowance to the aggrieved party for any delay occasioned by the repudiation.

§ 2–612. "Installment Contract"; Breach.

(1) An "installment contract" is one which requires or authorizes the delivery of goods in separate lots to be separately accepted, even though the contract contains a clause "each delivery is a separate contract" or its equivalent.

(2) The buyer may reject any installment which is non-conforming if the non-conformity substantially impairs the value of that installment and cannot be cured or if the non-conformity is a defect in the required documents; but if the non-conformity does not fall within subsection (3) and the seller gives adequate assurance of its cure the buyer must accept that installment.

(3) Whenever non-conformity or default with respect to one or more installments substantially impairs the value of the whole contract there is a breach of the whole. But the aggrieved party reinstates the contract if he accepts a non-conforming installment without seasonably notifying of cancellation or if he brings an action with respect only to past installments or demands performance as to future installments.

§ 2—613. Casualty to Identified Goods.

Where the contract requires for its performance goods identified when the contract is made, and the goods suffer casualty without fault of either party before the risk of loss passes to the buyer, or in a proper case under a "no arrival, no sale" term (Section 2—324) then

(a) if the loss is total the contract is avoided; and

(b) if the loss is partial or the goods have so deteriorated as no longer to conform to the contract the buyer may nevertheless demand inspection and at his option either treat the contract as avoided or accept the goods with due allowance from the contract price for the deterioration or the deficiency in quantity but without further right against the seller.

§ 2—614. Substituted Performance.

(1) Where without fault of either party the agreed berthing, loading, or unloading facilities fail or an agreed type of carrier becomes unavailable or the agreed manner of delivery otherwise becomes commercially impracticable but a commercially reasonable substitute is available, such substitute performance must be tendered and accepted.

(2) If the agreed means or manner of payment fails because of domestic or foreign governmental regulation, the seller may withhold or stop delivery unless the buyer provides a means or manner of payment which is commercially a substantial equivalent. If delivery has already been taken, payment by the means or in the manner provided by the regulation discharges the buyer's obligation unless the regulation is discriminatory, oppressive or predatory.

§ 2—615. Excuse by Failure of Presupposed Conditions.

Except so far as a seller may have assumed a greater obligation and subject to the preceding section on substituted performance:

(a) Delay in delivery or non-delivery in whole or in part by a seller who complies with paragraphs (b) and (c) is not a breach of his duty under a contract for sale if performance as agreed has been made impracticable by the occurrence of a contingency the nonoccurrence of which was a basic assumption on which the contract was made or by compliance in good faith with any applicable foreign or domestic governmental regulation or order whether or not it later proves to be invalid.

(b) Where the causes mentioned in paragraph (a) affect only a part of the seller's capacity to perform, he must allocate production and deliveries among his customers but may at his option include regular customers not then under contract as well as his own requirements for further manufacture. He may so allocate in any manner which is fair and reasonable.

(c) The seller must notify the buyer seasonably that there will be delay or non-delivery and, when allocation is required under paragraph (b), of the estimated quota thus made available for the buyer.

§ **2–616. Procedure on Notice Claiming Excuse.**

(1) Where the buyer receives notification of a material or indefinite delay or an allocation justified under the preceding section he may by written notification to the seller as to any delivery concerned, and where the prospective deficiency substantially impairs the value of the whole contract under the provisions of this Article relating to breach of installment contracts (Section 2–612), then also as to the whole,

    (a) terminate and thereby discharge any unexecuted portion of the contract; or

    (b) modify the contract by agreeing to take his available quota in substitution.

(2) If after receipt of such notification from the seller the buyer fails so to modify the contract within a reasonable time not exceeding thirty days the contract lapses with respect to any deliveries affected.

(3) The provisions of this section may not be negated by agreement except in so far as the seller has assumed a greater obligation under the preceding section.

PART 7

REMEDIES

§ **2–701. Remedies for Breach of Collateral Contracts Not Impaired.**

Remedies for breach of any obligation or promise collateral or ancillary to a contract for sale are not impaired by the provisions of this Article.

§ **2–702. Seller's Remedies on Discovery of Buyer's Insolvency.**

(1) Where the seller discovers the buyer to be insolvent he may refuse delivery except for cash including payment for all goods theretofore delivered under the contract, and stop delivery under this Article (Section 2–705).

(2) Where the seller discovers that the buyer has received goods on credit while insolvent he may reclaim the goods upon demand made within ten days after the receipt, but if misrepresentation of solvency has been made to the particular seller in writing within three months before delivery the ten day limitation does not apply. Except as provided in this subsection the seller may not base a right to reclaim goods on the buyer's fraudulent or innocent misrepresentation of solvency or of intent to pay.

(3) The seller's right to reclaim under subsection (2) is subject to the rights of a buyer in ordinary course or other good faith purchaser under this Article (Section 2–403). Successful reclamation of goods excludes all other remedies with respect to them.

§ **2–703. Seller's Remedies in General.**

Where the buyer wrongfully rejects or revokes acceptance of goods or fails to make a payment due on or before delivery or repudiates with respect to a part or the whole, then with respect to any goods directly affected and, if the breach is of the whole contract (Section 2–612), then also with respect to the whole undelivered balance, the aggrieved seller may

    (a) withhold delivery of such goods;

    (b) stop delivery by any bailee as hereafter provided (Section 2–705);

    (c) proceed under the next section respecting goods still unidentified to the contract;

    (d) resell and recover damages as hereafter provided (Section 2–706);

    (e) recover damages for non-acceptance (Section 2–708) or in a proper case the price (Section 2–709);

    (f) cancel.

§ 2–704. Seller's Right to Identify Goods to the Contract Notwithstanding Breach or to Salvage Unfinished Goods.

(1) An aggrieved seller under the preceding section may

    (a) identify to the contract conforming goods not already identified if at the time he learned of the breach they are in his possession or control;

    (b) treat as the subject of resale goods which have demonstrably been intended for the particular contract even though those goods are unfinished.

(2) Where the goods are unfinished an aggrieved seller may in the exercise of reasonable commercial judgment for the purposes of avoiding loss and of effective realization either complete the manufacture and wholly identify the goods to the contract or cease manufacture and resell for scrap or salvage value or proceed in any other reasonable manner.

§ 2–705. Seller's Stoppage of Delivery in Transit or Otherwise.

(1) The seller may stop delivery of goods in the possession of a carrier or other bailee when he discovers the buyer to be insolvent (Section 2–702) and may stop delivery of carload, truckload, planeload or larger shipments of express or freight when the buyer repudiates or fails to make a payment due before delivery or if for any other reason the seller has a right to withhold or reclaim the goods.

(2) As against such buyer the seller may stop delivery until

    (a) receipt of the goods by the buyer; or

    (b) acknowledgment to the buyer by any bailee of the goods except a carrier that the bailee holds the goods for the buyer; or

    (c) such acknowledgment to the buyer by a carrier by reshipment or as warehouseman; or

    (d) negotiation to the buyer of any negotiable document of title covering the goods.

(3) (a) To stop delivery the seller must so notify as to enable the bailee by reasonable diligence to prevent delivery of the goods.

    (b) After such notification the bailee must hold and deliver the goods according to the directions of the seller but the seller is liable to the bailee for any ensuing charges or damages.

    (c) If a negotiable document of title has been issued for goods the bailee is not obliged to obey a notification to stop until surrender of the document.

    (d) A carrier who has issued a non-negotiable bill of lading is not obliged to obey a notification to stop received from a person other than the consignor.

§ 2–706. Seller's Resale Including Contract for Resale.

(1)   Under the conditions stated in Section 2–703 on seller's remedies, the seller may resell the goods concerned or the undelivered balance thereof. Where the resale is made in good faith and in a commercially reasonable manner the seller may recover the difference between the resale price and the contract price together with any incidental damages allowed under the provisions of this Article (Section 2–710), but less expenses saved in consequence of the buyer's breach.

(2)   Except as otherwise provided in subsection (3) or unless otherwise agreed resale may be at public or private sale including sale by way of one or more contracts to sell or of identification to an existing contract of the seller. Sale may be as a unit or in parcels and at any time and place and on any terms but every aspect of the sale including the method, manner, time, place and terms must be commercially reasonable. The resale must be reasonably identified as referring to the broken contract, but it is not necessary that the goods be in existence or that any or all of them have been identified to the contract before the breach.

(3)   Where the resale is at private sale the seller must give the buyer reasonable notification of his intention to resell.

(4)   Where the resale is at public sale
  (a) only identified goods can be sold except where there is a recognized market for a public sale of futures in goods of the kind; and
  (b) it must be made at a usual place or market for public sale if one

is reasonably available and except in the case of goods which are perishable or threaten to decline in value speedily the seller must give the buyer reasonable notice of the time and place of the resale; and

  (c) if the goods are not to be within the view of those attending the sale the notification of sale must state the place where the goods are located and provide for their reasonable inspection by prospective bidders; and
  (d) the seller may buy.

(5)   A purchaser who buys in good faith at a resale takes the goods free of any rights of the original buyer even though the seller fails to comply with one or more of the requirements of this section.

(6)   The seller is not accountable to the buyer for any profit made on any resale. A person in the position of a seller (Section 2–707) or a buyer who has rightfully rejected or justifiably revoked acceptance must account for any excess over the amount of his security interest, as hereinafter defined (subsection (3) of Section 2–711).

§ 2–707. "Person in the Position of a Seller".

(1)   A "person in the position of a seller" includes as against a principal an agent who has paid or become responsible for the price of goods on behalf of his principal or anyone who otherwise holds a security interest or other right in goods similar to that of a seller.

(2)   A person in the position of a seller may as provided in this Article withhold or stop delivery (Section 2–705) and resell (Section 2–706) and recover incidental damages (Section 2–710).

§ 2–708. Seller's Damages for Non-acceptance or Repudiation.

(1) Subject to subsection (2) and to the provisions of this Article with respect to proof of market price (Section 2–723), the measure of damages for non-acceptance or repudiation by the buyer is the difference between the market price at the time and place for tender and the unpaid contract price together with any incidental damages provided in this Article (Section 2–710), but less expenses saved in consequence of the buyer's breach.

(2) If the measure of damages provided in subsection (1) is inadequate to put the seller in as good a position as performance would have done then the measure of damages in the profit (including reasonable overhead) which the seller would have made from full performance by the buyer, together with any incidental damages provided in this Article (Section 2–710), due allowance for costs reasonably incurred and due credit for payments or proceeds of resale.

§ 2–709. Action for the Price.

(1) When the buyer fails to pay the price as it becomes due the seller may recover, together with any incidental damages under the next section, the price

(a) of goods accepted or of conforming goods lost or damaged within a commercially reasonable time after risk of their loss has passed to the buyer; and

(b) of goods identified to the contract if the seller is unable after reasonable effort to resell them at a reasonable price or the circumstances reasonably indicate that such effort will be unavailing.

(2) Where the seller sues for the price he must hold for the buyer any goods which have been identified to the contract and are still in his control except that if resale becomes possible he may resell them at any time prior to the collection of the judgment. The net proceeds of any such resale must be credited to the buyer and payment of the judgment entitles him to any goods not resold.

(3) After the buyer has wrongfully rejected or revoked acceptance of the goods or has failed to make a payment due or has repudiated (Section 2–610), a seller who is held not entitled to the price under this section shall nevertheless be awarded damages for non-acceptance under the preceding section.

§ 2–710. Seller's Incidental Damages.

Incidental damages to an aggrieved seller include any commercially reasonable charges, expenses or commissions incurred in stopping delivery, in the transportation, care and custody of goods after the buyer's breach, in connection with return or resale of the goods or otherwise resulting from the breach.

§ 2–711. Buyer's Remedies in General; Buyer's Security Interest in Rejected Goods.

(1) Where the seller fails to make delivery or repudiates or the buyer rightfully rejects or justifiably revokes acceptance then with respect to any goods involved, and with respect to the whole if the breach goes to the whole contract (Section 2–612), the buyer may cancel and whether or not he has done so may in addition to recovering so much of the price as has been paid

(a) "Cover" and have damages under the next section as to all the goods affected whether or not they have been identified to the contract; or

(b) recover damages for non-delivery as provided in this Article (Section 2–713).

(2) Where the seller fails to deliver or repudiates the buyer may also

(a) if the goods have been identified recover them as provided in this Article (Section 2–502); or

(b) in a proper case obtain specific performance or replevy the goods as provided in this Article (Section 2–716).

(3) On rightful rejection or justifiable revocation of acceptance a buyer has a security interest in goods in his possession or control for any payments made on their price and any expenses reasonably incurred in their inspection, receipt, transportation, care and custody and may hold such goods and resell them in like manner as an aggrieved seller (Section 2–706).

§ 2–712. "Cover"; Buyer's Procurement of Substitute Goods.

(1) After a breach within the preceding section the buyer may "cover" by making in good faith and without unreasonable delay any reasonable purchase of or contract to purchase goods in substitution for those due from the seller.

(2) The buyer may recover from the seller as damages the difference between the cost of cover and the contract price together with any incidental or consequential damages as hereinafter defined (Section 2–715), but less expenses saved in consequence of the seller's breach.

(3) Failure of the buyer to effect cover within this section does not bar him from any other remedy.

§ 2–713. Buyer's Damages for Non-Delivery or Repudiation.

(1) Subject to the provisions of this Article with respect to proof of market price (Section 2–723), the measure of damages for non-delivery or repudiation by the seller is the difference between the market price at the time when the buyer learned of the breach and the contract price together with any incidental and consequential damages provided in this Article (Section 2–715), but less expenses saved in consequence of the seller's breach.

(2) Market price is to be determined as of the place for tender or, in cases of rejection after arrival or revocation of acceptance, as of the place of arrival.

§ 2–714. Buyer's Damages for Breach in Regard to Accepted Goods.

(1) Where the buyer has accepted goods and given notification (subsection (3) of Section 2–607) he may recover as damages for any non-conformity of tender the loss resulting in the ordinary course of events from the seller's breach as determined in any manner which is reasonable.

(2) The measure of damages for breach of warranty is the difference at the time and place of acceptance between the value of the goods accepted and the value they would have had if they had been as warranted, unless special circumstances show proximate damages of a different amount.

(3) In a proper case any incidental and consequential damages under the next section may also be recovered.

§ 2–715. Buyer's Incidental and Consequential Damages.

(1) Incidental damages resulting from the seller's breach include expenses

reasonably incurred in inspection, receipt, transportation and care and custody of goods rightfully rejected, any commercially reasonable charges, expenses or commissions in connection with effecting cover and any other reasonable expense incident to the delay or other breach.

(2) Consequential damages resulting from the seller's breach include

(a) any loss resulting from general or particular requirements and needs of which the seller at the time of contracting had reason to know and which could not reasonably be prevented by cover or otherwise; and

(b) injury to person or property proximately resulting from any breach of warranty.

§ 2–716. Buyer's Right to Specific Performance or Replevin.

(1) Specific performance may be decreed where the goods are unique or in other proper circumstances.

(2) The decree for specific performance may include such terms and conditions as to payment of the price, damages, or other relief as the court may deem just.

(3) The buyer has a right of replevin for goods identified to the contract if after reasonable effort he is unable to effect cover for such goods or the circumstances reasonably indicate that such effort will be unavailing or if the goods have been shipped under reservation and satisfaction of the security interest in them has been made or tendered.

§ 2–717. Deduction of Damages From the Price.

The buyer on notifying the seller of his intention to do so may deduct all or any part of the damages resulting from any breach of the contract from any part of the price still due under the same contract.

§ 2–718. Liquidation or Limitation of Damages; Deposits.

(1) Damages for breach by either party may be liquidated in the agreement but only at an amount which is reasonable in the light of the anticipated or actual harm caused by the breach, the difficulties of proof of loss, and the inconvenience or nonfeasibility of otherwise obtaining an adequate remedy. A term fixing unreasonably large liquidated damages is void as a penalty.

(2) Where the seller justifiably withholds delivery of goods because of the buyer's breach, the buyer is entitled to restitution of any amount by which the sum of his payments exceeds

(a) the amount to which the seller is entitled by virtue of terms liquidating the seller's damages in accordance with subsection (1), or

(b) in the absence of such terms, twenty per cent of the value of the total performance for which the buyer is obligated under the contract or $500, whichever is smaller.

(3) The buyer's right to restitution under subsection (2) is subject to offset to the extent that the seller establishes

(a) a right to recover damages under the provisions of this Article other than subsection (1), and

(b) the amount or value of any benefits received by the buyer directly or indirectly by reason of the contract.

(4) Where a seller has received payment in goods their reasonable value or the proceeds of their resale shall be treated as payments for the purposes of subsection (2); but if the seller has notice of the buyer's breach before reselling goods received in part performance, his resale is subject to the conditions laid down in this Article on resale by an aggrieved seller (Section 2–706).

§ 2–719. Contractual Modification or Limitation of Remedy.

(1) Subject to the provisions of subsections (2) and (3) of this section and of the preceding section on liquidation and limitation of damages,

    (a) the agreement may provide for remedies in addition to or in substitution for those provided in this Article and may limit or alter the measure of damages recoverable under this Article, as by limiting the buyer's remedies to return of the goods and repayment of the price or to repair and replacement of non-conforming goods or parts; and

    (b) resort to a remedy as provided is optional unless the remedy is expressly agreed to be exclusive, in which case it is the sole remedy.

(2) Where circumstances cause an exclusive or limited remedy to fail of its essential purpose, remedy may be had as provided in this Act.

(3) Consequential damages may be limited or excluded unless the limitation or exclusion is unconscionable. Limitation of consequential damages for injury to the person in the case of consumer goods is prima facie unconscionable but limitation of damages where the loss is commercial is not.

§ 2–720. Effect of "Cancellation" or "Rescission" on Claims for Antecedent Breach.

Unless the contrary intention clearly appears, expressions of "cancellation" or "rescission" of the contract or the like shall not be construed as a renunciation or discharge of any claim in damages for an antecedent breach.

§ 2–721. Remedies for Fraud.

Remedies for material misrepresentation or fraud include all remedies available under this Article for non-fraudulent breach. Neither rescission or a claim for rescission of the contract for sale nor rejection or return of the goods shall bar or be deemed inconsistent with a claim for damages or other remedy.

§ 2–722. Who Can Sue Third Parties for Injury to Goods.

Where a third party so deals with goods which have been identified to a contract for sale as to cause actionable injury to a party to that contract

    (a) a right of action against the third party is in either party to the contract for sale who has title to or a security interest or a special property or an insurable interest in the goods; and if the goods have been destroyed or converted a right of action is also in the party who either bore the risk of loss under the contract for sale or has since the injury assumed that risk as against the other;

    (b) if at the time of the injury the party plaintiff did not bear the risk of loss as against the other party to the contract for sale and there is no arrangement between them for disposition of the recovery, his suit or settlement is, subject to his own interest, as a fiduciary for the other party to the contract;

(c) either party may with the consent of the other sue for the benefit of whom it may concern.

§ 2–723. Proof of Market Price: Time and Place.

(1)   If an action based on anticipatory repudiation comes to trial before the time for performance with respect to some or all of the goods, any damages based on market price (Section 2–708 or Section 2–713) shall be determined according to the price of such goods prevailing at the time when the aggrieved party learned of the repudiation.

(2)   If evidence of a price prevailing at the times or places described in this Article is not readily available the price prevailing within any reasonable time before or after the time described or at any other place which in commercial judgment or under usage of trade would serve as a reasonable substitute for the one described may be used, making any proper allowance for the cost of transporting the goods to or from such other place.

(3)   Evidence of a relevant price prevailing at a time or place other than the one described in this Article offered by one party is not admissible unless and until he has given the other party such notice as the court finds sufficient to prevent unfair surprise.

§ 2–724. Admissibility of Market Quotations.

Whenever the prevailing price or value of any goods regularly bought and sold in any established commodity market is in issue, reports in official publications or trade journals or in newspapers or periodicals of general circulation published as the reports of such market shall be admissible in evidence. The circumstances of the preparation of such a report may be shown to affect its weight but not its admissibility.

§ 2–725. Statute of Limitations in Contracts for Sale.

(1)   An action for breach of any contract for sale must be commenced within four years after the cause of action has accrued. By the original agreement the parties may reduce the period of limitation to not less than one year but may not extend it.

(2)   A cause of action accrues when the breach occurs, regardless of the aggrieved party's lack of knowledge of the breach. A breach of warranty occurs when tender of delivery is made, except that where a warranty explicitly extends to future performance of the goods and discovery of the breach must await the time of such performance the cause of action accrues when the breach is or should have been discovered.

(3)   Where an action commenced within the time limited by subsection (1) is so terminated as to leave available a remedy by another action for the same breach such other action may be commenced after the expiration of the time limited and within six months after the termination of the first action unless the termination resulted from voluntary discontinuance or from dismissal for failure or neglect to prosecute.

(4)   This section does not alter the law on tolling of the statute of limitations nor does it apply to causes of action which have accrued before this Act becomes effective.

ARTICLE 3

COMMERCIAL PAPER

PART 1

SHORT TITLE, FORM AND INTERPRETATION

§ 3—101. Short Title.

This Article shall be known and may be cited as Uniform Commercial Code—Commercial Paper.

§ 3—102. Definitions and Index of Definitions.

(1)   In this Article unless the context otherwise requires

    (a) "Issue" means the first delivery of an instrument to a holder or a remitter.

    (b) An "order" is a direction to pay and must be more than an authorization or request. It must identify the person to pay with reasonable certainty. It may be addressed to one or more such persons jointly or in the alternative but not in succession.

    (c) A "promise" is an undertaking to pay and must be more than an acknowledgment of an obligation.

    (d) "Secondary party" means a drawer or endorser.

    (e) "Instrument" means a negotiable instrument.

(2)   Other definitions applying to this Article and the sections in which they appear are:

    "Acceptance". Section 3—410.
    "Accommodation party". Section 3—415.
    "Alteration". Section 3—407.
    "Certificate of deposit". Section 3—104.

    "Certification". Section 3—411.
    "Check". Section 3—104.
    "Definite time". Section 3—109.
    "Dishonor". Section 3—507.
    "Draft". Section 3—104.
    "Holder in due course". Section 3—302.
    "Negotiation". Section 3—202.
    "Note". Section 3—104.
    "Notice of dishonor". Section 3—508.
    "On demand". Section 3—108.
    "Presentment". Section 3—504.
    "Protest". Section 3—509.
    "Restrictive Indorsement". Section 3—205.
    "Signature". Section 3—401.

(3)   The following definitions in other Articles apply to this Article:

    "Account". Section 4—104.
    "Banking Day". Section 4—104.
    "Clearing house". Section 4—104.
    "Collecting bank". Section 4—105.
    "Customer". Section 4—104.
    "Depositary Bank". Section 4—105.
    "Documentary Draft". Section 4—104.
    "Intermediary Bank". Section 4—105.
    "Item". Section 4—104.
    "Midnight deadline". Section 4—104.
    "Payor bank". Section 4—105.

(4)   In addition Article 1 contains general definitions and principles of construction and interpretation applicable throughout this Article.

§ 3–103. Limitations on Scope of Article.

(1) This Article does not apply to money, documents of title or investment securities.

(2) The provisions of this Article are subject to the provisions of the Article on Bank Deposits and Collections (Article 4) and Secured Transactions (Article 9).

§ 3–104. Form of Negotiable Instruments; "Draft"; "Check"; "Certificate of Deposit"; "Note".

(1) Any writing to be a negotiable instrument within this Article must

(a) be signed by the maker or drawer; and

(b) contain an unconditional promise or order to pay a sum certain in money and no other promise, order, obligation or power given by the maker or drawer except as authorized by this Article; and

(c) be payable on demand or at a definite time; and

(d) be payable to order or to bearer.

(2) A writing which complies with the requirements of this section is

(a) a "draft" ("bill of exchange") if it is an order;

(b) a "check" if it is a draft drawn on a bank and payable on demand;

(c) a "certificate of deposit" if it is an acknowledgment by a bank of receipt of money with an engagement to repay it;

(d) a "note" if it is a promise other than a certificate of deposit.

(3) As used in other Articles of this Act, and as the context may require, the terms "draft", "check", "certificate of deposit" and "note" may refer to instruments which are not negotiable within this Article as well as to instruments which are so negotiable.

§ 3–105. When Promise or Order Unconditional.

(1) A promise or order otherwise unconditional is not made conditional by the fact that the instrument

(a) is subject to implied or constructive conditions; or

(b) states its consideration, whether performed or promised, or the transaction which gave rise to the instrument, or that the promise or order is made or the instrument matures in accordance with or "as per" such transaction; or

(c) refers to or states that it arises out of a separate agreement or refers to a separate agreement for rights as to prepayment or acceleration; or

(d) states that it is drawn under a letter of credit; or

(e) states that it is secured, whether by mortgage, reservation of title or otherwise; or

(f) indicates a particular account to be debited or any other fund or source from which reimbursement is expected; or

(g) is limited to payment out of a particular fund or the proceeds of a particular source, if the instrument is issued by a government or governmental agency or unit; or

(h) is limited to payment out of the entire assets of a partnership, unincorporated association, trust or estate by or on behalf of which the instrument is issued.

(2) A promise or order is not unconditional if the strument

(a) states that it is subject to or governed by any other agreement; or

(b) states that it is to be paid only out of a particular fund or source except as provided in this section.

§ 3–106. Sum Certain.

(1)   The sum payable is a sum certain even though it is to be paid

(a) with stated interest or by stated installments; or

(b) with stated different rates of interest before and after default or a specified date; or

(c) with a stated discount or addition if paid before or after the date fixed for payment; or

(d) with exchange or less exchange, whether at a fixed rate or at the current rate; or

(e) with costs of collection or an attorney's fee or both upon default.

(2)   Nothing in this section shall validate any term which is otherwise illegal.

§ 3–107. Money.

(1)   An instrument is payable in money if the medium of exchange in which it is payable is money at the time the instrument is made. An instrument payable in "currency" or "current funds" is payable in money.

(2)   A promise or order to pay a sum stated in a foreign currency is for a sum certain in money and, unless a different medium of payment is specified in the instrument, may be satisfied by payment of that number of dollars which the stated foreign currency will purchase at the buying sight rate for that currency on the day on which the instrument is payable or, if payable on demand, on the day of demand. If such an instrument specifies a foreign currency as the medium of payment the instrument is payable in that currency.

§ 3–108. Payable on Demand.

Instruments payable on demand include those payable at sight or on presentation and those in which no time for payment is stated.

§ 3–109. Definite Time.

(1)   An instrument is payable at a definite time if by its terms it is payable

(a) on or before a stated date or at a fixed period after a stated date; or

(b) at a fixed period after sight; or

(c) at a definite time subject to any acceleration; or

(d) at a definite time subject to extension at the option of the holder, or to extension to a further definite time at the option of the maker or acceptor or automatically upon or after a specified act or event.

(2)   An instrument which by its terms is otherwise payable only upon an act or event uncertain as to time of occurrence is not payable at a definite time even though the act or event has occurred.

§ 3–110. Payable to Order.

(1)   An instrument is payable to order when by its terms it is payable to the order or assigns of any person therein specified with reasonable certainty, or to him or his order, or when it is conspicuously designated on its face as "exchange" or the like and names a payee. It may be payable to the order of

(a) the maker or drawer; or

(b) the drawee; or

(c) a payee who is not maker, drawer or drawee; or

(d) two or more payees together or in the alternative; or

(e) an estate, trust or fund, in which case it is payable to the order of the representative of such estate, trust or fund or his successors; or

(f) an office, or an officer by his title as such in which case it is payable to the principal but the incumbent of the office or his successors may act as if he or they were the holder; or

(g) a partnership or unincorporated association, in which case it is payable to the partnership or association and may be indorsed or transferred by any person thereto authorized.

(2) An instrument not payable to order is not made so payable by such words as "payable upon return of this instrument properly indorsed."

(3) An instrument made payable both to order and to bearer is payable to order unless the bearer words are hand-written or typewritten.

§ 3—111. Payable to Bearer.

An instrument is payable to bearer when by its terms it is payable to

(a) bearer or the order of bearer; or

(b) a specified person or bearer; or

(c) "cash" or the order of "cash", or any other indication which does not purport to designate a specific payee.

§ 3—112. Terms and Omissions Not Affecting Negotiability.

(1) The negotiability of an instrument is not affected by

(a) the omission of a statement of any consideration or of the place where the instrument is drawn or payable; or

(b) a statement that collateral has been given to secure obligations either on the instrument or otherwise of an obligor on the instrument or that in case of default on those obligations the holder may realize on or dispose of the collateral; or

(c) a promise or power to maintain or protect collateral or to give additional collateral; or

(d) a term authorizing a confession of judgment on the instrument if it is not paid when due; or

(e) a term purporting to waive the benefit of any law intended for the advantage or protection of any obligor; or

(f) a term in a draft providing that the payee by indorsing or cashing it acknowledges full satisfaction of an obligation of the drawer; or

(g) a statement in a draft drawn in a set of parts (Section 3—801) to the effect that the order is effective only if no other part has been honored.

(2) Nothing in this section shall validate any term which is otherwise illegal.

§ 3—113. Seal.

An instrument otherwise negotiable is within this Article even though it is under a seal.

§ 3—114. Date, Antedating, Postdating.

(1) The negotiability of an instrument is not affected by the fact that it is undated, antedated or postdated.

(2) Where an instrument is antedated or postdated the time when it is payable is determined by the stated date if the instrument is payable on demand or at a fixed period after date.

(3) Where the instrument or any signature thereon is dated, the date is presumed to be correct.

§ 3–115. Incomplete Instruments.

(1) When a paper whose contents at the time of signing show that it is intended to become an instrument is signed while still incomplete in any necessary respect it cannot be enforced until completed, but when it is completed in accordance with authority given it is effective as completed.

(2) If the completion is unauthorized the rules as to material alteration apply (Section 3–407), even though the paper was not delivered by the maker or drawer; but the burden of establishing that any completion is unauthorized is on the party so asserting.

§ 3–116. Instruments Payable to Two or More Persons.

An instrument payable to the order of two or more persons

  (a) if in the alternative is payable to any one of them and may be negotiated, discharged or enforced by any of them who has possession of it;

  (b) if not in the alternative is payable to all of them and may be negotiated, discharged or enforced only by all of them.

§ 3–117. Instruments Payable With Words of Description.

An instrument made payable to a named person with the addition of words describing him

  (a) as agent or officer of a specified person is payable to his principal, but the agent or officer may act as if he were the holder;

  (b) as any other fiduciary for a specified person or purpose is payable to the payee and may be negotiated, discharged or enforced by him;

  (c) in any other manner is payable to the payee unconditionally and the additional words are without effect on subsequent parties.

§ 3–118. Ambiguous Terms and Rules of Construction.

The following rules apply to every instrument;

  (a) Where there is doubt whether the instrument is a draft or a note the holder may treat it as either. A draft drawn on the drawer is effective as a note.

  (b) Handwritten terms control typewritten and printed terms, and typewritten control printed.

  (c) Words control figures except that if the words are ambiguous figures control.

  (d) Unless otherwise specified a provision for interest means interest at the judgment rate at the place of payment from the date of the instrument, or if it is undated from the date of issue.

  (e) Unless the instrument otherwise specifies two or more persons who sign as maker, acceptor or drawer or indorser and as a part of the same transaction are jointly and severally liable even though the instrument contains such words as "I promise to pay."

(f) Unless otherwise specified, consent to extension authorizes a single extension for not longer than the original period. A consent to extension, expressed in the instrument, is binding on secondary parties and accommodation makers. A holder may not exercise his option to extend an instrument over the objection of a maker or acceptor or other party who in accordance with Section 3–604 tenders full payment when the instrument is due.

§ 3–119. Other Writings Affecting Instrument.

(1) As between the obligor and his immediate obligee or any transferee the terms of an instrument may be modified or affected by any other written agreement executed as a part of the same transaction, except that a holder in due course is not affected by any limitation of his rights arising out of the separate written agreement if he had no notice of the limitation when he took the instrument.

(2) A separate agreement does not affect the negotiability of an instrument.

§ 3–120. Instruments "Payable Through" Bank.

An instrument which states that it is "payable through" a bank or the like designates that bank as a collecting bank to make presentment but does not of itself authorize the bank to pay the instrument.

§ 3–121. Instruments Payable at Bank.

Note: *If this Act is introduced in the Congress of the United States this section should be omitted. (States to select either alternative)*

Alternative A—

A note or acceptance which states that it is payable at a bank is the equivalent of a draft drawn on the bank payable when it falls due out of any funds of the maker or acceptor in current account or otherwise available for such payment.

Alternative B—

A note or acceptance which states that it is payable at a bank is not of itself an order or authorization to the bank to pay it.

§ 3–122. Accrual of Cause of Action.

(1) A cause of action against a maker or an acceptor accrues

  (a) in the case of a time instrument on the day after maturity;

  (b) in the case of a demand instrument upon its date or, if no date is stated, on the date of issue.

(2) A cause of action against the obligor of a demand or time certificate of deposit accrues upon demand, but demand on a time certificate may not be made until on or after the date of maturity.

(3) A cause of action against a drawer of a draft or an indorser of any instrument accrues upon demand following dishonor of the instrument. Notice of dishonor is a demand.

(4) Unless an instrument provides otherwise, interest runs at the rate provided by law for a judgment

  (a) in the case of a maker, acceptor or other primary obligor of a demand instrument, from the date of demand;

  (b) in all other cases from the date of accrual of the cause of action.

PART 2

TRANSFER AND NEGOTIATION

§ 3–201. Transfer: Right to Indorsement.

(1) Transfer of an instrument vests in the transferee such rights as the transferor has therein, except that a transferee who has himself been a party to any fraud or illegality affecting the instrument or who as a prior holder had notice of a defense or claim against it cannot improve his position by taking from a later holder in due course.

(2) A transfer of a security interest in an instrument vests the foregoing rights in the transferee to the extent of the interest transferred.

(3) Unless otherwise agreed any transfer for value of an instrument not then payable to bearer gives the transferee the specifically enforceable right to have the unqualified indorsement of the transferor. Negotiation takes effect only when the indorsement is made and until that time there is no presumption that the transferee is the owner.

§ 3–202. Negotiation.

(1) Negotiation is the transfer of an instrument in such form that the transferee becomes a holder. If the instrument is payable to order it is negotiated by delivery with any necessary indorsement; if payable to bearer it is negotiated by delivery.

(2) An indorsement must be written by or on behalf of the holder and on the instrument or on a paper so firmly affixed thereto as to become a part thereof.

(3) An indorsement is effective for negotiation only when it conveys the entire instrument or any unpaid residue. If it purports to be of less it operates only as a partial assignment.

(4) Words of assignment, condition, waiver, guaranty, limitation or disclaimer of liability and the like accompanying an indorsement do not affect its character as an indorsement.

§ 3–203. Wrong or Misspelled Name.

Where an instrument is made payable to a person under a misspelled name or one other than his own he may indorse in that name or his own or both; but signature in both names may be required by a person paying or giving value for the instrument.

§ 3–204. Special Indorsement; Blank Indorsement.

(1) A special indorsement specifies the person to whom or to whose order it makes the instrument payable. Any instrument specially indorsed becomes payable to the order of the special indorsee and may be further negotiated only by his indorsement.

(2) An indorsement in blank specifies no particular indorsee and may consist of a mere signature. An instrument payable to order and indorsed in blank becomes payable to bearer and may be negotiated by delivery alone until specially indorsed.

(3) The holder may convert a blank indorsement into a special indorsement by writing over the signature of the indorser in blank any contract consistent with the character of the indorsement.

§ 3–205. Restrictive Indorsements.

An indorsement is restrictive which either

    (a) is conditional; or

    (b) purports to prohibit further transfer of the instrument; or

    (c) includes the words "for collection", "for deposit", "pay any bank", or like terms signifying a purpose of deposit or collection; or

    (d) otherwise states that it is for the benefit or use of the indorser or of another person.

§ 3–206. Effect of Restrictive Indorsement.

(1) No restrictive indorsement prevents further transfer or negotiation of the instrument.

(2) An intermediary bank, or a payor bank which is not the depositary bank, is neither given notice nor otherwise affected by a restrictive indorsement of any person except the bank's immediate transferor or the person presenting for payment.

(3) Except for an intermediary bank, any transferee under an indorsement which is conditional or includes the words "for collection", "for deposit", "pay any bank", or like terms (subparagraphs (a) and (c) of Section 3–205) must pay or apply any value given by him for or on the security of the instrument consistently with the indorsement and to the extent that he does so he becomes a holder for value. In addition such transferee is a holder in due course if he otherwise complies with the requirements of Section 3–302 on what constitutes a holder in due course.

(4) The first taker under an indorsement for the benefit of the indorser or another person (subparagraph (d) of Section 3–205) must pay or apply any value given by him for or on the security of the instrument consistently with the indorsement and to the extent that he does so he becomes a holder for value. In addition such taker is a holder in due course if he otherwise complies with the requirements of Section 3–302 on what constitutes a holder in due course. A later holder for value is neither given notice nor otherwise affected by such restrictive indorsement unless he has knowledge that a fiduciary or other person has negotiated the instrument in any transaction for his own benefit or otherwise in breach of duty (subsection (2) of Section 3–304).

§ 3–207. Negotiation Effective Although It May Be Rescinded.

(1) Negotiation is effective to transfer the instrument although the negotiation is

    (a) made by an infant, a corporation exceeding its powers, or any other person without capacity; or

    (b) obtained by fraud, duress or mistake of any kind; or

    (c) part of an illegal transaction; or

    (d) made in breach of duty.

(2) Except as against a subsequent holder in due course such negotiation is in an appropriate case subject to rescission, the declaration of a constructive trust or any other remedy permitted by law.

§ 3–208. Reacquisition.

Where an instrument is returned to or reacquired by a prior party he may cancel any indorsement which is not necessary to his title and reissue or further negotiate the instrument, but any intervening party is discharged as against the reacquiring party and subsequent holders not in due course and if his indorsement has been cancelled is discharged as against subsequent holders in due course as well.

PART 3

RIGHTS OF A HOLDER

§ 3–301. Rights of a Holder.

The holder of an instrument whether or not he is the owner may transfer or negotiate it and, except as otherwise provided in Section 3–603 on payment or satisfaction, discharge it or enforce payment in his own name.

§ 3–302. Holder in Due Course.

(1)   A holder in due course is a holder who takes the instrument

(a) for value; and

(b) in good faith; and

(c) without notice that it is overdue or has been dishonored or of any defense against or claim to it on the part of any person.

(2)   A payee may be a holder in due course.

(3)   A holder does not become a holder in due course of an instrument:

(a) by purchase of it at judicial sale or by taking it under legal process; or

(b) by acquiring it in taking over an estate; or

(c) by purchasing it as part of a bulk transaction not in regular course of business of the transferor.

(4)   A purchaser of a limited interest can be a holder in due course only to the extent of the interest purchased.

§ 3–303. Taking for Value.

A holder takes the instrument for value

(a) to the extent that the agreed consideration has been performed or that he acquires a security interest in or a lien on the instru-ment otherwise than by legal process; or

(b) when he takes the instrument in payment of or as security for an antecedent claim against any person whether or not the claim is due; or

(c) when he gives a negotiable instrument for it or makes an irrevocable commitment to a third person.

§ 3–304. Notice to Purchaser.

(1)   The purchaser has notice of a claim or defense if

(a) the instrument is so incomplete, bears such visible evidence of forgery or alteration, or is otherwise so irregular as to call into question its validity, terms or ownership or to create an ambiguity as to the party to pay; or

(b) the purchaser has notice that the obligation of any party is voidable in whole or in part, or that all parties have been discharged.

(2)   The purchaser has notice of a claim against the instrument when he has knowledge that a fiduciary has negotiated the instrument in payment of or as security for his own debt or in any transaction for his own benefit or otherwise in breach of duty.

(3)   The purchaser has notice that an instrument is overdue if he has reason to know

(a) that any part of the principal amount is overdue or that there is an uncured default in payment of another instrument of the same series; or

(b) that acceleration of the instrument has been made; or

(c) that he is taking a demand instrument after demand has been made or more than a reasonable length of time after its issue. A reasonable time for a check drawn and payable within the states and territories of the United States and the District of Columbia is presumed to be thirty days.

(4) Knowledge of the following facts does not of itself give the purchaser notice of a defense or claim

(a) that the instrument is antedated or postdated;

(b) that it was issued or negotiated in return for an executory promise or accompanied by a separate agreement, unless the purchaser has notice that a defense or claim has arisen from the terms thereof;

(c) that any party has signed for accommodation;

(d) that an incomplete instrument has been completed, unless the purchaser has notice of any improper completion;

(e) that any person negotiating the instrument is or was a fiduciary;

(f) that there has been default in payment of interest on the instrument or in payment of any other instrument, except one of the same series.

(5) The filing or recording of a document does not of itself constitute notice within the provisions of this Article to a person who would otherwise be a holder in due course.

(6) To be effective notice must be received at such time and in such manner as to give a reasonable opportunity to act on it.

§ 3–305. Rights of a Holder in Due Course.

To the extent that a holder is a holder in due course he takes the instrument free from

(1) all claims to it on the part of any person; and

(2) all defenses of any party to the instrument with whom the holder has not dealt except

(a) infancy, to the extent that it is a defense to a simple contract; and

(b) such other incapacity, or duress, or illegality of the transaction, as renders the obligation of the party a nullity; and

(c) such misrepresentation as has induced the party to sign the instrument with neither knowledge nor reasonable opportunity to obtain knowledge of its character or its essential terms; and

(d) discharge in insolvency proceedings; and

(e) any other discharge of which the holder has notice when he takes the instrument.

§ 3–306. Rights of One Not Holder in Due Course.

Unless he has the rights of a holder in due course any person takes the instrument subject to

(a) all valid claims to it on the part of any person; and

(b) all defenses of any party which would be available in an action on a simple contract; and

(c) the defenses of want or failure of consideration, nonperformance of any condition precedent, non-delivery, or delivery for a special purpose (Section 3–408); and

(d) the defense that he or a person through whom he holds the instrument acquired it by theft, or that payment or satisfaction to such holder would be inconsistent with the terms of a restrictive indorsement. The claim of any third person to the instrument is not otherwise available as a defense to any party liable thereon unless the third person himself defends the action for such party.

§ 3–307. Burden of Establishing Signatures, Defenses and Due Course.

(1)   Unless specifically denied in the pleadings each signature on an instrument is admitted. When the effectiveness of a signature is put in issue

(a) the burden of establishing it is on the party claiming under the signature; but

(b) the signature is presumed to be genuine or authorized except where the action is to enforce the obligation of a purported signer who has died or become incompetent before proof is required.

(2)   When signatures are admitted or established, production of the instrument entitles a holder to recover on it unless the defendant establishes a defense.

(3)   After it is shown that a defense exists a person claiming the rights of a holder in due course has the burden of establishing that he or some person under whom he claims is in all respects a holder in due course.

PART 4

LIABILITY OF PARTIES

§ 3–401. Signature.

(1)   No person is liable on an instrument unless his signature appears thereon.

(2)   A signature is made by use of any name, including any trade or assumed name, upon an instrument, or by any word or mark used in lieu of a written signature.

§ 3–402. Signature in Ambiguous Capacity.

Unless the instrument clearly indicates that a signature made in some other capacity it is an indorsement.

§ 3–403. Signature by Authorized Representative.

(1)   A signature may be made by an agent or other representative, and his authority to make it may be established as in other cases of representation. No particular form of appointment is necessary to establish such authority.

(2)   An authorized representative who signs his own name to an instrument

(a) is personally obligated if the instrument neither names the person represented nor shows that the representative signed in a representative capacity;

(b) except as otherwise established between the immediate parties, is personally obligated if the instrument names the person represented but does not show that the representative signed in a representative capacity, or if the instrument does not name the person represented but does show that the representative signed in a representative capacity.

(3) Except as otherwise established the name of an organization preceded or followed by the name and office of an authorized individual is a signature made in a representative capacity.

§ 3–404. Unauthorized Signatures.

(1) Any unauthorized signature is wholly inoperative as that of the person whose name is signed unless he ratifies it or is precluded from denying it; but it operates as the signature of the unauthorized signer in favor of any person who in good faith pays the instrument or takes it for value.

(2) Any unauthorized signature may be ratified for all purposes of this Article. Such ratification does not of itself affect any rights of the person ratifying against the actual signer.

§ 3–405. Impostors; Signature in Name of Payee.

(1) An indorsement by any person in the name of a named payee is effective if

(a) an impostor by use of the mails or otherwise has induced the maker or drawer to issue the instrument to him or his confederate in the name of the payee; or

(b) a person signing as or on behalf of a maker or drawer intends the payee to have no interest in the instrument; or

(c) an agent or employee of the maker or drawer has supplied him with the name of the payee intending the latter to have no such interest.

(2) Nothing in this section shall affect the criminal or civil liability of the person so indorsing.

§ 3–406. Negligence Contributing to Alteration or Unauthorized Signature.

Any person who by his negligence substantially contributes to a material alteration of the instrument or to the making of an unauthorized signature is precluded from asserting the alteration or lack of authority against a holder in due course or against a drawee or other payor who pays the instrument in good faith and in accordance with the reasonable commercial standards of the drawee's or payor's business.

§ 3–407. Alteration.

(1) Any alteration of an instrument is material which changes the contract of any party thereto in any respect, including any such change in

(a) the number or relations of the parties; or

(b) an incomplete instrument, by completing it otherwise than as authorized; or

(c) the writing as signed, by adding to it or by removing any part of it.

(2) As against any person other than a subsequent holder in due course

(a) alteration by the holder which is both fraudulent and material discharges any party whose contract is thereby changed unless that party assents or is precluded from asserting the defense;

(b) no other alteration discharges any party and the instrument may be enforced according to its original tenor, or as to incomplete instruments according to the authority given.

(3)   A subsequent holder in due course may in all cases enforce the instrument according to its original tenor, and when an incomplete instrument has been completed, he may enforce it as completed.

§ 3—408.   Consideration.

Want or failure of consideration is a defense as against any person not having the rights of a holder in due course (Section 3—305), except that no consideration is necessary for an instrument or obligation thereon given in payment of or as security for an antecedent obligation of any kind.   Nothing in this section shall be taken to displace any statute outside this Act under which a promise is enforceable notwithstanding lack or failure of consideration.   Partial failure of consideration is a defense pro tanto whether or not the failure is in an ascertained or liquidated amount.

§ 3—409.   Draft Not an Assignment.

(1)   A check or other draft does not of itself operate as an assignment of any funds in the hands of the drawee available for its payment, and the drawee is not liable on the instrument until he accepts it.

(2)   Nothing in this section shall affect any liability in contract, tort or otherwise arising from any letter of credit or other obligation or representation which is not an acceptance.

§ 3—410.   Definition and Operation of Acceptance.

(1)   Acceptance is the drawee's signed engagement to honor the draft as presented.   It must be written on the draft, and may consist of his signature alone.   It becomes operative when completed by delivery or notification.

(2)   A draft may be accepted although it has not been signed by the drawer or is otherwise incomplete or is overdue or has been dishonored.

(3)   Where the draft is payable at a fixed period after sight and the acceptor fails to date his acceptance the holder may complete it by supplying a date in good faith.

§ 3—411.   Certification of a Check.

(1)   Certification of a check is acceptance.   Where a holder procures certification the drawer and all prior indorsers are discharged.

(2)   Unless otherwise agreed a bank has no obligation to certify a check.

(3)   A bank may certify a check before returning it for lack of proper indorsement.   If it does so the drawer is discharged.

§ 3—412.   Acceptance Varying Draft.

(1)   Where the drawee's proferred acceptance in any manner varies the draft as presented the holder may refuse the acceptance and treat the draft as dishonored in which case the drawee is entitled to have his acceptance cancelled.

(2)   The terms of the draft are not varied by an acceptance to pay at any particular bank or place in the United States, unless the acceptance states that

the draft is to be paid only at such bank or place.

(3) Where the holder assents to an acceptance varying the terms of the draft each drawer and indorser who does not affirmatively assent is discharged.

§ 3–413. Contract of Maker, Drawer and Acceptor.

(1) The maker or acceptor engages that he will pay the instrument according to its tenor at the time of his engagement or as completed pursuant to Section 3–115 on incomplete instruments.

(2) The drawer engages that upon dishonor of the draft and any necessary notice of dishonor or protest he will pay the amount of the draft to the holder or to any indorser who takes it up. The drawer may disclaim this liability by drawing without recourse.

(3) By making, drawing or accepting the party admits as against all subsequent parties including the drawee the existence of the payee and his then capacity to indorse.

§ 3–414. Contract of Indorser; Order of Liability.

(1) Unless the indorsement otherwise specifies (as by such words as "without recourse") every indorser engages that upon dishonor and any necessary notice of dishonor and protest he will pay the instrument according to its tenor at the time of his indorsement to the holder or to any subsequent indorser who takes it up, even though the indorser who takes it up was not obligated to do so.

(2) Unless they otherwise agree indorsers are liable to one another in the order in which they indorse, which is presumed to be the order in which their signatures appear on the instrument.

§ 3–415. Contract of Accommodation Party.

(1) An accommodation party is one who signs the instrument in any capacity for the purpose of lending his name to another party to it.

(2) When the instrument has been taken for value before it is due the accommodation party is liable in the capacity in which he has signed even though the taker knows of the accommodation.

(3) As against a holder in due course and without notice of the accommodation oral proof of the accommodation is not admissible to give the accommodation party the benefit of discharges dependent on his character as such. In other cases the accommodation character may be shown by oral proof.

(4) An indorsement which shows that it is not in the chain of title is notice of its accommodation character.

(5) An accommodation party is not liable to the party accommodated, and if he pays the instrument has a right of recourse on the instrument against such party.

§ 3–416. Contract of Guarantor.

(1) "Payment guaranteed" or equivalent words added to a signature mean that the signer engages that if the instrument is not paid when due he will pay it according to its tenor without resort by the holder to any other party.

(2) "Collection guaranteed" or equivalent words added to a signature mean that the signer engages that if the instrument is not paid when due he will pay it according to its tenor, but only after the holder has reduced his claim against the maker or acceptor to judgment and execution has been returned unsatisfied, or after the maker or acceptor has become insolvent or it is otherwise apparent that it is useless to proceed against him.

(3) Words of guaranty which do not otherwise specify guarantee payment.

(4) No words of guaranty added to the signature of a sole maker or acceptor affect his liability on the instrument. Such words added to the signature of one of two or more makers or acceptors create a presumption that the signature is for the accommodation of the others.

(5) When words of guaranty are used presentment, notice of dishonor and protest are not necessary to charge the user.

(6) Any guaranty written on the instrument is enforceable notwithstanding any statute of frauds.

§ 3–417. Warranties on Presentment and Transfer.

(1) Any person who obtains payment or acceptance and any prior transferor warrants to a person who in good faith pays or accepts that

(a) he has a good title to the instrument or is authorized to obtain payment or acceptance on behalf of one who has a good title; and

(b) he has no knowledge that the signature of the maker or drawer is unauthorized, except that this warranty is not given by a holder in due course acting in good faith

(i) to a maker with respect to the maker's own signature; or

(ii) to a drawer with respect to the drawer's own signature, whether or not the drawer is also the drawee; or

(iii) to an acceptor of a draft if the holder in due course took the draft after the acceptance or obtained the acceptance without knowledge that the drawer's signature was unauthorized; and

(c) the instrument has not been materially altered, except that this warranty is not given by a holder in due course acting in good faith

(i) to the maker of a note; or

(ii) to the drawer of a draft whether or not the drawer is also the drawee; or

(iii) to the acceptor of a draft with respect to an alteration made prior to the acceptance if the holder in due course took the draft after the acceptance, even though the acceptance provided "payable as originally drawn" or equivalent terms; or

(iv) to the acceptor of a draft with respect to an alteration made after the acceptance.

(2) Any person who transfers an instrument and receives consideration warrants to his transferee and if the transfer is by indorsement to any subsequent holder who takes the instrument in good faith that

    (a) he has a good title to the instrument or is authorized to obtain payment or acceptance on behalf of one who has a good title and the transfer is otherwise rightful; and

    (b) all signatures are genuine or authorized, and

    (c) the instrument has not been materially altered; and

    (d) no defense of any party is good against him; and

    (e) he has no knowledge of any insolvency proceeding instituted with respect to the maker or acceptor or the drawer of an unaccepted instrument.

(3) By transferring "without recourse" the transferor limits the obligation stated in subsection (2) (d) to a warranty that he has no knowledge of such a defense.

(4) A selling agent or broker who does not disclose the fact that he is acting only as such gives the warranties provided in this section, but if he makes such disclosure warrants only his good faith and authority.

§ 3—418. Finality of Payment or Acceptance.

Except for recovery of bank payments as provided in the Article on Bank Deposits and Collections (Article 4) and except for liability for breach of warranty on presentment under the preceding section, payment or acceptance of any instrument is final in favor of a holder in due course, or a person who has in good faith changed his position in reliance on the payment.

§ 3—419. Conversion of Instrument; Innocent Representative.

(1) An instrument is converted when

    (a) a drawee to whom it is delivered for acceptance refuses to return it on demand; or

    (b) any person to whom it is delivered for payment refuses on demand either to pay or to return it; or

    (c) it is paid on a forged indorsement.

(2) In an action against a drawee under subsection (1) the measure of the drawee's liability is the face amount of the instrument. In any other action under subsection (1) the measure of liability is presumed to be the face amount of the instrument.

(3) Subject to the provisions of this Act concerning restrictive indorsements a representative, including a depositary or collecting bank, who has in good faith and in accordance with the reasonable commercial standards applicable to the business of such representative dealt with an instrument or its proceeds on behalf of one who was not the true owner is not liable in conversion or otherwise to the true owner beyond the amount of any proceeds remaining in his hands.

(4) An intermediary bank or payor bank which is not a depositary bank is not liable in conversion solely by reason of the fact that proceeds of an item indorsed restrictively (Sections 3—205 and 3—206) are not paid or applied consistently with the restrictive indorsement of an indorser other than its immediate transferor.

PART 5

PRESENTMENT, NOTICE OF DISHONOR AND PROTEST

§ 3–501. When Presentment, Notice of Dishonor, and Protest Necessary or Permissible.

(1)   Unless excused (Section 3–511) presentment is necessary to charge secondary parties as follows:

  (a) presentment for acceptance is necessary to charge the drawer and indorsers of a draft where the draft so provides, or is payable elsewhere than at the residence or place of business of the drawee, or its date of payment depends upon such presentment. The holder may at his option present for acceptance any other draft payable at a stated date;

  (b) presentment for payment is necessary to charge any indorser;

  (c) in the case of any drawer, the acceptor of a draft payable at a bank or the maker of a note payable at a bank, presentment for payment is necessary, but failure to make presentment discharges such drawer, acceptor or maker only as stated in Section 3–502(1) (b).

(2)   Unless excused (Section 3–511)

  (a) notice of any dishonor is necessary to charge any indorser;

  (b) in the case of any drawer, the acceptor of a draft payable at a bank or the maker of a note payable at a bank, notice of any dishonor is necessary, but failure to give such notice discharges such drawer, acceptor or maker only as stated in Section 3–502(1) (b).

(3)   Unless excused (Section 3–511) protest of any dishonor is necessary to charge the drawer and indorsers of any draft which on its face appears to be drawn or payable outside of the states, territories, dependencies, and possessions of the United States, the District of Columbia and the Commonwealth of Puerto Rico. The holder may at his option make protest of any dishonor of any other instrument and in the case of a foreign draft may on insolvency of the acceptor before maturity make protest for better security.

(4)   Notwithstanding any provision of this section, neither presentment nor notice of dishonor nor protest is necessary to charge an indorser who has indorsed an instrument after maturity.

§ 3–502. Unexcused Delay; Discharge.

(1)   Where without excuse any necessary presentment or notice of dishonor is delayed beyond the time when it is due

  (a) any indorser is discharged; and

  (b) any drawer or the acceptor of a draft payable at a bank or the maker of a note payable at a bank who because the drawee or payor bank becomes insolvent during the delay is deprived of funds maintained with the drawee or payor bank to cover the instrument may discharge his liability by written assignment to the holder of his rights against the drawee or payor bank in respect of such funds, but such drawer, acceptor or maker is not otherwise discharged.

(2) Where without excuse a necessary protest is delayed beyond the time when it is due any drawer or indorser is discharged.

§ 3—503. Time of Presentment.

(1) Unless a different time is expressed in the instrument the time for any presentment is determined as follows:

(a) where an instrument is payable at or a fixed period after a stated date any presentment for acceptance must be made on or before the date it is payable;

(b) where an instrument is payable after sight it must either be presented for acceptance or negotiated within a reasonable time after date or issue whichever is later;

(c) where an instrument shows the date on which it is payable presentment for payment is due on that date;

(d) where an instrument is accelerated presentment for payment is due within a reasonable time after the acceleration;

(e) with respect to the liability of any secondary party presentment for acceptance or payment of any other instrument is due within a reasonable time after such party becomes liable thereon.

(2) A reasonable time for presentment is determined by the nature of the instrument, any usage of banking or trade and the facts of the particular case. In the case of an uncertified check which is drawn and payable within the United States and which is not a draft drawn by a bank the following are presumed to be reasonable periods within which to present for payment or to initiate bank collection:

(a) with respect to the liability of the drawer, thirty days after date or issue whichever is later; and

(b) with respect to the liability of an indorser, seven days after his indorsement.

(3) Where any presentment is due on a day which is not a full business day for either the person making presentment or the party to pay or accept, presentment is due on the next following day which is a full business day for both parties.

(4) Presentment to be sufficient must be made at a reasonable hour, and if at a bank during its banking day.

§ 3—504. How Presentment Made.

(1) Presentment is a demand for acceptance or payment made upon the maker, acceptor, drawee or other payor by or on behalf of the holder.

(2) Presentment may be made

(a) by mail, in which event the time of presentment is determined by the time of receipt of the mail; or

(b) through a clearing house; or

(c) at the place of acceptance or payment specified in the instrument or if there be none at the place of business or residence of the party to accept or pay. If neither the party to accept or pay nor anyone authorized to act for him is present or accessible at such place presentment is excused.

(3) It may be made

(a) to any one of two or more makers, acceptors, drawees or other payors; or

(b) to any person who has authority to make or refuse the acceptance or payment.

(4)   A draft accepted or a note made payable at a bank in the United States must be presented at such bank.

(5)   In the cases described in Section 4—210 presentment may be made in the manner and with the result stated in that section.

§ 3—505. **Rights of Party to Whom Presentment is Made.**

(1)   The party to whom presentment is made may without dishonor require

   (a) exhibition of the instrument; and
   (b) reasonable identification of the person making presentment and evidence of his authority to make it if made for another; and
   (c) that the instrument be produced for acceptance or payment at a place specified in it, or if there be none at any place reasonable in the circumstances; and
   (d) a signed receipt on the instrument for any partial or full payment and its surrender upon full payment.

(2)   Failure to comply with any such requirement invalidates the presentment but the person presenting has a reasonable time in which to comply and the time for acceptance or payment runs from the time of compliance.

§ 3—506. **Time Allowed for Acceptance or Payment.**

(1)   Acceptance may be deferred without dishonor until the close of the next business day following presentment. The holder may also in a good faith effort to obtain acceptance and without either dishonor of the instrument or discharge of secondary parties allow postponement of acceptance for an additional business day.

(2)   Except as a longer time is allowed in the case of documentary drafts drawn under a letter of credit, and unless an earlier time is agreed to by the party to pay, payment of an instrument may be deferred without dishonor pending reasonable examination to determine whether it is properly payable, but payment must be made in any event before the close of business on the day of presentment.

§ 3—507. **Dishonor; Holder's Right of Recourse; Term Allowing Re-Presentment.**

(1)   An instrument is dishonored when

   (a) a necessary or optional presentment is duly made and due acceptance or payment is refused or cannot be obtained within the prescribed time or in case of bank collections the instrument is seasonably returned by the midnight deadline (Section 4—301); or
   (b) presentment is excused and the instrument is not duly accepted or paid.

(2)   Subject to any necessary notice of dishonor and protest, the holder has upon dishonor an immediate right of recourse against the drawers and indorsers.

(3)   Return of an instrument for lack of proper indorsement is not dishonor.

(4)   A term in a draft or an indorsement thereof allowing a stated time for re-presentment in the event of any dishonor of the draft by nonacceptance if a time draft or by nonpayment if a sight draft gives the holder as against any secondary party bound by the term an option to waive the dishonor without affecting the liability of the secondary party and

he may present again up to the end of the stated time.

§ 3–508. Notice of Dishonor.

(1)   Notice of dishonor may be given to any person who may be liable on the instrument by or on behalf of the holder or any party who has himself received notice, or any other party who can be compelled to pay the instrument.   In addition an agent or bank in whose hands the instrument is dishonored may give notice to his principal or customer or to another agent or bank from which the instrument was received.

(2)   Any necessary notice must be given by a bank before its midnight deadline and by any other person before midnight of the third business day after dishonor or receipt of notice of dishonor.

(3)   Notice may be given in any reasonable manner. It may be oral or written and in any terms which identify the instrument and state that it has been dishonored.   A misdescription which does not mislead the party notified does not vitiate the notice. Sending the instrument bearing a stamp, ticket or writing stating that acceptance or payment has been refused or sending a notice of debit with respect to the instrument is sufficient.

(4)   Written notice is given when sent although it is not received.

(5)   Notice to one partner is notice to each although the firm has been dissolved.

(6)   When any party is in insolvency proceedings instituted after the issue of the instrument notice may be given either to the party or to the representative of his estate.

(7)   When any party is dead or incompetent notice may be sent to his last known address or given to his personal representative.

(8)   Notice operates for the benefit of all parties who have rights on the instrument against the party notified.

§ 3–509. Protest; Noting for Protest.

(1)   A protest is a certificate of dishonor made under the hand and seal of a United States consul or vice consul or a notary public or other person authorized to certify dishonor by the law of the place where dishonor occurs. It may be made upon information satisfactory to such person.

(2)   The protest must identify the instrument and certify either that due presentment has been made or the reason why it is excused and that the instrument has been dishonored by nonacceptance or nonpayment.

(3)   The protest may also certify that notice of dishonor has been given to all parties or to specified parties.

(4)   Subject to subsection (5) any necessary protest is due by the time that notice of dishonor is due.

(5)   If, before protest is due, an instrument has been noted for protest by the officer to make protest, the protest may be made at any time thereafter as of the date of the noting.

§ 3–510. Evidence of Dishonor and Notice of Dishonor.

The following are admissible as evidence and create a presumption of dishonor and of any notice of dishonor therein shown:

    (a) a document regular in form as provided in the preceding section which purports to be a protest;

    (b) the purported stamp or writing of the drawee, payor bank or presenting bank on the instrument or accompanying it stating that acceptance or payment has been refused for reasons consistent with dishonor;

(c) any book or record of the drawee, payor bank, or any collecting bank kept in the usual course of business which shows dishonor, even though there is no evidence of who made the entry.

§ 3—511. Waived or Excused Presentment, Protest or Notice of Dishonor or Delay Therein.

(1)   Delay in presentment, protest or notice of dishonor is excused when the party is without notice that it is due or when the delay is caused by circumstances beyond his control and he exercises reasonable diligence after the cause of the delay ceases to operate.

(2)   Presentment or notice or protest as the case may be is entirely excused when

(a) the party to be charged has waived it expressly or by implication either before or after it is due; or

(b) such party has himself dishonored the instrument or has countermanded payment or otherwise has no reason to expect or right to require that the instrument be accepted or paid; or

(c) by reasonable diligence the presentment or protest cannot be made or the notice given.

(3)   Presentment is also entirely excused when

(a) the maker, acceptor or drawee of any instrument except a documentary draft is dead or in insolvency proceedings instituted after the issue of the instrument; or

(b) acceptance or payment is refused but not for want of proper presentment.

(4)   Where a draft has been dishonored by nonacceptance a later presentment for payment and any notice of dishonor and protest for nonpayment are excused unless in the meantime the instrument has been accepted.

(5)   A waiver of protest is also a waiver of presentment and of notice of dishonor even though protest is not required.

(6)   Where a waiver of presentment or notice or protest is embodied in the instrument itself it is binding upon all parties; but where it is written above the signature of an indorser it binds him only.

PART 6

DISCHARGE

§ 3—601. Discharge of Parties.

(1)   The extent of the discharge of any party from liability on an instrument is governed by the sections on

(a) payment or satisfaction (Section 3—603); or

(b) tender of payment (Section 3—604); or

(c) cancellation or renunciation (Section 3—605); or

(d) impairment of right of recourse or of collateral (Section 3—606); or

(e) reacquisition of the instrument by a prior party (Section 3—208); or

(f) fraudulent and material alteration (Section 3–407); or

(g) certification of a check (Section 3–411); or

(h) acceptance varying a draft (Section 3–412); or

(i) unexcused delay in presentment or notice of dishonor or protest (Section 3–502).

(2) Any party is also discharged from his liability on an instrument to another party by any other act or agreement with such party which would discharge his simple contract for the payment of money.

(3) The liability of all parties is discharged when any party who has himself no right of action or recourse on the instrument

(a) reacquires the instrument in his own right; or

(b) is discharged under any provision of this Article, except as otherwise provided with respect to discharge for impairment of recourse or of collateral (Section 3–606).

§ 3–602. Effect of Discharge Against Holder in Due Course.

No discharge of any party provided by this Article is effective against a subsequent holder in due course unless he has notice thereof when he takes the instrument.

§ 3–603. Payment or Satisfaction.

(1) The liability of any party is discharged to the extent of his payment or satisfaction to the holder even though it is made with knowledge of a claim of another person to the instrument unless prior to such payment or satisfaction the person making the claim either supplies indemnity deemed adequate by the party seeking the discharge or enjoins payment or satisfaction by order of a court of competent jurisdiction in an action in which the adverse claimant and the holder are parties. This subsection does not, however, result in the discharge of the liability

(a) of a party who in bad faith pays or satisfies a holder who acquired the instrument by theft or who (unless having the rights of a holder in due course) holds through one who so acquired it; or

(b) of a party (other than an intermediary bank or a payor bank which is not a depositary bank) who pays or satisfies the holder of an instrument which has been restrictively indorsed in a manner not consistent with the terms of such restrictive indorsement.

(2) Payment or satisfaction may be made with the consent of the holder by any person including a stranger to the instrument. Surrender of the instrument to such a person gives him the rights of a transferee (Section 3–201).

§ 3–604. Tender of Payment.

(1) Any party making tender of full payment to a holder when or after it is due is discharged to the extent of all subsequent liability for interest, costs and attorney's fees.

(2) The holder's refusal of such tender wholly discharges any party who has a right of recourse against the party making the tender.

(3) Where the maker or acceptor of an instrument payable otherwise than on demand is able and ready to pay at every place of payment specified in the instrument when it is due, it is equivalent to tender.

§ 3–605. Cancellation and Renunciation.

(1)   The holder of an instrument may even without consideration discharge any party

    (a) in any manner apparent on the face of the instrument or the indorsement, as by intentionally cancelling the instrument or the party's signature by destruction or mutilation, or by striking out the party's signature; or

    (b) by renouncing his rights by a writing signed and delivered or by surrender of the instrument to the party to be discharged.

(2)   Neither cancellation nor renunciation without surrender of the instrument affects the title thereto.

§ 3–606. Impairment of Recourse or of Collateral.

(1)   The holder discharges any party to the instrument to the extent that without such party's consent the holder

    (a) without express reservation of rights releases or agrees not to sue any person against whom the party has to the knowledge of the holder a right of recourse or agrees to suspend the right to enforce against such person the instrument or collateral or otherwise discharges such person, except that failure or delay in effecting any required presentment, protest or notice of dishonor with respect to any such person does not discharge any party as to whom presentment, protest or notice of dishonor is effective or unnecessary; or

    (b) unjustifiably impairs any collateral for the instrument given by or on behalf of the party or any person against whom he has a right of recourse.

(2)   By express reservation of rights against a party with a right of recourse the holder preserves

    (a) all his rights against such party as of the time when the instrument was originally due; and

    (b) the right of the party to pay the instrument as of that time; and

    (c) all rights of such party to recourse against others.

PART 7

ADVICE OF INTERNATIONAL SIGHT DRAFT

§ 3–701. Letter of Advice of International Sight Draft.

(1)   A "letter of advice" is a drawer's communication to the drawee that a described draft has been drawn.

(2)   Unless otherwise agreed when a bank receives from another bank a letter of advice of an international sight draft the drawee bank may immediately debit the drawer's account and stop the running of interest pro tanto. Such a debit and any resulting credit to any account covering outstanding drafts leaves in the drawer full power to stop payment or otherwise dispose of the amount and creates no trust or interest in favor of the holder.

(3)   Unless otherwise agreed and except where a draft is drawn under a credit issued by the drawee, the drawee of an international sight draft owes the drawer no duty to pay an unadvised draft but if it does so and the draft is genuine, may appropriately debit the drawer's account.

PART 8

MISCELLANEOUS

§ 3–801. Drafts in a Set.

(1) Where a draft is drawn in a set of parts, each of which is numbered and expressed to be an order only if no other part has been honored, the whole of the parts constitutes one draft but a taker of any part may become a holder in due course of the draft.

(2) Any person who negotiates, indorses or accepts a single part of a draft drawn in a set thereby becomes liable to any holder in due course of that part as if it were the whole set, but as between different holders in due course to whom different parts have been negotiated the holder whose title first accrues has all rights to the draft and its proceeds.

(3) As against the drawee the first presented part of a draft drawn in a set is the part entitled to payment, or if a time draft to acceptance and payment. Acceptance of any subsequently presented part renders the drawee liable thereon under subsection (2). With respect both to a holder and to the drawer payment of a subsequently presented part of a draft payable at sight has the same effect as payment of a check notwithstanding an effective stop order (Section 4–407).

(4) Except as otherwise provided in this section, where any part of a draft in a set is discharged by payment or otherwise the whole draft is discharged.

§ 3–802. Effect of Instrument on Obligation for Which It Is Given.

(1) Unless otherwise agreed where an instrument is taken for an underlying obligation

   (a) the obligation is pro tanto discharged if a bank is drawer, maker or acceptor of the instrument and there is no recourse on the instrument against the underlying obligor; and

   (b) in any other case the obligation is suspended pro tanto until the instrument is due or if it is payable on demand until its presentment. If the instrument is dishonored action may be maintained on either the instrument or the obligation; discharge of the underlying obligor on the instrument also discharges him on the obligation.

(2) The taking in good faith of a check which is not postdated does not of itself so extend the time on the original obligation as to discharge a surety.

§ 3–803. Notice to Third Party.

Where a defendant is sued for breach of an obligation for which a third person is answerable over under this Article he may give the third person written notice of the litigation, and the person notified may then give similar notice to any other person who is answerable over to him under this Article. If the notice states that the person notified may come in and defend and that if the person notified does not do so he will in any action against him by the person giving the notice be bound by any determination of fact common to the two litigations, then unless after seasonable receipt of the notice the person notified does come in and defend he is so bound.

§ 3–804. Lost, Destroyed or Stolen Instruments.

The owner of an instrument which is lost, whether by destruction, theft or otherwise, may maintain an action in his own name and recover from any party liable thereon upon due proof of his ownership, the facts which prevent his production of the instrument and its terms. The court may require security indemnifying the defendant against loss by reason of further claims on the instrument.

§ 3–805. Instruments Not Payable to Order or to Bearer.

This Article applies to any instrument whose terms do not preclude transfer and which is otherwise negotiable within this Article but which is not payable to order or to bearer, except that there can be no holder in due course of such an instrument.

ARTICLE 4

BANK DEPOSITS AND COLLECTIONS

PART 1

GENERAL PROVISIONS AND DEFINITIONS

§ 4–101. Short Title.

This Article shall be known and may be cited as Uniform Commercial Code—Bank Deposits and Collections.

§ 4–102. Applicability.

(1) To the extent that items within this Article are also within the scope of Articles 3 and 8, they are subject to the provisions of those Articles. In the event of conflict the provisions of this Article govern those of Article 3 but the provisions of Article 8 govern those of this Article.

(2) The liability of a bank for action or nonaction with respect to any item handled by it for purposes of presentment, payment or collection is governed by the law of the place where the bank is located. In the case of action or non-action by or at a branch or separate office of a bank, its liability is governed by the law of the place where the branch or separate office is located.

§ 4–103. Variation by Agreement; Measure of Damages; Certain Action Constituting Ordinary Care.

(1) The effect of the provisions of this Article may be varied by agreement except that no agreement can disclaim a bank's responsibility for its own lack of good faith or failure to exercise ordinary care or can limit the measure of damages for such lack or failure; but the parties may by agreement determine the standards by which such responsibility is to be measured if such standards are not manifestly unreasonable.

(2) Federal Reserve regulations and operating letters, clearing house rules, and the like, have the effect of agreements under subsection (1), whether or not specifically assented to by all parties interested in items handled.

(3) Action or non-action approved by this Article or pursuant to Federal Reserve regulations or operating letters constitutes the exercise of ordinary care

and, in the absence of special instructions, action or non-action consistent with clearing house rules and the like or with a general banking usage not disapproved by this Article, prima facie constitutes the exercise of ordinary care.

(4) The specification or approval of certain procedures by this Article does not constitute disapproval of other procedures which may be reasonable under the circumstances.

(5) The measure of damages for failure to exercise ordinary care in handling an item is the amount of the item reduced by an amount which could not have been realized by the use of ordinary care, and where there is bad faith it includes other damages, if any, suffered by the party as a proximate consequence.

§ 4–104. Definitions and Index of Definitions.

(1) In this Article unless the context otherwise requires

(a) "Account" means any account with a bank and includes a checking, time, interest or savings account;

(b) "Afternoon" means the period of a day between noon and midnight;

(c) "Banking day" means that part of any day on which a bank is open to the public for carrying on substantially all of its banking functions;

(d) "Clearing house" means any association of banks or other payors regularly clearing items;

(e) "Customer" means any person having an account with a bank or for whom a bank has agreed to collect items and includes a bank carrying an account with another bank;

(f) "Documentary draft" means any negotiable or nonnegotiable draft with accompanying documents, securities or other papers to be delivered against honor of the draft;

(g) "Item" means any instrument for the payment of money even though it is not negotiable but does not include money;

(h) "Midnight deadline" with respect to a bank is midnight on its next banking day following the banking day on which it receives the relevant item or notice or from which the time for taking action commences to run, whichever is later;

(i) "Properly payable" includes the availability of funds for payment at the time of decision to pay or dishonor;

(j) "Settle" means to pay in cash, by clearing house settlement, in a charge or credit or by remittance, or otherwise as instructed. A settlement may be either provisional or final;

(k) "Suspends payments" with respect to a bank means that it has been closed by order of the supervisory authorities, that a public officer has been appointed to take it over or that it ceases or refuses to make payments in the ordinary course of business.

(2) Other definitions applying to this Article and the sections in which they appear are:

"Collecting bank" Section 4–105.
"Depositary bank" Section 4–105.

"Intermediary bank" Section 4–105.

"Payor bank" Section 4–105.

"Presenting bank" Section 4–105.

"Remitting bank" Section 4–105.

(3)   The following definitions in other Articles apply to this Article:

"Acceptance" Section 3–410.

"Certificate of deposit" Section 3–104.

"Certification" Section 3–411.

"Check" Section 3–104.

"Draft" Section 3–104.

"Holder in due course" Section 3–302.

"Notice of dishonor" Section 3–508.

"Presentment" Section 3–504.

"Protest" Section 3–509.

"Secondary party" Section 3–102.

(4)   In addition Article 1 contains general definitions and principles of construction and interpretation applicable throughout this Article.

§ 4–105.   "Depository Bank"; "Intermediary Bank"; "Collecting Bank"; "Payor Bank"; "Presenting Bank"; "Remitting Bank".

In this Article unless the context otherwise requires:

(a) "Depository bank" means the first bank to which an item is transferred for collection even though it is also the payor bank;

(b) "Payor bank" means a bank by which an item is payable as drawn or accepted;

(c) "Intermediary bank" means any bank to which an item is transferred in course of collection except the depositary or payor bank;

(d) "Collecting bank" means any bank handling the item for collection except the payor bank;

(e) "Presenting bank" means any bank presenting an item except a payor bank;

(f) "Remitting bank" means any payor or intermediary bank remitting for an item.

§ 4–106.   Separate Office of a Bank.

A branch or separate office of a bank [maintaining its own deposit ledgers] is a separate bank for the purpose of computing the time within which and determining the place at or to which action may be taken or notices or orders shall be given under this Article and under Article 3.

Note: *The brackets are to make it optional with the several states whether to require a branch to maintain its own deposit ledgers in order to be considered to be a separate bank for certain purposes under Article 4.   In some states "maintaining its own deposit ledgers" is a satisfactory test.   In others branch banking practices are such that this test would not be suitable.*

§ 4–107.   Time of Receipt of Items.

(1)   For the purpose of allowing time to process items, prove balances and make the necessary entries on its books to determine its position for the day, a bank may fix an afternoon hour of two P.M. or later as a cut-off hour for the handling of money and items and the making of entries on its books.

(2)   Any item or deposit of money received on any day after a cut-off hour so fixed or after the close of the banking day may be treated as being received at the opening of the next banking day.

§ 4-108. Delays.

(1) Unless otherwise instructed, a collecting bank in a good faith effort to secure payment may, in the case of specific items and with or without the approval of any person involved, waive, modify or extend time limits imposed or permitted by this Act for a period not in excess of an additional banking day without discharge of secondary parties and without liability to its transferor or any prior party.

(2) Delay by a collecting bank or payor bank beyond time limits prescribed or permitted by this Act or by instructions is excused if caused by interruption of communication facilities, suspension of payments by another bank, war, emergency conditions or other circumstances beyond the control of the bank provided it exercises such diligence as the circumstances require.

§ 4-109. Process of Posting.

The "process of posting" means the usual procedure followed by a payor bank in determining to pay an item and in recording the payment including one or more of the following or other steps as determined by the bank:

(a) verification of any signature;

(b) ascertaining that sufficient funds are available;

(c) affixing a "paid" or other stamp;

(d) entering a charge or entry to a customer's account;

(e) correcting or reversing an entry or erroneous action with respect to the item.

PART 2

COLLECTION OF ITEMS: DEPOSITARY AND COLLECTING BANKS

§ 4-201. Presumption and Duration of Agency Status of Collecting Banks and Provisional Status of Credits; Applicability of Article; Item Indorsed "Pay Any Bank".

(1) Unless a contrary intent clearly appears and prior to the time that a settlement given by a collecting bank for an item is or becomes final (subsection (3) of Section 4-211 and Sections 4-212 and 4-213) the bank is an agent or sub-agent of the owner of the item and any settlement given for the item is provisional. This provision applies regardless of the form of indorsement or lack of indorsement and even though credit given for the item is subject to immediate withdrawal as of right or is in fact withdrawn; but the continuance of ownership of an item by its owner and any rights of the owner to proceeds of the item are subject to rights of a collecting bank such as those resulting from outstanding advances on the item and valid rights of setoff. When an item is handled by banks for purposes of presentment, payment and collection, the relevant provisions of this Article apply even though action of parties clearly establishes that a particular bank has purchased the item and is the owner of it.

(2) After an item has been indorsed with the words "pay any bank" or the like, only a bank may acquire the rights of a holder

(a) until the item has been returned to the customer initiating collection; or

(b) until the item has been specially indorsed by a bank to a person who is not a bank.

§ 4–202. **Responsibility for Collection; When Action Seasonable.**

(1)   A collecting bank must use ordinary care in

(a) presenting an item or sending it for presentment; and

(b) sending notice of dishonor or non-payment or returning an item other than a documentary draft to the bank's transferor [or directly to the depositary bank under subsection (2) of Section 4–212] (*see note to Section 4–212*) after learning that the item has not been paid or accepted as the case may be; and

(c) settling for an item when the bank receives final settlement; and

(d) making or providing for any necessary protest; and

(e) notifying its transferor of any loss or delay in transit within a reasonable time after discovery thereof.

(2)   A collecting bank taking proper action before its midnight deadline following receipt of an item, notice or payment acts seasonably; taking proper action within a reasonably longer time may be seasonable but the bank has the burden of so establishing.

(3)   Subject to subsection (1) (a), a bank is not liable for the insolvency, neglect, misconduct, mistake or default of another bank or person or for loss or destruction of an item in transit or in the possession of others.

§ 4–203. **Effect of Instructions.**

Subject to the provisions of Article 3 concerning conversion of instruments (Section 3–419) and the provisions of both Article 3 and this Article concerning restrictive indorsements only a collecting bank's transferor can give instructions which affect the bank or constitute notice to it and a collecting bank is not liable to prior parties for any action taken pursuant to such instructions or in accordance with any agreement with its transferor.

§ 4–204. **Methods of Sending and Presenting; Sending Direct to Payor Bank.**

(1)   A collecting bank must send items by reasonably prompt method taking into consideration any relevant instructions, the nature of the item, the number of such items on hand, and the cost of collection involved and the method generally used by it or others to present such items.

(2)   A collecting bank may send

(a) any item direct to the payor bank;

(b) any item to any non-bank payor if authorized by its transferor; and

(c) any item other than documentary drafts to any non-bank payor, if authorized by Federal Reserve regulation or operating letter, clearing house rule or the like.

(3)   Presentment may be made by a presenting bank at a place where the payor bank has requested that presentment be made.

§ 4–205. **Supplying Missing Indorsement; No Notice from Prior Indorsement.**

(1)   A depositary bank which has taken an item for collection may supply any indorsement of the customer which is necessary to title unless the item contains the words "payee's indorsement required" or the like. In the absence of such a re-

quirement a statement placed on the item by the depositary bank to the effect that the item was deposited by a customer or credited to his account is effective as the customer's indorsement.

(2) An intermediary bank, or payor bank which is not a depositary bank, is neither given notice nor otherwise affected by a restrictive indorsement of any person except the bank's immediate transferor.

§ 4–206. Transfer Between Banks.

Any agreed method which identifies the transferor bank is sufficient for the item's further transfer to another bank.

§ 4–207. Warranties of Customer and Collecting Bank on Transfer or Presentment of Items; Time for Claims.

(1) Each customer or collecting bank who obtains payment or acceptance of an item and each prior customer and collecting bank warrants to the payor bank or other payor who in good faith pays or accepts the item that

(a) he has a good title to the item or is authorized to obtain payment or acceptance on behalf of one who has a good title; and

(b) he has no knowledge that the signature of the maker or drawer is unauthorized, except that this warranty is not given by any customer or collecting bank that is a holder in due course and acts in good faith

   (i) to a maker with respect to the maker's own signature; or

   (ii) to a drawer with respect to the drawer's own signature, whether or not the drawer is also the drawee; or

   (iii) to an acceptor of an item if the holder in due course took the item after the acceptance or obtained the acceptance without knowledge that the drawer's signature was unauthorized; and

(c) the item has not been materially altered, except that this warranty is not given by any customer or collecting bank that is a holder in due course and acts in good faith

   (i) to the maker of a note; or

   (ii) to the drawer of a draft whether or not the drawer is also the drawee; or

   (iii) to the acceptor of an item with respect to an alteration made prior to the acceptance if the holder in due course took the item after the acceptance, even though the acceptance provided "payable as originally drawn" or equivalent terms; or

   (iv) to the acceptor of an item with respect to an alteration made after the acceptance.

(2) Each customer and collecting bank who transfers an item and receives a settlement or other consideration for it warrants to his transferee and to any subsequent collecting bank who takes the item in good faith that

(a) he has a good title to the item or is authorized to obtain payment or acceptance on behalf of one who has a good title and the transfer is otherwise rightful; and

(b) all signatures are genuine or authorized; and

(c) the item has not been materially altered; and

(d) no defense of any party is good against him; and

(e) he has no knowledge of any insolvency proceeding instituted with respect to the maker or acceptor or the drawer of an unaccepted item.

In addition each customer and collecting bank so transferring an item and receiving a settlement or other consideration engages that upon dishonor and any necessary notice of dishonor and protest he will take up the item.

(3)   The warranties and the engagement to honor set forth in the two preceding subsections arise notwithstanding the absence of indorsement or words of guaranty or warranty in the transfer or presentment and a collecting bank remains liable for their breach despite remittance to its transferor. Damages for breach of such warranties or engagement to honor shall not exceed the consideration received by the customer or collecting bank responsible plus finance charges and expenses related to the item, if any.

(4)   Unless a claim for breach of warranty under this section is made within a reasonable time after the person claiming learns of the breach, the person liable is discharged to the extent of any loss caused by the delay in making claim.

§ 4—208. Security Interest of Collecting Bank in Items, Accompanying Documents and Proceeds.

(1)   A bank has a security interest in an item and any accompanying documents or the proceeds of either

(a) in case of an item deposited in an account to the extent to which credit given for the item has been withdrawn or applied;

(b) in case of an item for which it has given credit available for withdrawal as of right, to the extent of the credit given whether or not the credit is drawn upon and whether or not there is a right of charge-back; or

(c) if it makes an advance on or against the item.

(2)   When credit which has been given for several items received at one time or pursuant to a single agreement is withdrawn or applied in part the security interest remains upon all the items, any accompanying documents or the proceeds of either. For the purpose of this section, credits first given are first withdrawn.

(3)   Receipt by a collecting bank of a final settlement for an item is a realization on its security interest in the item, accompanying documents and proceeds. To the extent and so long as the bank does not receive final settlement for the item or give up possession of the item or accompanying documents for purposes other than collection, the security interest continues and is subject to the provisions of Article 9 except that

(a) no security agreement is necessary to make the security interest enforceable (subsection (1) (b) of Section 9—203); and

(b) no filing is required to perfect the security interest; and

(c) the security interest has priority over conflicting perfected security interests in the item, accompanying documents or proceeds.

§ 4–209. When Bank Gives Value for Purposes of Holder in Due Course.

For purposes of determining its status as a holder in due course, the bank has given value to the extent that it has a security interest in an item provided that the bank otherwise complies with the requirements of Section 3–302 on what constitutes a holder in due course.

§ 4–210. Presentment by Notice of Item Not Payable by, Through or at a Bank; Liability of Secondary Parties.

(1) Unless otherwise instructed, a collecting bank may present an item not payable by, through or at a bank by sending to the party to accept or pay a written notice that the bank holds the item for acceptance or payment. The notice must be sent in time to be received on or before the day when presentment is due and the bank must meet any requirement of the party to accept or pay under Section 3–505 by the close of the bank's next banking day after it knows of the requirement.

(2) Where presentment is made by notice and neither honor nor request for compliance with a requirement under Section 3–505 is received by the close of business on the day after maturity or in the case of demand items by the close of business on the third banking day after notice was sent, the presenting bank may treat the item as dishonored and charge any secondary party by sending him notice of the facts.

§ 4–211. Media of Remittance; Provisional and Final Settlement in Remittance Cases.

(1) A collecting bank may take in settlement of an item

    (a) a check of the remitting bank or of another bank on any bank except the remitting bank; or

    (b) a cashier's check or similar primary obligation of a remitting bank which is a member of or clears through a member of the same clearing house or group as the collecting bank; or

    (c) appropriate authority to charge an account of the remitting bank or of another bank with the collecting bank; or

    (d) if the item is drawn upon or payable by a person other than a bank, a cashier's check, certified check or other bank check or obligation.

(2) If before its midnight deadline the collecting bank properly dishonors a remittance check or authorization to charge on itself or presents or forwards for collection a remittance instrument of or on another bank which is of a kind approved by subsection (1) or has not been authorized by it, the collecting bank is not liable to prior parties in the event of the dishonor of such check, instrument or authorization.

(3) A settlement for an item by means of a remittance instrument or authorization to charge is or becomes a final settlement as to both the person making and the person receiving the settlement

    (a) if the remittance instrument or authorization to charge is of a kind approved by subsection (1) or has not been authorized by the person receiving the settlement and in either case the person receiving the settlement acts seasonably before its midnight deadline in presenting, forwarding for collection or paying the instrument or authorization, — at the time the remittance instrument or authorization is finally paid by the payor by which it is payable;

(b) if the person receiving the settlement has authorized remittance by a non-bank check or obligation or by a cashier's check or similar primary obligation of or a check upon the payor or other remitting bank which is not of a kind approved by subsection (1) (b), —at the time of the receipt of such remittance check or obligation; or

(c) if in a case not covered by subparagraphs (a) or (b) the person receiving the settlement fails to seasonably present, forward for collection, pay or return a remittance instrument or authorization to it to charge before its midnight deadline, — at such midnight deadline.

§ 4–212. Right of Charge-Back or Refund.

(1)   If a collecting bank has made provisional settlement with its customer for an item and itself fails by reason of dishonor, suspension of payments by a bank or otherwise to receive a settlement for the item which is or becomes final, the bank may revoke the settlement given by it, charge back the amount of any credit given for the item to its customer's account or obtain refund from its customer whether or not it is able to return the items if by its midnight deadline or within a longer reasonable time after it learns the facts it returns the item or sends notification of the facts. These rights to revoke, charge-back and obtain refund terminate if and when a settlement for the item received by the bank is or becomes final (subsection (3) of Section 4–211 and subsections (2) and (3) of Section 4–213).

[(2) Within the time and manner prescribed by this section and Section 4–301, an intermediary or payor bank, as the case may be, may return an unpaid item directly to the depositary bank and may send for collection a draft on the depositary bank and obtain reimbursement. In such case, if the depositary bank has received provisional settlement for the item, it must reimburse the bank drawing the draft and any provisional credits for the item between banks shall become and remain final.]

Note: *Direct returns is recognized as an innovation that is not yet established bank practice, and therefore, Paragraph 2 has been bracketed. Some lawyers have doubts whether it should be included in legislation or left to development by agreement.*

(3)   A depositary bank which is also the payor may charge-back the amount of an item to its customer's account or obtain refund in accordance with the section governing return of an item received by a payor bank for credit on its books (Section 4–301).

(4)   The right to charge-back is not affected by

(a) prior use of the credit given for the item; or

(b) failure by any bank to exercise ordinary care with respect to the item but any bank so failing remains liable.

(5)   A failure to charge-back or claim refund does not affect other rights of the bank against the customer or any other party.

(6)   If credit is given in dollars as the equivalent of the value of an item payable in a foreign currency the dollar amount

of any charge-back or refund shall be calculated on the basis of the buying sight rate for the foreign currency prevailing on the day when the person entitled to the charge-back or refund learns that it will not receive payment in ordinary course.

§ 4–213. Final Payment of Item by Payor Bank; When Provisional Debits and Credits Become Final; When Certain Credits Become Available for Withdrawal.

(1)　An item is finally paid by a payor bank when the bank has done any of the following, whichever happens first:

(a) paid the item in cash; or

(b) settled for the item without reserving a right to revoke the settlement and without having such right under statute, clearing house rule or agreement; or

(c) completed the process of posting the item to the indicated account of the drawer, maker or other person to be charged therewith; or

(d) made a provisional settlement for the item and failed to revoke the settlement in the time and manner permitted by statute, clearing house rule or agreement.

Upon a final payment under subparagraphs (b), (c) or (d) the payor bank shall be accountable for the amount of the item.

(2)　If provisional settlement for an item between the presenting and payor banks is made through a clearing house or by debits or credits in an account between them, then to the extent that provisional debits or credits for the item are entered in accounts between the presenting and payor banks or between the presenting and successive prior collecting banks seri-

atim, they become final upon final payment of the item by the payor bank.

(3)　If a collecting bank receives a settlement for an item which is or becomes final (subsection (3) of Section 4–211, subsection (2) of Section 4–213) the bank is accountable to its customer for the amount of the item and any provisional credit given for the item in an account with its customer becomes final.

(4)　Subject to any right of the bank to apply the credit to an obligation of the customer, credit given by a bank for an item in an account with its customer becomes available for withdrawal as of right

(a) in any case where the bank has received a provisional settlement for the item,—when such settlement becomes final and the bank has had a reasonable time to learn that the settlement is final;

(b) in any case where the bank is both a depositary bank and a payor bank and the item is finally paid, —at the opening of the bank's second banking day following receipt of the item.

(5)　A deposit of money in a bank is final when made but, subject to any right of the bank to apply the deposit to an obligation of the customer, the deposit becomes available for withdrawal as of right at the opening of the bank's next banking day following receipt of the deposit.

§ 4–214. Insolvency and Preference.

(1)　Any item in or coming into the possession of a payor or collecting bank which suspends payment and which item is not finally paid shall be returned by the receiver, trustee or agent in charge of the closed bank to the presenting bank or the closed bank's customer.

(2)   If a payor bank finally pays an item and suspends payments without making a settlement for the item with its customer or the presenting bank which settlement is or becomes final, the owner of the item has a preferred claim against the payor bank.

(3)   If a payor bank gives or a collecting bank gives or receives a provisional settlement for an item and thereafter suspends payments, the suspension does not prevent or interfere with the settlement becoming final if such finality occurs automatically upon the lapse of certain time or the happening of certain events (subsection (3) of Section 4—211, subsections (1) (d), (2) and (3) of Section 4—213).

(4)   If a collecting bank receives from subsequent parties settlement for an item which settlement is or becomes final and suspends payments without making a settlement for the item with its customer which is or becomes final, the owner of the item has a preferred claim against such collecting bank.

PART 3

COLLECTION OF ITEMS: PAYOR BANKS

§ 4—301. Deferred Posting; Recovery of Payment by Return of Items; Time of Dishonor.

(1)   Where an authorized settlement for a demand item (other than a documentary draft) received by a payor bank otherwise than for immediate payment over the counter has been made before midnight of the banking day of receipt the payor bank may revoke the settlement and recover any payment if before it has made final payment (subsection (1) of Section 4—213) and before its midnight deadline it

(a) returns the item; or

(b) sends written notice of dishonor or nonpayment if the item is held for protest or is otherwise unavailable for return.

(2)   If a demand item is received by a payor bank for credit on its books it may return such item or send notice of dishonor and may revoke any credit given or recover the amount thereof withdrawn by its customer, if it acts within the time limit and in the manner specified in the preceding subsection.

(3)   Unless previous notice of dishonor has been sent an item is dishonored at the time when for purposes of dishonor it is returned or notice sent in accordance with this section.

(4)   An item is returned:

(a) as to an item received through a clearing house, when it is delivered to the presenting or last collecting bank or to the clearing house or is sent or delivered in accordance with its rules; or

(b) in all other cases, when it is sent or delivered to the bank's customer or transferor or pursuant to his instructions.

§ 4—302. Payor Bank's Responsibility for Late Return of Item.

In the absence of a valid defense such as breach of a presentment warranty (subsection (1) of Section 4—207), settlement effected or the like, if an item is presented on and received by a payor bank the bank is accountable for the amount of

(a) a demand item other than a documentary draft whether properly payable or not if the bank, in any case where it is not also the depositary bank, retains the item beyond midnight of the banking day of receipt without settling for it or, regardless of whether it is also the depositary bank, does not pay or return the item or send notice of dishonor until after its midnight deadline; or

(b) any other properly payable item unless within the time allowed for acceptance or payment of that item the bank either accepts or pays the item or returns it and accompanying documents.

§ 4–303. When Items Subject to Notice, Stop-Order, Legal Process or Setoff; Order in Which Items May Be Charged or Certified.

(1)   Any knowledge, notice or stop-order received by, legal process served upon or setoff exercised by a payor bank, whether or not effective under other rules of law to terminate, suspend or modify the bank's right or duty to pay an item or to charge its customer's account for the item, comes too late to so terminate, suspend or modify such right or duty if the knowledge, notice, stop-order or legal process is received or served and a reasonable time for the bank to act thereon expires or the setoff is exercised after the bank has done any of the following:

(a) accepted or certified the item;

(b) paid the item in cash;

(c) settled for the item without reserving a right to revoke the settlement and without having such right under statute, clearing house rule or agreement;

(d) completed the process of posting the item to the indicated account of the drawer, maker or other person to be charged therewith or otherwise has evidenced by examination of such indicated account and by action its decision to pay the item; or

(e) become accountable for the amount of the item under subsection (1) (d) of Section 4–213 and Section 4–302 dealing with the payor bank's responsibility for late return of items.

(2)   Subject to the provisions of subsection (1) items may be accepted, paid, certified or charged to the indicated account of its customer in any order convenient to the bank.

PART 4

RELATIONSHIP BETWEEN PAYOR BANK AND ITS CUSTOMER

§ 4–401. When Bank May Charge Customer's Account.

(1)   As against its customer, a bank may charge against his account any item which is otherwise properly payable from that account even though the charge creates an overdraft.

(2)   A bank which in good faith makes payment to a holder may charge the indicated account of its customer according to

(a) the original tenor of his altered item; or

(b) the tenor of his completed item, even though the bank knows the item has been completed unless the bank has notice that the completion was improper.

§ 4–402. Bank's Liability to Customer for Wrongful Dishonor.

A payor bank is liable to its customer for damages proximately caused by the wrongful dishonor of an item. When the dishonor occurs through mistake liability is limited to actual damages proved. If so proximately caused and proved damages may include damages for an arrest or prosecution of the customer or other consequential damages. Whether any consequential damages are proximately caused by the wrongful dishonor is a question of fact to be determined in each case.

§ 4–403. Customer's Right to Stop Payment; Burden of Proof of Loss.

(1)   A customer may by order to his bank stop payment of any item payable for his account but the order must be received at such time and in such manner as to afford the bank a reasonable opportunity to act on it prior to any action by the bank with respect to the item described in Section 4–303.

(2)   An oral order is binding upon the bank only for fourteen calendar days unless confirmed in writing within that period. A written order is effective for only six months unless renewed in writing.

(3)   The burden of establishing the fact and amount of loss resulting from the payment of an item contrary to a binding stop payment order is on the customer.

§ 4–404. Bank Not Obligated to Pay Check More Than Six Months Old.

A bank is under no obligation to a customer having a checking account to pay a check, other than a certified check, which is presented more than six months after its date, but it may charge its customer's account for a payment made thereafter in good faith.

§ 4–405. Death or Incompetence of Customer.

(1)   A payor or collecting bank's authority to accept, pay or collect an item or to account for proceeds of its collection if otherwise effective is not rendered ineffective by incompetence of a customer of either bank existing at the time the item is issued or its collection is undertaken if the bank does not know of an adjudication of incompetence. Neither death nor incompetence of a customer revokes such authority to accept, pay, collect or account until the bank knows of the fact of death or of an adjudication of incompetence and has reasonable opportunity to act on it.

(2)   Even with knowledge a bank may for ten days after the date of death pay or certify checks drawn on or prior to that date unless ordered to stop payment by a person claiming an interest in the account.

§ 4–406. Customer's Duty to Discover and Report Unauthorized Signature or Alteration.

(1)   When a bank sends to its customer a statement of account accompanied by items paid in good faith in support of the debit entries or holds the statement and items pursuant to a request or instructions of its customer or otherwise in a reasonable manner makes the statement and items available to the customer, the customer must exercise reasonable care and promptness to examine the statement and items to discover his unauthorized signature or any alteration on an item and must notify the bank promptly after discovery thereof.

(2)   If the bank establishes that the customer failed with respect to an item to comply with the duties imposed on the customer by subsection (1) the customer

is precluded from asserting against the bank

    (a) his unauthorized signature or any alteration on the item if the bank also establishes that it suffered a loss by reason of such failure; and

    (b) an unauthorized signature or alteration by the same wrongdoer on any other item paid in good faith by the bank after the first item and statement was available to the customer for a reasonable period not exceeding fourteen calendar days and before the bank receives notification from the customer of any such unauthorized signature or alteration.

(3) The preclusion under subsection (2) does not apply if the customer establishes lack of ordinary care on the part of the bank in paying the item(s).

(4) Without regard to care or lack of care of either the customer or the bank a customer who does not within one year from the time the statement and items are made available to the customer (subsection (1) discover and report his unauthorized signature or any alteration on the face or back of the item or does not within three years from that time discover and report any unauthorized indorsement is precluded from asserting against the bank such unauthorized signature or indorsement or such alteration.

(5) If under this section a payor bank has a valid defense against a claim of a customer upon or resulting from payment of an item and waives or fails upon request to assert the defense the bank may not assert against any collecting bank or other prior party presenting or transferring the item a claim based upon the unauthorized signature or alteration giving rise to the customer's claim.

§ 4–407. Payor Bank's Right to Subrogation on Improper Payment.

If a payor bank has paid an item over the stop payment order of the drawer or maker or otherwise under circumstances giving a basis for objection by the drawer or maker, to prevent unjust enrichment and only to the extent necessary to prevent loss to the bank by reason of its payment of the item, the payor bank shall be subrogated to the rights

    (a) of any holder in due course on the item against the drawer or maker; and

    (b) of the payee or any other holder of the item against the drawer or maker either on the item or under the transaction out of which the item arose; and

    (c) of the drawer or maker against the payee or any other holder of the item with respect to the transaction out of which the item arose.

PART 5

COLLECTION OF DOCUMENTARY DRAFTS

§ 4–501. Handling of Documentary Drafts; Duty to Send for Presentment and to Notify Customer of Dishonor.

A bank which takes a documentary draft for collection must present or send the draft and accompanying documents for presentment and upon learning that the draft has not been paid or accepted in due course must seasonably notify its customer of such fact even though it may have discounted or bought the draft or extended credit available for withdrawal as of right.

§ 4—502. Presentment of "On Arrival" Drafts.

When a draft or the relevant instructions require presentment "on arrival", "when goods arrive" or the like, the collecting bank need not present until in its judgment a reasonable time for arrival of the goods has expired. Refusal to pay or accept because the goods have not arrived is not dishonor; the bank must notify its transferor of such refusal but need not present the draft again until it is instructed to do so or learns of the arrival of the goods.

§ 4—503. Responsibility of Presenting Bank for Documents and Goods; Report of Reasons for Dishonor; Referee in Case of Need.

Unless otherwise instructed and except as provided in Article 5 a bank presenting a documentary draft

(a) must deliver the documents to the drawee on acceptance of the draft if it is payable more than three days after presentment; otherwise, only on payment; and

(b) upon dishonor, either in the case of presentment for acceptance or presentment for pay-

ment, may seek and follow instructions from any referee in case of need designated in the draft or, if the presenting bank does not choose to utilize his services, it must use diligence and good faith to ascertain the reason for dishonor, must notify its transferor of the dishonor and of the results of its effort to ascertain the reasons therefor and must request instructions. But the presenting bank is under no obligation with respect to goods represented by the documents except to follow any reasonable instructions seasonably received; it has a right to reimbursement for any expense incurred in following instructions and to prepayment of or indemnity for such expenses.

§ 4—504. Privilege of Presenting Bank to Deal With Goods; Security Interest for Expenses.

(1)   A presenting bank which, following the dishonor of a documentary draft, has seasonably requested instructions but does not receive them within a reasonable time may store, sell, or otherwise deal with the goods in any reasonable manner.

(2)   For its reasonable expenses incurred by action under subsection (1) the presenting bank has a lien upon the goods or their proceeds, which may be foreclosed in the same manner as an unpaid seller's lien.

ARTICLE 9

SECURED TRANSACTIONS; SALES OF ACCOUNTS AND CHATTEL PAPER

PART 1

SHORT TITLE, APPLICABILITY AND DEFINITIONS

§ **9–101. Short Title.**

This Article shall be known and may be cited as Uniform Commercial Code—Secured Transactions.

§ **9–102. Policy and Subject Matter of Article.**

(1) Except as otherwise provided in Section 9–104 on excluded transactions, this Article applies

    (a) to any transaction (regardless of its form) which is intended to create a security interest in personal property or fixtures including goods, documents, instruments, general intangibles, chattel paper or accounts; and also

    (b) to any sale of accounts or chattel paper.

(2) This Article applies to security interests created by contract including pledge, assignment, chattel mortgage, chattel trust, trust deed, factor's lien, equipment trust, conditional sale, trust receipt, other lien or title retention contract and lease or consignment intended as security. This Article does not apply to statutory liens except as provided in Section 9–310.

(3) The application of this Article to a security interest in a secured obligation is not affected by the fact that the obligation is itself secured by a transaction or interest to which this Article does not apply. Amended in 1972.

Note: *The adoption of this Article should be accompanied by the repeal of existing statutes dealing with conditional sales, trust receipts, factor's liens where the factor is given a non-possessory lien, chattel mortgages, crop mortgages, mortgages on railroad equipment, assignment of accounts and generally statutes regulating security interests in personal property.*

Where the state has a retail installment selling act or small loan act, that legislation should be carefully examined to determine what changes in those acts are needed to conform them to this Article. This Article primarily sets out rules defining rights of a secured party against persons dealing with the debtor; it does not prescribe regulations and controls which may be necessary to curb abuses arising in the small loan business or in the financing of consumer purchases on credit. Accordingly there is no intention to repeal existing regulatory acts in those fields by enactment or re-enactment of Article 9. See Section 9–203(4) and the Note thereto.

§ **9–103. Perfection of Security Interests in Multiple State Transactions.**

(1) Documents, instruments and ordinary goods.

(a) This subsection applies to documents and instruments and to goods other than those covered by a certificate of title described in subsection (2), mobile goods described in subsection (3), and minerals described in subsection (5).

(b) Except as otherwise provided in this subsection, perfection and the effect of perfection or nonperfection of a security interest in collateral are governed by the law of the jurisdiction where the collateral is when the last event occurs on which is based the assertion that the security interest is perfected or unperfected.

(c) If the parties to a transaction creating a purchase money security interest in goods in one jurisdiction understand at the time that the security interest attaches that the goods will be kept in another jurisdiction, then the law of the other jurisdiction governs the perfection and the effect of perfection or nonperfection of the security interest from the time it attaches until thirty days after the debtor receives possession of the goods and thereafter if the goods are taken to the other jurisdiction before the end of the thirty-day period.

(d) When collateral is brought into and kept in this state while subject to a security interest perfected under the law of the jurisdiction from which the collateral was removed, the security interest remains perfected, but if action is required by Part 3 of this Article to perfect the security interest,

(i) if the action is not taken before the expiration of the period of perfection in the other jurisdiction or the end of four months after the collateral is brought into this state, whichever period first expires, the security interest becomes unperfected at the end of that period and is thereafter deemed to have been unperfected as against a person who became a purchaser after removal;

(ii) if the action is taken before the expiration of the period specified in subparagraph (i) the security interest continues perfected thereafter;

(iii) for the purpose of priority over a buyer of consumer goods (subsection (2) of Section 9–307), the period of the effectiveness of a filing in the jurisdiction from which the collateral is removed is governed by the rules with respect to perfection in subparagraphs (i) and (ii).

(2) Certificate of title.

(a) This subsection applies to goods covered by a certificate of title issued under a statute of this state or of another jurisdiction under the law of which indication of a security interest on the certificate is required as a condition of perfection.

(b) Except as otherwise provided in this subsection, perfection and the effect of perfection or non-perfection of the security interest are governed by the law (including the conflict of laws rules) of the jurisdiction issuing the certificate until four months after the goods are removed from that jurisdiction and thereafter until the goods are registered in another jurisdiction, but in any event not beyond surrender of the certificate. After the expiration of that period, the goods are not covered by the certificate of title within the meaning of this section.

(c) Except with respect to the rights of a buyer described in the next paragraph, a security interest, perfected in another jurisdiction otherwise than by notation on a certificate of title, in goods brought into this state and thereafter covered by a certificate of title issued by this state is subject to the rules stated in paragraph (d) of subsection (1).

(d) If goods are brought into this state while a security interest therein is perfected in any manner under the law of the jurisdiction from which the goods are removed and a certificate of title is issued by this state and the certificate does not show that the goods are subject to the security interest or that they may be subject to security interests not shown on the certificate, the security interest is subordinate to the rights of a buyer of the goods who is not in the business of selling goods of that kind to the extent that he gives value and receives delivery of the goods after issuance of the certificate and without knowledge of the security interest.

(3) Accounts, general intangibles and mobile goods.

(a) This subsection applies to accounts (other than an account described in subsection (5) on minerals) and general intangibles and to goods which are mobile and which are of a type normally used in more than one jurisdiction, such as motor vehicles, trailers, rolling stock, airplanes, shipping containers, road building and construction machinery and commercial harvesting machinery and the like, if the goods are equipment or are inventory leased or held for lease by the debtor to others, and are not covered by a certificate of title described in subsection (2).

(b) The law (including the conflict of laws rules) of the jurisdiction in which the debtor is located governs the perfection and the effect of perfection or non-perfection of the security interest.

(c) If, however, the debtor is located in a jurisdiction which is not a part of the United States, and which does not provide for perfection of the security interest by filing or recording in that jurisdiction, the law of the jurisdiction in the United States in which the debtor has its major executive office in the United States governs the perfection and the effect of perfection or non-perfection of the security interest through filing. In the alternative, if the debtor is located in a jurisdiction which is not a part of the United States or Canada and the collateral is accounts or general intangibles for money due or to become due, the security interest may be perfected by notification to the account debtor. As used in this paragraph, "United States" includes its territories and possessions and the Commonwealth of Puerto Rico.

(d) A debtor shall be deemed located at his place of business if he has one, at his chief executive office if he has more than one place of business, otherwise at his residence. If, however, the debtor is a foreign air carrier under the Federal Aviation Act of 1958, as amended, it shall be deemed located at the designated office of the agent upon whom service of process may be made on behalf of the foreign air carrier.

(e) A security interest perfected under the law of the jurisdiction of the location of the debtor is perfected until the expiration of four months after a change of the debtor's location to another jurisdiction, or until perfection would have ceased by the law of the first jurisdiction, whichever period first expires. Unless perfected in the new jurisdiction before the end of that period, it becomes unperfected thereafter and is deemed to have been unperfected as against a person who became a purchaser after the change.

(4) Chattel paper.

The rules stated for goods in subsection (1) apply to a possessory security interest in chattel paper. The rules stated for accounts in subsection (3) apply to a non-possessory security interest in chattel paper, but the security interest may not be perfected by notification to the account debtor.

(5) Minerals.

Perfection and the effect of perfection or non-perfection of a security interest which is created by a debtor who has an interest in minerals or the like (including oil and gas) before extraction and which attaches thereto as extracted, or which attaches to an account resulting from the sale thereof at the wellhead or minehead are governed by the law (including the conflict of laws rules) of the jurisdiction wherein the wellhead or minehead is located. Amended in 1972.

§ 9–104. Transactions Excluded From Article.

This Article does not apply

(a) to a security interest subject to any statute of the United States, to the extent that such statute governs the rights of parties to and third parties affected by transactions in particular types of property; or

(b) to a landlord's lien; or

(c) to a lien given by statute or other rule of law for services or materials except as provided in Section 9–310 on priority of such liens; or

(d) to a transfer of a claim for wages, salary or other compensation of an employee; or

(e) to a transfer by a government or governmental subdivision or agency; or

(f) to a sale of accounts or chattel paper as part of a sale of the business out of which they arose, or an assignment of accounts or chattel paper which is for the purpose of collection only, or a transfer of a right to payment under a contract to an assignee who is also to do the performance under the contract or a transfer of a single account to an assignee in whole or partial satisfaction of a preexisting indebtedness; or

(g) to a transfer of an interest in or claim in or under any policy of insurance, except as provided with respect to proceeds (Section 9–306) and priorities in proceeds (Section 9–312); or

(h) to a right represented by a judgment (other than a judgment taken on a right to payment which was collateral); or

(i) to any right of set-off; or

(j) except to the extent that provision is made for fixtures in Section 9–313, to the creation or transfer of an interest in or lien on real estate, including a lease or rents thereunder; or

(k) to a transfer in whole or in part of any claim arising out of tort; or

(l) to a transfer of an interest in any deposit account (subsection (1) of Section 9–105), except as provided with respect to proceeds (Section 9–306) and priorities in proceeds (Section 9–312). Amended in 1972.

§ 9–105. Definitions and Index of Definitions.

(1) In this Article unless the context otherwise requires:

(a) "Account debtor" means the person who is obligated on an account, chattel paper or general intangible;

(b) "Chattel paper" means a writing or writings which evidence both a monetary obligation and a security interest in or a lease of specific goods, but a charter or other contract involving the use or hire of a vessel is not chattel paper. When a transaction is evidenced both by such a security agreement or a lease and by an instrument or a series of instruments, the group of writings taken together constitutes chattel paper;

(c) "Collateral" means the property subject to a security interest, and includes accounts and chattel paper which have been sold;

(d) "Debtor" means the person who owes payment or other performance of the obligation secured, whether or not he owns or has rights in the collateral, and includes the seller of accounts or chattel paper. Where the debtor and the owner of the collateral are not the same person, the term "debtor" means the owner of the collateral in any provision of the Article dealing with the collateral, the obligor in any provision dealing with the obligation, and may include both where the context so requires;

(e) "Deposit account" means a demand, time, savings, passbook or like account maintained with a bank, savings and loan association, credit union or like organization, other than an account evidenced by a certificate of deposit;

(f) "Document" means document of title as defined in the general definitions of Article 1 (Section 1–201), and a receipt of the kind described in subsection (2) of Section 7–201;

(g) "Encumbrance" includes real estate mortgages and other liens on real estate and all other rights in real estate that are not ownership interests;

(h) "Goods" includes all things which are movable at the time the security interest attaches or which are fixtures (Section 9–313), but does not include money, docments, instruments, accounts, chattel paper, general intangibles, or minerals or the like (including oil and gas) before extraction. "Goods" also includes standing timber which is to be cut and removed under a conveyance or contract for sale, the unborn young of animals, and growing crops;

(i) "Instrument" means a negotiable instrument (defined in Section 3–104), or a security (defined in Section 8–102) or any other writing which evidences a right to the payment of money and is not itself a security agreement or lease and is of a type which is in ordinary course of business transferred by delivery with any necessary indorsement or assignment;

(j) "Mortgage" means a consensual interest created by a real estate mortgage, a trust deed on real estate, or the like;

(k) An advance is made "pursuant to commitment" if the secured party has bound himself to make it, whether or not a subsequent event of default or other event not within his control has relieved or may relieve him from his obligation;

(l) "Security agreement" means an agreement which creates or provides for a security interest;

(m) "Secured party" means a lender, seller or other person in whose favor there is a security interest, including a person to whom accounts or chattel paper have been sold. When the holders of obligations issued under an indenture of trust, equipment trust agreement or the like are represented by a trustee or other person, the representative is the secured party;

(n) "Transmitting utility" means any person primarily engaged in the railroad, street railway or trolley bus business, the electric or electronics communications transmission business, the transmission of goods by pipeline, or the transmission or the production and transmission of electricity, steam, gas or water, or the provision of sewer service.

(2)　Other definitions applying to this Article and the sections in which they appear are:

"Account". Section 9–106.
"Attach". Section 9–203.

"Construction mortgage". Section 9–313(1).

"Consumer goods". Section 9–109(1).

"Equipment". Section 9–109(2).

"Farm products". Section 9–109(3).

"Fixture". Section 9–313(1).

"Fixture filing". Section 9–313(1).

"General intangibles". Section 9–106.

"Inventory". Section 9–109(4).

"Lien creditor". Section 9–301(3).

"Proceeds". Section 9–306(1).

"Purchase money security interest". Section 9–107.

"United States". Section 9–103.

(3) The following definitions in other Articles apply to this Article:

"Check". Section 3–104.

"Contract for sale". Section 2–106.

"Holder in due course". Section 3–302.

"Note". Section 3–104.

"Sale". Section 2–106.

(4) In addition Article 1 contains general definitions and principles of construction and interpretation applicable throughout this Article. Amended in 1966, 1972.

§ 9–106. Definitions: "Account"; "General Intangibles".

"Account" means any right to payment for goods sold or leased or for services rendered which is not evidenced by an instrument or chattel paper, whether or not it has been earned by performance. "General intangibles" means any personal property (including things in action) other than goods, accounts, chattel paper, doc-uments, instruments, and money. All rights to payment earned or unearned under a charter or other contract involving the use or hire of a vessel and all rights incident to the charter or contract are accounts. Amended in 1966, 1972.

§ 9–107. Definitions: "Purchase Money Security Interest".

A security interest is a "purchase money security interest" to the extent that it is

(a) taken or retained by the seller of the collateral to secure all or part of its price; or

(b) taken by a person who by making advances or incurring an obligation gives value to enable the debtor to acquire rights in or the use of collateral if such value is in fact so used.

§ 9–108. When After-Acquired Collateral Not Security for Antecedent Debt.

Where a secured party makes an advance, incurs an obligation, releases a perfected security interest, or otherwise gives new value which is to be secured in whole or in part by after-acquired property his security interest in the after-acquired collateral shall be deemed to be taken for new value and not as security for an antecedent debt if the debtor acquires his rights in such collateral either in the ordinary course of his business or under a contract of purchase made pursuant to the security agreement within a reasonable time after new value is given.

§ 9–109. Classification of Goods; "Consumer Goods"; "Equipment"; "Farm Products"; "Inventory".

Goods are

(1) "consumer goods" if they are used or bought for use primarily for

personal, family or household purposes;

(2) "equipment" if they are used or bought for use primarily in business (including farming or a profession) or by a debtor who is a non-profit organization or a governmental subdivision or agency or if the goods are not included in the definitions of inventory, farm products or consumer goods;

(3) "farm products" if they are crops or livestock or supplies used or produced in farming operations or if they are products of crops or livestock in their unmanufactured states (such as ginned cotton, wool-clip, maple syrup, milk and eggs), and if they are in the possession of a debtor engaged in raising, fattening, grazing or other farming operations. If goods are farm products they are neither equipment nor inventory;

(4) "inventory" if they are held by a person who holds them for sale or lease or to be furnished under contracts of service or if he has so furnished them, or if they are raw materials, work in process or materials used or consumed in a business. Inventory of a person is not to be classified as his equipment.

§ 9–110. Sufficiency of Description.

For the purposes of this Article any description of personal property or real estate is sufficient whether or not it is specific if it reasonably identifies what is described.

§ 9–111. Applicability of Bulk Transfer Laws.

The creation of a security interest is not a bulk transfer under Article 6 (see Section 6–103).

§ 9–112. Where Collateral Is Not Owned by Debtor.

Unless otherwise agreed, when a secured party knows that collateral is owned by a person who is not the debtor, the owner of the collateral is entitled to receive from the secured party any surplus under Section 9–502(2) or under Section 9–504(1), and is not liable for the debt or for any deficiency after resale, and he has the same right as the debtor

(a) to receive statements under Section 9–208;

(b) to receive notice of and to object to a secured party's proposal to retain the collateral in satisfaction of the indebtedness under Section 9–505;

(c) to redeem the collateral under Section 9–506;

(d) to obtain injunctive or other relief under Section 9–507(1); and

(e) to recover losses caused to him under Section 9–208(2).

§ 9–113. Security Interests Arising Under Article on Sales.

A security interest arising solely under the Article on Sales (Article 2) is subject to the provisions of this Article except that to the extent that and so long as the debtor does not have or does not lawfully obtain possession of the goods

(a) no security agreement is necessary to make the security interest enforceable; and

(b) no filing is required to perfect the security interest; and

(c) the rights of the secured party on default by the debtor are governed by the Article on Sales (Article 2).

§ 9–114. Consignment.

(1) A person who delivers goods under a consignment which is not a security interest and who would be required to file under this Article by paragraph (3)(c)

of Section 2–326 has priority over a secured party who is or becomes a creditor of the consignee and who would have a perfected security interest in the goods if they were the property of the consignee, and also has priority with respect to identifiable cash proceeds received on or before delivery of the goods to a buyer, if

(a) the consignor complies with the filing provision of the Article on Sales with respect to consignments (paragraph (3) (c) of Section 2–326) before the consignee receives possession of the goods; and

(b) the consignor gives notification in writing to the holder of the security interest if the holder has filed a financing statement covering the same types of goods before the date of the filing made by the consignor; and

(c) the holder of the security interest receives the notification within five years before the consignee receives possession of the goods; and

(d) the notification states that the consignor expects to deliver goods on consignment to the consignee, describing the goods by item or type.

(2) In the case of a consignment which is not a security interest and in which the requirements of the preceding subsection have not been met, a person who delivers goods to another is subordinate to a person who would have a perfected security interest in the goods if they were the property of the debtor. Added in 1972.

PART 2

VALIDITY OF SECURITY AGREEMENT AND RIGHTS OF PARTIES THERETO

§ 9–201. General Validity of Security Agreement.

Except as otherwise provided by this Act a security agreement is effective according to its terms between the parties, against purchasers of the collateral and against creditors. Nothing in this Article validates any charge or practice illegal under any statute or regulation thereunder governing usury, small loans, retail installment sales, or the like, or extends the application of any such statute or regulation to any transaction not otherwise subject thereto.

§ 9–202. Title to Collateral Immaterial.

Each provision of this Article with regard to rights, obligations and remedies applies whether title to collateral is in the secured party or in the debtor.

§ 9–203. Attachment and Enforceability of Security Interest; Proceeds; Formal Requisites.

(1) Subject to the provisions of Section 4–208 on the security interest of a collecting bank and Section 9–113 on a security interest arising under the Article on Sales, a security interest is not enforceable against the debtor or third parties with respect to the collateral and does not attach unless

(a) the collateral is in the possession of the secured party pursuant to agreement, or the debtor has signed a security agreement which contains a description of the collateral and in addition, when the security interest covers crops growing or to be grown or timber to be cut, a description of the land concerned; and

(b) value has been given; and

(c) the debtor has rights in the collateral.

(2) A security interest attaches when it becomes enforceable against the debtor with respect to the collateral. Attachment occurs as soon as all of the events specified in subsection (1) have taken place unless explicit agreement postpones the time of attaching.

(3) Unless otherwise agreed a security agreement gives the secured party the rights to proceeds provided by Section 9–306.

(4) A transaction, although subject to this Article, is also subject to . . . . . . *, and in the case of conflict between the provisions of this Article and any such statute, the provisions of such statute control. Failure to comply with any applicable statute has only the effect which is specified therein. Amended in 1972. **Note:** *At* in subjection (4) insert reference to any local statute regulating small loans, retail installment sales and the like.*

The foregoing subsection (4) is designed to make it clear that certain transactions, although subject to this Article, must also comply with other applicable legislation.

This Article is designed to regulate all the "security" aspects of transactions within its scope. There is, however, much regulatory legislation, particularly in the consumer field, which supplements this Article and should not be repealed by its enactment. Examples are small loan acts, retail installment selling acts and the like.

Such acts may provide for licensing and rate regulation and may prescribe particular forms of contract. Such provisions should remain in force despite the enactment of this Article. On the other hand if a retail installment selling act contains provisions on filing, rights on default, etc. such provisions should be repealed as inconsistent with this Article except that inconsistent provisions as to deficiencies, penalties, etc., in the Uniform Consumer Credit Code and other recent related legislation should remain because those statutes were drafted after the substantial enactment of the Article and with the intention of modifying certain provisions of this Article as to consumer credit.

§ 9–204. After-Acquired Property; Future Advances.

(1) Except as provided in subsection (2), a security agreement may provide that any or all obligations covered by the security agreement are to be secured by after-acquired collateral.

(2) No security interest attaches under an after-acquired property clause to consumer goods other than accessions (Section 9–314) when given as additional security unless the debtor acquires rights in them within ten days after the secured party gives value.

(3) Obligations covered by a security agreement may include future advances or other value whether or not the advances or value are given pursuant to commitment (subsection (1) of Section 9–105). Amended in 1972.

§ 9–205. Use or Disposition of Collateral Without Accounting Permissible.

A security interest is not invalid or fraudulent against creditors by reason of liberty in the debtor to use, commingle or dispose of all or part of the collateral (including returned or repossessed goods) or to collect or compromise accounts or chattel paper, or to accept the return of goods or make repossessions, or to use, commingle or dispose of proceeds, or by reason of the failure of the secured party to require the debtor to account for proceeds or replace collateral. This section does not relax the requirements of possession where perfection of a security interest depends upon possession of the collateral by the secured party or by a bailee. Amended in 1972.

§ 9–206. Agreement Not to Assert Defenses Against Assignee; Modification of Sales Warranties Where Security Agreement Exists.

(1) Subject to any statute or decision which establishes a different rule for buyers or lessees of consumer goods, an agreement by a buyer or lessee that he will not assert against an assignee any claim or defense which he may have against the seller or lessor is enforceable by an assignee who takes his assignment for value, in good faith and without notice of a claim or defense, except as to defenses of a type which may be asserted against a holder in due course of a negotiable instrument under the Article on Commercial Paper (Article 3). A buyer who as part of one transaction signs both a negotiable instrument and a security agreement makes such an agreement.

(2) When a seller retains a purchase money security interest in goods the Article on Sales (Article 2) governs the sale and any disclaimer, limitation or modification of the seller's warranties. Amended in 1962.

§ 9–207. Rights and Duties When Collateral is in Secured Party's Possession.

(1) A secured party must use reasonable care in the custody and preservation of collateral in his possession. In the case of an instrument or chattel paper reasonable care includes taking necessary steps to preserve rights against prior parties unless otherwise agreed.

(2) Unless otherwise agreed, when collateral is in the secured party's possession

(a) reasonable expenses (including the cost of any insurance and payment of taxes or other charges) incurred in the custody, preservation, use or operation of the collateral are chargeable to the debtor and are secured by the collateral;

(b) the risk of accidental loss or damage is on the debtor to the extent of any deficiency in any effective insurance coverage;

(c) the secured party may hold as additional security any increase or profits (except money) received from the collateral, but money so received, unless remitted to the debtor, shall be applied in reduction of the secured obligation;

(d) the secured party must keep the collateral identifiable but fungible collateral may be commingled;

(e) the secured party may repledge the collateral upon terms which do not impair the debtor's right to redeem it.

(3) A secured party is liable for any loss caused by his failure to meet any obligation imposed by the preceding subsections but does not lose his security interest.

(4)   A secured party may use or operate the collateral for the purpose of preserving the collateral or its value or pursuant to the order of a court of appropriate jurisdiction or, except in the case of consumer goods, in the manner and to the extent provided in the security agreement.

§ 9–208. Request for Statement of Account or List of Collateral.

(1)   A debtor may sign a statement indicating what he believes to be the aggregate amount of unpaid indebtedness as of a specified date and may send it to the secured party with a request that the statement be approved or corrected and returned to the debtor. When the security agreement or any other record kept by the secured party identifies the collateral a debtor may similarly request the secured party to approve or correct a list of the collateral.

(2)   The secured party must comply with such a request within two weeks after receipt by sending a written correction or approval. If the secured party claims a security interest in all of a particular type of collateral owned by the debtor he may indicate that fact in his reply and need not approve or correct an itemized list of such collateral. If the secured party without reasonable excuse fails to comply he is liable for any loss caused to the debtor thereby; and if the debtor has properly included in his request a good faith statement of the obligation or a list of the collateral or both the secured party may claim a security interest only as shown in the statement against persons misled by his failure to comply. If he no longer has an interest in the obligation or collateral at the time the request is received he must disclose the name and address of any successor in interest known to him and he is liable for any loss caused to the debtor as a result of failure to disclose. A successor in interest is not subject to this section until a request is received by him.

(3)   A debtor is entitled to such a statement once every six months without charge. The secured party may require payment of a charge not exceeding $10 for each additional statement furnished.

PART 3

RIGHTS OF THIRD PARTIES; PERFECTED AND UNPERFECTED SECURITY INTERESTS; RULES OF PRIORITY

§ 9–301. Persons Who Take Priority Over Unperfected Security Interests; Rights of "Lien Creditor".

(1)   Except as otherwise provided in subsection (2), an unperfected security interest is subordinate to the rights of

(a) persons entitled to priority under Section 9–312;

(b) a person who becomes a lien creditor before the security interest is perfected;

(c) in the case of goods, instruments, documents, and chattel paper, a person who is not a secured party and who is a transferee in bulk or other buyer not in ordinary course of business or is a buyer of farm products in ordinary course of business, to the extent that he gives value and receives delivery of the collateral without knowledge of the security interest and before it is perfected;

(d) in the case of accounts and general intangibles, a person who is not a secured party and who is a transferee to the extent that he gives value without knowledge of the security interest and before it is perfected.

(2) If the secured party files with respect to a purchase money security interest before or within ten days after the debtor receives possession of the collateral, he takes priority over the rights of a transferee in bulk or of a lien creditor which arise between the time the security interest attaches and the time of filing.

(3) A "lien creditor" means a creditor who has acquired a lien on the property involved by attachment, levy or the like and includes an assignee for benefit of creditors from the time of assignment, and a trustee in bankruptcy from the date of the filing of the petition or a receiver in equity from the time of appointment.

(4) A person who becomes a lien creditor while a security interest is perfected takes subject to the security interest only to the extent that it secures advances made before he becomes a lien creditor or within 45 days thereafter or made without knowledge of the lien or pursuant to a commitment entered into without knowledge of the lien. Amended in 1972.

§ 9–302. When Filing Is Required to Perfect Security Interest; Security Interests to Which Filing Provisions of This Article Do Not Apply.

(1) A financing statement must be filed to perfect all security interests except the following:

(a) a security interest in collateral in possession of the secured party under Section 9–305;

(b) a security interest temporarily perfected in instruments or documents without delivery under Section 9–304 or in proceeds for a 10 day period under Section 9–306;

(c) a security interest created by an assignment of a beneficial interest in a trust or a decedent's estate;

(d) a purchase money security interest in consumer goods; but filing is required for a motor vehicle required to be registered; and fixture filing is required for priority over conflicting interests in fixtures to the extent provided in Section 9–313;

(e) an assignment of accounts which does not alone or in conjunction with other assignments to the same assignee transfer a significant part of the outstanding accounts of the assignor;

(f) a security interest of a collecting bank (Section 4–208) or arising under the Article on Sales (see Section 9–113) or covered in subsection (3) of this section;

(g) an assignment for the benefit of all the creditors of the transferor, and subsequent transfers by the assignee thereunder.

(2) If a secured party assigns a perfected security interest, no filing under this Article is required in order to continue the perfected status of the security interest against creditors of and transferees from the original debtor.

(3) The filing of a financing statement otherwise required by this

Article is not necessary or effective to perfect a security interest in property subject to

(a) a statute or treaty of the United States which provides for a national or international registration or a national or international certificate of title or which specifies a place of filing different from that specified in this Article for filing of the security interest; or

(b) the following statutes of this state; [list any certificate of title statute covering automobiles, trailers, mobile homes, boats, farm tractors, or the like, and any central filing statute*.] ; but during any period in which collateral is inventory held for sale by a person who is in the business of selling goods of that kind, the filing provisions of this Article (Part 4) apply to a security interest in that collateral created by him as debtor; or

(c) a certificate of title statute of another jurisdiction under the law of which indication of a security interest on the certificate is required as a condition of perfection (subsection (2) of Section 9–103).

(4) Compliance with a statute or treaty described in subsection (3) is equivalent to the filing of a financing statement under this Article, and a security interest in property subject to the statute or treaty can be perfected only by compliance therewith except as provided in Section 9–103 on multiple state transactions. Duration and renewal of perfection of a security interest perfected by compliance with the statute or treaty are governed by the provisions of the statute or treaty; in other respects the security interest is subject to this Article. Amended in 1972.

*Note: *It is recommended that the provisions of certificate of title acts for perfection of security interests by notation on the certificates should be amended to exclude coverage of inventory held for sale.*

§ 9–303. When Security Interest Is Perfected; Continuity of Perfection.

(1) A security interest is perfected when it has attached and when all of the applicable steps required for perfection have been taken. Such steps are specified in Sections 9–302, 9–304, 9–305 and 9–306. If such steps are taken before the security interest attaches, it is perfected at the time when it attaches.

(2) If a security interest is originally perfected in any way permitted under this Article and is subsequently perfected in some other way under this Article, without an intermediate period when it was unperfected, the security interest shall be deemed to be perfected continuously for the purposes of this Article.

§ 9–304. Perfection of Security Interest in Instruments, Documents, and Goods Covered by Documents; Perfection by Permissive Filing; Temporary Perfection Without Filing or Transfer of Possession.

(1) A security interest in chattel paper or negotiable documents may be perfected by filing. A security interest in money or instruments (other than instruments which constitute part of chattel paper) can be perfected only by the secured party's taking possession, except as provided in subsections (4) and (5) of this section and subsections (2) and (3) of Section 9–306 on proceeds.

(2) During the period that goods are in the possession of the issuer of a negotiable document therefor, a security interest in the goods is perfected by perfecting a security interest in the document, and any security interest in the goods otherwise perfected during such period is subject thereto.

(3) A security interest in goods in the possession of a bailee other than one who has issued a negotiable document therefor is perfected by issuance of a document in the name of the secured party or by the bailee's receipt of notification of the secured party's interest or by filing as to the goods.

(4) A security interest in instruments or negotiable documents is perfected without filing or the taking of possession for a period of 21 days from the time it attaches to the extent that it arises for new value given under a written security agreement.

(5) A security interest remains perfected for a period of 21 days without filing where a secured party having a perfected security interest in an instrument, a negotiable document or goods in possession of a bailee other than one who has issued a negotiable document therefor

(a) makes available to the debtor the goods or documents representing the goods for the purpose of ultimate sale or exchange or for the purpose of loading, unloading, storing, shipping, transshipping, manufacturing, processing or otherwise dealing with them in a manner preliminary to their sale or exchange, but priority between conflicting security interests in the goods is subject to subsection (3) of Section 9–312; or

(b) delivers the instrument to the debtor for the purpose of ultimate sale or exchange or of presentation, collection, renewal or registration of transfer.

(6) After the 21 day period in subsections (4) and (5) perfection depends upon compliance with applicable provisions of this Article. Amended in 1972.

§ 9–305. When Possession by Secured Party Perfects Security Interest Without Filing.

A security interest in letters of credit and advices of credit (subsection (2)(a) of Section 5–116), goods, instruments, money, negotiable documents or chattel paper may be perfected by the secured party's taking possession of the collateral. If such collateral other than goods covered by a negotiable document is held by a bailee, the secured party is deemed to have possession from the time the bailee receives notification of the secured party's interest. A security interest is perfected by possession from the time possession is taken without relation back and continues only so long as possession is retained, unless otherwise specified in this Article. The security interest may be otherwise perfected as provided in this Article before or after the period of possession by the secured party. Amended in 1972.

§ 9–306. "Proceeds"; Secured Party's Rights on Disposition of Collateral.

(1) "Proceeds" includes whatever is received upon the sale, exchange, collection or other disposition of collateral or proceeds. Insurance payable by reason of loss or damage to the collateral is proceeds, except to the extent that it is payable to a person other than a party to the security agreement. Money, checks, de-

posit accounts, and the like are "cash proceeds". All other proceeds are "noncash proceeds".

(2)   Except where this Article otherwise provides, a security interest continues in collateral notwithstanding sale, exchange or other disposition thereof unless the disposition was authorized by the secured party in the security agreement or otherwise, and also continues in any identifiable proceeds including collections received by the debtor.

(3)   The security interest in proceeds is a continuously perfected security interest if the interest in the original collateral was perfected but it ceases to be a perfected security interest and becomes unperfected ten days after receipt of the proceeds by the debtor unless

(a) a filed financing statement covers the original collateral and the proceeds are collateral in which a security interest may be perfected by filing in the office or offices where the financing statement has been filed and, if the proceeds are acquired with cash proceeds, the description of collateral in the financing statement indicates the types of property constituting the proceeds; or

(b) a filed financing statement covers the original collateral and the proceeds are identifiable cash proceeds; or

(c) the security interest in the proceeds is perfected before the expiration of the ten day period.

Except as provided in this section, a security interest in proceeds can be perfected only by the methods or under the circumstances permitted in this Article for original collateral of the same type.

(4)   In the event of insolvency proceedings instituted by or against a debtor, a secured party with a perfected security interest in proceeds has a perfected security interest only in the following proceeds:

(a) in identifiable non-cash proceeds and in separate deposit accounts containing only proceeds;

(b) in identifiable cash proceeds in the form of money which is neither commingled with other money nor deposited in a deposit account prior to the insolvency proceedings;

(c) in identifiable cash proceeds in the form of checks and the like which are not deposited in a deposit account prior to the insolvency proceedings; and

(d) in all cash and deposit accounts of the debtor in which proceeds have been commingled with other funds, but the perfected security interest under this paragraph (d) is

(i) subject to any right to set-off; and

(ii) limited to an amount not greater than the amount of any cash proceeds received by the debtor within ten days before the institution of the insolvency proceedings less the sum of (I) the payments to the secured party on account of cash proceeds received by the debtor during such period and (II) the cash proceeds received by the debtor during such period to which the secured party is entitled under paragraphs (a) through (c) of this subsection (4).

(5) If a sale of goods results in an account or chattel paper which is transferred by the seller to a secured party, and if the goods are returned to or are repossessed by the seller or the secured party, the following rules determine priorities:

    (a) If the goods were collateral at the time of sale, for an indebtedness of the seller which is still unpaid, the original security interest attaches again to the goods and continues as a perfected security interest if it was perfected at the time when the goods were sold. If the security interest was originally perfected by a filing which is still effective, nothing further is required .to continue the perfected status; in any other case, the secured party must take possession of the returned or repossessed goods or must file.

    (b) An unpaid transferee of the chattel paper has a security interest in the goods against the transferor. Such security interest is prior to a security interest asserted under paragraph (a) to the extent that the transferee of the chattel paper was entitled to priority under Section 9–308.

    (c) An unpaid transferee of the account has a security interest in the goods against the transferor. Such security interest is subordinate to a security interest asserted under paragraph (a).

    (d) A security interest of an unpaid transferee asserted under paragraph (b) or (c) must be perfected for protection against creditors of the transferor and purchasers of the returned or repossessed goods. Amended in 1972.

§ 9–307. Protection of Buyers of Goods.

(1) A buyer in ordinary course of business (subsection (9) of Section 1–201) other than a person buying farm products from a person engaged in farming operations takes free of a security interest created by his seller even though the security interest is perfected and even though the buyer knows of its existence.

(2) In the case of consumer goods, a buyer takes free of a security interest even though perfected if he buys without knowledge of the security interest, for value and for his own personal, family or household purposes unless prior to the purchase the secured party has filed a financing statement covering such goods.

(3) A buyer other than a buyer in ordinary course of business (subsection (1) of this section) takes free of a security interest to the extent that it secures future advances made after the secured party acquires knowledge of the purchase, or more than 45 days after the purchase, whichever first occurs, unless made pursuant to a commitment entered into without knowledge of the purchase and before the expiration of the 45 day period. Amended in 1972.

§ 9–308. Purchase of Chattel Paper and Instruments.

A purchaser of chattel paper or an instrument who gives new value and takes possession of it in the ordinary course of his business has priority over a security interest in the chattel paper or instrument

    (a) which is perfected under Section 9–304 (permissive filing and temporary perfection) or under

Section 9—306 (perfection as to proceeds) if he acts without knowledge that the specific paper or instrument is subject to a security interest; or

(b) which is claimed merely as proceeds of inventory subject to a security interest (Section 9—306) even though he knows that the specific paper or instrument is subject to the security interest. Amended in 1972.

§ 9—309. Protection of Purchasers of Instruments and Documents.

Nothing in this Article limits the rights of a holder in due course of a negotiable instrument (Section 3—302) or a holder to whom a negotiable document of title has been duly negotiated (Section 7—501) or a bona fide purchaser of a security (Section 8—301) and such holders or purchasers take priority over an earlier security interest even though perfected. Filing under this Article does not constitute notice of the security interest to such holders or purchasers.

§ 9—310. Priority of Certain Liens Arising by Operation of Law.

When a person in the ordinary course of his business furnishes services or materials with respect to goods subject to a security interest, a lien upon goods in the possession of such person given by statute or rule of law for such materials or services takes priority over a perfected security interest unless the lien is statutory and the statute expressly provides otherwise.

§ 9—311. Alienability of Debtor's Rights: Judicial Process.

The debtor's rights in collateral may be voluntarily or involuntarily transferred (by way of sale, creation of a security interest, attachment, levy, garnishment or other judicial process) notwithstanding a provision in the security agreement prohibiting any transfer or making the transfer constitute a default.

§ 9—312. Priorities Among Conflicting Security Interests in the Same Collateral.

(1) The rules of priority stated in other sections of this Part and in the following sections shall govern when applicable: Section 4—208 with respect to the security interests of collecting banks in items being collected, accompanying documents and proceeds; Section 9—103 on security interests related to other jurisdictions; Section 9—114 on consignments.

(2) A perfected security interest in crops for new value given to enable the debtor to produce the crops during the production season and given not more than three months before the crops become growing crops by planting or otherwise takes priority over an earlier perfected security interest to the extent that such earlier interest secures obligations due more than six months before the crops become growing crops by planting or otherwise, even though the person giving new value had knowledge of the earlier security interest.

(3) A perfected purchase money security interest in inventory has priority over a conflicting security interest in the same inventory and also has priority in identifiable cash proceeds received on or before the delivery of the inventory to a buyer if

(a) the purchase money security interest is perfected at the time the debtor receives possession of the inventory; and

(b) the purchase money secured party gives notification in writing to the holder of the conflicting security interest if the holder had filed a financing statement covering the same types of inventory (i) before the date of the filing made by the purchase money secured party or (ii) before the beginning of the 21 day period where the purchase money security interest is temporarily perfected without filing or possession (subsection (5) of Section 9–304); and

(c) the holder of the conflicting security interest receives the notification within five years before the debtor receives possession of the inventory; and

(d) the notification states that the person giving the notice has or expects to acquire a purchase money security interest in inventory of the debtor, describing such inventory by item or type.

(4)   A purchase money security interest in collateral other than inventory has priority over a conflicting security interest in the same collateral or its proceeds if the purchase money security interest is perfected at the time the debtor receives possession of the collateral or within ten days thereafter.

(5)   In all cases not governed by other rules stated in this section (including cases of purchase money security interests which do not qualify for the special priorities set forth in subsections (3) and (4) of this section), priority between conflicting security interests in the same collateral shall be determined according to the following rules:

(a) Conflicting security interests rank according to priority in time of filing or perfection.   Priority dates from the time a filing is first made covering the collateral or the time the security interest is first perfected, whichever is earlier, provided that there is no period thereafter when there is neither filing nor perfection.

(b) So long as conflicting security interests are unperfected, the first to attach has priority.

(6)   For the purposes of subsection (5) a date of filing or perfection as to collateral is also a date of filing or perfection as to proceeds.

(7)   If future advances are made while a security interest is perfected by filing or the taking of possession, the security interest has the same priority for the purposes of subsection (5) with respect to the future advances as it does with respect to the first advance.   If a commitment is made before or while the security interest is so perfected, the security interest has the same priority with respect to advances made pursuant thereto.   In other cases a perfected security interest has priority from the date the advance is made.   Amended in 1972.

§ 9–313. Priority of Security Interests in Fixtures.

(1)   In this section and in the provisions of Part 4 of this Article referring to fixture filing, unless the context otherwise requires

(a) goods are "fixtures" when they become so related to particular real estate that an interest in them arises under real estate law

(b) a "fixture filing" is the filing in the office where a mortgage on the real estate would be filed or recorded of a financing statement covering goods which are or are to become fixtures and conforming to the requirements of subsection (5) of Section 9–402

(c) a mortgage is a "construction mortgage" to the extent that it secures an obligation incurred for the construction of an improvement on land including the acquisition cost of the land if the recorded writing so indicates.

(2) A security interest under this Article may be created in goods which are fixtures or may continue in goods which become fixtures, but no security interest exists under this Article in ordinary building materials incorporated into an improvement on land.

(3) This Article does not prevent creation of an encumbrance upon fixtures pursuant to real estate law.

(4) A perfected security interest in fixtures has priority over the conflicting interest of an encumbrance or owner of the real estate where

(a) the security interest is a purchase money security interest, the interest of encumbrancer or owner arises before the goods become fixtures, the security interest is perfected by a fixture filing before the goods become fixtures or within ten days thereafter, and the debtor has an interest of record in the real estate or is in possession of the real estate; or

(b) the security interest is perfected by a fixture filing before the interest of the encumbrancer or owner is of record, the security

interest has priority over any conflicting interest of a predecessor in title of the encumbrancer or owner, and the debtor has an interest of record in the real estate or is in possession of the real estate; or

(c) the fixtures are readily removable factory or office machines or readily removable replacements of domestic appliances which are consumer goods, and before the goods become fixtures the security interest is perfected by any method permitted by this Article; or

(d) the conflicting interest is a lien on the real estate obtained by legal or equitable proceedings after the security interest was perfected by any method permitted by this Article.

(5) A security interest in fixtures, whether or not perfected, has priority over the conflicting interest of an encumbrancer or owner of the real estate where

(a) the encumbrancer or owner has consented in writing to the security interest or has disclaimed an interest in the goods as fixtures; or

(b) the debtor has a right to remove the goods as against the encumbrancer or owner. If the debtor's right terminates, the priority of the security interest continues for a reasonable time.

(6) Notwithstanding paragraph (a) of subsection (4) but otherwise subject to subsections (4) and (5), a security interest in fixtures is subordinate to a construction mortgage recorded before the goods become fixtures if the goods become fixtures before the completion of the con-

struction. To the extent that it is given to refinance a construction mortgage, a mortgage has this priority to the same extent as the construction mortgage.

(7) In cases not within the preceding subsections, a security interest in fixtures is subordinate to the conflicting interest of an encumbrancer or owner of the related real estate who is not the debtor.

(8) When the secured party has priority over all owners and encumbrancers of the real estate, he may, on default, subject to the provisions of Part 5, remove his collateral from the real estate but he must reimburse any encumbrancer or owner of the real estate who is not the debtor and who has not otherwise agreed for the cost of repair of any physical injury, but not for any diminution in value of the real estate caused by the absence of the goods removed or by any necessity of replacing them. A person entitled to reimbursement may refuse permission to remove until the secured party gives adequate security for the performance of this obligation. Amended in 1972.

§ 9–314. Accessions.

(1) A security interest in goods which attaches before they are installed in or affixed to other goods takes priority as to the goods installed or affixed (called in this section "accessions") over the claims of all persons to the whole except as stated in subsection (3) and subject to Section 9–315(1).

(2) A security interest which attaches to goods after they become part of a whole is valid against all persons subsequently acquiring interests in the whole except as stated in subsection (3) but is invalid against any person with an interest in the whole at the time the security interest attaches to the goods who has not

in writing consented to the security interest or disclaimed an interest in the goods as part of the whole.

(3) The security interests described in subsections (1) and (2) do not take priority over

  (a) a subsequent purchaser for value of any interest in the whole; or
  (b) a creditor with a lien on the whole subsequently obtained by judicial proceedings; or
  (c) a creditor with a prior perfected security interest in the whole to the extent that he makes subsequent advances

if the subsequent purchase is made, the lien by judicial proceedings obtained or the subsequent advance under the prior perfected security interest is made or contracted for without knowledge of the security interest and before it is perfected. A purchaser of the whole at a foreclosure sale other than the holder of a perfected security interest purchasing at his own foreclosure sale is a subsequent purchaser within this section.

(4) When under subsections (1) or (2) and (3) a secured party has an interest in accessions which has priority over the claims of all persons who have interests in the whole, he may on default subject to the provisions of Part 5 remove his collateral from the whole but he must reimburse any encumbrancer or owner of the whole who is not the debtor and who has not otherwise agreed for the cost of repair of any physical injury but not for any diminution in value of the whole caused by the absence of the goods removed or by any necessity for replacing them. A person entitled to reimbursement may refuse permission to remove until the secured party gives adequate security for the performance of this obligation.

§ 9–315. Priority When Goods Are Commingled or Processed.

(1) If a security interest in goods was perfected and subsequently the goods or a part thereof have become part of a product or mass, the security interest continues in the product or mass if

(a) the goods are so manufactured, processed, assembled or commingled that their identity is lost in the product or mass; or

(b) a financing statement covering the original goods also covers the product into which the goods have been manufactured, processed or assembled.

In a case to which paragraph (b) applies, no separate security interest in that part of the original goods which has been manufactured, processed or assembled into the product may be claimed under Section 9–314.

(2) When under subsection (1) more than one security interest attaches to the product or mass, they rank equally according to the ratio that the cost of the goods to which each interest originally attached bears to the cost of the total product or mass.

§ 9–316. Priority Subject to Subordination.

Nothing in this Article prevents subordination by agreement by any person entitled to priority.

§ 9–317. Secured Party Not Obligated on Contract of Debtor.

The mere existence of a security interest or authority given to the debtor to dispose of or use collateral does not impose contract or tort liability upon the secured party for the debtor's acts or omissions.

§ 9–318. Defenses Against Assignee; Modification of Contract After Notification of Assignment; Term Prohibiting Assignment Ineffective; Identification and Proof of Assignment.

(1) Unless an account debtor has made an enforceable agreement not to assert defenses or claims arising out of a sale as provided in Section 9–206 the rights of an assignee are subject to

(a) all the terms of the contract between the account debtor and assignor and any defense or claim arising therefrom; and

(b) any other defense or claim of the account debtor against the assignor which accrues before the account debtor receives notification of the assignment.

(2) So far as the right to payment or a part thereof under an assigned contract has not been fully earned by performance, and notwithstanding notification of the assignment, any modification of or substitution for the contract made in good faith and in accordance with reasonable commercial standards is effective against an assignee unless the account debtor has otherwise agreed but the assignee acquires corresponding rights under the modified or substituted contract. The assignment may provide that such modification or substitution is a breach by the assignor.

(3) The account debtor is authorized to pay the assignor until the account debtor receives notification that the amount due or to become due has been assigned and that payment is to be made to the assignee. A notification which does not reasonably identify the rights assigned is ineffective. If requested by the account debtor, the assignee must seasonably furnish reasonable proof that the assignment has been made and unless

he does so the account debtor may pay the assignor.

(4) A term in any contract between an account debtor and an assignor is ineffective if it prohibits assignment of an account or prohibits creation of a security interest in a general intangible for money due or to become due or requires the account debtor's consent to such assignment or security interest. Amended in 1972.

PART 4
FILING

§ 9–401. Place of Filing; Erroneous Filing; Removal of Collateral.

First Alternative Subsection (1)

(1) The proper place to file in order to perfect a security interest is as follows:

(a) when the collateral is timber to be cut or is minerals or the like (including oil and gas) or accounts subject to subsection (5) of Section 9–103, or when the financing statement is filed as a fixture filing (Section 9–313) and the collateral is goods which are or are to become fixtures, then in the office where a mortgage on the real estate would be filed or recorded;

(b) in all other cases, in the office of the [Secretary of State].

Second Alternative Subsection (1)

(1) The proper place to file in order to perfect a security interest is as follows:

(a) when the collateral is equipment used in farming operations, or farm products, or accounts or general intangibles arising from or relating to the sale of farm products by a farmer, or consumer goods, then in the office of the . . . . in the county the debtor's residence or if the debtor is not a resident of this state then in the office of the . . . . in the county where

the goods are kept, and in addition when the collateral is crops growing or to be grown in the office of the . . . . in the county where the land is located;

(b) when the collateral is timber to be cut or is minerals or the like (including oil and gas) or accounts subject to subsection (5) of Section 9–103, or when the financing statement is filed as a fixture filing (Section 9–313) and the collateral is goods which are or are to become fixtures, then in the office where a mortgage on the real estate would be filed or recorded;

(c) in all other cases, in the office of the [Secretary of State].

Third Alternative Subsection (1)

(1) The proper place to file in order to perfect a security interest is as follows:

(a) when the collateral is equipment used in farming operations, or farm products, or accounts or general intangibles arising from or relating to the sale of farm products by a farmer, or consumer goods, then in the office of the . . . . in the county of the debtor's residence or if the debtor is not a resident of this state then in the office of the . . . . in the county where the goods are kept, and in addition when the collateral is crops growing or to be grown in the office of the .... in the county where the land is located;

(b) when the collateral is timber to be cut or is minerals or the like (including oil and gas) or accounts subject to subsection (5) of Section 9–103, or when the financing statement is filed as a fixture filing (Section 9–313) and the collateral is goods which are or are to become fixtures, then in the office where a mortgage on the real estate would be filed or recorded;

(c) in all other cases, in the office of the [Secretary of State] and in addition, if the debtor has a place of business in only one county of this state, also in the office of .... of such county, or, if the debtor has no place of business in this state, but resides in the state, also in the office of .... of the county in which he resides.

Note: *One of the three alternatives should be selected as subsection (1).*

(2)   A filing which is made in good faith in an improper place or not in all of the places required by this section is nevertheless effective with regard to any collateral as to which the filing complied with the requirements of this Article and is also effective with regard to collateral covered by the financing statement against any person who has knowledge of the contents of such financing statement.

(3)   A filing which is made in the proper place in this state continues effective even though the debtor's residence or place of business or the location of the collateral or its use, whichever controlled the original filing, is thereafter changed.

Alternative Subsection (3)

[(3)   A filing which is made in the proper county continues effective for four months after a change to another county of the debtor's residence or place of business or the location of the collateral, whichever controlled the original filing. It becomes ineffective thereafter unless a copy of the financing statement signed by the secured party is filed in the new county within said period. The security interest may also be perfected in the new county after the expiration of the four-month period; in such case perfection dates from the time of perfection in the new county. A change in the use of the collateral does not impair the effectiveness of the original filing.]

(4)   The rules stated in Section 9–103 determine whether filing is necessary in this state.

(5)   Notwithstanding the preceding subsections, and subject to subsection (3) of Section 9–302, the proper place to file in order to perfect a security interest in collateral, including fixtures, of a transmitting utility is the office of the [Secretary of State]. This filing constitutes a fixture filing (Section 9–313) as to the collateral described therein which is or is to become fixtures.

(6)   For the purposes of this section, the residence of an organization is its place of business if it has one or its chief executive office if it has more than one place of business. Amended in 1962 and 1972.

Note: *Subsection (6) should be used only if the state chooses the Second* *or Third Alternative Subsection (1).*

§ 9–402. Formal Requisites of Financing Statement; Amendments; Mortgage as Financing Statement.

(1)   A financing statement is sufficient if it gives the names of the debtor and the secured party, is .signed by the debtor, gives an address of the secured party from which information concerning the security interest may be obtained, gives a mailing address of the debtor and contains a statement indicating the types, or describing the items, of collateral. A financing statement may be filed before a security agreement is made or a security interest otherwise attaches. When the financing statement covers crops growing or to be grown, the statement must also contain a description of the real estate concerned. When the financing statement covers timber to be cut or covers minerals or the like (including oil and gas) or accounts subject to subsection (5) of Section 9–103, or when the financing statement is filed as a fixture filing (Section 9–313) and the collateral is goods which are or are to become fixtures, the statement must also comply with subsection (5). A copy of the security agreement is sufficient as a financing statement if it contains the above information and is signed by the debtor. A carbon, photographic or other reproduction of a security agreement or a financing statement is sufficient as a financing statement if the security agreement so provides or if the original has been filed in this state.

(2)   A financing statement which otherwise complies with subsection (1) is sufficient when it is signed by the secured party instead of the debtor if it is filed to perfect a security interest in

(a) collateral already subject to a security interest in another jurisdiction when it is brought into this state, or when the debtor's location is changed to this state. Such a financing statement must state that the collateral was brought into this state or that the debtor's location was changed to this state under such circumstances; or

(b) proceeds under Section 9–306 if the security interest in the original collateral was perfected. Such a financing statement must describe the original collateral; or

(c) collateral as to which the filing has lapsed; or

(d) collateral acquired after a change of name, identity or corporate structure of the debtor (subsection (7)).

(3)   A form substantially as follows is sufficient to comply with subsection (1):

Name of debtor (or assignor). . . . . . .
Address . . . .
Name of secured party (or assignee) . .
Address . . . .

1. This financing statement covers the following types (or items) of property: (Describe) . . . .

2. (If collateral is crops) The above described crops are growing or are to be grown on:
(Describe Real Estate) . . . .

3. (If applicable) The above goods are to become fixtures on*

*Where appropriate substitute either "The above timber is standing on . . . . " or "The above minerals or the like (including oil and gas) or accounts will be financed at the wellhead or minehead of the well or mine located on . . . . "

(Describe Real Estate) . . . . and this financing statement is to be filed [for record] in the real estate records. (If the debtor does not have an interest of record) The name of a record owner is . . . . . .

4. (If products of collateral are claimed) Products of the collateral are also covered.

(use whichever is applicable)
. . . .
Signature of Debtor (or Assignor)
. . . .
Signature of Secured Party (or Assignee)

(4) A financing statement may be amended by filing a writing signed by both the debtor and the secured party. An amendment does not extend the period of effectiveness of a financing statement. If any amendment adds collateral, it is effective as to the added collateral only from the filing date of the amendment. In this Article, unless the context otherwise requires, the term "financing statement" means the original financing statement and any amendments.

(5) A financing statement covering timber to be cut or covering minerals or the like (including oil and gas) or accounts subject to subsection (5) of Section 9–103, or a financing statement filed as a fixture filing (Section 9–313) where the debtor is not a transmitting utility, must show that it covers this type of collateral, must recite that it is to be filed [for record] in the real estate records, and the financing statement must contain a description of the real estate [sufficient if it were contained in a mortgage of the real estate to give constructive notice of the mortgage under the law of this state]. If the debtor does not have an interest of record in the real estate, the financing statement must show the name of a record owner.

(6) A mortgage is effective as a financing statement filed as a fixture filing from the date of its recording if
(a) the goods are described in the mortgage by item or type; and
(b) the goods are or are to become fixtures related to the real estate described in the mortgage; and
(c) the mortgage complies with the requirements for a financing statement in this section other than a recital that it is to be filed in the real estate records; and
(d) the mortgage is duly recorded. No fee with reference to the financing statement is required other than the regular recording and satisfaction fees with respect to the mortgage.

(7) A financing statement sufficiently shows the name of the debtor if it gives the individual, partnership or corporate name of the debtor, whether or not it adds other trade names or names of partners. Where the debtor so changes his name or in the case of an organization its name, identity or corporate structure that a filed financing statement becomes seriously misleading, the filing is not effective to perfect a security interest in collateral acquired by the debtor more than four months after the change, unless a new appropriate financing statement is filed before the expiration of that time. A filed financing statement remains effective with respect to collateral transferred by the debtor even though the secured party knows of or consents to the transfer.

(8) A financing statement substantially complying with the requirements of this section is effective even though it contains minor errors which are not seriously misleading. Amended in 1972.

Note: *Language in brackets is optional.*

Note: *Where the state has any special recording system for real estate other than the usual grantor-grantee index (as, for instance, a tract system or a title registration or Torrens system) local adaptations of subsection (5) and Section 9–403(7) may be necessary. See Mass. Gen. Laws Chapter 106, Section 9–409.*

§ **9–403. What Constitutes Filing; Duration of Filing; Effect of Lapsed Filing; Duties of Filing Officer.**

(1)   Presentation for filing of a financing statement and tender of the filing fee or acceptance of the statement by the filing officer constitutes filing under this Article.

(2)   Except as provided in subsection (6) a filed financing statement is effective for a period of five years from the date of filing. The effectiveness of a filed financing statement lapses on the expiration of the five year period unless a continuation statement is filed prior to the lapse. If a security interest perfected by filing exists at the time insolvency proceedings are commenced by or against the debtor, the security interest remains perfected until termination of the insolvency proceedings and thereafter for a period of sixty days or until expiration of the five year period, whichever occurs later. Upon lapse the security interest becomes unperfected, unless it is perfected without filing. If the security interest becomes unperfected upon lapse, it is deemed to have been unperfected as against a person who became a purchaser or lien creditor before lapse.

(3)   A continuation statement may be filed by the secured party within six months prior to the expiration of the five year period specified in subsection (2).

Any such continuation statement must be signed by the secured party, identify the original statement by file number and state that the original statement is still effective. A continuation statement signed by a person other than the secured party of record must be accompanied by a separate written statement of assignment signed by the secured party of record and complying with subsection (2) of Section 9–405, including payment of the required fee. Upon timely filing of the continuation statement, the effectiveness of the original statement is continued for five years after the last date to which the filing was effective whereupon it lapses in the same manner as provided in subsection (2) unless another continuation statement is filed prior to such lapse. Succeeding continuation statements may be filed in the same manner to continue the effectiveness of the original statement. Unless a statute on disposition of public records provides otherwise, the filing officer may remove a lapsed statement from the files and destroy it immediately if he has retained a microfilm or other photographic record, or in other cases after one year after the lapse. The filing officer shall so arrange matters by physical annexation of financing statements to continuation statements or other related filings, or by other means, that if he physically destroys the financing statements of a period more than five years past, those which have been continued by a continuation statement or which are still effective under subsection (6) shall be retained.

(4)   Except as provided in subsection (7) a filing officer shall mark each statement with a file number and with the date and hour of filing and shall hold the statement or a microfilm or other photographic copy thereof for public inspection.

In addition the filing officer shall index the statement according to the name of the debtor and shall note in the index the file number and the address of the debtor given in the statement.

(5)   The uniform fee for filing and indexing and for stamping a copy furnished by the secured party to show the date and place of filing for an original financing statement or for a continuation statement shall be $ . . . . if the statement is in the standard form prescribed by the [Secretary of State] and otherwise shall be $ . . . . , plus in each case, if the financing statement is subject to subsection (5) of Section 9–402, $ . . . . The uniform fee for each name more than one required to be indexed shall be $ . . . . The secured party may at his option show a trade name for any person and an extra uniform indexing fee of $ . . . . shall be paid with respect thereto.

(6)   If the debtor is a transmitting utility (subsection (5) of Section 9–401) and a filed financing statement so states, it is effective until a termination statement is filed.   A real estate mortgage which is effective as a fixture filing under subsection (6) of Section 9–402 remains effective as a fixture filing until the mortgage is released or satisfied of record or its effectiveness otherwise terminates as to the real estate.

(7)   When a financing statement covers timber to be cut or covers minerals or the like (including oil and gas) or accounts subject to subsection (5) of Section 9–103, or is filed as a fixture filing, [it shall be filed for record and] the filing officer shall index it under the names of the debtor and any owner of record shown on the financing statement in the same fashion as if they were the mortgagors in

a mortgage of the real estate described, and, to the extent that the law of this state provides for indexing of mortgages under the name of the mortgagee under the name of the secured party as if he were the mortgagee thereunder, or where indexing is by description in the same fashion as if the financing statement were a mortgage of the real estate described. Amended in 1972.

Note: *In states in which writings will not appear in the real estate records and indices unless actually recorded the bracketed language in subsection (7) should be used.*

§ 9–404.   Termination Statement.

(1)   If a financing statement covering consumer goods is filed on or after . . . . . then within one month or within ten days following written demand by the debtor a after there is no outstanding secured obligation and no commitment to make advances, incur obligations or otherwise give value, the secured party must file with each filing officer with whom the financing statement was filed, a termination statement to the effect that he no longer claims a security interest under the financing statement, which shall be identified by file number. In other cases whenever there is no outstanding secured obligation and no commitment to make advances, incur obligations or otherwise give value, the secured party must on written demand by the debtor send the debtor, for each filing officer with whom the financstatement was filed, a termination statement to the effect that he no longer claims a security interest under the financing statement, which shall be identified by file number.   A termination statement signed by a person other than the secured party of record must be accompanied by

a separate written statement of assignment signed by the secured party of record complying with subsection (2) of Section 9–405, including payment of the required fee. If the affected secured party fails to file such a termination statement as required by this subsection, or to send such a termination statement within ten days after proper demand therefor, he shall be liable to the debtor for one hundred dollars, and in addition for any loss caused to the debtor by such failure.

(2) On presentation to the filing officer of such a termination statement he must note it in the index. If he has received the termination statement in duplicate, he shall return one copy of the termination statement to the secured party stamped to show the time of receipt thereof. If the filing officer has a microfilm or other photographic record of the financing statement, and of any related continuation statement, statement of assignment and statement of release, he may remove the originals from the files at any time after receipt of the termination statement, or if he has no such record, he may remove them from the files at any time after one year after receipt of the termination statement.

(3) If the termination statement is in the standard form prescribed by the [Secretary of State], the uniform fee for filing and indexing the termination statement shall be $ . . . . . . , and otherwise shall be $ . . . . . . , plus in each case an additional fee of $ . . . . . . for each name more than one against which the termination statement is required to be indexed. Amended in 1972.

Note: *The date to be inserted should be the effective date of the revised Article 9.*

§ 9–405. Assignment of Security Interest; Duties of Filing Officer; Fees.

(1) A financing statement may disclose an assignment of a security interest in the collateral described in the financing statement by indication in the financing statement of the name and address of the assignee or by an assignment itself or a copy thereof on the face or back of the statement. On presentation to the filing officer of such a financing statement the filing officer shall mark the same as provided in Section 9–403(4). The uniform fee for filing, indexing and furnishing filing data for a financing statement so indicating an assignment shall be $ . . . . . if the statement is in the standard form prescribed by the [Secretary of State] and otherwise shall be $ . . . . . , plus in each case an additional fee of $ . . . . . . for each name more than one against which the financing statement is required to be indexed.

(2) A secured party may assign of record all or part of his rights under a financing statement by the filing in the place where the original financing statement was filed of a separate written statement of assignment signed by the secured party of record and setting forth the name of the secured party of record and the debtor, the file number and the date of filing of the financing statement and the name and address of the assignee and containing a description of the collateral assigned. A copy of the assignment is sufficient as a separate statement if it complies with the preceding sentence. On presentation to the filing officer of such a separate statement, the filing officer shall mark such separate statement with the date and hour of the filing. He shall note the assignment on the index of the financing statement, or in the case of

a fixture filing, or a filing covering timber to be cut, or covering minerals or the like (including oil and gas) or accounts subject to subsection (5) of Section 9—103, he shall index the assignment under the name of the assignor as grantor and, to the extent that the law of this state provides for indexing the assignment of a mortgage under the name of the assignee, he shall index the assignment of the financing statement under the name of the assignee. The uniform fee for filing, indexing and furnishing filing data about such a separate statement of assignment shall be $ . . . . . . if the statement is in the standard form prescribed by the [Secretary of State] and otherwise shall be $ . . . . . . , plus in each case an additional fee of $ . . . . . . for each name more than one against which the statement of assignment is required to be indexed. Notwithstanding the provisions of this subsection, an assignment of record of a security interest in a fixture contained in a mortgage effective as a fixture filing (subsection (6) of Section 9—402) may be made only by an assignment of the mortgage in the manner provided by the law of this state other than this Act.

(3) After the disclosure or filing of an assignment under this section, the assignee is the secured party of record. Amended in 1972.

§ 9—406. Release of Collateral; Duties of Filing Officer; Fees.

A secured party of record may by his signed statement release all or a part of any collateral described in a filed financing statement. The statement of release is sufficient if it contains a description of the collateral being released, the name and address of the debtor, the name and address of the secured party, and the file number of the financing statement. A statement of release signed by a person other than the secured party of record must be accompanied by a separate written statement of assignment signed by the secured party of record and complying with subsection (2) of Section 9—405, including payment of the required fee. Upon presentation of such a statement of release to the filing officer he shall mark the statement with the hour and date of filing and shall note the same upon the margin of the index of the filing of the financing statement. The uniform fee for filing and noting such a statement of release shall be $ . . . . . . if the statement is in the standard form prescribed by the [Secretary of State] and otherwise shall be $ . . . . . . , plus in each case an additional fee of $ . . . . . . for each name more than one against which the statement of release is required to be indexed. Amended in 1972.

[§ 9—407. Information From Filing Officer].

[(1) If the person filing any financing statement, termination statement, statement of assignment, or statement of release, furnishes the filing officer a copy thereof, the filing officer shall upon request note upon the copy the file number and date and hour of the filing of the original and deliver or send the copy to such person.]

[(2) Upon request of any person, the filing officer shall issue his certificate showing whether there is on file on the date and hour stated therein, any presently effective financing statement naming a particular debtor and any statement of assignment thereof and if there is, giving the date and hour of filing of each such statement and the names and addresses of each secured party therein. The uniform fee for such a certificate shall be $. . . . . . if the request for the certificate is in the standard form prescribed by the [Secretary of State] and otherwise shall be $ . . . . . . Upon request the filing officer shall furnish a copy of any filed financing statement or statement of assignment for a uniform fee of $ . . . . . . per page.] Amended in 1972.

Note: *This section is proposed as an optional provision to require filing officers to furnish certificates. Local law and practices should be consulted with regard to the advisability of adoption.*

§ 9–408. Financing Statements Covering Consigned or Leased Goods.

A consignor or lessor of goods may file a financing statement using the terms "consignor," "consignee," "lessor," "lessee" or the like instead of the terms specified in Section 9–402. The provisions of this Part shall apply as appropriate to such a financing statement but its filing shall not of itself be a factor in determining whether or not the consignment or lease is intended as security (Section 1–201(37)). However, if it is determined for other reasons that the consignment or lease is so intended, a security interest of the consignor or lessor which attaches to the consigned or leased goods is perfected by such filing. Added in 1972.

PART 5

DEFAULT

§ 9–501. Default; Procedure When Security Agreement Covers Both Real and Personal Property.

(1)   When a debtor is in default under a security agreement, a secured party has the rights and remedies provided in this Part and except as limited by subsection (3) those provided in the security agreement. He may reduce his claim to judgment, foreclose or otherwise enforce the security interest by any available judicial procedure. If the collateral is documents the secured party may proceed either as to the documents or as to the goods covered thereby. A secured party in possession has the rights, remedies and duties provided in Section 9–207. The rights and remedies referred to in this subsection are cumulative.

(2)   After default, the debtor has the rights and remedies provided in this Part, those provided in the security agreement and those provided in Section 9–207.

(3)   To the extent that they give rights to the debtor and impose duties on the secured party, the rules stated in the subsections referred to below may not be waived or varied except as provided with respect to compulsory disposition of collateral (subsection (3) of Section 9–504 and Section 9–505) and with respect to redemption of collateral (Section 9–506) but the parties may by agreement determine the standards by which the fulfillment of these rights and duties is to be measured if such standards are not manifestly unreasonable:

(a) subsection (2) of Section 9–502 and subsection (2) of Section 9–504 insofar as they require accounting for surplus proceeds of collateral;

(b) subsection (3) of Section 9–504 and subsection (1) of Section 9–505 which deal with disposition of collateral;

(c) subsection (2) of Section 9–505 which deals with acceptance of collateral as discharge of obligation;

(d) Section 9–506 which deals with redemption of collateral; and

(e) subsection (1) of Section 9–507 which deals with the secured party's liability for failure to comply with this Part.

(4)   If the security agreement covers both real and personal property, the secured party may proceed under this Part as to the personal property or he may proceed as to both the real and the personal property in accordance with his rights and remedies in respect of the real property in which case the provisions of this Part do not apply.

(5)   When a secured party has reduced his claim to judgment the lien of any levy which may be made upon his collateral by virtue of any execution based upon the judgment shall relate back to the date of the perfection of the security interest in such collateral. A judicial sale, pursuant to such execution, is a foreclosure of the security interest by judicial procedure within the meaning of this section, and the secured party may purchase at the sale and thereafter hold the collateral free of any other requirements of this Article. Amended in 1972.

§ 9–502. Collection Rights of Secured Party.

(1)   When so agreed and in any event on default the secured party is entitled to notify an account debtor or the obligor on an instrument to make payment to him whether or not the assignor was theretofore making collections on the collateral, and also to take control of any proceeds to which he is entitled under Section 9–306.

(2)   A secured party who by agreement is entitled to charge back uncollected collateral or otherwise to full or limited recourse against the debtor and who undertakes to collect from the account debtors or obligors must proceed in a commercially reasonable manner and may deduct his reasonable expenses of realization from the collections. If the security agreement secures an indebtedness, the secured party must account to the debtor for any surplus, and unless otherwise agreed, the debtor is liable for any deficiency. But, if the underlying transaction was a sale of accounts or chattel paper, the debtor is entitled to any surplus or is liable for any deficiency only if the security agreement so provides. Amended in 1972.

§ 9–503. Secured Party's Right to Take Possession After Default.

Unless otherwise agreed a secured party has on default the right to take possession of the collateral. In taking possession a secured party may proceed without judicial process if this can be done without breach of the peace or may proceed by action. If the security agreement so provides the secured party may require the debtor to assemble the collateral and make it available to the secured party at a place to be designated by the secured party which is reasonably convenient to both parties. Without removal a secured party may render equipment unusable, and may dispose of collateral on the debtor's premises under Section 9–504.

§ 9–504. Secured Party's Right to Dispose of Collateral After Default; Effect of Disposition.

(1)   A secured party after default may sell, lease or otherwise dispose of any or all of the collateral in its then condition or following any commercially reasonable preparation or processing. Any sale of goods is subject to the Article on Sales (Article 2). The proceeds of disposition shall be applied in the order following to

(a) the reasonable expenses of retaking, holding, preparing for sale or lease, selling, leasing and the like and, to the extent provided for in the agreement and not prohibited by law, the reasonable attorneys' fees and legal expenses incurred by the secured party;

(b) the satisfaction of indebtedness secured by the security interest under which the disposition is made;

(c) the satisfaction of indebtedness secured by any subordinate security interest in the collateral if written notification of demand therefor is received before distribution of the proceeds is completed. If requested by the secured party, the holder of a subordinate security interest must seasonably furnish reasonable proof of his interest, and unless he does so, the secured party need not comply with his demand.

(2)   If the security interest secures an indebtedness, the secured party must account to the debtor for any surplus, and, unless otherwise agreed, the debtor is liable for any deficiency. But if the underlying transaction was a sale of accounts or chattel paper, the debtor is entitled to any surplus or is liable for any deficiency only if the security agreement so provides.

(3)   Disposition of the collateral may be by public or private proceedings and may be made by way of one or more contracts. Sale or other disposition may be as a unit or in parcels and at any time and place and on any terms but every aspect of the disposition including the method, manner, time, place and terms must be commercially reasonable. Unless collateral is perishable or threatens to decline speedily in value or is of a type customarily sold on a recognized market, reasonable notification of the time and place of any public sale or reasonable notification of the time after which any private sale or other intended disposition is to be made shall be sent by the secured party to the debtor, if he has not signed after default a statement renouncing or modifying his right to notification of sale. In the case of consumer goods no other notification need be sent. In other cases notification shall be sent to any other secured party from whom the secured party has received (before sending his notification to the debtor or before the debtor's renunciation of his rights) written notice of a claim of an interest in the collateral. The secured party may buy at any public sale and if the collateral is of a type customarily sold in a recognized market or is of a type which is the subject of widely distributed standard price quotations he may buy at private sale.

(4)   When collateral is disposed of by a secured party after default, the disposition transfers to a purchaser for value all of the debtor's rights therein, discharges the security interest under which

it is made and any security interest or lien subordinate thereto. The purchaser takes free of all such rights and interests even though the secured party fails to comply with the requirements of this Part or of any judicial proceedings

(a) in the case of a public sale, if the purchaser has no knowledge of any defects in the sale and if he does not buy in collusion with the secured party, other bidders or the person conducting the sale; or

(b) in any other case, if the purchaser acts in good faith.

(5) A person who is liable to a secured party under a guaranty, indorsement, repurchase agreement or the like and who receives a transfer of collateral from the secured party or is subrogated to his rights has thereafter the rights and duties of the secured party. Such a transfer of collateral is not a sale or disposition of the collateral under this Article. Amended in 1972.

§ 9—505. Compulsory Disposition of Collateral; Acceptance of the Collateral as Discharge of Obligation.

(1) If the debtor has paid sixty per cent of the cash price in the case of a purchase money security interest in consumer goods or sixty per cent of the loan in the case of another security interest in consumer goods, and has not signed after default a statement renouncing or modifying his rights under this Part a secured party who has taken possession of collateral must dispose of it under Section 9—504 and if he fails to do so within ninety days after he takes possession the debtor at his option may recover in conversion or under Section 9—507(1) on secured party's liability.

(2) In any other case involving consumer goods or any other collateral a secured party in possession may, after default, propose to retain the collateral in satisfaction of the obligation. Written notice of such proposal shall be sent to the debtor if he has not signed after default a statement renouncing or modifying his rights under this subsection. In the case of consumer goods no other notice need be given. In other cases notice shall be sent to any other secured party from whom the secured party has received (before sending his notice to the debtor or before the debtor's renunciation of his rights) written notice of a claim of an interest in the collateral. If the secured party receives objection in writing from a person entitled to receive notification within twenty-one days after the notice was sent the secured party must dispose of the collateral under Section 9—504. In the absence of such written objection the secured party may retain the collateral in satisfaction of the debtor's obligation. Amended in 1972.

§ 9—506. Debtor's Right to Redeem Collateral

At any time before the secured party has disposed of collateral or entered into a contract for its disposition under Section 9—504 or before the obligation has been discharged under Section 9—505(2) the debtor or any other secured party may unless otherwise agreed in writing after default redeem the collateral by tendering fulfillment of all obligations secured by the collateral as well as the expenses reasonably incurred by the secured party in retaking, holding and preparing the collateral for disposition, in arranging for the sale, and to the extent provided in the agreement and not prohibited by law, his reasonable attorneys' fees and legal expenses.

§ 9–507. Secured Party's Liability for Failure to Comply With This Part.

(1)   If it is established that the secured party is not proceeding in accordance with the provisions of this Part disposition may be ordered or restrained on appropriate terms and conditions. If the disposition has occurred the debtor or any person entitled to notification or whose security interest has been made known to the secured party prior to the disposition has a right to recover from the secured party any loss caused by a failure to comply with the provisions of this Part. If the collateral is consumer goods, the debtor has a right to recover in any event an amount not less than the credit service charge plus ten per cent of the principal amount of the debt or the time price differential plus 10 per cent of the cash price.

(2)   The fact that a better price could have been obtained by a sale at a different time or in a different method from that selected by the secured party is not of itself sufficient to establish that the sale was not made in a commercially reasonable manner. If the secured party either sells the collateral in the usual manner in any recognized market therefor or if he sells at the price current in such market at the time of his sale or if he has otherwise sold in conformity with reasonable commercial practices among dealers in the type of property sold he has sold in a commercially reasonable manner. The principles stated in the two preceding sentences with respect to sales also apply as may be appropriate to other types of disposition. A disposition which has been approved in any judicial proceeding or by any bona fide creditors' committee or representative of creditors shall conclusively be deemed to be commercially reasonable, but this sentence does not indicate that any such approval must be obtained in any case nor does it indicate that any disposition not so approved is not commercially reasonable.

Appendix B

APPENDIX B

UNIFORM PARTNERSHIP ACT

(Adopted in 43 jurisdictions: Alaska, Arizona, Arkansas, California, Colorado, Connecticut, Delaware, District of Columbia, Guam, Idaho, Illinois, Indiana, Kentucky, Maryland, Massachusetts, Michigan, Minnesota, Missouri, Montana, Nebraska, Nevada, New Jersey, New Mexico, New York, North Carolina, North Dakota, Ohio, Oklahoma, Oregon, Pennsylvania, Rhode Island, South Carolina, South Dakota, Tennesee, Texas, Utah, Vermont, Virginia, Virgin Islands, Washington, West Virginia, Wisconsin, and Wyoming.)

An Act to Make Uniform the Law of Partnerships

Be it enacted, etc.,

PART I

Preliminary Provisions

Sec. 1. (Name of Act.) This act may be cited as Uniform Partnership Act.

Sec. 2. (Definition of Terms.) In this act, "Court" includes every court and judge having jurisdiction in the case.

"Business" includes every trade, occupation, or profession.

"Person" includes individuals, partnerships, corporations, and other associations.

"Bankrupt" includes bankrupt under the Federal Bankruptcy Act or insolvent under any state insolvent act.

"Conveyance" includes every assignment, lease, mortgage, or encumbrance.

"Real property" includes land and any interest or estate in land.

Sec. 3. (Interpretation of Knowledge and Notice.) (1) A person has "knowledge" of a fact within the meaning of this act not only when he has actual knowledge thereof, but also when he has knowledge of such other facts as in the circumstances shows bad faith.

(2) A person has "notice" of a fact within the meaning of this act when the person who claims the benefit of the notice.

(a) States the fact to such person, or

(b) Delivers through the mail, or by other means of communication, a written statement of the fact to such person or to a proper person at his place of business or residence.

Sec. 4. (Rules of Construction.) (1) The rule that statutes in derogation of the common law are to be strictly construed shall have no application to this act.

(2) The law of estoppel shall apply under this act.

(3) The law of agency shall apply under this act.

(4) This act shall be so interpreted and construed as to effect its general pur-

pose to make uniform the law of those states which enact it.

(5) This act shall not be construed so as to impair the obligations of any contract existing when the act goes into effect, nor to affect any action or proceedings begun or right accrued before this act takes effect.

Sec. 5. (Rules for Cases Not Provided for in this Act.) In any case not provided for in this act the rules of law and equity, including the law merchant, shall govern.

PART II

Nature of Partnership

Sec. 6. (Partnership Defined.) (1) A partnership is an association of two or more persons to carry on as co-owners a business for profit.

(2) But any association formed under any other statute of this state, or any statute adopted by authority, other than the authority of this state, is not a partnership under this Act, unless such association would have been a partnership in this state prior to the adoption of this act; but this act shall apply to limited partnerships except in so far as the statutes relating to such partnerships are inconsistent herewith.

Sec. 7. (Rules for Determining the Existence of a Partnership.) In determining whether a partnership exists, these rules shall apply:

(1) Except as provided by Section 16 persons who are not partners as to each other are not partners as to third persons.

(2) Joint tenancy, tenancy in common, tenancy by the entireties, joint property, common property, or part ownership does not of itself establish a partnership, whether such co-owners do or do not share any profits made by the use of the property.

(3) The sharing of gross returns does not of itself establish a partnership, whether or not the persons sharing them have a joint or common right or interest in any property from which the returns are derived.

(4) The receipt by a person of a share of the profits of a business is prima facie evidence that he is a partner in the business, but no such inference shall be drawn if such profits were received in payment:

(a) As a debt by installments or otherwise,

(b) As wages of an employee or rent to a landlord,

(c) As an annuity to a widow or representative of a deceased partner,

(d) As interest on a loan, though the amount of payment vary with the profits of the business.

(e) As the consideration for the sale of a good-will of a business or other property by installments or otherwise.

Sec. 8. (Partnership Property.) (1) All property originally brought into the partnership stock or subsequently acquired by purchase or otherwise, on account of the partnership, is partnership property.

(2) Unless the contrary intention appears, property acquired with partnership funds is partnership property.

(3) Any estate in real property may be acquired in the partnership name. Title so acquired can be conveyed only in the partnership name.

(4) A conveyance to a partnership in the partnership name, though without words of inheritance, passes the entire estate of the grantor unless a contrary intent appears.

PART III

Relations of Partners to Persons Dealing with the Partnership

Sec. 9. (Partner Agent of Partnership as to Partnership Business.) (1) Every partner is an agent of the partnership for the purpose of its business, and the act of every partner, including the execution in the partnership name of any instrument, for apparently carrying on in the usual way the business of the partnership of which he is a member binds the partnership, unless the partner so acting has in fact no authority to act for the partnership in the particular matter, and the person with whom he is dealing has knowledge of the fact that he has no such authority.

(2)   An act of a partner which is not apparently for the carrying on of the business of the partnership in the usual way does not bind the partnership unless authorized by the other partners.

(3)   Unless authorized by the other partners or unless they have abandoned the business, one or more but less than all the partners have no authority to:

(a)   Assign the partnership property in trust for creditors or on the assignee's promise to pay the debts of the partnership,

(b)   Dispose of the good-will of the business,

(c)   Do any other act which would make it impossible to carry on the ordinary business of a partnership.

(d)   Confess a judgment,

(e)   Submit a partnership claim or liability to arbitration or reference.

(4)   No act of a partner in contravention of a restriction on authority shall bind the partnership to persons having knowledge of the restriction.

Sec. 10. (Conveyance of Real Property of the Partnership.) (1) Where title to real property is in the partnership name, any partner may convey title to such property by a conveyance executed in the partnership name; but the partnership may recover such property unless the partner's act binds the partnership under the provisions of paragraph (1) of section 9 or unless such property has been conveyed by the grantee or a person claiming through such grantee to a holder for value without knowledge that the partner, in making the conveyance, has exceeded his authority.

(2)   Where title to real property is in the name of the partnership, a conveyance executed by a partner, in his own name, passes the equitable interest of the partnership, provided the act is one within the authority of the partner under the provisions of paragraph (1) of section 9.

(3)   Where title to real property is in the name of one or more but not all the partners, and the record does not disclose the right of the partnership, the partners in whose name the title stands may convey title to such property, but the partnership may recover such property if the partners' act does not bind the partnership under the provisions of paragraph (1) of section 9, unless the purchaser or his assignee, is a holder for value, without knowledge.

(4)   Where the title to real property is in the name of one or more or all the partners, or in a third person in trust for the partnership, a conveyance executed by a partner in the partnership name, or in his own name, passes the equitable interest of the partnership, provided the act is one within the authority of the partner under the provisions of paragraph (1) of section 9.

(5) Where the title to real property is in the names of all the partners a conveyance executed by all the partners passes all their rights in such property.

Sec. 11. (Partnership Bound by Admission of Partner.) An admission or representation made by any partner concerning partnership affairs within the scope of his authority as conferred by this act is evidence against the partnership.

Sec. 12. (Partnership Charged with Knowledge of or Notice to Partner.) Notice to any partner of any matter relating to partnership affairs, and the knowledge of the partner acting in the particular matter, acquired while a partner or then present to his mind, and the knowledge of any other partner who reasonably could and should have communicated it to the acting partner, operate as notice to or knowledge of the partnership, except in the case of a fraud on the partnership committed by or with the consent of that partner.

Sec. 13. (Partnership Bound by Partner's Wrongful Act.) Where, by any wrongful act or omission of any partner acting in the ordinary course of the business of the partnership or with the authority of his co-partners, loss or injury is caused to any person, not being a partner in the partnership, or any penalty is incurred, the partnership is liable therefor to the same extent as the partner so acting or omitting to act.

Sec. 14. (Partnership Bound by Partner's Breach of Trust.) The partnership is bound to make good the loss:

(a) Where one partner acting within the scope of his apparent authority receives money or property of a third person and misapplies it; and

(b) Where the partnership in the course of its business receives money or property of a third person and the money or property so received is misapplied by any partner while it is in the custody of the partnership.

Sec. 15. (Nature of Partner's Liability.) All partners are liable

(a) Jointly and severally for everything chargeable to the partnership under sections 13 and 14.

(b) Jointly for all other debts and obligations of the partnership; but any partner may enter into a separate obligation to perform a partnership contract.

Sec. 16. (Partner by Estoppel.) (1) When a person, by words spoken or written or by conduct, represents himself, or consents to another representing him to any one, as a partner in an existing partnership or with one or more persons not actual partners, he is liable to any such person to whom such representation has been made, who has, on the faith of such representation, given credit to the actual or apparent partnership, and if he has made such representation or consented to its being made in a public manner he is liable to such person, whether the representation has or has not been made or communicated to such person so giving credit by or with the knowledge of the apparent partner making the representation or consenting to its being made.

(a) When a partnership liability results, he is liable as though he were an actual member of the partnership.

(b) When no partnership liability results, he is liable jointly with the other persons, if any, so consenting to the contract or representation as to incur liability, otherwise separately.

(2) When a person has been thus represented to be a partner in an existing

partnership, or with one or more persons not actual partners, he is an agent of the persons consenting to such representation to bind them to the same extent and in the same manner as though he were a partner in fact, with respect to persons who rely upon the representation. Where all the members of the existing partnership consent to the representation, a partnership act or obligation results; but in all other cases it is the joint act or obligation of the person acting and the persons consenting to the representation.

Sec. 17. (Liability of Incoming Partner.) A person admitted as a partner into an existing partnership is liable for all the obligations of the partnership arising before his admission as though he had been a partner when such obligations were incurred, except that this liability shall be satisfied only out of partnership property.

PART IV

Relations of Partners to One Another

Sec. 18. (Rules Determining Rights and Duties of Partners.) The rights and duties of the partners in relation to the partnership shall be determined, subject to any agreement between them, by the following rules:

(a) Each partner shall be repaid his contributions, whether by way of capital or advances to the partnership property and share equally in the profits and surplus remaining after all liabilities, including those to partners, are satisfied; and must contribute towards the losses, whether of capital or otherwise, sustained by the partnership according to his share in the profits.

(b) The partnership must indemnify every partner in respect of payments made

and personal liabilities reasonably incurred by him in the ordinary and proper conduct of its business, or for the preservation of its business or property.

(c) A partner, who in aid of the partnership makes any payment or advance beyond the amount of capital which he agreed to contribute, shall be paid interest from the date of the payment or advance.

(d) A partner shall receive interest on the capital contributed by him only from the date when repayment should be made.

(e) All partners have equal rights in the management and conduct of the partnership business.

(f) No partner is entitled to remuneration for acting in the partnership business, except that a surviving partner is entitled to reasonable compensation for his services in winding up the partnership affairs.

(g) No person can become a member of a partnership without the consent of all the partners.

(h) Any difference arising as to ordinary matters connected with the partnership business may be decided by a majority of the partners; but no act in contravention of any agreement between the partners may be done rightfully without the consent of all the partners.

Sec. 19. (Partnership Books.) The partnership books shall be kept, subject to any agreement between the partners, at the principal place of business of the partnership, and every partner shall at all times have access to and may inspect and copy any of them.

Sec. 20. (Duty of Partners to Render Information.) Partners shall render on demand true and full information of all things affecting the partnership to any partner or the legal representative of any deceased partner or partner under legal disability.

Sec. 21. (Partner Accountable as a Fiduciary.) (1) Every partner must account to the partnership for any benefit, and hold as trustee for it any profits derived by him without the consent of the other partners from any transaction connected with the formation, conduct, or liquidation of the partnership or from any use by him of its property.

(2) This section applies also to the representatives of a deceased partner engaged in the liquidation of the affairs of the partnership as the personal representatives of the last surviving partner.

Sec. 22. (Right to an Account.) Any partner shall have the right to a formal account as to partnership affairs:

(a) If he is wrongfully excluded from the partnership business or possession of its property by his co-partners,

(b) If the right exists under the terms of any agreement,

(c) As provided by section 21,

(d) Whenever other circumstances render it just and reasonable.

Sec. 23. (Continuation of Partnership Beyond Fixed Term.) (1) When a partnership for a fixed term or particular undertaking is continued after the termination of such term or particular undertaking without any express agreement, the rights and duties of the partners remain the same as they were at such termination, so far as is consistent with a partnership at will.

(2) A continuation of the business by the partners or such of them as habitually acted therein during the term, without any settlement or liquidation of the partnership affairs, is prima facie evidence of a continuation of the partnership.

PART V

Property Rights of a Partner

Sec. 24. (Extent of Property Rights of a Partner.) The property rights of a partner are (1) his rights in specific partnership property, (2) his interest in the partnership, and (3) his right to participate in the management.

Sec. 25. (Nature of a Partner's Right in Specific Partnership Property.) (1) A partner is co-owner with his partners of specific partnership property holding as a tenant in partnership.

(2) The incidents of this tenancy are such that:

(a) A partner, subject to the provisions of this act and to any agreement between the partners, has an equal right with his partners to possess specific partnership property for partnership purposes; but he has no right to possess such property for any other purpose without the consent of his partners.

(b) A partner's right in specific partnership property is not assignable except in connection with the assignment of rights of all the partners in the same property.

(c) A partner's right in specific partnership property is not subject to attachment or execution, except on a claim against the partnership. When partnership property is attached for a partnership debt the partners, or any of them, or the representatives of a deceased partner, cannot claim any right under the homestead or exemption laws.

(d) On the death of a partner his right in specific partnership property vests in the surviving partner or partners, except where the deceased was the last surviving partner, when his right in such property vests in his legal representative. Such surviving partner or partners, or the legal representative of the last surviving partner, has no right to possess the partnership property for any but a partnership purpose.

(e) A partner's right in specific partnership property is not subject to dower, curtesy, or allowances to widows, heirs, or next of kin.

Sec. 26. (Nature of Partner's Interest in the Partnership.) A partner's interest in the partnership is his share of the profits and surplus, and the same is personal property.

Sec. 27. (Assignment of Partner's Interest.) (1) A conveyance by a partner of his interest in the partnership does not of itself dissolve the partnership, nor, as against the other partners in the absence of agreement, entitle the assignee, during the continuance of the partnership to interfere in the management or administration of the partnership business or affairs, or to require any information or account of partnership transactions, or to inspect the partnership books; but it merely entitles the assignee to receive in accordance with his contract the profits to which the assigning partner would otherwise be entitled.

(2) In case of a dissolution of the partnership, the assignee is entitled to receive his assignor's interest and may require an account from the date only of the last account agreed to by all the partners.

Sec. 28. (Partner's Interest Subject to Charging Order.) (1) On due application to a competent court by any judgment creditor of a partner, the court which entered the judgment, order, or decree, or any other court, may charge the interest of the debtor partner with payment of the unsatisfied amount of such judgment debt with interest thereon; and may then or later appoint a receiver of his share of the profits, and of any other money due or to fall due to him in respect of the partnership, and make all other orders, directions, accounts and inquiries which the debtor partner might have made, or which the circumstances of the case may require.

(2) The interest charged may be redeemed at any time before foreclosure, or in case of a sale being directed by the court may be purchased without thereby causing a dissolution:

(a) With separate property, by any one or more of the partners, or

(b) With partnership property, by any one or more of the partners with the consent of all the partners whose interests are not so charged or sold.

(3) Nothing in this act shall be held to deprive a partner of his right, if any, under the exemption laws, as regards his interest in the partnership.

PART VI

Dissolution and Winding up

Sec. 29. (Dissolution Defined.) The dissolution of a partnership is the change in the relation of the partners caused by any partner ceasing to be associated in the carrying on as distinguished from the winding up of the business.

Sec. 30. (Partnership Not Terminated by Dissolution.) On dissolution the partnership is not terminated, but continues until the winding up of partnership affairs is completed.

Sec. 31. (Causes of Dissolution.) Dissolution is caused: (1) Without violation of the agreement between the partners,

(a) By the termination of the definite term or particular undertaking specified in the agreement,

(b) By the express will of any partner when no definite term or particular undertaking is specified,

(c) By the express will of all the partners who have not assigned their interests or suffered them to be charged for their separate debts, either before or after the termination of any specified term or particular undertaking.

(d) By the expulsion of any partner from the business bona fide in accordance with such a power conferred by the agreement between the partners;

(2) In contravention of the agreement between the partners, where the circumstances do not permit a dissolution under any other provision of this section, by the express will of any partner at any time;

(3) By any event which makes it unlawful for the business of the partnership to be carried on or for the members to carry it on in partnership;

(4) By the death of any partner;

(5) By the bankruptcy of any partner or the partnership;

(6) By decree of court under section 32.

Sec. 32. (Dissolution by Decree of Court.) (1) On application by or for a partner the court shall decree a dissolution whenever:

(a) A partner has been declared a lunatic in any judicial proceeding or is shown to be of unsound mind,

(b) A partner becomes in any other way incapable of performing his part of the partnership contract,

(c) A partner has been guilty of such conduct as tends to affect prejudicially the carrying on of the business,

(d) A partner wilfully or persistently commits a breach of the partnership agreement, or otherwise so conducts himself in matters relating to the partnership business that it is not reasonably practicable to carry on the business in partnership with him,

(e) The business of the partnership can only be carried on at a loss,

(f) Other circumstances render a dissolution equitable.

(2) On the application of the purchaser of a partner's interest under sections 27 or 28:

(a) After the termination of the specified term or particular undertaking.

(b) At any time if the partnership was a partnership at will when the interest was assigned or when the charging order was issued.

Sec. 33. (General Effect of Dissolution on Authority of Partner.) Except so far as may be necessary to wind up partnership affairs or to complete transactions begun but not then finished, dissolution terminates all authority of any partner to act for the partnership,

(1) With respect to the partners,

(a) When the dissolution is not by the act, bankruptcy or death of a partner; or

(b) When the dissolution is by such act, bankruptcy or death of a partner, in cases where section 34 so requires.

(2) With respect to persons not partners, as declared in section 35.

Sec. 34. (Right of Partner to Contribution From Copartners After Dissolution.) Where the dissolution is caused by the act, death or bankruptcy of a partner, each partner is liable to his copartners for his share of any liability created by any partner acting for the partnership as if the partnership had not been dissolved unless

(a) The dissolution being by act of any partner, the partner acting for the partnership had knowledge of the dissolution, or

(b) The dissolution being by the death or bankruptcy of a partner, the partner acting for the partnership had knowledge or notice of the death or bankruptcy.

Sec. 35. (Power of Partner to Bind Partnership to Third Persons After Dissolution.) (1) After dissolution a partner can bind the partnership except as provided in Paragraph (3)

(a) By any act appropriate for winding up partnership affairs or completing transactions unfinished at dissolution;

(b) By any transaction which would bind the partnership if dissolution had not taken place, provided the other party to the transaction

(I) Had extended credit to the partnership prior to dissolution and had no knowledge or notice of the dissolution; or

(II) Though he had not so extended credit, had nevertheless known of the partnership prior to dissolution, and, having no knowledge or notice of dissolution, the fact of dissolution had not been advertised in a newspaper of general circulation in the place (or in each place if more than one) at which the partnership business was regularly carried on.

(2) The liability of a partner under paragraph (1b) shall be satisfied out of partnership assets alone when such partner had been prior to dissolution.

(a) Unknown as a partner to the person with whom the contract is made; and

(b) So far unknown and inactive in partnership affairs that the business reputation of the partnership could not be said to have been in any degree due to his connection with it.

(3) The partnership is in no case bound by any act of a partner after dissolution

(a) Where the partnership is dissolved because it is unlawful to carry on the business, unless the act is appropriate for winding up partnership affairs; or

(b) Where the partner has become bankrupt; or

(c) Where the partner has no authority to wind up partnership affairs; except by a transaction with one who

(I) Had extended credit to the partnership prior to dissolution and had no knowledge or notice of his want of authority; or

(II) Had not extended credit to the partnership prior to dissolution, and, having no knowledge or notice of his want of authority, the fact of his want of authority has not been advertised in the manner provided for advertising the fact of dissolution in paragraph (1bII).

(4) Nothing in this section shall affect the liability under section 16 of any person who after dissolution represents himself or consents to another representing him as a partner in a partnership engaged in carrying on business.

Sec. 36. (Effect of Dissolution on Partner's Existing Liability.) (1) The dissolution of the partnership does not of itself discharge the existing liability of any partner.

(2) A partner is discharged from any existing liability upon dissolution of the partnership by an agreement to that effect between himself, the partnership creditor and the person or partnership continuing the business; and such agreement may be inferred from the course of dealing be-

tween the creditor having knowledge of the dissolution and the person or partnership continuing the business.

(3) Where a person agrees to assume the existing obligations of a dissolved partnership, the partners whose obligations have been assumed shall be discharged from any liability to any creditor of the partnership who, knowing of the agreement, consents to a material alteration in the nature or time of payment of such obligations.

(4) The individual property of a deceased partner shall be liable for all obligations of the partnership incurred while he was a partner but subject to the prior payment of his separate debts.

Sec. 37. (Right to Wind Up.) Unless otherwise agreed the partners who have not wrongfully dissolved the partnership or the legal representative of the last surviving partner, not bankrupt, has the right to wind up the partnership affairs; provided, however, that any partner, his legal representative or his assignee, upon cause shown, may obtain winding up by the court.

Sec. 38. (Rights of Partners to Application of Partnership Property.) (1) When dissolution is caused in any way, except in contravention of the partnership agreement, each partner as against his copartners and all persons claiming through them in respect of their interests in the partnership, unless otherwise agreed, may have the partnership property applied to discharge its liabilities, and the surplus applied to pay in cash the net amount owing to the respective partners. But if dissolution is caused by expulsion of a partner, bona fide under the partnership agreement and if the expelled partner is discharged from all partnership liabilities,

either by payment or agreement under section 36(2), he shall receive in cash only the net amount due him from the partnership.

(2) When dissolution is caused in contravention of the partnership agreement the rights of the partners shall be as follows:

(a) Each partner who has not caused dissolution wrongfully shall have,

(I) All the rights specified in paragraph (1) of this section, and

(II) The right, as against each partner who has caused the dissolution wrongfully, to damages for breach of the agreement.

(b) The partners who have not caused the dissolution wrongfully, if they all desire to continue the business in the same name, either by themselves or jointly with others, may do so, during the agreed term for the partnership and for that purpose may possess the partnership property, provided they secure the payment by bond approved by the court, or pay to any partner who has caused the dissolution wrongfully, the value of his interest in the partnership at the dissolution, less any damages recoverable under clause (2aII) of the section, and in like manner indemnify him against all present or future partnership liabilities.

(c) A partner who has caused the dissolution wrongfully shall have:

(I) If the business is not continued under the provisions of paragraph (2b) all the rights of a partner under paragraph (1), subject to clause (2aII), of this section,

(II) If the business is continued under paragraph (2b) of this section the right as against his co-partners and all claiming through them in respect of their interests in the partnership, to have the value of his interest in the partnership, less any damages caused to his co-partners by the dissolution, ascertained and paid to him in cash, or the payment secured by bond approved by the court, and to be released from all existing liabilities of the partnership; but in ascertaining the value of the partner's interest the value of the goodwill of the business shall not be considered.

Sec. 39. (Rights Where Partnership is Dissolved for Fraud or Misrepresentation.) Where a partnership contract is rescinded on the ground of the fraud or misrepresentation of one of the parties thereto, the party entitled to rescind is, without prejudice to any other right, entitled,

(a) To a lien on, or right of retention of, the surplus of the partnership property after satisfying the partnership liabilities to third persons for any sum of money paid by him for the purchase of an interest in the partnership and for any capital or advances contributed by him; and

(b) To stand, after all liabilities to third persons have been satisfied, in the place of the creditors of the partnership for any payments made by him in respect of the partnership liabilities; and

(c) To be indemnified by the person guilty of the fraud or making the representation against all debts and liabilities of the partnership.

Sec. 40. (Rules for Distribution.) In settling accounts between the partners after dissolution, the following rules shall be observed, subject to any agreement to the contrary:

(a) The assets of the partnership are;

(I) The partnership property,

(II) The contributions of the partners necessary for the payment of all the liabilities specified in clause (b) of this paragraph.

(b) The liabilities of the partnership shall rank in order of payment, as follows:

(I) Those owing to creditors other than partners,

(II) Those owing to partners other than for capital and profits,

(III) Those owing to partners in respect of capital,

(IV) Those owing to partners in respect of profits.

(c) The assets shall be applied in the order of their declaration in clause (a) of this paragraph to the satisfaction of the liabilities.

(d) The partners shall contribute, as provided by section 18(a) the amount necessary to satisfy the liabilities; but if any, but not all, of the partners are insolvent, or, not being subject to process, refuse to contribute, the other parties shall contribute their share of the liabilities, and, in the relative proportions in which they share the profits, the additional amount necessary to pay the liabilities.

(e) An assignee for the benefit of creditors or any person appointed by the court shall have the right to enforce the contributions specified in clause (d) of this paragraph.

(f) Any partner or his legal representative shall have the right to enforce the contributions specified in clause (d) of this paragraph, to the extent of the amount which he has paid in excess of his share of the liability.

(g) The individual property of a deceased partner shall be liable for the contributions specified in clause (d) of this paragraph.

(h) When partnership property and the individual properties of the partners are in possession of a court for distribution, partnership creditors shall have priority on partnership property and separate creditors on individual property, saving the rights of lien or secured creditors as heretofore.

(i) Where a partner has become bankrupt or his estate is insolvent the claims against his separate property shall rank in the following order:

(I) Those owing to separate creditors,

(II) Those owing to partnership creditors,

(III) Those owing to partners by way of contribution.

Sec. 41. (Liability of Persons Continuing the Business in Certain Cases.) (1) When any new partner is admitted into an existing partnership, or when any partner retires and assigns (or the representative of the deceased partner assigns) his rights in partnership property to two or more of the partners, or to one or more of the partners and one or more third persons, if the business is continued without liquidation of the partnership affairs, creditors of the first or dissolved partnership are also creditors of the partnership so continuing the business.

(2) When all but one partner retire and assign (or the representative of a deceased partner assigns) their rights in partnership property to the remaining partner, who continues the business without liquidation of partnership affairs, either alone or with others, creditors of the dissolved partnership are also creditors of the person or partnership so continuing the business.

(3) When any partner retires or dies and the business of the dissolved partnership is continued as set forth in paragraphs (1) and (2) of this section, with the consent of the retired partners or the representative of the deceased partner, but without any assignment of his right in partnership property, rights of creditors of the dissolved partnership and of the creditors of the person or partnership continuing the business shall be as if such assignment had been made.

(4) When all the partners or their representatives assign their rights in partnership property to one or more third persons who promise to pay the debts and who continue the business of the dissolved partnership, creditors of the dissolved partnership are also creditors of the person or partnership continuing the business.

(5) When any partner wrongfully causes a dissolution and the remaining partners continue the business under the provisions of section 38(2b), either alone or with others, and without liquidation of the partnership affairs, creditors of the dissolved partnership are also creditors of the person or partnership continuing the business.

(6) When a partner is expelled and the remaining partners continue the business either alone or with others, without liquidation of the partnership affairs, creditors of the dissolved partnership are also creditors of the person or partnership continuing the business.

(7) The liability of a third person becoming a partner in the partnership continuing the business, under this section, to the creditors of the dissolved partnership shall be satisfied out of partnership property only.

(8) When the business of a partnership after dissolution is continued under any conditions set forth in this section the creditors of the dissolved partnership, as against the separate creditors of the retiring or deceased partner or the representative of the deceased partner, have a prior right to any claim of the retired partner or the representative of the de-

ceased partner against the person or partnership continuing the business, on account of the retired or deceased partner's interest in the dissolved partnership or on account of any consideration promised for such interest or for his right in partnership property.

(9) Nothing in this section shall be held to modify any right of creditors to set aside any assignment on the ground of fraud.

(10) The use by the person or partnership continuing the business of the partnership name, or the name of a deceased partner as part thereof, shall not of itself make the individual property of the deceased partner liable for any debts contracted by such person or partnership.

Sec. 42. (Rights of Retiring or Estate of Deceased Partner When the Business is Continued.) When any partner retires or dies, and the business is continued under any of the conditions set forth in section 41 (1, 2, 3, 5, 6), or section 38(2b), without any settlement of accounts as between him or his estate and the person or partnership continuing the business, unless otherwise agreed, he or his legal representative as against such persons or partnership may have the value of his interest at the date of dissolution ascertained, and shall receive as an ordinary creditor an amount equal to the value of his interest in the dissolved partnership with interest, or, at his option or at the option of his legal representative, in lieu of interest, the profits attributable to the use of his right in the property of the dissolved partnership; provided that the creditors of the dissolved partnership as against the separate creditors, or the representative of the retired or deceased partner, shall have priority on any claim arising under this section, as provided by section 41(8) of this act.

Sec. 43. (Accrual of Actions.) The right to an account of his interest shall accrue to any partner, or his legal representative, as against the winding up partners or the surviving partners or the person or partnership continuing the business, at the date of dissolution, in the absence of any agreement to the contrary.

PART VII

Miscellaneous Provisions

Sec. 44. (When Act Takes Effect.) This act shall take effect on the _____ day of _____ one thousand nine hundred and _____ .

Sec. 45. (Legislation Repealed.) All acts or parts of acts inconsistent with this act are hereby repealed.

Appendix C

APPENDIX C

UNIFORM LIMITED PARTNERSHIP ACT

(Adopted in 47 jurisdictions: Alaska, Arizona, Arkansas, California, Colorado, Connecticut, District of Columbia, Florida, Georgia, Hawaii, Idaho, Illinois, Indiana, Iowa, Kansas, Maine, Maryland, Massachusetts, Michigan, Minnesota, Mississippi, Missouri, Montana, Nebraska, Nevada, New Hampshire, New Jersey, New Mexico, New York, North Carolina, North Dakota, Ohio, Oklahoma, Oregon, Pennsylvania, Rhode Island, South Carolina, South Dakota, Tennessee, Texas, Utah, Vermont, Virginia, Virgin Islands, Washington, West Virginia, Wisconsin.)

An Act to Make Uniform the Law Relating to Limited Partnerships

Be it enacted, etc., as follows:

Sec. 1. (Limited Partnership Defined.) A limited partnership is a partnership formed by two or more persons under the provisions of Section 2, having as members one or more general partners and one or more limited partners. The limited partners as such shall not be bound by the obligations of the partnership.

Sec. 2. (Formation.) (1) Two or more persons desiring to form a limited partnership shall

(a) Sign and swear to a certificate, which shall state

I. The name of the partnership,

II. The character of the business,

III. The location of the principal place of business,

IV. The name and place of residence of each member; general and limited partners being respectively designated.

V. The term for which the partnership is to exist,

VI. The amount of cash and a description of and the agreed value of the other property contributed by each limited partner,

VII. The additional contributions, if any, agreed to be made by each limited partner and the times at which or events on the happening of which they shall be made.

VIII. The time, if agreed upon, when the contribution of each limited partner is to be returned.

IX. The share of the profits or the other compensation by way of income which each limited partner shall receive by reason of his contribution,

X. The right, if given, of a limited partner to substitute an assignee as contributor in his place, and the terms and conditions of the substitution,

XI. The right, if given, of the partners to admit additional limited partners,

XII. The right, if given, of one or more of the limited partners to priority over other limited partners, as to contributions or as to compensation by way of income, and the nature of such priority,

XIII. The right, if given of the remaining general partner or partners to continue the business on the death, retirement or insanity of a general partner, and

XIV. The right, if given, of a limited partner to demand and receive property other than cash in return for his contribution.

(b)   File for record the certificate in the office of [here designate the proper office].

(2)   A limited partnership is formed if there has been substantial compliance in good faith with the requirements of paragraph (1).

Sec. 3. (Business Which may be Carried On.)   A limited partnership may carry on any business which a partnership without limited partners may carry on, except [here designate the business to be prohibited].

Sec. 4.   (Character of Limited Partner's Contribution.) The contributions of a limited partner may be cash or other property, but not services.

Sec. 5.   (A Name Not to Contain Surname of Limited Partner; Exceptions.) (1) The surname of a limited partner shall not appear in the partnership name, unless

(a)   It is also the surname of a general partner, or

(b)   Prior to the time when the limited partner became such the business had been carried on under a name in which his surname appeared.

(2)   A limited partner whose name appears in a partnership name contrary to the provisions of paragraph (1) is liable as

a general partner to partnership creditors who extend credit to the partnership without actual knowledge that he is not a general partner.

Sec. 6. (Liability for False Statements in Certificate.) If the certificate contains a false statement, one who suffers loss by reliance on such statement may hold liable any party to the certificate who knew the statement to be false.

(a)   At the time he signed the certificate, or

(b)   Subsequently, but within a sufficient time before the statement was relied upon to enable him to cancel or amend the certificate, or to file a petition for its cancellation or amendment as provided in Section 25(3).

Sec. 7. (Limited Partner Not Liable to Creditors.) A limited partner shall not become liable as a general partner unless, in addition to the exercise of his rights and powers as a limited partner, he takes part in the control of the business.

Sec. 8. (Admission of Additional Limited Partners.)   After the formation of a limited partnership, additional limited partners may be admitted upon filing an amendment to the original certificate in accordance with the requirements of Section 25.

Sec. 9. (Rights, Powers and Liabilities of a General Partner.) (1) A general partner shall have all the rights and powers and be subject to all the restrictions and liabilities of a partner in a partnership without limited partners, except that without the written consent or ratification of the specific act by all the limited partners, a general partner or all of the general partners have no authority to

(a)   Do any act in contravention of the certificate,

(b)   Do any act which would make it impossible to carry on the ordinary business of the partnership,

(c)   Confess a judgment against the partnership,

(d)   Possess partnership property, or assign their rights in specific partnership property, for other than a partnership purpose,

(e)   Admit a person as a general partner,

(f)   Admit a person as a limited partner, unless the right so to do is given in the certificate,

(g)   Continue the business with partnership property on the death, retirement or insanity of a general partner, unless the right so to do is given in the certificate.

Sec. 10. (Rights of a Limited Partner.) (1) A limited partner shall have the same rights as a general partner to

(a)   Have the partnership books kept at the principal place of business of the partnership, and at all times to inspect and copy any of them,

(b)   Have on demand true and full information of all things affecting the partnership, and a formal account of partnership affairs, whenever circumstances render it just and reasonable, and

(c)   Have dissolution and winding up by decree of court.

(2)   A limited partner shall have the right to receive a share of the profits or other compensation by way of income, and to the return of his contribution as provided in Sections 15 and 16.

Sec. 11. (Status of Person Erroneously Believing Himself a Limited Partner.) A person who has contributed to the capital of a business conducted by a person or partnership erroneously believing that he has become a limited partner in a limited partnership, is not, by reason of his exercise of the rights of a limited partner, a general partner with the person or in the partnership carrying on the business, or bound by the obligations of such person or partnership; provided that on ascertaining the mistake he promptly renounces his interest in the profits of the business, or other compensation by way of income.

Sec. 12. (One Person Both General and Limited Partner.) (1) A person may be a general partner and a limited partner in the same partnership at the same time.

(2)   A person who is a general, and also at the same time a limited partner, shall have all the rights and powers and be subject to all the restrictions of a general partner; except that, in respect to his contribution, he shall have the rights against the other members which he would have had if he were not also a general partner.

Sec. 13. (Loans and Other Business Transactions with Limited Partner.) (1) A limited partner also may loan money to and transact other business with the partnership, and, unless he is also a general partner, receive on account of resulting claims against the partnership, with general creditors, a pro rata share of the assets. No limited partner shall in respect to any such claim

(a)   Receive or hold as collateral security any partnership property, or

(b)   Receive from a general partner or the partnership any payment, conveyance, or release from liability, if at the time the assets of the partnership are not sufficient to discharge partnership liabilities to persons not claiming as general or limited partners,

(2)   The receiving of collateral security, or a payment, conveyance, or re-

lease in violation of the provisions of paragraph (1) is a fraud on the creditors of the partnership.

Sec. 14. (Relation of Limited Partners Inter Se.) Where there are several limited partners the members may agree that one or more of the limited partners shall have a priority over other limited partners as to the return of their contributions, as to their compensation by way of income, or as to any other matter. If such an agreement is made it shall be stated in the certificate, and in the absence of such a statement all the limited partners shall stand upon equal footing.

Sec. 15. (Compensation of Limited Partner.) A limited partner may receive from the partnership the share of the profits or the compensation by way of income stipulated for in the certificate; provided, that after such payment is made, whether from the property of the partnership or that of a general partner, the partnership assets are in excess of all liabilities of the partnership except liabilities to limited partners on account of their contributions and to general partners.

Sec. 16. (Withdrawal or Reduction of Limited Partner's Contribution.) (1) A limited partner shall not receive from a general partner or out of partnership property any part of his contribution until

(a) All liabilities of the partnership, except liabilities to general partners and to limited partners on account of their contributions, have been paid or there remains property of the partnership sufficient to pay them,

(b) The consent of all members is had, unless the return of the contribution may be rightfully demanded under the provisions of paragraph (2), and

(c) The certificate is cancelled or so amended as to set forth the withdrawal or reduction.

(2) Subject to the provisions of paragraph (1) a limited partner may rightfully demand the return of his contribution

(a) On the dissolution of a partnership, or

(b) When the date specified in the certificate for its return has arrived, or

(c) After he has given six months' notice in writing to all other members, if no time is specified in the certificate either for the return of the contribution or for the dissolution of the partnership,

(3) In the absence of any statement in the certificate to the contrary or the consent of all members, a limited partner, irrespective of the nature of his contribution, has only the right to demand and receive cash in return for his contribution.

(4) A limited partner may have the partnership dissolved and its affairs wound up when

(a) He rightfully but unsuccessfully demands the return of his contribution, or

(b) The other liabilities of the partnership have not been paid, or the partnership property is insufficient for their payment as required by paragraph (1a) and the limited partner would otherwise be entitled to the return of his contribution.

Sec. 17. (Liability of Limited Partner to Partnership.) (1) A limited partner is liable to the partnership

(a) For the difference between his contribution as actually made and that stated in the certificate as having been made, and

(b) For any unpaid contribution which he agreed in the certificate to make in the future at the time and on the conditions stated in the certificate.

(2)   A limited partner holds as trustee for the partnership

(a)   Specific property stated in the certificate as contributed by him, but which was not contributed or which has been wrongfully returned, and

(b)   Money or other property wrongfully paid or conveyed to him on account of his contribution.

(3)   The liabilities of a limited partner as set forth in this section can be waived or compromised only by the consent of all members; but a waiver or compromise shall not affect the right of a creditor of a partnership, who extended credit or whose claim arose after the filing and before a cancellation or amendment of the certificate, to enforce such liabilities.

(4)   When a contributor has rightfully received the return in whole or in part of the capital of his contribution, he is nevertheless liable to the partnership for any sum, not in excess of such return with interest, necessary to discharge its liabilities to all creditors who extended credit or whose claims arose before such return.

Sec. 18.   (Nature of Limited Partner's Interest in Partnership.)   A limited partner's interest in the partnership is personal property.

Sec. 19.   (Assignment of Limited Partner's Interest.)   (1) A limited partner's interest is assignable.

(2)   A substituted limited partner is a person admitted to all the rights of a limited partner who has died or has assigned his interest in a partnership.

(3)   An assignee, who does not become a substituted limited partner, has no right to require any information or account of the partnership transactions or to inspect the partnership books; he is only entitled to receive the share of the profits or other compensation by way of income, or the return of his contribution, to which his assignor would otherwise be entitled.

(4)   An assignee shall have the right to become a substituted limited partner if all the members (except the assignor) consent thereto or if the assignor, being thereunto empowered by the certificate, gives the assignee that right.

(5)   An assignee becomes a substituted limited partner when the certificate is appropriately amended in accordance with Section 25.

(6)   The substituted limited partner has all the rights and powers, and is subject to all the restrictions and liabilities of his assignor, except those liabilities of which he was ignorant at the time he became a limited partner and which could not be ascertained from the certificate.

(7)   The substitution of the assignee as a limited partner does not release the assignor from liability to the partnership under Sections 6 and 17.

Sec. 20.   (Effect of Retirement, Death or Insanity of a General Partner.)   The retirement, death or insanity of a general partner dissolves the partnership, unless the business is continued by the remaining general partners

(a)   Under a right so to do stated in the certificate, or

(b)   With the consent of all members.

Sec. 21.   (Death of Limited Partner.) (1) On the death of a limited partner his executor or administrator shall have all the rights of a limited partner for the purpose of settling his estate, and such power as the deceased had to constitute his assignee a substituted limited partner.

(2)   The estate of a deceased limited partner shall be liable for all his liabilities as a limited partner.

Sec. 22.   (Rights of Creditors of Limited Partner.) (1) On due application to a court of competent jurisdiction by any judgment creditor of a limited partner, the court may charge the interest of the indebted limited partner with payment of the unsatisfied amount of the judgment debt; and may appoint a receiver, and make all other orders, directions, and inquiries which the circumstances of the case may require.

In those states where a creditor on beginning an action can attach debts due the defendant before he has obtained a judgment against the defendant it is recommended that paragraph (1) of this section read as follows:

On due application to a court of competent jurisdiction by any creditor of a limited partner, the court may charge the interest of the indebted limited partner with payment of the unsatisfied amount of such claim; and may appoint a receiver, and make all other orders, directions, and inquiries which the circumstances of the case may require.

(2)   The interest may be redeemed with the separate property of any general partner, but may not be redeemed with partnership property.

(3)   The remedies conferred by paragraph (1) shall not be deemed exclusive of others which may exist.

(4)   Nothing in this act shall be held to deprive a limited partner of his statutory exemption.

Sec. 23.   (Distribution of Assets.) (1) In Settling accounts after dissolution the liabilities of the partnership shall be entitled to payment in the following order:

(a)   Those to creditors, in the order of priority as provided by law, except those to limited partners on account of their contributions, and to general partners,

(b)   Those to limited partners in respect to their share of the profits and other compensation by way of income on their contributions,

(c)   Those to limited partners in respect to the capital of their contributions,

(d)   Those to general partners other than for capital and profits,

(e)   Those to general partners in respect to profits,

(f)   Those to general partners in respect to capital.

(2)   Subject to any statement in the certificate or to subsequent agreement, limited partners share in the partnership assets in respect to their claims for capital, and in respect to their claims for profits or for compensation by way of income on their contributions respectively, in proportion to the respective amounts of such claims.

Sec. 24.   (When Certificate Shall be Cancelled or Amended.) (1) The certificate shall be cancelled when the partnership is dissolved or all limited partners cease to be such.

(2)   A certificate shall be amended when

(a)   There is a change in the name of the partnership or in the amount or character of the contribution of any limited partner,

(b)   A person is substituted as a limited partner,

(c)   An additional limited partner is admitted,

(d)   A person is admitted as a general partner,

(e) A general partner retires, dies or becomes insane, and the business is continued under section 20.

(f) There is a change in the character of the business of the partnership,

(g) There is a false or erroneous statement in the certificate,

(h) There is a change in the time as stated in the certificate for the dissolution of the partnership or for the return of a contribution,

(i) A time is fixed for the dissolution of the partnership, or the return of a contribution, no time having been specified in the certificate, or

(j) The members desire to make a change in any other statement in the certificate in order that it shall accurately represent the agreement between them.

Sec. 25. (Requirements for Amendment and for Cancellation of Certificate.) (1) The writing to amend a certificate shall

(a) Conform to the requirements of Section 2(1a) as far as necessary to set forth clearly the change in the certificate which it is desired to make, and

(b) Be signed and sworn to by all members, and an amendment substituting a limited partner or adding a limited or general partner shall be signed also by the member to be substituted or added, and when a limited partner is to be substituted, the amendment shall also be signed by the assigning limited partner.

(2) The writing to cancel a certificate shall be signed by all members.

(3) A person desiring the cancellation or amendment of a certificate, if any person designated in paragraphs (1) and (2) as a person who must execute the writing refuses to do so, may petition the [here designate the proper court] to direct a cancellation or amendment thereof.

(4) If the court finds that the petitioner has a right to have the writing executed by a person who refuses to do so, it shall order the [here designate the responsible official in the office designated in Section 2] in the office where the certificate is recorded to record the cancellation or amendment of the certificate; and where the certificate is to be amended, the court shall also cause to be filed for record in said office a certified copy of its decree setting forth the amendment.

(5) A certificate is amended or cancelled when there is filed for record in the office [here designate the office designated in Section 2] where the certificate is recorded

(a) A writing in accordance with the provisions of paragraph (1), or (2) or

(b) A certified copy of the order of court in accordance with the provisions of paragraph (4).

(6) After the certificate is duly amended in accordance with this section, the amended certificate shall thereafter be for all purposes the certificate provided for by this act.

Sec. 26. (Parties to Actions.) A contributor, unless he is a general partner, is not a proper party to proceedings by or against a partnership, except where the object is to enforce a limited partner's right against or liability to the partnership.

Sec. 27. (Name of Act.) This act may be cited as The Uniform Limited Partnership Act.

Sec. 28. (Rules of Construction.) (1) The rule that statutes in derogation of the common law are to be strictly construed shall have no application to this act.

(2) This act shall be so interpreted and construed as to effect its general

purpose to make uniform the law of those states which enact it.

(3)   This act shall not be so construed as to impair the obligations of any contract existing when the act goes into effect, nor to affect any action on proceedings begun or right accrued before this act takes effect.

Sec. 29.   (Rules for Cases Not Provided for in this Act.)   In any case not provided for in this act the rules of law and equity, including the law merchant, shall govern.

Sec. 30.[1]   (Provisions for Existing Limited Partnerships.) (1) A limited partnership formed under any statute of this state prior to the adoption of this act, may become a limited partnership under this act by complying with the provisions of Section 2; provided the certificate sets forth

(a)   The amount of the original contribution of each limited partner, and the time when the contribution was made, and

(b)   That the property of the partnership exceeds the amount sufficient to discharge its liabilities to persons not claiming as general or limited partners by an amount greater than the sum of the contributions of its limited partners.

(2)   A limited partnership formed under any statute of this state prior to the adoption of this act, until or unless it becomes a limited partnership under this act, shall continue to be governed by the provisions of [here insert proper reference to the existing limited partnership act or acts], except that such partnership shall not be renewed unless so provided in the original agreement.

Sec. 31.[1]   (Act [Acts] Repealed.) Except as affecting existing limited partnerships to the extent set forth in Section 30, the act (acts) of [here designate the existing limited partnership act or acts] is (are) hereby repealed.

---

[1] Sections 30, 31, will be omitted in any state which has not a limited partnership act.

Acknowledgments

Technical Reviewers: S. Richard Levin and Terence E. Shanley

Consulting Editor,
  Midmanagement/Marketing Series: Gary R. Schornack

The staff at Delmar Publishers
Director of Publications: Alan N. Knofla
Divisional Editor: William N. Sprague
Supervising Editor,
  Midmanagement/Marketing Series: Mary R. Grauerholz
Editoral Assistant: Mary L. Wright
Copy Editors: Angela LaGatta, Judith Cerminaro
Photo Editor: Sherry Patnode
Director of Manufacturing and Production: Frederick Sharer
Illustrators: Anthony Canabush, Georgy Dowse, Tanya Little, John Orozco
Production Specialists: Jean LeMorta, Debbie Monty, Sharon Lynch, Betty Michelfelder, Margaret Mutka, Lee St. Onge

A substantial part of the material in BUSINESS LAW: A PRACTICAL APPROACH was classroom tested at Syracuse University, Syracuse, New York.

Contributions of Content and Illustration:

Julius Blumberg, Incorporated, figures 2-4A and B, 11-1, 11-2, 11-3, and 11-5

Corpex Banknote Company, figures 15-3 and 15-5.

Mutual of Omaha Insurance Company (Terry Calek), figure 3-2.

General Motors Corporation (Dale Ann Cooper), figure 15-2.

The Union-Sun Journal, Lockport, New York, photograph of courtroom scene, Chapter 2.

Index

A

Abstract of title, 194
Acceptance and rejection, in contract of sale, 105
Acceptance of offer
by corespondence, 65-66
by performance, 65
by words or actions, 64
Acceptance of sale, on approval, 103
Act for the Prevention of Frauds and Perjuries, 44
Act of God, 162
Act of public authority, 163
Act of public enemy, 163
Acts of Congress. *See* Federal statutes
Administration Regulations
agencies of, 10-11
definition of, 10
division of public law, 32
example, 11
Adverse possession, 186
Advertisements
for bids, 59-60
as invitation, 57
Lefkowitz v. Great Minneapolis Surplus Store, Inc., 57-59
for rewards, 57, 61
Age of majority, 68-69
Agency
creation of, 257-260
definition of, 252-253
express, 258-259
implied, 259-260
of necessity, 259
by ratification, 262-263
Agency, termination of
agreement, 271-272
by law, 272-273
renouncement by agent, 272
revocation by principal, 272
Agency law, historical development of, 254
Agents
in agency relationship, 253-254
authority of, 260-267
duties of, 268
minor, 257
qualifications of, 257-258
torts and crimes of, 267
unauthorized action of, 262
Agents, types of
employees, 254-255

general, 255
professional, 256
special, 255-256
Agreement
in contract termination, 87
definition of, 31
legal, categories of, 33
Alteration
as cause of termination, 87
material, 350-351
American Bar Association, 2, 19, 297
American law
administrative, 10-11
business, 13
categories of, 4
civil, 11
common, 4-7
constitutional, 7-8
criminal, 12
statutory, 9-10
subdivisions of, 12
Answer, legal definition of, 28
Appeal process, 23
Appellate courts, 18-19
Arrest, false. *See* Imprisonment, false
Assault and battery, 230-231
Assets
definition of, 80
distribution of, in partnerships, 288
liquidation, 285
Assignable contracts, 79-80
Assignee
definition of, 78
liability of, 213-214
rights of, 80
Assignment
of contracts, 78-80
imposed by law, 80
of lease, 213
Assignor, 78
Auctions, 60
Authority
apparent, 261-262
case example, 264-267
express, 260
implied, 260-261
incidental, 260-261
scope of, 260

B

Bailee
definition of, 147
extraordinary, 162, 164-165

Bailments, 96, 147, 148, 149
Bailments, contract
  case example, 155-160
  for hire, 153
  for hiring of custody, 154-155
  pledge of pawn, 152-153
  for service or repair, 153-154
Bailments, elements of, 147-148
  extraordinary, 149
Bailments, gratuitous
  benefit of bailee, 151-152
  benefit of bailor, 149-151
  termination of, 152
Bailments, mutual benefit, 152-161
Bailments, sole benefit of bailee, 151-152
Bailments, special
  fungible goods, 161
  hotel owners and innkeepers, 165-167
  transporation of merchandise, 161-164
  transportation of passengers, 164-165
Bailor, 147
Balfour v. Balfour, 52-56
Bankruptcy, 80, 273
Bates v Dresser, 316
Battery. *See* Assault and battery
Bearer paper, 338, 342
Bid, definition of, 59
Bidding, 59-60
Bilateral contract, 39
Bill of exchange, 331
Bill of sale, 47
Black Beret Lounge and Restaurant v. Meisnere,
  148
Bonds, definition of, 304
Breach
  case example, 89-91
  definition of, 88
  of duty, 227-228
  of fiduciary duty, 269
  of lease, 216
Breach, remedies for
  damages, 88-89
  injunction, 91-92
  specific performance, 89-91
Breach of contract
  buyer's remedies, 107-109
  in contract of sale, 105
  seller's remedies, 105-107
Breach of peace, 119
Brokers
  commission, 191
  role of, 191
  and stock transfer, 305
Bulk transfer, 104
Business
  definition of, 251
  types of organization, 251-252
Business law, scope of, 13. *See also* Law

Bylaws, of corporation, 299

C

Canons of Judicial Ethics, 19
Capital stock, 301
Carlill v. Carbolic Smoke Ball Co., 35-39, 57
Carriers
  baggage responsibilities of, 165
  common, 161-162
  liability of, 162
  private, 161
  regulation of, 162
Case, legal, definition of, 1
Case law. *See* Common law
Case title, 25
Cause, proximate, 228-229
Caveat emptor, 123-124, 142
Certainty of terms, definition of, 60
Certificate of deposit, 333
Chapin's Estate v Long, 287
Charge accounts, as unsecured credit, 112
Charitable subscriptions, 68
Charter. *See* Incorporation, certificate of
Checks, 330, 332, 338
Circuits, of Federal Court System, 20
Civil law, 11-12
Civil wrong, *See* Torts
Client, definition of, 1
Closing statement, 201-204
Collateral
  definition of, 113
  disposing of, 120-121
  identification of, 116
  kinds of, 113
  redemption of, 120-121
  sale of, 116
Commercial paper
  alteration of, 350-351
  basic benefit of, 340
  cancellation of, 350
  correct methods of writing, 339
  and credit, 327
  dishonored, 344
  incorrect methods of writing, 339-340
  negotiability of, 330
  overdue, 344
  payment of, 350
  requirements of, 334-338
  transfer of, 331, 340
  types of, 331-334
Commission
  for brokers, 191
  for professional agents, 256
Common law, 4-7, 225
Communication
  between agent and principal, 270
  as necessary part of offer, 60
Compensation, 181
  of agent, 270

Competent parties, 68-70
Competition, illegal, 243
Complaint, 25
Concurrent jurisdiction, 21
Condominium, as ownership form, 184
Conforming goods, 107
Consideration
  adequacy of, 66-67
  of charitable subscriptions, 68
  definition of, 66
  kinds of, 66
  and past performance, 67
  and pre-existing obligation, 67
Consolidation, of corporations, 320
Constitutional law, 7-8
Construction ordinances, 10
Consumer, and business law, 95
Consumer education, 140
Consumer Product Safety Commission, 140
Consumer protection laws
  federal, 140-142
  state and local, 139-140
Contract law, 32
Contractor
  independent, 256-257
  third parties and, 256
Contracts
  assignment of, 78-80, 331
  bilateral, 39
  breaking statutory laws, 70
  in consideration of marriage, 47
  definition of, 32
  delegated, 79
  enforceable, 151
  executed and executory, 43
  express, 39-41
  formal, 34
  in gratuitous bailment, 149
  harmful to public welfare, 71-72
  implied, 41
  long-term, 45
  made by promoter, 297
  oral, 44-45, 99-102
  partnerships, 278, 284
  to pay debts of another, 46
  promises of executors, 46
  ratification of by minors, 69
  of sale, 97-98, 104-105
  sale of a specified value, 47-48
  for sale or lease of real property, 46
  to sell, 97-98
  simple, 34-44
  with time limitations, 49
  types, 97, 101
  unassignable, 78-79
  under seal, 34
  unenforceable, 43
  unilateral, 35

  usurious, 71
  valid, 42
  violations not covered by, 224
  void, 42, 68, 71-72
  written, 44-45, 98-99, 101
Contracts, binding, elements of, 51
Contracts, termination of, 80-92
  by agreement, 87
  by alteration, 87
  by breach, 88
  by destruction of subject matter, 86
  by impossibility of performance, 85-86
  by performance, 80-85
  by statute of limitations, 88
  by waiver, 87-88
Conversion, 233-234
Copyright
  definition of, 244
  duration of, 244-246
  request to print, 245
  violation of, 243
Corporation
  avoiding disadvantages of, 321
  characteristics, 295
  compared with partnerships, 321
  consolidation of, 320
  creation of, 296-297
  definition of, 252
  dissolution of, 320-321
  distinguishing features of, 321
  financing of, 300-304
  historical development of, 295
  insolvency in, 320
  management of, 311-320
  merger of, 320
  powers of, 299-300
  termination of, 320-321
  types of, 295-296
  voting power in, 303-304
Correspondence, 65-66
Counteroffers, 64
Court, circuits, 19, 20
Court of appeal. *See* Appellate courts
Court of Claims, 19
Court of Customs, 19
Court of Patent Appeals, 19
Courts, 15
  appellate, 18-19
  district, 21-22
  federal, 19-21
  inferior, 24
  justice of the peace, 24
  municipal, 24
  procedure, 24-29
  for special purposes, 19
  state, 23-24
  system, 19-24
  trial, 18, 21

Covenant, 201, 205
Cover
  definition of, 105
  in recovery of damages, 106
Credit
  categories of, 112-113
  and commercial paper, 327
  definition of, 96, 112
Credit risk, 112-113
Creditors, 280
Criminal law, 11-12, 32
Cross-examination, 29
Curtice Bros. Co. v. Catts, 89-91
Custody, hiring of, 154-155

D

Damages, 25, 26, 88, 89
  defective goods, 108
  incidental, 106
  liquidated, 88
  nondelivery, 107-108
  recovery of, 105-107
  and torts, 229-230
Darryl v. Ford Motor Co., 239-241
Davis v. Gibson Products Company, 236-243
Death
  in agency termination, 272
  effect on contract, 86
  effect on offer, 62
Debtor, 113, 119
Debts, and bulk transfer, 104
Deeds
  bargain and sale, 201
  definition of, 182, 195
  delivery of, 195
  forms of, 195
  quitclaim, 198-199, 200
  recording of, 200
  statutory form for, 195-197
  under seal, 34
  warranty, full covenant in, 201
Defamation
  definition of, 231
  privilege, 232
  and true accusations, 232
  types of, 231-232
Default
  definition of, 116, 119
  reasons for, 114-115
  remedies for, 115, 119-121
Defendant, definition of, 1
Defenses
  absolute, 348-349
  case example, 345-347
  personal, 345-349
  real, 348-349
Deficiency, definition of, 121
Delegated contracts, 79

Delivery
  of commercial paper, 340
  in contract of sale, 104
  of deeds, 195
  reclaiming, 107
  stopping, 107
Demurrage, 164
Department of Agriculture, 142
Department of Health, Education and Welfare, 11
Directors
  board of, 311-312
  case example, 312-314, 316-320
  of corporation, 311
  inside, 311
  obligations of, 312-315
  outside, 311, 312
Disability, effect on contract, 86
Discharged contract. *See* Contracts, termination of
Disclaimer, 128
Discovery period, 28-29
Dispossess, definition of, 213
Dividends
  cash, 309-310
  definition, 309
  stock, 310
Donee, in acquiring ownership, 186
Donor, in acquiring ownership, 186
Dowries, 47
Drafts, 331
Drawee, and drawer, 331, 332
Driving regulations, 9
Due care, definition of, 150
Duty, 225-227
  breach of, 227-228

E

Easement, 175, 176-180
  types, 175-176
Education, legal, 1-2
Egyptian law, 3
Elmore v. American Motors Corp., 239
Eminent domain
  definition of, 181
  and lease termination, 215
  problems of, 181
Employee and employer, 254-255
Encumbrance, definition of, 201
Endorsee, of commercial paper, 341
Endorsement, 340-341
  full, 341
  qualified, 343, 349-350
  restrictive, 342
  special, 341-342
Endorser, misspelling of, 340-341
English law, 4
Entity, legal, 277-278, 295
Estate, definition of, 174

Eviction, 216
Exclusion
conspicuous, 128
of implied warranties, 138
Exclusive jurisdiction, 21-22
Executed and executory contract, 43
Executor, definition of, 46
Express contract, 39-41
Express powers, of corporations, 299-300
Express warranty, 124-126

F

Face value. *See* Par value
Family law suits, 7
FCC. *See* Federal Communications Commission
FDA. *See* Food and Drug Administration
Federal Communications Commission (FCC), 10
Federal courts
circuits of, 19-20
jurisdiction of, 19-21
special, 19
Federal Food, Drug and Cosmetic Act, 11
Federal statutes, 9
Federal Trade Commission (FTC), 10 and Magneson-Mass Warranty Act, 141
rights of holder, 348
role of, 140-141
Fee simple absolute, 174-175
Fiduciary duty
of agents, 268-269
breach of, 269
of directors, 312
of partners, 282
of promoter, 297
Financing statement, 116
Fire, effect on lease, 216
Fixtures
definition of, 174
in purchase offer, 194
and real property, 214
reasonable man standard, 174
trade, 214-215
Food and Drug Administration (FDA), 10-11, 141
Food quality, liability for, 127
Formal contract, form of, 34
Fraud, effect on contracts, 42
Free enterprise system, 251
FTC. *See* Federal Trade Commission
Full-covenant deed. *See* Deed, warranty

G

Good faith, definition of, 344
Goods
conforming, 107
defective, 108
fungible, 161
nature of, 163
nonacceptance of, 106

reclaiming, 107
recovering, 108
unique, 108-109
Grantee, definition of, 195
Grantor, 195
and bargain and sale deed, 201
and quitclaim deed, 200

H

Henningsen v. Bloomfield Motors, Inc., 129-138
Holder, 340, 345-347
real defenses, 348-349
Holder in due course
definition of, 343
personal defenses of, 345
requirements of, 343-344
rights of, 344-348
value, 344
Hotel owners, responsibilities of, 165-166

I

ICC. *See* Interstate Commerce Commission
Illegality, effect on contract, 86
Implied contract, 41
Implied powers, of corporations, 300
Implied warranty, 124, 128-137
types, 127-128, 137-138
Impossibility of performance, 85, 86
Imprisonment, false, 231
Incorporation, 297-299
Industrial pirates, 9
Infants. *See* Minors
Inferior courts, 24
Inheritance, of real property, 187
Injunction, 91-92, 244
Injured party, in breach of contract, 88
Innocence, proof of, 12
Insanity, 62
and contract law, 70
Insolvency
caused by dividends, 309
of corporations, 320
definition of, 107
by partnership, 280
Inspection, in contract of sale, 104
Instruments. *See* Commercial paper
Insurance policies, as express contracts, 40-41
Insurers of property, 162
Intent, 52-60
Balfour v. Balfour, 52-56
in determining fixtures, 174
Interest, on security deposits, 215
Interstate carriers, regulation of, 162
Interstate Commerce Commission, and common carriers, 162
Intervention, in offer, 63
Intestate death, 187
Intoxication, and contract law, 70
Intrastate carriers, regulation of, 162
Inventory, 104

J

Jacob & Young v. Kent, 82-85, 88
Judges, role of, 19
Jurisdiction
  concurrent, 21
  definition of, 16
  exclusive, 21-22
  original, 18, 22
  personal, 16-18
  subject matter of, 16
Justice of the Peace (J.P.) courts, 24
Justices. *See* Judges

K

Kroger Co. v. Bowman, 240

L

Landlord
  definition of, 204
  liability of, 208-213
  rights and duties, 205-213
  as trespasser, 205
  warrants, 205
Law, 1, 3-4
  basic divisions of, 172
  business, 243-246
  categories of, 32
  common, 205, 208
  tort, 221-246
Lease
  commercial, 205
  covenants in, 205
  definition of, 204
  effect of death on, 215
  long-term, 205
  residential, 205
  short-term, 205-207
  in Statute of Fraud, 46
  termination of, 215-216
  under seal, 34
Lefkowitz v. Great Minneapolis Surplus Store, Inc., 57-59
Legal practice, regulation of, 1-2
Legal purpose, and binding contracts, 70-72
Legal system, 2, 3-13
Legislation, 9
  for consumer protection, 139-142
Legislature, definition of, 9
Lessee and Lessor, definition of, 204
Liability, 80, 236-243
  of assignee, 213-214
  contract, 284
  of corporation directors, 312, 315
  criminal, 284-285
  in fire, 214
  of landlords, 208
  of limited partnerships, 288-289
  strict, 236
  of sublessee, 214
  tort, 284

Libel, 231-232
License, definition of, 176
Lien, 154
  of taxes, 187
  as used by hotels, 167
Life estate, 175
Life tenant, 175
Liquidation, of partnership assets, 285
Listing agreement, 191
Litigate, definition of, 29
Local statutes, 10
Long Island Trust Company v. Porta Aluminum, Inc., 119-120
Long-term contracts, 45
Loss. *See also* Damages; Risk of loss in partnerships, 281-282
Loyalty, of agents, 268-269
L.S. *See* Place of seal
Lucas v. Auto City Parking, 158
Lucy v. Zehmer, 74-77

M

McKisson v. Sales Affiliates, Inc., 238-239
Magneson-Mass Warranty Act, 141
Malicious intent, in libel and slander, 231
Management of corporations
  directors, 311-315
  officers, 315-320
Maturity date, 116
Media, and legal profession, 2
Meeting of minds
  definition of, 62
  in mutual assent, 66
Memorandum
  bill of sale, 48
  elements of, 99
  enforceable, 98-99
  order blank, 47-48
  requirements for, 48-49
  sample of, 99
Merchant, definition of, 98
Merger, corporate, 320
Methyl salicylate, FDA ruling on, 11
Miranda Rights card, 5
Miranda v. Arizona, 4-5, 6, 23
Miranda Warnings, 5
Minors
  and appointment of agents, 257-258
  contract ratification by, 69
  and cosigning adults, 70
  definition of, 68
  examples in contracts, 69-70
  legal responsibility of, 68
  in partnerships, 278
Minutes, 312
Model, definition of, 126
Model Act. *See* Model Business Corporation Act
Model Business Corporation Act, 299, 305, 308-309

Mundy v. Holden, 286-288
Muncipal courts, 24
Mutual assent, characteristics of, 66

N

National Conference of Commissioners on
    Uniform State Laws, 10
Negligence
    of bailee, 152
    in breach of duty, 227-228
    comparative, 235-236
    contributory, 235
    definition of, 234
    reasonable man standard, 235
    of shipper, 163
    as unintentional tort, 234-235
Negotiability, explanation of, 330-331
Negotiation, methods of, 340-341
Nonmerchant, 98, 128, 138
Notes
    antedated and postdated, 339
    definition of, 332-333
    items included in, 338-339
    negotiable, 339
    samples, 332, 334
Notice, of shareholder's meeting, 305
Nuisance, definition of, 234

O

Obedience, of agents, 268
Offer
    acceptance of, 64-66
    · counteroffers, 64
    definition of, 52
    determining factors of, 52-60
    intervening illegality, 63
    lapsed, 62
    public, 61
    rejection of, 63
    termination of, 60-64
Offeree, 52, 63
Offeror, 52
Officers, corporate, 299
    liability and responsibilities of, 315-320
Option, 61, 62
Oral contracts, 44-45
Order blank, example of, 47-48
Order paper, 338, 342
Order to pay, 332, 335
Ordinances, zoning, 180-181. *See also* Local
    statutes
Ordinary care. *See* Due care
Original jurisdiction, 18, 21
Osterlind v. Hill. 225-227
Ownership, acquistion of
    adverse possession, 186-187
    inheritance, 187
    purchase, 185-186
    tax sale, 187
Ownership in bailment, 147
Ownership, forms of
    community property, 183-184
    concurrent, 185
    condominiums, 184-185

tenancy, 181-183

P

Pailet v. Guillory, 264-267
Palsgraf v. The Long Island Railroad, 228
Par value, of stocks, 303
Parking Management Incorporated v. Jacobson,
    158
Partners
    capacity to be, 278
    compensation of, 281
    definition of, 277
    duties of, 282-283
    general, 279
    incoming, 280
    liability of, 279-280, 282-283
    powers of, 283-284
    silent, 279-280
Partnerships
    articles of, 278-279
    avoiding disadvantages of, 321
    and bankruptcy of partner, 285
    capital, 281
    case example, 286-288
    compared with corporations, 321
    creation of, 278-279
    creditors of, 280
    definition of, 252, 277
    distinguishing features of, 321
    as entity, 277-278
    insolvent, 289
    liability, 284-285
    limited, liability of, 288-289
    management of, 281
    and minors, 278
    nontrading, 283-284
    profit and loss in, 281-282
    property ownership by, 278
    reasons for, 278
    termination of, 285-286, 288
    trading, 283-284
    unwritten, 278
Passengers, transporation of, 164-165
Past performance, and consideration, 67
Patent, duration of, 244
Pawn and pawnbroker, 153
Payee, 331, 332, 333
Payment
    according to written word, 335-336
    to bearer, 338
    case example, 336-337
    of commercial paper, 350
    in contract of sale, 104
    on demand, 337-338
    to order, 338
    at specific time, 337-338
Performance
    of contract of sale, 104-105
    as form of acceptance, 65
    impossibility of, 85-86
    satisfactory, 81
    substantial, 81-85
    to terminate contract, 80-81

Perjury, 44
Personal jurisdiction, 16-17
Personal property, 95-96
Personal rights, wrongs affecting, 230-233
Place of seal, 34
Plaintiff, definition of, 1
Pleadings, 25-26
Pledge and pledgee, 152
Pledges, 68
Pledger, 152
Picker v. Searcher's Detective Agency, Inc.,
    155-160
Pines v. Perssion, 208-213
Possession, in bailment, 147
Possessory interest. *See* Estate
Power of attorney, 258, 259
Precedents
    in common law, 4-7
    for contract cases, 35
Pre-existing obligation, and consideration, 66
Present sale. *See* Contract, of sale
Principal
    disclosed and undisclosed, 270-271
    duties of, 270
    liability of, 262-263, 267
    qualifications of, 257
Principal-agent relationships, 260-270
Principal-third party relationships, 270-271
Privacy, right of, 233
Private law, definition of, 32
Privilege, in defamation cases, 232
Probate court, jurisdiction of, 16
Process. *See* Summons
Product liability, responsibility for, 139
Product reliability, responsibility for, 124
Profit
    in corporations, 296
    in partnerships, 281-282
Promise to pay, 334, 335
Promisee and promisor, 31
Promises
    in bilateral contract, 39
    of executors, 46
    to pay debts of another, 46
Promissory note. *See* Notes
Promoter, duties and functions, 296-297
Property
    affixed to real, 174
    category in private law, 171-172
    classifications of, 95
    community, 183-184
    corporation ownership of, 295
    definition of, 95
    insurers of, 162
    legal definition of, 171
    partners' rights in, 280-281
    personal, 95-96
Property, real

concurrent ownership of, 185
    deeds for, 200
    leasing of, 204-216
    purchasing of, 191-204
Property rights, wrongs affecting, 233-234
Proprietorship, 251-252
Prosecution, malicious, 233
Proxy, voting, 307
Public law, definition of, 32
Public welfare, contracts harmful to, 71-72
Puffing, 124, 126
Purchase offer. *See also* Contract, of sale
    elements of, 191-194
    and Statute of Frauds, 191
    property description, 195
Purchase price, recovery of, 105

Q
Quasi-contract, examples of, 41
Quorum, at board meeting, 311

R
Real property, 46, 95-96, 258
Reasonable man standard
    in breach of duty, 227-228
    in determining fixtures, 174
    in negligence, 235
Receiver, and partnership dissolution, 288
Records, court, 18, 24
Records, financial, as agent's
    duty, 269
Remainder interest, definition of, 175
Remedies, 88
    for breach of contract
        buyer's, 107-109
        seller's, 105-107
Remote purchaser, 139
Renouncement of agency, 272
Rent, 204, 213
Repairs, tenant's responsibility for, 213
Reply, definition of, 28
Repossession, 119-120
    profit from sale of, 121
Republic, definition of, 9
Reputation, citizen's right to, 231-232
Respondeat superior, definition of, 236
Responsibility, cycle of, 260, 261, 262
Retailer, responsibility of, 139
Retained earnings, 301
Return, in bailment, 148
Revocation, of agency, 272
Rights, personal, violations of, 224
Risk of loss
    and recovery of purchase price, 105
    in sale on approval, 103
    in sale or return, 103
    UCC ruling on, 102
Robert N. Brown Associates, Inc. v. Fileppo,
    312-314
Rogers v. Karem, 240-241

S

Salaries, for partners, 281
Sale, 97. *See also* Contracts, of sale
Sale of specified value, 47-48
Sale on approval, 103
Sale or return, 103
Sample, definition of, 126
Seal, 34
SEC. *See* Securities and Exchange Commission
Secured party, definition of, 113
Securities
  debt. *See* Bonds
  equity. *See* Stock
  types, 301
Securities and Exchange Commission
    (SEC), 10, 142
Security, definition of, 215
Security agreement, 113, 114-115, 116
Security interest, 113
Security payments, 116
Services, categories of, 147
Shareholders
  meetings of, 305
  role of, 305-309
  ways to become, 304-305
Shurtleff v. Giller, 345-347
Signature, definition of, 335
Silence, and acceptance, 64
Simple contracts, 34, 44
Slander, 231-232
Specific performance, 89-91
Speculation, by corporation, 300
Standard UCC Form – 1
  for financing statement, 116
  sample of, 117
  for termination of financing
    statement, 116, 118
State administration agencies, 10-11
State constitutions, 8
State courts, organization and jurisdiction of,
    23-24
State statutes, 9, 10
State Supreme Court, 24
Statute of frauds
  application of, 44-45
  contracts for agents, 258
  contracts included in, 45-49
  enforceable purchase offer, 191-194
  and partnerships, 278
  technical requirements of, 44
  in United States, 44
Statute of limitations
  and contract termination, 88
  definition and examples of, 49
Statutory form, for deeds, 195
Statutory law
  contracts which break, 70
  definition of, 9

established from case law, 23
Statutory regulations, and agency relationships,
    258
Stock
  assignment form, 304-305
  capital, 301
  certificate, 301-303, 304
  common, 303
  cumulative and noncumulative, 303
  issued and nonissued, 301
  par value of, 303
  preferred, 303
  purchasing, 305
  reverse split, 310-311
  split, 310
  transfer of, 305-306
  treasury, 301
Stock certificates, under seal, 34
Story v. Hefner, 176-180
Subject matter jurisdiction, 16-18
Sublessee, liability of, 214
Sublessor, 214
Subletting, liability in, 214
Suit, against partnership, 284
Sum certain, definition of, 335-336
Summons
  definition of, 16, 25
  illustrations of, 26-27
Survey, definition of, 194-195
Survivorship, right of, 183
Swicegood v. State, 5-6
  influence of *Miranda* case on, 5-6

T

Tax Court, 19
Tax sale, state regulation of, 187
Tenancy, types, 182-183
Tenant
  definition of, 204
  liability for assignee, 213-215
  rights and duties of, 213-215
Tender, definition of, 85
Termination. *See also* Contracts, termination
    of
  of agency, 271-273
  of corporations, 320-321
  form of, 273
  notice of, 273-274
  of partnerships, 285-288
Termination notice, 116, 118
Termination of offer, reason for
  counteroffers, 64
  death or insanity, 62-63
  destruction of subject matter, 63
  intervening illegality, 63
  rejection by offerer, 63
  revocation, 61
  time lapse, 62

Third party
in agency relationship, 253-254
and disclosed principal, 270-271
and independent contractors, 256
and partially disclosed principal, 271
and termination notice, 273
and undisclosed principal, 271
Time lapse, effect on offer, 62
Title
abstract of, 194
acquisition of, 204
company, role of, 194
deed for transfer of, 200
definition of, 102
search, 194
of stolen goods, 103
transfer of, 102-103, 191
Title closing, definition of, 201
Tort law, 221, 229
Tortfeasor, definition of, 224
Torts
of agent, 267
case examples, 225-227, 236-243
classifications of, 224, 246
definition of, 221
elements of, 225-230
meaning of, 224
partnership liability for, 284
Torts, business
deceitful practices, 243
types, 224, 243
unlawful copying, 243-246
violated, 243
Torts, intentional
affecting personal rights, 230-233
affecting property rights, 233-234
definition of, 224
Torts, unintentional
definition of, 224
negligence, 234-236
strict liability, 236
Trade secret, definition of, 244
Trademarks, illegal use of, 243
Transients, definition of, 165
Transportation
of merchandise, 161-164
of passengers, 164-165
Trespass, 234
and common law, 225
Trial, process of, 29
Trial courts, 18. *See also* United States
District Courts
Trustee, in bankruptcy, 80
Truth-in-Lending Act, requirements and
penalties of, 141-142

U

UCC. *See* Uniform Commercial Code
ULPA. *See* Uniform Limited Partnership Act

Ultra vires, and corporations, 300
Under seal. *See* Contracts, under seal
Unenforceable contract, 43
Uniform Commercial Code (UCC), 381-497
acceptance of, 64
and auctions, 66
breach of implied warranty, 128
collateral definitions, 113
collateral disposal, 120
commercial paper transfer, 340
contract assignment, 78
and contract seals, 34
correspondence, 66
and credit, 96, 113
deficiency, 121
establishment of, 10
exclusion of implied warranties, 138
express warranty, 124-126
and financing statement, 116
implied warranty classification, 127-138
and injured party, 88
memorandums, 48
merchantable goods, 127
performance of contract of sale, 104-105
and product liability, 139
reclaiming goods, 107
revocation of offer, 61
rights of buyers and sellers, 97
sale of goods, 98
and security agreements, 113
signatures, 335
and statute of fraud, 44, 98
and stock transfer, 304
Uniform Limited Partnership Act (ULPA),
288, 511-518
Uniform Partnership Act (UPA), 498-510
limitations on partners, 283
and partnership records, 283
and partnership termination, 285
scope of, 277-279
Unilateral contract, 35-39
UPA. *See* Uniform Partnership Act
U.S. Court of Appeals, 19, 22
U.S. District Courts, 19
jurisdiction of, 21-22
U.S. Patent Office, 244
U.S. Postal Service, as agent of offeror, 65
U.S. Supreme Court, 4, 22-23
Usurius contracts, 71
Usury, definition of, 71

V

Valid contract, definition of, 42
Value, reasonable, 344
Value received, on negotiable paper, 339
Void contract, 42, 68, 71-72
Voidable contract, definition of, 42
Voting
cumulative, 307-308

Voting (continued)
by proxy, 307

W

Waiver, 87-88
Wall v. East Texas Teachers Credit Union, 336-337
Warranties
breach of, 208
definition of, 124
of endorsers and transferors, 349-350
express, 124-126
of fitness for particular purpose, 137-138
for habitable premises, 208
history of, 123-124
implied, 127
kinds of, 124
of merchantability, 127-137
disclaimer for, 128
of title, 127
Warrants
and false imprisonment, 231
of landlords, 205
Wintergreen oil. *See* Methyl salicylate
Wire tapping, as invasion of privacy, 233
Words and actions, as form of acceptance, 64

Z

Zoning ordinances. *See* Ordinances, zoning